INT

PHILOSOPHY

A TEXT-BOOK
FOR COLLEGES AND
HIGH SCHOOLS

BY

CHARLES A. DUBRAY, S.M., PH. D.

PROFESSOR OF PHILOSOPHY AT THE
MARIST COLLEGE, WASHINGTON, D.C.

Nihil Obstat:

J. F. SOLLIER, S.T.D.,
Provincial S.M.

Imprimatur:

✠ JOHN CARDINAL FARLEY,
Archbishop of New York.

February 7th, 1912.

PREFACE

The efforts which have been made in recent years to provide the beginner in philosophy with a text-book suited to his needs are justified both by the importance of the subject and by the requirements of educational method. It is obvious that an introduction should really introduce, in other words that it should present philosophy in such a way as to arouse the student's interest, give him a firm grasp of essentials, and encourage him to further study. But how these results are to be secured is still an open question. The books that have so far appeared have, each from its own point of view, distinct advantages either as outlining the history of philosophical problems, or as setting forth the claims of rival systems, or as explaining the principles which serve as the foundation of some special system and a basis of criticism in discussing variant theories. An introduction that will combine these several utilities seems to be our present need.

Dr. Dubray's aim in this volume is to lead the student by easy approaches into the field of philosophy and to show him its divisions with their several problems and the solutions which these have received. In accordance with the principles of correct method, the knowledge which the student has already acquired is made to serve as the starting-point, and from this he is led on to the consideration of more abstract philosophical concepts and theories. These again are presented in clear statement and orderly sequence, with sufficient indication of outstanding questions, yet without the excess of detail which sometimes destroys proportion or results in narrowness of view. At the same time, definite conclusions are presented with the evidence on which they rest, so that the student may get from his use of the book not merely a lot of vague questionings, but a certain amount of positive knowledge and critical direction for later investigation.

PREFACE

Students of Catholic philosophy will appreciate both the form and the content of this manual. While adhering to the principles of Scholasticism, the author has kept steadily in view the development of modern philosophy and the recent advances of science. It is not possible of course to effect a conciliation all along the line where the aim is rather to open up the whole subject. But important service can be rendered by illustrating the method by which the old and the new may be combined. This feature of the book is the more helpful because the student, working simultaneously in other departments of knowledge, is sure to come upon problems which lead up to philosophy. This is true not only of the physical and biological sciences, but also of the social and historical. In each of these, whatever be the special subject of study, there is needed a certain seasoning of philosophical principle and method in order that the student may see scientific facts, not in their first crudeness or isolation, but as parts of a larger truth. In this way he will not only give to each item of knowledge its proportionate value, but will also form the habit of philosophical thinking, which in itself is the best result that can be derived from an introductory course.

In Catholic colleges, importance has always been attached to the study of philosophy both as a means of culture and as a source of information regarding the great truths which are influential in supporting Christian belief and in shaping character. It is rightly considered essential for every graduate to have a training in logic and in the fundamentals of psychology, ethics, and metaphysics. But if this training is to be successful, philosophy must be presented not as a complex of abstruse speculations on far-off inaccessible topics, but as a system of truths that enter with vital consequence into our ordinary thinking and our everyday conduct. For beginners especially it is not the best plan to take up first the science and art of reasoning where the formal treatment predominates. On the other hand, the study of logic itself becomes more attractive when it follows that of ethics or psychology. There is yet considerable difference of opinion as to which of the philosophical disciplines should have precedence; but if the choice is to be made with due regard to the scientific subjects which have previously been studied, psychology would seem to have the strongest claim. The recognition of the value of its empirical methods is quite compatible with the philosophical discussion of its central problems, and its own conclusions find numerous applications in other fields of research.

Teachers of philosophy realize that the difficulties encountered in an introductory course can, in part at least, be overcome by the use of a suitable text-book. As it is not desirable that the student should memorize a set of formulæ for the purpose of recitation or examination, it is also unwise to expand each topic in such lengthy fulness that no margin is left for individual thinking. The conciseness that marked the writings of the great Schoolmen is an art that may yet be revived. It leaves the teacher scope to develop the text, to suggest new points of view, and to select special topics for discussion. The best features of the lecture method may in this way be added to the ordinary class exercise and the student be gradually led on to examine each statement in the light of established principles and with a single eye for the truth — which is the attitude and temper of the really critical mind.

Dr. Dubray has profited by his experience as a teacher, and in this volume he offers the results with the hope that they may be useful to others. He has certainly contributed his share toward encouraging the beginner in philosophy and has indicated a line of approach which is neither too steep nor too easy. If it smoothes out some of the hard places, it leaves ample room for hard thinking.

EDWARD A. PACE

THE CATHOLIC UNIVERSITY OF AMERICA
March 7, 1912

CONTENTS

GENERAL INTRODUCTION

PSYCHOLOGY, OR THE EMPIRICAL STUDY OF THE MIND

INTRODUCTION

CHAPTER I

KNOWLEDGE

Article I. Sense Presentation

CHAPTER II

FEELING

CHAPTER III

ACTING AND WILLING

Article I. Action and Modes of Action

Article II. Determinants and Freedom of the Will

CHAPTER IV

SUPPLEMENTARY — SOME SPECIAL RELATIONS AND MODES OF MENTAL PROCESSES

LOGIC, OR THE NORMATIVE SCIENCE OF THE INTELLECT

CHAPTER I

REASONING

Article I. The Idea

CHAPTER II

METHOD

CONTENTS

ÆSTHETICS, OR THE NORMATIVE SCIENCE OF THE FEELINGS OF THE BEAUTIFUL

CHAPTER I

BEAUTY

CHAPTER II

THE FINE ARTS

ETHICS, OR THE NORMATIVE SCIENCE OF THE WILL

INTRODUCTION

CHAPTER I

FUNDAMENTAL ETHICS

ARTICLE I. THE MORAL NORMS OR LAWS

CHAPTER II

APPLIED ETHICS

CONTENTS

EPISTEMOLOGY, OR THE THEORY OF KNOWLEDGE

INTRODUCTION

CHAPTER I

IS CERTITUDE JUSTIFIED?

CHAPTER II

CERTITUDES

CHAPTER III

WHAT IS KNOWLEDGE?

CHAPTER IV

THE CRITERIA OF VALID KNOWLEDGE

COSMOLOGY, OR THE METAPHYSICAL STUDY OF THE PHYSICAL WORLD

CHAPTER I

INORGANIC SUBSTANCES

CHAPTER II

LIVING BEINGS

CHAPTER III

ORIGIN AND EVOLUTION

CONTENTS

CHAPTER IV

THE COSMOS

RATIONAL PSYCHOLOGY, OR PHILOSOPHY OF THE HUMAN MIND

CHAPTER I

SUBSTANTIALITY

CHAPTER II

SPIRITUALITY

CHAPTER III

THE UNION OF THE SOUL WITH THE BODY

CHAPTER IV

ORIGIN OF THE SOUL AND OF MAN

CHAPTER V

IMMORTALITY OF THE SOUL

THEODICY, OR THE STUDY OF GOD

CHAPTER I

THE EXISTENCE AND NATURE OF GOD

CONTENTS

CHAPTER II

GOD AND THE WORLD

OUTLINES OF HISTORY OF PHILOSOPHY

CHAPTER I

ANCIENT PHILOSOPHY

CHAPTER II

MEDIÆVAL PHILOSOPHY

CONTENTS

CHAPTER III

MODERN PHILOSOPHY

GENERAL CONCLUSION

INTRODUCTORY PHILOSOPHY

GENERAL INTRODUCTION

I. THE NATURE OF PHILOSOPHY

AS the study of philosophy takes place at the end of the college course, it will be useful to outline the relations of philosophy to the knowledge already acquired by the student.

I. What Has Been Done Already

1. **Special Results.**—During the college years numerous studies have been pursued, and little by little the physical universe has unfolded its secrets.

(*a*) *Chemistry* has reduced material substances to their finest elements and revealed the laws by which their various combinations are governed. *Biology* has manifested the special properties of living beings, and the human organism has been the special subject-matter of *anatomy* and *physiology*. The whole earth has been described in the sciences of *geography* and *geology*, while *astronomy* pointed to millions of other worlds which, in their constitution and evolution, bear a striking resemblance to the world which we inhabit. From *physics* we also know that, however near or distant they may be, all the beings of the universe are ruled by natural laws which all obey and which produce order and harmony in the world.

(*b*) *Mathematical* and *geometrical* sciences deal with the properties and laws of quantity; namely of numbers, surfaces, and volumes. Wherever applied, these relations, once ascertained, will always be verified.

(*c*) Events of the past recorded in *history* have also been memorized, and from the comparison of the present with the past the mind is now able to draw useful lessons. We know the deeds of great men in war and peace, and we are able to follow the successive steps by which nations have reached their actual standing in the world.

(*d*) Not only knowledge has been acquired, but also the aptitude to express it by speech and writing. The study of *grammar* and of the various *languages* and *literatures* enables man not only to manifest his own thoughts to others, but also to profit by the thoughts of other men and to admire the beauties found in the various forms of literature.

(*e*) *Religious* science has taught us how to revere and serve God. The principles of *morality* are the guides of human actions and behavior.

2. **More General Results.** — In addition to the mastering of the various sciences, another result has been attained. Gymnastic exercises do not merely develop one muscle or another; their purpose is not only to make man go through a certain series of motions, but chiefly to strengthen and develop the whole organism. So also the mental efforts made in the different studies have contributed to the general and harmonious *growth of the mind.* Memory is stronger; the power of attention has been increased; habits of study and reflection have been developed. The faculties of judgment and reasoning have been strengthened. The discipline of college life, the obligation to follow a rule, the constant relations with other students, have been important factors in the formation of character and the acquisition of social virtues.

Hence if we had to summarize in a few words the mental results of college years, we might say that the mind has been furnished with a numerous array of facts grouped and classified, and that it has grown or increased in power and energy.

II. What Remains to be Done

Great and important as it is, the knowledge acquired so far is insufficient. Certain things have been neglected altogether and the knowledge of the others needs a complement.

1. **New Knowledge to be Acquired.** — (*a*) There is a whole world, as varied and as complex as the physical world, which has been left aside almost completely, or, at least, has not been the

object of any systematic study. It is the inner world of the *self*, of *our own mind*, with its constant changes, its successive states, its growth and development, and its conditions of activity. You have learned your lessons, but what is it to learn? What is the power of acquiring knowledge with which the mind is endowed, and how is such a power exercised? How should it be exercised? What is knowledge itself? And when judgments and conclusions are called true or false, questions are suggested immediately concerning the nature of truth, the possibility of reaching it and of distinguishing it from error, and the method of doing this most effectively.

(*b*) In your studies you made use of your *memory*, *judgment*, *reasoning*, *reflection*, etc., so many words which now call for further explanation, and which suggest numerous problems concerning the functions of the senses, the memory, and the intellect. Frequently you have relied on the testimony of others; you have learned a text-book and taken it for granted that the author was right. How could you do otherwise, for instance, for historical or geographical statements? But this method, which was the only possible one, must not now lead to an exaggerated reverence for all that is found in books or newspapers. For, how many errors are published and how many fallacies are taken for truths simply because they appear in print, or even because they are spoken in brilliant language accompanied by fine gestures. It is necessary to learn how to use one's own reason and to practise the difficult art of criticism so as to distinguish truth from falsity, and thus to become able to steer one's own mental life, to think for oneself, and no longer depend too exclusively on the thinking of others.

(*c*) Other questions may be raised which so far have received no answer. You have made *efforts* and *acted* for the best: herein are included such notions as those of end, purpose, motive, choice, activity, habit, etc., which have to be elucidated.

(*d*) When the working of man's organic and mental life is understood, when we know its conditions and laws, there still remain the problems of *our own constitution*. We speak of body and mind. What are they and what are their mutual relations? What is the origin and what will be the destiny of the human soul? What is the end of man? Even if our Christian faith has given us answers to these questions, what is the attitude of reason toward our belief?

These are a few of the many problems which so far have received no solution.

2. **The Knowledge already Acquired must be Completed.** — Even in sciences that have been mastered, there remain many incomplete conclusions. They are good as far as they go, but they do not go far enough.

(*a*) At the very outset, when we learn to *read* and *write*, and when later we learn to *express our thoughts* correctly, accurately, and clearly, how many problems present themselves: the nature of thought, of correct and consistent thought; the possibility of expressing it by means of symbols and of understanding others; the general relations of body ând mind, since, in speaking, writing, or making signs, bodily movements are supposed to be controlled by the mind and to represent mental processes or ideas.

(*b*) *Historical* and *social* sciences lead to such problems as the conditions, motives, and value of human activity. We pass judgments on the actions of others, approve them as right or condemn them as wrong; what, then, is right and wrong? We rely on human testimony and historical records; what is their value as signs of truth?

(*c*) Sciences that deal with the *material* world leave also many notions unexplained. The very word "matter" is an enigma, and "force" is hardly clearer. We are told of a being acting on another in a certain way and under certain conditions, and producing such or such results. Because these are everyday occurrences which have become familiar, they seem clear, and we do not even think that they may need an explanation. And yet if we are asked to define what is meant by activity, action, and cause in general, and how action and causality are possible, we find that the task is not an easy one, and that, at every step, many obscurities and difficulties are met with. If all this were understood, there would still remain questions which are altogether beyond the reach of natural science; namely, those concerning the first origin and cause of the world, the nature and necessity of the laws that govern it.

(*d*) **Religion** requires a basis. It does not consist in blindly believing certain things as true or following certain arbitrary practices. To reason belongs the task of proving the existence of God and of explaining his attributes as far as possible.

To sum up: The task of philosophy is *to complete and unify knowledge* by showing how all the things which we know are related together, and by examining certain notions which have a wide range of application and cover numerous cases, such as those of substance, cause, activity, matter, mind, etc.

III. Definition of Philosophy

If we consider the name itself, we find that philosophy means the love of wisdom (φίλος friend, σοφία wisdom). The first Greek philosophers did not call themselves "friends of wisdom," but "wise" (σοφοί). Cicero says that Pythagoras was the first to take the name of philosopher because, according to him, the gods alone should be called wise.

1. **For the ancients** philosophy included both *science*, i.e. the knowledge and explanation of things, and *wisdom*, i.e. prudence, the practice of virtue, and the right conduct of life. As a science it was not limited to any special object, but included the sum total of all knowledge. Thus Cicero: "Nec quidquam aliud est philosophia, si interpretari velis, quam studium sapientiae. Sapientia autem est (ut a veteribus philosophis definitum est) rerum divinarum et humanarum causarumque quibus hae res continentur scientia" (De Offic. II. ii).

2. **To-day**, owing to the increase of human knowledge and the multiplication of sciences, philosophy can no longer be a universal science in the same sense as formerly. (1) Sometimes the word is still applied to any reasoned doctrine or science, the main surviving use being the name "natural philosophy," which is sometimes given to the science of physics. (2) More frequently to say of a man that he is a philosopher, or that he takes things philosophically, indicates a habit or disposition, especially in practical matters, to refer things to higher principles and to govern

the senses and the feelings by reason. (3) Strictly speaking, however, the name philosophy applies to *the science of the higher principles of things*, to the elucidation of those concepts and laws which are common to several sciences and which are used by them without being subjected to any special investigation.

It is not a mere classification of the sciences, it has special questions to answer and special problems to solve. Sciences reduce phenomena to general laws; philosophy tries to further *unify the various sciences* by taking a higher point of view and going to the *principles* common to many or to all sciences.

3. **Relation of Philosophy to the Other Sciences.** — Hence it is easy to understand the relations of philosophy to the other sciences. It considers the same objects, but from a different and higher standpoint. It uses the same methods, at least essentially, although the processes of observation and experiment have a considerably smaller importance, whereas reasoning is given greater prominence.

(*a*) Philosophy *completes the other sciences*. (1) It considers higher principles and causes which are neglected by them. (2) It examines critically the value of the principles which they presuppose, e.g. the principle of causality which is used by all natural sciences, but tested by none. (3) It links and connects the different sciences, because it considers the common principles that pervade them all and on which they rest.

(*b*) On the other hand philosophy *depends on the other sciences*, for it must constantly keep in touch with the facts and laws which they manifest. Otherwise it would be a mere random play of the mind, in which any vagary could find a place.

(*c*) The relation of philosophy to the sciences may be conceived diagrammatically as follows. If we have a large circle the circumference of which represents the facts of experience, its surface will represent the sciences dealing with different groups of facts, and more or less closely related. These sciences may be represented by sectors the number and dimensions of which vary with the progress of sciences and their differentiations. The circle itself is constantly being enlarged as new facts are discovered. Within this circle let us draw another concentric with it which will represent philosophy. It may also vary in size; originally it was co-extensive with the circle of sciences, but is now considerably smaller. Beginning at the outer circumference, sciences may go higher and higher, be more or less general, give a more immediate or a more remote explanation of the facts, stop at one or the other of the dotted circles; all converge toward philosophy. Can we reach a centre O which would give us one general principle, or one key applying to all sciences? This is a question which we cannot attempt to answer at present. The human mind craves unity; sciences are subordinate to one another and lead to a higher science. All finally lead to philosophy, which always, whatever be the extension of the questions assigned to it, occupies a central position and from this vantage-ground surveys in its own general way the whole field of human knowledge.

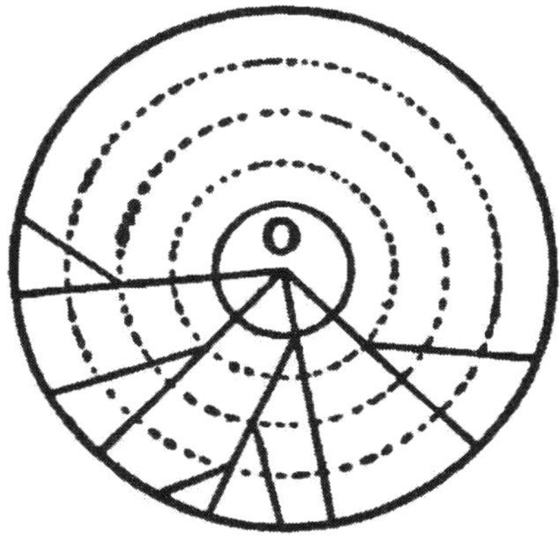

IV. Division of Philosophy

1. **The Various Branches of Philosophy.** — (*a*) Since the extension of the field of philosophy has varied so much in history, and since even to-day not all philosophers are agreed on this point, it is impossible to give a division of philosophy into its various branches that will be acceptable to all and that may claim to be finally and forever settled. Not long ago logic, psychology, and ethics had still an undisputed place in philosophy. To-day many look upon them as independent sciences, and only some of their higher problems are turned over to philosophy.

For our purpose in the present course it matters little how much ground philosophy strictly so-called should cover. Our point of view is a practical one, and hence we shall treat of those questions which have been neglected heretofore and yet are necessary to complete the knowledge acquired so far and prepare the student for further studies.

(*b*) Philosophy comes after the study of physical sciences; hence the name "metaphysics" (μετὰ τὰ φυσικά, after-physics), which is frequently given to philosophy or to a branch of it.

(1) The philosophical study of *realities*, i.e. of existing objects, includes *cosmology*, or the general study of the world; *biology*, or the more special study of living organisms; *psychology*, or the still more special study of the human mind; *theodicy*, or the study of God as the first cause of the world. (2) Besides the real we have to consider the *ideal*, i.e. the rules to which thought must conform in order to be consistent (*logic*); the expression of ideals to realize something beautiful (*æsthetics*); the guidance of our actions in conformity with the rules of morality (*ethics*). (3) *Epistemology* holds an intermediate place between the science of the real and that of the ideal. It examines whether and how far our ideas correspond to external reality. Hence the following synopsis:

Philosophical study of the	real	world = cosmology.
		man = psychology and philosophy of the mind.
		God = theodicy.
	relations of knowledge with reality = epistemology.	
	ideal	of thought = logic.
		of expression = æsthetics.
		of action = ethics.

2. Division of this Course. — In itself the order just mentioned would seem to be the best. But it is not the most practical nor the most useful because it requires too many a priori postulates and obliges one to admit too many presuppositions which are to be justified only later. Moreover it is true that the mind is first objective, that it knows other things before knowing itself. But, in order precisely to develop habits of reflection, it seems preferable to begin with psychology. Hence the following order is better adapted to our present purpose, because it enables the mind to proceed step by step without supposing and taking too much for granted at the outset. We shall begin with the *psychological processes* of knowledge, feeling, and action; then proceed to examine the *rules* of these three groups of processes. After examining the *value of knowledge* we shall pass to the study of the *world*, of *man*, and of *God*. The synopsis of the present course is therefore as follows:

I. The empirical study of the self = psychology.
   1. Cognitive consciousness = knowledge.
   2. Affective consciousness = feeling.
   3. Conative or active consciousness = activity and will.

II. The normative sciences
   1. of the intellect = logic.
   2. of expression of ideals to arouse certain feelings = æsthetics.
   3. of will and action = ethics.

III. Epistemology, or the study of the relations of cognitive processes to real world; a transition to the following.

IV. Philosophical study = metaphysics.
   1. of the world = cosmology.
   2. of man = philosophy of mind.
   3. of God = theodicy.

V. The Method of Philosophy

The central rule to be observed for the profitable study of philosophy is: *Use your own judgment and reason* under the guidance of your professor and text-book.

1. **Eagerness to Know.** — (*a*) The *main cause* that prompts men to philosophize, as Plato and Aristotle already pointed out, is wonder or admiration. The mind wonders as long as a given fact has not been given an explanation and assigned adequate causes. It endeavors to discover causes and principles so as to account for experience. Out of this desire philosophy was born; in this desire it finds its incentive.

(*b*) Hence an *essential quality* of the mind is to be inquisitive, to question and investigate, and never to feel at rest so long as a satisfactory explanation has not been found. It must compare facts, gather solutions, discuss, criticise, and harmonize them.

2. **Personal Reflection.** — (*a*) This work must be a *personal work of understanding*, not the mere memorizing of the words of the professor or of books. It is true that without books or pro-

fessor the student could do very little; he would grope in the dark, uncertain of the direction to be taken and of the value of the progress already made. But nevertheless these are only aids for the student's thinking, and their teaching would be of little value if the mind did not verify it and appropriate it. If exaggerated self-confidence is a serious defect, if man must listen to the opinions of others, be somewhat diffident of his own intellect, and proceed cautiously, it is also a serious defect for the mind to remain inactive and to take for granted everything that is said without understanding the truth of it.

A lesson in philosophy is not like a lesson in geography or history. When I am told that Peking is in China and London in England, I believe it at once; my activity consists only in memorizing a fact which I cannot verify and on which all agree. But in philosophy it is always necessary first to understand and verify the truth of a statement; the work of memorizing comes last. *Never try to memorize anything which is not understood thoroughly.* A nurse is a help to the child who begins to walk; she guides his first steps, but cannot take the place of the child's own activity; the walking process must be that of the child. So also the beginner in philosophy needs guidance, but this can never dispense with his own activity. To be genuine and to deserve its name, *philosophy must be the mind's own philosophy;* not in the sense that the mind has discovered all the truths which it possesses, but in the sense that it has appropriated and digested them and thought them for itself.

(*b*) Habits of *reflection* must be acquired. Man is not, or should not be, a machine to be moved at will by an engineer; he must act for himself. This is not a book of ready made formulas, but rather a book of suggestions for the student's thought.

(*c*) The study of philosophy should make man *cautious* in affirming and denying, in approving and condemning the opinions of others. If those men are not to be admired and imitated who are never able to take a resolution, to side for or against a proposition, and to give a straight answer, still less are those to be commended who have ready made ideas on all questions, unchangeable and categorical solutions for all problems, and whom no amount of proofs, however cogent, can ever induce to modify their views. The most affirmative are also frequently the most ignorant.

In one word, at the time when the body is acquiring its full development, let the mind also grow, and, by its own efforts under the guidance of those who are more skilful and experienced, proceed in the acquisition, or rather in the building up for itself, of a sound philosophy.

II. GENERAL VIEW OF THE WORLD AND OF MAN

I. The Self and the Not-Self

Sciences group and classify the various beings of the world according to their resemblances and differences. But there is one division which they overlook; a division which, though it is most important and should be most striking, is frequently neglected or receives little attention; a division the members of which are most unequal in number and extension, for it opposes one individual to the rest of the world. On one side I place myself; on the other, all the other beings of the world. The division of the universe into self and not-self is a primary one, as it brings into opposition beings that are endowed with irreducible characters.

1. **Their Opposition.** — (*a*) What I call *myself* is that centre around which the whole world seems to be grouped. I am constantly acting, perceiving, imagining, thinking, feeling, etc.; yet this conscious activity, this inner life, is directly perceivable only for myself. It is my inalienable property which no amount of effort will enable me to transfer to another. I may, by certain gestures, speech, or writing, manifest my thoughts to others, but they remain mine, and are experienced by me alone. Nothing but a sign or a symbol of them can reach another mind.

(*b*) Far different are the *objects of the world;* any number of observers may study and examine them; they are not "private," but "public" property. If I know the existence of other minds like mine, of other selves, it is only because I see elsewhere the same manifestations by which I make mine known, but I am not aware of them directly. In themselves they have the same strict privacy which I enjoy.

(*c*) My self is a sanctum into which I alone can penetrate, a *within* which I constantly oppose to a *without*, i.e. to the world which reflects itself in my mind.

2. **The Self is Primary.** — (*a*) Although it is so small when compared to the universe, yet my self is for me the *primary* and *most important reality* in the whole world, and, in a certain sense, coextensive with it, since all the knowledge which I have of the world is in my mind. All other things and selves act on my self and are acted on by my self. I thus become a *centre* toward which, from my point of view, all converge. I know, it is true, of the interaction between them, but the chief point of interest is how they behave, not toward one another, but toward me. In this sense, we are all, and we cannot help being, egoists. I move and act amid other material beings and amid other persons, but my own motion and action is what concerns me most. *The world is my world* as I know it and as it affects me.

(*b*) Nor does it take long for me to notice that *my world*, i.e. the world as known by me, is not perfectly identical with *the world of my neighbor*. My views differ from his; the thoughts and feelings aroused by one and the same object are not the same for my mind and for his. In the same circumstances we are not affected in the same manner, and the ensuing actions are different. In all such cases I cannot but place myself first; for what I am primarily interested in is my own, and not anybody else's, knowledge and activity.

3. **The Objective World is Known First.** — Self and not-self form an antithesis which is not known clearly to the individual at the beginning of his mental life. The child lives almost exclusively in an objective world. His power of reflection is not strong enough to be concentrated on the subject or self. The distinction is for him vague and indistinct, but becomes clearer as the mind develops.

A similar remark applies to the beginnings of philosophy. The first philosophers of Greece deal with the objective, not the subjective, world. Their theories are cosmologic, cosmogonic, theogonic; the self is neglected. They are concerned primarily with the origin of things, the constitution and the elements of the universe, not with the nature and functions of the self. We must wait till the time of Socrates to find the attention directed toward the subject, toward the internal world of ideas, feelings, and activities, together with the rules these ought to obey: "Socrates autem primus philosophiam evocavit e coelo, et in urbibus collocavit, et in domos etiam introduxit, et coegit de vita et moribus, rebusque bonis et malis quaerere." (Cicero, Tusc., V. iv.)

II. The Not-Self and its Obvious Characteristics

1. **Diversity.** — If we consider the not-self, i.e. the material world around us, we are amazed at the *number, variety, and complexity* of the beings that compose it. Their multitude is beyond our power of understanding. Moreover, all have different natures, sizes, qualities, etc. Whether we can find in the whole world two beings exactly and in all details alike is a question which cannot be answered. Try to find in nature two things perfectly similar, even if they are the most common, like two leaves, or two blades of grass, or even two particles of dust, and you will at once find it very difficult. Even when you think you have succeeded, a more minute examination, a dissection, the use of the microscope, or certain modes of analysis will reveal numerous differences.

2. **Likeness.** — At the same time we observe many common features, many points of similarity which enable us to classify things.

(*a*) In the first place, there are *other men* to whom I attribute a nature essentially *similar to mine*. I believe that they also are selves. Not that it is possible for me to be directly aware of the fact, for, although I see their organisms, their minds are, as stated already, their own private property; but, in their whole behavior, these organisms are so similar to mine that, by analogy, I cannot fail to infer that they are also related to minds like my own. I hold myself responsible for my actions, and worthy of praise or blame; I experience a number of feelings and impulses, and I attribute the same to my fellow-men. I cannot believe that they are governed by the same laws as physical things. I do not blame the stone that hurts me by its fall, but I condemn the man who throws it at me; I judge his motives and intentions, and treat him differently from any other being. The physical laws that govern matter are fatal and inevitable, but man is capable of education; he subjugates nature and uses it for his own purposes.

(*b*) Below man in nature I find *animals* with their infinite varieties. To them also I attribute a mind with sensations, memory, feelings of pain and pleasure, etc. But their mind is of an inferior order; they manifest no ideas by speech or writing, and are capable of but little progress.

(*c*) Men, animals, and plants, however different, may nevertheless be classed together as *living organisms*. They possess certain common properties of nutrition, growth, and reproduction, and by these differ from inorganic substances. An organism originates from a similar organism; it assimilates foreign substances and transforms them into its own substance.

(*d*) In opposition to organisms we find the manifold beings which belong to the *inorganic world*. They exist in three different states, liquid, solid, and gaseous, and present many different properties and activities.

(*e*) Obvious as are these main classifications theoretically, since they are based on marked differences between the classes, and on marked similarities among members of the same class, their *concrete applications* sometimes offer great difficulties. If I compare a higher animal with a tree or a mineral, the points of difference are clear. But when we come to the confines of two kingdoms, it may be impossible to determine whether a given specimen is an animal or a plant, a plant or a mineral. The principle of the continuity of nature finds an application everywhere. In many respects nature is like the spectrum, the colors of which pass insensibly from one to the other. I see the different colors, and yet cannot point out the exact limit where one begins and the other ends. Between two extremes clearly differentiated are to be found numerous transitional forms.

3. **Change.** — All beings, organic and inorganic, undergo manifold changes.

(*a*) *They pass from place to place*, sometimes with slow and hardly perceptible motion, and sometimes with great rapidity.

There are motions of the smallest particles of matter and of the tiniest microscopical organisms, and there are motions of the earth, of the stars, and of the whole universe, carrying with them all things, even those that seem to be at rest.

(*b*) *Changes in size and quantity, in quality, color, temperature, activity*, etc., also take place constantly. And besides the changes which we may observe ourselves, many others are recorded in history or inferred from science. At all times and in all things change is a law of the world.

(*c*) Nevertheless the *order, harmony, and unity of the world* are preserved. It is important to keep in mind this unity of nature. We are obliged to study things separately, to analyze, divide, and dissect, but we must not lose sight of the unity which results from the various relations between all these elements of the universe.

Changes are not produced at random, but form a continuous and uninterrupted chain of events, each link of which depends on the preceding and contributes to the production of the following; or rather it is a continuous network ramifying in all directions. This is another aspect of the unity of nature, a unity resulting from harmonious *succession*, and which must be added to that which was mentioned above resulting from the harmonious *coexistence* of manifold realities. Not only do the beings of the world form a series the members of which are close to one another, they also form one continuous network of activity and causality. Every event is determined by antecedent events. Sometimes the thread which links them is plainly visible; sometimes also we become lost in the investigation and are unable to trace the manifold ramifications of causes and effects. Yet we never doubt that such connections exist, even if they are unknown to us. The task of science is to discover them.

III. Relations of the Self with the External World

1. **Knowledge and Action.** — All the relations which the self has with the various objects of the world may be reduced to two groups: knowledge of, and action on, them. These two terms are

not mutually exclusive, for I am conscious that, in knowing, I am not merely passive and receptive, but that I also exercise some activity, and that I contribute my share to the final result. But such an activity is essentially immanent, that is, it remains within myself and in no way modifies the known object.

(*a*) The object is perceived through its substitute, the idea, but my invincible inclination is to suppose that, known or unknown, it remains permanent and identical. I alone, not the object, undergo a change when I acquire a new idea. *In cognition the primary direction of activity is from the known object to the knowing mind*, since the object is appropriated in the form of an idea within the mind under the action or stimulation coming from the object. We naturally and spontaneously believe that we know things as they are; yet, a little reflection suffices to convince us that exaggeration is very easy on this point, and that, since frequently men have different views of the world or of parts of it, all views cannot correspond exactly to the supposedly identical reality. This problem will be examined in epistemology.

(*b*) Besides immanent activity such as that of the mind in knowing, there is another form, namely, transitive activity, when the modification is received in a being different from the agent. This is what is meant by action as opposed to knowledge. *In action the primary direction is from the self to other things or persons.* That we have many such relations is evident, for every use which we make of things implies for them changes of place, shape, qualities, relations, etc. We adapt them to our purposes, and in many ways, voluntarily or involuntarily, modify them.

2. **Further Determination of Knowledge and Action.** — The self's twofold relation with the world is obvious. We know some realities of the world, and are known by some, namely, by other minds. We act on them and are acted upon by them. There are many forms of knowledge, from sense-perception to the highest form of reasoning, from the weakest opinion or belief to the strongest certitude. There are also many forms of action, from those which we accomplish without, or even against, our will to the highly deliberative and intentional actions. But the essential characteristics of knowledge and action remain the same.

One is an *acquisition*, an *incoming*, the other, *a giving out* or *outgoing*. The two, however, are closely related. As stated already, some kind of action is implied in knowledge; one transitive, from the object to the mind; the other immanent in the mind. Moreover, knowledge is frequently a principle or motive of human actions.

Thus *in knowledge, the object is to be looked upon as a centre* acting in different directions, and its activity, when received in a responsive mind, produces knowledge. The sun sends its light all around; it is perceived by a number of minds which might be increased or decreased without changing the nature or amount of the light itself, and without modifying the perception of any individual mind. *In action*, on the contrary, *the self is considered as a centre* radiating its energy in various directions, sometimes at random, sometimes also for a purpose and in a chosen direction in order to obtain a certain response and produce a determined result.

IV. Obvious Characteristics of the Self

The obvious characteristics of the self may be reduced to the following: (1) Its states are manifold, complex, ever flowing, and ever changing. (2) Something one, permanent, and identical is the common centre of all mental states.

1. **Diversity.** — (*a*) The *variety* which is observed in the material world is little when compared to that of the spiritual world of the mind. Since knowledge is but the mental representation of things, it is clear that every *difference between objects* perceived in the external world is accompanied by a correlative *difference in the ideas* that represent them. It is true that there is in the world more variety than can be known by the mind, since our knowledge is necessarily limited. But of unnoticed variety nothing can be said, and all the variety which is noticed has its correlative in the mind. In other words, if we assume — as commonsense obliges us to assume — that ideas are representations of things, it must be admitted that, on this ground, there is at least as much diversity in the representing mind as in the represented objects.

But the mind offers another kind of diversity which is not

shared by things and is the mind's exclusive feature. Consciousness is not limited to representative states; it extends to imaginary ideas, to feelings of pleasure and pain, emotions of fear and anger, pride and sympathy, hope and despair, etc., to moral, æsthetic, and religious sentiments, to attention, effort, mental struggle, will, etc. A little reflection suffices to show in all these an endless variety. At times, the field of consciousness is large and varied, but, at other times, it is more restricted and uniform. Consciousness itself may become more and more feeble till apparently it disappears altogether in a dreamless sleep, or in certain abnormal states such as epilepsy or swoons.

(*b*) Moreover, mental processes are always very *complex* and depend on many factors, as will be made clearer when we study them in detail. Their elements cannot be taken apart in the same way that an organism is dissected, but reflection reveals their presence by showing that a mental state, even after it has disappeared, nevertheless influences those that follow. This is clear for memory, imagination, and habit. It is hardly less evident that mental processes are *conditioned* by past experience, surroundings, and education. Here the complexity of the mind baffles all attempts at analysis. Common language seems to recognize this normal complexity and diversity of the mind, since the name "simple-minded" is applied to those whose minds are weak and defective.

(*c*) To be constantly *flowing* and *changing* is also a law of the human mind, and this feature is even more striking in the mind than in the outer world. Things change, it is true, sometimes rapidly and sometimes imperceptibly. Yet many things seem to have great permanence; they may be observed year after year without noticing the slightest change in place, color, shape, size, or any other respect. As to mental processes, all are short-lived. Ideas are in constant flux; they succeed one another rapidly, and no sooner has one appeared than it is pushed out of consciousness by another. A persistent idea is not normal. Try to keep the same idea for some time in the field of consciousness, and you will see how short an interval elapses before a distracting thought enters the mind.

2. **Unity.** — Under the complexity, variety, and flux of mental states are found *unity, identity, and permanence.* There is unity, for all these states belong to the same self; however diverse they may be, all are referred to the same centre, and attributed to the same ego from whose activity they proceed. There is identity and endurance, for, under the constant flux of its conscious states, the self remains, and, under the undulating surface, a deeper reality is found. Such facts as memory and recognition of the past, responsibility for past deeds, remorse and self-approval, just reward and punishment, show that after the passing away of one state something remains, more stable and more enduring; something related to, yet distinct from, the ever-changing surface of consciousness.

PSYCHOLOGY OR THE EMPIRICAL STUDY OF THE MIND

INTRODUCTION

I. THE NATURE OF PSYCHOLOGY

I. Definition and Subject-Matter

1. **The Meaning of Psychology.**—Psychology (ψυχή and λόγος) means etymologically the science of the psyche or soul. Formerly it embraced all the knowledge concerning the soul, its manifestations or processes, its nature, origin, and destiny. Nor was it restricted to the soul as the principle of conscious life; it extended to all vital activities, and dealt with life in all its forms.

But the meaning of psychology, like that of a number of sciences, has been more and more restricted. Psychology is *the study of mental processes*. The higher questions concerning the nature of the mind or soul are referred to what is known as rational psychology or the philosophy of mind. Psychology is an *empirical science*, that is, its statements and laws may be tested and verified by an appeal to some form of experience. Like physics and chemistry, which deal with material facts and laws without considering the essence and origin of matter, it considers only mental processes, but not the first principle from which they originate.

When the term "psychology" is used without qualification, (1) it applies only to the study of the *human* mind. When applied to the study of lower minds, such terms as "animal psychology" or "comparative psychology" are used. (2) It applies only to the study of *mental* life, and does not extend to the functions of organic life. Organic processes, however, may be considered as influencing and determining conscious processes, and this gives rise to the various problems of physiological psychology. (3) It deals chiefly with the *normal* manifestations of the human mind, the others being considered in abnormal psychology or mental pathology.

2. **The Subject-Matter of Psychology** is what is called consciousness, mind, mental processes, or mental states. These terms cannot be defined; they denote facts which must be experienced. All that can be done is to call attention to these facts, classify them and explain them.

(*a*) *Consciousness* is internal or subjective experience. It includes all those states which a man calls his own, and which are experienced by him alone. It is the fact of being aware of something. It includes the complex and manifold experiences by which the state of wakefulness is different from that of a dreamless sleep. Seeing, hearing, thinking, feeling, wishing, desiring, willing, etc., are states of consciousness. However different they may be, all share the common characteristic of being internal experiences. Even in what is called external experience two elements must be distinguished, one, objective or common, the other, subjective or private. A multitude of persons may see the same picture or listen to the same concert. All *perceive the same object*, but each has *his own perception* of it in his own consciousness, distinct from the perception in every other consciousness. This perception of the same thing arouses in one mind ideas, judgments, feelings, and appreciations different from those aroused in other minds. How different the world would appear to a man if it were possible to substitute for his own consciousness the consciousness of another man.

(*b*) The terms *conscious process* and *conscious state* are often used synonymously; their meaning, however, is not quite identical. Conscious or mental *state* applies to the contents of the mind at any given time and apart from their essential flux (static point of view). Conscious or mental *process* represents better the ever-moving and ever-changing character of consciousness (dynamic point of view).

(*c*) *Variations* are observed in the extension of the field of consciousness, the intensity of mental processes, and the rapidity of their succession.

(1) The *field of consciousness*, i.e. the number of ideas actually

present, varies greatly. One idea only may be present, or perhaps a multitude of ideas try to crowd themselves together in the mind. Sometimes consciousness is concentrated on a very narrow field, whereas at other times it is, as it were, diffused over a number of objects.

(2) The *intensity of consciousness*, both as a whole and in its several processes, undergoes marked changes. We may pass almost insensibly from vivid consciousness to unconsciousness, and vice versa. It is like the bright light of the evening sun which decreases little by little till finally it leaves us in the complete darkness of night. As to individual conscious processes, they may at first occupy the very focus or centre of the field of consciousness, and gradually move toward the border till they finally disappear altogether out of consciousness; or, on the contrary, they may move from the dim borders of the field toward its bright centre. Thus at any time the field of consciousness is composed of a central bright part or focus, and of a multitude of other more obscure elements which have been termed the fringe of consciousness. It is a fact of frequent experience that an idea, and especially a feeling, even when not actually thought of, continues nevertheless to influence, tinge, or shade subsequent mental processes.

(3) The *rapidity* with which mental processes succeed one another is also variable. Sometimes the stream seems to pass through a level region; the current is slow and weak, and constant efforts, frequently unsuccessful, are necessary to stimulate the mind and bring up ideas. In other cases, on the contrary, one has to deal with a mighty torrent which no effort can stay. Ideas succeed one another with amazing rapidity, and it is almost impossible to stop any of them. Not only may every one notice these variations in his own consciousness, but certain minds are habitually and naturally slow and sluggish, whereas others are quick, impetuous, and precipitate.

(*d*) The term *mind* (and the corresponding adjective *mental*) has several meanings. In general it is opposed to matter, which is external and located in space, while mind is internal, subjective, and without spatial relations. A body is always located somewhere, and has definite relations with other material substances. An idea, on the contrary, has no size, and, for instance, cannot be said to be on the right or the left of another. "Mind" has a greater extension than "consciousness," for it includes not only actual conscious processes, but also whatever has been or may become conscious, and, in general, it is the capacity for experiencing conscious processes. A narrower signification is given to the term "mind" when we say of a man that he is strong or weak minded, or that he has a great mind.

3. **Relations of Psychology to Other Sciences.** — Psychology endeavors to determine the laws, conditions, relations, etc., of conscious processes. From this are derived its differences from other sciences.

(*a*) It is needless to mention how psychology *differs* from sciences which consider the *world external* to man; what was said above concerning its subject-matter is sufficient. The distinction from the sciences which consider the *human organism*, such as anatomy, physiology, morphology, histology, hygiene, is also obvious. The organism is an object external to the mind, although intimately connected with it. Hence psychology is not directly interested in it, but only indirectly: in general, because the organism influences the mind and is in some manner united with it, and, in particular, because some of its processes are accompanied by, and are indispensable conditions of, consciousness.

As to other sciences which also deal with *internal* and *conscious facts*, they differ from psychology primarily in the points of view from which they regard these facts. Psychology alone considers conscious processes in themselves, *as events*, to find out their nature and the conditions of their appearance. The other mental sciences compare them with something else to which they have to conform. They do not examine what these processes are in themselves and *how they happen*, but *how they should happen* in order to reach intended results. Thus *logic* teaches us how to use rational faculties, deals with intellectual processes only, and lays down the rules that must be observed in order to have consistent thinking. *Epistemology* examines the relations between knowledge and external reality, and endeavors to indicate whether and how far the former is the representation of the latter. *Ethics* considers voluntary processes with the purpose of determining their conformity with certain laws and rules, i.e. of ascertaining whether they are right or wrong. Thus the same mental process, as studied by psychology, may be, for logic, good or fallacious reasoning; for epistemology, true knowledge or error; for ethics, worthy of praise or blame. For psychology, it is simply a mental event.

(*b*) Psychology, however, *needs* the other sciences in so far as they may throw some light on mental processes. The sciences that study the human organism are especially very useful, as they explain some of the essential conditions of consciousness. Hence it will be necessary to study, or at least to recall to mind, the essentials of physiology, especially concerning the brain, the nervous system, and the sense-organs.

4. **The Utility and Importance** of psychology need not be insisted upon. The maxim, "Know thyself," which was inscribed in the temple of Apollo at Delphi, is a fundamental one. *Self-knowledge* is indispensable both for one's private conduct and for one's dealings with other men. *Many sciences and arts*, such as logic, ethics, pedagogy, rhetoric, medicine, politics, history, etc., are based on, or largely indebted to, psychology. All need a thorough acquaintance with the working of the human mind. *Success* in social or business relations, even those of the most ordinary nature, will always be found to depend greatly on the practical and applied knowledge of psychological laws.

II. Method of Psychology

Psychology uses a twofold method, one subjective or introspective, based on the observation of one's own mental states, the other objective, based on the observation of the mental states of other men.

(*a*) *The introspective method is primary and fundamental*, because the experience of a mental process is the only way we have of knowing its nature. Thus no amount of explanation and description will ever give the faintest idea of a sensation of color to the man born blind, or of hearing to the man born deaf. If, from the actions, words, and signs of other men we are enabled to know —

always imperfectly — what mental states they experience, it is only in an indirect manner, from the analogy with those we have experienced ourselves. Hence an important remark for the student. *Nowhere is reflection more essential than in the study of psychology*. To try to understand psychology by merely reading a description of mental states, without verifying this description by introspection, as far as possible, is preposterous. The text-book and the professor are useful guides in directing introspection, but they cannot take its place. The first and most indispensable text-book of psychology is one's own mind.

(*b*) *Introspection must be supplemented and controlled by the objective method*, i.e. by the study of other minds. In psychology, as in every other science, the observation of one instance — and we can observe directly one mind only — is not always a sufficient basis for a valid generalization. The mental processes of others are inferred from the oral or written account which is given of them, or from more or less decisive physiological manifestations. Physiology, pathology, and medicine may give valuable assistance in gathering data.

(*c*) These two sources of information must be used together. Psychology starts from observed facts and endeavors to formulate the laws that govern them. It uses, therefore, what will be called in logic the inductive method.

III. Division of Mental Processes

The classification of mental processes, and the division of psychology which depends on it, may be made from a philosophical or from a psychological point of view.

1. **Philosophical Point of View.** — (*a*) If the distinction and opposition of mind and body were taken for granted, and if it were presupposed that some processes are at once and essentially *both organic and mental*, whereas others are essentially and exclusively *mental* and *spiritual*, we might be justified in distinguishing and opposing also these two groups of processes. But this distinction, even if true and legitimate in itself, is not legitimate as a starting-point because it is far from self-evident. Later on we shall see whether it is a valid conclusion based on observed facts.

Here we are not justified in presupposing a dividing line between sense (organic) and intellect (spiritual), or between lower tendencies (organic) and will (spiritual).

(*b*) If the distinction of *faculties* as *specific energies* of the mind were admitted, we might again be led to a bipartite division into what the scholastics called knowledge and tendency (*appetitus*), or what others term intellectual and active powers. According to this, feelings, emotions, and sentiments do not form a separate group, but share in the nature of both knowledge and *appetitus* without being adequately distinct from *appetitus*. The pleasantness or unpleasantness of a known object is nothing but its conformity or disagreement with tendencies, i.e. a special aspect of *appetitus*. The whole affective life is a resultant of the two specific energies, knowledge and *appetitus*. But here again it must be noted that the doctrine of faculties, when assumed to mean anything beyond the mere classification and grouping of mental processes, is not empirical, and hence cannot be used at the outset of psychology.

2. **Psychological Point of View.** — Modern psychology does not attempt to explain philosophically, but simply to classify, mental processes. The classification which it offers may be more or less superficial and arbitrary, and nevertheless be more useful for, and better adapted to, a mere description of facts without any underlying philosophical assumption.

Although exceptions are to be found, psychologists generally reduce mental processes to three groups: processes of *cognition*, of *feeling*, and of *conation*. The prominence given to feelings by making them a separate class is due to the recognition of their special characteristics and of their importance in the whole psychological life. Feeling is the outcome of the exercise of all forms of activity, and, on the other hand, exercises a very great influence on action.

(*a*) *Knowledge* is the presence in the mind of the idea of an external object; it has both an active and a passive phase; the mind must be first acted upon, and then exercise its own activity. *Feeling* is subjective; it manifests no external reality, and is chiefly passive. Yet it is a powerful incentive to action. If it is too intense, it tends to exclude knowledge and intellectual application.

Moreover, feeling is of itself concerned chiefly with the present, and is largely spontaneous and necessary. *Conation* is essentially active and directed toward the future in order to produce, preserve, or remove a mental state according as it is found desirable or undesirable.

(*b*) These feelings may undergo different variations. The same sound or song (knowledge), at first agreeable (feeling), may, if prolonged (same knowledge), become tedious and thoroughly annoying and painful (different feeling). As a consequence, and according to the complex motives and circumstances influencing human actions, the will may assume diverse attitudes, e.g. it may determine the listener to stay or to leave, to encourage or stop the singer, to make this or that remark, etc.

(*c*) Knowledge of the same thing, because it is more objective, and especially sense-perception, will be more similar in the same and in different minds. Affections are more subjective and changing. Volition is also less permanent and more variable because it may struggle with different feelings.

Such are the main reasons for distinguishing, in psychology, three groups of mental processes; but this is merely a working psychological classification, useful for purposes of study; and it must be remembered that there is a constant overlapping of one group upon the others.

II. THE GENERAL LAWS OF THE MIND

I. A Danger to be Avoided

1. **Necessity of Analysis.** — (*a*) The human intellect cannot reach at once the complete knowledge of anything. Every reality is so complex, its aspects and relations are so numerous, that the mind is always obliged to decompose it, to proceed by analysis, and to take successively different points of view. The physicist, the chemist, the geologist, have to examine separately the various properties and energies of material substances. The historian and the sociologist must consider one after another the different phases of human events. In proportion as an object is more

complex, the necessity of analysis becomes greater. See, for instance, how the human organism has to be analyzed, and how its parts and organs must be studied successively, in order to reach even a superficial knowledge of its functions. We cannot acquire a thorough knowledge of the human organism as a whole without studying first separately the different organs that compose it.

(*b*) Nowhere is this necessity of analysis greater than in psychology. (1) The mind is more *varied* and more *complex* than any material reality. Yet recourse to dissection or actual separation is impossible. Nor can we take apart for single consideration one mental process and hold it in the mind for special examination. A mental process, as it occurs actually, is said to be complex and composed of elementary processes. But these cannot be really separated in the same manner that it is possible to dissect an organism. (2) Material substances are permanent, whereas mental processes are essentially *fleeting* and disappear rapidly. Mental analysis can only be an abstraction and a process of inference. Unlike chemical elements, which are really set apart when the compound is analyzed, elementary mental processes, though influencing actual complex processes, are not experienced by themselves in consciousness.

2. **Danger of Analysis.** — Such a necessity for the human intellect to proceed analytically is not without danger. The danger consists in resting satisfied with partial views, without reconstructing again by synthesis the complete reality, and *in studying the parts* chosen more or less arbitrarily as units, *without perceiving their relations to the whole.* This danger again is greater in the study of the mind than in any other study because solidarity and continuity are most striking in the mental world. One might be led to consider a mental process such as sensation, memory, pleasure, love, anger, desire, choice, action, as isolated, as taking place apart from the others, and even sometimes independently of them, and thus to view, so to say, a dead and unreal mind, not the living, complex, and ever-changing mind. The mind is one. Even if it is endowed with distinct energies or faculties, it must be remembered that these are energies of one and the same mind, that they do not act independently of one another, but that the

activity of one is always mixed with, and influenced by, that of the others.

It is in order to obviate these difficulties, and guard the student against these dangers, that a short outline is given here of some general laws of the mind which must never be lost sight of while studying separately the different mental processes. On this condition only is the knowledge of the real living mind possible.

II. General Processes and Attitudes of the Mind

Several mental attitudes and processes, which will receive a more extensive treatment elsewhere, run through the three groups of mental processes and influence all. Hence a few words will be said of them here. They are attention and association, which are of a most general nature; memory and imagination, which refer especially to the cognitive aspect of consciousness; habit, which refers chiefly to activity in all its forms.

1. **Attention.** — (*a*) By attention is meant the *focussing* of the mind on a special object or conscious process. It includes primarily a mental and sometimes also secondarily an organic attitude, like "stretching the ears," "fixing the gaze," "holding the breath" in expectation. In attention the energy of the mind is more concentrated, less diffused, and hence intensified with regard to the object to which it is applied. This attitude may be compared to the focussing of the sun-rays with a lens. *Distraction*, therefore, is not the contrary of attention, but rather a form of it, for it is attention to an object against the will, the inclination or intention. Distraction, however, may bear on many ideas and thus be equivalent to *diffusion* or *dispersion of mental energy*, which is the mental attitude opposed to attention. In attention the mind looks at one thing intensely; in dispersion it looks at many things, but less intensely at each one.

Attention is not restricted to knowledge, but extends to feelings and actions. Thus a man may concentrate his mind on his sorrows, sufferings, or joys; he may act with or without care, and carefulness is but a form of attention. The power of attention is an indispensable condition of success in any pursuit. The man who cannot pay attention to his own thoughts, actions, or feelings, and to surrounding objects or persons, is doomed to failure.

(*b*) The capacity for arousing attention is called *interest*. Interest depends both on certain conditions of the *object* and on the dispositions of the *subject*. Thus I may study a lesson because I like it and find it interesting; or because, although I dislike it, I am prompted by a sense of duty, or I feel that this study, uninteresting though it may be in itself, is useful or necessary.

Hence, if we consider the cause that produces it, attention is of two kinds: (1) One is the result of *objective interest* alone. The will has no part in it, or may even oppose it. A concert may be found very interesting, and attention is naturally given to it; or an idea may be present in the focus of consciousness in spite of the efforts of the will to banish it. (2) The other is *voluntary;* the interest may be partly in the object, but it is chiefly subjective. The will itself influences the mental activity, and applies it to the consideration of an idea or to a certain action. Thus even things which are found uninteresting in themselves are paid attention to for subjective reasons of utility, necessity, duty, etc.

(*c*) The most important *laws of attention* are the following: (1) *Attention is proportional to interest*, objective and subjective. Sometimes one, and sometimes the other, is predominant. The presence of the subjective factor accounts for the fact that one and the same thing will be of interest to one man and not to another, nor even to the same man at different times. The object remains identical, but the mental dispositions are different. (2) *In the object* interest results from several qualities or properties, among which may be mentioned newness, unusualness in size, color, intensity, change, etc. *In the subject* it depends on education, habits, character, actual dispositions of the mind, ideals, aspirations, etc. When a man wants to call the attention of others to anything, he has to take all these into account. A good illustration may be found in the art of advertising. (How? . . . Where? . . When? . . . By what means? . . . is advertising done?) A more particular instance is that of the orator who varies the intensity and pitch of his voice and the nature of his gestures. Sometimes a thundering voice and sometimes a low whisper will be effective in making the listener attentive. (Why?) (3) *Attention does not remain constant* in the same direction for a long period of time. Little by little it decreases and disappears unless its object changes or some new aspect is discovered in it (e.g. . . . ?). (4) *The intensity of attention varies in inverse ratio to the number of objects* attended to: "Pluribus intentus minor est ad singula sensus." Jugglers know how to divert the spectator's attention so that the way in which they perform their tricks of legerdemain will not be detected. Pickpockets choose the psychological moment at which their prospective victim's attention is absorbed. . . . (Why? . . . Find other instances.)

(*d*) From these principles it is clear that, besides *physical and physiological obstacles* to attention, such as surroundings, temperament, health, etc., which it is not always possible to remove, there are *psychological obstacles*, such as mental restlessness or the incapacity for the mind of applying itself to one object, mental sluggishness or the incapacity of making an effort in order to bring the energy of the mind into play. It is important to correct these defects and to cultivate the power of attention. For children the only source of attention is objective interest, and the teacher must always remember it in his lessons and explanations. As the mind develops it becomes capable also of voluntary attention, which is the more important since by it we attend for a purpose and in order to reach an end. The power of attention must be increased by daily practice. How many fail in life because they "notice" nothing, and are unable to concentrate their mental energy on the objects which should be of interest to them!

2. **Memory and Imagination.** — After it has been experienced, a mental state can be recalled into the mind. Not that the same identical process which took place in the past can again take place at present; in this sense that which is passed never comes back. But I may be aware that the process which I now experience is similar to the one which I experienced yesterday; that I now see, hear, consider, or feel the same thing as formerly. This power of reproduction is exercised in memory (when the mind is aware of

the fact of reproduction), and in imagination (when in fact there is reproduction, but without the consciousness of the fact that it is a reproduction). Not only knowledge, but also feelings and conscious activities, may be reproduced in the mind.

3. **Association of Ideas.** — Memory and imagination depend on association. We know from personal experience that an idea is not recalled at random, but is suggested by others which call it back to consciousness. Ideas seem to be linked together so that, if one is reproduced, it has a tendency to reproduce another. Like memory and imagination, association refers chiefly to knowledge, yet an idea will recall not only another idea with which it is connected, but also the feeling or action by which it was accompanied. The sight of an enemy yesterday was accompanied by a feeling of anger. To-day the thought of the event tends to call forth not merely the idea that I was angry, but also this feeling itself.

4. **Habit.** — What association does for ideas habit does for actions. In fact, habit and association present the same essential features, and association is but one form of habit. The action which has become habitual is performed automatically, without effort, frequently even without distinct consciousness. Before acquiring the habit of piano-playing, for instance, every single action (vision, hearing, appropriate motions) of which the complete series is composed, required a distinct effort. When the action has become habitual, the result is more perfect and obtained more easily. Once the series is started, all the other complex elements follow in their order. Habit has also a close resemblance with that form of memory which consists in learning by rote. The schoolboy who repeats his lesson several times in order to memorize it establishes a number of associations between words as written or spoken, and between the physiological processes necessary to utter them, so that words uttered by him follow one another in order and automatically. Both mental and organic activities are subject to the law of fixation or habit. We not only have habits of movement, but also habitual views, associations, and mental attitudes.

III. General Laws of the Mind

Besides the general processes and attitudes just mentioned, there are general laws that govern processes belonging to different groups. They are the laws of solidarity, continuity, and unity amid multiplicity. These laws should be constantly kept in mind, as applications of them will be found at every step.

1. **Solidarity.** — By solidarity is meant the mutual dependence of all mental processes.

(*a*) The use of the analytical process in psychology may be the source of great errors, if one fails to notice that it isolates artificially that which is in reality always connected and associated. The mind is like an organism or a well-ruled society in which all organs or all classes depend on the others for their functions or their subsistence. *Mental life, in its various manifestations, is one*, and none of its manifestations is independent of the others.

(*b*) All psychical phenomena are *dependent on*, and *influenced by*, the general processes and attitudes mentioned above: attention, memory, association, and habit. The whole progress and development of the mind is conditioned by them.

(*c*) All mental processes *influence* one another. (1) *Cognition* is the basis of most feelings. We are pleased or displeased, and experience various emotions according to the ideas that are present in the mind. Moreover, to know, or to study in order to know, is in itself an important source of feelings. The will is essentially guided by motives, i.e. by the results of reflection and reasoning. The actions which are not voluntary are frequently the consequences of impulses resulting from inferior forms of knowledge. (2) *Feelings*, being a source of interest, are also a source of attention and application, and hence very important in acquiring knowledge. They also often influence opinions and beliefs. What a man likes is readily accepted by him as true; he is willing to believe the calumnies which he hears about an enemy, but admits his good qualities more reluctantly. It is no less clear that feelings influence activity, since we act in order to obtain some good and for the satisfaction of some desire. How much greater and more effective is our activity for a task which we like than for one which we are compelled to do against our inclination. (3) *The will* is the power that rules — more or less perfectly — the other mental energies. It controls attention, commands a patient and impartial research, or, by its precipitation, causes the mind to assent without sufficient grounds, and is thus partly responsible for resulting errors. On the other hand, man endeavors to conform his actions to his thoughts. Although the will has not perfect control over the feelings, it nevertheless exercises a great power in checking, suppressing, or fostering them.

(*d*) Finally, there is a *solidarity between the mind and the organism.* (1) The conditions of the organism, age, sex, temperament, food and drink, health or disease, present physiological condition and disposition, have their counterpart in the activities of the mind. (2) The mind influences the organism in many ways, e.g. emotions are accompanied by various physiological phenomena; mental application may cause a headache; the will controls many movements of the body, etc.

2. **Continuity.** — (*a*) In the perpetual flux of mental life we distinguish certain waves as more prominent, and consider them separately. This conception of mental states may be misleading, and it must be remembered that *consciousness is not made up of parts*, but is always flowing like a stream. In the state of wakefulness at least, mental processes are always going on without intermission, even if, for purposes of study, only the most prominent and those that are better characterized are attended to. The break which seems to occur in a dreamless sleep, epilepsy, fainting, and similar states, is bridged over by memory which connects the part preceding with the part following the interruption.

(*b*) At any one time *the contents of consciousness are complex*, including a focus and a fringe. Thus while I am writing, my mind is concentrated upon the ideas to be expressed — the schoolboy's mind might be concentrated on the manner in which he has to hold the pen and form every letter; at the same time I have an indistinct consciousness of papers and books around me, of the little noise of the pen as it runs over the paper, the ticking of the clock, the singing of the birds outside; of sensations of touch in the fingers holding the pen, the arm resting on the table, the parts of the body that are in contact with other objects; of temperature; of my whole organic disposition; of images fleeting through my mind; of an emotion experienced a short time ago, etc.

(*c*) Generally the contents of consciousness *are not renewed all at once;* its elements pass from the focus to the fringe, and vice versa; some disappear altogether, while others persist and enter the succeeding complex mental state. As an instance of such persistence may be mentioned a violent emotion, e.g. of anger, which may remain in the background of consciousness for a long time and continue to influence more or less apparently many successive processes. In this respect, the mind is somewhat like the organism, the whole of which is renewed after a certain length of time, but through changes that take place gradually, more rapidly in some parts, more slowly in others.

(*d*) As a consequence of this fact, it follows that the nature of the contents of consciousness *depends on previous contents.* This is true even where the direction of the stream seems to be modified suddenly. The new state is different according as it follows different thoughts, emotions, or mental efforts. For instance, the impression produced by a sudden clap of thunder varies according to the circumstances in which I find myself when I hear it. Differences in the contents of my mind will cause me to experience different feelings when a friend calls on me unexpectedly.

Not only is there continuity between immediately succeeding states, but habit, memory, and generally subconsciousness, are like so many permanent *links of continuity*, making mental life one uninterrupted whole, or like so many reservoirs into which all mental activities bring some modifying element, and owing to which, accordingly, every new mental activity is modified. Thus the mind may be compared to a water reservoir into which all ingoing streams would bring their own special and constantly changing qualities, and from which outgoing streams would in consequence derive these new qualities. We cannot experience two mental states perfectly identical, since, on the one hand, the actual mental background is always different in some respects, and, on the other, the new state is modified by past influences.

(*e*) When in a series of objects arranged according to gradually increasing diversity two extremes are compared, the differences are striking; but if two objects placed in immediate succession are compared, the differences are hardly noticeable. Between any two colors, intermediate tinges may be inserted passing insensibly from one to the other; between a giant and a dwarf a series of men with slowly decreasing sizes make an easy transition, etc. The same is true of the mind: between extremes a number of transitional forms are found. The abstract definitions of mental attention and mental dispersion are easily understood, and their concrete applications also are easily verified when two attitudes far apart in this respect are compared. But if the diffusion be restricted gradually, it is impossible to point out the beginning of the attentive attitude. Sensations of vision, sound, taste, smell, temperature, etc., may be arranged in series varying imperceptibly according to quality or intensity. Perfect memory and complete forgetfulness are extremes between which may be inserted an infinite number of partial, more or less vague and obscure, remembrances. In a more complex sphere, the insane man in an asylum has mental defects by which he clearly differs from what he was when normal; yet if his condition has developed gradually, we cannot indicate the precise moment where insanity began. And in a series of minds passing from a normal to an abnormal condition, extremes alone are recognizable; the limit separating the normal from the abnormal cannot be indicated. Examples could be multiplied for all transitions from one process or series of processes to another.

3. **Unity amid Multiplicity.** (*a*) *From what is manifold in nature one conscious state may result*, e.g. a large number of vibrations of ether, air, or molecules, produces in consciousness one sensation of light, sound, or temperature. Moreover, the mind strives to unify external experiences by constantly reducing them to more general laws and principles.

(*b*) *The mind tends to homogeneity and consistency.* Self-contradiction, i.e. the presence in the mind of irreconcilable judgments, is painful. Attempts are made to find the means of reconciling them or to see which should be eliminated. Moreover, the mind strives after harmony between itself and the external world of things and persons, either by trying to conform its ideas to the reality of things and to adapt itself to surroundings, or by trying to conform the environment to its own desires and purposes. Consistency, harmony, uniformity, are sources of pleasure; dissension is a source of unhappiness.

(*c*) Attention has been called to the *complexity, variety, changes, and succession* of mental states. It is a fact of experience, however, that *these always form a part of a group* which is personal. There is no mental process which is not somebody's, and which is not claimed by some person as his own. Isolated as they are from mental processes which belong to other minds, my own mental processes are all within the unity of my own self.

(*d*) Hence *the thinking subject is one*. Consciousness is not simply the existence of thought, but also of *my* thinking, and *I* am the centre to which all thoughts are referred and attributed as their source and as the subject toward which all converge. This holds for past as well as for present states. The self appears not only as one, but also as identical under many changes. To say "*I think*" is true, but it is also true to say "*I thought*." Obviously there is something underlying the stream of consciousness. A man remembers his past, feels responsible for his actions, prepares his future. Memory, responsibility, foresight, are signs that, even if the states of mind disappear, the mind itself is a more permanent and a deeper reality.

CHAPTER I

KNOWLEDGE

Preliminary Remarks

1. **What is Knowledge?** — (*a*) The mental state called knowing cannot be defined strictly. It is obvious to all men, and a definition would be useful only inasmuch as it would be known, i.e. inasmuch as it would imply the experience of the very state to be defined. The following explanations are given only to make this experience clearer. *To know is to be aware of something* which is called the object of knowledge. In every cognitive process is implied essentially an antithesis of something (object) which faces or lies opposite to (*ob-iacere*) the mind and of the knowing mind or subject (*sub-iacere*) which is modified by the knowing process, that is, which acquires a new idea or the perception of a new relation.

(*b*) The *object of knowledge* may be internal or external; it includes not only external things, but also mental states. Thus a feeling or an emotion may not only be experienced as such, i.e. felt, but it may be analyzed, studied, recognized, and known; and the same is true of actions. It may be impossible in many cases to draw a well-defined line separating knowledge from other mental processes which are objects of knowledge, but nevertheless we understand the distinction between feeling and knowing that we feel, acting and knowing that we act. And even in cases of intense feeling or activity, the awareness or knowledge of them may almost disappear; a man feels and acts, and his whole consciousness seems to be absorbed in these processes so that he does not even reflect that he is experiencing them.

(*c*) In knowledge, subject and object are opposed, yet closely related. In fact, the known object must, in some manner, be present within the knowing subject, not according to its natural reality, but in a special mental or ideal form. To know a thing is to have in the mind an idea or representation of it. The fact of its being known changes in no way the reality of the object; the mind alone is modified by the acquisition of an idea which it did not possess previously.

2. **There are Several Kinds of Knowledge.** — (*a*) Knowledge is *actual* when the idea is present in consciousness; *habitual* when the idea which has disappeared from consciousness can be recalled. In the former case a man actually thinks of what he knows; in the latter, he does not actually think of it, but can do so. Immediately upon completing the demonstration of a geometrical theorem I have the actual knowledge of its truth. The following day, when my mind is occupied with other matters, I still know it although actually thinking of something else.

(*b*) (1) To know may mean simply to be *acquainted with*, to be able to recognize. Thus I know a man by sight after meeting him more or less frequently; I know his character after a more or less prolonged intercourse with him. This form of knowledge reaches the object *directly;* it implies perception and recognition. (2) To know means also to *understand*. In this sense knowledge reaches the object *indirectly;* it supposes the work of intellectual comparison, judgment, and reasoning. Thus I may know many things about a man whom I have never seen. A blind man who never perceived light may nevertheless know several things about it, like its laws of reflection or refraction.

(*c*) The term "knowledge" is applied sometimes to the *process of knowing* (subjective sense), and sometimes to the *known object* (objective sense). I may speak of my knowledge of chemistry, and of the science of chemistry as a body of knowledge.

(*d*) *Knowledge* is frequently opposed to *opinion* and *belief*. The former is more certain and has a stronger and firmer objective basis; the latter is more subjective and depends also on personal mental dispositions.

(*e*) The cognitive faculties are (1) presentation (sensation and perception), (2) representation (memory and imagination), (3) conception or abstract representation, (4) judgment, which is obtained either immediately (intuitive) or mediately by reasoning. Hence the division of the present chapter into four articles, to which a fifth will be added on language, which is the expression of knowledge.

A simple representation as such is neither true nor false, but only in so far as it is truly or falsely affirmed or denied to be the accurate representation of such or such an object. Hence knowledge proper is found only in judgment.

3. **Complexity of Knowledge.** — It must be kept in mind that the cognitive processes just mentioned are not isolated, but work together. A simple and commonplace instance may be given to illustrate the complexity of knowledge and of the many processes which it implies. "I see my friend speaking to a policeman." This is about as simple an experience as can be imagined. It takes place all at once. Without reflection or hesitation, in what seems to be one single act of perception, I affirm that "I see my friend talking to a policeman." What is so simple now is in reality very complex in its analysis and genesis. If the many elementary processes are not now present in consciousness, it is owing to habit and to what will be called later the education of the senses. As we shall see more clearly in the following articles, it has not always been so. Let us now briefly analyze our statement; the analysis will be justified later.

"*I see.*" Directly and primitively vision gives to the mind only *sensations* of light and color. In the present case, if by "I see" I mean a sensation, i.e. a primitive and elementary process, what I see is a certain surface colored in this or that way. But the educated eye reports much more than this. There are additions to the primitive fact, that make the present mental state much more complex.

"*My friend.*" A certain familiarity and habit make me recognize the form of a man, and, although I see only about one half, my *imagination* readily supplies the part which I do not see. Moreover, certain signs, e.g. the fact of his being in the street, of moving the limbs or lips, of facing another person, etc. (facts which are also perceived owing to a number of past associations and to the education of the senses), make me infer that I have before my eyes a real man, and not a mere image or statue of a man. My imagination again supplies implicitly a whole group of sensations of sound, touch, etc., of which this man, under certain circumstances, would be the cause for me. All this supposes that I have seen, heard, etc., other men before.

When I refer to this man as "my friend," I suppose an act of *recognition*. This is not simply a man, but it is this man with whom I had such or such relations, with whom I am in sympathy, who did this or that, etc. Many signs may help me to recognize him, but, strictly speaking, I do not see my friend; I see only certain colors and shape, I perceive a man, and I recognize or infer that it is my friend. It is evident that the relation of friendship cannot be perceived by any sense: it is an implicit *judgment* supposing many mental elements past and present.

"*Speaking*." I may hear a sound, I cannot see it. Here I perceive certain attitudes, gestures, and motions which, in my experience, are associated with sensations of hearing. We have here again an *inference*, an *induction*, an *implicit reasoning*, which, stated explicitly, would run thus: "Such or such visual sensations in the past have always been accompanied by corresponding auditory sensations when I was within hearing distance. Now I experience the same visual sensations. Therefore the man is speaking, although, on account of the distance, I do not hear him."

"*To a policeman*." Here again we have a very complex perception, as may be gathered from the preceding remarks.

This is a very short and summary analysis of a simple statement, and every statement which we make is of the same complex nature. Let us now proceed to examine the various stages of cognition, and thereby see how the mind passes from simple to complex processes of knowledge.

ARTICLE I. SENSE PRESENTATION

I. SENSATION

I. Sensation in General

1. **The Nature of Sensation.** — Sensation is the *first* or *elementary mental process;* first, because mental life begins with sensation; elementary, because other mental states are based on and suppose sensation. Sensations are therefore real constituents of complex states, but they are only abstractions when considered in themselves as simple, and apart from the complex states. The normal adult does not experience simple sensations; his so-called sensations are always complex processes, and are influenced by other past or present sensations of the same or of different kind.

Perception is the *reference of sensations to an external object.* It supposes several presentative and representative elements, and includes not only primitive data of the senses, but also results from the education of the senses. The knowledge which we have of sensations is not obtained directly from introspection, but rather from inferences based on introspection. Frequently, however, the distinction between sensation and perception is not observed in ordinary language, and both terms are used indifferently.

2. **Definition of Related Terms.** — (1) *Sense* denotes the ability to experience a certain class of sensations. Thus we speak of the sense of vision or of the sense of touch. (2) The being which is capable of experiencing sensations is called *sentient* or *sensitive*, and this is opposed to inanimate or vegetal. There are evidently many degrees of perfection in sensitive life. In a more general way, sentient and sensitive are synonymous with conscious, and refer to any form of consciousness. (3) *Sensitive* frequently refers also to one who is excitable, impressionable, or who is easily affected by external influences. When applied to a special sense, it denotes a special keenness. (4) The adjective *sensible* is more ambiguous on account of its several meanings. It may be synonymous with sentient; or it denotes a sound judgment and a prudent estimate of things, persons, and events. Again, a man is sensible

of a thing when he is aware or persuaded of it. Finally, the term "sensible" may be used objectively of a thing that can be perceived by the senses. (5) *Sensuous* means that which pertains to the senses. Thus we speak of sense-perception or of sensuous perception. (6) *Sensual* applies especially to one who indulges in the lower tendencies and pleasures of the senses. (7) *Sensibility*, *sentiency*, *sensitivity* and *sensitiveness* may be used to denote the capacity of experiencing sensations, but sensibility signifies more particularly a special susceptibility to pleasure, pain, and emotion, while sensitiveness denotes a special mental or nervous excitability or keenness of the senses.

3. **Internal and External Sensations.** — Sensations are commonly classified into internal and external, but the meaning given to internal sensations to-day is not the same as formerly. *External sensations* are those by which the mind enters into direct relation with external things, e.g. seeing, hearing, etc. They are exercised through sense-organs located at the periphery of the organism.

Formerly, *internal sensations* meant the mental processes by which the mind enters into relation directly with something mental, and indirectly with external concrete realities. Their organ is internal, namely, the brain. Thus memory and imagination were called internal senses because they deal immediately with mental images, and only mediately with the things of which they are images. To these two internal senses two others were added, the *sensus communis* or central sense which gathers together the various impressions received from the external senses, and the *aestimativa* which enables the mind to discern the good or bad, useful or harmful qualities of objects (akin to instinct in animals).

To-day, by *internal sensations* are meant those sensations which do not refer to the external world, but to some internal states, especially of the organism, like hunger, thirst, fatigue, etc. They are vague, hard to localize, and generally indicative of physical conditions and needs. Hence they are also more subjective than external sensations. The division of sensations into internal and external almost coincides with the division into special and general or organic sensations. Internal sensations are closely related to the affective life, and in many cases they are feelings rather than cognitions.

II. Internal or General Sensations

1. **Characteristics.** — These sensations are called *internal* and *organic* because the information which they give refers to states and changes within the body; *general* or *common* because they have no special end-organs and are hard to localize. *Cœnesthesis* is a more technical term to express the same idea. Internal sensations are numerous, complex, vague, difficult to analyze, localize, and discriminate. As cognitions they are in themselves of but little value; yet habit and experience enable us to assign to them external or internal causes, e.g. we may know what food has caused a painful digestion, where nervousness or fatigue comes from, etc.

2. **The Main Groups** of internal sensations are: (1) The *vital sense*, or general sensations of life, of the whole living organism, of its position and changes of position, its general condition of strength or weakness, activity or sleepiness, etc. (2) Sensations connected with the *nervous* system, its excitability and tension, or, on the contrary, inactivity and laziness, nervousness and neurasthenia. (3) Sensations connected with the *muscular* system. Some are more general, like the tension or relaxation of the muscles, and general fitness or fatigue. Others are more special, like local fatigue, or the sensations experienced in executing various movements. (4) Sensations connected with the *digestive* system; hunger, thirst, repletion, nausea, easy or difficult digestion. (5) Sensations connected with the *respiratory* system, such as facility or difficulty in breathing, abundance or scarcity of air, its qualities, like purity or foulness, choking, stifling, etc. (6) Sensations connected with the *circulatory* system, like those of blushing or growing pale, of active circulation in the whole organism or in some of its parts.

III. External Sensations

(*a*) External sensations are experienced through the *sense-organs*. A sense-organ includes three essential elements: (1) a peripheral apparatus, like the eye, ear, nerve-endings in the skin, etc.; (2) a sensory or afferent nerve connecting the peripheral structure with (3) the centre, which is some determined portion of the brain. The study of the anatomy and functions of these belongs to physiology, and, while studying sensations, it will be useful to review the physiology of the senses as well as the physics of sound, light, etc.

(*b*) The *factors of sensation* are: (1) *Physical*, i.e. something external (e.g. vibrations of ether or air) which acts on the organism. It is called the stimulus of sensation, and its action on the appropriate organ is the stimulation. (2) *Physiological*. The organ at the periphery is especially adapted to receive the stimulation proper to each sense, and the impression thus received is transmitted to the brain by the afferent nerve. (3) *Psychological*. Consciousness is intimately connected with, and depends on, the physiological processes. Yet it cannot be identified with them, for consciousness is something altogether different from a movement, a vibration, or a chemical change, such as take place in the organism.

External senses are reduced to five classes: smell, taste, touch, hearing, and vision.

A. Smell and Taste

1. **Common Features.** — (1) These two senses are closely connected and generally work together. Smell, however, is more independent of taste than taste of smell. It has been ascertained that when the sense of smell is impaired taste is also less perfect, and in some cases it is difficult to say whether a sensation is due primarily to smell or to taste, e.g. spices are "tasted" chiefly through the sense of smell. (2) In both cases the sensations are vague and lack definiteness. Feeling, i.e. their pleasantness or unpleasantness, is the predominant feature. (3) These sensations are not easily classified, and the reason why a substance smells or tastes differently from another is not known. (4) As verbs, the terms "smell" and "taste" are transitive or intransitive; as substantives, they apply to both the sensation or mental state and to the physical stimulus. I speak not only of my sensa-

tions of smell and taste, but also of the smell of a rose or the taste of an orange. (5) Smell and taste are not so useful for intellectual life as the other sensations, but are very useful for organic life, especially in animals. Their very position at the entrance of the respiratory and digestive systems is suggestive of these functions. Thus the sense of smell may give warning of the presence of impure or poisonous air; that of taste, of the presence of some injurious element in food.

2. **Smell.** — Its organ is the mucous membrane lining the upper part of the nasal cavity where the olfactory nerves are distributed.

(*a*) *Odors* are the object of the sense of smell. It is impossible to classify them and to give definitions of the several odors. When we speak of them, we refer them to the substances to which they generally belong. Thus we say of a substance that it smells like the rose or the violet, or we use general terms like "fragrant," "nauseous," etc.

(*b*) In order to have sensations of smell, emanations from odorous substances must be carried to the olfactory organs through the air. Liquids as such, if they come in contact with the organs of smell without air, produce no olfactory sensation. Breathing draws these emanations through the nasal fossæ, and this is done more effectively by sniffing. A very small amount of an odorous substance is sufficient to produce a sensation of smell. Thus the smallest particle of musk will give its characteristic smell to clothes for years. The action of the odorous substance on the olfactory organs is probably of a chemical nature.

(*c*) One of the important features of the sense of smell is that it easily becomes *fatigued*. The same continuous stimulation makes it dull with regard to this special odor. When entering a kitchen or a room filled with foul air, we are conscious at first of certain sensations which we cease to experience after some time spent there.

3. **Taste.** — *Organ:* The papillæ of the mucous membrane covering the superior surface of the tongue. The circumvallate papillæ at the base of the tongue seem to be the most important.

(*a*) *Savors* or *flavors* are the object of the sense of taste. For want of a better division they are commonly reduced to four types: sweet, bitter, acid, and salt. Their action on the organ of taste is also probably of a chemical nature.

(*b*) In order to have sensations of taste, the sapid substance must be soluble. Only fluids, i.e. dissolved substances, are perceived. The saliva, and the act of pressing the substance against the palate or the gums with the tongue, help the process of solution.

(*c*) Like the sense of smell, the sense of taste is subject to *fatigue*. It is also greatly affected by *contrast*. Every one may notice, for instance, that the same cup of tea which has a very sweet taste while eating meat, bread, or pickles, seems almost bitter while eating candy or sweets.

B. Touch

The sense of touch includes three main groups of sensations: sensations of contact and pressure, sensations of temperature, and kinesthetic sensations. For contact and pressure, and for temperature, its organ consists of the papillæ of the derma or true skin. For kinesthetic sensations, it consists of the numerous nervous fibrillæ found in the muscular system. The distinction of the organs of contact and pressure from those of temperature is not clear physiologically, that is, organs special to each group cannot be pointed out. Yet they seem to be distinct, for, in certain diseases, the sense of touch proper may disappear while the sense of temperature persists, and vice versa.

1. **Contact and Pressure.** — These two sensations go together. Evidently there can be no pressure without contact, and most sensations of contact are also accompanied by some pressure.

(*a*) The *qualities* perceived by contact are hardness and softness, roughness and smoothness. All these may be reduced to resistance; hardness and softness are degrees of resistance; roughness and smoothness are its qualities and its localization on the same surface.

(*b*) The different parts of the body are not equally sensitive. The points of a pair of dividers kept at the same distance from each other will be felt as two or as one according to the place to which they are applied. This has been called *discriminative sensibility*, or the skin's sense of locality. It varies from about 1 mm. (0.039 inch) for the tip of the tongue to about 68 mm. for the skin of the middle of the back, the upper arm and leg. Discriminative sensibility may be greatly improved by exercise.

2. **Temperature.** — (*a*) "Hot" and "cold" are terms used in relation to our own temperature. Sensations of temperature depend on the physiological zero, i.e. the temperature of the skin on the part of the body where the sensation is experienced. An object having this temperature is felt as neither hot nor cold. The physiological zero is not identical with blood temperature, but may be higher or lower.

(*b*) *Contrast* is an important factor in the appreciation of temperature. The temperature of a room which one enters seems colder or warmer according as one comes from a warmer or a colder place. The same water may be almost burning for a cold hand, and only warm for the hand which has just experienced a higher temperature.

(*c*) Within certain limits, the sense of temperature is subject to *adaptation*. The water which at first seemed very hot to the hand becomes more tolerable if the contact be prolonged. Some heat being imparted to the organism, the contrast disappears, and thus it is seen that this phenomenon is connected with the one just mentioned.

(*d*) Temperatures most readily appreciated are those between 10 and 45 degrees Centigrade (50–111 Fahrenheit). Extreme heat and cold produce painful sensations in many respects similar. The finger dipped in boiling water or in liquid air experiences a sensation which might be called "burning" in both cases.

(*e*) The organs for heat seem to be different from those for cold. There are "cold spots" and "heat spots," as may be ascertained easily by pressing gently on the skin with the point of a lead pencil. In some spots no distinct sensation of temperature is experienced; in other spots there is a sensation of cold. Or if the point be previously warmed, sensations of heat are experienced only in some spots.

3. **Kinesthetic or Muscular Sensations** may be reduced in part to internal sensations (e.g. muscular tension), and in part to

external sensations (when they give information concerning the external world, e.g. weight). They include two main groups: sensations of movement, including the sensations of skin, joints, muscles, and tendons; sensations of strain or resistance, e.g. muscular effort in lifting a weight.

C. Hearing

1. **The Organs of Hearing** consist of the ear; external ear (*pinna* or auricle, and auditory canal or *meatus*); middle ear or *tympanum*, separated from the external ear by the *membrana tympani* and including the three auditory bones; internal ear or labyrinth (vestibule, semicircular canals, and *cochlea*) communicating with the middle ear by the two *foramina*.

The external ear gathers air vibrations and transmits them to the middle ear by vibrating the *membrana tympani*. The middle ear serves for the transmission of vibrations, the ossicles diminishing their amplitude but increasing their intensity. The organ proper of hearing is the internal ear where the acoustic nerve is distributed, partly in the semicircular canals, and partly in the *cochlea* in which the complex and interesting organ of Corti is found.

2. **Sound** is the stimulus of the sense of hearing. Physically it consists of air vibrations. According as these follow one another in regular or irregular succession, we have musical sounds or noises.

(*a*) Sound possesses: (1) *Intensity* or loudness, which depends on the force or amplitude of the vibrations. (2) *Pitch*, which depends on the number of vibrations in a given unit of time. The number of perceivable vibrations, i.e. the range of hearing, is from about 16 to 38,000 a second for an ordinary ear. (3) *Quality*, timbre, or, as it is sometimes called, the color of the tone, which depends on the combination of secondary vibrations or overtones with the fundamental tone.

(*b*) The *discrimination of sounds* of different pitch is susceptible of great improvement by exercise. For simultaneous sounds the sensitiveness is not so great as for successive sounds. With a little exercise the average ear may perceive the difference in pitch between two successive sounds whose number of vibrations are in the ratio 200: 201. A very keen ear may perceive the difference when the number of vibrations is in the ratio 1000: 1001.

D. Vision

1. **The Organ of Vision is the Eye.**—(1) The *enclosing membranes*, protective and nutritive, are the sclerotic (in front, cornea) and the choroid (in front, iris). (2) The *refracting media* are the aqueous humor, the crystalline lens, and the vitreous humor. (3) *Accessory structures* are the various muscles both of the eyeball and the interior eye (especially those which regulate the convexity of the lens and the aperture of the pupil), the eyelids, and the lachrymal glands. (4) The *organ proper* of vision is the retina, and among the eight or nine layers which are distinguished in the retina that of rods and cones is the most important. The retina is the expansion of the optic nerve spreading within the eyeball close to the choroid. The *macula lutea* or yellow spot, and chiefly the pit in its centre or *fovea centralis*, is the place where the rays of light fall in clear vision. The blind spot is the entrance itself of the optic nerve in the eyeball. Rays of light falling there are not perceived.

2. **The Stimulus of Vision** is *light*, which physically consists of ether vibrations.

By *refraction* the white light of the sun is decomposed into the seven colors of the spectrum. The differences in color depend on the rapidity and length of the waves, these two being in inverse ratio. Substances are white or black according as they reflect all or none of the rays of light. They are variously colored according as they absorb some rays of the spectrum and reflect others.

The union of the seven spectral colors is not necessary to produce white. Two colors, called *complementary*, give the same result: red and bluish-green, orange and greenish-blue, yellow and ultramarine blue, greenish-yellow and violet.

3. **Special Features.** — (*a*) The sensation of vision does not disappear immediately after the stimulus is withdrawn, but continues for a short time; e.g. the fiery trail of a shooting-star; a luminous point rotating rapidly, as the end of a kindled stick,

produces the impression of a luminous disk. If you look intensely at a bright lamp for a few seconds, and put out the light, you will continue to see the flame in the dark.

(*b*) *Color blindness*, or the incapacity of the eye to discern one or several colors, is more frequent than is commonly supposed. Red is the color for which blindness is more generally found. Hence the necessity of careful tests for locomotive engineers and others who have to distinguish colored signals.

(*c*) An *after-image* is a phenomenon of vision produced after the stimulus has disappeared. The after-image may be positive, as in the cases mentioned above (under *a*), or negative, due to the fatigue of the retina. The negative after-images of dark objects are relatively bright, and vice versa; those of colored objects present the complementary color. After gazing fixedly at the bright window about a half minute, turn your eyes toward the white wall or ceiling, and you will see the window again, but the pane will be darker than the frame. After looking intensely at a bright and glossy red cardboard triangle, look again at the white ceiling; a green triangle will be seen, the dimensions of which will vary according to the distance of the wall which is used as a screen. If the wall or ceiling is not white, the color of the after-image will be different.

(*d*) *Contrast* in brightness and colors is very important, and the harmonious arrangement of colors is to be observed in painting, decorating, dressing, etc.

IV. Number and Comparison of the Senses

1. **Number.** — The question of the number of the senses is limited to external senses. On account of their complexity and vagueness, no attempt is made to number internal senses, and psychologists follow different classifications. For the external senses, on the contrary, we have the traditional division into five senses as mentioned above. Some psychologists, however, pay little or no attention to this classification which they find inadequate. The present question is secondary and of minor importance, yet it may be of interest to see how solutions have been attempted.

(*a*) If we take a *psychological* basis of division, namely, the different qualities of sensations as mental states, we are at once confronted with the difficulty of determining the meaning of quality when applied to sensations. A sensation of red is qualitatively different from a sensation of blue; the sound of the flute from that of thunder, etc. It is asserted even that every change in intensity is also a change in quality. Hence on this basis alone a classification is impossible. Perhaps quality may be used in a generic sense, all colors forming one kind of quality; all sounds, another, and so on. But this is not purely psychological; sensations here are said to have the same generic quality because they are experienced through the same sense organ (physiology), or because their stimuli are of the same nature (physics).

(*b*) If we take a *physiological* basis of division, namely, the number of the different sense organs, we have first to define what is meant by a special organ. Double organs like eyes and ears are counted as one. Why? Partly because they have the same structure and functions, partly also because they are affected by the same stimuli (this is not physiological, but physical). Moreover, what is one special organ? Physiologists commonly hold that there are within the eye special organs for the perception of each of the fundamental colors, that the organs of touch are distinct from those of temperature, that different qualities of taste are perceived through different papillæ, etc. Hence the number of sense organs can hardly be determined. We may, however, admit five generic kinds of organs, counting as one those that are close together and have the same outer and accessory structures. For instance, even if every fundamental color is perceived through different retinal endings, the eye is one organ with only one set of enclosing membranes, refracting media, etc.

(*c*) To argue from the number of distinct *physical* stimuli is to beg the question, since we are aware of the stimulus only through the sensation. To say that there are five groups of irreducible stimuli simply means that we experience five kinds of sensations, and this is the very question at issue. Physical sciences, however, lend us assistance by reducing all colors to ether vibrations, heat to molecular vibrations, etc.

(*d*) Let us conclude that the commonly received division of the external senses may be retained on condition that it be understood as a generic division under which are found distinct subclasses. As such it corresponds to the generic division of physical stimuli and of organs. All colors are referred to the sense of vision because, although blue differs from red, both are ether vibrations, and, although each may have special organs in the retina, these organs belong to the same structure and are parts of the whole complete organ, which is the eye. The same remarks apply to the other sensations.

(*e*) As to the *possibility* of some other sense altogether different from those we have now, it has been asserted by some; but it can be neither proved nor disproved. The question is an idle one. (1) To have a new sense, there should be another stimulus different from those that are known at present. Its existence can only be asserted gratuitously. (2) In certain abnormal states, like somnambulism or hypnotism, a man may perceive things which he does not perceive normally, or in a manner different from that of the normal mind. But no new quality of things is manifested; there is only a special keenness of the senses, or a new mode of perceiving the same qualities. (3) Granting this supposition of another sense, it could not be inferred that things would seem different from what they are now. The new information would not contradict, but complete, the information which we have at present. In the same way, if the power of vision is given to the man born blind, he becomes aware of qualities hitherto unknown to him, but this knowledge does not contradict or invalidate that which he has acquired through the other senses.

2. **The Comparison of the Senses** may be made from different points of view.

(*a*) In reference to *usefulness*. (1) Taste and smell are more closely related to organic sensations and less definite. They give less information concerning the external world. Hence, whereas they may be very useful for organic life, especially in some kinds of animals, they are of little use for intellectual life. (2) Touch, hearing, and sight are the "intellectual" senses; from them are derived the data necessary for the higher mental functions.

Through hearing we receive oral information, which is essential both in early education and in the whole course of life. Touch is the sense on which, in many cases, the other senses depend for the confirmation of the reality of their perceptions; it is of great value in educating them, as will be seen hereafter. In adult life, however, sight seems to be the chief sense, because it enables the mind to receive written information, and, as will be shown when we speak of perception, it embodies the results of touch and the other senses.

(*b*) With regard to the *mode of stimulation*, it may be said that some kind of actual contact is required of the appropriate stimulus with the sense organ. Ether waves, air vibrations, emanations, etc., must act on the organ. Yet a distinction is to be made, if not for the simple sensation, at least for perception. An object cannot be tasted or touched without actual contact with it. On the contrary, it is possible to smell, hear, or see distant odorous, sounding, or luminous bodies, the reach of sight being far greater than that of any other sense.

(*c*) As to the *evolution* of the senses, touch comes first. (1) It is the foundation of the other senses, since all require some contact. (2) It is the most universal. Lower animals which do not have all the other senses have at least the sense of touch. There is no known instance of the presence of other senses where this one is absent. (3) In the same individual man, touch is the first sense to be exercised.

V. Psychophysics and Psychophysiology

1. **Facts of Common Experience.** — (*a*) Sensations are called weak, strong, moderate, etc., i.e. *their intensity varies*. A sound may be loud or hardly perceptible; temperature may be increased or decreased; and thus for all the senses. (1) Generally to an increase in the *stimulus* corresponds an increase in the *intensity of the sensation*. Fifty candles give more light than one; lifting a hundredweight gives a more intense sensation of muscular tension than lifting twenty pounds, etc. (2) Yet ordinary experience shows also that the sensation does not increase in the same absolute proportion as the stimulus. One singer's voice added to a

numerous chorus does not produce the same increment of sensation as if it were added to one or two singers only. In a very bright room, the addition of one candle is not so striking as it would be in a dimly lighted room, etc. Therefore, in order to produce a noticeable difference in the sensation, the necessary *increment of stimulus*, must be proportioned to the *already existing stimulus*, i.e. it must be greater or smaller according as the original stimulus is itself greater or smaller.

(*b*) A certain amount of physical stimulus is required to produce a sensation. A violin string may be vibrating without my hearing any sound, either because the vibrations are too feeble, or because, owing to the distance, they do not reach my ear. At a certain distance, the ticking of a clock may be heard whereas that of a watch is not. A small amount of a given substance diluted in a glass of water may not give it a noticeable taste; if it be increased a little the taste will be perceived. The initial point of sensation is called its *threshold* or its *lower limit*. There is also an *upper limit* or *acme* of sensation, but it cannot be determined, because some perceptible stimuli (e.g. some odors and savors) cannot be increased beyond certain limits, and chiefly because the sensations become too painful and dangerous; e.g. too high a temperature, too bright a light, too intense a sound, too great a contact and pressure are productive of pain rather than of external sensation, and injure the organism.

2. **Experimental Science** tries to determine more accurately these facts of common experience.

(*a*) Sensations cannot be measured *directly* and in themselves. Evidently no physical unit can be applied to mental states. Nor can any mental process be taken as a unit, because mental states are of widely different nature (a sensation of color or smell cannot be estimated in sound-units); and also because, even within the same class of processes, no unit can be applied. I may know that a sound is louder than another, but it is impossible for consciousness to determine whether it is exactly three or four times louder. The relative intensity of sensations cannot be measured by introspection.

(*b*) Only an *indirect measurement* is possible. A sensation can be measured, not in itself, but in its relation to something else which is under control and which can be measured accurately. (1) I cannot, it is true, say whether a sensation of sound is three or four times more intense than another, but I can know that the number of vibrations producing it is three or four times larger than another. This relation of the sensation to the physical stimulus is the problem which *psychophysics* undertakes to solve. Its two main questions are those of the threshold of sensations, i.e. the minimum quantity of stimulus that can be perceived, and of the smallest differences of sensations, i.e. the minimum increment of stimulus necessary to produce a difference in consciousness. (2) All mental states are accompanied by organic processes. *Physiological psychology* endeavors to measure these organic changes in blood-circulation, secretion, muscular activity, temperature, etc., in order to see how they are correlated to various mental states. (3) Mental processes require time. Between the application of a given stimulus and a corresponding reaction an interval of time elapses which *psychometry* tries to analyze and measure.

N.B. Of these various problems, the first applies only to sensation and perception, for the stimulus must be external and under control, and such is not the case in other mental states like memory, emotion, volition. The second applies to all mental states, for all have correlates in the organism; but it is impossible to measure all organic processes. Some, like nervous processes, are central and cannot be reached. All are variable; what affects the circulation in one may affect the secretions in another; one grows pale where another would blush or tremble, etc. The third applies also to all mental states, but it is difficult to analyze and measure exactly every one of the elementary processes of a reaction.

3. **Methods.** — (*a*) To determine the *threshold of sensation* two methods are followed. (1) Begin with too weak or too distant a stimulus, and gradually increase it or bring it nearer until it is perceived. (2) Begin with a certainly perceivable stimulus, and gradually decrease it or move it farther until it ceases to be perceived. N.B. The latter method will generally give a lower

threshold than the former, i.e. weaker or more distant stimuli will be perceived; hence averages must be taken.

(*b*) To determine the *smallest perceptible difference*, three methods are used. (1) The method of *least observable difference*, which is applied in four ways. Begin with two equal stimuli, and gradually (*a*) increase or (*b*) decrease one till the precise moment when the difference is noticed. Begin with stimuli perceived as unequal, and gradually (*c*) increase the weaker or (*d*) decrease the stronger till no difference is felt. (2) The method of *correct and mistaken cases*. Slightly different stimuli are used, and after comparing them the subject pronounces on their relative differences. (3) The method of *average error*. One fixed stimulus is taken, and others more or less different are tried until one is found which appears to be equal to the first.

N.B. In all these methods, which it is advisable to use together whenever possible in order to correct one by another, several experiments are made and averages taken. Without complicated apparatus they can be easily applied to certain sensations, e.g. weight, temperature, taste.

(*c*) The methods of *physiological psychology* are very complex and require an elaborate apparatus to record and measure organic changes.

(*d*) The same must be said of experiments in *reaction-time*. The general procedure, however, is as follows: In simple reaction-time or physiological time, the subject reacts by an easy and familiar movement — generally cutting off an electric current by pressing on a key — to a simple sensation which he expects. In complex reaction-time, which is longer, there is a choice in the mode of reaction according to the nature of the stimulus, or there is uncertainty as to the nature or quality of the sensation which will be experienced. The duration of the complex mental process is calculated by subtracting the physiological time from the total duration of the whole process.

4. **Results.** — (*a*) Special results and numerical formulæ which have been arrived at in these various experiments cannot be given here. Only some of the most general points will be mentioned.

(*b*) Experiments on the *threshold of sensation* give different results according to the nature and distance of the stimuli used. Experiments on the minimum of *perceptible increase* have led to the formulation of the law known as "Weber's law," which is but a formula for both common and scientific experience: "The intensity of a sensation increases by absolute magnitudes when the stimulus increases by relatively constant magnitudes." Or: "Equal increments of sensation result from relatively equal increments of stimulus." Absolute increment means the addition of the same quantity; relative increment means the addition of a quantity compared to the already existing amount to which it is added. This law was given a more mathematical formulation by Fechner: "If the sensation must increase in arithmetical progression, the stimulus must increase in geometrical progression." Or: "The sensation increases as the logarithm of the stimulus."

Thus, for instance, to say that the smallest perceptible increment is, for sound $\frac{1}{3}$, for weight $\frac{1}{17}$, and for light $\frac{1}{100}$, means that, in order to perceive the increment of stimulus, we must add $\frac{1}{3}$, $\frac{1}{17}$, $\frac{1}{100}$, of the preceding stimulus. The difference between 100 and 101 candles will be the minimum perceptible. If the first stimulus be 200 or 300, then we must have, in order to perceive a difference, not 201 or 301 candles, but $200 + \frac{200}{100}$, or 202, and $300 + \frac{300}{100}$, or 303.

(*c*) Experiments in *physiological psychology* show the influence of various mental states on organic processes, the effects of fatigue, emotions, dispositions, etc.

(*d*) *Reaction-time* has led to determine the rate of transmission of the nervous current, and hence the duration of more complex cerebral processes. Even so-called simple reaction-time is in reality complex, for it includes the action of the stimulus on the end-organs, the transmission to the nervous centre, either to the brain directly or to the brain through the cord, the passage from a sensory to a motor process in the brain centre, the transmission of the motor excitation through the brain, cord, and motor nerves, and the production of muscular contraction.

5. **Value of the Results of Experiments.** — We shall limit ourselves to a general appreciation.

(*a*) *Weber's law* has been discussed and criticised, and the conclusion seems to be that it holds good provided it be accepted only as an approximation and applied only to sensations of moderate intensity. Hence Fechner's formula is too strict and too mathematical.

(*b*) Experiments give different results according to the methods used, the aptitudes of the subject, his training, power of attention, habits and disposition. Hence the results obtained by different psychologists do not always agree, and they must always be understood as *averages*, not as invariable formulæ.

(*c*) Experimental psychology is a young science. The first psychological laboratory was founded by Wundt at Leipzig (1878), but Weber's and Fechner's investigations had taken place before that time. It has developed rapidly, and to-day psychological laboratories are found in all leading universities. By some, experimental psychology has been hailed as the only true psychological science in which alone progress is possible. By others, it has been condemned unreservedly as a vain and fruitless attempt from which no results useful to psychology have been obtained, and from which none are to be expected. It is not psychology at all, but physiology. It has even been identified with materialistic psychology.

(*d*) The truth is to be found between these two extreme views. Experimental psychology in itself is not materialistic. It has nothing or little to do with the metaphysical problem of the nature of the mind. It is only one branch or one method of psychology. It does not reach all mental processes, and considers only some aspects of those which it does reach. Its limitations are in its range of application, in the restricted value of the results, and in the need which it has of other psychological methods to coördinate its results.

Its value is both theoretical and practical. It makes of psychology a more exact science, helps us to understand better the nature and effects of certain mental attitudes and processes, like attention, emotions, expectation, and shows more clearly the relations of mind and organism. The influence of sex, fatigue, heredity, drugs, etc., is ascertained more accurately and verified. The laws of habit, education, training, distraction, etc., are also determined more strictly. Hence experimental psychology is useful to medicine, physiology, and may become very valuable for pedagogy by finding better methods of teaching, in stricter accordance with the laws of the mind and the organism. The results so far obtained are imperfect, but they are sufficient to give hopes of greater, better, and more useful results in the future.

II. PERCEPTION

I. Analysis and Genesis of Sense Perception

1. **Analysis.** — (*a*) *Perception is the consciousness of things*, whereas sensation is merely the consciousness of qualities. Perception refers these qualities to objects. Thus in adult life I do not merely hear a sound, but I hear the church bell or the whistle of the engine, I see a man, I smell a rose, I touch the table, etc.

(*b*) Perceptions have not always the same degree of *clearness*. I may hear a sound without being able to ascertain its source; perceive an unknown tree, or a machine which I never saw before and the use of which I do not know, or an animal different from all those with which I am familiar. In such cases there is perception, although indistinct, for I am conscious not only of a quality, but also in some manner of a distance, direction, etc., and chiefly of an object to which I refer such qualities. Perceptions become more and more perfect with age, education, and mental development, because they embody a more accurate and more complete knowledge of the perceived objects.

(*c*) Consequently it is in perception that sensations acquire a *meaning*. If I hear somebody speaking in a language unknown to me, his words have no meaning for me; they are simply sounds, since I cannot grasp the underlying thought which they are intended to manifest. In the same manner sensations by themselves are meaningless, and perception unites them into a coherent whole.

(*d*) Perception is *synthetic* and coördinates several sensations. In the statement "I see the dog asleep over there," are implied many sensations past and present. I see simply a certain color, and I supply the rest from past associations. Many sensory, and perhaps intellectual, elements enter into my complete perception of the dog, and only a few of these are actually given in my act of vision. All are now synthetized in the one perception of the sleeping dog.

(*e*) Hence perception implies: (1) *A synthesis of several simultaneous sensations*, although sometimes only one sense is used. Thus I refer to the same bell the sensations of vision, sound, hardness, etc. (2) *A synthesis of present sensations with past sensations* of the same or of other senses, i.e. memory and recognition. Thus, although I have no actual experience of it, I know how the boiling water which I see would affect my sense of touch if I dipped my finger in it, and the knowledge that it is boiling is itself the result of past experiences. Imagination and habit may even prevent us from perceiving things as they are really, for instance, when a word in which a letter is missing is read without the misprint being noticed. Or they complete the perception, as when I see a ball and perceive that it is spherical, although I really see only half of it. (3) *The substitution of one sense for another*, or of one sense for a more complex act of judgment and inference. For instance, I *see* that the table is hard and the pillow soft (touch), or I *see* that the dog is living (inference from its behavior).

(*f*) We may recall an old distinction which applies here.

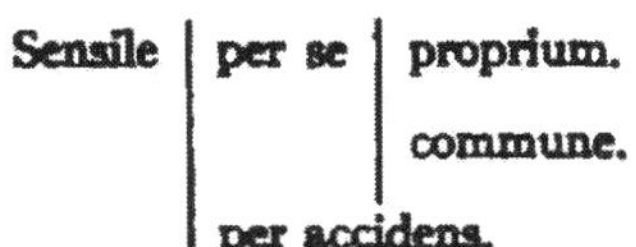

By *sensile* or *obiectum sensibile* is meant the object about which the senses give information. The *sensile per se* is perceived directly. The *sensile per accidens* is not perceived in itself, but only because of some connection with the sense to whose perception it is attributed. Color, sound, odor, taste, tactile qualities, are *sensilia per se* and *propria*, i.e. special to each sense. Size, number, shape, movement, rest, are *sensilia per se* but *communia*, as they may be perceived by more than one sense. Thus distance may be perceived by touch, vision, hearing, and even smell. To see the hardness of an object; to see a friend; to see that a dog is alive or dead, that a man is sad or joyful, healthy or sick; to hear that the bell is broken; to know by taste that a fruit is of such or such a kind; to enter a room and learn by smell that the windows have not been opened for a long time, etc., are examples of *sensilia per accidens*. These qualities or objects are not perceived directly by the sense to which they are attributed, but inferred by habitual association.

2. **Genesis.** — The first sensations are very vague, but, little by little, images left by them in the mind associate with sensations and images of the same or of different kind so as to enable the mind to identify and discern objects. The senses become educated. Applied to the senses, education means: (1) Their *development* and perfection for their immediate and original sensations. By exercise they acquire a greater keenness and accuracy. (2) The *acquisition* by a given sense of perceptions which are not original (*sensilia communia* and *sensilia per accidens*). (3) The *correction of errors and illusions*. The main psychological factors in the education of the senses are attention, association, imagination and memory, intellect and will. Physiological factors are the habituation of the nervous system and the whole organism, the development, growth, and adaptation of sense organs, the development of the brain, hygiene, and the proper care and use of the sense organs.

3. **The Most Important Perceptions** are those of sight, for, in the adult, sight is in many cases a substitute for the other senses, and reaches objects at a greater distance. It enables the mind to communicate with others by gestures and writing. Touch, as we shall see, contributes greatly to the education of the other senses, especially of sight. Hearing has a great importance because it makes it possible to exchange ideas by means of speech. Smell and taste occupy the lowest place.

II. Perceptions of Smell and Taste

Both senses can be developed so as to reach a wonderful degree of *keenness*, e.g. in professional tasters. But even when educated, they give but little information concerning the external world. By experience, however, we learn to associate many odors and savors with the *objects* from which they proceed, and thus can recognize certain substances by these senses alone. Smell may also indirectly, and more or less accurately, give information concerning the *distance*, *direction*, and even *size* of the odorous object.

III. Auditory Perceptions

1. **Nature of Objects.** — By association, sensations of hearing are ascribed to their causes and referred to such or such objects. A certain sound becomes the sound of a bell, and even of the church bell, the engine bell, the school bell . . . , because this sensation of hearing has been associated with other visual or tactual sensations, and because it has been noticed in what respects the sound of a bell in general differs from every other sound, and the sound of a particular bell from that of other bells. In the same way I come to know that a certain tune is played on the violin, the cornet, or the trombone, even when I do not see these instruments. (Let the student endeavor to indicate more in detail and more concretely the genesis of such perceptions.) Mention must also be made of the auditory perceptions of tempo, rhythm, and cadence in music, speech, poetry, etc., which are the sources of so much enjoyment.

2. **The Localization of Sounds** in space includes the perceptions of direction and distance.

(*a*) *Perception of Direction*. (1) The use of the senses of sight and touch is fundamental in acquiring and developing this perception, and, even for the educated ear, these senses are frequently necessary to ascertain the direction accurately and to confirm the auditory perception. (2) Binaural perception is an index of direction, because the intensity of sounds coming from the right or the left is different for the right and the left ear. Hence it is that in order to perceive the direction of a sound we generally turn the head around. Experience shows that the direction of sounds coming from the right or the left is more readily ascertained than that of sounds coming from objects in front or back of the hearer. (3) It is probable that the sensitiveness of the skin of the external ear and meatus, and the position of the semicircular canals, have something to do with the perception of direction.

(*b*) *Perception of Distance*. The distance of a sonorous object is known by comparing the intensity of the present sound with the intensity of the same sound at greater or shorter known distances. To this end, the nature of the sonorous object and the intensity of its sound at a given distance must be already known. Atmospheric conditions, like the direction of the wind, the presence of fog, etc., must be taken into consideration. The distance of unusual or unfamiliar sounds is much more difficult to determine.

IV. Tactual Perceptions

The information received from the sense of touch concerns the primary qualities of matter which are most fundamental, namely, quantity, extension, number, shape, etc. Moreover, touch is the sense to which appeal is generally made when other senses do not seem to agree, e.g. by grasping the object, walking toward or around it. Through cultivation it is capable of acquiring a wonderful and almost incredible degree of perfection, as, for instance, in persons born blind. In all cases active touch, e.g. "feeling" with the hands, is much more useful than mere passive touch, because to the simple contact of the latter it adds sensations of muscular activity and movement, and it gives several simultaneous and successive sensations. The knowledge of the shape, dimensions, and qualities of a knife will be more accurate after handling it than after merely touching it. Tactual perceptions may be reduced to those of our own body and those of other material substances.

1. **Perception of One's Own Organism.** — (*a*) There seems to be some native but very vague consciousness of the organism. In the beginning, tactual sensations — including contact and pressure, temperature, sensations of muscles and joints — are vaguely localized in the organism, and discriminative sensibility is very imperfect. The numerous and complex vital sensations, the various contacts of the organism with surrounding objects, the experience of pain, etc., contribute to make the perception more definite. So also the fact that objects produce different impressions according to their size and qualities, and according to the parts of the body with which they come in contact.

(*b*) More effective are the sensations of *double contact*. When a part of the organism, e.g. the hand, touches another, a double sensation of touch is experienced, and thus by passive and chiefly by active touch the limits and parts of the organism are soon ascertained.

(*c*) The sense of sight is a help in localizing more accurately the sensations of touch.

2. **Perception of Other Material Substances.** — (*a*) Sensations of *single contact*, as opposed to those of double contact, contribute to the consciousness of the distinction between one's organism and other bodies. The same is true of the pain felt in one part of the organism or in two according as the child strikes some external substance or his own body.

(*b*) *Size*, *figure*, and *distance* are perceived chiefly by active touch, and by the muscular sensations experienced in passing the hands on or around the object, and in walking toward or around it. Measurements of size and distance are effected by a comparison with a known unit, with parts of our own body, or with our bodily movements. It is noteworthy that the interpretation of visual sensations of size and distance is frequently done in terms of touch. A thing is so many "steps" away, so many "feet" or "cubits" long; it is at the distance of "a stone's throw," of "a two-hour walk," etc. In such expressions the standard unit is taken from the human body and its movements.

(*c*) *Weight* depends largely on the strength, exercise, and education of the muscular sense. In consequence it is greatly relative, unless the habit has been acquired of referring it to a fixed unit, such as ounce, pound, etc. Active touch especially is important in the determination of the *number* and the *movements* of objects.

(*d*) Combined sensations and perceptions of touch may in some cases give the knowledge of the very *nature* of an object. Thus a certain group of sensations will indicate a metal, and even this or that metal; another group will indicate marble or wood, oil or water, etc.

V. Visual Perceptions

1. **Erect and Single Vision.** — The phenomena of erect vision although the image formed on the retina is inverted, and of single vision although we have two eyes, belong chiefly to the domain of physiology.

(*a*) With regard to *erect vision*, habit may be an important factor, for, even if originally we had a tendency to see things inverted, habit acquired by touch would correct this tendency. It is possible also that, in the transmission from the retina to the brain, spatial relations are not preserved. But the more probable explanation is that the image on the retina is not perceived at all, and in fact we are not directly aware of it. The rays of light are perceived in the direction from which they come because in vision there seems to be a double movement, one of the object toward the eye through the refracting media, producing the inverted image on the retina, the other from the eye, projecting the image in its erected position. This activity from the eye is manifest in projected after-images. In photography, on the contrary, the object is simply received on the film, which is passive, and hence is found inverted.

(*b*) As to *single perception:* (1) The greater part of the field of vision is common to both eyes, as can be easily verified by using each separately. The same is not true of fishes, birds, or other animals whose eyes are found on the sides of the head. (2) If we look simultaneously at two objects unequally distant from the eye, for instance, at two pencils held vertically before the eyes, one at a distance of seven or eight inches, the other seven or eight inches farther, the nearer pencil will appear double if the eyes are accommodated for and fixed upon the more distant, and vice versa. Or hold a finger before your eyes, and look at the ceiling or sky: two fingers will be seen, although vaguely. (3) Some animals certainly have single perceptions from the beginning, e.g. the chick, which immediately pecks the grain of corn. But they are precisely those whose eyes are divergent, and for which therefore the majority of objects perceived simultaneously are perceived by one eye only. (4) Physiologists commonly hold that single perception is based on the corresponding points of the retina, i.e. points situated in the same relative position with regard to the *fovea centralis*, both being on the right of it, or on the left, or up, or down. Hence, for instance, the nasal half of one retina has no corresponding point in the nasal half of the other retina, but in its temporal half. Rays of light falling on corresponding points are perceived as single, otherwise as double. — From what precedes it would seem that both a native disposition and also education and exercise are factors in the phenomenon of single vision.

2. **Perception of Surface.** — Against pure empiricists who claim that the perception of surface is not original and primitive, but acquired by experience, it seems certain that original perceptions of vision include in a vague manner that of surface and extension. (1) It seems impossible to perceive a color without perceiving at once some colored extension. (2) In fact, in the few instances of persons born blind and made to see in adult age, these persons perceive at once some colored surface, but no distance or solidity. (3) Some animals, e.g. the chick which does not miss its aim, as already mentioned, have originally not only the perception of extension, but also that of distance.

The superficial shape, if small, is perceived at one glance; if large, by the movements of the eye around the object.

3. **Perception of Distance.** — (*a*) The perception of distance is not original, but acquired. A nativistic view cannot be accepted here, as it was for the perception of surface. (1) A man born blind and operated upon for cataract reports objects as being in contact with the eye, or at most perhaps at a vague distance which cannot be estimated. (2) A child shows that it cannot appreciate distances, e.g. when it tries to grasp objects, like the moon, which are far beyond its reach. — These reasons show at least that distances cannot be estimated at first, even should the object be perceived as vaguely distant and distinct from the eye.

(*b*) The main *factors* in the perception of distance are: (1) The *sensations of accommodation*, as various structures of the eye adapt themselves differently according as the object is far or near. (2) The *visual angle*, that is, the apparent size of an object when its real size is known. A man appears smaller at the distance of one mile than at the distance of ten feet, i.e. the visual angle — the angle formed from the eye as vertex between lines directed toward the extremities of the perceived object — is smaller. Hence illusions of distance will produce illusions of size, e.g. in panoramas. (3) The fact that an object covers another totally or in part, and the number of *intervening objects*, are signs of their relative distances.

(4) The *apparent brightness* of the object, the distinctness of its parts and outlines. (5) The *changes in the relative positions* of different objects, and the rapidity with which these changes take place when one moves the head or the whole body. On a train, nearer objects seem to "move" much faster than the more distant ones. (6) The *degree of convergence* of the axes of both eyes, which is greater for near objects. This applies only to distances under one fourth of, or perhaps half, a mile. For greater distances the convergence is the same. (7) The *similarity and dissimilarity of the separate vision of each eye*, which vary according to the distance of the object. (8) *Touch* and *locomotion*, which make it possible to estimate distances accurately and are necessary to train the eye.

With the use of one eye only, vertically hold a pin or a pencil in each hand, one higher, the other lower, and without the help of the sense of touch try to bring the point of the higher pencil or pin exactly on top of the point of the lower, and see how you will succeed. Try again. Try with the use of both eyes. Do you succeed better? Why?

4. **The Perception of Solidity, Relief, and Depth** is but an application of the perception of distance. It depends chiefly on binocular vision helped by touch. Monocular perception of solidity is always imperfect. Unless an object, e.g. a book, is at too great a distance (of over twenty or thirty feet), one eye does not perceive it in exactly the same way as the other. The right eye perceives more on the right side of the object, and the left eye more on the left side. Hold a pencil or rod about one foot long horizontally before the eyes, the nearer end being about six inches from the face, and at the height of the mouth; look at it with the right eye, it is seen as /; look with the left eye, it is seen as \ ; look with both eyes fixed on the nearer end, it is seen as V; fixed on the farther end, it is seen as Λ; fixed on the middle, it is seen as X. The factors in the perception of relief are the same as for distance. In paintings and drawings many illusions of distance, solidity, and relief are produced by the proper arrangement of light, colors, shades, perspective, sizes, etc. Two pictures may be taken of the same object, but slightly different, one as it appears to the right, the other as it appears to the left eye. In the stereo-

scope, by means of lenses, both are made to be seen in the same place as one picture, and thus produce the illusion of solidity and relief.

5. **The Perception of the Size or Magnitude** of surfaces and solids is acquired in different ways.

(*a*) Near objects may be compared to the human body or to parts of it, and this comparison is facilitated by touch and locomotion. Or they may be compared to other bodies the size of which is already known. Hence in drawing the sketch of a building, an architect will place near it drawings of men, trees, carriages, or other familiar objects, so as to make it easier to estimate the height of the building.

(*b*) By means of the visual angle, the distance, if known, makes it possible to form an idea of the real size of objects. Thus I may know that the man twenty feet away is taller than another at a distance of ten feet, although the latter, judged only by the visual angle, seems taller.

(*c*) Important also are the muscular sensations experienced in moving the eyeball or head in order to follow the outlines of the object.

ARTICLE II. SENSE REPRESENTATION

I. THE MENTAL IMAGE

I. Nature of the Image

1. **Psychological.** — (*a*) Representation does not mean that the same object or quality which has been perceived is again presented and perceived in the same way, but only as a likeness, a copy, or, better, an image (*imago*, from the root *im* in *imitor*). It is a fact of daily experience that we can "imagine" absent things, that is, recall to mind the images of things perceived in the past. *Image*, which in common usage refers to the sense of vision, applies here to all senses. Not only are there visual images, but auditory, tactual, etc., images as well. *Mental imagery* is the collection of images in the mind.

(*b*) An image necessarily implies that something has been left over by the preceding perception which it represents. Where there has been no sensation, there is no image; a blind man may form images of sounds, but not of colors. This residue of the preceding perception is not the image itself, for image applies only to the representation actually present in consciousness, not to the unconscious retention of something intermediary between the perception and the image. This residue is therefore more commonly called a *disposition*, i.e. a capacity or aptitude resulting from a permanent modification, which enables the mind to revive images of things perceived formerly. Three stages are included in representation: (1) *perception;* (2) *retention* of an unconscious disposition, sometimes called latent image; (3) *actual revival* and presence of the image in the mind.

(*c*) The following *characteristics* differentiate the image from the percept, i.e. from the result of the act of perception. — We shall speak later of abnormal cases in which images are taken for percepts (hallucination) — (1) The percept is *antecedent* in time, and *independent of* the resulting image; the image is *posterior to*, and *dependent on*, perception. (2) The percept is *vivid* and attributed to the presence of a *real object;* the image is *fainter*, and is *not referred* to an object actually present. (3) Perception is dependent on the *presence* of external objects for its possibility, nature, appearance, or disappearance. The image is possible in the *absence* of the external object; it appears or disappears of itself, or under the influence of the will; its nature even may be modified so as to be either a true or a more or less fanciful representation. If my eyes are normal and open, I cannot help seeing objects within my field of vision, and I can see no other. But even in the dark or with my eyes closed, some visual images may come spontaneously or be called to the mind; others may be excluded or modified purposely.

(*d*) A few remarks will be useful on the meaning of certain terms used in connection with the present question. "*Idea*" applies to both images and concepts, i.e. to all mental representations, whether concrete or abstract. By the scholastics any image or mental picture was called *phantasma*, and the faculty of retaining images was the *phantasia* (φαίνω, to appear). To-day the terms "phantasm" and "phantasy" are seldom, if ever, used in this sense. *Phantasy* or fancy indicates something illusory, odd or whimsical, "fanciful" or "fantastic." *Phantasm* is applied especially to forms or spectres of an hallucinatory nature which appear in various forms of mental excitation and exaltation, or under the influence of certain drugs. Sometimes, chiefly in spiritistic literature, it is restricted to the true or supposed apparitions of disembodied spirits.

2. **Physiological.** — (*a*) Certain facts make it clear that the mental image has a physiological basis. (1) Experimental researches and pathological observations have shown that injury to, and disease of, certain parts of the brain destroy or impair the power of reviving certain groups of mental images. (2) The restoration or cure of these parts has been followed by the restitution of the missing images. (3) The easier acquisition of images in early age is generally explained, in part at least, by the fact that the nervous centres are more plastic than in old age. (4) On the other hand, physiological experiments show that a nerve, once it has been excited, acquires some facility for receiving again the same excitation, that is, every excitation leaves some trace or residue in the nervous system. Whether this is a persisting movement and vibration, or a permanent impression and modification, or a latent disposition, is secondary. These three hypotheses are not mutually exclusive. Persisting vibrations and persisting imprints may coexist, and both account for the resulting aptitude or disposition. Sensations produce some modification in the nervous substance, and hence leave special dispositions.

(*b*) Physiological dispositions cannot dispense with mental dispositions. A movement, vibration, or chemical change in the organism can no more account for the image than for the perception itself. Consciousness cannot be reduced to material properties. To speak of organic memory, or of the memory of a violin, because it improves by usage, is objectionable because memory is a psychological term implying consciousness.

II. Properties of the Image

The image is representative (psychological), and motor (physiological).

1. **The Image is Representative.** — (*a*) According as it repre-

sents an object as it was really perceived, or is combined with other images, the image is called *simple* or *complex*. In a certain sense, it is true that all images are complex, since perception itself is complex. But simplicity and complexity here refer to the image considered either as reproducing only one perception, or as reproducing together several, or parts of several, perceptions. The complexity of images results from the combination of several images into one, or from the dissociation of the elements of one image, and their grouping with parts of other images. I may imagine, for instance, a dog with feathers, or a bird with hair and four feet. In the simple image no new elements are introduced, but it may be a more or less complete representation of the object.

(*b*) Images become *fused*, that is, images partly similar and partly dissimilar may be, as it were, superposed in the mind so as to strengthen common features, and blur individual features. By taking successively on the same plate photographs of, let us say, six members of a family, each one receiving only one sixth of the total necessary exposure, a composite photograph is obtained in which common features are reinforced, whereas individual characteristics are weak. The fusion of images has a similar result. For instance, the features common to all dogs, like the facts of having two ears and eyes, four legs, a certain general appearance, etc., remain prominent; but individual features, like size, definite color, etc., are in the background. These are included in the image of an individual dog, but are generally replaced by averages, or are hardly noticed, when we simply think of a dog without referring the image to this or that individual.

(*c*) Complexity and fusion give one simultaneous result, namely, one composite or vague image. *Association* gives a successive result. It means a linking together of two or more images in a series as antecedents and consequents, so that the revival of an image is likely to produce the revival of another image with which it is associated. Of association we shall soon speak more in detail.

(*d*) An image has *intensity*. Not in the same sense as sensation, for the images of thunder or of a dazzling light may be fainter than those of a whisper or a candle; but in the sense that it is more or less vivid, clear, distinct, and similar to the original.

(*e*) Complexity, fusion, association, and vividness of images sometimes require no effort of the will, sometimes also are under the control of the will and are intended for special purposes.

2. **The Image is Motor.** — This important aspect of ideas has a more direct reference to the chapter on conative faculties than to the present chapter on cognitive faculties.

(*a*) All perceptions are accompanied by various organic processes which are more or less conscious. Hence by association mental images are accompanied by the images of these processes. In playing the piano, or the trombone, or any other instrument, the sensations of sound are accompanied by the movements of the arms, hands, and fingers, necessary to produce these sounds. In listening to music played by others, the performer's motions may also be perceived and associated with the auditory sensations. Or the listener may be aware of certain definite or indefinite motions in his own organism, e.g. of the tendency to dance, beat time, mark the rhythm by certain gestures, etc. In reproduction all these images tend to come back together.

(*b*) A perception or image of a movement is accompanied by an inchoative execution of such a movement, which in many cases is conscious. When I follow the pianist's motions with the eyes, my hands themselves have a tendency to move with those of the player. I feel a beginning of the necessary innervation and muscular adaptation, the strength of which varies with the nature of the stimulus, and with subjective dispositions and habits. When I recall a tune which I have played, there is some inchoation of those movements which were required to play it. If it is a march or a dance, there is a tendency to take a certain bodily attitude and to execute appropriate movements. The image of a circle includes certain eye changes in order to follow its outline. The image of a word produces inchoative movements in the organs of speech to utter it, or in the hands and fingers to write it, etc. Hence, in general, an image always implies a motor tendency to realization.

(*c*) This tendency may be so strong, for instance in the case of habits, that an idea is immediately and almost automatically accompanied by complete motor processes. Or it may be reduced to a feeble and imperceptible change in the nerve centres, without any external manifestation. If there is only one idea in the mind, as happens in a hypnotized subject, the tendency to realization is irresistible, because the mind is deprived of other ideas which normally would hold this one in check. If, for instance, while the subject is in reality eating something sweet and agreeable, the idea is suggested to him that he is eating something loathsome, his face will show an expression of disgust, and his stomach may be so upset as to cause vomiting. When, on the contrary, several ideas are present in the mind, either they will evoke a series of coördinated movements, if they are in harmony, or, if they are opposed, they will remain in equilibrium, or form antagonistic groups, one of which will finally prevail. Higher mental faculties also contribute to foster or check the motor tendencies of ideas.

(*d*) Not only does the idea suggest the movement, but the movement or attitude suggests the idea. Thus the attitude of prayer suggests the idea of praying, clenching the fist is suggestive of revenge, etc.

(*e*) This motor property of ideas accounts for many facts attributed to imitation. The perception of actions performed by another suggests the idea of this action, which is in turn followed by the appropriate movements. It also accounts for many facts attributed to mind-reading. Slight movements and muscular contractions are real, although unconscious, and they can be detected by a skilled and sensitive person. Thus, for instance, an object is concealed, and only one person knows where. This person is taken by the hand and led almost immediately to the hiding-place. Such mind-reading amounts simply to perceiving and interpreting some slight muscular contractions performed unconsciously and involuntarily by the subject, as he is led toward or away from the place where the object is to be found. The whole expression of the face, especially of the eyes, is also of great help in such experiments.

III. Association and its Laws

1. **Meaning.** — (*a*) As already remarked, association does not mean a process of combination by which several images would

unite so as to become one. It refers to the *succession* of ideas in the mind, and means that images are not revived independently and at random, but that their revival depends on actual perceptions or on the presence of other ideas in the mind. Images are grouped or linked together so that the revival of one tends to bring about the revival of another or of several others.

(*b*) Sometimes we are clearly aware of this connection; we can follow the "train" of ideas and perceive their nexus. In other cases we are unable to see why one idea is revived; it seems to flash into the mind without being called for and of its own accord. But frequently in such cases further reflection reveals the hidden thread which bound ideas together. After a conversation, the beginning and the end of which deal with totally different subjects that seem to have nothing in common, it is very interesting to trace back the trend of the conversation in order to see the connection between the various topics, and examine how one led to another.

(*c*) Association has no *laws* properly so-called. Every individual mind has its own associations, and the same idea or perception will revive different ideas in different minds; it "reminds" one of one thing, and another of another thing. Moreover, even in the same mind, manifold associations exist, and it is impossible beforehand to say which idea will be revived. Hence it occurs frequently that we fail when trying to "give the clue" to another, and that a "hint" is not always taken. The so-called laws of association simply indicate how groups of ideas are formed, and how one idea suggests another.

2. **The Laws of Association** have been enumerated in various ways. Some psychologists mention three, others two, and others one, reducing all to the law of contiguity in consciousness. Here the various modes of association are indicated without any attempt to examine whether they are reducible to one or two laws.

(*a*) An idea may be revived owing to the *likeness* which it has with another already present in consciousness. The similarity may be total or partial, and the common features are more or less numerous. Examples: likeness of two tunes, of two words in spelling or pronunciation, of a copy and its original, of two houses, of two smells or tastes, etc.

(*b*) *Contrast* contributes to the revival of images, e.g. a hot summer day and a cold winter day, a giant and a dwarf, a good and a bad action. It is clear that contrast in some respects and similarity in other respects frequently exist together between the same objects.

(*c*) Association also takes place on account of the *contiguity in space or time*. Thus my thought of a building in a city may recall that of another building in the same city; a state may suggest a neighboring state. The thought of a historical event may recall other contemporary or immediately preceding and following events or personages.

Similarity, contrast, and contiguity are the three main laws of association.

(*d*) Among other important factors of association must be mentioned: (1) The *vividness* of the impression or impressions, and hence their interest, the attention voluntarily or involuntarily given to them, their emotional aspect, etc. (2) *Recentness;* generally images fade away with time unless they are recalled. (3) General and special *dispositions*, organic and mental, permanent and transitory, acquired and natural.

(*e*) An idea may be linked with others in more than one way, and in this case the chances of its being recalled are greater.

(*f*) Associations and groupings of ideas may be coöperative or conflicting. In the struggle for persistence and revival, the law which, for organisms, has been called the law of "the survival of the fittest," applies to ideas. An idea may have several advantages over its competitors, both in itself and on account of the group to which it belongs. In this case it stands a better chance of survival. Others, on the contrary, being weak, soon become weaker still; they fall into subconsciousness, never perhaps to be revived.

II. IMAGINATION

I. Nature of Imagination

1. Meaning of the Term. — Imagination sometimes means the power, sometimes the process itself, of forming mental images, and sometimes the result of this activity, namely, the mental image.

The term "imagination" is also used in a more restricted sense for the constructive imagination, i.e. the forming of images that are not in conformity with reality, as when, after listening to a yarn, we say; "That's all imagination." This last meaning is more properly that of fancy, which is more superficial, playful, false, and artificial.

2. **Kinds of Imagination.** — (*a*) Imagination is called *passive* or *active* according as images recur spontaneously, or as an effort is made to recall them.

(*b*) Imagination is simply *reproductive*, or *constructive*, according as it merely represents (more or less completely) the object as perceived, or combines images into one composite image. The "construction" may be merely mechanical and spontaneous, or it may be purposive, for instance, in inventions and works of art. To the constructive imagination may be reduced the power of magnifying and minimizing things.

(*c*) Constructive imagination includes two main processes, isolating and combining. By the former ideas are dissociated into several parts; by the latter the parts thus obtained are united in different ways to form composite images.

(*d*) Imagination deals with reproduction, but not necessarily, nor even primarily, with faithful reproduction. Nevertheless all the elements of a composite image are found scattered in preceding sense-perceptions.

II. Importance of Imagination

The importance of imagination, both for good and for bad, can hardly be overestimated; it is a useful, yet dangerous power.

1. **For Organic Life.** — Imagination exercises a great influence on the health of the organism because ideas are not only representative but also motor. Many illustrations of this could be given. Do we not see frequently imaginary ills leading to real sickness? To imagine that you are sick is one of the best ways to become truly sick, and to avoid thinking of your real sickness frequently proves to be a powerful help in the cure. The use of an appropriate remedy is in itself very beneficial, but the conviction that it is beneficial and that it will produce a certain result makes it twice

as effective. Imagination without the remedy may even produce the desired result. Cases might be cited of persons who felt sure they had taken a certain medicine, and indeed experienced the results of it, and who later found the pill which, in fact, they had forgotten to take. There is a better chance for the man who has made up his mind to get well than for the one who imagines that he will die and despairs.

2. **Intellectual Life.** — (*a*) *General.* Perception supposes imagination; it is from images left by past experiences that we supply the elements of the object which are not actually perceived by the senses. The higher forms of mental life, conception, judgment, and reasoning, are dependent on imagination, as will be shown later. To a certain extent the imagination helps to concentrate the mind on an object; but it may also be the source of fickleness and of a constant wandering of the mind.

(*b*) *Special.* Imagination helps the understanding of abstract truths because it furnishes concrete examples and illustrations. It may also become a danger, because thought cannot always take the form of images, and some are inclined to identify understanding with imagining. Under the guidance of reason, imagination is the principle of inventions, for it furnishes the mind with the complex images of certain effects to be expected and realized. It helps to frame and test hypotheses, and here it is very important to imagine all possible cases, e.g. for a general to think of all the possible movements of the enemy, since to omit one may cause defeat; or for a scientist to think of all the possible causes of a phenomenon, otherwise he is in danger of being mistaken.

The danger of attaching too much importance to imaginary conceptions, and of mistaking them for realities, is to be avoided. One must beware especially of "complementary" imagination by which things are perceived, not as they really are, but as they should be in order to meet one's expectations and views. See, for instance, in how many different ways the same fact is interpreted and reported by different observers, every one coloring it according to his own fancy.

(*c*) In arts, imagination creates ideals, types, fictions, etc., which the artist endeavors to realize and express.

3. **In Daily Practical Life**, imagination has a very complex rôle. Success depends largely on imagination and forethought, since it requires the idea of the end to be reached and of the means to reach it, the prevision of the possible good and bad results of an enterprise, etc. Failure is frequently due to an excess or a lack of imagination. Imagination exercises a great influence in making human life happy or miserable, for it causes us to magnify or minimize its goods and evils, and to compare our lot with the worse or the better lot of others. It thus gives an optimistic or a pessimistic view of the world and of life, and changes the aspect of things. In the relations with others, it may so blind one to reality that nothing but good will be seen in certain persons, and nothing but evil in others. Motives will be supplied rightly or wrongly, and "complementary" imagination will make it almost impossible to pass a sound judgment on the actions of others.

4. **In Moral Life**, imagination may usurp the place of reason as the guide of human actions, but it may also be used to construe the means of doing good, and to form ideals and examples.

5. **In Religious Life**, imagination helps to grasp the highest spiritual truths and to express them by appropriate symbols. But it is also the source of errors, prejudices, and superstitions.

III. Training of the Imagination

1. **General Principles**. — (*a*) As imagination may be both very useful and very harmful according to the use which is made of it, it is important to pay attention to its development. Imagination must be *cultivated* on account of its utility, and *controlled* on account of its dangers. Certain features must be strengthened, others must be checked.

(*b*) The main principle is that *imagination should be a useful servant*. Hence it should never be allowed to reign over other faculties and activities, or to guide human actions and behavior; it must remain under the guidance and control of reason. To do this is a serious task which requires constant effort and vigilance, and, notwithstanding these, imagination from time to time will still work mischief in the mind; it will still deceive and mislead man. With persevering attention it is possible to train and control the imagination, to increase its usefulness by developing it along certain lines and checking its excessive activity. Imagination must not be allowed free scope to wander at random. Images which should not occupy the mind — remember that they are motor — must be banished and held in check by calling forth other images and ideas.

2. **The General Factors** in the development of the imagination are psychological and physiological. (1) Acquired or innate dispositions, temperament, sex, character, age, etc. (2) The relative development and keenness of the senses. (3) Surroundings, mode of life, occupations, business, etc. (4) Habits. (5) The use of narcotics and stimulants.

(*a*) From these result the various *types of imagination:* visual, auditory, tactual, and motor. A type of imagination consists in a special tendency to revive images of one sense in preference to those of other senses. Thus in reciting a lesson which they have memorized, some pupils will see it on their books, follow it line after line, remember the first words of each page and paragraph, etc. Others are led rather by the sequence of sounds; others, by the motions necessary to utter the words. In consequence, some will learn their lesson by simply reading it with the eyes; others, by reading it aloud; others, by going through the motions of the organs of speech, especially of the lips and tongue, without uttering any sound. The revival of the image of a band concert may consist primarily of the visual images of the players, their respective positions, their uniforms, motions, etc.; or of the various sounds and tunes; or of certain motor phenomena, marching or dancing, which lead to remember the tunes.

(*b*) *More special features* may be developed for certain purposes according to various conditions of life, for business, arts, and sciences. This is effected by attention and concentration of mind. Thus the chauffeur has to remember roads; the car conductor, persons; the business man, merchandise, etc. The musician imagines sounds in preference to colors; the painter, colors and visual features in preference to sounds, etc.

To conclude: Keep the faculty of imagination alive, but apply it according to reason. Develop it, but control and direct it, and do not be led by it in your judgments and actions.

III. MEMORY

I. Nature of Memory

1. **Distinction of Memory and Imagination.** — It is difficult to draw a strict dividing line between memory and imagination. The main differences, however, are the following:

(*a*) *Imagination* is more *fanciful* and *constructive*, whereas *memory* reproduces the image of an experience *as it really occurred*. Whatever is added or changed, whether consciously or unconsciously, belongs to imagination. It must be noted, however, that, in order to belong to memory, it is not necessary for the image to represent all details. This is generally impossible, and the memory of some features co-exists with the oblivion of some others. The image may be true without being complete. Yet it cannot be called a faithful reproduction if essential features are left out; but, according to different points of view, different features may be looked upon as essential.

(*b*) *Memory* implies a reference to the *past*, and includes *recognition*; *imagination* refers chiefly to the *present* or *future*, and includes no recognition. An image may be present in the mind without the awareness that it is an image and therefore a reproduction. Or I may perceive a thing for the second or third time without remembering former perceptions; it is altogether "new" to me. This is true not only of images that are built up by the constructive imagination, and the elements of which are found scattered in past perceptions, but even of simple images. The mind may be incapable of referring them to the original, and is not conscious that they are copies. Or it may stop at the consideration of the present image, without thinking at all of the past perception. Or finally it may apply itself chiefly to the future realization of such an image or ideal. This is not enough for memory, which requires that the image be referred to its original, and that the mind recognize it as a representation of some past perception.

(*c*) Hence memory supposes at least the implicit knowledge

that the ego or subject who now recognizes the image is the same who experienced the original corresponding perception. It leads one to acknowledge the fact of the persistence of the self and of self-identity, since the same mind is at once forming the present image and referring it to its own past experience.

2. **Two Kinds of Memory.** — According to the mode of this reference two kinds of memory must be distinguished. (1) One is the recall of an *individual event* which has occurred only once or a few times, at such or such a date, in these or those circumstances. Thus I may clearly remember an event which I witnessed, an action which I performed, a conversation which I held, a speech which I heard, etc. (2) The other is acquired by a *series of repetitions* made for the purpose of learning. The child who memorizes his lesson for the next day reads it and repeats it to himself one, two, . . . ten times, in succession, or at several intervals of time, and on the next day, when he recites it, the individual readings are of no importance for him; he is attentive only to the present conformity of his words with those of the book. This memory is very close to habit and consists of many habitual associations.

3. **The Three Stages of Memory** are retention, reproduction, and recognition. The former two are common to memory and imagination, the latter is special to memory:

(*a*) Images are *retained* in the mind as unconscious dispositions. Images must not be conceived as "stored up" in the mind or the brain, as though the mind or brain were like a storehouse, box, or receptacle in which they can be gathered and preserved. Since image means a conscious representation, the retention of images is but a metaphorical expression. What is retained is the latent disposition or aptitude to call forth an image.

(*b*) *Reproduction*, or the actual revival in consciousness, depends on (1) association with, or suggestion from, present perceptions or images; (2) recollection, that is, the voluntary effort to recall an idea that has been partially forgotten, and some elements of which are now present in consciousness. In recollection we endeavor to reach back in the past and to recall the whole idea or group of ideas by the use of the laws of association.

(*c*) *Recognition*, or the reference of the present to the past, is of two kinds, as already indicated. The child who recites a lesson learned by successive repetitions endeavors to reproduce the ideas or words of the book. This implies some recognition, namely, the recognition of the similarity of the present recitation with the original. Yet this recognition is rather secondary, for now the child is hardly aware of the past, he is all intent on the present recitation, and recognition is, in this case, little more than a general and vague sense of familiarity. Perfect and properly so-called recognition will occur only if there is a special reason directing the attention to the past. Thus, if a child be asked why he does not know the lesson, whether he has studied it, or how many times he has read it, his mind will begin to think of the past. Each attempt at learning, with its circumstances of time, space, succession, success or difficulty, etc., will be brought back to the mind. This is recognition proper, i.e. the identification of a present image with its corresponding original, and it may be more or less perfect, more or less accurate and complete. Thus, for the time, I may recall the day, or the week, or the month, or the year in which an event took place; for the place and circumstances, details may be remembered with varying degrees of perfection.

II. Qualities and Conditions of a Good Memory

1. **The Main Qualities of Memory are:** (*a*) *Ease and facility in acquiring* knowledge, i.e. in receiving in the mind ideas capable of future recall.

(*b*) *Tenacity in retaining.* The forgetful mind easily loses the traces of past experiences, of promises made, and of advice received. Once an experience has disappeared from consciousness, its recall is difficult. Some learn rapidly, but forget almost immediately. Others need a longer time to learn, but the knowledge once acquired is not so easily forgotten.

(*c*) *Readiness of revival.* It is not enough to have many ideas in the mind. In order to be serviceable, these ideas must be at the mind's disposal, ready to come back when called for.

(*d*) *Faithfulness of revival*, that is, the absence of purely imaginary elements, and the completeness of the mental representation. Many memories are defective in this respect. Sometimes, even in perfect good faith, events, chiefly when complex, are distorted and misrepresented owing to subjective additions and changes.

2. **Conditions of Memory.** — Memory depends chiefly on: (1) The plasticity of the brain; hence in old age it is more difficult to learn, or to change ideas acquired formerly. (2) Natural endowments and mental education, including the various types of imagination and memory. (3) The laws of association, and consequently the interest of the event, the intensity, vividness, recentness, and repetition of mental processes. (4) The influence of intellect and will.

III. Culture of Memory

1. **General Principles.** — (*a*) Important as it may be to have a good memory, care must be taken not to develop it at the expense of judgment; the two must go together, and be developed and exercised together. This is true especially of rational sciences, in which the work of the understanding, not that of memory, is of primary importance. Nothing must be committed to memory before seeing whether it is worth retaining and before understanding it.

(*b*) The development of memory coincides in a great measure with the development of the thinking powers, the growth of attention, the faculty of properly correlating events, etc. Hence, to improve memory, special attention should be given to these faculties.

(*c*) In general we must remember the law of "the survival of the fittest" ideas. The training of memory must have for its object to make ideas which we want to survive "fitter" than the others. Do what we may, it is certain that we shall forget a great many things; we must know what may be allowed to fall into oblivion and what should be preserved. The art of forgetting goes along with the art of remembering. The fitness of an idea consists in its strength, vividness, interest, and in its association with strong groups of ideas by strong ties, for then it has the strength of the whole group to which it belongs.

2. **Special Rules.** — (*a*) *Attention* and *concentration of mind* contribute to make a deeper impression, a more vivid and better defined perception and image.

(*b*) *Do not begin with something too complex*, because the mind is puzzled by too great an abundance of details. This is why to a child who, for instance, has to learn the whole course in grammar, history, or geography, a primer is given first, containing only the essentials without the encumbering minor details, rules, and exceptions which cannot yet be mastered. In the same way, for private study, try to analyze a complex lesson into simpler elements. The degree of simplification and analysis which is required depends on the stage of mental development and on personal aptitudes. What is simple enough for one mind may be far too complex for another.

(*c*) *Associate*, i.e. *organise ideas*. An idea by itself is weak, but associated with others it acquires strength and vitality. The motto might apply here: "United we stand, divided we fall." In reading, study the objective sequence of ideas, and subjectively associate them in your mind.

(*d*) *Repetition strengthens ideas*. A certain number of repetitions is required to learn a lesson, but it will be found preferable, after going over the lesson attentively several times, to allow some interval to elapse between following repetitions. To revive ideas at intervals of time, the duration of which varies with the nature of these ideas and the special dispositions of mind, is better than to revive them the same number of times in immediate succession.

(*e*) *Use as many faculties as possible* so as to form several images of the same object. An idea which, at the same time, belongs to an auditory, a visual, and a logical group is more firmly seated in the mind and has more numerous associations. Real, not merely verbal, knowledge should be insisted on; learn ideas primarily, not words. Simple and obvious as this is, it is too often forgotten in practice. Of the several senses sight seems to be the most important, as it is a substitute for the other senses, especially for the sense of touch.

(*f*) *Use simultaneously reason and the senses*. Know what to retain and what to forget. Group ideas logically around a central idea which is the most important, and which, when recalled, will tend to recall the whole group. In a speech, article, or lesson, see the logical connections, the main ideas, their organization and sequence. One attentive and intelligent reading will do much more than many mechanical repetitions.

N.B. All so-called mnemonic systems and methods of never forgetting are but applications of the above rules.

IV. Time-Perception

Since memory refers the present to the past and implies succession, a few words will be said here of time-perception. Evidently we are not concerned at present with the abstract idea of time and its definition; nor even with the concrete, but objective and artificial, division of time into years, months, days, hours, minutes, and seconds. We deal only with the concrete subjective experience of time or duration; with time as recorded in the mind, not as recorded in nature by the course of the sun or the revolutions of the hands of a watch.

(*a*) In the very beginning of mental life there is a succession of processes which, however, is hardly conscious. It takes some time to notice by reflection the facts of change, endurance, and recurrence, and thus to acquire the conscious distinction of a *now*, or present, and a *then*, or past. The memory of rhythmic changes like respiration, pulse, need of food or sleep, is probably of great importance in the development of time-perception. Little by little the vague notion of time or succession becomes clearer and develops into a time-appreciation.

(*b*) *The appreciation of time is to a great extent relative.* It is a fact of daily experience that certain lapses of time objectively equal pass more or less rapidly. We are surprised that an hour has already passed in a conversation with a friend, the reading of an interesting book, or some amusement; and we are equally surprised that it is only ten minutes since we began studying an uninteresting lesson or listening to a tedious speech.

These variations depend on: (1) *The number of intervening experiences.* When these are many and varied, time passes away more rapidly than when they are few. In retrospect, on the contrary, intervals almost empty of experiences, as a week spent in bed, seem shorter because we have no memory of any events with which to fill up the interval. This is the source of a frequent historical fallacy which consists in jumping from century to century without distinction, because we have only a few events to record; hence the beginning and the end of a century seem nearer than they are in reality, and men who lived at great intervals of time are looked upon as contemporary. (2) *The interest of intervals;* if they are pleasant, time passes more rapidly. (3) *Suspense, expectation, and anticipation;* a future event which is desired anxiously and has to be waited for does not come quickly enough; but once it has come, it passes off very rapidly. The youth sees a long, long life before him; behind him the old man sees only a short duration. Any one may compare the day or year that precedes an expected and desired event with the day or year that follows it, and see how much shorter the latter seems.

(*c*) Localization in time may be vague or accurate, definite or indefinite. It seems to depend chiefly on the importance of events and on associations between ideas.

IV. ILLUSIONS OF THE SENSES

I. Nature of Illusions and Hallucinations

Illusions and hallucinations are generally dependent on reproductive activity. They may be partly presentative and partly representative phenomena.

1. **Definitions.** — (*a*) Frequently common-sense draws a sharp distinction between illusion and normal perception, as if illusion were always something abnormal and indicative of a special defect in the mind. This meaning is inaccurate; there are illusions that are natural, ordinary, and common to all men.

(*b*) *Illusion* may be defined in general as the acceptance as real by the mind of anything which is unreal. In this broad sense it includes delusion, error, and hallucination. More strictly, illusion is the acceptance as real by the mind of something unreal, but on the basis of some real data. *Sense illusion* is commonly restricted to errors of sense perception that are normal, regular, persistent, and common to all. *Delusion* applies rather to a false belief which implies reasoning processes, is persistent, and can be removed only with great difficulty.

(*c*) *Hallucination* cannot always be distinguished from illusion. In general it differs from illusion because it lacks the basis of real data which is present in illusion, or at least because real data contribute but little and remotely to the present mental state which is mistaken for a perception. To see a stick where there is no stick at all is a hallucination; to see a stick as broken in the water, when in reality it is straight, is an optical illusion. To see the moon when there is none would be a hallucination; to see the moon as gliding behind the clouds is an illusion.

2. **Classification.** — Sense illusions can hardly be classified except by referring them to the different senses. The most frequent are optical illusions of color, shape, distance, size, and movement. Hallucination is (1) *positive or negative*, according as it makes one perceive the unreal, or prevents one from perceiving the real which under normal conditions should be perceived; (2) *simple or complex*, according as it affects only one sense or several senses. The senses most subject to hallucinations are sight and hearing and also cœnesthesis.

II. Main Causes of Illusions and Hallucinations

We speak of the causes of these two phenomena together because many are common to both. By indicating their causes, the means of correcting illusions and hallucinations will also be indicated. In general an illusion or hallucination is corrected by removing its causes when possible, and by testing the report of one sense by the use of other senses.

1. **The Constitution, Keenness, and Fatigue of the Sense Organs**; their defects, either special to some or common to all individuals, are sources of illusions. After-images, lack of discriminative sensibility of the skin, color blindness, double vision, etc., come from such causes. Thus if a man with his eyes closed is touched gently on the hand with the point of a pencil, and is asked, always without looking, to indicate the exact spot with the point of another pencil, he will generally fail, and, if he succeeds, the success will

be purely accidental. The reason is that, on the back of the hand, the discriminative sensibility is about $1\frac{1}{8}$ inches; hence within that distance the two impressions are felt as one.

2. **Nature of the Surroundings.** — (*a*) The newness of an object and the lack of familiarity with it tend to make imagination complete and interpret it.

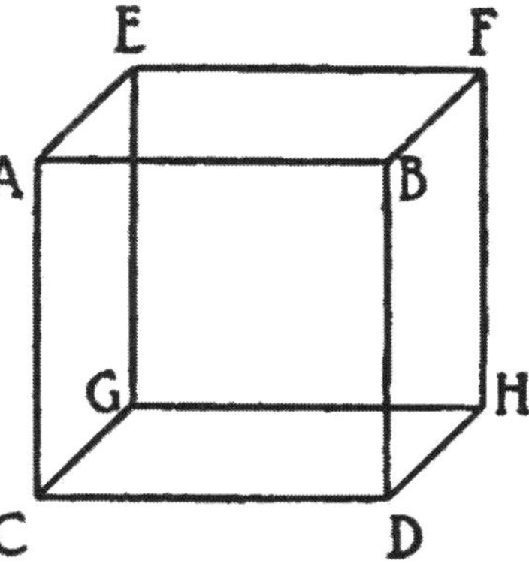

(*b*) Various circumstances, such as incompleteness, e.g. equivocal figures which are capable of being interpreted in different ways, thus the planes ABCD or EFGH may be seen in the front or in the back of the figure; amount of light, e.g. with a clear atmosphere a mountain seems nearer than with a misty atmosphere; in the fog, a lamp post may be mistaken for something else; darkness is the source of many illusions; intervening objects; presence or absence of materials for comparison. Compare a straight line crossed by perpendiculars with its continuation of the same length but without such cross lines. Which part seems longer?

Or again compare and

The moon seems larger at the horizon than at the zenith because the number of intervening objects makes it look more distant, and consequently the same visual angle is interpreted as corresponding to a larger object; the angles are equal, but their sides seem to extend farther.

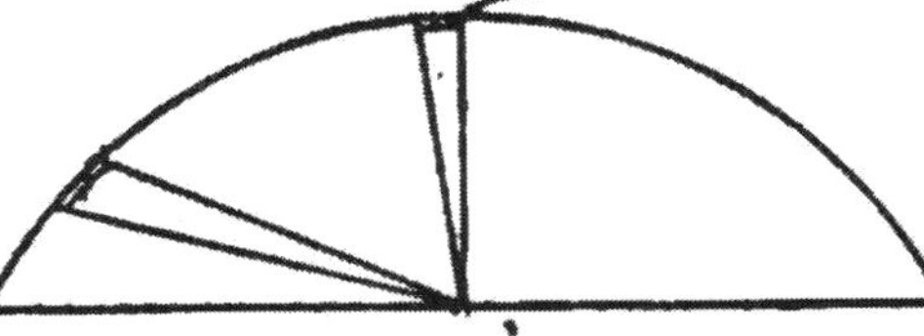

In a picture, the eyes always seem to follow the spectator because the pupil is always in view as if directed toward him (absence of relief).

(*c*) Contrast in sizes, colors, shapes, etc., is likely to influence the judgment. (Instances. . . .)

(*d*) The use of instruments like colored glasses, lenses, mirrors, etc.

3. **Mental Influences.** — (1) Memory, inference, association, suggestion, and habit. It is well known how sensations can be affected by these influences. (2) Lack of attention. (3) Expectation, desire, and fear.

4. Diseases, strong emotions, weakness, exhaustion, delirium, epilepsy, insanity, the use of certain drugs, hypnosis, etc., produce illusions and hallucinations.

ARTICLE III. CONCEPTION

I. CHARACTERISTICS OF THE CONCEPT

I. Various Terms Explained

Before describing the distinctive features of the concept, it will be useful to compare this term with some other closely related terms.

1. **Thought.** — (1) Frequently the term "thought" is applied to all conscious activities and representations. To think of the events of yesterday is to bring them back to memory. When asked for information which I do not actually remember, I am likely to say: "Let me think a little." To think is also used to express mere opinion as distinct from certitude; for instance, when I say: "I think so." (2) Yet other current expressions point to another more restricted meaning. When we say of a man: "He never thinks," or of another: "He is or was a great thinker," we refer to something different from the mere power of memory and imagination. To think is to examine, compare, judge, classify, elaborate the data of the senses so as to see their logical relations. It is from present and past experiences to foresee and prepare the future; to find out the laws that govern events and the conditions of phenomena; to rise from the concrete instance which is experienced to the abstract law or principle common to this and to similar instances.

2. **Intellect.** — In this narrower sense, thinking is generally attributed to man alone, and referred to the faculty known as

intellect. Animals are frequently called more or less intelligent, and by this we refer to their greater or smaller aptitude to adapt means to an end, or to be trained. But it will be seen in another place that this requires no thought in the stricter meaning; it is explainable by the senses and the retentive powers. In fact we do not speak of the intellect of animals, and thus we make a difference between intelligence, or the taking of means appropriate to an end, and the intellect, or the superior mode of knowledge by abstraction, generalization, and logical sequence. Thought proper, or intellectual knowledge, includes three steps: the formation of abstract and general ideas, judgment, and reasoning. From these spring other manifestations, especially language, written or spoken.

3. **Concept.** — Abstract and general ideas are properly called concepts. "Idea" is thus a more general term applying to all forms of mental representations, images, and judgments. I say, for instance: "I have no idea how that building looks; I never saw it;" or "I have no clear idea on this matter," that is, "I cannot form a satisfactory judgment, or reach certitude." As percept corresponds to perception, so the concept is the result of the process of conception.

We have seen that sensations are gradually elaborated into perceptions. The perception, for instance, of a horse, resulting from many presentations and representations, is always *concrete*. I see this horse, with this color, size, etc., in this direction and at this distance. When I say: "It is a horse," I apply to this concrete object an *abstract and general idea*, or a *concept*. For not only of this, but of any other animal of the same kind, wherever it may be, and whatever its color and size, I may also say: "It is a horse." I therefore am led to distinguish something which is common to all horses and which I consider by itself apart from individual determinations. As a percept, horse is always an individual concrete reality; as a concept it is an idea common and applicable to all horses, and it can be so only because it is abstract, namely, because it does not include all the distinctive features of this or that individual. Hence abstraction is the fundamental process in the formation of the concept.

II. The Essential Characteristics of the Concept

1. **Abstraction.** — The first characteristic of the concept is to be abstract. The concept does not represent the object as it exists in nature, with all its individual qualities and determinations, but it considers certain features and leaves out the others (*abs-trahere*). Here evidently the question is not that of a physical, but only of a mental or ideal separation.

Mental abstraction is of several kinds. (*a*) In the same object there are many qualities, each of which may be perceived by a special sense, the color by the eye, the sound by the ear, the resistance by touch, etc. Hence by its very nature *every sense is abstractive;* it perceives only one out of many qualities belonging to the same object. Or sense-abstraction may be due to voluntary attention, when, in an object, a quality or group of qualities is of special interest, e.g. the taste of an apple, the sound of a musical instrument.

(*b*) There is also a process of abstraction in *imagination* and its various types, in the association and fusion of images, and in memory. Some features of the images are considered while others are left out.

(*c*) In *language*, spoken or written, one may consider the ideas represented, i.e. the meaning of words and sentences, or one's attention may be directed to the words themselves from the different points of view of etymology, declension, spelling, pronunciation, etc.

(*d*) The *concept* is called abstract in a stricter sense. That which it represents is, or should be, only the features that are absolutely essential to the object and therefore common to all objects of the same kind, leaving out all unessential and particular features. The concept, for instance, will represent something essential and common to all movements (change of place), to all causes (production), to all squares (the fact of having four equal sides and four right angles). The individual determinations, conditions, circumstances, . . . of this or that movement, cause, and square are left out of consideration. In the same concrete object, however, we may consider different aspects and find different concepts. Thus in my free action I may find the concepts of freedom, cause, motion, action, responsibility, and change.

2. **Derived Characteristics.** — Because the concept is abstract, it also possesses three other main characteristics.

(*a*) It is not restricted to one individual, but may be applied to several; it is *universal* because it does not include individualizing determinations. My perception of a man, because it is concrete, applies only to the one man whom I perceive; my concept of man applies to all men; — the same is true of the concepts of color, weather, circle, etc., as compared to perceptions.

(*b*) The concept is not restricted to individuals actually existing. If it represents only that which is really essential — in many cases, as we shall see, it is not so — it is *necessary*, and independent of actual existence which is contingent. The acquisition of it depends on the perception of concrete existing things, but, in some cases, no concrete object may be found in which the concept thus formed is actually realized. Thus my concepts of a circle, of a triangle, of two parallels, represent in my mind that which is the essential and necessary constituents of these, although perhaps such elements are neither represented nor perfectly representable physically on the blackboard or on paper. I have the concept of a man perfect physically and mentally, although such a man may never be found. The formation of the concept of life supposes the perception of living beings, but this concept, once acquired, is indifferent to the various forms according to which life is actually realized, and even to any realization of life in the world.

(*c*) Hence it follows that the concept is not dependent on the conditions of *space and time*, which are always determinations of concrete things.

3. **Various Degrees of these Characteristics.** — These characteristics of the concept, and primarily its abstraction, are not always found in the same degree nor in the same manner.

(*a*) By *intension* or *connotation* of a concept are meant its constituent notes. By its *extension* or *denotation* is meant the number of individuals to which it applies. Thus I may have the concept of a plane geometrical figure limited by four equal straight lines parallel two by two and intersecting at right angles. This is the *intension* of my concept of a square, and this concept *denotes* all squares. If in the definition I leave out the idea "equal," I decrease the intension, but the concept will apply to a greater number of figures, namely, to all rectangles. The connotation may be further decreased by leaving out the condition of intersection at right angles; the denotation will be increased, since the concept will apply to all parallelograms. Further still the condition of parallelism may be omitted, and the concept applies to all quadrilaterals, and so on. Thus it is seen that *intension and extension vary in opposite directions*. To increase one is to decrease the other, and vice versa.

(*b*) This also shows that the concept may be *more or less complete*, accurate, and comprehensive. It is true but incomplete to say that the essence of the square is to be a rectangle or a parallelogram. In these latter concepts we reach a higher degree of abstraction, a lessening of the connotation, and an addition to the extension. Again, I may conceive the cow as a large herbivorous animal; this is true but insufficient. By the complete essence of a thing is meant that which includes all the constituent elements of the species to which it belongs, and that which distinguishes it from anything belonging to any other class.

(*c*) In many, if not in most cases, we know the essences of things very imperfectly. For the child, a cat may be essentially black or white, and it is only later, after seeing cats of different colors, that this notion is corrected. The same frequently occurs in sciences; tentative and provisional definitions are used which must be revised by future progress along the same line of investigation.

4. **The Concept and the Image Compared.** — From what precedes, and from what has been said on imagination, the differences between the concept and the image may be inferred. Since the concept is general, it is clear that it differs essentially from the simple image, which represents a single perception. Some claim that the concept is but a generic image in which the essential features, because they are common to many images, are prominent, whereas individual features are blurred. This account, however, is insufficient.

(*a*) Like the composite photograph, *the generic image is concrete.* It is true that it does not represent exclusively this or that individual which has been perceived before. To some extent it is vague and indetermined, but yet it is an individual picture, representing perfectly one individual only, which, it is true, has not been perceived and probably does not exist, but which is one and concrete. Because it is vague, it may be applied to several individuals, but to all imperfectly and only in part; to none perfectly. The concept, on the contrary, is applicable perfectly to all the individuals. As a concept, movement means simply a change of place; as an image, it is always this movement with this special direction and velocity. The concept of a circle includes no definite dimensions; the image of a circle cannot be without them. In other words, the composite image is an average picture, and an average here, as in mathematics, is always something concrete. In fact, every image, however complex, represents an object with certain dimensions, shape, size, color, etc.

(*b*) Hence an image can always be outlined, or painted, or described in some manner; the concept cannot. The concepts of triangle, man, or color apply to *all* triangles, men, and colors. An image always represents *one* triangle, *one* man, *one* color. It is true that the concept is generally accompanied by some shadowy, vague, and indistinct mental image. But as soon as we turn the attention to it, the image becomes clearer and assumes definite determinations. It was vague because attention was not concentrated upon it.

(*c*) A concept may be clear and distinct while the corresponding image is obscure or even impossible. I understand perfectly what is meant by a chiliagon or a geometrical figure of a thousand sides, and how it differs from another figure with a thousand and one sides. Yet my imagination is powerless to give me a mental picture of these. The same may be said in general of very large and of very small things, like the distance between the sun and the earth, and the size of a cell $\frac{1}{5000}$ of an inch in diameter. I understand what the mathematician tells me when he says that a quantity may be multiplied and divided ad infinitum, but I can imagine it in no concrete case. A familiar instance may be taken from those animals which are called myriapods (etymologically 10,000 feet), among which are centipeds (etymologically 100 feet). To understand is not to imagine; intellect is not imagination.

(*d*) We have concepts of things immaterial which can in no way be represented by imagination, like virtue, justice, duty, truth, etc. There are virtuous and just actions, but I do not perceive at all with the senses the goodness or justice of a concrete action. This concept, therefore, though derived from, and realized only in, individual actions, has a source distinct from the senses and the imagination. Or again, I see one thing succeeding another, but I do not see the causality or production, and yet I have not only the concept of succession, but also that of cause.

II. GENESIS OF THE CONCEPT

I. Various Proposed Systems

The systems proposed to explain the origin of concepts may be reduced to three, two extreme and one intermediate. (1) At one extreme are found those who claim that the formation of the concept can be accounted for completely by the senses — presentation and representation — and their various complex functions; no special activity is required. (2) At the other extreme are found those who claim that the senses have nothing to do with the formation of the concept. It must be attributed to a special independent mental power. (3) Between these two are found those who claim that the senses are both necessary and insufficient to account for the concept. Intellectual knowledge begins with the senses, but rises higher and cannot be completed by them.

1. **First Extreme or Generally Sensism.** — (*a*) It is clear that if no other existence than that of matter is admitted, every form of knowledge must be reduced to the properties of matter. This was the conclusion of the older and cruder *materialists*, Empedocles, Leucippus, Democritus, Epicurus, who explained knowledge by the entering into the sense organs, of small material particles coming from the objects themselves. It is also the conclusion of the new and more elaborate materialism of the latter half of the eighteenth century in France and of the middle of the nineteenth

century in Germany. Thought in all its forms is the manifestation of some material energy.

(*b*) The name of *Sensationalism* is given especially to the systems of Locke and Condillac. According to Locke, all ideas come from experience, and experience is twofold: sensation by which external objects are perceived, and reflection by which we are aware of concrete mental processes. Ideas thus acquired are complex or simple according as they are repeated and combined with others or not. Condillac rejects reflection as a distinct source of knowledge. For him there is only one source, sensation together with its various transformations, which are attention or application to sensations, reflection or attention to successive sensations, memory or the power of recall, comparison or attention to simultaneous sensations and memories, judgment or perception of their relations of likeness and difference, imagination or the combination of ideas, reasoning or the inference of a judgment from other judgments.

(*c*) More recently the theory reducing all ideas to images has been and is still advocated, but as a more complete and more elaborate system. (1) The main point which is insisted on is the fusion of images by which, as in composite photographs, common features are made to stand prominent, while individual features are not apparent. There is thus a double process, dissociation and combination, the causes of which are either external and involuntary, especially the identity and dissimilarity of certain features, or internal, like elective attention, mental types, and special purpose. This process of addition and subtraction, or, perhaps better, of multiplication and division, gives the abstract and general idea which represents only common features. This is *Associationism* (Stuart Mill, Bain). (2) Others say that the idea remains really concrete, but we look upon it as abstract and general when it is expressed by a universal term, or common name, applying to a group of similar images. The label only, not the real content of the mind, is abstract and universal. This is *Nominalism* (Taine). (3) Finally, the process may be completed by accumulating the experiences and associations not only of the individual, but of his ancestors. Thus the individual is born, if not with ready-made ideas, at least with the capacity and aptitude for forming them immediately, because he profits by the work of mental combination of images which has taken place before and the results of which he inherits. This is *Evolutionism* added to *Associationism* (Spencer). And here, as in so many other instances, extremes meet, and this view comes close to innatism, which belongs to the aprioristic group of theories.

2. **Second Extreme or Generally Apriorism.** — It has four chief forms: Innatism, Transcendentalism, Ontologism, Traditionalism.

(*a*) According to *innatism* concepts are not acquired. All, or at least some, are inborn in the mind. (1) For Plato, this world is essentially changing and contingent; consequently our necessary ideas cannot be derived from sense-perception. There exists another world of which this visible world is only a participation, an appearance and a shadow, namely the world of ideas, in which are found, for instance, justice-in-itself, beauty-in-itself, virtue-in-itself, etc., whereas in our world are found only things that partake of these in various degrees, i.e. just things, beautiful things, virtuous actions, etc. Before being united with a body in this world, the soul preëxisted as a pure spirit in the world of ideas, and had the intuition of them. Its union with the organism — which is a punishment — deprives the soul of this intuition. The perception of things by the senses revives in the mind ideas acquired previously, but forgotten. Pure ideas are really remembrances.

(2) Descartes recognizes three kinds of ideas: adventitious, (from sense-perceptions), fictitious (built up by the imagination), and innate (universal and purely intellectual ideas). What Descartes means by innate ideas is not clear. Sometimes he speaks of them as actual and ready-made ideas or representations; sometimes, when pressed by the objections of his adversaries, he speaks of them as faculties or virtualities or even unconscious ideas.

(3) According to Leibniz, the soul having "neither doors nor windows," i.e. being incapable of communicating in any way with the external world, all ideas must be innate. But, of themselves, innate ideas are not yet conscious, not yet "apperceptions." They

are rather inclinations, dispositions, habits, or, better, germs which will evolve into conscious perceptions.

(*a*) Rosmini claimed that one idea at least, namely, the idea of being which is implied in every concept, must be innate.

(*b*) According to Kant, the mind must find in itself the "forms" according to which it knows things. The characters of universality and necessity which are found in some ideas cannot be derived from individual contingent objects; hence they come from the mind alone. Things-in-themselves exist, but, as such, are unknowable. They are necessarily known according to the mind's natural and inborn "a priori forms." We know things-as-they-appear to the mind (*phenomena*); to reach the thing-in-itself (*noumenon*) is impossible. This system is known as *transcendentalism.*

(*c*) For *ontologism* — Malebranche and a few Catholic philosophers of the nineteenth century — we know all things in God, the source not only of all being, but also of all knowledge. God alone is intelligible, and things are intelligible only through the divine intelligence.

(*d*) *Traditionalism* — another system of some Catholic philosophers: De Bonald, Lamennais, etc., in the nineteenth century — supposes that general ideas cannot be formed by the mind; they must be taught and transmitted by tradition, and therefore traditionalists have recourse to a primitive divine revelation.

3. **Intermediate System.** — The formation of concepts depends on, and begins with, the senses, but is completed by a special faculty, the intellect, distinct from them. (1) We have no innate ideas, and, in forming concepts, the intellect depends on sense-perception and images. The senses are thus the necessary point of departure of intellectual knowledge. (2) All sense-perceptions and images are representations of concrete and individual objects. To be elaborated into concepts they require a special operation, namely, abstraction, by which the material, individual, and concrete features of the image are, so to say, removed so as to leave only the essential and consequently common features. (3) Hence the formation of abstract and general ideas requires in the intellect a double function, one of activity, the other of receptivity.

By the former the sense-products are elaborated; by the latter the act itself of intellectual knowledge is performed.

II. Discussion of the Systems

It will be easier to begin with the last-mentioned system. Its very position between two extremes seems already to be in its favor. If it is true that "*In medio stat virtus*," it is frequently true also that "*In medio stat veritas.*" A system is not advocated by serious thinkers without good reasons, and when serious thinkers advocate systems that are diametrically opposed, it is generally safe to infer that there is some misunderstanding and some one-sidedness in their respective points of view. If another system can avail itself of the reasons in favor of both extremes, and avoid their shortcomings, it has a chance to stand nearer to the truth.

1. **Intellectual Knowledge Begins with, but is not Completed by, the Senses.** — Let us briefly give reasons for this proposition.

(*a*) Intellectual knowledge *depends on the senses*. In this we agree with the first extreme system and differ from most of the advocates of the second. By senses here we mean chiefly images with their various associations and fusions. The formation itself of the concept seems to depend ultimately on some corresponding image. For instance, to form the concept of a dog, I must have had the perception of a dog, or of animals closely akin to it, or I must have its appearance and nature explained to me. But once the concept has been acquired, any sign or image may recall it by association. Thus the word itself, "dog," which is a purely arbitrary and conventional term, is sufficient to recall my concept. Again, although the concept of a circle may be acquired without having ever seen a perfect geometrical circle, yet the elements which compose this complex concept depend ultimately on sense-perception from which the ideas of point, line, curve, etc., are formed.

The main reasons for asserting this dependence are based on the following facts: (1) The condition of the organism, especially of the brain, influences the highest mental functions, and, in many cases, mental disorders are traced back to organic, and especially cerebral, lesions and diseases. The influence of certain drugs and intoxicants is also too well known. (2) When some sense is lacking, no concept of things referring to this sense is possible. The man born blind may have ideas of mechanical vibrations, but not of colors as such. (3) Experience shows that the highest conceptions are greatly facilitated by the use of images, symbols, diagrams, etc.

(*b*) If the materials for forming concepts are found in perceptions and images, *these materials must be elaborated*. This is but the conclusion of what was said above (p. 96) on the impossibility of reducing the concept to the image. The senses always give representations that have individual, contingent, and concrete characters. A special power of abstraction must be used to elaborate these into a necessary and universal concept. The universal is radically in things, since they have an essence which may be looked upon as common when considered apart from the individual notes with which it is really found in nature; but, as a universal, it exists only in the mind. The image gives the necessary basis on which the concept can be formed.

(*c*) Knowing the starting-point, i.e. the senses, and the result, i.e. the concept, the question remains: How can the bridging over be effected? Here we need a special activity, or "intellectus agens," whose function is abstraction and the elaboration of the data of the senses into some higher idea whose nature is purely intellectual. This process of abstraction is also called illumination, as it throws light on certain features and leaves others in darkness. Thus is formed the abstract concept, which is a special mental representation deprived of the material and individual features found in the mental image, and which consequently may be applied to all individuals that belong to the same class.

2. **Sensism.** — (*a*) In general sensism rightly recognizes the necessity of the senses for intellectual knowledge; but it does not go far enough in its account, for it denies the radical distinction which exists between the concept and the image. A defect in the method used may be pointed out: Sensists generally try to explain the origin of concepts without examining first their specific characteristics. They seem to take it for granted a priori that the

concept must be reduced to some activity of the senses. It is true that the general law of continuity applies here, and that the passage from the image to the concept is gradual, but this does not prevent the two from being different and irreducible. Sometimes even metaphysical preoccupations — concerning the nature of the soul and its spirituality — seem to be found at the start of this investigation. It may also be noted that sensists often implicitly assume the existence of a special faculty of elaboration, even when they deny it.

To all forms of sensism the following objections apply: (1) They fail to recognize the distinction between concept and image. (2) Either, if they are consistent, they cannot account for the special characteristics of the concept; or, if they do, it is by introducing tacitly the special activity which they deny. In fact, when carefully considered, sensistic theories are seen to introduce special activities, reflection, the power of transforming the sensations, the power of elective attention or elaboration, and the like. (3) Frequently sensism is only a consequence or application of a wider philosophical view, materialism, positivism, etc.

(*b*) The features special to some systems do not obviate these difficulties. (1) *Reflection* is only the consciousness of the mind's own individual and concrete activities. (2) The *transformation* of the sensation either does not account for the formation of the concept, or, if it accounts for it, requires a special elaborative faculty. (3) The *association*, or, better, fusion, of images may give a composite image; but this cannot be identified with the concept, even if we give it the accumulated associations of centuries. (4) The *name*, it is true, may be common and applicable to all individuals of the same class. Yet the name as written or uttered is always concrete; it is abstract and common only because it expresses an abstract and general idea. Suppress the abstract idea which it manifests, and the word is then a mere concrete utterance, at such a time, with such a sound, and in such circumstances. Far from giving to the image its abstract character, the name must itself receive it from the idea for which it stands. When I apply the name "triangle" to all triangles, it is because I have already recognized that which is essential to a triangle, and considered this apart from the determinations with which it is always accompanied in the perceived or imagined triangle, of such an area, right-angled or otherwise, scalene or otherwise, with sides of a definite length, angles of definite dimensions, etc.

3. **Apriorism.** — As aprioristic systems are widely different, they must be considered separately. In general, all rightly recognize the impossibility of deriving the concept from mere sense-experience, but wrongly fail to recognize the dependence of the concept on the senses.

(*a*) *Ontologism* and *traditionalism* were systems designed by Catholic philosophers to counteract extreme materialistic, sensistic, and rationalistic tendencies in the past century. Both were condemned by the Church and soon disappeared. Hence a few remarks will suffice here. Ontologism is gratuitous and in opposition to the testimony of consciousness. Ontologists took a great deal of trouble to explain the intuition of God, which, according to them, we must necessarily possess; but their explanation is satisfactory neither to the philosopher nor to the theologian.

Traditionalism contains much that must be accepted. Undoubtedly tradition transmitted by language is a great help in acquiring ideas. For the most part, our ideas are received from others, and, if our individual minds were left to their own activity, all ideas would remain very imperfect. But it does not follow that no idea can be acquired otherwise. In fact, in order to convey ideas to the hearer or reader, language must be understood, and understanding supposes in the hearer or reader the ideas which the words represent. If words presuppose ideas, it is clear that they cannot be the exclusive source of ideas.

(*b*) *The theory of innate ideas* is a purely gratuitous and lazy theory, since there is no consciousness of them, and their innateness is not the only way of accounting for their presence in the mind. On the contrary, we are conscious of the mental activity by which we elaborate concepts from the data of the senses, and of a continuity, not of a break, between the senses and the intellect. To say that ideas are ready-made and conscious is obviously false. To say that they are ready-made, yet unconscious, is to say nothing intelligible. To say that they are mere faculties and virtualities is to deny that they are innate and to fall back into another system admitting only the power of forming concepts.

(c) *Kant's special views* on the present problem are but parts of his whole philosophy, and cannot be discussed fully here. His solution cannot be proved to have any real value, as it may be nothing but a result of a priori forms of the mind. It is difficult to understand the meaning of these a priori forms which are empty until they receive experiences from the external world, and, after receiving them, form with them the complete knowledge. Nor does it seem possible to demonstrate the necessity of their existence. The principle: "Whatever is necessary and universal in knowledge must come from the mind, and not from the object," is gratuitous until it has been shown that these characteristics are not radically in objects themselves, and therefore can in no way be found in them. Thus we are told that, since all things are perceived in space, and all mental processes in time, space and time are presupposed to any perception; they must preëxist in the mind as a priori forms of external and of internal sensibility. It would be equally reasonable to say that they do not preexist, but simply coexist, and, in this case, the ideas of space and time may be derived from things and processes themselves. From the fact that all things are perceived in space, I may simply conclude that all things are in space, and are perceived as they are. The same may be said of all a priori forms; their existence is not to be admitted if facts can be accounted for otherwise.

4. **Conclusion.** — From what has been said we conclude that, of the two extreme systems proposed to explain the origin of concepts, one starts rightly but stops too low, the other ends rightly but starts too high. The intermediate system has the advantage of being in better conformity with experience, and of giving a sufficient explanation with a minimum of a priori elements.

ARTICLE IV. JUDGMENT

I. NATURE OF THE JUDGMENT

I. The Psychological Process

1. **What is Judgment?** — (*a*) Human thinking essentially takes the form of judgments; judgment alone has a meaning and is true or false. I may have the idea of four miles, and the idea of the distance from a place *A* to another place *B*. There is no meaning, no truth or falsity, in these ideas taken separately, but only when I compare them and think or say that the distance from *A* to *B* is, or is not, four miles. This is a judgment, and the new essential element which has been introduced is the connecting link between two ideas, by which I pronounce on their agreement or disagreement. A mere list of words gives no meaning, unless these words are so connected as to form judgments. Conversations, writings, scientific formulæ, speeches, etc., all express judgments, and not merely ideas, although idea is sometimes used in the sense of judgment (cf. p. 93). Strictly, an idea is a mere representation of an object. When we speak of a true or of a false idea according as it does or does not correspond to reality, we really speak of an implicit judgment pronouncing on this conformity. *Judging is essentially affirming the relations between things or ideas*, relations which may be of agreement or disagreement, of affirmation or negation.

(*b*) Hence the distinction between positive and negative judgments, however true it may be from a certain point of view, and useful for certain purposes, is not strictly applicable to the psychological act of judging, which is always essentially positive. The judgment: "Peter is not attentive," is negative from the point of view of grammar and logic; yet, if I consider only the nature of the mental process, it consists essentially of the positive act by which I pronounce or judge that there is a lack of attention in Peter's mind. The mental attitude opposed to this would be rather ignorance or doubt.

2. **Elements and Conditions of a Judgment.** — A judgment

always implies: (1) The presence of *two ideas* in the mind, namely, the subject, of which something is affirmed or denied, and the attribute or predicate, which is affirmed or denied of the subject. (2) A *comparison* of these two ideas. (3) The *affirmation* of their agreement or disagreement, which is the judgment itself.

The judgment may be reached very rapidly as soon as the two ideas are brought in presence of each other. The comparison is only implicit and needs no special attention, as, for instance, when I say that the whole is greater than any of its parts. Or it may necessitate a more or less complex process of comparison of the ideas with other ideas and judgments, as, for instance, when I say that the sum of the three angles of a triangle is equal to two right angles. This cannot be affirmed immediately, but only after demonstrating it.

3. **Judgment and Concept Compared.** — We may now understand the relations between judgment and conception. A concept is one notion standing apart from other notions. A judgment necessarily implies at least two notions or groups of notions, and the perception of their relation. But a notion which is the necessary element of a judgment depends itself on previous judgments. Our first concepts are vague and most general; they become clearer and clearer, more and more connotative, in proportion as they embody the results of more judgments. Thus my primitive idea of "water" as a flowing something, or a transparent liquid, may be perfected by the judgment that it is composed of oxygen and hydrogen, or that it has certain definite physical properties. These new elements in my idea of water are the results of a great many comparisons and judgments. The botanist's notion of a plant is more complex and more accurate than that of the ordinary man because it embodies many elements acquired by study, i.e. by a series of judgments.

II. Various Kinds of Judgments

N.B. We mention only the most important divisions of judgments from the psychological point of view. Other divisions belong to logic.

1. **Singular and General.** — According as the subject is an individual or a class, a concrete or an abstract idea, the judgment is singular or general, concrete or abstract. Thus, "This man is tall," or "This rose is red," are individual and concrete judgments. "Man is made to live in society," or "Roses are fragrant," are judgments referring to a class, and their predicates are attributed, not to any special individual, but to all. General judgments are also abstract, since the class as such does not exist, but is realized only in the concrete individuals. Universal judgments refer to all concrete individuals of a class, e.g. "All men are made to live in society," "All roses are fragrant." Partial judgments pronounce only on a part of the whole class. Thus, "Some men are white."

2. **Analytic and Synthetic.** — When the predicate is already contained in the nature or essential relations and properties of the subject, the judgment is called analytical; the predicate may be inferred from the consideration of the subject. When the predicate adds something new to the subject, that is, something which no amount of analysis of the subject would reveal, the judgment is synthetical. The analytic judgment unfolds the subject, and states explicitly that which was already implied in it and in its essential relations. The synthetic judgment gives a knowledge which could not be derived from the essence of the subject.

We must distinguish between the subject itself of the judgment and the knowledge which we have of it. A judgment may be analytic in itself, and yet synthetic for a given individual; and a judgment which is synthetic for one may be analytic for another who possesses a more complete knowledge of the subject. Thus the judgments "Two and two are four," or "The whole is greater than any of its parts," are obvious for all those who understand the meaning of the terms used. The same cannot be said of these judgments: "11 multiplied by 12 is 132," or "The sum of the angles of a triangle equals two right angles." In themselves these judgments are analytic, yet all men do not see why the predicate belongs essentially to the subject. On the contrary, such judgments as "This man is six feet tall," or "This iron is hot," are synthetic, because the predicate is not essentially contained in the analysis of the subject.

Hence *analytical* judgments are also called *necessary*, because they suffer no exception; *absolute*, because they do not depend on any condition; *a priori*, because they need not be known by experience before their truth is accepted. Thus, after demonstration, the theorem "The sum of the three angles of a triangle is equal to two right angles," is seen to express an essential property of all kinds of triangles, true of all triangles without exception and under all circumstances. It is not necessary to measure the angles of any given triangle to see that the theorem applies to it. *Synthetical* judgments are called *contingent*, *hypothetical*, and *a posteriori*, because they are based directly on experience, and are true only of the cases observed, or within the limits of a valid generalization. Experience alone can justify the statements: "This book has five hundred pages;" "This man is learned;" "This triangle is isosceles."

3. **Intuitive and Deliberative.** — Considering the manner in which they are arrived at, judgments are intuitive or deliberative. An intuitive or immediate judgment is a judgment which is reached immediately as soon as both terms are compared. The intuition may be a sense intuition, as in the judgment "This iron is hot," or a direct perception of consciousness, as "I am suffering," or a rational intuition, as "The whole is greater than its part." A deliberative or mediate judgment is a judgment which cannot be passed at once, but requires a more or less prolonged consideration, study, and reasoning, e.g. the formulation of physical and chemical laws and properties.

II. GENESIS OF THE JUDGMENT

I. General

N.B. We do not speak here of extra-intellectual factors in the formation of judgments, such as feelings, prejudices, personal dispositions, etc. They will be mentioned later.

1. **Analysis and Synthesis in the Judgment.** — (*a*) Judgment supposes the power of abstraction. Frequently the subject is abstract and stands, not for something individual and concrete, but for an abstract quality or a class, as "Virtue is to be prac-

tised," "Iron is a metal." Generally the predicate is abstract, the only exception being for judgments in which there is a perfect identity between the subject and the predicate, as when I say, "This man is Peter Smith." In other cases the predicate is the concept of a class to which the subject belongs or not, of a quality which is affirmed or denied of it.

(*b*) The same judgment may often be considered both as an analysis and a synthesis of the subject. I say, for instance, "This paper is white." As explained above, this is a synthetic judgment; the mere analysis of the notion "paper" will not give me the predicate "white," but I have to verify it by experience. This judgment is therefore the synthesis of two terms, "paper" and "white." Yet, in another sense, this same judgment is really the result of my one perception of white paper, which I have first to disjoin or analyze into two elements in order to form the above judgment, i.e. in order to synthetize them again. However, a judgment based immediately on sense-perception differs from this perception, because the perception is concrete, "this-white-paper," whereas in the judgment "This paper is white" the predicate is abstract and general.

2. **Experience and Reason in the Judgment.** — In all synthetic judgments some perception or experience is required to ascertain the relation between the subject and the predicate. Not that the experience need be repeated in every individual case; it is not necessary to decompose all drops of water to pronounce with certitude that they are composed of the same definite proportions of hydrogen and oxygen. Natural laws like those of physics and chemistry are universal, although they have not been verified experimentally for all individual cases. But all rest on some experience interpreted with the help of reason. They never reach the same degree of certitude which we attribute to certain other principles, for we conceive that the laws that govern the world might be different, whereas we cannot conceive of a whole not being equal to the sum of its parts. This leads us to examine the genesis of a priori and necessary principles.

II. Genesis of Necessary Judgments

1. **Meaning.** — Necessary judgments as understood here are those that are simple, clear, primitive, and immediate, needing no demonstration, and self-evident as soon as their terms are understood. They are *a priori* and *analytical* — admitted independently of their verification by experience; *necessary* — the negation of them is absurdity; *universal* both in regard to the knowing mind, which cannot fail to perceive their truth, and in regard to their range of application, for they admit of no possible exception at any time or in any place. Hence we do not speak here of all analytic judgments, but only of those that are obvious and require no demonstration. That is, we speak of principles, or judgments that stand in the very beginning of intellectual life, and that are admitted even before or without verification by experience. Thus the principles of identity: "*A* is *A*," or "A thing is what it is"; of excluded middle: "*A* is or is not"; of contradiction: "The same thing cannot be and not be at the same time"; of sufficient reason: "Whatever exists has a sufficient reason accounting for its existence or happening." Thus also in geometry such principles as: "The whole is greater than any of its parts, and equal to the sum of its parts"; "Two things which are equal to the same third are equal to each other;" "A straight line cannot enclose a space."

These principles are not formulated explicitly by all minds, but they are implicitly recognized by all. The child may know nothing of the explicit statement called the principle of contradiction, yet he does not fail to recognize that one of two assertions which he knows to be contradictory is a falsehood. A man may not be aware that he is applying the principle of causality and of sufficient reason when he concludes that the house has not built itself, but requires an architect; yet he will consider it absurd to require proofs for his assertion. Ask a child to give you half his apple, and try to convince him that he will lose nothing by it and that what will be left is as big as the whole apple.

Now the question is: Wherefrom do such principles derive their characters of necessity and universality so as to admit of no exception?

2. **Theories.** — We need not discuss theories of apriorism and innatism. If there is no reason for asserting the existence of innate ideas, still less is there any for asserting the innateness of principles. Two main systems remain, *intuitionalism* and *empiricism*. (1) According to the former, the senses furnish the mind with the concrete materials out of which are elaborated abstract ideas, or concepts, representing the essences of things. The mind is thus enabled to perceive and affirm their essential and necessary relations. Thus the concepts of whole and of part are not given in pure experience; they are abstractions and elaborations from experience. The relation between them is at once clear to the mind independently of the actual concrete perception of a whole and its parts. (2) According to the empirical theory, or associationism, principles are simply the results of many associated experiences in which they have been constantly verified. The individual's experience is strengthened by the experiences of his ancestors, which were accumulated in the course of ages and transmitted by heredity. Such judgments may perhaps seem intuitive to us now, but their formation has required many concrete experiences of instances in which they were applied.

3. **Criticism of Associationism.** (*a*) A mere empirical theory is inadequate to give a satisfactory account of necessary judgments and axioms. Experience manifests only that which exists, but does not reveal whether things are *necessarily* or not. We are not concerned at present simply with what happens or is true, nor even with what always happens or is always true, but with what happens and is true *necessarily* so that it could never be otherwise. *This character of necessity cannot be found in experience.* A man may not have seen many or even any straight lines, yet he knows a priori that two straight lines cannot enclose a space. He may never have seen parallels, yet he will not hesitate to pronounce that parallels can never meet, because the principle of contradiction is implied here: Lines always at the same distance cannot at the same time change their respective distances.

(*b*) In order to have any reliable, orderly, and organized experience, certain *principles*, like those of identity and contradiction, are already required; they cannot therefore result exclusively from experience. How is any experience possible if the same thing can at the same time be and not be, be perceived and not perceived, true and not true, white and not white, etc.?

(*c*) Finally, it may be noted that, for such principles, no trace whatever of any increase of evidence or firmness is found either in the individual or the race. At all times they are accepted as clear and self-evident, and repeated experience does not strengthen them. Ever since men have been, their thinking has implied certain principles admitted as necessary and universal; their experience has constantly testified to the regular succession of day and night resulting from the apparent revolution of the sun around the earth. Yet such constant experience does not show this regular succession every twenty-four hours as necessary and universal. The empiricist may say that this is due to the known possibility of different experiences on the earth or on other planets, as revealed by science. But his explanation implies the very distinction of the necessary and the contingent which is not given in experience, but derived from some other source. In experience we never find necessity, but at most universal contingency.

4. **Conclusion.** — Hence we say that principles are neither *a priori*, if by this we mean innate and without any empirical factor, nor yet *a posteriori*, if by this we exclude the rational factor. They are both. Experience is necessary to form the abstract ideas the relations of which are affirmed by these principles; and it is useful for their reflex knowledge, formulation, and application to concrete instances. But this experience is not necessarily so frequent and repeated as to produce invincible associations, as empiricists claim. The terms being known, the mind has at once the intuition of their necessary relation of agreement or disagreement. Knowing things, not only in their individual and concrete existence, but in their abstract, general, and essential aspects, the mind is also capable of perceiving the essential relations which exist between them.

III. Genesis of Mediate Judgments. Inference. Reasoning

1. **Nature of the Reasoning Process.** — (*a*) Thinking consists essentially in judging, and is complete only when we can affirm or deny. We frequently say: "I think so," by which we implicitly formulate a judgment. We also say: "Let me think a minute," by which we mean that a little reflection and consideration is needed before we can express an opinion, make an assertion, and see the relation between ideas, i.e. pass a judgment. In this latter sense thought is equivalent to inference or reasoning. The immediate or intuitive judgments of sense or reason are few when compared to the number of judgments obtained by explicit or implicit reasoning. *In an intuitive and immediate judgment, no reason can be given* except that the truth is seen at once, and that the judgment is self-evident. *In the mediate judgment*, obtained by reasoning — reasoning is only a means toward judging — *a reason can be given on which it rests and on which its truth depends;* the link between two or several judgments is perceived.

(*b*) Hence we see the *difference between reasoning and association*. Ih association also one idea or judgment is linked with another, but *without dependence* as far as the truth of the second judgment is concerned. One idea gives rise to another, but it is a mere succession. Thus, if I see John sick with a cold, a number of ideas may be recalled to my mind by association; of boys running, drinking cold water, being careless . . . ; of remedies and drug stores . . . ; of coughing, staying in bed . . . ; of other diseases, other persons . . . etc. This is not reasoning. But, if I say: "John is sick because he remained in a draught of cold air," or: "This remedy will cure him because it has cured Peter and Henry in the same circumstances," then I perceive a *relation of dependence* between two judgments; I conceive one as being the foundation of another. This is reasoning.

(*c*) It is clear that the great majority of our judgments are based on some inference, sometimes explicit, sometimes also existing implicitly in the mind, and ready to express itself in the form of a "because." When a judgment is not immediate, it is always accepted *because* of something else. Whether the psychological process be valid or not from the point of view of logic and epistemology, the psychological process is the same.

2. **Elements of the Reasoning Process.** — (*a*) From what has just been said, it is easy to understand that the elements of reasoning are not only several ideas, but *several judgments*, which must be present explicitly or implicitly in the mind, and one of which is considered as a consequence of the others. This consequence may be expressed last: "He who wilfully injures his neighbor is worthy of blame; Peter has stolen, and to steal is wilfully to injure one's neighbor; consequently Peter is blameworthy." Or it may be expressed first: "Peter is blameworthy because he has stolen, thereby injuring his neighbor." Or it may find an intermediate place: "Peter has stolen; he is therefore blameworthy, since whoever wilfully injures his neighbor is blameworthy." In Logic we shall see how these may be reduced to perfect syllogisms. For the present we are concerned with the process of syllogism as we generally use it.

(*b*) The foregoing examples show that reasoning always includes a *universal element* or law, and a more *special instance* or application. Even in cases in which we seem to pass from one particular or individual instance to another a general statement is implied. Thus: "This remedy is likely to do good to John because it did good to Peter," implies that in both cases the diseases are of the same nature, and that in the same circumstances the same remedy will produce the same effect. Again, when I say: "We shall have rain because such clouds are forming and the wind comes from such a direction," I seem to derive my conclusion from concrete facts of past experience. Yet I suppose the general principle that such a direction of the wind and such clouds are generally followed by rain.

3. **Inductive and Deductive Reasoning.** — (*a*) When the general principle or law is the *goal* reached or the conclusion, the reasoning is *inductive*. When it is the *starting-point* or the reason, the reasoning process is called *deductive*. If I have been deceived by one, then by another, and by a third man with whom I dealt, I say — rightly or wrongly, it matters not for our present purpose

—"All men, or at least all men of this class, are liars" (induction). Now when I say: "Beware of *A*, he will tell you all sorts of stories, for, you know, he is engaged in such or such a profession," I proceed deductively. Again, it is by induction or generalization that the chemist pronounces that all water is composed of oxygen and hydrogen. It is by deduction that he applies this to a glass of water which he has never analyzed. These two processes complete each other. We proceed from the observed facts to the law, and from the law to the unobserved facts.

(*b*) *Induction is primarily analytic; deduction, primarily synthetic.* By *analysis* is meant the resolution of the complex into that which is more simple; by *synthesis*, the combination of simple elements into something more complex. A general proposition is simpler than the individual fact, because it does not include the concrete determinations special to each instance. "All bodies attract one another in direct ratio to their masses and in inverse ratio to the square of the distances" is a simpler statement than that which determines all the particulars in the case of this body whose mass is *A*, and this other body whose mass is *B*, the distance between the two being *C*.

IV. The Processes of Judging and Reasoning in Ordinary Life

1. There are Three Ways of Forming Judgments. — (1) As stated already, some judgments are *intuitive*, i.e. accepted in view of their self-evidence. I say that snow is white because I see that it is so; that two and two are four because I understand that it cannot be otherwise. (2) Other judgments are *accepted on the authority of other men*. I know that Napoleon was emperor of the French, that Columbus discovered America, and that Peking is a city in China. For these and a multitude of other judgments I depend on the testimony, and therefore on the knowledge and truthfulness of other men who either exist now or have existed in the past. The same is true of many scientific statements. Empirical science need not always be a science based on one's own experience. Little progress would be made if, before accepting the report of an experiment, one always had to perform the same experiment. There are facts that occur only once or a few times, and cannot be observed by all. (3) A third way of forming a judgment is *to reason it out*. For instance, I find two contradictory statements, say, on a political or religious question. I endeavor to get the data on both sides, weigh the arguments, use my own intelligence, and form my own judgment. In all sciences and in daily life many statements are based on personal inference. And even when a truth is based on authority, its acceptance supposes inferences concerning the value of the testimony of others.

It is evident that judgments reached by these methods are not considered as having always the same value; and, within the same method, judgments are more or less certain, probable, or doubtful. The process by which they are reached may be short and simple, or require long and difficult demonstrations.

2. **Prejudices.** — (*a*) Reflection shows that frequently assent is given to judgments that do not deserve it. Things considered as certainly true, and never before suspected of being even doubtful, may be rejected later as certainly false. As a result of more careful study and greater mental development, it is found that a number of judgments must be revised. Statements that were not self-evident were accepted without reason, or for insufficient reasons. Early education gives the child a number of ideas and beliefs which are accepted on authority or insufficient inference, and even are the results of misunderstanding and misinterpretation. One may find many misrepresentations in former beliefs now outgrown, arising from various causes and circumstances. See how many popular maxims, proverbs, and sayings concerning health, happiness, social life, and even the weather, are accepted without reflection. Even when disproved by science and personal experience, they still hold their ground; favorable occurrences strengthen them; contrary occurrences are looked upon as exceptions. Surroundings, daily intercourse with other men, bodily and mental dispositions, contribute to form a nucleus of knowledge which, little by little, is developed and increased, and which is the centre toward which all knowledge converges.

(*b*) We become accustomed to these judgments. Like all habits they become stronger, and take a deeper root by daily acceptance and by the uses or applications — at least implicit — which are made of them. They form a bulk of supposedly known and ascertained truths, and become the standard to which we refer and by which we judge new propositions offered for our acceptance. If we reach a pleasant conclusion, little or no trouble is taken to verify it. Mere hearsay becomes the highest source of certitude. But sometimes the most cogent arguments do not succeed in leading to the acceptance of an unpleasant conclusion. See, for instance, how ready a man is to accept as true the slanders he hears about his enemy, and how reluctantly he admits the good qualities that are attributed to him. An obvious fact or argument against one's fixed ideas may convince for the time being. If it does not frequently reënter the mind so as to strengthen its impression, it soon loses its hold on the mind. A few days or months later it may have been forgotten, and the conviction may have vanished. The new and unexpected takes root with difficulty; it rather tends to remain at the surface and wither, because the mental soil is already occupied by deep-rooted judgments which are not easily torn away.

(*c*) In all cases the value of new judgments is tested by comparing them with other judgments accepted as certain and used as norms. And as man is loath to break with inveterate habits and to discard long-standing opinions, so is he likely to reject, or at least to suspect a priori, whatever conflicts with his previous views.

(*d*) Because these judgments are habitual and familiar they attract no attention or reflection. It hardly occurs to the mind to question or test them until some strong evidence is offered against their validity. Even in this case they cling to the mind until obliged to retreat — a step which, like the breaking of an old habit, is always more or less painful. Because they are unnoticed they are the more dangerous.

(*e*) A large number of habitual views and opinions are true, but many also are narrow and belong to an individual man or a special group of men as a result of their education. They arouse the curiosity, sometimes the suspicion and hatred, of other individuals or groups of men. They are sources of misunderstanding, frequently without any ill-will on either side, but too often with the imputation of ill-will on the part of those whose opinions are different. A man cannot be educated by, or associate with, other men without reflecting in some degree their views and opinions. This is true especially of children and young people, because their minds are more receptive and more easily influenced. Hence the importance of a good early intellectual education cannot be overestimated; its influence extends to the whole life. All judgments acquired without sufficient justification, whether they be true or false, influence following judgments. *For good or for bad, they are prejudices.*

3. **Knowledge and Belief.** — (*a*) This leads us to recognize an important distinction between what may be called *impersonal* and *personal* truths. *Impersonal truth* is that which is so evident that it imposes itself on all. The reasons for accepting it are cogent, and appeal to all minds to whom they are presented. *Personal truths* have not the same evidence; they are accepted owing to both objective and subjective influences. Generally they are truths which carry with them practical consequences and are the sources of certain rules of conduct. To this class belong many judgments in the religious, moral, political, and social orders.

(*b*) This distinction corresponds to a distinction which is frequently made between knowledge and belief. *Knowledge* is based on immediate or mediate evidence and is essentially rational. *Belief* refers to that which is not evident, or at least not clearly so; thus it is partly rational, partly emotional, and partly volitional in its causes. In the acceptance of a statement, the proportion of objective and subjective influences may vary; a truth is more or less impersonal and more or less personal.

(*c*) With truths of the first class, e.g. a theorem of geometry, only the *intellect* is concerned. In truths of the second class the *whole man* is interested, and all the faculties contribute to influence the judgment. "Thy wish was father, Harry, to that thought" (Henry IV, P. II, act iv, sc. iv) is applicable to many thoughts, and, at times, all of us are so many Harries. As a matter of fact — we are not concerned at present with what should be, but with what is — judgments are influenced by motives which do not come simply from reason, but from prejudices, feelings, desires, and will. These blind man, and either prevent him from accepting reasons at all, or act as convex or concave lenses through which reasons are seen in such a way that their real value is exaggerated or minimized. Even in truths that are of themselves impersonal it may happen that, because a man has a theory which he cherishes, he will rather close his eyes than examine facts which, if admitted, would be irreconcilable with the theory accepted so far.

To sum up: *In the majority of our assents we are not simply drawn by objective light and evidence, but also impelled and prompted by subjective and internal motives which may or may not be explicitly recognized in consciousness.*

4. **Three Uses of Reasoning.** — Man, being reasonable, is not satisfied until he can give to himself and to others a reason for his judgments. Reasoning and proving may be used for three purposes, to form judgments, to test those that are already accepted, and to convince others.

(*a*) When the truth is not known, we endeavor to *find* it by investigating, comparing, and weighing the evidence for and against it. This is chiefly the work of reason; but, as mentioned already, reason is sometimes guided — or rather misguided and blinded — by preconceived ideas and prejudices.

(*b*) When a judgment is already accepted, and we want to examine whether it is sufficiently justified, reasoning is again used as a *test* to revise the motives and arguments and estimate their value. Too frequently again, especially in matters of practical interest, reasoning is used to justify rather than to test. An opinion is already accepted, and only motives that can make it appear reasonable are considered, or their value is magnified, while the value of antagonistic motives is lessened. In such cases, judgments are not based on reasons, but rather reasons are adapted to suit our judgments. They are like the pretexts which are sometimes found to justify in one's own eyes, and, if possible, in the eyes of others, a course of action which one has already determined to follow.

(*c*) When reasoning is used to *convince* other men, two things must be kept in mind: the nature of the truth itself, and the mental dispositions of the man or of the audience addressed. According as the statement which is presented has an impersonal or a personal character in the sense explained above, the process of argumentation will assume a more rigid and more formal aspect, or a warmer and more highly colored tone. In one case, reason alone, in the other case, all human activities and feelings, will be appealed to. A political principle is not demonstrated in the same way as a theorem of geometry. According as the audience is well disposed or hostile, fair or prejudiced, the speaker will again assume different attitudes. In every case, since the truth must enter the mind, it is necessary first to remove obstacles, then to prepare the mind for its reception and assimilation, and finally to present the truth in the best adapted manner. The same truth presented differently, by different persons, to different hearers, in different ways, and different circumstances, will produce an innumerable variety of results. Hear, for instance, the simple statement: "Miss So-and-So was in church yesterday," and listen to the comment started by the mention of such a fact.

ARTICLE V. LANGUAGE

I. THE FUNCTION OF LANGUAGE

I. Signs in General. Signs of Mental Processes

Mental processes are essentially private and personal. They are not manifested directly by the action of one mind upon another, but indirectly by means of signs. I know the opinion of another man because he told me or because I read it. I know his grief or joy because I see him weeping or laughing. Words, spoken or written, tears, laughter, are so many signs of mental processes.

1. **Meaning of Sign.** — A sign is whatever manifests something else because of some relation between the two, like similarity, causality, association, or convention among men. A certain position of the semaphore is a sign of danger for the engineer. A certain form of clouds, direction of the wind, peculiarity of the

atmosphere, are signs of an impending storm. The sign is perceived directly, and the thing signified, indirectly. The same thing may be a sign for one man and not for another, according as the relation between it and something else is known or not. The interpretation of signs is the work of mental association and judgment.

2. **Division of Signs.** — (*a*) A sign is *natural* when its relation with the thing it signifies comes from nature itself. When this relation is one of similarity the sign is called *formal*. Thus certain clouds are the natural signs of coming rain; smoke is the natural sign of fire; a picture is the natural and formal sign of the individual whom it represents. On the contrary, the sign is *conventional* when its signification is based merely on an agreement between men. Such are the signals for trains or vessels, the telegraphic codes, the flags of the different nations, the red, white, and blue striped pole to indicate a barber shop, etc. A sign may be neither strictly natural nor strictly conventional but share in the nature of both. Thus a sword is the emblem of war; a crown, the emblem of royalty, etc.

(*b*) Signs are more or less *certain*, or *equivocal*, according as they are clear and refer to one thing only, or are vague and may refer to several things. Thus a symptom may be the certain sign of a special disease; smoke the certain sign of fire; a sentence the certain sign of a meaning. But a tower is not certainly the sign of a church; perspiration not necessarily a sign of hot weather; constant reading not always a sign of science or of studiousness. Different signs may signify the same thing, or the same sign different things.

(*c*) Signs may be perceived by any of the five senses. I see a certain badge and I know that the man wearing it is a policeman; I hear a bell and become aware that the church service is about to begin; I touch a patient and his temperature is a sign of fever; I smell tobacco smoke and am sure it is coming from a good cigar; I taste an apple and am sure that it may do me harm because it is not ripe.

3. **The Signs of Mental Processes may be:** (*a*) *Natural or conventional*, or partly natural and partly conventional. Thus

crying is the natural sign of pain; laughing the natural sign of mirth; clenching the fist the natural sign of anger. Some words — in onomatopœia — may also be considered as natural signs, but they are exceptions, for words generally have a purely conventional meaning. The form of letters, the spelling and pronunciation of words are also conventional. Some gestures are natural, e.g. pointing toward a certain direction to call attention to an object; others are artificial, e.g. the language-signs of the deaf and dumb; others seem to depend both on nature and convention, e.g. many of the gestures of an orator.

(*b*) *Certain or doubtful.* Some words and sentences have a clear meaning; others are equivocal. The expression on the face is not always easy to interpret, and the corresponding feelings cannot always be inferred. The modes of salutation vary with different countries; the same gesture or action may be a sign of respect in one place, and an insult in another. Signs are frequently misunderstood owing either to the nature of the sign itself, and the circumstances in which it is used, or to the ignorance, distraction, and mental preoccupation of the man to whom it is given.

(*c*) *Visual, auditory, and tactual.* Touch is not a frequent sign of mental processes except for the blind. Hence normally there remain two classes of signs: auditory, like cries, speech, singing; visual, like certain physiognomical expressions, gestures, writing.

II. Special Signs of Intellectual Ideas. Language

1. **Nature of Language.** — The term "language" applies to *a system of rational and conventional signs which express abstract and general ideas and the various relations between these ideas.* It manifests thought in the strict sense, and thus does not refer to the manifestations of emotions and feelings, such as crying, laughing, or blushing. Animals may give signs of their mental states, but language proper belongs to man alone. The same words may be uttered by a man and a parrot, but in the former case only do they manifest ideas; in the latter they are the results of sensory associations and have no conscious meaning. Man alone has devised

rational means of communication with other men. Bugle calls, cannon and gun reports, ringing of bells, blowing of whistles, etc., are, or may be, so many auditory signs of orders and ideas. Semaphores, flag signals, lights of certain colors, bodily gestures, etc., are so many visual signs which manifest thoughts or inferences; for instance, that a train has passed the station recently and consequently is still within a short distance, thus making it dangerous for the present train to proceed.

However important these signs may be, there are two means of communication which are more common, more usual, and of greater value: one auditory, *spoken language;* the other visual, *written language.* In fact, all the others may be reduced to these. The signs of the deaf and dumb stand for alphabetical letters, the bugle call for a definite sentence or order, the red lantern for a warning of danger, etc.

2. **Speech and Writing Compared.** — (*a*) *Speech has several advantages over writing.* (1) The visual field extends only in a certain direction and is intercepted by opaque bodies. Sounds can be heard from any direction, and are not so easily intercepted. Hence sound attracts the attention more easily. (2) Visual signs depend on light; sounds are heard even in obscurity. (3) Speech, especially when combined with facial expression and gestures, is more living than writing, and expresses better the feelings that accompany the ideas.

(*b*) On the other hand, *writing has several advantages over speech.* (1) It is more permanent. (2) It can be transmitted more easily, and with less danger of alteration. (3) Hence it can reach a greater number of persons, especially by printing.

(*c*) In certain modes of writing, such as hieroglyphics, the sign is directly the sign of the thing or rather of the idea of the thing. But in modern writing, the sign represents directly the sound. Thus a certain group of signs stands for the sound "cat," which in turn stands for the idea.

3. **Acquisition of Language.** — In the acquisition of language the child is helped greatly by the fact that there are other speaking men to teach him. At first the exercise of the limbs and of the vocal organs is spontaneous; movements and cries manifest only

sensations and feelings. These signs become rational little by little as reason itself develops. The main factors in this acquisition of language are:

(*a*) *Natural signs*. The attention of the child is called to certain objects by appropriate gestures, and their names are pronounced until the association between the sound and the thing is established. Easy names are learned first, like "papa," "bow-wow," etc.

(*b*) On the part of the child there are also certain *natural manifestations* of painful or agreeable states, and to these correspond certain actions on the part of the mother or the nurse. Another association is formed, and the desire to have his mother come may induce the child to cry or utter certain sounds.

(*c*) The child tends to *imitate* both rational beings and the phenomena of inanimate nature.

(*d*) Little by little, from purely emotional, and, we might say, concrete expressions, the child passes to *rational language*. Signs are used to manifest concepts and their relations. Definitions, reading, intercourse with other men, constantly perfect the knowledge and use of language.

(*e*) Even without the help of others, man, endowed with reason and reflection, would soon find the means to communicate his thoughts, however imperfect these might be at first.

II. LANGUAGE AND THOUGHT

I. In the Speaker or Writer

1. **Language Presupposes Thought.** — (*a*) Since the function of language is to express and communicate thought, it follows that language is not the source of ideas, but presupposes them. The child has ideas before being able to express them, and even the adult frequently has thoughts for which he can hardly find any expression. The child at first uses natural signs to express his desires and feelings, and later is gradually initiated to conventional language which he learns from others. This process of learning evidently supposes ideas in the child's mind, for otherwise *language would be absolutely unintelligible*, and words would have no mean-

ing. Nature gives only, so to speak, the instruments of speech; it is reason that gives to words their soul and their real intellectual value.

(*b*) It is true, however, that *thought and speech develop together* and in close dependence, and that we hardly ever think without speaking to ourselves within our own mind. In Greek, the word λόγος means both reason and speech, and in scholastic philosophy, the mental word or *verbum mentale* means the idea itself or concept. To think is really to speak to oneself; to speak is to think aloud and for others.

(*c*) Hence the importance of clear and methodical thought. Without clear thought it is impossible to express oneself clearly, and what is clear in the mind is usually clear in the expression.

2. **Language Perfects Thought.** — If language is the instrument of reason and reflection, it must be admitted also that it greatly contributes to improve thought and reason.

(*a*) By *transmitting thought*, it is the basis of all social relations. It is also the means of preserving the knowledge accumulated by the individual and by generations.

(*b*) It *facilitates attention* by giving stability and permanence to the thought, which is naturally transient and unstable. Hence it also *facilitates memory* by embodying the idea in a sensible symbol, which is the condition of thought, since, as we have seen, we never think without some image or some sense-perception. The best way to master ideas is to endeavor to express them, and this attempt frequently shows that ideas which seemed clear are really far from being so. A compendium of philosophy made by the student himself is not only a memorandum; it also contributes to the understanding of the subject. Reading is much more profitable when it is done with a pencil or pen in hand to take notes.

(*c*) Language is an *instrument of analysis*, for it serves to decompose the complex thought into its various elements, and to fixate every one of these elements. By the very fact that we can speak only successively we are obliged to express separately ideas which are together in the mind. When I say: "Peter is coming," I decompose the one act of perception, by which I see at once "Peter-and-his-coming," into two elements.

(*d*) At the same time it is an *instrument of synthesis*, combination, and classification. A word, because it is general, applies to a multitude of individuals. It includes in one single expression all their common features which are found scattered in many individuals amid a multitude of other features.

II. In the Hearer or Reader

We shall simply call attention to a few general principles, easily understood, yet too frequently forgotten in practice.

1. **Speech Signifies the Ideas of the Speaker,** not those of the hearer. The word or sentence, in the mind and intention of the man who uses it, may not always stand for exactly the same idea which it stands for in the mind of the man who hears or reads it. Hence arise frequent misrepresentations. Hence also frequent complaints on the part of writers and speakers that they have been misunderstood and misquoted.

2. **Changes in the Meaning of Words.** — Language is sometimes equivocal, that is, the meaning may be uncertain. Meaning may also vary with the various countries, regions, and times. Like a living organism, a language is constantly changing. Many influences are always at work to modify it with regard to the signification of words, their pronunciation and spelling, the rules of grammar, etc. The language that does not change and is crystallized is rightly called a dead language.

3. **Consequences.** — It is important to keep these principles in mind. The word is only a symbol of the speaker's mind; it must not therefore be interpreted in the light of the hearer's or reader's ideas. How many discussions, oral or written, would be avoided if, on one side, the speaker were careful to make his meaning clear, and, on the other, the hearer were careful to get the right meaning. How many long and bitter controversies end or should end by: "If this is what you mean, I agree with you." Perhaps there is mental agreement all the time, and the disagreement is only a verbal one. Be sure then of the meaning of those to whom you listen or whose writings you read. Interpret expressions according to their obvious meaning, but always taking into account by whom and in what circumstances

they were used. Ask for further explanation, when possible, especially in cases of different opinions, and you will frequently avoid many difficulties and discussions.

CLOSING REMARKS ON THIS CHAPTER

I. General Conspectus of Cognitive Faculties

1. **Summary.** — (*a*) The present chapter has led us through the various successive steps of cognition. Beginning with the simplest elements we have risen to more and more complex acts. The elaboration of knowledge requires a multitude of processes of ever-increasing complexity, each process depending on those that have preceded. Analysis and synthesis, separation and combination, resolution and construction, go together and give each other mutual help. The highest mental processes of the intellect pervade, complete, and perfect the data of the senses, and the senses are necessary to the highest mental processes.

(*b*) Continuity and solidarity are found at every stage. Sensation, perception, retention and reproduction, conception, judgment and reasoning, are all interwoven in cognitive processes. What is now a direct perception may have been in the beginning a judgment and an act of reasoning now embodied in one and the same act. When I say that I see my friend Peter, think how many acts of sensation, perception, comparison, and judgment, perhaps even scientific conclusions reached by a long process of reasoning, are summed up in that one word "friend."

(*c*) Yet it must be kept in mind that continuity does not necessarily mean that all cognitive acts come from and must be attributed to the same principle. If we admit, as common-sense leads us to admit, a radical distinction between inorganic and organic substances, and between plants and animals, we must also admit that there is in the plant a special mode of activity which is not found in inorganic matter, and in the animal some special property which is not found in the plant. Nevertheless it may be impossible to determine, in concrete cases, where one kingdom begins and where the other ends. From what has been said especially on the origin and the formation of concepts, one may already suspect that sense and intellect are two distinct and irreducible faculties. This point must now be made clearer.

2. **Senses and Intellect.** — Man is endowed with two kinds of faculties or powers, irreducible to each other, the senses and the intellect. At present we shall simply indicate the main reasons for this assertion, as we intend to come back to the same subject and determine the nature of intellectual processes when we study the philosophy of the human mind.

(*a*) We acquire *concepts* that are abstract and universal, not determined therefore by the concrete circumstances of space and time. The concept has been shown already to be irreducible to the image. Through an organic or material process we can know only the material, concrete, and actual reality. The senses, therefore, however complex or composite the image may be, can give only the knowledge of concrete objects determined in space and time.

(*b*) The *judgment* supposes the concept. It does not simply consist in a juxtaposition, in a resemblance or a difference between two ideas, but it consists essentially in the perception and affirmation of such relations. In the case of necessary judgments, that is, of judgments which not only *are* true as matters of fact, but *must be* true at all times, everywhere, and for all minds, no sense can ever give to any judgment, or perceive in any reality, this character of necessity. It comes from a higher source.

(*c*) Probably the most marvellous power of the human mind is the power of *reflection* or *self-consciousness*. The mind not only thinks objects external to itself, but thinks its own thought, observes its own sensations, emotions, volitions, and desires, compares them with one another, and notices their differences or resemblances. Under all these we are aware of the identity of the agent from whose activity they proceed and to whom all are attributed. An organic or material action cannot thus perceive itself. Vision does not see itself, hearing does not hear itself, etc. An organ cannot be reflected, or folded back on itself. If this feature belongs to higher mental manifestations, it points to a power superior to the senses. It is only a supra-sensuous power of thought that can bind together the passing states of mind, and recognize the identity and permanence of the self under its passing processes.

II. Genesis of Some Ideas and Principles

We give here a short outline of the way in which we acquire some fundamental concepts and judgments which others imply, or which are of most frequent use. The present point of view is exclusively psychological. Some of these ideas and principles will have to be examined elsewhere from other points of view, in Logic, Epistemology, Cosmology, etc.

1. **Ideas.** — The most important ideas to be mentioned are those of being, self, substance and accident, cause and effect, finite and infinite, relative and absolute.

(*a*) The notion of *being* is the first which the human mind acquires. It is the most general since it applies to everything, hence also the most indetermined and the most imperfect. It is at the basis of all other notions, for, whatever is known is known as something, i.e. as some form of being.

(*b*) The knowledge of *self* is acquired by reflection. The facts of memory and recognition lead to the idea of self-identity. Comparison and the perception of difference and similarity between mental processes indicate a judging unity under the multiplicity of mental states. Moreover, the consciousness of power manifests the self as an active principle. It is not merely a centre or support for its passing states, but an agent from which they spring.

(*c*) Consciousness gives me the testimony that I am a *substance*, namely, that I exist in myself as an individual. On the contrary, it gives the testimony that the ideas, feelings, emotions, desires, etc., which I experience are mine. They do not stand by themselves, and I cannot think of a thought which is not some mind's thought. Another contrast is apparent, namely, the contrast of the permanent ego with the transitory states of the ego, which again leads to the recognition of a distinction between the ego as a substance, and its states as accidents. This is also verified in external objects. The same thing changes in various respects. These two ideas of sameness and yet of successive variety are indications that, in external things, a distinction must also be made between substance and accidents or properties.

(*d*) Internal experience reveals the self as an *agent*. There are changes and successions of mental states, or even bodily movements, whose happening is the result of volition. We feel that, sometimes at least, we are not merely spectators, but agents and causes of the sequence of our mental processes; that we dispose of and use a certain energy which is in ourselves, and that we are capable of effort. Through external experience we observe similar facts of change and succession in the outside world. These changes take place according to laws which science endeavors to discover. In the same circumstances, the same antecedent is always followed by the same consequent. Reason is naturally led to inquire why these changes are produced, and to attribute them to the activity of causes from which they proceed. A *cause* is not merely an antecedent; it not only precedes in time, but it exercises an influence in the production of the consequent.

(*e*) The senses of vision and touch give perceptions of surface and solidity, that is, of concrete extension and dimension. By abstraction, the concepts of *extension*, *matter*, and *body* in general are formed. Moreover, we perceive the various relations of distance, the respective positions of bodies and their changes of place, and we look upon space as one immense receptacle in which all things are and move.

(*f*) The perception of succession, i.e. of the fact that events, internal and external, do not all take place at once, but one after the other, leads to the idea of *time*, or of a present instant preceded by a past and to be followed by a future.

(*g*) Everywhere in the world we find limitations in extension, power, activity, and perfection. From these we form the idea of *limitation;* and by removing all limitations we form the idea — always imperfect — of the unlimited, of the perfect and the *infinite*. I can do only certain things, the Omnipotent or Infinite Power can do all things. My knowledge is imperfect and limited, the Infinite Knower reaches perfectly every truth, etc. In the same manner, knowing that we are dependent on many other persons and things, both for our very existence and for our activity; knowing that all beings are thus dependent on one another and that they have manifold relations, we conceive the idea of the perfectly *independent* or *Absolute.*

2. **Principles.** — From primitive concepts are formed primary judgments or principles which are necessary, universal, and fundamental in experimental and rational sciences. The most important are: The principle of *identity:* "What is is," or "*A* is *A*." The principle of *contradiction:* "The same thing cannot be and not be at the same time;" or, applied to cognition: "The same thing cannot be affirmed and denied at the same time and in the same sense." The principle of *substantiality:* "There is no mode or phenomenon without a substance." The principle of *causality* and *sufficient reason:* "Nothing begins to exist without an adequate cause." The principles of *space and time:* "All bodies are in space," and "All events take place in time." The principle of the *absolute:* "The relative supposes an absolute; the imperfect supposes the perfect; the finite supposes the infinite." The principle of *morality:* "Right and wrong differ essentially," "Moral obligation must be fulfilled, and moral evil must be avoided."

III. Development of Intellectual Cognition

1. **Intellectual Development.** — Let us first ask the question: In what does intellectual development consist? As has been indicated already, the first notions acquired by the intellect are very vague, indistinct, and general. The intellect is developed and perfected little by little, and its perfection consists mainly in the three following qualities:

(*a*) The *extension of knowledge*, that is, the number of things that are known, of sciences that are mastered, and of facts, laws, and details with which the mind is acquainted.

(*b*) Far more important than the quantity of knowledge is its *quality*, its distinctness, clearness, accuracy, and thoroughness. To know *much* is good; to know *well* is better. Persons are found who have acquired varied and extensive information on a number of subjects; they have a smattering of everything. But it is all vague and hazy, all à-peu-près, without any clearness or definiteness. They may astonish the ignorant, but to the really learned their display of knowledge appears as an addition of conceit to ignorance.

(c) More important still and more fruitful is what may be called the *synthesis of knowledge*, that is, the perception, not merely of individual objects, but of their relations, both ontological and logical. Things and events are related by similarity, difference, analogy, causality, etc., and, both in speculative and in practical thinking, success depends on the power of the mind to grasp these relations. What are scientific and popular classifications but groupings of things according to likeness and difference? On what does the success of an enterprise depend, if not on the power of grasping beforehand the possible sources of success and failure, and the relations of one event to another? In business, in science, in war, in politics, in commerce, everywhere, the powerful mind is the mind that does not see or foresee merely one side of reality, but that embraces at once all its complex aspects. Look not only at the individual; look at the whole to which it belongs and with which it has manifold relations. It is necessary for the mind to analyze, but it must later replace every object of knowledge in its true relations.

2. **Main Factors in Intellectual Development.** — (a) *Much assistance is received from others*, but it is necessary to control human testimony and authority. I make no difficulty in believing my friend, whom I know to be truthful, when he tells me of things he has seen and of events he has witnessed. If, however, he speaks to me on other matters, before I assent I must weigh his reasons and test their value. To act differently would be to renounce the highest and noblest human prerogative.

(b) Besides this external assistance, several *internal helps* must be mentioned. (1) The intellect depends on the *senses;* therefore it is necessary to give to the senses the greatest possible perfection, and, within proper limits, to cultivate memory and imagination. Hence also the importance of explaining and illustrating abstract notions by concrete examples. (2) *Attention* must be given to the various aspects of sense-experience. Judgment and reasoning are to be used with caution and prudence. Care must be taken not to be misled by prejudices and habits of thought. The principle or law must be based on facts, and the facts must not be denied or distorted in order to fit in with a preconceived theory. (3) The habits of *introspection* and *reflection* are necessary, as self-knowledge is essential in all aspects of life. (4) The *connections* and *relations* between objects of knowledge are to be examined. The endeavor should not be so much to acquire manifold and varied information as to group it and arrange it in the mind. On this condition only will knowledge be available. A business man who has many things in his store but without any order, and who does not keep his accounts carefully, is not likely to succeed. The same is true of a mind in which many ideas are scattered at random without order and method.

3. **Main Dangers to be Guarded Against.** — (*a*) *The illusion of clearness* is frequent. A word or sentence is heard or read frequently, and, because it becomes familiar, the mind never stops to consider its accurate meaning. A word altogether new will strike the mind and lead us to consult the dictionary. Yet many familiar words are not thoroughly understood; we have only a vague and hazy idea of their signification. Try to read a page of a novel or of any easy book. Stop carefully to ponder every word and try to give a definition of it, and you will see how many do not convey a clear and distinct idea to your mind.

(*b*) *Imagination, prejudices, a priori theories*, blind the intellect, prevent it from seeing things in their true light, and even make it incapable of observing facts without bias. They are like colored glasses which change the visual appearance of everything, or like lenses which, according as they are convex or concave, magnify or reduce the apparent size of objects.

(*c*) Some have an *exaggerated credulity* with regard to the statements of a favorite author, orator, friend, etc., without even examining their value; or, on the contrary, a disposition to *disbelieve* anything which another man may state. A priori the former are always right; the latter always wrong.

(*d*) In general, *mental passivity* and laziness make the mind merely receptive instead of active. An easy-going intellectual life, satisfied with any kind of reason, frightened at the very idea of research, scrutiny, questioning, and reflection, incapable of advancing one step unless it is pushed, is the surest sign of mental weakness and atrophy.

CHAPTER II

FEELING

Introductory Remarks

1. **Meanings of the Term "Feeling."** — The term "feeling" has several meanings. (1) Sometimes it is used to denote *general* or *internal sensations:* a man feels hungry, tired, nervous, unwell, etc. (2) It is also applied to *specific external sensations*, especially those of touch: a man feels the contact and qualities of an external object, or he feels cold. (3) It expresses a *form of cognition* or belief which it is difficult to account for and justify by reason: a man feels that a certain action is right or wrong, that a certain man is not reliable or friendly, although the reasons therefor may not be clear and defined. (4) As opposed to knowing and willing, it denotes in general what is called the *affective life*, i.e. certain states of consciousness, or mental attitudes, known as pleasure and displeasure, satisfaction and dissatisfaction, etc., which result from the manner in which objects affect us. (5) It has a more restricted meaning applying only to *pleasure and pain*, that is, to the elementary processes of affective life.

Here we speak of feelings in meanings (4) and (5). In meaning (4) it includes, and in meaning (5) it is opposed to, the other manifestations of affective life, namely, emotions and sentiments.

2. **Meaning of Other Terms.** — An *emotion* is a mental state of an affective nature, more complex than the mere feeling of pleasure and pain. It is the way in which the mind is affected by a complex situation which it apprehends. By *passion* is generally meant a strong emotion or emotional tendency, uncontrolled and violent. A *sentiment* is of a higher and still more complex nature. It has its source in the higher mental processes of knowledge. *Appetite* implies a tendency, craving, or desire, and applies

especially to organic and periodical needs, chiefly the need of food, which refer to the preservation of the individual and the species. Thus the modern use of this term is far more restricted than that of the term *appetitus* in mediæval philosophy, where *appetitus* included the whole affective and active life. Love, anger, enjoyment, desire, satisfaction, will, etc., were all reduced to *appetitus*.

These definitions, or rather descriptions, may be made clearer by an example. A wound on my body produces a feeling of pain. If I am aware that it has been inflicted intentionally by an enemy, I may feel an emotion of anger which will prompt me to take revenge. But just then I may experience a moral or religious sentiment which will make me forgive. Pain is felt by the infant, but he does not experience any emotion when slandered or insulted, since this requires understanding. Some emotions, however, are experienced in very-early childhood; the sentiments develop later.

3. **Classification.** — No classification of the processes of the affective life is perfectly satisfactory. It is difficult to analyze these processes. They are very complex, and frequently it would be impossible to say whether a concrete affective process belongs to feelings, or emotions, or sentiments. Each group generally includes elements which belong to another group. However, for purposes of study a classification is needed, and the following will be used with the understanding that it is not adequate:

I. Feelings proper, in the strict sense.

II. Emotions: (1) self-regarding, personal, or individual; (2) altruistic, sympathetic, or social.

III. Sentiments: (1) of truth, intellectual; (2) of beauty, æsthetic; (3) of right and wrong, moral; (4) of relations with God, religious.

ARTICLE I. FEELINGS OF PLEASURE AND PAIN

I. NATURE AND LAWS OF THESE FEELINGS

I. Nature of the Feelings

1. **Definitions.** — The term "pain" and the term "pleasure" cannot be defined; their meaning can only be experienced. As no idea of color can be imparted to the man born blind, so no idea of pleasure and pain could ever be imparted to a man who had never felt them. But no definition is necessary since, in a general way at least, everybody knows the general character of each feeling and the difference between them. With regard to the use of these two terms it may be noted that "pain" applies chiefly to feelings resulting from certain organic conditions, for instance, a wound, a soreness, an ache. Yet some other mental states due to other causes are also called painful. "Unpleasantness" is a more general term and applies to all phases of mental life. It indicates less than pain, and many states of consciousness to which we could hardly apply the term "painful" may be called "unpleasant." The same distinction is also applied, but less generally, to the terms "pleasure" and "pleasantness." "Agreeable" and "disagreeable" have a meaning which is very close to that of pleasant and unpleasant.

2. **Psychological Nature.** — (*a*) Whatever be said concerning their cause and their ontological nature, from the point of view of psychology both pleasure and pain are *positive* feelings. Even if pain be considered as negative in itself, i.e. as resulting from the lack of a due perfection, from a defect or a privation; if, for instance, a stomach ache results from the absence of certain normal conditions necessary for the proper functioning of this organ; or if the unpleasantness of a sensation is caused by the lack of adaptation of the sense organ to a certain stimulation, it is true, nevertheless, that, in consciousness, the feeling of pain or unpleasantness is a feeling no less positive than pleasure and pleasantness.

(*b*) Pleasure *results from* the healthy, vigorous, normal, and harmonious exercise of the various activities. Inactivity and rest, as such, are not pleasurable. The most agreeable rest is a change in the nature and intensity of activity. Pain and unpleasantness result from excessive exercise or excessive restraint. The complete inactivity of a faculty — like the eye, the ear, the muscles, imagination, etc. — especially if prolonged, becomes very painful. Think of being always in complete darkness or remaining with closed eyes, of making no motion, of not thinking of anything; it would be unbearable. On the other hand, excessive exercise is also painful. Too bright a light, too loud a sound, too great a muscular effort are sources of pain. Moderate and appropriate efforts are rather pleasurable, and to assert, with pessimists like Schopenhauer, that activity and effort are essentially painful is to go directly against the clear testimony of consciousness.

3. **Variations.** — Feelings vary in intensity, and their variations depend both on *subjective conditions* and on *objective factors.* (1) *According as the mind is disposed*, the same perception or image may be pleasant or unpleasant. The present occupation, the mental contents, the preceding sensations, etc., exercise an influence on the way in which the mind is affected. We also know that the same stimulus may produce an agreeable feeling in one individual and a disagreeable feeling in another. (2) On the other hand, *certain objects* naturally produce an agreeable, others a painful feeling. Some sensations of taste, sound, etc., are pleasant, while others are unpleasant, for practically all individuals. The following laws will specify this general principle.

II. Laws of Feelings

1. **Law of Stimulation.** — The stimulus may be suitable for the sense, or unsuitable; proportioned, or too great, or too small. Too weak a stimulus — for instance, too feeble a light, a scarcely audible whisper — requires too much effort and tension. Too great a stimulus — for instance, a dazzling light, a shrill sound, a suffocating odor, extremes of heat and cold — is also painful. A sensation is agreeable only when the stimulation remains within certain limits of intensity.

2. **Law of Duration, Change, and Contrast.** — When pleasure is prolonged unduly it ceases to be felt, and even may be succeeded

by unpleasantness. The same activity which was agreeable in the beginning becomes tedious. The same piece of music which was pleasing when heard for the first time becomes tiresome if it is repeated too frequently. See how rapidly the popularity of a song, even of a "hit," decreases and dies. The same dainty food becomes unbearable. We have "too much of a good thing." Hence the necessity of variety and of change: (1) *In the kind of stimulus*, even if we remain within the same group of sensations, e.g. change of visual surroundings. (2) *In the degree of stimulation;* in many cases the pleasure will continue up to a certain level if the stimulus be increased. The persistent admiration of real masterpieces is due to some kind of change. The more we see or hear them, the more also do we appreciate them, because we understand them better and find new beauties in them. (3) *In the kind of activity*. The monotony due to repeating certain actions is painful; hence the importance of varying exercises, and of passing from one mode of occupation to another.

Contrast affects the nature and intensity of the feelings. Pleasure following pain is more keenly felt, and vice versa.

3. **Law of Accommodation.** — This law works in two ways, either toward pleasure or toward pain, as will be verified easily from personal experience. (1) Things which at first were very disagreeable may become indifferent and even pleasurable; smoking, eating certain foods or condiments, studying according to certain methods, may serve as illustrations. Taste for what is disagreeable may be acquired. We first "get used to" them, and later derive real pleasure from them. This is due largely to the influence of habit. (2) But accommodation may also lessen the pleasure. After a certain time of constant use, more condiment, more cigars, more amusements, etc., may be required to cause the same amount of pleasure. An activity which at first was accompanied by a pleasurable feeling, by repetition may become indifferent and tedious. (3) When an action or a stimulation has become habitual, even if it is the source of no special pleasure, the interruption of it, or interference with it, is painful. If I am used to the ticking of the clock in my room, I "miss" it when it stops. The interference with habitual activities, move-

ments, religious or moral opinions and accustomed modes of thought, is disagreeable.

4. **Laws of Mutual Furtherance or Hindrance of Activities, and of Harmony or Antagonism between Mental States.** — As was said above, pleasure and pain depend largely on subjective dispositions. The same behavior toward me may be agreeable or disagreeable according as I am dealing with a man whom I like or with one whom I dislike. In the same manner, when working in behalf of a friend, I find pleasure in actions which would cause me annoyance if I had to perform them under other conditions. When a man is occupied with an important or interesting task, interruption, even in the form of an otherwise agreeable conversation or recreation, will be unwelcome. What furthers the present purpose and is in harmony with the present state of mind and disposition will, as the case may be, cause more pleasure or less displeasure than what is antagonistic to them and hinders them.

II. IMPORTANCE OF FEELINGS

All men naturally and without exception crave for happiness. They may differ as to the means of obtaining it; they may look merely for present enjoyment, or work for future pleasure; they may seek the pleasures of the senses or those of the mind and the moral aspirations; they may work for happiness in this life or in the next; but the innate desire to be happy is universal. Hence the importance of feelings as springs of action.

1. **For Happiness.** — Pleasure and pain are the main factors in human happiness and misery. The amount of happiness in life is measured by the amount of pleasure found in it. But such pleasure must not be estimated in reference to the present alone. An action which would be otherwise painful may become agreeable on account of the pleasure to which it is expected to lead. Frequently the same complex process will have pleasant and unpleasant aspects, for instance, the satisfaction of the senses, and remorse of conscience; present pleasure, and anticipation of future pain.

2. **For Mental Life.** — Pleasure and pain are very important

in intellectual life and affect the whole mental attitude and behavior. Pleasure or the anticipation of pleasure is a powerful incentive to study. What the mind likes is much more easily attended to and assimilated. From this fact important pedagogical conclusions may be inferred. The child's reason is not yet sufficiently developed to control his feelings and direct his conduct. It is necessary, therefore, to give him lessons and exercises that will interest him, and from which he will derive some pleasure. He must be made to like his work and studies; and means, such as change, variety, concrete applications, etc., must be adapted to this end. Even for the adult, agreeable work is much easier. A great amount of will power is required to overcome repugnances and become proficient in a science for which one feels nothing but dislike. Pleasantness facilitates and quickens attention, and increases mental energy.

3. **For Ordinary Behavior.** — Feelings play an important part in daily life. (1) Pleasure is often a *guide*, but not an infallible one, to the real good. Certain agreeable sensations of smell and taste may be signs of the healthfulness of aliments, and repugnance is frequently a sign of danger. This is true especially of animals; man depends more on artificial conventions, and less on nature. Even for higher activities, pleasures to be obtained or pains to be avoided are ordinary motives of action. (2) Bodily pain is a *warning* and calls attention to a diseased organism. Were it not for pain, how many would die before knowing that they were sick at all. It also tells us when to stop the exercise of certain activities; a soreness of the eyes or a headache may be a warning that continuing to read will be injurious. (3) Pleasure and pain influence man's whole *behavior and character*. Suffering and enjoyment, whether transitory or permanent, affect the ordinary mental attitude. Reflection will show that the influence of feelings on the whole human conduct is much greater than is commonly supposed.

4. **For Development and Progress.** — Pleasure and pain are prominent factors in the progress and development both of the individual and of the race. (1) What is the best educator for the child? His own experience. According as it is pleasurable or

unpleasant there will be a tendency to repeat or to avoid it. Burning his fingers will make him very careful when he sees fire again. Receiving a reward or a punishment will tend to make him perform or refrain from certain actions. In adult age, reason becomes more important, yet reflection will show that the motives derived from reason are generally reducible to the obtaining of what is pleasurable and the avoiding of what is painful. (2) Civilization, that is, the progress realized by mankind in useful sciences and arts, is due to a constant effort toward decreasing pain, fatigue, and whatever else is disagreeable, and toward increasing pleasure and comfort. Inventions tend to make life easier and more agreeable.

5. **For Morality.** — In the higher sphere of moral life we shall mention only the following: (1) Pleasure and pain, whether immediate or future, supply motives of conduct, good or bad. Theft and almsgiving, murder and disinterested love, etc., have reference to present or future pleasure and pain of the agent or of his fellowmen. (2) They contribute to the practice of individual virtues, the development of the will, courage, self-respect, etc., and (3) of social virtues, charity, sympathy, self-sacrifice, almsgiving, etc.

6. **For Religion.** — Religion and religious practices depend greatly on the feelings of pleasure and pain. Reward or punishment is always presented as the outcome of a good or a bad life. During life, suffering shows man his nothingness and the vanity of pleasures, and it makes him look forward to a future and better life. Evil and the fear of evil are incentives to prayer and divine worship so as to obtain the divine assistance. Christian religion is full of references to happiness, riches, and pleasures, to misery, poverty, and sufferings. It supplies higher motives and views both in the examples and in the teachings of its Founder.

ARTICLE II. EMOTIONS

As already indicated, the emotions are more complex than the feelings of pleasure and pain. They always include pleasurable or painful elements, and sometimes a mixture of both; these vary with different individuals, and even with different manifestations of the same emotion in the same individual. Hence it is difficult to analyze an emotion, because its elements are closely interwoven and form a very complex and intricate state of mind. To this may be added that, at least when an emotion is strong and violent, the power of reflection is lessened or suppressed. After the emotion has abated or ceased, what remains is the memory of it, not the emotion itself as it appeared in consciousness. And in the memory of an emotion it is almost impossible to distinguish from the purely emotional elements the ideational and volitional processes which preceded, accompanied, or followed them.

We shall consider successively the egoistic or self-regarding emotions — referring to and centring around the self; and the altruistic emotions — referring to, caused by, or tending to others.

I. SELF-REGARDING EMOTIONS

1. **Their Nature.** — These emotions refer to the *personal good* of the individual. When they are called egoistic, this term is not given the odious meaning which it frequently has, namely, that of an excessive self-love which makes one forget other men; it only indicates that these emotions refer primarily to the self. All are based on the innate tendency to self-preservation, self-assertion, and development. Man wants to preserve himself, that is, he wants to protect his life, not only the life of the body, but also his mental faculties, reputation, and character. Man wants to assert and develop his life and his faculties, to manifest his various energies, to increase and perfect them. Hence two general features of these emotions. Some refer to things that are conducive to the fundamental ends of man, and therefore objects of love; others refer to things that are antagonistic to them, and therefore objects of aversion. We shall mention the most important.

Bodily appetites need not detain us; they are physiological needs which manifest themselves in consciousness by a painful craving, like hunger, thirst, need of air or of exercise, etc., and the satisfaction of which causes a special pleasure. They refer primarily to the conservation of individual organic life.

2. **Self-Importance** is a fundamental emotion which takes an explicit form with the power of reflection, clear germs of which, however, manifest themselves in very early childhood. It assumes several forms. (1) *Self-esteem* and *self-love;* man knows his own qualities, true or apparent, and is aware of the good there is, or he thinks there is, in himself. This leads to (2) *self-complacency*, that is, pleasure at the thought of his excellence, and (3) *self-respect*, which influences conduct in an honorable direction so as to preserve his dignity. (4) *Self-reliance* results from the consciousness of power, intellectual, moral, social, political, muscular, etc. It is based on self-esteem, that is, on the good opinion which a man has of himself. (5) *Pride*, in its ordinary meaning, is an excessive self-esteem, and a desire for superiority, which are not justified by real merits and excellence.

These emotions are mostly pleasurable, but they may be closely associated with displeasure, if others do not concur in the opinion which we have of ourselves. *Self-pity* is a feeling of weakness and inferiority experienced when the lack of a desirable attainment is recognized. It may assume many forms and is chiefly painful.

3. **The Love of Approbation** is the natural consequence of self-assertion and self-importance. It refers to the self, and includes also a social element. We want others to recognize our excellence or our superiority; we want their esteem and respect; we feel pleasure when we succeed and pain when we fail. Frequently pleasure and pain will be experienced together, because the approval of all men, and even the approval of the same person for all actions, cannot be obtained. According as one is held in greater esteem, his approval gives greater satisfaction, and his disapproval greater pain. The esteem and love for a person may be so great that his approval alone seems sufficient, and what others may think is indifferent.

This emotion easily leads to vanity or vainglory, which seeks undue praise or esteem, and deems very important that which is really worth little or nothing, like birth, dress, ornaments, wealth, etc.

4. **Love of Activity.** — (*a*) The love of activity and power follows from the natural desire to exercise our faculties, that is, from the emotions of self-importance and self-esteem. The consciousness of power manifests itself especially in successful efforts to overcome obstacles which are met when endeavoring to reach an end (*ambition*). A social influence frequently manifests itself, namely, the love of superiority over others. The feelings of restraint of activity, or of incapacity to overcome a difficulty, are painful.

(*b*) The love of activity and superiority produces *emulation* and *rivalry*, which are so important in all concerns of life, in intellectual development, in business, in politics, etc. Individuals and nations in all their various pursuits, serious or sportive, seek to display their activity and power, and to outshine one another. There is pleasure in the hope and anticipation of victory and approval, and in the conflict itself that is expected to lead to them. Pain may result from failure and from the consciousness of inferiority. This emotion, in itself, is legitimate and noble. It stimulates the ardor and multiplies the activity. But it may also be the source of envy, hatred, anger, antipathy, and injustice in the use of the means.

5. **Fear** is primarily egoistic, yet it may also refer to others. It is produced by the *painful anticipation of some evil*. This emotion depends on some previous painful experience which has been stored up in memory, or on a complexity of experiences which have been associated or constructed by imagination. I am afraid of fire because I have experienced sensations of burning. I am afraid of a strange animal, of darkness, of an unknown object, of a sudden and unexpected noise or sight, because they suggest danger.

The *physical effects* of fear vary with individuals. In general, they are *depressive* and consist of a lowering of vitality and control — paleness, trembling, perspiration, chattering of the teeth, etc. Fear may have very serious, and even fatal, results. Mental functions are also impaired. Judgment, reasoning, reflection, and attention are suspended or disordered. In some cases the will, or rather the impulse to act, will be quickened, and strength increased in order to escape the object of fear. In other cases fear will paralyze every effort. It must not be forgotten that the fear of punishment simply deters from evil, and that, while it is a useful means of education, other means must be taken to promote good aspirations.

Fear is legitimate and unavoidable, but must not be allowed to turn into cowardice, that is, groundless or exaggerated fear, out of proportion with the impending evil. The objective causes of it are generally beyond control, but its subjective causes — frequently ignorance, ill-health, nervousness, laziness, imagination — may be removed little by little.

6. **Anger**, like fear, is primarily egoistic, but may also refer to others. It results from a *sense of injury*, either bodily or mental. Hence it includes a painful element, namely, the consciousness of a wrong which is suffered, and of a failure on the part of others to respect our own persons or possessions. Anger is a *stimulant for activity*, and creates a desire to retaliate. It multiplies the energy, accelerates the circulation and respiration, quickens the heart, etc., but prevents the exercise of attention, judgment, and reason. It may include a pleasurable element in the exercise of activity, and the success in retaliating. Anger takes several forms. It may be a sudden involuntary outburst, or premeditated anger. It may lead to revenge, or take the form of a natural, persistent antipathy, and even hatred. Malevolence takes pleasure in inflicting pain on others.

7. **Remorse, Shame, and Self-Condemnation** are painful feelings resulting from the consciousness of having done something wrong which lowers us in our own eyes or in the eyes of others. They are therefore opposed to the pleasurable feelings of self-importance and love of approbation. Remorse comes especially from self-disapproval, while shame is rather the result of feeling oneself disapproved by other men.

II. ALTRUISTIC EMOTIONS

1. **Their Existence.** — (*a*) Man does not suffice to himself, he needs others and is made to live in society. He is also endowed by nature with certain feelings that refer to his fellowmen. The

distinct existence of these feelings has been denied or doubted by some psychologists. For them every feeling is essentially selfish. When we do good to others, it is because we expect a return and thus have in view our own good. When we feel sympathy for others, we imagine how we should suffer if their afflictions were thrown upon ourselves. When we revere and respect others, it is self-regard and the desire of esteem and approval that prompt us. Whatever feeling is experienced toward other men is always reducible to a self-regarding emotion.

(*b*) This view cannot be accepted. A man, it is true, may perform charitable actions, give alms or encouragement, for selfish motives and in the hope of deriving therefrom certain personal advantages. (1) But the inner feelings of compassion, respect, and sympathy are frequently experienced without being manifested at all, and therefore without being able to bring any return. (2) It is a fact of consciousness that sometimes disinterested feelings are experienced, and that actions springing from motives of compassion or of the love of others are performed without any expectation or prospect of reward or personal satisfaction. (3) Such feelings are universal, found in all men, beginning at an early age, extending not only to our fellowmen, but even to the imaginary characters described in novels or plays.

(*c*) It must be admitted that in many cases personal satisfaction accompanies these feelings, but what is claimed here is that this satisfaction is not always what the agent has in view, and that there are sympathetic emotions which are completely orientated toward others, not toward self. Altruistic emotions may presuppose personal experience without being selfish in their nature. The love of others does not exclude self-love, but self-love does not account for all emotions and is not always primary. The assertion that there are altruistic emotions does not exclude their close contact with egoistic emotions. Emotions referring to others are more or less developed, but one of the worst insults that can be addressed to a man is to say that he has no feeling, no regard, and no sympathy for others.

We shall not speak here of the blameworthy feelings toward others, such as hard-heartedness, hatred, cruelty, scorn, etc. These come rather from a lack of feeling for others, from exaggerated and overbearing self-love and self-conceit, and from egoism, in the bad sense in which this word is generally used.

2. **Sympathy.** — The fundamental altruistic emotion is sympathy. Etymologically this word means a "feeling with"; it indicates, therefore, an understanding and a sharing of the feelings of others, of their pleasures and pains, of their joys and afflictions. *Its chief factors* are: (1) A natural and instinctive tendency from the earliest age. (2) Association and imagination. We associate certain modes of expression with certain feelings, recall similar feelings experienced by ourselves, and imagine feelings which we have not experienced. Thus a man who never had his meal delayed more than a few hours will nevertheless imagine the feelings of a man whom he sees starving. Imagination is frequently misleading, because it interprets the feelings of others according to the dispositions of the sympathizer himself, and hence may magnify or minimize them. (3) The intellect also is an important factor in the observation and interpretation of the manifestation of feelings.

3. **The Main Determinants of Sympathy** are the following: (1) Its intensity varies with both the subjective dispositions — temperament, friendship, love, etc. — and the objective conditions, that is, the greatness, real or imagined, of the feeling experienced by others. (2) It always supposes some similarity and community between the sympathizer and the object of his sympathy. This community may be merely one of nature, between all human beings; or of interests, between members of the same civil, industrial, commercial, society; or of purposes; or of family relations. In proportion as it is closer, the feelings of sympathy are more easily aroused and more intense. Differences and contrasts in education, religion, social position, and character are frequently obstacles to sympathy. (3) Sympathy has a tendency to increase in proportion to the activity used in expressing it. Works generate love. Thus — all things being otherwise the same — a mother will frequently love the more a sickly child who has required more care. (4) Sympathy is communicative and, as it were, contagious. The best means to win the sympathy of a person is to manifest sympathy toward him.

4. **The Main Effects of Sympathy** are the following: (1) It not only makes man share the joys and sorrows of his fellowmen, but tends to make him increase the former and lessen the latter. Hence arise *benevolence*, which is the desire of the good of others, and *beneficence*, charity, commiseration, etc., which are practical endeavors to procure it. (2) There is a tendency, sometimes unconscious, to *imitate* those for whom sympathy is felt, to love what they love, and to share their interests. Members of the same family and the same community generally have many common features. (3) *Respect* and *reverence* are manifestations of sympathy toward persons who have some special merit and perfection. Respect is due to all in various degrees. Reverence is due to those who have some superiority in virtue, position, character, etc. Both imply some affection, otherwise they pass into mere formality, wonder, awe, and even fear.

5. **Forms of Sympathy.** — Sympathetic feelings take several forms according to their range and nature. They are less intense in proportion as they refer to a greater number of individuals at the same time.

(*a*) *Love* and *friendship* are selective; a special choice is made of the person who is their object. The former is generally more intense, less durable, more sensitive, more blind; the latter more reflective, more intellectual, more lasting. Friendship is always reciprocal and requires mutual esteem; love may be one-sided. Besides this meaning as an emotion, love has also a more general meaning applicable to feelings which we should have toward all men: "Thou shalt love thy neighbor as thyself."

(*b*) *Family affections* bind together by mutual sympathy husband and wife, parents and children, and children among themselves. There is a natural sympathy for members of the same family, which, unhappily, certain uncongenialities of temperament, or other causes, may sometimes prevent.

(*c*) Local interests, business, and neighborhood bring men into special contact with some other men, and unite them for certain purposes, especially those referring to the good of the *community*. Thus in the cases of members of the same church, of the same political party, of the same commercial enterprise, etc.

(*d*) *Patriotism*, or love of one's country, is still more extensive. It is based on a common consent to promote the interests of the nation. The community of tongue, religion, authority, laws, customs, history, etc., cements the wills of the citizens and unites their efforts.

(*e*) *Philanthropy* is sympathy for mankind in general. On the mere ground of their community of nature, all men are entitled to the sympathy and respect of their fellowmen.

ARTICLE III. SENTIMENTS

Their Nature. — Sentiments are superior, more rational, more complex, and also more disinterested feelings.

(*a*) *They are based on higher needs*, and hence can hardly ever be satiated. They manifest aspirations toward ideals which are never fully realized. The ideals of truth, beauty, goodness, and religion seem always to recede from us in our search for them. For instance, for the satisfaction and pleasure of discovering one truth, there is the pain and anxiety of finding several new unsolved problems and unanswered difficulties. As we proceed, new horizons are opened before us. Based on the higher mental processes, they are also the best incentives to the perfection of these processes.

(*b*) Because they are of a more refined nature, they are also *less common*, at least in their nobler manifestations. They depend more on education and general culture than the feelings proper and the emotions. The same wound will produce about the same pain in several individuals. An insulting remark is likely to produce emotions of anger in all men, although, for emotions, the variations are already of great importance, and the laws much less strict. In the sentiments still greater variations will be observed. Some men will experience no æsthetic sentiment when looking at a perfect painting, or reading a beautiful poem. Some may even prefer the ragtimes of the street-organ to a classical piece played by a first-class orchestra, and the funny pictures of the Sunday paper to a masterpiece of a great artist. Sentiments are so complex that the whole mental structure of every individual must be taken into account.

I. INTELLECTUAL SENTIMENTS

1. **Love of Truth.** — The basis of the intellectual sentiments is the love of truth. Man is naturally eager to know, and although this tendency is not explicit at first, it manifests itself in many ways, such as questions, investigations, attempts at generalization and explanation. Men do not always require the same accurate and scientific explanation, but all want to link facts and events together under the same general laws. In its highest form, the love of truth is disinterested, pursuing knowledge for its own sake, and apart from practical and utilitarian motives like the love of fame, the hope of remuneration, the satisfaction of ambition, and the like. In its earlier stages, especially, this sentiment is associated with, and results from, other feelings. The child learns his lesson in order to please his teacher and parents, or in order to avoid punishment and obtain reward. Later he may come to see the necessity of learning in order to attain success in life, and, later still, he will learn because of the pleasure which he finds in knowing.

2. **Ignorance.** — (*a*) Since man likes to know, it follows that the *awareness of ignorance* and perplexity is painful. To see something which cannot be understood creates a certain feeling of want and a sense of uneasiness, especially if that thing is of interest. This general feeling of ignorance and confusion, however, may sometimes be accompanied by pleasurable elements, like novelty, surprise, and wonder.

(*b*) *Novelty* implies either an objective change, or the discovery by the mind of a new aspect in the object. It is likely to produce a certain amount of pleasure. *Surprise* indicates not only a change, but a sudden and unexpected change. *Wonder* refers to something which is unexpected because it is out of the ordinary, or which seems strange on account of its unusually large or small size, its peculiar unwonted characteristics, its excellence or depravity, etc. Hence it is a very complex state, in which pleasurable and unpleasurable elements may be combined.

(*c*) Ignorance, perplexity, wonder, naturally arouse the *curiosity* and the desire to know. Curiosity is one of the mainsprings of mental activity. It prompts to inquire, investigate, and question. At a more developed stage it can be sustained longer, because the love of truth is deeper. In the child the feeling of curiosity would soon be forgotten, were not the interest kept up and revived. Curiosity is very useful; it must be encouraged, and, as much as possible, satisfied. It is the sign of an inquisitive mind and of eagerness to know. Hence, in repressing the excessive and objectionable forms of this feeling, care must be taken not to discourage or rebuke the child, or in any way to repress the natural and useful tendency of the mind to know what it has the duty or right to know.

3. **Curiosity Leads to Investigation.** — At this stage are experienced various feelings of pursuit, discovery, assimilation, and possession; or of incapacity, disappointment, and failure.

(*a*) *Pursuit*, as an exercise of activity, is a source of pleasure. This character, however, may be modified at every step by the hope of success or the fear of failure, the sense of power or of incapacity.

(*b*) *Discovery* is a source of great pleasure, and, when confusion and perplexity have preceded, when the pursuit has been arduous and strenuous, the pleasure of final success is enhanced by contrast. How much greater is the joy of finding a solution for oneself than that of being told without having made any effort. A success which has cost more labor is more pleasurable. The failure to find a solution is always unpleasant.

(*c*) The knowledge thus acquired is assimilated with the knowledge already at hand. It is compared to and incorporated with the other mental possessions. The feeling of *logical consistency*, that is, of agreement with previous experience and knowledge, is very pleasant. On the contrary, the awareness of *contradiction* and *inconsistency* is distressing and produces a new state of perplexity; either the new knowledge is invalid and the mind has gone astray, or previously acquired knowledge has to be rejected.

Besides the feelings of which we have spoken may be mentioned some others that have both an intellectual and an ethical aspect, like fairness, impartiality, disinterestedness, or, on the contrary, intellectual bias, prejudice, and prepossession. When these are experienced in ourselves or perceived in others, they naturally produce complex agreeable or disagreeable sentiments.

II. ÆSTHETIC SENTIMENTS

Certain persons, things, and actions which we call beautiful, pretty, graceful, sublime, harmonious, melodious, witty, ludicrous, etc., produce in the mind a pleasurable impression, whereas others recognized as ugly, inharmonious, improportionate, etc., produce a disagreeable feeling. This is called the æsthetic sentiment, and the special faculty for experiencing it, or the susceptibility to it, is called the æsthetic taste. The beautiful is always agreeable, but the agreeable is not always beautiful.

1. **Elements of the Æsthetic Sentiment.** — The objective elements of beauty will be examined in Æsthetics. *On the subjective side*, the one of interest to psychology, the elements of the æsthetic sentiments are:

(*a*) *Sensory.* Objects that produce æsthetic sentiments are perceived by two senses: (1) sight — natural objects, such as landscapes, sceneries, rivers, seas, mountains, etc.; artificial objects, such as paintings, monuments, sculptures, etc.; (2) hearing — singing of birds, music, rhythm, poetry, etc. Some sensations of color, light, sound, etc., in themselves are agreeable and pleasant for all men. This purely sensuous feeling which results from a suitable stimulation of the sense-organ disposes and contributes to the æsthetic pleasure, but stops at its lowest degree.

(*b*) *Perceptive and intellectual.* Details must be perceived in their mutual relations, so as to give rise to the perception of the object as a whole. The æsthetic sentiment is due chiefly to this perception of details or units forming one harmonious whole.

(*c*) *Associative and ideal.* Things which of themselves might not arouse any special æsthetic sentiment do so on account of the memories which they recall or the ideas which they suggest. Historical places where important events have occurred, or places associated with legends, will, on account of these associations, arouse sentiments more readily. Or again, a certain scenery will suggest ideas of danger, power, or strength, which contribute to the production and special aspects of sentiments. It is not so much on account of their melodies as on account of the associations which they suggest that the national hymn or patriotic songs are able to arouse enthusiastic feelings.

2. **Special Features.** — Among the special features of the æsthetic sentiments two must be mentioned.

(*a*) *Æsthetic taste is capricious*, and the old proverb "De gustibus non disputandum" does not only apply to the sense of taste, but indicates also that diverse feelings may be aroused in several individuals by the perception of the same object. These differences come partly from native dispositions, emotional tendencies and character, and partly from the cultivation of taste in a certain direction.

(*b*) However, *there is a standard of taste* which varies within broader or narrower limits according as it is applied to a more or less numerous class of men. Thus there are things which cannot be considered as æsthetic in any place or at any time, but they are few. The standard is more uniform for the same epoch, still more so when applied only to a nation, a class having the same education, a school within the class, a closely related group within the school.

These questions will be developed more at length in Æsthetics. Some points concerning the subjective or psychological aspect of the æsthetic feelings will find there a more suitable place, as they will help to determine the nature of objective beauty.

3. **Forms of the Æsthetic Sentiment.** — The sentiments thus far analyzed in their generality take several forms according to the nature of the object by which they are aroused. (1) *Sublimity* implies greatness, superiority, and power. Hence the corresponding feeling is mingled with awe, fear, admiration, and a sense of inferiority and weakness. Thus something immense and imposing in space or time, the power of the sea in a tempest, an heroic deed, etc. (2) *Prettiness*, on the contrary, refers to something small, tiny, or weak. (3) The feeling of the *ludicrous*, wit, humor, is produced by something unexpected, surprising, incongruous, or undignified. It is expressed by laughter and mirth.

III. MORAL SENTIMENTS

1. **Their Nature.** — The moral sentiments refer to voluntary human actions in so far as they are good or bad, right or wrong. (1) *Voluntary* actions are the only ones which we call moral. Merely physical happenings have no moral aspect, and the same must be said of accidental results produced unintentionally, and of spontaneous actions in man, like the organic vital functions. The will has no control over these. We condemn as wrong the mere intention and desire to do wrong, even if it be not carried out. (2) *In so far as they are right or wrong.* Other feelings may refer to the same actions in other respects; other sciences may try to give them another special direction. The point of view here is that of the moral value, i.e. of the *rightness* or *wrongness* of the actions, their comparison with a rule, a standard, and an ideal to which they ought to conform.

2. **The Fundamental Form of the Moral Sentiment** is the feeling of *right* and *wrong* in conscience, that is, a feeling of obligation to do or avoid certain actions. It imposes a reference to some law, authority, and command which tell us absolutely: "Thou shalt," or "Thou shalt not." Whatever source be assigned to this categorical imperative, and however great be the differences in the standards of morality among different nations and at different times, all men recognize that some actions must, and others must not, be performed. Hence this sentiment is a powerful spring of action.

The sentiment of right and wrong must be distinguished from that of mere *utility* or from the *conditional imperative.* If I fail to profit by a good business opportunity, I may blame myself, but not as having done wrong morally. According to the moral character of the action a man feels satisfaction, pleasure, and self-approval, or remorse, shame, guilt, and self-condemnation. All this supposes the sentiment of responsibility and free-will. We experience satisfaction and remorse only for those actions which we feel we could perform or avoid. If I kill a man accidentally and unavoidably, I may, of course, be very sorry, but I do not feel responsible for it.

3. **Factors in the Concrete Sentiment of Morality.** — This is not the place to speak of the value of the moral law, which will be explained in Ethics. But one cannot fail to notice a great diversity of standards according to individuals, places, and times. What one would be thoroughly ashamed of will be indifferent for another. What is considered wrong in one locality, or at one time, may be considered right elsewhere and at another time. Few, if any, are the actions which have been regarded as wrong at all times and by all men. Without speaking of the objective value of actions, and of the true rule to which they ought to conform, we merely enumerate the main psychological factors that influence concrete moral feelings. (1) The importance of *intellectual faculties* in supplying motives and intentions, and in determining the moral value of actions, is self-evident. (2) *Custom, association, imagination, and habit* exercise a very great influence. What a man has been accustomed to do, even if known intellectually to be wrong, will hardly excite any feeling of shame or remorse. The inveterate drunkard or criminal are good illustrations of this. Again, what is customary in a locality arouses no surprise and no moral feeling for those who live there, though it may shock outsiders. (3) *Human passions* may blind man's understanding and pervert his will. Thus avarice and greed will easily lead to theft, hatred to murder, and so on. The feeling experienced may vary in nature and intensity according to the prompting passions and the derived advantages.

IV. RELIGIOUS SENTIMENTS

1. **Their Nature.** — Religious sentiments, manifestations, and practices are found in all places and at all times, but take many different forms. The conceptions regarding the attributes of the object or objects of religious worship, and the nature of religious practices, have been and are still varied almost beyond imagination. One has but to recall the practices of polytheism and fetichism to understand the truth of this statement. In some religions, the dominant feeling is that of fear, and, in order to placate the terrible divinities, practices of an inconceivable cruelty are

frequently adopted. In others the dominant feeling is love, and all good gifts are lavished by the Creator on His creatures. These feelings may assume numberless forms and give rise to many others. It would be an endless task to go through their analysis, and to enter into the enumeration of the actions performed for religious motives. Some elements, however, are common to all forms of the religious sentiment.

Independently of particular creeds, there is in all religions a *sentiment of dependence*, a recognition of God's greatness and power, and of man's littleness and weakness when compared to God. According to the nature which is ascribed to God, this feeling will take the forms of love, confidence, fear, resignation, prayer, etc., and express itself in the offering of various sacrifices. In its highest stage of development, the feeling of the greatness of God becomes that of the divine Infinity which brings man face to face with an unfathomable mystery.

2. **Main Forms of Religious Sentiments.** — The religious sentiment will tend to make man view things in their relations to God, as coming from Him, directed by Him, returning to Him, and, in the case of man, accountable to Him. It ennobles our views of things and events by referring them to their source and ultimate goal. It even creates the desire of a union with God by knowledge and possession. Hence come many of the ideas of reward and punishment in the next life. Hence also the ideas of being in peace with God when we have not offended Him, and of enmity when we have not complied with His law. It is easy to see how complex these feelings are, how numerous their elements, and how difficult their analysis. They vary in nature, elevation, and refinement according to the nature and elevation of the ideas concerning God, the divine attributes, and the divine laws and sanctions.

3. **Psychological Factors.** — These feelings manifest themselves by religious worship, that is, by a multitude of religious practices which in turn are the sources of many other feelings. The main factors in the determination of these practices are: (1) *Reason*, which examines the foundation of beliefs and the value of religious practices. (2) *Habit*; what we are used to seems right, whereas

novelty arouses suspicion. A new belief that contradicts accustomed ways of thinking, or which is merely added to them, is sometimes difficult to accept. Unwonted practices are generally unwelcome until the sense of novelty has passed. On the contrary, an unfounded or superstitious belief and practice, if habitual, stands firm. It is easy to notice how great a difficulty is found in changing the habitual religious ideas and customs of thoroughly religious people. (3) *The senses, association, and imagination;* certain surroundings, times, and places are more favorable to religious practices and to religious manifestations. Looking at religious pictures, statues, symbols, etc., hearing or singing religious hymns, are incentives to the religious feelings. (4) *Other emotions and sentiments;* thus suffering and need are motives for having recourse to God by prayer. How much more fervent is prayer in time of danger! The beauty of religious temples, and the solemnity of rites and ceremonies, also contribute to the experience of religious sentiments.

CONCLUSION

IMPORTANCE AND CULTURE OF AFFECTIVE LIFE

I. Importance of Affective Life

Affective life is very important both for the individual himself and in his relations with other men. In general it may be said that feelings give to human life its distinctive character, its tone, its happiness or unhappiness, its enjoyment or irksomeness. Hence judgments passed on other men refer in a large measure to their character and their various modes of feeling. The esteem in which some men are held, and the reprobation which is given others, are due to their conduct in so far as this conduct manifests their sentiments.

1. **In the Development of Intellectual Life,** as already pointed out, feelings are important factors. (1) They incite to the search of truth, the enjoyment of the pursuit and of the success. They may also be the sources of error and bias, when interest is found

in one solution rather than in its opposite. They magnify or minimize reasons that tend to prove a conclusion which a priori is found to be favorable or unfavorable, and which accordingly one desires to have demonstrated or disproved. (2) Feelings are frequently made use of in convincing others. In many cases an appeal to pure reason, though it be cogent, will fail, whereas an appeal to the feelings will be successful. If a speaker wants to bring his audience to practical conclusions, he has not only to convince but to move and touch them; hence he must appeal to their ambitions, desires, interests, egoistic or altruistic emotions, and higher sentiments. (Cf. p. 117 ff.)

2. **In Regard to Moral Life.** — (1) *Feelings themselves may have a moral value* according as they are or are not regulated and controlled. One may be blameworthy for failing to repress certain emotions or passions. (2) *Feelings are powerful springs of action.* As a motive of action, a mere intellectual idea is weak; its strength is greatly increased by feelings. The notion that an action is good or bad will not go far toward making one perform or avoid it, unless there is at the same time in consciousness the love of the good and the hatred of the bad, the sense of duty, and the pleasure in complying with the rules of morality. (3) *Feelings exercise a great influence on responsibility.* A murder committed coolly and deliberately is judged more severely than a murder committed in a passion. Certain feelings blind the understanding and prevent it from throwing its searching light on the value of an action.

3. **Religious Life** is largely dependent on the affective life. A revealed creed, especially one that includes mysteries to be believed, will be accepted with difficulty by a proud intellect. Under the influence of feelings, how frequently is the accidental in religion preferred to the essential, the optional to the obligatory! The choice of religious practices which are not regarded as obligatory will be largely a matter of feelings prompting to one mode of prayer, devotion, offering, sacrifice, rather than to another. Some saints are austere and unsympathetic; others are mild, and excite not only our admiration, but also our sympathy and love. The former are directed chiefly by fear of the judgments of God, the latter by

confidence in His mercy. According to our own feelings, we are inclined to imitate the former or the latter.

4. **For Success and Happiness.** — The importance of affective life in daily affairs and for general happiness is very great.

(*a*) Feelings are not all of the same importance, nor are they necessary to all men in the same degree — this depends on the special conditions of life and culture, — yet some are fundamental, especially those of joy, hope, cheerfulness, fear, grief, gloominess, etc., since they are the main factors of happiness or misery in life, and contribute so much to man's character, and to his view of things. Emotions, and especially passions, are the source of the greatest good, and of the greatest evil. A good conscience makes a man happy, remorse leaves him no rest.

(*b*) Personal moods and dispositions, inclinations, or aversions are due to feelings, and experience teaches how much influence they exercise for success and failure.

(*c*) Other men are to be dealt with according to their temper and character, that is, chiefly according to their affective peculiarities. Success in dealing with others depends principally on a certain insight into the propensities of those with whom we come in contact. The successful man knows that each individual must be treated differently from all others, that each has a special "touchy" or "sensitive" spot, etc.

(*d*) General happiness is partly objective, and due to the enjoyment of external goods; but it is chiefly subjective. Frequently we see the poor happier than the rich, the man who has only the necessaries of life more cheerful than the one who has all possible luxuries. Happiness is the satisfaction of desires. Desire little, and little will suffice to make you happy. Be resigned to the inevitable, and accept cheerfully that which, however painful, cannot be averted. Let your mind be hopeful, and always strive for better things, but let it not lose courage and equanimity if failure follows your efforts. All things, even the worst, have some brighter aspect; look at them from this point of view, and this brightness will be a source of light for your reason and of agreeable warmth for your heart. In all circumstances, cultivate "happy" feelings and dispositions, throw away melancholy and gloomy views; life will bring you greater comfort, pleasure, and success.

II. Cultivation of Affective Life

1. **Its Necessity.** — The importance of feelings in general sufficiently shows the necessity of cultivating them.

(*a*) This culture is *general* — of the affective life in its most general manifestations, — or *special* — of particular feelings and emotions, for instance, of the religious sentiment, æsthetic taste, sympathy, etc. All feelings are not equally necessary in all conditions of life.

(*b*) Nor are all feelings capable of the same degree of culture and control. This varies with subjective dispositions, natural endowments, character, and temperament, which cannot be changed altogether. The more refined feelings are not accessible to all classes in their perfection. Yet for all, within variable limits, progress is possible. Even physical suffering which seems inevitable can be alleviated by physical and mental means.

(*c*) The culture of affective life is *negative* when it has for its object the repression or suppression of feelings; *positive* when it tends to increase or acquire them.

(*d*) It may also be *personal*, for the individual himself who applies himself to it; or it may be the culture of feelings *in others*, especially in children, by education. The child's affective life must be cultivated very early. Even when objectionable, feelings may be utilized, transformed, and elevated by making them serve nobler purposes and giving them worthy objects.

2. **General Principles.** — (*a*) Difficult though it is, cultivation is possible and necessary. Feelings can and must be regulated, acquired or suppressed, increased or decreased, according to the dictates of reason, and within just limits. Some are praiseworthy, others shameful. Even feelings that are good may be excessive, e.g. self-love, sympathy, etc. Hence *all must be controlled*.

(*b*) *No fixed standard can be assigned*, for it varies within extensive limits according to conditions in life. In the case of more fundamental and more necessary feelings, like sympathy, love, fairness, etc., the limits, though wide, are narrower than for the others. Moreover, it is impossible for all men to be moulded according to the same pattern. Every individual's personality must be preserved. This world would be a dull world if it were otherwise.

(*c*) Generally speaking, the *egoistic feelings tend to excess* and should rather be repressed; *altruistic feelings tend to defect* and should rather be developed. Higher sentiments are to be cultivated according to education and special dispositions.

(*d*) *Feelings are connected.* Hence cultivating one group will also affect the others; cultivating the more general will affect the more special. Thus developing sympathy will develop compassion, esteem, and respect.

(*e*) Feelings arise from ideas, hence *controlling the ideas will naturally modify the resulting feelings.* Feelings are also closely associated with their physical expression; *control of the physical expression* will be a help in controlling the feeling itself. The law of adaptation and habit and the law of change have been mentioned already.

(*f*) *Feelings are contagious.* For instance, to be with a congregation praying fervently helps the attitude of prayer; panic is a fear which spreads rapidly; the indignation and cruelty of a mob are communicated sometimes without any reason.

(*g*) A *special illusion* must be guarded against, that of mistaking the strong expression of a feeling for strenuous action. The man who vents his displeasure and inveighs vehemently against this or that evil, may come to the belief that he is doing much to relieve the situation, whereas he merely expresses his dissatisfaction without trying to find the causes of the evil or the suitable remedies.

3. **A Few Special Applications** of these general principles will be mentioned here.

(*a*) To *repress* a feeling: (1) Avoid occasions in which you know from experience that it would be aroused. (2) If it is aroused, combat it by positive efforts of reason and will. (3) Give rise to contrary feelings by calling to mind contrary ideas. In most cases this is the most effective means. (4) Procure yourself diversion and distraction by thinking of other things which have enough interest to keep the mind's attention. (5) Control the emotional expression, or create an antagonistic one. To check all manifestations of anger helps to decrease the feeling itself. To whistle at night will help to remove fear. A noble and proud behavior will tend to do away with excessive timidity. Expressions of sympathy will reduce excessive selfishness, and so on.

(*b*) To *create* or *stimulate* a feeling: (1) Call forth suitable ideas, objects, circumstances, or situations. (2) Cultivate certain modes of attention, reflection, and imagination. (3) Produce the suitable expression. Clenching the fist is likely to stimulate anger; trembling, fear; kneeling, prayer; an humble deportment, humility. Actors have been seen to feel really and with great intensity the sentiments and emotions which they merely sought to express.

In all this the purpose is to make the affective life an auxiliary in striving for the noblest aims.

CHAPTER III

ACTING AND WILLING

ARTICLE I. ACTION AND MODES OF ACTION

I. INTRODUCTION

I. Meaning of Action

1. **Definition of Terms.** — It would be as impossible to explain action to one who had never exercised any activity — were such a case possible — as it is to explain color to the man born blind, or sound to the man born deaf. No definition of action can be given. Nor is a definition necessary, for all men understand what it is to "do" and to "be active" and to "exercise one's energy." The term *conation* denotes all the active aspects of consciousness, or rather that which is common to them all, namely, a tendency to induce, preserve, or change a state of mind or body. Thus conation applies to those processes which we call desiring, craving, longing, endeavoring, trying, making effort, striving, wishing, willing, and the like.

2. **Meaning of Action.** — (*a*) In a broad sense — first extreme — activity is a general condition of all our faculties, and all mental states have an active aspect. To think, to judge, to perceive, to reason, to feel . . . are actions, or, perhaps better, reactions. The mind is not exclusively passive; it is first acted on, but must also, in response, exercise its own activity. Thus knowledge has a twofold aspect, one representative, and the other active. So far we have considered only its representative aspect. Even feelings and passions, though primarily passive, are also in this sense active.

(*b*) In a very strict sense — second extreme — action refers only to external actions, i.e. to movements of the organism. Thus we oppose action to thought and feeling, both of which are internal and subjective. Thus also we oppose the man of science, thought, contemplation, meditation, . . . to the man of action, who uses his energy in some external and visible manner, and for tangible results. The man who spends his days in study and reflection, although he is at work, and hence really active all the time, is not called a man of action.

(*c*) Between these two extremes, terms denoting exercise and activity are applied to a multitude of processes. My stomach acts on the food to digest it. My brain and my mind are active during study, reflection, reasoning, deliberation, and choice. I am active in interpreting or paying attention to my sensations and perceptions, but I should rather be inclined to call myself inactive when simply receiving sensations and perceptions without making any effort to interpret and understand them. Thus we say of a boy in class that he is merely passive and does nothing, when he is present without making any personal effort.

II. General Modes of Action

N.B. What we say here of positive action must be applied also to inhibition, i.e. the checking of an activity which would naturally manifest itself. Inhibition is but another form of effort and activity.

1. **Personal and Impersonal.** — There are actions which I am conscious of as coming from, and attributable to, myself. They may be called *personal*. Others, on the contrary, take place within myself, but do not spring from my own ego. They may be called *impersonal*. Thus my digestion, my winking of the eye when some object suddenly approaches too near, my wounding or killing a man accidentally and unavoidably, the thoughts that come to my mind of themselves and inadvertently, etc., are not my own doings. Applying my mind purposely to a certain object or study, my killing a man premeditately and intentionally, my voluntarily going to a certain place, etc., spring from my own personal activity.

2. **Actions are Conscious or Unconscious.** — (*a*) While I am now conscious of reading and writing, I am not conscious of a multitude of processes that take place within the organism, and that

might be conscious, like breathing; nor of the pain which I felt a moment ago, and which I know I should feel if I were not absorbed in something else; nor of the ticking of my clock, although I must hear it in some way, since, if it stops, I become immediately aware of the fact.

(*b*) Conscious actions are not always personal. For instance, I may be conscious of the beating of my heart, of my respiration, of the winking of my eyes, the stretching forward of my arms when I feel I am going to fall, or of thoughts suddenly occurring to my mind. Yet I know that I am not the cause, but only the witness, of such actions. They take place within me, but I am not accountable for them. Conscious actions therefore may be impersonal.

On the other hand, in order to be personal, must an action be conscious? Or can there be personal, yet unconscious, actions? An action cannot actually spring from myself and be personal without my being aware of it. The man who is so thoroughly intoxicated, or in such a passion that he no longer knows what he is doing, does not perform any personal actions. Not himself, but his state and condition, are the true agents if, for instance, he kills another man. Such an action is not *actually* and *immediately* personal. Yet it may be called *indirectly*, *remotely*, and *causally* personal, if the man consciously and voluntarily induced the state of intoxication or the passion, and at the same time had some consciousness or prevision of what was likely to happen when he would no longer be himself and no longer capable of acting as a person. Hence all personal actions suppose consciousness, if not actual, at least antecedent.

3. **Voluntary, Non-Voluntary, and Involuntary.** — From what precedes we see that there are *three degrees* in our mode of acting. Some actions are unconscious; others are simply conscious but without personal will; others finally are volitional.

With regard to the attitude of the person toward the action, we may have (1) voluntary, (2) non-voluntary, (3) involuntary action, according as it (1) is intended, and proceeds from a positive act of the will; or (2) is independent of the will, the will neither producing nor opposing it; thus I may let my mind wander at leisure without doing anything to induce or check the train of thought; or (3) finally takes place against the will. My arm may be moved by force notwithstanding my efforts to the contrary; I may be obliged to stay in some place because of paralysis; or I may be unable to banish a certain thought or feeling from my mind.

II. NON-VOLITIONAL ACTION

We shall speak here only of organic activity and movement. There are also many non-voluntary mental actions such as perception, reproduction of images, association, feeling, etc., but these have been examined elsewhere. They are the spontaneous or automatic working of the mind. Non-volitional movements may be divided into two general classes according as (1) they are performed not only without a command and direction of the will, but, even, as sometimes happens, without preceding or accompanying consciousness of purpose (random, automatic, and reflex movements); or, on the contrary, (2) are performed for an end and with some consciousness of a purpose (impulsive and instinctive movements). There is no strict line of demarcation between the two classes; actions pass gradually from the former to the latter. It may be noted also that authors do not always agree in defining the terms mentioned here.

I. Random, Automatic, and Reflex Movements

1. **Spontaneous or Random Movements** include a great number of movements of the limbs in the child, and few in the adult. As far as can be known, they are not provoked by external impressions or internal states of mind, but are *purposeless*, and seem to be merely spontaneous overflows of energy.

2. **Automatic Movements** are *purposive* and necessary for life, although the purpose may be unconscious. They require no stimulation from without, but are spontaneous discharges of energy from the nerve-centres. The most common examples are those of the regular beating of the heart, respiratory movements, the processes of digestion and assimilation. These are automatic from the beginning. Some are or may be conscious; others are unconscious.

To these may be added others that become *automatic by habit.* In the beginning they require consciousness, attention, and effort; but, later on, these factors are no longer necessary, and, as soon as the series is initiated, all the movements follow of themselves, being perfectly automatic in some cases, and in others, nearly so. As examples may be mentioned walking, dancing, speaking, etc. These have also been called *acquired reflexes.* More will be said about them when we speak of habit.

3. **Reflex Action** differs from automatic action chiefly in this, that, whereas the latter has its origin within the organism itself, the reflex action is due to a *stimulation from without.* It is a motor process due directly to a sensory process, but without will, desire, conscious effort, or conscious purpose. The action itself, however, may be performed consciously or unconsciously. Thus if the sole of the foot be tickled, the foot is immediately withdrawn from its place, whether the person be asleep or awake. In both cases the action is reflex; in the former it is unconscious, in the latter conscious. Reflexes are due to motor centres which are excited by an external sensory stimulation, the afferent nerve and the efferent nerve being connected in the nerve-centres of the brain or of the spinal cord.

Some reflexes are *original* and *natural;* they tend chiefly to the preservation of life, like sneezing, swallowing, winking. Others are *acquired* and depend on association and education. These suppose generally some conscious state to start the whole series. Thus the sight of the notes by the pianist determines immediately the appropriate movements for striking the keys.

Animals, the spinal cord of which has been severed, or the brain removed, perform reflex actions. A decapitated frog will jerk away its leg or scratch it if some acid be put on it. These actions depend on the nerve-centres in the cord, and, although they are not conscious, they are nevertheless seemingly purposive. They correspond directly and immediately to the stimulation, just as if there had been a conscious sensation.

In normal life, such actions as sneezing, winking, vomiting, secreting saliva, withdrawing the hand from a burning object, extending the arms forward when in danger of falling, etc., are reflex actions. Although they are generally accompanied and even preceded by consciousness, they are not determined by any effort, nor produced under the guidance of the will.

II. Impulsive and Instinctive Movements

1. **Impulsive Actions** are those which proceed *immediately from the presence of an idea in the mind*, and from the consciousness of an end to be reached. There is no deliberation, no reflection, no multiplicity of tendencies, and no choice. The primary impulses are toward pleasure and freedom from pain. But, as the work of education proceeds and habits are contracted, impulses are diversified, and become as numerous as the things themselves from which pleasure and pain are derived in the physical, the intellectual, the moral, and the religious spheres. Hence the impulses of several men in the same circumstances will be widely different. For instance, a murder may be committed impulsively when the mind is so obsessed by one idea that the action follows immediately without any deliberation. Again, upon hearing a noise in my room at night, my impulse may be to run away, or to speak and ask questions, or to grasp my revolver and fire, etc.

To impulsive movements may be reduced *imitative movements* which originate from an impulse excited by the perception of these movements as performed by others. Children especially have a tendency to imitate the actions of others, like smiling, pouting, talking, etc.

2. **Instinctive Actions** are found chiefly in animals; their number is small in man. They are more complex than impulsive actions, do not always suppose the clear idea of the end to be reached, have a more remote purpose, and do not vary so much with the individuals, but are common to the species, and are transmitted by heredity. Thus the migratory habits of birds, their building of nests, the constructing of wax cells by bees, the swimming of the young duck, etc. These actions are prompted by sensations or images of some kind, and tend to a purpose, but sometimes — for instance, when the bird builds a nest for the first time — the representation of this purpose can only be a vague one.

Summary

We may sum up briefly the main characteristics of the various forms of action mentioned so far. *All agree in being fatal and necessary*, that is, there is no conflict of motives and no deliberation. The tendency to act is all in one direction. The will may sometimes interfere with them, foster or inhibit them, but, in this case, the action becomes more or less voluntary.

(*a*) *Random movements* are purposeless, and centrally initiated. *Automatic movements* are purposive, and adapted to an end which, however, is not a determinant of the movement; they also are centrally initiated. *Reflex movements* are purposive, but peripherally initiated. Their purpose is an immediate one, and hence reflex differ from instinctive actions.

(*b*) *Impulsive movement* supposes only one idea in the mind, and generally follows this idea immediately; it varies with the individuals. *Instinctive action* is not always accompanied by the distinct consciousness of the end; it implies a greater complexity of ideas and elements, and is the same for all individuals of the same species. Both impulsive and instinctive actions are ordinarily more complex than random, automatic, and reflex actions, and involve a series of movements coördinated in order to reach an end. They always suppose some consciousness, whereas the others may be conscious or unconscious. They are not so mechanical, but require some intelligent adaptation and coördination.

(*c*) In the young child we find only the forms of movement mentioned so far. *Voluntary* or *controlled movements*, that is, movements consciously directed and adapted to a known end, are evolved little by little as the mental and the organic faculties become more developed. The main factor in this development seems to be the mental association of certain uncontrolled actions with the sensations of pleasure or pain resulting from them. Some random, impulsive, automatic, and instinctive actions yield a pleasant result; others are unpleasant. Hence the tendency to repeat the former, and to abstain from the latter. Hence also arise tentative efforts to do so; and little by little the control of more and more complex movements is secured.

III. VOLITIONAL ACTION

1. **Elements of Volitional Actions.** — Volitional action is *directed to an end known and intended*. Hence it implies the following steps which, however, have not the same importance in all actions, and may require more or less time according to the different cases. Some even may not be explicit at all, but merely implied in others or presupposed, because they have already taken place at other times.

(*a*) The mind must have the *idea of an end* to be reached, i.e. of a good to be obtained or of an evil to be avoided. To become rich, successful, learned, or influential; to enjoy oneself, to be upright and virtuous, etc., may be so many ends. They appear as good, and create in the mind the desire of reaching them. There may be in the mind several alternatives of ends to be reached or of means to reach them, of actions to be performed or omitted, of means to be taken or rejected, of conduct to be followed or avoided.

(*b*) The *reasons for choosing* one end rather than another, for instance, duty rather than pleasure; and, when the end has been chosen, the reasons for taking some means in preference to others, are examined, compared with one another, and weighed. In some cases, this takes a long time; in other cases, it is a short process, because either the merits of the various alternatives are clear enough, or it is urgent to act at once, or the decision is imprudent and hasty. This process is called *deliberation*.

(*c*) *Choice* follows the examination of motives. A course of action is selected, and an alternative accepted. This is *decision* or *volition*.

(*d*) Finally comes the *execution*. At the command of the will, the mental or organic faculties are applied to perform the action that has been chosen.

From this analysis it is easy to see how voluntary actions differ from those mentioned above. Example: A young man has to choose a profession . . . must learn . . . goes to college . . . applies himself to study, etc. See how many alternatives present themselves at every step, and how every step is taken in accordance with the analysis just made.

2. **Desire.** — (*a*) We have mentioned the term "desire." Desire must be distinguished from volition; it is the transitional step from knowledge to volition. Desire is a *tendency to*, or *craving for*, something which appears good. It includes cognitive elements, presentative and chiefly representative, by which the idea of the object arouses the idea of some pleasurable feeling connected with it. Hence it contains also elements of feelings, and the intensity of the desire is in proportion to the greatness of the pleasure which is anticipated.

(*b*) (1) Desire is blind and fatal. We cannot help finding certain things good and agreeable. (2) Desire may refer to things that are independent of the will — e.g. good weather — and even to unattainable things which one would like to possess — e.g. good health. (3) With regard to the same thing, we may have contradictory desires, desire in one respect, and aversion in another. I may at the same time desire to enjoy a certain pleasure because it is agreeable, and to turn away from it because it is forbidden. Two things may be desired at the same time — e.g. a walk outside and an entertainment indoors — although one only is possible.

(*c*) In opposition to these characteristics of desire, (1) the will is reasonable and controllable. (2) It applies only to things that seem attainable and that are in our power. (3) Of several incompatible alternatives one only can be willed. (4) It may be added that the will is not always proportioned to the desire. Some men seem to be almost incapable of carrying out their plans. Their desires may be strong, but their will is weak. They "would like" to do certain things, but have not enough determination to say: "I will do it."

3. **Decision** concerning a certain action may be positive or negative, a volition or a nolition; it may produce or inhibit a movement. As psychological processes, however, both are positive, and nolition is called negative only with regard to the result. Inhibition is as frequent and as necessary as the initiation of action. It may check the desire and impulse to action, as when we desire to perform certain actions which, for better reasons, we decide not to perform. It is implied in any decision where a choice is

made between conflicting desires. It may also interrupt an action already begun, and prevent it from being completed. Like action, arrest of action is more or less volitional, sometimes being entirely or almost automatic, and sometimes resulting from deliberation.

IV. HABIT

Recall to mind your first lessons in writing, and compare them with the facility which you have at present. Writing has now become habitual. In examining the nature, genesis, and importance of habits, constantly keep before your mind the instance just given, or any other habit which you have acquired.

1. **Nature of Habit.** — (*a*) Experience shows that, after being performed several times, organic and mental actions become easier, and require less attention and effort. Hence habit is *a disposition to reproduce certain actions and to act in the same way under the same circumstances*. The perfectly habitual action is not actually voluntary in the strict sense, because it is performed without reflection and deliberation, and even with little or no consciousness. This, however, is true only of actions that proceed exclusively from habit. In many cases habit and will together play a more or less important part. Habitual actions differ also from instinctive actions because they are not results of innate dispositions, but acquired by repetition. They are more diverse, and are not perfect from the beginning, but become more and more so by repetition.

(*b*) A habit may be contracted voluntarily or involuntarily. In the former case, the resulting action, although presently non-voluntary, is nevertheless voluntary in its cause. In the latter case, the action cannot be voluntary since the habit itself is not.

2. **Genesis of Habits.** — (*a*) Habit *begins* with the first act, and grows with every repetition. If no disposition were left by the first act, there would be no reason why habit should begin with the second or any subsequent act. Every action leaves a trace or disposition, which, however, may disappear if it is not again excited within a certain time. The trace left is more important in proportion to the interest, attention, application, etc.

(*b*) The strength of the habit *increases* in proportion to the frequency of the actions, their duration, their intensity, the interval between them, and chiefly the accompanying attention and feelings. How frequent, how long, and how intense the actions and repetitions should be cannot be determined except by experience. This varies with the nature of the actions, and the subjective dispositions.

(c) Habits *decrease* in strength, or even disappear, through lack of exercise, and chiefly, when possible, through opposite actions. Will and effort to resist the habit are more or less effective according to the strength of the habit and the amount of effort.

3. **Importance.** — (a) Habit is important because of the range of its application and influence which include every aspect of human life. The organism becomes habituated to certain modes of activity, to foods, stimulants, narcotics, climate, diet, etc. Its various movements are perfected, or vitiated, by habit. On the mental side, we find habits of perception, memory, imagination, association, judgment, conduct, feelings, will, etc., all this framing man's character and personality.

(b) *The effects of habit* are chiefly the following: (1) Habitual actions, good and bad, are more perfect and easier than others. (2) They require less attention, and are performed, so to say, automatically. (3) Habit is a great economy of energy and time; instead of having to make an effort for every detail of the action, the series of details follows of itself, and meanwhile attention may be directed to something else. (4) Habits enable one to do things which would be otherwise impossible.

(c) If you examine your daily actions, you will see how many are performed by force of habit and routine, without consciousness or attention, whereas in the beginning they required many distinct efforts. Dressing, eating, walking, speaking, writing, in fact, every ordinary action has been made as easy as it is by habit. Hence habit has rightly been called a second nature, and man has been termed a bundle of habits. Hence also the importance of learning to do all things well from the beginning, for a bad habit is hard to overcome, and every false step means a great waste of energy.

ARTICLE II. DETERMINANTS AND FREEDOM OF THE WILL

I. Determinants and Motors of the Will

1. **Motives.** — (*a*) A motive is that for which we act. It is always *the idea of something good*, i.e. of something useful, pleasurable, noble, honest, etc., which we want to obtain. Motives may be subordinated to one another. Thus I take my umbrella to avoid getting wet. I want to avoid getting wet in order not to fall sick, or not to spoil my new straw hat, or not to feel uncomfortable, etc. I want to preserve my health in order to do my work, and so on. Whatever is done voluntarily is done on account of some good to be derived from the action. It is impossible for man to act otherwise; he cannot choose to do something which appears altogether, and from all points of view, evil and unpleasurable. He may be mistaken in his estimate, and pursue an apparent for a real good, but there is at least the appearance, that is, the idea, of something good.

(*b*) *The first motor of the will, therefore, is the tendency to happiness*, which is implied in every action. Happiness is the ultimate goal which all men want to reach. They do not agree in their conception of the concrete realization of happiness. Some may place it in riches, others in glory, others in pleasure, others in the fulfilment of duty, etc. Some may expect it in this life, others in a future life. But the desire of happiness in general is always the mainspring of every form of activity. Hence the most general and the most uniform tendencies of man are toward those things that are conceived as necessary to happiness: life, health, reputation, the normal exercise of faculties, etc.

(*c*) If all men had the same conception of concrete happiness, and if there were only one possible means of reaching it, all would be determined to act in the same way. Thus, whenever a man has chosen to reach a certain end, and he has only one possible way of doing so, he necessarily takes this one means. If I have determined to go to Europe, there is as yet no other means but to take a vessel. Hence to do this is necessary, although there are several vessels to be chosen from. If I really want to learn, and see that the only means is to study, I certainly will study. To neglect study is a sure sign that one has at most a desire, not the will, of acquiring science. As *concrete ends vary*, and as even the same end may be reached by *different means* — e.g. I may earn a living in different ways; I may, as a Christian, sanctify myself by the practice of different virtues — a great variety of actions will result, but all with the same underlying motive of reaching some form of happiness.

(*d*) Ends may be conflicting, like acquiring wealth by whatever means, and observing the rules of justice. In such a case the will abandons one in so far as it is incompatible with the other. Some will abandon honesty and become rich by whatever means; others will remain poor rather than go against the dictates of their conscience.

2. **Relative Force of Motives.** — Thus we see that we follow a certain line of action because the motives for it appear preponderant, and because it seems to be a greater good than another. What makes a motive preponderant? To a great extent it is its *objective worth*. But it is also, and perhaps to a greater extent, the *subjective dispositions* of the agent. Both internal experience and the observation of other men make it clear that we act as we are, and that we are what we are on account of heredity, temperament, habit, surroundings, education, etc. When we know a man, we generally can guess pretty accurately how he will behave under certain circumstances. The views entertained of things during deliberation, and the attention given to one motive — for instance, the religious or moral aspect of an action — rather than to another — for instance, personal interest or gratification of the senses — are due largely to circumstances, to personal character, and to the manner in which a man has been educated. We may not be aware of it at all times, but to a great extent we are what all these circumstances have made us, and our actions follow our nature.

II. Freedom of the Will

1. **Meaning of the Question.** — When we ask whether the will is free, we ask whether the motors mentioned above so completely

determine the will that the choice which it makes is always made necessarily; or whether the will, notwithstanding these, can determine itself, choose freely, and subtract itself from the necessity of acting in one way only. (1) Hence we do not speak here of *physical liberty*, or liberty of execution, for it is certain that I may choose to do a thing and be prevented by force. I may want to go out and may be locked in, or refuse to go out and be carried out by force. Here we speak of the volition itself. (2) Nor do we speak of various liberties, *political or economic*, as when we speak of a free citizen, a free nation, a free country, free thought, free trade, free port, free goods, free of cost, etc. These liberties imply the absence of some external obligation, restraint or duty. (3) By *freedom of the will* we mean the power of the will to be its own determinant and to originate action. The question, therefore, is this: Are objective motives and subjective influences the only adequate causes of all actions, or is the will itself a power, capable of self-determination?

2. **Limits of Freedom.** — (*a*) (1) From what has been said above it is clear that freedom *does not mean caprice*, or the power of acting without motives. On the contrary, only those actions can be free that are voluntary, and imply some implicit or explicit deliberation and weighing of the motives. Hence habitual actions, and actions proceeding from a violent passion or from ignorance, are not free unless there is nevertheless enough attention and reflection given to them. (2) *Many organic actions* are not and can never be free because they are not under the influence of the will. (3) We can be free only with respect to what seems *possible and attainable*. Thus the strong or the learned may attempt what is not possible for the weak or the ignorant. Hence freedom is limited both in regard to the nature itself of freedom which is present or absent, greater or less in different individuals, and in the same individual with regard to different actions.

(*b*) From habits, education, temperament, etc., life has a general direction which, however, may have been taken freely to some extent, and perhaps even now may be changed. Because a man is engaged in a certain business in which he wants to succeed, he will not act in the same manner as the man who is in another line of business. Certain actions are determined by the end one wants to reach. But the end itself may have been chosen freely in the past. The will is like a vessel sailing on a river and kept between the two banks so that she can move only within them; or like a man walking on the deck of a steamer, having his own limited movement, and, at the same time, carried on by the general movement of the vessel. Every individual has to steer his own vessel, but the general direction toward happiness cannot be changed, although all do not expect to find happiness in the same port.

3. **The Consciousness of Freedom.** — (*a*) When we *deliberate*, we are conscious that we can choose one of two or more alternatives that are offered to the mind. The power of choice supposes the absence of determinism. The stone thrown up in the air has no choice between staying up or falling down; it falls necessarily. Moreover, we are conscious that we are not mere spectators, but actors, in the deliberation; that, by voluntary attention, we may strengthen one motive or underrate its value, and that we may even suspend the deliberation, shorten it, or exclude certain reasons and considerations. Thus all the time we are conscious that the final decision is in our power. The motives are weighed in the balance, but their weight depends partly on the mind.

(*b*) The *decision* itself comes from the individual, and the resulting action seems to be free. Not only are we conscious of no determination, but we are conscious of indetermination. We make a clear distinction between a necessary and a free volition, between the cases where we can choose freely and those where we cannot, between an action performed in a passion and one performed calmly and deliberately. We do not deliberate and decide whether we shall try to be happy, but we do deliberate and decide by what means we shall endeavor to reach happiness.

(*c*) Sometimes deliberation manifests an action as obligatory; there is a *sense of duty and obligation*. Duty is an imperative independent of pleasure and usefulness, and duty supposes freedom. I cannot feel obliged to respect my fellowmen, or to abstain from theft and murder, unless it is in my power to do so. To act necessarily against what I feel to be now my duty is an impossibility. If I must, I can; if I can, I have the power and am free.

(*d*) *After acting* we feel that we have been prudent or imprudent, and that we might have done otherwise. If the action has a moral character, we feel worthy of praise or blame. This again is inexplicable if the action was not free. I deserve neither esteem nor blame for what I could not have done otherwise. I clearly distinguish between a just and an unjust punishment according as I failed voluntarily and freely, or, on the contrary, "could not help it." We deplore and regret actions that are evil and necessary as we deplore and regret accidents or bodily deformities. These do not cause any feeling of shame nor any desert of blame.

(*e*) That *all men have the same consciousness* of freedom is evidenced by their behavior, especially in their deliberations, and in the blame or praise which they give to others. A man cannot be blamed unless it is supposed that he acted freely. I do not blame the stone that hits me, but I blame the man who threw it, inasmuch as such an action was free and could have been avoided. All men have the idea of a just punishment, and a just punishment supposes freedom. Indeed, even if committed necessarily, a crime might be punished to deter others from committing it, or to train the wrongdoer as we train an animal. Such a punishment is only useful, not just. It is intended to have good results in the future, but cannot be merited by the past deed. In fact, the law makes a difference between free and necessary actions; it punishes the criminal, but not the insane.

In a word, the testimony of consciousness is summed up in the awareness that certain actions are personal, that they come from me, that I am their cause, that the ego is, in part at least, responsible for the occurrence, that the action is really mine, not only because it takes place *in me*, but because it originates *from me*.

(*f*) *The reason why the will is free* is found in the relations of concrete goods to perfect happiness. All concrete goods are limited and imperfect; they even have some evil aspects, such as the difficulty of obtaining them, the uncertainty of the success, the necessity of parting with them perhaps in life, and certainly at death, and the fact that we cannot have all at once. Hence none satisfies the will fully, for the will craves for perfect happiness.

4. **Value of this Testimony of Consciousness.** — This testimony

seems clear, and, if we are really free, it is difficult to see how the fact could be perceived with greater evidence. We must say immediately that a clear testimony of direct consciousness cannot easily be invalidated, and should not be rejected except for cogent reasons. Yet, in the present instance, it has been rejected by some psychologists.

(*a*) Stuart Mill asserts that the consciousness of freedom is *impossible*. We have the consciousness only of what occurs, not of what perhaps could, but in fact does not, take place. The consciousness of actual processes alone is possible, and the consciousness of freedom would be the consciousness of processes which could be, but are not actually, performed.

Answer: Consciousness does not perceive what is not, but it perceives the actual power which the individual possesses of determining himself, namely, it perceives the act as it is, as indetermined and as coming from an agent who acts as he chooses.

(*b*) The consciousness of freedom is *illusory;* it is simply the ignorance of determinant motives. Not being conscious of the motives that determine us necessarily, we believe falsely that we determine ourselves.

Answer: We are not only unconscious of determining motives, but positively conscious of our own active power in the decision. Moreover, if the objection were true, the sense of freedom would be in inverse ratio to the knowledge we have of the motives. But, on the contrary, it is when there has been no deliberation and when we do not know why we have acted that the action seems necessary and that we feel no responsibility for it.

(*c*) In fact, we know that a hypnotized subject acts necessarily and cannot refuse to execute the command of the hypnotizer. Yet he feels and asserts that he is free. Consciousness of freedom is again *illusory*.

Answer. The following remarks will answer this difficulty. (1) The subject may *assert* his freedom, but he shows no sign of the *consciousness* of freedom; there is no deliberation before the action, and no joy or shame after it. Moreover, he will not always assert his freedom; in some cases he will say that he acted necessarily, although he may be unable to account for this necessity.

When he falsely asserts it, he may do so by force of habit, because he generally has the real sense of freedom, or because the answer has been suggested to him, or finally because he knows what answer is wanted. Many excuses of irresistible hypnotic influences have been brought before the courts. (2) From *abnormal* and exceptional cases one cannot validly base an inference applying to all, even *normal*, cases. Because a man is sick or insane, it cannot be inferred that all men are in the same condition. The objection, therefore, consists in depriving a man of his freedom and concluding that no men are free. The illusion of the subject who is made to believe that he is an emperor does not prove that there are no real emperors, although he is not one. And the fact that some men have not the use of their legs does not prove that no men can walk. The reason why the hypnotized subject is deprived of his freedom is easy to find. For him there can be no choice of motives, since only such ideas enter his mind as are allowed by the hypnotizer. (3) The question of the existence of freedom in a hypnotized person, and his power to resist the orders that are given to him, is one on which there is no complete agreement.

(*d*) Character, habits, temperament, education, and in general subconscious factors determine the will. The actions of other men can be foreseen with enough accuracy, and, were our knowledge of other minds more perfect all actions could be foreseen with certainty. In a word, as was admitted above, *we act as we are.*

Answer. To the first statement we say that: (1) All these may *sometimes* be necessitating, but *not always*. We feel that we can resist them and we do resist. A man struggles against himself and changes his natural dispositions. (2) They give a *general impulse* which does not determine all concrete actions, but leaves some room for freedom. (3) Subconscious factors exercise an influence only when they appear *at the surface* in consciousness, and their action results in a conscious impulse.

To the second statement we say that: (1) We may foresee a free action of other men, because *men act for reasonable motives*, have the same essential nature, and are influenced by their character. (2) This foresight is in most cases only a *conjecture*, and we are frequently mistaken. (3) Our foreknowledge generally bears on external, spontaneous, indeliberate, and hence *necessary actions*. (4) Our behavior toward other men in bestowing praise or blame shows that we recognize some of their actions as *free*. (5) "We act as we are." Even if this were true, we must say that we are not only what circumstances make us, but also *what we make ourselves*. Emotional tendencies, dispositions, character, strength or weakness of will, etc., depend greatly on ourselves, on the will, and on the good or bad use which is made of it.

(*e*) It is affirmed that *the strongest motive determines the will*. It would be unreasonable to act without a motive, or to choose a less good when a greater good is offered.

Answer. As was said above, it must be admitted that a free action is always performed for a motive, but it does not necessarily follow that the greatest objective good is always and necessarily chosen. (1) We may also admit that the strongest motive determines the will, for we have no other means of determining which motive is the strongest except that it finally prevails. There is no common measure to estimate objectively the weight of different motives such as duty and pleasure. Evidently the preponderant motive is the one according to which we act. But do we act necessarily or freely? This is the question. (2) The will contributes to make a motive preponderant, and gives it its final victory over the others. As already stated, the will is not like the indicator of a balance, inert and passive, but living and active. It makes a given motive stronger and prevalent. But, it may be asked, why does it do so? Sometimes, because we have already "made up our minds," either deliberately and freely, or indeliberately and necessarily. Sometimes, owing to the influence of subjective dispositions and habits which may, more or less, be dependent on the past or present exercise of the free will. Sometimes, with the full consciousness that it is doing right or wrong, yielding to the call of duty or to that of pleasure, and doing it freely.

(*f*) The objection taken from the constancy of human statistics — births, marriages, crimes, etc. — need not detain us. Statistics apply to communities, not to individuals; nor are they absolutely constant. They simply point to a uniformity of motives by which men in general are prompted to act; whether freely or necessarily, statistics cannot indicate.

Hence, although it is true that the large majority of human actions are not *actually* free, in a number of cases the consciousness of freedom remains a valid testimony.

CONCLUSION

CULTIVATION OF THE WILL

I. The Qualities and Defects of the Will

1. **Importance of the Will.** — (1) A man is himself in proportion as he is *his own master*, has control of his actions, and withdraws himself from external determining influences to command his own actions. (2) A man who has *self-control*, who possesses a strong, persevering, and well-directed will, is not only his own master, he will also subdue inanimate nature, succeed in his undertakings, and be the leader of his fellowmen. To be the master of others, a man must first be master of himself. Nothing resists a strong will. The man who has taken a firm resolution, and takes the proper means to carry it out, will seldom fail, or, after a first failure, he will try again until his efforts are rewarded with success. (3) Even *intellectual value* depends to a great extent on the will. Application, attention, perseverance, are so many conditions of success, and the will is the power that commands them. (4) *Moral character*, habits, even feelings, and hence personality, are largely dependent on the will. The will is the supreme power, the mainspring of human activities, and the governing authority. To it must be attributed to a great extent man's success or failure in his various undertakings, and in general, man's worth.

No man, it is true, can ever be independent of external surroundings and of internal dispositions, innate or acquired, permanent or temporary, which influence his thought and action.

Nor is such an independence what we mean by freedom and mastery over oneself. But, whereas the weak will is the tool of these influences and is unable to resist them, the strong will utilizes some, resists others, directs and controls all. Influences known to be good are accepted knowingly and willingly; those that are misleading are excluded. Thus the man who is his own master does not blindly follow the example of others or his own impulses, but he examines first whether they are worth following. He is able to check the natural impulse to act until he has reached a prudent decision based on calm judgment, and, when the occasion requires it, he is also able to muster all his energies and make them subservient to the realization of his ideals.

2. **The Main Qualities of the Will** are the following: (1) *There should be no hastiness* in the deliberation or decision, but the whole process should be calm and without passion. Be slow, take as much time as is required and as circumstances will allow according to the importance of the step which you want to take and the difficulty which you experience. Precipitation in speaking or acting is often the source of subsequent regrets. (2) Yet the necessity of reflection *must not cause one to postpone* the decision and action indefinitely. Do not remain all the time hesitating, fluctuating, and deferring. When all the evidence is at hand, take your decision accordingly, and carry it out. (3) *Execute your decision promptly.* Be not satisfied with desires that are never realized. When you have seen what you ought to do, do it without useless delay. Remember that "desires kill the slothful, for his hands have refused to work at all. He longeth and desireth all the day." (Prov. xxi, 25.) He will keep his resolution "to-morrow," or the "next time," and the more he procrastinates, the weaker he becomes. (4) Do not "change your mind" on the slightest pretext, but *be constant and persevering*. To abandon one's prudent plans without sufficient reason is a sign of fickleness and a presage of failure.

3. **The Defects of the Will** come from two causes, and are in two opposite directions, excess and defect. (1) *The will may be too strong*, when it shows, not prudent, but imprudent firmness, constancy, and perseverance. This is obstinacy and stubborn-

ness. A man who is stubborn will abide by his former decision in spite of new contrary and convincing evidence. (2) *The will may be too hasty,* impulsive, rash, and impatient. Instead of reflecting attentively, a man will at once rush into action on the impulse of the moment. The power of inhibition seems insufficient to apply the brakes in time and to prevent impulses from passing at once into action. (3) *Some, on the contrary, have not enough will power.* Without speaking of extreme cases of aboulia which are pathological, some persons are unable to take a decision. They are always hesitating and cannot resolve to adopt a plan. Others "want to do," but always find an excuse. "I know," they will say, "that I ought to do it, but I can't." In every pursuit man needs light and intelligence, but he needs also a good, strong, and persevering will. Truly and sincerely to say "I will" implies generally "I can," whereas to say "I cannot" is to make an action almost impossible.

II. Some Principles to be Used in Will Culture

In general, try to acquire the qualities and to avoid the defects mentioned above. Here we must limit ourselves to a few of the most general principles regarding the intellect, the feelings, and the will itself.

1. **Intellect.** — The common principles "Nil volitum nisi praecognitum," and "Ignoti nulla cupido," express the evident truth that the will does not tend to any unknown good, but must necessarily have something apprehended as good presented to it. But the intellect by itself is a weak motor, and mere ideas have but little influence on the determination. How many know what is good, noble, and right, and yet seem to have no inclination for it, or, if they have an inclination, seem incapable of making it pass into action. They know their duty, but do not love it. They may even *desire* to fulfil it, but do not *will* it.

2. **Feelings.** — Therefore *ideas must be associated with feelings.* What we ardently love and want sets the energy into action. The meditation on the motives must not be cold and purely rational; it must be warm, and tend to excite not only the knowledge, but also the love of the good. Consider not only the truth, but also

the utility, pleasure, peace, etc., that will result. See the examples of heroes and saints, and let them instil in you courage, confidence, and enthusiasm. At every step, keep in mind the necessity and advantages of your action. Attention to the end, attention to the means, attention to the results, will lead to strength and perseverance. It has been said that ideas lead the world. This is not exact; what leads the world is not so much the ideas as the love for certain ideas. Hence the necessity of feelings and of enthusiasm.

If you find it impossible to perform an action or conquer a habit immediately, proceed gradually and step by step, but always take clear-cut resolutions bearing on a well-determined point. The resolution to do good in general is too abstract, and does not excite a concrete love. But take the resolution to do this specified kind of good, in this special circumstance, under these special conditions.

3. **Will.** — (*a*) As to the will itself, see what should be developed and what should be repressed, where there is excess and where there is defect. It is very important to *acquire good habits*, for a habit is a ready mechanism which needs only a first impulse to unfold immediately a whole series of actions. Habit prevents the diffusion of energy in various useless directions, and the dispersion of strength. The whole energy goes straight to performing the action. How much conscious and organic energy is dispersed, for instance, in the first piano lesson. Later on, it is concentrated unconsciously and tends to the perfect result. Hence the importance of acquiring immediately the habit of performing a series of movements in the manner which is the shortest and the best adapted to the intended result. Watch constantly lest you should acquire bad habits, for it is very difficult to uproot them. Apply yourself chiefly to the acquisition of those habits which you need most, and especially of the four moral habits that have such an importance in the whole course of life: prudence, justice, temperance, and courage.

(*b*) *Always keep your will on edge;* exercise it constantly; find something to do that requires effort. If you simply let yourself go down the stream, carried along by the current of your habits and character, even if they do not lead you astray, you will find that you will not have strength enough to overcome obstacles and change your course if it becomes necessary to do so. Like our muscles, our will weakens if it is not exercised. Hence every day impose on yourself some task and effort. A great fault to be avoided is to fail to carry out a good resolution once it has been taken, for every voluntary failure is a weakening defeat. It is better to take no resolutions than to take them reluctantly and without trying to keep them by all possible means. Yet let not your failures discourage you, but rise again, strengthen your resolution, and try to do better. Let not a single day pass without making some useful effort, without using your will, and using it well.

CHAPTER IV

SUPPLEMENTARY. — SOME SPECIAL RELATIONS AND MODES OF MENTAL PROCESSES

I. MIND AND ORGANISM

I. Mutual Relations of Dependence and Influence

Although the mind is distinct from the organism, and consciousness cannot be reduced to any form of movement, it is certain that the two are very closely united and influence each other.

1. **Influence of the Organism on the Mind.** — (*a*) In general, mental processes depend on the conditions of the organism. (1) *Sensations* depend on the transmission through an afferent nerve to the brain, of an impression received by the peripheral apparatus. Cut the transmitting nerve, or let the nerve or the brain centre be diseased, and no sensation is experienced. (2) *Imagination, memory, intelligence*, depend on brain centres; if these are destroyed or impaired, there follows a loss or a disturbance of these faculties. Moreover, intellectual faculties cannot be exercised until the brain reaches a certain minimum of development. (3) *Feelings* depend largely on organic dispositions, especially of the nervous system. (4) *The exercise of activity* commanded by the will can be carried out only if the organism is in the normal condition. Thus the paralytic is unable to execute a volition of movement.

(*b*) In a more special manner, we mention the concomitant variations of mental processes with the dispositions of the organism: (1) health and illness; (2) food and drink; (3) special organic modifications caused by mental processes like memory, imagination, emotions, etc.

(*c*) Finally we note the following influences: (1) *Age;* the child, the adult, and the old man have not the same views, the same sensibility, and the same constancy. The youth is more impetuous and more changing, the mature man more circumspect and prudent, the old man generally weaker. These differences are due largely to differences in the irritability of the nerves, the strength of the muscles, the plasticity of the whole system, the quality of the blood, and the vital functions. (2) *Sex;* women have generally more sensitiveness, more delicacy, more changeableness; men, more strength, constancy, and intelligence. (3) *Temperament;* strong or weak according as the mental energy is greater or smaller, and in consequence the mental states are more or less intense; quick or slow according as the mental states succeed one another rapidly or slowly. The strong temperaments are the choleric and melancholic; the weak temperaments, the sanguine and phlegmatic; the quick temperaments, the choleric and sanguine; the slow temperaments, the melancholic and phlegmatic. Strong temperaments are inclined to great emotions, and yield more easily to painful impressions. Weak temperaments have little emotion, and are rather disposed to enjoyment. Quick temperaments have rapid changes, are intent on the present, and require additional strength to do more work. Slow temperaments change slowly, are rather inclined to look toward the future, and require additional time to do more work. We may also note that the choleric and phlegmatic temperaments chiefly refer to action; the sanguine and melancholic, chiefly to feelings. Temperaments are seldom found with these exclusive features; they include elements belonging to several groups, and are determined by their predominant features. (4) *Climate;* mental dispositions vary with different atmospheric conditions, and there is a noticeable difference between the inhabitants of cold and those of hot countries. (5) *Heredity* of certain organic traits.

2. **Influence of Mental Processes on the Organism** — (*a*) *Ideas and images of movements* tend to produce those movements. In general, as explained above, the image is both representative and motor. The thought of something terrible may cause trembling; the thought of something disgusting may cause vomiting, etc. Imagination may contribute to induce and increase sickness, and many an apparent remedy has acted with as

much efficacy as a real one. In such cases, there is generally a combination of images and feelings.

(*b*) *Feelings*, and chiefly strong emotions, *are naturally expressed in the organism* by certain modifications; circulatory — blushing, turning pale, acceleration or decrease of pulsations, etc.; respiratory — cries, moanings, acceleration of respiration, etc.; movements of eyes; secretions, e.g. tears; facial nerves, physiognomy; and other nerves — trembling, spasms, etc. Moreover, emotions may affect all vital functions, secretion, digestion, etc. If too violent, they may cause serious troubles, swoonings, and even death.

(*c*) *The will causes motions* in the organism; some are directly under its control, but it can reach indirectly all organs and functions, for instance, digestion by allowing only a certain quantity or quality of food.

Hence, in a general way, organic habits, health, features, etc., are to a certain extent signs of habits of mind. Physiognomy is frequently an unsafe and misleading guide, yet its value, especially in certain cases, cannot be denied. Although unsafe when used alone, and when relied on too securely, judging a person "by his looks" may sometimes be of great utility.

II. Cerebral Localization

Besides the general relations of mind and body, there are others of a more special nature. Certain mental functions have their seat, or are localized, in certain parts of the organism.

1. **Phrenology** generally applies to the systems of Gall and Spurzheim, in the beginning of the nineteenth century. They suppose the innateness of all mental faculties or qualities, and their adequate manifestation through the brain, which, according to them, has as many special organs as there are distinct faculties. Hence, according as a certain area of the brain is more developed — this is manifested externally by the shape of the skull — a mental aptitude will be predominant. The number of distinct faculties varies from twenty-six, according to Gall, to thirty-five, according to Spurzheim, and even more according to others.

Phrenology is completely discredited to-day. The methods

used are unscientific, and some of the fundamental principles are false, for instance, that the development of a mental power always depends on the size of the corresponding organ — it depends rather on qualitative properties; that mental tendencies are innate and unmodifiable; that the shape of the skull always manifests the relative development of the corresponding parts of the brain, — the convolutions of the brain, which are very important, cannot be manifested by the shape of the skull. The division of faculties is arbitrary and fanciful; and to assign a special part of the brain to every faculty is impossible. The main objection against phrenology, however, is the progress of modern psychological and physiological sciences which have disproved the tenets of phrenologists concerning the functions of the brain, and, in some cases, have established cerebral localizations different from those which phrenology mapped out.

2. **Scientific Localization.** — (*a*) The *methods* used to determine the localization of functions in the brain are: (1) *Experimentation.* Either stimulate — chiefly by an electric current — certain areas of the brain cortex, and see what movements take place or what results are obtained. Or extirpate certain portions of the brain, and see what loss or disturbance in motion or in sensory processes follows. Such experiments are performed on animals, and, by analogy, the results are applied to man. (2) *Pathology.* Man does not experiment on the human brain. But it happens that lesions or pathological affections occur which are observed in post-mortem examinations, and thus the cause of the motor or sensory troubles which had been manifested is ascertained. In some cases the skull has been trepanned, and a tumor, piece of bone, or lesion has been found where it was supposed to be. (3) *Comparative anatomy and histology.* The higher the organization of animals, the greater the number of localized functions. Hence localizations verified in the highest vertebrates are applied to man with great probability. Histology is making progress toward following the nerve-tracts through the brain to the cortex. (4) These methods are generally used cumulatively, and the evidence is compared.

(*b*) The student is referred to text-books of physiology for the details of cerebral localization. The most general and best established are the following: (1) The motor centres are found on both sides of the fissure of Rolando. It is noteworthy that motor centres of one hemisphere are related to the other side of the body — the right hemisphere controls the left limbs, and the left hemisphere, the right limbs. (2) The sensory centres are not all ascertained. The visual centre is in the occipital lobes; the auditory, in the temporal lobes, as also probably the olfactory and the gustatory. The tactile centres are probably in the parietal lobes.

(*c*) These localizations are not restricted to a well-defined spot, mathematically circumscribed. Neighboring centres, so to speak, interpenetrate. Moreover, if one part becomes incapable of performing its functions, other parts — either corresponding parts of the other hemisphere, or neighboring parts in the same hemisphere — sometimes may take its place.

II. SOME SPECIAL MENTAL CONDITIONS

The following mental conditions are related to special organic conditions, many of which are but very imperfectly known.

1. **Insanity.** — The mind as well as the body has its diseases. They form the object of the sciences known as abnormal psychology; mental pathology, i.e. the science of the diseases of the mind; psychiatry (etymologically, the healing of the soul). Some of these diseases, like hallucination and aboulia, are partial and affect a special faculty. Others are of a more general nature and seem to affect the whole or almost the whole mental life. Again, some are of small importance and little apparent. Others are more manifest and deeper. The term "insanity"—although etymologically meaning any disease (*in-sanitas*) — is restricted to the most general and best characterized forms of mental disease. Hardly any definition or classification of its various forms can be given. In general, insanity is not applied to temporary mental derangement, like that due to a strong emotion; yet this usage seems to become current in criminal courts where temporary insanity is made the plea for the defence. Nor is it applied to a slight dis-

turbance or irregularity of functions, but to a serious defect of thought, emotion, or rational activity.

Dementia is a weakened condition of the mental powers. It denotes feebleness, inactivity, and incapacity, rather than abnormal functioning. It supposes that the faculties have been stronger before, whereas idiocy and imbecility or feeble-mindedness are congenital.

The causes of insanity may be general dispositions or accidental events. The most important are heredity, worry, a melancholic temperament, various hereditary and acquired dispositions and defects of the organism, and especially of the nervous system. Many accidents, bodily injury, strong emotions, intemperance, drug-habits, etc., may bring about insanity.

2. **Sleep and Dream.** — Sleep is a temporary dementia, and insanity has been termed the dream of the waking man. In fact, there is more than one point of resemblance between these two states. In dream and in insanity we observe the same incoherence, irrational sequence of ideas and images, and the same absence of control of the inferior mental powers by the higher faculties.

(*a*) Psychologically, *sleep is the suspension or, at least, the lowering of consciousness.* If we rely on the testimony of memory, we may think that consciousness is totally suspended at least during some periods of sleep, for we are not aware of dreaming all the time. However, this testimony is not necessarily reliable, for we have dreams which we do not remember, or which are recalled later owing to some accidental association. It seems also that whenever we wake up, if we can take immediate cognizance of our state we are conscious of waking from a dream which may be weak, and the memory of which, after a few instants, disappears beyond recall.

(*b*) *The physiological causes of sleep* are not certain. To a great extent they seem to be changes in the blood circulation in the brain. The work of the day fatigues the brain and accumulates waste-matter. Hence the need of rest, during which this is eliminated. The main conditions contributing to induce sleep are fatigue, monotonous impressions, the influence of cold and heat, certain organic functions like digestion, or organic morbid dispositions, and chiefly the absence of ordinary sensory stimuli, that is, darkness, silence, and tranquillity. Waking may result from the sufficiency of rest, from a stimulus, either internal, like pain, or external, like sound, light, or touch, especially if the stimulus is strong, or if, though weak, it corresponds to a special attention of the subject. Thus a mother perceives the slightest cry of a sick child, the fireman hears the sound of the alarm bell, etc. The stopping of accustomed regular movements or noises may also cause one to arouse from sleep.

(*c*) Conscious processes during sleep are called *dreams*. Between the state of wakefulness and the dreaming state we may mention "rêverie," in which little or no attention is paid to external things, and free play is allowed to the imagination. As all mental faculties may be, or at least may seem to be, suspended during sleep, so also all may be exercised. There is imagination and memory; feeling — e.g. fear in a nightmare; judgment and reasoning, no matter how uncouth and unreasonable these may be; will, or at any rate something akin to it, for instance, when one wants to run away, speak, etc. There is even some kind of sensation, as we shall see when we speak of the causes of dreams. However, a dream is a continuous hallucination. Images, no matter how ridiculous from the point of view of the waking state, are taken for realities. This is due to the fact that such images are not corrected by perceptions or by reason. They are not under the control of attention and will, and follow their own capricious course. No account is taken of time. Observations have shown that, in a few seconds, one may dream of a succession of events that would occupy a very long time.

(*d*) *The main causes of dreams* are: (1) Sensations. Thus a little touch or smart may be magnified and represented in consciousness by huge weights or wounds. (2) Organic conditions like indigestion, difficult breathing, etc. (3) Mental states going on before sleep and continued during it. (4) General tendencies and preoccupations which contribute to modify the dreaming tendencies.

3. **Somnambulism** — etymologically, walking asleep — is a state of mental activity during sleep, or perhaps quasi-sleep, accompa-

nied by perceptions, movements, and purposive actions. It has been called the acting of one's dream. In somnambulism there is activity and coördinated movement, e.g. walking, speaking, writing. Frequently there is also sequence and coherence in the ideas. The somnambulist may speak or write very sensibly, and even do intellectual work, solve problems, write essays, and find solutions which had been sought in vain during the state of wakefulness. The senses are awake, and the somnambulist walks and avoids obstacles on his way, or carries on a conversation. The senses are even generally keener than in the waking state, especially the muscular sense. The somnambulist performs dangerous actions which he would never be able to perform when awake. At the same time, the senses are selective, and their field is narrower. Frequently certain objects only are perceived, namely, those that are connected with the train of ideas, while the others are overlooked. There is thus an exaggerated form of what, in the waking state, would be called distraction. Whereas we may have a very vivid recollection of dreams, actions performed in the somnambulistic state are not remembered in the state of wakefulness, but may be recalled in a new somnambulism.

4. **Duality or Multiplicity of "Selves" or "Personalities"** is a term frequently used, although what it expresses is in reality a dissociation of the centres, chiefly of the memory centres.

(*a*) In some cases, a person has had, so to speak, two or three different *successive* or *alternating* personalities which, though succeeding one another, form in consciousness two continuous series and are generally more or less independent:

$$A—A_1—A_2\text{———}A_3—A_4—A_5\text{————}A_6\ldots\ldots$$
$$B—B_1—B_2—B_3—B_4\text{———}B_5—B_6—B_7—B_8\ldots\ldots$$

In the series A, the events of the series B are not remembered, nor are those of the series A in the series B. Sometimes, however, one series is privileged, and includes the other, but not vice versa. Something, e.g. language, knowledge of persons, etc., may be, but is not always, common to both series. If one "personality" has any knowledge of the other, it will generally refer to it in the third person. It also may happen that in one series the character and aptitudes are greatly different from those in the other series.

(*b*) Two *simultaneous* "personalities" may also be found. For instance, while the subject is engaged in conversation with another person, a third person may ask questions which will be answered rationally by automatic writing. In more general terms, two simultaneous series of rational actions will go on independently. It is remarkable that, when the subject writes automatically while carrying on a conversation, the "writer" will refer to the "speaker" in the third person, and even may refer to him as a stranger or an enemy.

Such facts — which of course are rare — occur chiefly in cases of hysteria. Hysteria is a very complex organic and mental disease, having several points in common with somnambulism, chiefly the hyperæsthesia of certain senses.

5. **Suggestion** is very closely allied to imagination.

(*a*) *In a broad sense*, to suggest is to impart an idea, especially with a view to determine some action. It is of daily occurrence and use. A striking instance will be found in advertising. The purpose of advertising is to arouse in the mind the idea of certain wants, and hence the desire to satisfy them by buying the recommended article. The symptoms of a disease will be described so as to suggest that you have that disease. Conclusion: buy the patent medicine. The more completely an idea takes possession of the mind and is prominent, the greater is its motor power, and the greater the chances of its being effective. Hence if it is the only idea present in the mind, or if other ideas are made to strengthen it, or if, finally, other antagonistic ideas have no time to counteract it, the suggested action is certain to follow.

(*b*) This *necessary* determination of an action by an idea is suggestion *in the strict sense*. The determined process may be sensory — hallucination, illusion, etc., — motor, inhibitory, emotional, or ideal. Suggestibility in the broad sense is common to all men. In the strict sense it is found chiefly in certain abnormal states, especially in hypnotism. Hetero-suggestion, or simply suggestion, is given by the words, gestures, or signs of some one else. Auto-suggestion comes consciously or unconsciously from the agent himself.

6. **Hypnotism** (ὕπνος, sleep) is the art, theory, or practice of hypnosis. Hypnosis is a mental state in many respects similar to somnambulism.

(*a*) Hypnosis is produced in many different ways: gazing at a bright object, listening to a monotonous sound, passes before the eyes and on the body, suggestion or command to go to sleep.

(*b*) The main *psychological features* of the deep and complete hypnosis are: (1) Suggestibility. All kinds of illusions and hallucinations occur at the will of the hypnotizer. Present things or persons are not perceived, or absent things and persons are imagined to be present. The subject changes his attitude and behavior accordingly. Actions are performed when and as commanded — whether always irresistibly seems uncertain. Post-hypnotic suggestions are suggestions made during the hypnotic state, but to be carried out only at an appointed time, after the subject has been aroused. (2) Alterations of memory. Actions performed during hypnosis generally are not recalled in the normal state, but may be recalled in a subsequent hypnosis. (3) The "rapport" of the subject with the hypnotizer is a special relation of the two, to the exclusion of every other person unless the hypnotizer allows the subject to communicate also with others.

(*c*) The causes and mechanism of hypnotism are very uncertain. Some analogies and hints are found in other mental conditions already mentioned; but an adequate explanation is not possible with our actual knowledge.

(*d*) All serious psychologists and hypnotists agree that the practice of hypnotism is dangerous. It weakens the intellect and will, and generally has a harmful influence on the nervous system, not to mention the immoral or criminal influences that may be exercised by unscrupulous hypnotizers. In some cases, however, hypnotism may be useful to correct mental or organic defects. Only competent and upright physicians should be allowed to practice hypnotism, and under restrictions and conditions which obviate its dangers.

7. **Clairvoyance, Mental Suggestion, Telepathy.** — (*a*) *Clair-*

voyance is the alleged power to see things through opaque bodies, or at great distances. If the facts alleged are true, perhaps other facts, such as radio-activity, wireless telegraphy, and wireless telephony, may throw some light on these abnormal phenomena. Certain rays penetrate opaque bodies, and can affect special photographic plates. Is it impossible that the eye should be adapted to receive and perceive them? All that is required is that the eye should allow such rays to pass through its various refracting media — which it does not ordinarily — and that the retina be sensitive to them. As to the vision of past and future events, if true, it can be explained to some extent by memory — even though the event was not consciously known, — or by guesses and inferences from known causes.

(*b*) *Mental suggestion* is a suggestion made immediately from mind to mind without any sensible sign, word, or gesture. Several hypotheses have been proposed to explain such facts, supposing them to be authentic. None seems satisfactory, or, at least, sufficiently based on known mental or physical properties. Is it possible for an idea to correspond to certain brain processes which would be transmitted to and interpreted by another brain? Here again recent discoveries in physical sciences must make us hesitate in denying this possibility. As we do not know all the properties of matter, so we do not know all the properties of organized matter, nor of mind. Investigations seem to point out that mental work produces something like emanations or radiations. At certain times two brains may be in special relations of sympathy, so that one of them is apt to receive and interpret the other's messages.

(*c*) *Telepathy* is the communication between two minds without the help of the senses, and generally at a great distance. The alleged facts consist chiefly of apparitions of persons dying far away, of a sense of uneasiness when some absent relative or friend meets with an accident, and of certain premonitions of danger. Whether and how such facts can be explained, it is not possible at present to say. The indications given for mental suggestion or thought-transference apply also to some of the facts of telepathy.

8. **Spiritism**, sometimes called spiritualism, which is to-day so much in evidence, includes many marvellous facts: table-turning in order to receive answers to questions asked, motions of furniture, light or sounds coming from unknown and unseen causes, apparitions, etc. It is noteworthy that the presence of a medium is required, that is, of a specially sensitive person through whom the "spirits" manifest themselves. Frequently the medium gives answers by speech or automatic writing.

(*a*) Many of the so-called spiritistic phenomena are frauds which have been exposed more than once. However, there seems to remain a certain number of well-ascertained facts, and, even if there is much more fraud than truth, this is not a sufficient reason for denying everything, especially when we have honest, serious, and competent witnesses. These facts are not at present explicable. We simply note that the facts of objectivated dreams, hallucinations, hypnotism, double personality, and somnambulism can probably account for some of the medium's powers, and perhaps *for all* those which he *really* possesses. Thought-transference, if possible, would also be a clue toward an explanation. It is significant that the same "spirit" does not speak in the same manner, nor are his opinions the same, when given through different mediums, and that the medium impersonates the "spirits" and transmits messages purporting to come from them according to the knowledge he has of such "spirits." Significant also is the fact of the "trance" of the medium during his supposed communication with the spirit, as we know that hypnotism predisposes one to play a rôle or a second personality.

(*b*) What has been said of the dangers of hypnotism applies to spiritism, and here even the dangers are much greater, as experience teaches. Moreover, there may be moral and religious reasons for avoiding all spiritistic practices. As a religious system based on supposed revelations of the "spirits," spiritism is in open contradiction with the Christian religion.

N.B. It is impossible to enter here into a more detailed account of these extraordinary facts. We caution the student against too great a credulity with regard to the multitude of stories circulated on these topics, and against hasty inferences and theories.

It may also be noticed that these facts form a continuous series. The passage from one to the other is gradual; there is no sudden jump and no gap. But psychology is unable at present to explain them all. Finally, it must be recalled that continuity does not necessarily mean identity in nature or in the causes of the extremes that are linked by many intermediaries.

CONCLUSION

CHARACTER AND PERSONALITY

1. **Character.** — (*a*) Etymologically, character signifies a distinctive mark, and accordingly means the most salient features in every individual's mental structure and functions, that which makes him to be so or so. *In this broad sense* it denotes something very complex, namely, the general relations between mental tendencies, their relative importance, the inferiority or predominance of some. The most obvious distinctive feature in man is his conduct, his mode of acting, especially in such actions as are voluntarily purposive. Hence character refers chiefly to the active aspect of life, that is, to the tendencies and feelings, inasmuch as they prompt to certain lines of action.

(*b*) *In a narrower signification*, as when we speak of a man of character, or say that a man has no character, we refer especially to the unity and consistency of his mental processes, together with some independence and strength of will. A character is thus dependent on the qualities of intelligence, especially reflection, and on the emotional nature, especially the control of the emotions by the will. Although character depends largely on heredity, environment, early education, and surroundings, it refers chiefly to the acquired habits of will. We act according to our habits. The early formation of character is very important. Parents and teachers can never give too much attention and care to it. They must use innate tendencies to help the formation of right habits and the uprooting of wrong ones, and to suggest noble motives and ideals.

(*c*) *Temperament* and *disposition* are closely related to character. Temperament is chiefly dependent on inherited organic conditions, and can be reformed less easily than character. Disposition is also mostly innate and hereditary. It refers to emotional and active tendencies. Thus a man is said to have a happy disposition, an excitable disposition, a sluggish disposition, etc. We have spoken above (p. 191) of the four temperaments; characters cannot be classified satisfactorily; according to their dominant features they are referred to as weak, obstinate, inconstant, selfish, etc.

2. **Personality.** — In its psychological — not philosophical — sense, personality is almost the same as character; it denotes a strong and marked individuality. Man alone is a person, and he is personal when he performs certain actions that spring from himself. To be a person is to emerge above the universal determinism of matter, to conquer and not be conquered, to possess oneself. The self is the centre of attribution of voluntary activities, the responsible agent, that which in us is worthy of respect and which, therefore, is the foundation of social ethics. The psychological self changes and is modified by circumstances and chiefly by effort. We say of a man: "He is not what he used to be;" and of the man who acts according to his character, and according to our expectation, we say: "That is just like him." Of a man whom we suppose to have acted under such a strong or sudden impulse that his will was prevented from inhibiting the action, we say: "He was not himself." To be oneself is to be one's own master. Hence let your primary and chief endeavor be to develop in you good habits, good dispositions, and a good character. Always strive after what is worth your best effort. Ascertain the direction to be taken, and, when you know that your efforts are directed toward right and noble ideals, be strong, constant, and invincible. *In all things and actions, be a personality; be yourself.*

LOGIC OR THE NORMATIVE SCIENCE OF THE INTELLECT

INTRODUCTION

1. **Main Conclusions from Psychology**, which it is necessary to recall here. (1) Truth is found in the judgment, that is, in the affirmation or negation of the agreement of two notions. A simple idea in itself has no truth, but only when its relation to another is asserted (p. 107). (2) Judgments are immediate and self-evident, or mediate and reached through a process of reasoning (p. 112, 115 ff.). (3) Judgments are true or false according as they affirm that which is or is not in conformity with reality. Men reform some of their judgments, considering as false what they previously considered as true, and vice versa. Again, they look upon the judgments of other men as true or false, and as more or less certain or uncertain (p. 117 ff.). (4) The mind may be in a state of ignorance, when it has no knowledge whatever of an object, and hence can form no judgment; of error, when a false judgment is accepted; of doubt, when the mind, although knowing something about an object, finds no sufficient reason for affirming or denying; of opinion, when the mind assents to a judgment, but does not give a firm assent because there are reasons to fear lest such a judgment be false; of certitude, when the truth appears with evidence, and a judgment is assented to unreservedly. It may be noticed that in common usage ignorance is often used for doubt and error, and doubt for opinion, or rather for the fear of error. (5) We have also called attention to the distinction between assent and consent, convincing and persuading, knowing intellectually and practically accepting the truth with all its consequences. The former regards the intellect alone, the latter concerns the whole man (p. 120 ff.).

2. **Meaning of Logic.** — (*a*) The names of many sciences end in -logy — psychology, cosmology, geology, etc. The term λόγος signifies primarily word, and secondarily thought, and also science. "Logic" comes from the same Greek term. *In ordinary language* it refers to the power of reasoning, and to the consistency either between the thoughts of an individual, or between his thoughts and his mode of action. *To be logical is to be reasonable.*

(*b*) As used here, the term "logic" means *the normative science of the intellectual faculties.* Certain modes of thought are invalid. There are judgments that are incompatible and exclude one another. Others are compatible, but independent of one another, and have no logical relation. Others are compatible and logically related as principles and conclusions, one being inferred from others. The purpose of logic is to indicate the rules of valid inference so as to facilitate the progress of the mind in the pursuit of truth and the freedom from error. In other words, logic tries to dispose the materials found in the mind into harmonious structures, and to indicate the way toward the acquisition of new knowledge.

3. **Definition of Logic.** — The truth which is considered here is logical truth. The intrinsic value of the materials used is not examined, but only their valid sequence in the mind. For instance, "All men are white; Peter is a man; therefore Peter is white," is a true and valid syllogism from the point of view of logic, although the first proposition is not in conformity with reality. The logical value of a syllogism is independent of the truth of its propositions, as will be explained more in detail later on. Hence logic has frequently been defined as *the science of the formal laws of thought.*

By "thought" is meant chiefly discursive thought or reasoning. The "laws of thought" are the norms of valid reasoning, and of inference in general. By "formal" laws is meant that logic deals with the process of reasoning apart from its contents or materials, considering only the validity of the process, no matter what the contents may be.

Hence logic differs from *psychology*, which studies also the processes of thought, but in their nature and genesis apart from their validity; from *epistemology*, which examines the value of the contents of judgments; from *oratory*, which tries not only to convince but chiefly to persuade; from *grammar*, which deals with the correct expression of thought.

4. **Utility of Logic.** — Logic is a very useful science, since it teaches the proper use of intellectual faculties in finding and teaching the truth and in guarding against error. It has been called rightly the science of sciences, or the instrument of sciences. All men have a natural logic; all know what it is to contradict oneself; all use arguments and detect fallacies. Scientific logic develops this natural aptitude. It strengthens the intellectual faculties by exercising them methodically and contributing to the acquisition of good habits of thought. It assists the mind in finding the truth and testing the value of judgments. It makes it easier to detect the numerous fallacies which, consciously or unconsciously, creep into books, conversations, speeches, and articles. The logical mind is not drawn so irresistibly by an appeal to prejudices, passions, and emotions. It looks for the reasons and the inner value of the arguments used.

5. **Division of Logic.** — This treatise will be divided into two chapters. The first will consider the instruments which the mind uses to reach truth, the most important of which is reasoning. The second will deal with the proper use of these instruments, their value, and orderly arrangement.

CHAPTER I

REASONING

Knowledge is generally discursive. Except in the case of self-evidence, truth is acquired by proceeding from some known judgment to another. This is called reasoning, by means of which a judgment, unknown or less known before, is reached. Hence reasoning is the main instrument by which knowledge is acquired, and consequently the primary object of this chapter. However, as reasoning supposes judgments, and judgments suppose ideas, it is also necessary to consider these elements of reasoning. Beginning with the simplest, we have the three following articles: (1) Idea. (2) Judgment. (3) Reasoning.

ARTICLE I. THE IDEA

I. NATURE OF IDEAS

I. The Idea in Logic

1. **How Logic Considers Ideas.** — From what has been said in psychology we know that an idea is a simple mental representation, i.e. something in the mind, holding the place of or representing some object. This representation is called simple because it includes no affirmation or negation, and in this differs from the judgment. Logic does not consider the idea in all its aspects; it leaves its genesis to psychology, and its conformity with the object to epistemology. It considers the idea only *as the element — subject or predicate — of the judgment.* An idea may be attributed to another according to various modes, and their connection may be more or less necessary. On the other hand, all possible ideas are reducible to certain higher classes in which they are contained.

Hence the necessity of speaking of predicables and of predicaments or categories. To predicate (praedicare) means to affirm the relation of an attribute to a subject.

2. **Predicables.** — (*a*) An idea may be conceived: (1) *As constituting the complete essence*, and only the essence of a class of individuals, e.g. the idea of man as applied to Peter, Paul, John, etc., or the idea of a plane figure bounded by four straight lines as applied to all quadrilaterals. (*Species.*) (2) *As common to several classes of individuals* and constituting their essence *incompletely*. Thus I say that a man, a horse, a robin, a fly, etc., are animals. (*Genus.*) (3) *As something differentiating* this common idea or genus. Thus every class of animals just mentioned has essential characteristics by which it differs from the others. (*Specific difference.*) (4) *As necessarily connected with*, and flowing from, the essence, although not constituting it. Thus in man the power of expressing ideas by speech or writing. (*Property.*) (5) As present *in fact*, but with *no necessary connection*, so that it might be absent. Thus for man to be white, learned, tall, strong, etc. (*Accident.*)

(*b*) Hence *we have five predicables*, that is, five modes according to which ideas may be predicated of others: species, genus, specific difference, property, and accident. The predicates of all judgments are attributed to the subject in one of these five ways. Hence the following synopsis.

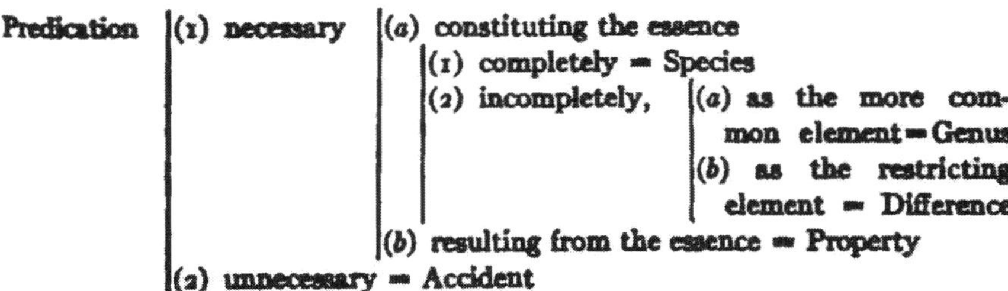

Predication
- (1) necessary
  - (*a*) constituting the essence
    - (1) completely = Species
    - (2) incompletely,
      - (*a*) as the more common element = Genus
      - (*b*) as the restricting element = Difference
  - (*b*) resulting from the essence = Property
- (2) unnecessary = Accident

(*c*) Hence several individuals may agree or differ specifically. Individuals within the same species necessarily agree in species, genus, specific difference, and properties. Individuals within the same genus always have some common essential note.

N.B. We speak here of property in the strict sense, as that which belongs to all individuals of the same class, and to these individuals alone. In common language other meanings are frequently used.

(*d*) The same idea may often be considered both as genus and as species from different points of view. Thus *animal* is a *species of living substances* — specifically different from plants which are also living, — and at the same time it is the *genus of man and of irrational animals.* The *genus supremum* is the first division of the most general notion, that of being. The *species infima* is the last species under which individuals only are found. The following list is known as the tree of Porphyry (a philosopher, A.D. 233–304).

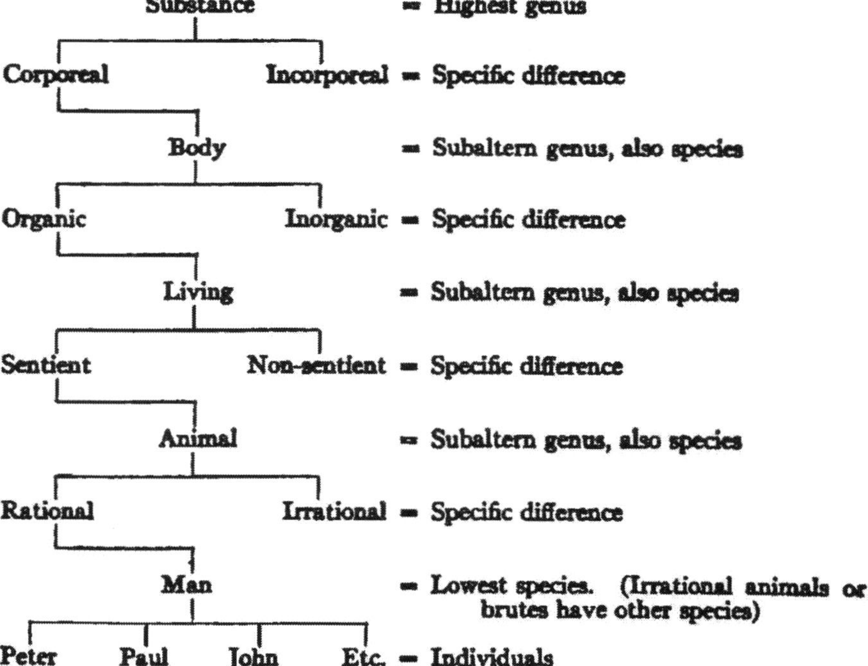

N.B. We suppose that there is no genus above substance. The idea of being alone is above it, and this is not a genus, since, whatever difference that might be added to it is something or some being, and therefore already contained in the notion of being.

Ideas may be within the same proximate, or only within the same remote genus. Thus man and stone are within the same genus of material substances or bodies, but not within the same proximate genus.

3. **Predicaments** or **Categories** are the *genera suprema*, or highest genera to which all possible ideas are reducible. Aristotle numbered ten categories: substance, quantity, quality, relation, action, passion, place, time, situation or posture, habit or bearing. All ideas certainly can be reduced to one of these groups. The nine last together form the group known as accident. Accidents are conceived, not as existing in themselves, but as being received in and modifying the substance. Probably a further reduction of the categories is possible into: substance, quantity, quality, and relation, all other accidents being reduced to relations; or into: substance — existing in itself, — as man, gold, etc.; accident — existing in the substance — as science, color, size, etc.; and relation — referring a thing to another — as cause and effect, similarity, right or left, etc. N.B. Notice the difference in the meaning of accident as a predicament and as a predicable.

4. **Terms.** — *A term is a word*, spoken or written, *used to express an idea.* The function of language has been explained in psychology (p. 122 ff.). Since it is a sign, the term stands for something else. This is called its *supposition*. The term may stand for itself as written or spoken, for instance, "man is spelt m-a-n," or "man is a monosyllable." This is called *material supposition*. Or the term may stand for an idea that exists only in the mind, e.g. a genus or species, for instance, "Man is a species of animal." This is called *logical supposition*. Or, finally, it may stand for a reality existing outside of the mind, e.g. "This man is wise." This is called *real supposition*.

II. Intension and Extension of Ideas and Terms

1. **Meaning.** — In the Porphyry tree above, higher notions are not so complex as lower ones. Thus animal includes the ideas of substance, material, organic, and sentient; living includes only the ideas of substance, material, and organic; body includes only the ideas of substance and material. On the

contrary, as we go higher, the number of individuals contained under the notion grows larger. There are more living substances than animals, and more bodies than living substances. *The totality of the necessary elements of an idea*, that is, of the simpler ideas that are implied in it, is called its *connotation*, *comprehension*, *intension*, or *contents*. *The totality of the individuals to which such an idea applies* is called its *denotation*, *extension*, or *sphere of application*.

2. **Law.** — From what precedes it is apparent that *extension and intension vary in opposite directions*, that is, the greater the extension, the smaller the intension, and vice versa. Since increasing the intension means adding a new difference, it means forming two or several sub-classes, each of which cannot include the same number of individuals as all taken together. And since widening the extension means enlarging the number of individuals, it means removing some barrier, i.e. some difference by which the former class was separated from neighboring classes. Thus, there are more men than white men, more books than bound books, etc. "White" and "bound" are new differences or new ideas introduced in the connotation, and restricting men and books to fewer applications. The addition of "tallness" to white men or of "leather binding" to bound books would still further reduce their extension, and so on. We suppose, however, that such connotative additions are not already contained essentially in the former idea so as to apply to all individuals; e.g. "trilateral triangle" has the same extension as triangle. (Cf. p. 95.)

III. Division of Ideas and Terms

1. **Division of Ideas.** — An *idea* is: (1) *Clear*, if the object which it represents can be discerned from every other; *obscure*, if this is not possible. For instance, I know clearly a bird in general, but I may not be able to distinguish certain kinds of birds from certain others. My generic knowledge is clear, but my specific knowledge is obscure. (2) *Distinct*, if the distinctive essential notes are known; *vague*, if they are not known. Thus I may know the scientific characteristics of a bird, or simply know it as an animal that flies in the air. N.B. A distinct notion is always clear,

but a clear notion may be vague, because accidental features may be sufficient to distinguish clearly one thing from another. Closely connected with this division is the division of ideas into generic, specific, and individual, the nature of which results from what has been said on the genus, species, and individual. (3) *Adequate*, if it represents all the object's features; *inadequate*, if it does not. In the strict sense no human idea is adequate, i.e. none represents all that can be known about an object. In a relative sense an adequate idea is one that represents as much about an object as the present state of science allows.

2. **Division of Terms.** — The main division special to terms is into univocal, equivocal, and analogous.

(*a*) A term is *univocal* when it applies to several things in exactly the same sense, i.e. without any change in its connotation. Thus "man" is applied univocally to all individual men.

(*b*) It is *equivocal* when it stands for two or several different ideas, i.e. when the connotation is not at all the same. Terms may be equivocal (1) in sound only — equivocation in speech — e.g. "right," "rite," "wright"; (2) in spelling only — equivocation in writing — e.g. "lĕad" and "lēad," "tĕar" and "teăr"; (3) in both sound and spelling, e.g. "pen" (writing instrument, and cattle enclosure), "mean" (average, and vulgar).

(*c*) It is *analogous* when the sense is neither totally different nor totally identical, i.e. when there is some connection between the several meanings of a term, and hence its connotation is partly the same and partly different. Such a relation may be one of causality; thus we speak of a healthy man (enjoying health), of a healthy food or climate (producing health), and of a healthy appearance (caused by health). Or it may be a relation of similarity, as when the term "fox" is applied to an animal, or to a man because of his cunning. Such terms as "sweet, brilliant, terrible, awful, smart," etc., have many analogous uses.

3. **Division of Both Terms and Ideas.** — (*a*) *Considering their object*, we have the following: (1) *Positive* and *negative*, according as they mean the presence or the absence of a reality. "Good," "man," "organic," . . . are positive. "Immature," "abnormal," "inorganic," . . . are negative. If the reality which is

absent ought to be present, the term is called privative, e.g. "deaf," "dumb," or "blind," when applied to man. It must be noted that certain terms are positive in appearance, yet really negative, like "bad," "blind," etc. Others are negative in appearance, — i.e. preceded by a negation or by negative prefixes like *im*, *in*, *a*, *dis*, etc., or followed by negative suffixes like *less* — and yet in reality positive, because they are the negation of a negation, e.g. "immortal." "Death" (*mors*) is the cessation of a reality (life), hence negative; and "immortal" is thus really positive. Some terms may be regarded as positive or negative according to the point of view. Thus "unpleasant" may mean simply "that which is not pleasant," or "that which produces a painful feeling." (2) *Categorematic* or *syncategorematic*, according as they can or cannot stand alone as subjects or predicates in a judgment. "Man," "good," white," . . . are categorematic; "very," "with," "through," . . . and in general, conjunctions, adverbs, prepositions, and interjections are syncategorematic. (3) *Concrete* or *abstract*, according as they mean a subject, or a determination without its subject. "Man," "white," . . . are concrete; "humanity," "whiteness," . . . are abstract. N.B. Adjectives are always concrete, for they apply to a subject. (4) *Substantive* or *adjective*, according as they represent a thing as existing in itself, e.g. "man," "blueness," "humanity," or in a subject, e.g. "blue," "human." (5) *Real* or *logical*, according as the object represented can or cannot exist independently of the mind. Names of individuals are real; genera and species are logical.

(*b*) *Considering their relations to other terms*, some terms may be *associated* together, like "man" and "wise," "man" and "white," "paper" and "blue." Others are *opposed to and exclude* one another, like "white" and "black," "cold" and "hot," "square" and "circle." Opposition may be (1) *contradictory*, when a term simply denies the other, i.e. when one is positive and the other negative, e.g. "white" and "not-white"; (2) *privative*, in the sense already explained; (3) *contrary*, when one implies more than is necessary to deny the other, e.g. "white" and "black," "good," and "bad." Between contradictory terms there is no middle; a thing is white or not-white. Between contrary terms there are intermediates. Between white and black there are various shades of gray; between good and bad there is indifference.

(*c*) *Considering their extension.* (1) *Singular* terms apply only to one individual, and are indicated by a proper name, or by a demonstrative with a common name; *particular* terms apply to a part of a whole class, and are indicated by such particles as "some," "those," "a part of," . . . ; *universal* terms apply to all individuals of the same class. (2) A distinction must also be made between the *distributive* term, applying to all taken individually, e.g. "soldier," "book," . . . and the *collective* term, applying to all taken together, e.g. "army," "library." . . . A collective term may also be used universally: "All armies are composed of soldiers"; particularly: "Some armies are composed of volunteers"; or singularly: "This army is commanded by General *X*." But with regard to the soldiers that compose it, army is always a collective term. Not the individual soldiers, but only the aggregate can be called an army.

II. DEFINITION AND DIVISION

In psychology attention has been called to the confusion that may arise from language. It is very important both to understand the meaning intended by other men, and to use expressions that will manifest clearly one's own ideas. The use of definition and division is intended to make the meaning of terms clearer, and also to make the ideas themselves more distinct.

I. Definition

1. **Meaning of Definition.** — In general, to define (*de-finire, finis*) is to assign limits. Hence to define a thing is to say what it is, so as to distinguish it from everything else. To define a word is to explain its meaning by indicating its comprehension. Complex ideas become clearer when their total comprehension is analyzed and reduced to simpler ideas.

2. **Kinds of Definition.** — A definition is *nominal* when it expresses the meaning of a term; *real*, when it expresses the nature of an object.

(*a*) Nominal definition is (1) *Private* and *conventional* when a man uses a new term, or when he assigns a special meaning to an already existing term; (2) *common* when it gives the accepted meaning or meanings as found in dictionaries. A nominal definition consists in describing the idea which a term expresses in such a way that it will be distinguished from all others. To the nominal definition are reduced *etymology* — which is sometimes misleading, e.g. in "physiology," "geology," "geometry," — *the use of synonyms* the meaning of which is better known, and *the translation into another language* in which the meaning of the equivalent term is known.

(*b*) Real definition is *perfect* or *essential* when it indicates completely the essential elements of an idea and of the things which the idea represents, i.e. the genus proximum and differentia specifica. These elementary ideas in turn, if not clear, may have to be defined again until some simple and therefore indefinable idea is reached. Hence some ideas cannot be defined because of their simplicity; others, on the contrary, because of their complexity and of the great number of elements entering into their comprehension. Thus individuals cannot be defined perfectly. In such cases we have to be satisfied with some of the following imperfect modes of definition, which are frequently used, because a perfect definition supposes that the thing to be defined is known completely and definitely, which is seldom the case.

A *descriptive* definition gives a certain number of accidental features sufficient to make the object distinctly recognizable, e.g. shape, color, density, properties, etc.

A *genetic* definition indicates the process by which a thing is produced, e.g. the materials and manufacturing process of alcohol, paper, cigars, etc., or the factors of a psychological process.

An *analytic* definition indicates the materials out of which a thing is made. Chemistry commonly uses such definitions.

A definition *by the effects* indicates what a thing is capable of doing, e.g. the explosion of a chemical substance, or the purpose of a mechanism.

All kinds of definitions agree in pointing out *some feature common to several things*, and *some specific characteristics*, that is, some agreement and some difference which in the perfect definition are expressed by the genus proximum and the differentia specifica. Thus I define water as a compound (common notion) of oxygen and hydrogen in certain definite proportions (difference); or a pen as an instrument (common notion) to write with (difference which is also common to pencils) by letting the ink flow regularly on the paper (more special difference), etc.

3. **Rules of Definitions.** — (*a*) Definitions must be *reciprocal*, i.e. there must be a complete identity of the thing defined with its definition. In other words, the definition must apply "omni et soli definito," and be coextensive with the object. Examples. . . .

(*b*) Definitions must be *clear*, i.e. convey a definite idea of the term to be defined. Hence, as far as possible, (1) Do not use merely negative terms which indicate, not what a thing is, but what it is not. (2) Use neither metaphors, nor obscure, ambiguous, and vague expressions. (3) Avoid the "circulus in definiendo," i.e. in the definition do not use the term itself to be defined. Examples. . . .

4. **Place of Definition.** — What is the place of the definition in the process of knowledge? Nominal definitions are presupposed in the beginning of any investigation. As to the essential definition, it is the very purpose of the investigation. Hence, except in cases in which the definition is clear, and used as a principle (e.g. in geometry), its place is at the end, since it supposes a complete and perfect knowledge of the object. If it is placed at the beginning, it is only as a hypothesis to be verified.

II. Division

1. **Meaning of Division.** — (*a*) *To define is to analyze or unfold the comprehension of a term*, and to go up to less complex, but more extensive, notions. *To divide is to analyze or unfold the extension of a term*, and to go down to more complex — because new differentiæ are added — but less extensive notions. If "man" is defined by the genus "animal," and the differentia "rational," divisions will be obtained by adding new differences like white and colored, young and old, etc.

(*b*) We speak here of the *logical division*, by which a logical whole, an abstract representation, a genus or class, is divided into the species or sub-classes which are contained under it, and which are formed by adding new specific or accidental differences. Thus I divide the class "book" into bound or unbound; scientific and non-scientific; quartos, octavos, etc. "Scientific books" again may be subdivided into books dealing with theoretical and books dealing with practical sciences, and so on. Hence we do not speak here of (1) *physical division* by which the actual physical whole, made up of parts really united in the physical world, is divided into its component parts, e.g. the dissection of an organism; (2) *metaphysical division* by which the actual metaphysical whole, made up of ideas that are not separate except in our conception, is divided into these ideas; e.g. the division of "animal" into life and sensation. If these ideas are the essence of the object, metaphysical division is the same as perfect definition, otherwise it is the same as imperfect descriptive definition.

2. **Main Rules of Logical Divisions.** (1) *Each process of division must have only one basis or principle*, i.e. the differentia which is added must be the same. Thus "man" should not be divided into "white, learned, and tall." The basis of division varies with the purposes for which the division is made. (2) As a consequence, the *sub-classes of the same degree must be mutually exclusive* according as the new difference is present or absent. (3) *The division must be adequate*, i.e. all the parts must be mentioned, and no individual of the general class must be found which will not have a place in one of the sub-classes. In other words, the parts taken together must be coextensive with the whole, and none separately must be coextensive with it. (4) *The processes of division and subdivision must be gradual*, proceed without jumps, always going to the immediately following sub-classes. (Find instances.)

ARTICLE II. THE JUDGMENT

I. Nature of the Judgment and Proposition

In Psychology (p. 107 ff) we have spoken of the process of judging. It consists in pronouncing on the agreement or disagreement of two ideas. Hence its elements are (1) two ideas, the *subject* — that of which something is affirmed or denied — and the *predicate* — which is affirmed or denied; these two ideas are called the *matter* of the judgment; (2) the copula, that is, the affirmation or denial; it is called the *formal* element of the judgment.

A proposition is the expression of a judgment, and hence has, at least implicitly, the same three elements as the judgment. The one Latin word "amo" expresses a judgment: "ego" (subject) "sum" (copula) "amans" (predicate). All grammatical sentences are not logical propositions; for instance, interrogative, imperative, optative sentences, as such, express no judgment.

From the point of view of logic the subject and predicate are not always the same as from the point of view of grammar. Logically, a proposition contains nothing but the subject, the predicate, and the copula, and always contains these. Thus in "Dogs bark," "bark" is not the predicate, but contains both the copula "are" and the predicate "beings that bark." When I say: "The boy who learns his lesson is worthy of praise," the logical subject is "the boy who learns his lesson," and the predicate is "worthy of praise." Whatever is found in a proposition besides the copula, which is invariably the verb "to be," is always logically reducible to the subject or the predicate.

II. Division of Judgments and Propositions

1. **If we Consider the Quantity**, i.e. the extension of the subject, judgments are *singular*, *particular*, *collective*, or *universal*. Examples: "Paul is tall." "Some men are virtuous." "The family is numerous." "All men are mortal." N.B. In logic, the singular proposition is considered as universal, since the subject is

in fact taken in its total extension. Hence it has the same properties as the universal proposition.

2. **If we Consider the Connection between the Subject and the Predicate:** — (*a*) Judgments are *contingent* or *necessary* according as the relation which is affirmed between the subject and the predicate can or cannot be otherwise. Thus, "The part is not so large as the whole" is necessary. "The part is one-third of the whole" is contingent.

(*b*) In a closely related sense, but with special reference to the mode of acquisition, a judgment is *a priori*, when it is not based directly on sense-perception, e.g. "The whole is greater than its part," or *a posteriori*, when experience is required, e.g. "This line is four inches long."

(*c*) If the relation between the subject and the predicate is perceived immediately, either by reason or by experience, the judgment is *intuitive;* if mediately, the judgment is *discursive*. "I am suffering," "This paper is white," "Two and two are four," are intuitive. "The soul is immortal" is discursive. For further development, and for the distinction between analytic and synthetic judgments, see Psychology (p. 109).

(*d*) The *absolute* judgment simply affirms or denies. In the *conditional* judgment, the affirmation or denial depends on a supposition. "I am pleased" is absolute; "If he comes back I shall be pleased" is conditional. To the conditional proposition may be reduced the *disjunctive* proposition, when it is affirmed or denied that the subject is this, *or* that, *or* . . . ; and the *conjunctive* proposition, when it is affirmed that this, *and* that, *and* . . . cannot belong to the subject at the same time. For instance, "To-day is either Sunday, or Monday, or Tuesday, or . . ." is disjunctive. "A man cannot be sitting and standing at the same time" is conjunctive. More will be said on these propositions when we speak of the syllogism.

3. **From the Point of View of Unity and Simplicity.** — (*a*) *Simple* propositions are those in which there is only one subject and one predicate, e.g. "The rose is fragrant."

(*b*) If various explicative or restrictive terms or propositions are used to qualify the one subject or predicate, the proposition becomes *complex*. It may include several propositions, one principal, and the others subordinate. For instance: "The rose which you gave me" (subject) is "the most beautiful I have ever seen" (predicate).

(*c*) If the proposition has two or several principal subjects or predicates, it is called *compound*, and is equivalent to a number of propositions equal to the number of the subjects multiplied by the number of the predicates. Thus: "Exercise and pure air are necessary to health" is equivalent to two propositions, each with one of the two subjects. "Peter and Paul are tall and strong" is equivalent to four propositions: "Peter is tall," "Paul is tall," "Peter is strong," "Paul is strong." A proposition may be both complex and compound.

4. **If we Consider their Quality**, i.e. their formal element or copula, propositions are *affirmative* or *negative*.

Looking at both the *quantity* and *quality* of propositions, we have four kinds of propositions symbolized by four vowels:

Universal affirmative, A (*a*ffirmo)
Universal negative, E (n*e*go)
Particular affirmative, I (aff*i*rmo)
Particular negative, O (neg*o*)

As already noted, individual propositions are reduced to universal.

5. **Intension and Extension of the Terms in Propositions.** — It is very important to know what are the extension and intension of the terms in a proposition.

(*a*) In a proposition *A* like "All birds are vertebrates," it is clear that the subject is taken according to its complete extension. But it is not taken according to its whole intension, for there are elements in it — e.g. living, animal, egg-laying, etc. — to which the predicate "vertebrate" cannot be attributed.

As to the predicate "vertebrates," it is taken according to its whole intension, since, in order to be truly called vertebrates, birds must have all the essential characteristics of vertebrates. But it is not taken according to its whole extension, for, besides birds, there are other vertebrates. In other words, birds do not exhaust the extension of vertebrates; they are only *some* of the vertebrates.

It would be easy to show similarly that in a proposition *I* as "Some men are prudent," the subject is taken according to its partial extension and comprehension, and the predicate according to its partial extension, but according to its whole comprehension.

Hence the first general rule of the predicate: *In affirmative propositions the predicate is undistributed*, i.e. not universal in extension, *but must be taken according to its complete intension.* This is always true in formal logic. However, if we consider the contents or matter of the proposition, it may happen that the predicate has the same extension as the subject, namely, in cases of definitions. E.g. "Logic is the science of the formal laws of thought," "A triangle is a plane figure bounded by three straight lines."

(*b*) If we take a proposition *E*, as "No mollusks are vertebrates," the subject is universal in extension, but its comprehension is limited — e.g. the idea of "animal," which is an essential element of it, does not exclude the predicate "vertebrates."

The predicate is taken according to its whole extension — "mollusks are none of the vertebrates," i.e. the whole class of vertebrates is excluded, — but not according to its whole comprehension, for certain ideas included essentially in that of "vertebrates" — e.g. the idea of "animal" — may also belong to mollusks.

In the same manner, in a proposition *O*, as "Some elements are not metals," the subject is taken according to a part of its extension and comprehension; the predicate, according to its whole extension, but not according to its whole comprehension.

Hence the second general rule of the predicate: *In negative propositions, the predicate is distributed*, i.e. universal in extension, *but taken only according to a part of its comprehension.*

III. Related Propositions

Propositions are related in several manners, namely, as opposed, obverted, converted, contraposed, and immediately inferrible.

1. **Opposition.** — In the strict sense, propositions are opposed when the same predicate is affirmed in one and denied in the

other, of the same subject, in the same sense, and from the same point of view. In a broader sense, propositions are opposed when they differ in quantity, or in quality, or in both. If they differ in both, they are contradictory, *A* and *O*, *E* and *I*. If they differ in quality only, when universal, they are contrary, *A* and *E;* when particular, they are subcontrary, *I* and *O*. If they differ in quantity only, they are subalterns, *A* and *I*, *E* and *O*, the universal *A* or *E* being the "subalternans," and the particular *I* or *O* being the "subalternate."

There is a strict opposition only between contradictories and between contraries. Subalterns have the same quality. In subcontraries, there is not necessarily identity of subject, for the part of which the predicate is affirmed may not be the same as that of which it is denied. The following diagram shows the various kinds of opposition.

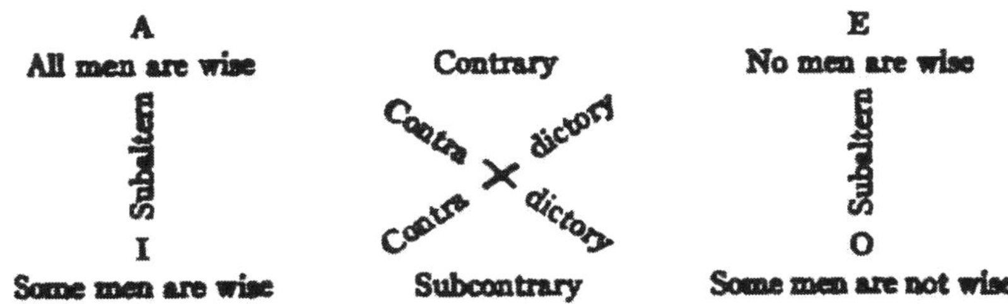

2. **Obversion** consists in negativing both the copula and the predicate of a proposition, i.e. in changing the quality of the proposition, and giving it as predicate the term contradictory of the former predicate. Thus, *Obvertend:* "All men are mortal"; *Obverse:* "No men are not-mortal." Again, *Obvertend:* "No birds are quadruped"; *Obverse:* "All birds are not-quadruped." *Obvertend:* "Some men are unhappy." *Obverse:* "Some men are not not-unhappy," or "Some men are not happy."

3. **Conversion** consists in transposing the subject to the place of the predicate, and the predicate to the place of the subject, without changing the quality of the proposition, and without distributing an undistributed term. A distributed term in the convertend may be undistributed in the converse, for what was affirmed or denied of the whole may evidently be also affirmed

or denied of its various parts. N.B. In the following, S stands for Subject, P for Predicate.

(*a*) A proposition E is susceptible of *simple* conversion, i.e. of a conversion in which the same quantity is retained. $SP(e)$ becomes $PS(e)$, for both terms are universal in both propositions, one as the subject of a universal proposition, the other as the predicate of a negative proposition.

A proposition I also is susceptible of *simple* conversion. $SP(i)$ becomes $PS(i)$, for both terms are particular in both propositions, one as the subject of a particular proposition, the other as the predicate of an affirmative proposition.

(*b*) A proposition A cannot be converted except *by limitation*, i.e. from a universal $SP(a)$ (convertend) it becomes a particular $PS(i)$ (converse). For, in the convertend, P is particular as the predicate of an affirmative proposition, and it must remain particular in the converse.

(*c*) A proposition O cannot be converted at all, because S is particular, and if it became the predicate of a negative proposition it would become universal. $SP(o)$ can only be contraposed.

N.B. Let the student find applications and concrete instances of these and of other rules of formal logic.

4. **Contraposition** consists in negativing the copula and the predicate, and then converting the proposition. In other words: First obvert, then convert. E.g. "All men are mortal"; "No men are not-mortal"; "No immortal beings are men" (contraposed). "Some men are not just"; "Some men are not-just"; "Some unjust beings are men" (contraposed). From what precedes it follows that a proposition I has no contrapositive, since by obversion it becomes O, which is not convertible.

5. **Immediate Inference** is the immediate passage from one proposition to another. Knowing or supposing the truth or falsity of a proposition we may be able to infer at once the truth or falsity of certain others.

(*a*) *Inferences owing to the opposition of propositions.* (1) *Of two contradictories one must be true and the other false.* Hence if one is known or supposed to be true, the other is false. If one is known to be false, the other is true. If, for instance, it is true to say that "some men are just" (*I*), it is false to say that "no men are just" (*E*). If it is false to say that "all men are just" (*A*), it is true to say that "some are not just" (*O*).

(2) *Of two contraries one must be false, and both may be false.* If one is known to be true, the other is false; but if one is known to be false, the truth of the other cannot be inferred. If I know the truth of "All men are mortal" (*A*), I know the falsity of "No men are mortal" (*E*). But if I know the falsity of "All men are just" (*A*), I cannot infer the truth of "No men are just" (*E*). The reason is that, between these two extreme propositions, there is room for a third assertion in which alone perhaps truth is to be found, namely, "Some men are just" (*I*).

(3) In the case of two subalterns, *the truth of the subalternans implies the truth of the subalternate*, and *the falsity of the subalternate implies the falsity of the subalternans*, because what is true of the whole is a fortiori true of the part, and what is false of the part is a fortiori false of the whole. But we cannot say that what is true of the part is also true of the whole, nor that what is false of the whole, is also false of the part. From the truth of "Some men are just" (*I*), I cannot infer the truth of "All men are just" (*A*). From the falsity of "All men are unjust" (*A*), I cannot infer the falsity of "Some men are unjust" (*I*). It must be remarked that logically, in such sentences as "Some men are just," we consider only that which is affirmed, not that which is frequently implied and meant, namely, that some others are not just.

(4) *Of two subcontraries one must be true, and both may be true.* If one is known to be false, the other is true; but if one is known to be true, it cannot be inferred that the other is false. If it is false to say "Some men are immortal" (*I*), it is true to say "Some men are not immortal" (*O*). The first proposition *I* is false, as we suppose; then *E* is true as being its contradictory, and also a fortiori *O* as the subalternate of *E*. But both *I* and *O* may be true, for the predicate which is affirmed or denied does not necessarily apply to the same subject in each proposition. The part of which it is affirmed in *I* may be different from the part of which it is denied in *O*. E.g. "Some men are virtuous"; "Some men are not virtuous."

(*b*) *From the obvertend, the obverse may be inferred, and vice versa.*

(*c*) *From the convertend, the converse may be inferred, and vice versa;* except in the conversion by limitation, for $SP(a)$ gives $PS(i)$, which can be converted only into $SP(i)$.

(*d*) *From a proposition its equivalent is inferred,* for instance, when synonyms are used, e.g. "Peter is not just," and "Peter is unjust."

(*e*) *Inferences are also obtained by the use of determinants,* "All metals are chemical elements," "All heavy metals are heavy chemical elements"; *and by complex conception,* "All metals are elements," "A mixture of metals is a mixture of elements." Great care must be taken in this process of inference, as frequently the determinant has not the same relative meaning when added to the predicate and when added to the subject. For instance, "Voters are men," "The majority of voters is the majority of men"; "Flies are animals," "Big flies are big animals."

ARTICLE III. REASONING

I. THE PERFECT SYLLOGISM

I. Nature of the Syllogism

1. **Reasoning and Syllogism.** — As explained in Psychology (p. 115 ff), *reasoning is a mediate inference.* It consists in proceeding from two or several known judgments to another unknown or less known judgment. It may be defined: The logical inference of a judgment from two or several others. An argument means either the mental process of reasoning or its expression. We have seen also in psychology that, if the mind proceeds from a general law or principle to particular or individual instances, the process is deductive, i.e. the individual or sub-class is derived (de-duco) from the more general class in which it is contained. If the mind proceeds from individual or particular instances to a general law or principle, the process is inductive, i.e. individuals or sub-classes are classified under, or put in (in-duco), a more general class.

A syllogism is a perfect form of deductive reasoning. The present article will deal only with the syllogism, and with other forms of reasoning reducible to it. The laws of the syllogism are generally applicable to inductive reasoning. But the latter is a more complex process in which the series of steps to be taken is more numerous. We shall speak of it in the second chapter.

2. **Elements of the Syllogism.** — *The formal element* of the syllogism and of any reasoning is the consequence, that is, the right to assert the conclusion, owing to the nexus between the inferred proposition and those from which it is inferred.

The material elements of the syllogism are:

proximate:	three propositions	major proposition minor proposition	antecedent or premises
		conclusion,	consequent
remote:	three terms	major term, the predicate of the conclusion minor term, the subject of the conclusion middle term, not found in the conclusion, but in both premises	

The conclusion expresses the relation of a predicate with a subject after they have been compared with the same third (middle) term in the premises. The predicate of the conclusion, having generally a greater extension than the subject, is called the major term, and the subject is called the minor term. The premise in which the third or middle term is compared with the major term is called the major premise, and that in which it is compared with the minor term, the minor premise.

All virtues are praiseworthy;	Major premise	Antecedent
Prudence is a virtue;	Minor premise	
Therefore prudence is praiseworthy.		Conclusion

II. Figures and Moods of the Syllogism

1. **Figures.** — Syllogisms are divided into four figures *according to the four places which the middle term may occupy in the premises*, namely, as (1) Subject in the major and predicate in the minor. (2) Predicate in both. (3) Subject in both. (4) Predicate in the major and subject in the minor. Or as a Latin mnemonic

verse expresses it: "Sub prae, tum prae prae, tum sub sub, denique prae sub." (*Sub* stands for *subiectum*, *prae* for *praedicatum*.) Representing the major term by *P*, the minor by *S*, the middle by *M*, we have:

	1st fig.	2d fig.	3d fig.	4th fig.
Major premise	MP	PM	MP	PM
Minor premise	SM	SM	MS	MS
Conclusion	SP	SP	SP	SP

2. **Moods.** — The moods of the syllogism are *the various manners according to which the three propositions in a syllogism may be arranged considering their quantity and quality.* If for the present no attention is paid to the validity of the syllogism, the four kinds of propositions (*A*, *E*, *I*, *O*) may occupy one of three positions (major, minor, conclusion). With a proposition *A* as major, we may have a minor *A* and four conclusions, *A*, *E*, *I*, or *O*; or a minor *E* and the same four conclusions; or a minor *I* and four conclusions; or a minor *O* and four conclusions, giving us sixteen moods for this one major. The same will be true for majors *E*, *I*, and *O*, giving a total of sixty-four moods. Combining these now with the four figures we find a total of two hundred and fifty-six moods. But the majority of these are against the rules of the syllogism. Only nineteen are valid, some of which are seldom used:

1st fig. AAA, AII, EAE, EIO
2d fig. AEE, AOO, EAE, EIO
3d fig. AAI, AII, EAO, EIO, IAI, OAO
4th fig. AAI, AEE, EAO, EIO, IAI

N.B. Let the student construct syllogisms according to the various moods and figures, and, after studying the rules of the syllogism, indicate why the other moods are not valid.

III. Rules of the Syllogism

There are eight rules of the syllogism, four of which refer to the terms, and four to the propositions.

1. **Rules for the Terms:**

(*a*) 1st. *Terminus esto triplex, maior, mediusque, minorque.*

There must be three terms, only three, and they must be used with the same meaning. From the very nature of the syllogism two terms only are not sufficient, and if there are more than three, there can be no comparison of two with the same third. Hence it is necessary to pay attention to the meaning of the terms to see whether it is the same, since a term used with two different meanings is equivalent to two terms; e.g. "All men are mankind; Peter is a man; therefore Peter is mankind." "All men," i.e. taken together. Peter is only "one" man.

(*b*) 2d. *Latius hos quam praemissae conclusio non vult.* No term must have a greater extension in the conclusion than in the premises, otherwise the conclusion contains a surplus which is not justified by the premises, since this surplus was not compared with the middle term. E.g. "Liars are not to be believed; liars are men; men are not to be believed."

(*c*) 3d. *Nequaquam medium capiat conclusio fas est.* The middle term must be found only in the premises, not in the conclusion, where it has nothing to do. It can only vitiate the conclusion. "This boy is poor; this boy is a ball player; this boy is a poor ball player."

(*d*) 4th. *Aut semel aut iterum medius generaliter esto.* Once at least the middle term must be taken according to its whole extension. Otherwise the two parts to which it refers might be different in each premise, and thus there would be in reality no common middle term. The syllogism would have four terms. "Thieves are men; saints are men; therefore saints are thieves."

2. Rules for the Propositions:

(*a*) 5th. *Ambae affirmantes nequeunt generare negantem.* If both premises assert the agreement of the subject and of the predicate with the same middle term, the conclusion must evidently assert the agreement of the subject with the predicate.

(*b*) 6th. *Utraque si praemissa neget nil inde sequetur.* No conclusion can be inferred from two negative premises, because two ideas disagreeing with the same third may or may not agree with each other.

(*c*) 7th. *Peiorem sequitur semper conclusio partem.* The "peior" or weaker part is the negative as compared to the affirmative, and the particular as compared to the universal. (1) If one premise is negative and the other affirmative, the conclusion must be negative. One extreme is in agreement with the middle term, and the other is not; hence they cannot agree together. (2) If one premise is particular and the other universal, the conclusion must be particular because a partial agreement in the premise cannot be the valid ground of a total agreement in the conclusion. If the premises are *A* and *I*, there is only one universal term, and this must be the middle term (4th rule). Both extremes are therefore particular, and the conclusion must also be particular (2d rule). If the premises are *A* and *O*, or *E* and *I*, there are two universal terms, one of which must be the middle term (4th rule), and the other the major term as predicate of a negative conclusion. Hence the minor term or subject must be particular in the conclusion, since it is in the antecedent (2d rule).

(*d*) 8th. *Nil sequitur geminis ex particularibus unquam.* Two particular premises give no conclusion, for (1) both cannot be negative (6th rule); (2) if both are affirmative, all terms are particular (4th rule); (3) if one is affirmative (*I*), and the other negative (*O*), the conclusion will be negative (7th rule), and consequently the major term, universal. But the premises have only one universal term, namely, the predicate of the negative premise. If this is the middle term, the syllogism is against the second rule; if it is the major term, the syllogism is against the fourth rule.

II. VARIOUS KINDS OF ARGUMENTS

Perfect syllogisms are not used so frequently as imperfect forms of reasoning. Reasonings are expressed in abbreviated or lengthened forms. Hence we shall speak here of hypothetical syllogisms, and of certain incomplete or irregular arguments.

1. **Hypothetical, Conjunctive, and Disjunctive Arguments.**— (*a*) A *hypothetical syllogism* is one in which one proposition — generally the major — is conditional, i.e. consists of two propositions, the antecedent or condition, — preceded by such particles as "if," "in case," "suppose that," etc., — and the consequent or conditioned.

Rules: Either *affirm the condition in the minor, and the conditioned in the conclusion;* or *deny the conditioned in the minor and the condition in the conclusion.* In other words, in the first figure — in which the minor contains the antecedent — the affirmative mood is valid, but not the negative mood. In the second figure — in which the minor contains the consequent — the negative mood is valid, but not the affirmative mood. E.g. "If John studies, he will know his lesson." *First fig.*, "He studies; therefore he will know his lesson." *Second fig.*, "He will not know his lesson; therefore he does not study."

A conditional proposition may be reduced to a categorical proposition, not always, as some logicians have claimed, to a universal proposition, but to a universal, particular, or singular proposition, according to the nature of the condition itself. "If a man runs he is moving" is equivalent to "All running men are moving." "If John studies he will know his lesson" is equivalent to "John's studying means the future knowledge of his lesson"; other individuals might study their lesson without being able to understand and to know it. To change a conditional argument into a perfect syllogism may sometimes be useful to test its validity.

(*b*) A *conjunctive syllogism* has a conjunctive proposition as major. The rule is *to affirm one member in the minor and deny the other in the conclusion.* The "modus ponendo tollens" is valid, not the "modus tollendo ponens." For instance, "You cannot play and study at the same time; you are playing; therefore you are not studying," or "you are studying; therefore you are not playing." The major states only the incompatibility of its members, but these may not exhaust all the possible cases. Hence we cannot say: "You are not playing; therefore you are studying." This syllogism may be reduced to a hypothetical and a categorical syllogism, the major propositions of which are: "If you are playing, you are not studying at the same time," and "Your playing implies your not-studying at the same time."

(*c*) In the *disjunctive syllogism*, the major is a disjunctive proposition. *Both the "modus ponendo tollens" and the "modus tollendo ponens" are valid*, since the disjunction must be exhaustive in order to be true. But, if there are more than two members, and one member is affirmed or denied in the minor, all the others must be denied or affirmed *disjunctively* in the conclusion. E.g. "To-day is either Sunday, or Monday, or . . . Saturday; it is Sunday; therefore it is neither Monday, nor Tuesday, nor . . . "; or, "it is not Sunday; therefore it is either Monday, or Tuesday, or . . . ." The disjunctive syllogism may also be reduced to the conditional and the categorical syllogism.

(*d*) A *dilemma* is a disjunctive argument in which, whichever member of the disjunction be selected, something is inferred against an adversary. E.g. "Speaking irreverently of Holy Scripture is done either in jest or in earnest; if in jest, it is not respectful; if in earnest, it is not good." *Rules:* (1) The disjunction must be complete. (2) The consequences inferred from each member must be valid.

2. **Imperfect and Incomplete Syllogisms.** (*a*) The *enthymeme* is an abbreviated argument, either one of the premises or the conclusion being understood. E.g. "He must be sick, for he has not come."

(*b*) The *epicheirema* is an argument in which to one or both of the premises its reason or proof is added immediately. E.g. "Order requires an intelligence, for chance does not produce order; there is order in the world, otherwise it could not continue to exist as it is; therefore the world requires an intelligence."

(*c*) The *polysyllogism* is a series of complete syllogisms in which the conclusion of one is assumed immediately as the major of the following. "*A* is *B*; *B* is *C*; therefore *A* is *C*; *C* is *D*; therefore *A* is *D*."

(*d*) The *sorites* is a series of incomplete syllogisms or enthymemes in which only one conclusion, the last, is expressed. It includes as many complete syllogisms as there are propositions minus two. To test its validity, it is useful to reduce it to complete syllogisms. "*A* is *B*; *B* is *C*; *C* is *D*; *D* is *E*; therefore *A* is *E*." There are two special rules for the sorites: (1) Only one particular premise is allowable, namely, the first; otherwise the argument is against the 4th rule of the syllogism. (2) Only one negative premise is allowable, namely, the last major; otherwise the argument is against the 2d rule. The student may verify for himself that, if any premise except the first is particular, the middle term will be undistributed in one of the syllogisms, and, if any premise except the last is negative, the major term will have a greater extension in one of the conclusions than in the major premise of the same syllogism.

N.B. Sometimes in order to reduce an argument to a perfect syllogism it is necessary to use equivalent propositions. E.g. "Those who are not good will not be rewarded; Peter is not good; therefore Peter will not be rewarded." Both premises are apparently negative, and yet the syllogism is certainly valid, because in reality the minor, as compared to the major, is affirmative. Again this syllogism contains apparently four terms: (1) "those who are not good," (2) "rewarded," (3) "Peter," (4) "good." By using equivalents, we have "Men in the class not-good will not be rewarded; Peter is in the class not-good; therefore he will not be rewarded." Again "*Iron* (1) is *a useful metal* (2); *this bridge* (3) is *made of iron* (4); therefore *this bridge* (3) is *made of a useful metal* (5)." Here we have apparently five terms. But it must be noticed that besides the mediate inference by reasoning, we have an immediate inference by complex conception (p. 226) and the argument is perfectly valid. This type of reasoning is used very frequently.

III. PRINCIPLES OF THE SYLLOGISM

1. **Points of View of Extension and of Comprehension.** — In a syllogism, the propositions may be considered from the point of view of comprehension or from that of extension. The *predicate* may be looked upon as *an idea contained in the comprehension of the subject*, or as *a class containing the subject*. "All men are mortal," interpreted from the point of view of comprehension means "Mortal is an attribute of all men," or "Man owing to his nature is mortal." Interpreted from the point of view of extension it means "Man is a sub-class of the class mortal," or "Man is one of the mortal beings." In the former case it is meant that man has a greater comprehension than mortal; in the latter, that

mortal has a greater extension than man. This is in agreement with what has been mentioned concerning the relations of intension and extension.

2. **Principles of the Syllogism.** — (*a*) *From the point of view of comprehension* the eight rules of the syllogism are based on the following principle: "Quod dicitur de continente dicitur etiam de contento." That which is predicated — affirmatively or negatively — of that which contains must be predicated also of that which is contained. If "mortal" is contained explicitly or implicitly in the comprehension of "man," and "man" in the comprehension of "Peter," "mortal" is also contained in the comprehension of "Peter."

(*b*) *From the point of view of extension*, the principle of the syllogism is stated briefly as "Dictum de omni" and "Dictum de nullo." Whatever is predicated — affirmatively or negatively — of the genus or class must also be predicated of the species, subclasses, and individuals under this genus or class. If "man" is a sub-class of "mortal," and "Peter" is an individual man, Peter is also mortal.

(*c*) More generally the principles of the syllogism are three. (1) Two terms agreeing with one and the same third agree with each other. (2) Two terms one of which agrees and the other disagrees with the same third disagree with each other. (3) Two terms neither of which agrees with the same third cannot be said to agree or to disagree with each other. It would be easy to show that all the rules of the syllogism are but applications of these principles.

N.B. It may be found useful to represent syllogistic processes by means of circles which diagrammatically show their value (see on opposite page two illustrations showing how this can be done). By applying the rules given for the quantity of the predicate, one may verify which inferences are valid, and which are invalid.

3. **Quantitative Syllogisms.** — So far we have spoken only of the logical or qualitative syllogism. There is also a mathematical or quantitative syllogism based on quantity, succession, equality of relations, etc. For instance: "*A* is equal to *B*; *B* is equal to *C*; therefore *A* is equal to *C*." "*A* is greater than *B*;

B is greater than *C;* therefore *A* is greater than *C.*" "*A* (a musical instrument) is in tune with *B; B* with *C*. . . ." "*A* is a brother of *B*. . . ." "*A* lived before *B*. . . ." In each of these arguments we have four terms. Yet they are valid, because they are based on quantitative self-evident relations: "Two things equal to the same third are equal to each other"; "The greater than the

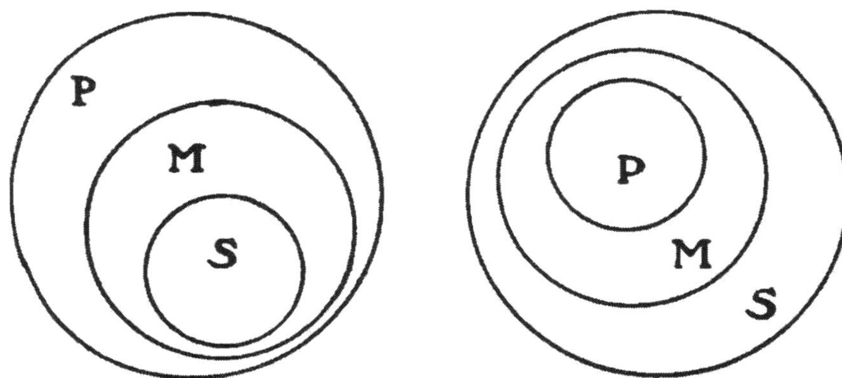

Point of view of extension Point of view of comprehension

MP(*a*); SM(*a*); Conclusion: SP(*a*)

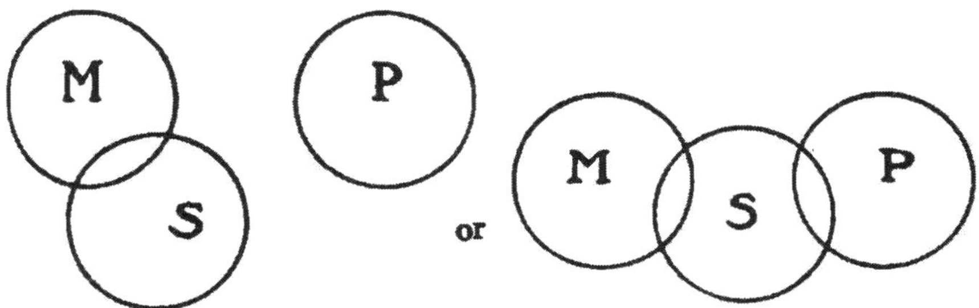

MP(*e*); SM(*i*); Conclusion: SP(*o*)

greater is greater than the great," etc. In the syllogism: "*A* is greater than *B; B* greater than *C;* therefore *A* is greater than *C*," if *A*'s greatness is *a*, *B*'s greatness *b*, and *C*'s greatness *c*, we have: $a = b + x$; $b = c + y$; therefore $a = c + y + x$.

4. **Primary Laws of Thought.** — All the principles and rules of the syllogism are ultimately reducible to three primary laws of thought implied in all affirmations, negations, and processes of

reasoning. (1) *Law of identity:* "A thing is what it is." Or logically: "Every subject is its own predicate"; "*A* is *A*." (2) *Law of contradiction:* "The same thing cannot at the same time and from the same point of view be and not be." Or logically: "The same predicate cannot at the same time and in the same sense be affirmed and denied of the same subject." (3) *Law of excluded middle:* "A thing is or is not." Or logically: "Of two contradictory attributes one must be affirmed and the other denied of the same subject." These laws are the basis on which the syllogism rests, and are implied in every process of thinking and judging.

CHAPTER II

METHOD

Object of this Chapter

1. **Meaning.** — Method (ὁδὸς μετά, road or way toward) in general signifies the adaptation of means in order to do something and to reach safely a determined end. In logic, it signifies the adaptation of means in order to reach scientific truth, i.e. the knowledge of things from their causes and in their relations to other things. To know, in the strict sense, is not simply to apprehend a fact or an event, but also to perceive the reasons, laws, causes, and relations of facts and events. Methodology teaches how to proceed in order to acquire science. In every syllogism there is a progress from the premises to the conclusion. Knowledge is generally acquired by a series of reasonings. Hence, although a method is required for one single reasoning, method as understood here applies to a more complex progress in which arguments of different value and from different sources are used.

2. **Importance.** — It is important to proceed methodically. (1) Unless the road is known, one is likely to go astray, or at least to lose much time in finding the way. This will be made clear if you compare, with regard to both quantity and quality, the work of two men, one of whom proceeds methodically, and the other does not. (2) It is necessary to proceed gradually, not by jumps; precipitation is likely to mislead the mind. (3) What is acquired with method, and orderly arranged, is more easily memorized, and only such a methodical arrangement of ideas deserves the name of knowledge.

Thus, whereas the first chapter of logic indicated how to make a valid formal syllogism, and as such is indispensable, there remains to show (1) the value of the premises used; if the form be correct, but the materials weak, the whole edifice lacks solidity;

(2) the use to be made of the syllogism, and the mode of proceeding step by step from one conclusion to another; (3) the danger of fallacies which may come either from the form or the matter of the syllogism.

3. **Division of this Chapter.** — Method being a progress supposes two extremes: one, the starting-point; the other, the end to be reached. As the direction of any movement or progress is derived from the term to which it tends, — "motus specificatur a termino" — we must begin with the end to be reached, for it is from this end that the process derives its orientation. As to the process itself from the starting-point to the terminus, it supposes that we know the value of the instruments to be used, the various kinds of methods, and the wrong ways, fallacies or errors. Hence our division: (1) The extremes; (*a*) the *terminus ad quem*, or end to be reached, (*b*) the *terminus a quo*, or starting-point. (2) The progress itself; (*a*) the value of the arguments, (*b*) the two main general methods, (*c*) the obstacles.

ARTICLE I. THE TERMINI

I. THE END TO BE REACHED

Man's intelligence strives after science, that is, a certain mode of knowledge to which his innate curiosity instinctively impels him. Man not only wants to see things and events, but he is anxious to know their "how" and "why" — two words which are frequently used by both the child and the adult.

I. The Nature of Science

The term "science" is used with both a subjective and an objective meaning. It signifies the knowledge and the object of knowledge, and we speak of the science which a man possesses, and of the various sciences which he studies.

1. **Characteristics of Scientific Knowledge.** — Science is always knowledge, but knowledge in its broad sense is not always science. (1) Sense-perception, of itself, is not scientific knowledge. (2) Things known directly and immediately by the intellect, i.e.

self-evident principles, are not said to be known scientifically, but are the bases of science. Scientific knowledge is essentially *the knowledge of things through their causes and their common principles.* It possesses the three following characteristics:

(*a*) *It is certain.* It starts from something certain, and uses valid inferences that lead to certitude. This certitude is based on reasons and justified by proofs. Unscientific knowledge is frequently doubtful and accepted without proof.

(*b*) *It is general.* The fact or individual as such is not the object of science. Science has for its object the causes common to several happenings, the types common to several beings, the laws common to several phenomena. To know that a man died is not science; to know that he died on account of his swallowing a certain poison which, under the same circumstances, is capable of killing not only this man, but any other man, because it has such or such effects on the organism, is scientific. To see a dog is not science; to know its nature and essential features belongs to science. To perceive that the stone thrown up in the air falls down is not science; the law of gravitation gives a scientific explanation of the fact.

(*c*) *It is systematic.* Facts are only the materials of science. They are not science itself any more than the materials of a house are a house. The materials become a house by their adjustment according to certain relations. So also facts become science only when their connections and relations are perceived, and when they are reduced to common principles and laws.

2. **Two Meanings of Science.** — (*a*) If stress is laid on the *knowledge of causes* and on *certitude*, it may be insisted that such causes give necessary conclusions, i.e. conclusions which, under existing circumstances, the mind conceives as incapable of being otherwise. Mathematical sciences are the best types of this meaning of science.

(*b*) If stress is laid on the element of *systematisation*, the limits of science are widened and may be made to include not only conclusions that are certain, but also others that are more or less conjectural and hypothetical. These, it is true, do not constitute science in the strict sense; they are called scientific because they are obtained methodically, connected with strictly ascertained conclusions, and, for the present, offer a plausible explanation of facts. Many such conclusions are found in empirical sciences.

3. **Advantages of Scientific Knowledge.** — From the characteristics of scientific knowledge its advantages are easily derived.

(*a*) It enables the mind to *understand* and explain things; to know not only what happens, but also *why* it happens.

(*b*) It makes it possible to *foresee the future*, so that measures may be taken accordingly. Certain events, like an eclipse of the sun or an explosion of dynamite, may be foreseen and predicted with certitude. Others, like a storm, human actions, political events, etc., can be foreseen only with varying degrees of probability. Besides freedom which is found in human actions, the reason of this difference is the complexity of the causes that contribute to produce a given phenomenon, and the difficulty of knowing them all in their various relations.

(*c*) It increases our *power over nature*, for, when the causes that produce a thing are known, they may be brought about, or avoided, or combined in a thousand ways, so as to give rise to intended results. Machinery is an obvious instance. It is the adaptation of many causes, laws, and principles for certain purposes. To know the cause of a disease is the first step toward curing it. To know the character of a man is of great importance in dealing with him.

II. Classification of Sciences

1. **Distinction and Subordination.** — (*a*) *Sciences are distinguished and classified according to their formal objects*, that is, not according to the object itself of which they treat considered in its totality (material object), but according to the special point of view which they take of it (formal object). Thus many sciences have the human body for their material object: anatomy, physiology, pathology, histology, hygiene, etc. They are distinct sciences because they do not study the human body under the same aspect.

(*b*) Sciences may be *subordinated* in several ways. (1) *If we consider their objects*, some are more general, and the knowledge of them is supposed by the more special. Thus ethics supposes psychology; trigonometry supposes geometry, etc. This does not mean that the higher sciences must always be studied first; sometimes the inferior and more special sciences may be a necessary means toward the superior. (2) *If we consider their utility*, some sciences are speculative, and others more immediately practical. As a rule practical sciences are based on theoretical sciences. (3) *If we consider their origin*, empirical sciences come or should come first, since psychologically experience comes before generalization. (4) *If we consider their excellence*, the higher the object, the nobler the science. Thus the knowledge of God and of the human soul is higher than that of nature.

2. **Classification.** — It is difficult, not to say impossible, to give a satisfactory classification of sciences. (1) In fact, scientists do not agree in all details. (2) The number of distinct sciences increases with experience, and mere chapters of former sciences little by little become special sciences. (3) The limits separating distinct sciences are largely artificial. Since all the objects of nature, and all aspects of these objects, are in close connection, it is not possible for any science to be independent; it must necessarily go beyond its own limits into the domain of other sciences.

Without stopping to consider the merits of other classifications, the following seems sufficiently complete and satisfactory. Generic sciences alone will be mentioned, and these again may be subdivided.

I. Physical and natural sciences, i.e. sciences of the material world.

1. Inorganic	(*a*) General properties of matter,	*Physics*
	(*b*) Nature, composition, and special properties of elements and compounds,	*Chemistry*
	(*c*) Minerals,	*Mineralogy*
	(*d*) Description of the earth,	*Physical Geography*
	(*e*) Constitution of the earth,	*Geology*
	(*f*) Other mundane bodies,	*Astronomy*, *Cosmogony*, etc.

2. Organic	(a) Life in general,	*Biology*
	(b) Plant life,	*Botany*
	(c) Animal life,	*Zoology*

N.B.—Both botany and zoology are subdivided into the study of

(a) General structure of organisms,	*Anatomy*
(b) Minute structure,	*Histology, Cystology*
(c) Functions,	*Physiology*
(d) Diseases,	*Pathology*
(e) Early development,	*Embryology*
(f) Fossil remains,	*Paleontology*

II. Sciences of man considered as intelligent, free, and social, either as an individual or in his social relations.

1. Individual	(a) Conscious processes,		*Psychology*
	(b) Normative sciences of	truth,	*Logic and Epistemology*
		duty,	*Ethics*
		beauty,	*Æsthetics*

2. Social	(a) Language,	*Philology*
	(b) Wealth,	*Political Economy*
	(c) Social ethics and politics,	*Law and Jurisprudence*
	(d) Description of States,	*Political Geography*
	(e) Past events, *History* and *Historical Sciences*, e.g.	*Epigraphy, Archeology*, etc.
	(f) Early human development,	*Anthropology*
	(g) Human races,	*Ethnology*

III. Mathematical sciences, i.e. sciences of abstract quantity.

1. Of numbers,	*Arithmetic, Algebra*
2. Of extension,	*Geometry, Trigonometry*
3. Of movement and force,	*Mechanics*

IV. Metaphysical sciences, i.e. higher constitution and nature,

1. Of material substances,	*Cosmology*
2. Of the human soul,	*Philosophy of mind*
3. Of God,	*Theodicy*

II. THE STARTING POINT

1. **Doubt.** — Any question and any desire for learning suppose in the mind both knowledge and doubt; namely, the knowledge, however vague and imperfect, of something concerning the object we want to study, for, if man were altogether ignorant of it, he would not even suspect that any question may be asked about it; and a doubt with regard to the special points to be examined and the answer to the questions proposed. This doubt, however, bears on a special point. It is not universal, for, if everything, including sense-experience, the value of the faculties of knowledge, and the first principles be doubted, it becomes absolutely impossible ever to reach anything certain. Since they are primary, self-evident facts and principles cannot be reconstructed out of anything else.

Descartes began by a universal doubt, but did not reach certitude except through inconsistencies, implicitly admitting later on what he had formerly rejected as doubtful. He warns us himself that his example is not to be followed indiscriminately. Logically, certitude can come only from certitude, universal doubt can beget only doubt, since the conclusion must be contained in the premises. Moreover, it is impossible to demonstrate everything, for, if a proposition *M* be demonstrated by *L*, *L* by *K*, *K* by *J*, and so on, without ever reaching a proposition standing by itself and on its own merits, no certitude can ever be obtained.

2. **Positive Data.** — The process may be analytical or synthetical. In the former case, the positive starting-point will be a fact or a series of facts; in the latter, it will be self-evident and indemonstrable principles. *Facts* will be gathered from internal or external experience. *Principles* will be either general, or special to each science. Thus the principle of sufficient reason is general; the axioms and definitions of geometry are more special. In all these are contained implicitly or explicitly the fact of the subject's existence, which is implied in every conscious process; the subject's power to know which is implied in the act itself of knowledge; the primary laws of thought — identity, contra-

diction, and excluded middle — without which consistent thinking is an impossibility.

ARTICLE II. THE PROGRESS

I. THE VALUE OF THE ARGUMENTS

Method is the way to make progress from the known to the unknown, or from the better known to the less known. Hence the importance of knowing the value of inferences and reasonings. These may be (1) *certain*, i.e. start from premises that are certain, and lead to conclusions that are also certain; (2) more or less *probable* and worthy of assent; (3) *false*, either because the premises are false, or because the rules of the syllogism are not observed. Only the first two classes belong here as instruments of science, and as yielding scientific results, permanent or provisional. The last class, on the contrary, is an obstacle to science, and will be considered later.

I. Demonstration

1. **Nature of Demonstration.** — Demonstration is a process of reasoning in which from premises known to be certain a conclusion which is also certain is inferred. Hence two conditions are required: (1) The *formal validity* of the process of reasoning; (2) the *certainty of the premises*, either because they are self-evident, or because they are ultimately reducible to self-evident facts and principles, since, as was said above, the process of demonstration requires indemonstrable principles. Thus the last theorems of Euclidean geometry are based on the preceding ones, and ultimately on principles, axioms, and definitions.

2. **Various Kinds of Demonstration.** — A demonstration is: (*a*) (1) *Direct*, when it proceeds by positive arguments, and shows positively that the predicate does or does not belong to the subject. (2) *Indirect*, when it shows the falsity of the contradictory or of opposite propositions. To prove the freedom of the will from consciousness is to proceed directly; to prove it from the consequences of determinism is to proceed indirectly.

(*b*) (1) *A priori*, *synthetic*, or *deductive*, when it proceeds from that which is in reality prior, namely, from the cause to the effect, from the essence to the property, from the law to the phenomenon. (2) *A posteriori*, *analytic*, or *inductive*, when it proceeds from that which is in reality posterior, namely, from the effect to the cause, from the property to the essence, from the phenomenon to the law. To prove the immortality of the soul from the soul's spirituality is to proceed a priori; to prove the existence of God from the world is to proceed a posteriori. In natural sciences, these two methods are generally combined. We proceed first from the effects to the cause, and the knowledge of the cause leads again to the knowledge of other effects.

N.B. Prioriness and posterioriness here are taken in the *natural*, not in the *logical*, order, since logically the premises, whatever be their natural relation to the conclusion, are always prior to the conclusion. In the a posteriori demonstration, the fact is better known than, or *logically* prior to, the law, although in the *natural order* it is but an application of the existing law.

(*c*) (1) *Perfect* — *propter quid*, διότι, "*why*" — when it gives the necessary, proximate, special, and adequate reasons or principles of the conclusion. Hence it is always a priori. (2) *Imperfect* — *quia*, ὅτι, "*that*" — when it shows simply the existence of a thing, or does not give its intrinsic, special, or proximate reasons.

N.B. Causes and reasons are necessary when they make it impossible for the conclusion to be otherwise; proximate and special when there is no link omitted between the conclusion and its premises; adequate when they give the complete reason of the conclusion. The perfect demonstration is possible chiefly in mathematics, logic, and metaphysics, where it can start from the axioms of quantity, and from self-evident principles considered either as laws of thought or as principles of being and existence.

(*d*) (1) *Absolute* when the premises are true in themselves and for all men. (2) *Relative*, or *ad hominem*, when the premises are admitted by an adversary, although they may not be certain. The former is valid for all, not the latter. To base a demonstration on principles or facts which are admitted by an opponent, but known to be false by the one who uses them, is a lack of intellectual honesty. Probabilities are frequently used in this way.

II. Probable Arguments

1. **Nature of Probable Arguments.** — (*a*) Probable arguments are those in which one of the premises is, or both premises are, probable, and lead to a probable conclusion. *Probability* means likelihood, approach to truth, or greater force of argument. It refers to the object, and produces in the mind the state of *opinion*, that is, an assent without the firmness of certitude. Degrees of probability are numberless, and the corresponding states of opinion are more or less firm, nearer to, or farther from, doubt and certitude. In fact, doubt and certitude exist only in one point, at each extreme of the line of mental assent; doubt is the absence of assent; certitude is full, complete, and unrestricted assent. Opinion with its various degrees occupies the whole range between these two extremes. Probability is much more frequent than certitude, especially in practical matters, in historical, moral, social, political, and even natural sciences. But in many cases, as explained in psychology, subjective motives are added to objective evidence, and make one consider as certain that which prudently and logically should be considered only as probable (p. 117 ff.).

(*b*) The general rule of probable arguments is that *the conclusion cannot have a greater probability than the weaker premise.* We must understand in this sense also the general rules: "Latius hos quam . . . ." and: "Peiorem sequitur semper. . . ." If in a series of arguments, or in the same argument, two or several propositions are only probable, the conclusion represents their combined weakness. A mathematical example will illustrate this: In tossing a coin, the chances of turning tails are $\frac{1}{2}$; the chances of turning tails twice in succession are $\frac{1}{2} \times \frac{1}{2}$, i.e. $\frac{1}{4}$, for there are four chances in all, two for tails and two for heads. In the same way probability means a chance for truth. If to this be added another chance, the probability of both chances coinciding with truth is smaller than it would be if only one proposition were probable.

However, probabilities, *when independent*, form a *cumulative evidence*, and may produce certitude. Thus a coincidence of independent facts, each one only probable in itself, may show the guilt of an accused person, because his guilt is the only sufficient reason of this coincidence. Cumulative evidence is frequently used in all sciences.

The main probable arguments are analogy and example, statistics, hypothesis, and authority.

2. **Analogy and Example.** — (*a*) *Analogy* applies to an object what is known to apply to another object having with the former one or several points of resemblance. From certain features known to be common certain other features are inferred to be also common. *Example* and analogy are closely related, and these terms are frequently used for each other. Strictly speaking, however, analogy argues from one instance to another by passing through a general law; it is inductive and deductive. Example goes directly and conjecturally from one instance to another. Thus, knowing that a certain disease is produced by micro-organisms, I infer by *analogy* that another disease having some similar symptoms is also due to a similar cause. Here is implied the general principle that the same symptoms are due to the same cause. To deter a man from excess in drinking, I may point out to him the *example* of this or that man who is an habitual drunkard.

(*b*) Analogy and example are of frequent use in all sciences and in daily life. They are the starting-point of many discoveries, by suggesting solutions which later on may be proved true. Their value depends on the number and character of the observed resemblances, and thus ranges anywhere from certitude to zero. Hence extreme caution is necessary in using and admitting these arguments. They are sources of metaphors and allegories which must not be taken as true beyond the legitimate value of the inference. Points of resemblance must not cause one to overlook the differences.

3. **Statistics** consist in noting the absolute and relative frequency of certain happenings. All happenings of a certain nature and within a certain period are numbered, and averages are taken and compared with various circumstances which are conjectured to be the causes of these happenings. Thus I may note the number of divorces for a whole nation or for a certain class of people during a certain period of time, compare their increasing or decreas-

ing rate with changes in social, political, and religious conditions, and thus find out the causes which influence their frequency. Statistics are of frequent use in social sciences, for mortality, births, diseases, crimes, accidents, suicides, etc., and also in many other sciences, e.g. for harvests, money circulation, mineral and agricultural products, etc. Statistics are very useful because observed coincidences help to find the causes of phenomena, or at least the various influences under which they happen. But they are difficult both to make and to interpret correctly because the causes and influences of events may be very complex and varied. There is danger of mistaking a mere fortuitous coincidence for the true cause, and of overlooking some important factors.

4. **Hypothesis** (Greek, "placing under") in general consists in supposing (Latin, *sub-positio*) or presuming the solution looked for, and dealing with it as if it were known. It is, therefore, a tentative explanation to be verified.

(*a*) When a fact or a series of facts has been observed, we may not know its law immediately. Or even if the law is known in its generality, we may not know all its determinations. A hypothesis consists in *supposing the law to be true*, and in working on this assumption so as to ascertain whether it is true and justified. The principle which impels to frame hypotheses is the principle of sufficient reason which applies to all phenomena. The faculty that frames them is the imagination under the guidance of reason.

(*b*) The main *utilities of hypotheses* are, (1) to offer a more or less probable solution of a problem which perhaps cannot be solved definitively, or which has not yet received a satisfactory solution; (2) to coördinate and group results already obtained, and to systematize them into a class that will be more or less permanent; (3) to incite to work in a certain direction in order to ascertain if the hypothesis is verifiable; (4) to throw many side-lights on the problem, even if the hypothesis is disproved, and to point the way to a true solution.

(*c*) The *conditions* of a scientific hypothesis are the following: (1) It must not be taken as an end, but as a means; not as a proposition to be *proved*, but as a proposition to be *tested*. (2) It must not contradict any well-ascertained facts, conclusions, or principles, but sometimes may overthrow conclusions hitherto accepted as certain. (3) It must not be gratuitous, but based on facts. (4) It must be adequate, i.e. applicable to all the observed phenomena, and assign to them what is, or seems to be, a sufficient explanation. A hypothesis which certainly contradicts one fact which is certain, ceases to be valid. (5) It must be capable of some verification or disproof, for its value consists chiefly in the hope of testing it.

5. **Authority**. — Historical sciences are based on human authority. In all other sciences, as well as in daily life, men frequently rely on the authority of others. Few are the beliefs and actions prompted exclusively, and even principally, by personal reflection, when compared with the number of those prompted by the authority of others, common opinion, education, individual advice and suggestion.

(*a*) In general it may be said that the value of human authority as such ordinarily does not go beyond probability, for any man may be deceived or be a deceiver. Yet there may be found such guarantees in one single witness or in several independent witnesses — cumulative probability — as to give a moral certitude. *On questions of facts*, especially of facts that are easily observable, it is possible in many cases to reach certitude, but in other cases probability alone can be obtained. *On questions of doctrine* and systems, a competent man has greater authority; yet none is infallible, and for a man who can appreciate and weigh the reasons that are given, an authority is worth these reasons.

(*b*) Hence two extremes must be avoided: (1) Making of science a mere study and repetition of the opinions of others. This does not give a scientific knowledge; it is a lazy process dispensing with private research and progress. (2) Neglecting completely what others have said. We may profit by their discoveries and discussions, avoid doing the same work twice, proceed more safely where they have groped and, perhaps, lost their way, appropriate the conclusions of science already acquired.

II. THE TWO GENERAL METHODS

1. **Induction and Deduction.** — The two general methods are induction and deduction. *Induction* goes from the particular to the universal, from the effect to the cause, from the phenomenon to the law. It tries to generalize, to find uniformities and general truths. *Deduction* follows the reverse process. Hence, considering the real order of things, induction is regressive; deduction, progressive. The cause is prior to the effect, but the effect may be known better than the cause (cf. p. 116.). The chief instrument of induction is analysis; of deduction, synthesis.

2. **Analysis and Synthesis.** — By analysis (*re-solutio*) is meant a decomposing, a passing from the more complex to the simpler. By synthesis (*com-positio*) is meant a putting together, a passing from the simpler to the more complex. The whole which is decomposed by analysis, and the parts that are put together by synthesis, are to be understood, not according to extension, but according to comprehension. Thus the human organism is more complex than a single organ, since it includes this organ, and others besides. The fact is more complex than the law, since it is a concrete application of the law, i.e. it is the law plus some individual determinations. In general, analysis proceeds from the conditioned to the condition; synthesis, from the condition to the conditioned.

(*a*) In the case of *facts* or of *concrete realities*, analysis reduces the whole to its parts or components; either really, as, for instance, water to oxygen and hydrogen; white light to the colors of the spectrum; the organism, plant or animal, to its organs, tissues, etc.; or mentally, as, for instance, in psychology we have tried to analyze the complex mental states into their elements which do not exist separately as simple. Synthesis proceeds in the opposite direction.

(*b*) In the case of *ideas* or *mental truths*, e.g. in mathematics, analysis proceeds from a more complex to a more simple statement until known principles are reached. Synthesis starts from the principles, and deduces consequences from them. Thus when I consider the theorem "The sum of the angles of a triangle is equal to two right angles," I may ascend from it to simpler principles (analysis), or, as is commonly done in learning geometry, descend toward it from the simpler principles (synthesis).

I. Induction

We do not speak here of complete induction, or induction *per enumerationem simplicem*, which consists in affirming of the whole in the conclusion that which has been affirmed of *all the parts* enumerated separately in the premises. E.g. "It rained Sunday, Monday, Tuesday . . and Saturday; but these are all the days of the week; therefore it rained every day of the week." "Peter, Paul, John . . . are under thirty; but Peter, Paul, John . . are all the men here present; therefore . . . ." Such an induction is not scientific, and leads to no new result. It is a mere process of addition based on the principle that the totality equals the sum of its parts. We speak only of incomplete induction, e.g. "This water is composed of oxygen and hydrogen; therefore all water is composed of oxygen and hydrogen."

1. **Description of the Inductive Process.** — The inductive process includes three steps: knowledge of individual facts, generalization, verification.

(*a*) *The knowledge of facts*, internal or external, is acquired by *observation* and *experiment*. Experiment is a special mode of, and includes, observation. To observe is to watch attentively phenomena as they occur in nature when it is left to itself. To experiment is to question nature. It consists in varying and controlling circumstances so as to see what results will follow. Whenever possible, experiment is superior to simple observation, because it creates circumstances, and consequently results which otherwise might never occur. I may simply observe the behavior of an animal, or experiment with drugs to see how the animal's behavior will be affected by them. Observation and experiment are very important. If the facts are not observed correctly, the theory based on them cannot fail to be weak for lack of sufficient foundation.

The qualities required are: (1) *On the object's side* (*a*) precision as to the circumstances; (*b*) the variation of these circumstances in a precise manner; (*c*) the isolation, as far as possible, of the phenomenon under observation from other phenomena. (2) *On the observer's side*, (a) physiological and physical conditions: health and normal state of organs; use of good instruments; (b) intellectual: attention to all circumstances and to analogies; desire to know; (c) moral: patience, impartiality, carefulness to discriminate accurately between what is observed and what is inferred, between what is really perceived and what is imagined.

(b) When a fact or a sufficient number of facts have been observed, their *uniformities* are noted, and their laws assigned, first generally in a tentative way.

(c) The theory must be *verified* by new observations and experiments.

2. **Methods of Induction.** — Observation and experiment are made according to four methods known as the four inductive methods. All inductions, both in science and in daily life, depend on the use of one or several of these methods by which experience is interpreted.

(a) *Method of agreement.* When a phenomenon occurs in two or several cases which agree only in one circumstance, this circumstance is probably the cause of, or at least causally related to, the phenomenon. In other words, if, in several instances where a phenomenon occurs, there is only one common antecedent, this antecedent is the cause. The value of the conclusion depends on the constancy and multiplicity of coincidences under varying circumstances. Thus, if after eating a certain food — whatever other food I may also take with it — I invariably feel sick, this article of food is very likely the cause of my sickness.

(b) *Method of difference.* Two or several instances are observed, one in which the phenomenon occurs, and the others in which it does not. If all the circumstances except one are the same in all cases, this one circumstance is probably the cause. In other words, the one difference in the antecedent is the cause of the difference in the result. Thus sickness or death is ascribed to a certain poison because, everything else being identical, the taking of the poison is followed by sickness or death.

N.B. *The joint method of agreement and difference* combines these two methods.

(c) *Method of residues.* It is a modification of the method of difference. When in a group of consequents, *a*, *b*, *c*, *d*, some, for instance, *a*, *b*, *c*, are known to be due to certain antecedents *A*, *B*, *C*, the residual consequent *d* is probably caused by a residual antecedent *D*. If I have bought three articles, *a*, *b*, *c*, and know how much I have spent in all and how much *a* and *b* cost, I can find the cost of *c*. Knowing what effects are due to the presence of certain elements in a compound, a new effect is ascribed to the presence of a new element.

(d) *Method of concomitant variations.* If variations of a phenomenon occur simultaneously with variations in the antecedent, it is probable that these two variations are causally related. Thus the concomitant variations of the number of vibrations with the pitch of a sound, or of the thermometer with the temperature, show that these phenomena are causally related.

N.B. As much as possible these methods must be used together to test, correct, verify, and strengthen one another. The experiments in each must be varied and multiplied according to the nature of the case.

3. **The Principle of Induction.** — (*a*) In induction, the conclusion has a greater extension than the premises, since from observed particular instances a general conclusion is drawn applying to unobserved instances. If the process is valid, there must be some principle that makes this passage legitimate. Observation and experiment are always limited to few cases, and, by themselves, justify only the affirmation of the facts observed. Nor is the association of ideas sufficient to justify this passage.

According to associationists, as mentioned in Psychology (p. 113), because several times a man has observed that the same antecedents were followed by the same consequents, he is led to expect this succession in every case. Little by little these associations and partial uniformities lead to the formation by the mind of the general principle of the uniformity of the laws of nature: "Nature always acts in the same manner under the same circumstances." In addition to its psychological difficulties, this view is open to the following objections: (1) This principle would have only a subjective and relative value; it could be changed by subsequent experiences and habits. (2) A law is frequently discovered after one observation, or very few observations, and hence not through constant associations. On the contrary, sometimes induction corrects long-standing prejudices due to associations and habits of thought. (3) The number of cases in which constant uniformities are perceived by the senses is very small when compared to the number of cases in which they are not observed.

(*b*) Some other criterion is needed since *experience* can never account for the *universality* and *necessity* of knowledge. In fact, the principle of induction is *the principle of the uniformity of nature:* "The same causes produce the same effects," or "Causal relations are constant," or "Nature is governed by constant laws." This principle is not derived from mere sense association, but rests immediately on the principle of sufficient reason, which in turn is but an application of the principle of contradiction. Not only does every single fact require a sufficient reason without which it could not occur, but a series of coincidences, or harmonious and constant occurrences, must be assigned an adequate reason. A single fact requires a proportionate cause. The recurrence of the same fact requires the sameness of natural inclination and of energy, which alone can explain the observed uniformities, and from which we are led to know future and unobserved uniformities. Wherever there is the same nature, i.e. the same source of activity, there also the same effects will necessarily occur.

II. Deduction

1. Description of the Deductive Process. — (*a*) Deduction starts from principles, and goes to their special applications. These principles may either be self-evident, like the axioms and definitions of geometry, or result from a previous inductive process, like the various laws of natural sciences. Deduction is used especially in abstract sciences, the best types of which are mathematics and geometry. In physical sciences it is used to demonstrate that which has been found to be the truth. The professor may sometimes proceed deductively in proving what he has discovered by induction. Generally speaking, however, the method of demonstration should be essentially the same as the method of invention.

(*b*) Deduction includes *three steps:* (1) *Definition*, i.e. the unfolding of the intension of the terms, and the indication of the exact meaning in which they are used. (2) *Division*, i.e. the unfolding of the extension of the terms, and classification. (3) *Proof*, i.e. the assigning of the reasons, or demonstration proper.

2. **Utility of Deduction.** — Two main objections are raised by Stuart Mill against the usefulness of the deductive syllogism.

(*a*) It is *sterile*, and teaches nothing new, since the major already contains the conclusion. In the following syllogism, "All men are mortal; Socrates is a man; therefore Socrates is mortal," in order to be able to affirm the major, I must already be certain of the conclusion, for, the major would not be true if Socrates were not mortal.

Answer: (1) The conclusion may be contained only *virtually* and *implicitly* in the premises. The syllogistic process makes it *explicit*. Who can say that deduction is sterile in geometry, and that he who knows the principles knows also all the theorems which these principles serve to prove? (2) Deduction teaches the *reason* why the conclusion is true. I might know that Socrates was mortal because in fact he died, that the number 275 is divisible by 5 because I have tried the division, and that the square built on the hypothenuse of a right-angled triangle is equal to the sum of the squares built on both its sides because I have measured them. But demonstration will give me the reason of these truths, show not only *that* they are so, but *why* they are so, and why they are universal.

(*b*) The syllogism is a *petitio principii;* in affirming the major we already suppose the truth of the conclusion.

Answer. (1) In the example given by Mill, the major is not taken extensively, but *comprehensively*. "All men are mortal" does not mean primarily "All men *numerically* are mortal," but "mortal" belongs to the *comprehension* of "man," or "Human nature implies mortality," an assertion which is based on the knowledge of human nature acquired by an inductive process. (2) Hence induction does not require the complete enumeration of all cases.

(*c*) Mill also says that, in fact, we do not argue from the general to the individual, but from the individual to the individual. For instance, a matron unhesitatingly prescribes a remedy for her neighbor's child simply because it has cured her own child.

Answer. Universal principles are *implied* here; that the same symptoms are signs of the same disease; and that what has cured the disease in one case is likely to cure it in all cases. The matron would give the same advice to anybody else, thus showing that, in the case of her neighbor's child, she only applies a general principle.

3. **Induction and Deduction Compared.** — In conclusion we may briefly compare the uses of induction and of deduction.

(*a*) Induction gives to deduction many of its principles. It is the main method of the sciences of nature. But with the progress of sciences, more laws are discovered, and deduction of particular instances from these known laws is more frequent.

(*b*) Deduction is necessary even in the inductive process. It is by deduction that hypotheses are verified, and laws applied to particular cases.

(*c*) Some sciences are chiefly deductive; others, chiefly inductive; others, like politics, political economy, ethics, make frequent use of both processes. Thus I may demonstrate the advantages of a certain form of government either from facts or from principles.

N.B. Find concrete applications of these methods in the sciences which you have studied.

III. OBSTACLES

Besides the difficulties inherent in the problems themselves, the main obstacles met with in an investigation are fallacies, which, together with other causes to be mentioned later, are sources of error. As to controversy, contradiction, and discussion, they may also be obstacles, or may become great helps, according to the use which is made of them.

I. Fallacies

1. **Nature of Fallacies.** — (*a*) A *fallacy* (*fallacia, fallere*, to deceive) is an erroneous argument, or a reasoning which, for some reason, fails to lead to a valid conclusion. The term "fallacy" is more general than the terms "paralogism" and "sophism." A

paralogism supposes in the logical form of the reasoning a defect which is apt to deceive the reasoner himself. As generally used, the term *sophism*, and its derivatives, have an ethical implication, namely, that the reasoner is aware of the weakness of the argument, but nevertheless uses it with an intention to deceive.

(*b*) It is difficult to give a satisfactory *classification of fallacies*. The following, though imperfect, is sufficient for the present practical purpose.

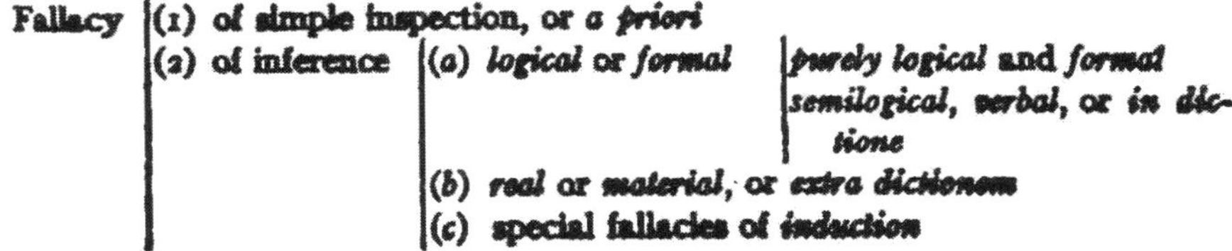

Fallacy
- (1) of simple inspection, or *a priori*
- (2) of inference
  - (*a*) *logical* or *formal*
    - *purely logical* and *formal*
    - *semilogical*, *verbal*, or *in dictione*
  - (*b*) *real* or *material*, or *extra dictionem*
  - (*c*) special fallacies of *induction*

2. Fallacies of Simple Inspection, or a priori fallacies, in general consist in the acceptance of certain principles, maxims, and generalizations without sufficient evidence. By some these fallacies are said to be wholly a priori, i.e. accepted without any reasoning. It seems truer, at least in most cases, to say that such principles are accepted on the strength of an implicit reasoning, hasty and insufficient induction, or common acceptance and authority. They are looked upon as self-evident and as requiring no proof, and many inferences are based on them.

Many are popular, like omens, the interpretation of dreams, prognostics, superstitions, lucky or unlucky days or numbers, prejudices, etc. They are found in the most ordinary assents of daily life, and in the highest pursuits like religion and morality. Others have a higher character in science, philosophy, and religion, like such ambiguous principles as: "All men are born equal;" "Progress and evolution are the law of nature"; "Man is essentially truthful"; "Nature and the supernatural cannot meet"; "All religions are equally good"; "It is enough for man to live honestly"; and a multitude of other maxims either admitted almost universally or special to a certain region or class of men. To avoid them it is necessary to exercise constant watchfulness. Because they are common to all or to many, and because they are habitual, they attract no attention. Yet they need to be explained, tested, and verified. Observe the conversation of certain persons, and see how many principles of this kind are appealed to. (Cf. p. 118 ff.)

3. **The Formal or Purely Logical Fallacies** are those which result from violating any of the logical rules of propositions and reasonings. The most frequent are: (1) *In immediate inferences:* the confusion of contrary and contradictory terms and propositions; the violation of the rules of opposition, conversion, and contraposition. (2) *In mediate inferences:* the fallacy of four terms, of undistributed middle, of the illicit process or undue extension of either the major or the minor term, of negative premises, and of the consequent, i.e. the violation of the rules of hypothetical syllogisms.

4. **Verbal Fallacies** — fallacies *in dictione*, or fallacies of language — arise from the use of terms. They include a defect in the form of the syllogism, and consequently a violation of its rules, but this defect comes from the matter, that is, from the terms which are used. Hence they are also called semilogical fallacies. The most important are:

(*a*) *Amphibology*, or the use of ambiguous grammatical structures and sentences, e.g. "The noble hound the wolf hath slain," or this sign at the entrance of a store: "Why go elsewhere to be cheated? Come in here."

(*b*) *Equivocation*, or the use of a term — more frequently of the middle term — in two senses, so that the syllogism has really four terms: "What produces intoxication is evil, and should be prohibited; the use of alcoholic liquors produces intoxication; therefore it should be prohibited." Distinctions should be made between the various alcoholic beverages, their various uses, and the various circumstances in which they may be used.

(*c*) *Composition*, or affirming of the totality that which is true only of the parts taken distributively; "All the angles of a triangle are less than two right angles" is true of any angle taken separately, not of their sum.

(*d*) *Division*, or affirming of the parts distributively that which is true only of the totality. "All the angles of a triangle are equal to two right angles" is true of the totality, not of any one angle. From the collective vote, i.e. the vote of the majority of Congress, or from the verdict of a jury, I cannot infer the votes of the various members taken individually.

(*e*) *Accent*, or the ambiguity arising from the difference in the stress laid on a particular syllable of a word, or on a special word in the sentence.

5. **Real Fallacies** — fallacies *extra dictionem*, or material fallacies — depend not so much on the form as on the matter of the syllogism. Hence they suppose the knowledge, not only of the rules of syllogism, but also of the subject with which the syllogism deals.

(*a*) *The fallacy of accident — a dicto simpliciter ad dictum secundum quid* — consists in the erroneous inference of a special or conditional statement from a general and unconditional statement. "In a republican government, subjects have the right to vote; criminals are subjects; therefore they have the right to vote."

(*b*) *The converse fallacy of accident — a dicto secundum quid ad dictum simpliciter* — is the reverse of the preceding. "We must avoid intoxication; wine produces intoxication ; therefore we must not drink wine." Only a certain use, or rather abuse, of wine produces intoxication.

(*c*) *Begging the question — petitio principii* — is a fallacy in which the truth of the conclusion itself is presupposed in the premises, that which is to be proved being assumed as the very ground of proof. This occurs frequently when the principle of proof is a popular axiom accepted a priori and without questioning. "Nothing exists but what the senses can perceive; the senses cannot perceive God; therefore God does not exist." The major cannot be true unless we already suppose the conclusion that an invisible God does not exist. This fallacy is also called *circulus in probando*, vicious circle, or argument in a circle. The really identical propositions are generally separated by several intermediate steps, and expressed in different forms, so that the fallacy is not always easy to detect.

(*d*) *Irrelevant reasoning*, or evading the question — *ignoratio elenchi* — consists in arguing — perhaps validly — to the wrong point; in proving a conclusion which was not in question, in such a way that the right conclusion seems to have been proved. If a man is accused before the court, the lawyer may praise his family, his moral and civic virtues and qualities, or appeal to feelings, instead of proving that he is not guilty of the offence for which he is tried. It is the great resource of those who have a weak cause to defend, and is used in many ways.

6. **Special Fallacies of Induction.** — (*a*) *Referring to observation.* (1) *Non-observation of instances.* We are inclined to notice affirmative rather than negative instances, coincidences rather than their absence, especially when they suit a preconceived theory. Or certain relevant facts or groups of facts may be overlooked. (2) *Non-observation of circumstances.* One may neglect the circumstance which is the true cause, or which is important for the explanation of a fact. (3) *Mal-observation*, either because of the imperfection of the senses and instruments, or because of intellectual dispositions which make man see what he is anxious to find, and prevent him from seeing what he does not want to find. This leads to the fallacy of the false cause — *non causa pro causa, post hoc ergo propter hoc* — which considers as the true cause a fact or circumstance which is a mere accidental coincidence. One must always be careful to distinguish between what is really perceived or observed, and what is inferred from such observations.

(*b*) *False analogy and example*, or the exaggeration of the points of likeness or difference, as "*Ab uno disce omnes.*"

(*c*) *The wrong application of inductive methods;* hastiness; the exaggeration of the value of theories and hypotheses.

II. Error

1. **Causes.** — Error is a false judgment. Its main causes may be assigned as follows:

(*a*) *External causes.* (1) *In the object:* The difficulty and complexity of the object under investigation. Hence the necessity of a long, complex, and manifold process of inference at any step of which error may creep in and vitiate all subsequent results. (2) *In the means used to reach the object:* The reliance on incompetent authority and on customary views; language, which may be ambiguous, and hence a source of many misunderstandings; the impossibility of reaching the same certitude and of using the same methods in all sciences.

(*b*) *Internal or subjective causes* (see Psychology). (1) *Intellectual:* (*a*) In general, the weakness and fallibility of the human mind; its dependence on organic conditions; preconceived ideas, prejudices, and intellectual surroundings; education and the resulting habits of thought. (*b*) In a more special manner, the senses and imagination which should be, but are not always, guided by the understanding; the defects of memory, forgetfulness and inaccurate memory; the lack of attention and of the power of observation and inference; irreflection and hastiness in judging things and persons. (2) *Moral:* In general, the passions, which prevent us from seeing things in their true light; especially pride and exaggerated self-confidence, which cause a man to affirm or deny rashly, and make him loath to abandon a position once he has taken it; love and hatred, that make him exaggerate or minimize; the will, in things that are practical; the desire to prove instead of investigating, owing to which the value of reasons is overestimated, and facts are adapted so as to fit in with a preconceived theory.

2. **Remedies.** — The main remedies of error are easily inferred from what has just been outlined concerning its causes. (1) Try to apply the rules of logic, both of induction and deduction. Use definitions and divisions. (2) Pay attention to the validity of every step you take. (3) Without falling into scepticism, be careful in receiving information from others, and be not always ready to swear by it. In matters where proofs are possible and where you can appreciate them, ask for them. Always examine the value of a testimony before you accept it. (4) Acquire habits of reflection, calmness of judgment, steadiness and seriousness of study. They are indispensable to success. (5) Endeavor to develop intellectual feelings, especially a great disinterestedness and a sincere love of truth.

CONCLUSION

Main Rules to be Observed in Controversies and Discussions. — Discussions arise from the diversity of opinions. They are very useful when carried on with the proper spirit and disposition. But in many cases, a discussion becomes a dispute and an intolerant altercation, in which the purpose is not so much to find the truth or inculcate it as to triumph over and to down an opponent, cost what may, and even should the truth suffer thereby. In some cases, on certain subjects, or with certain persons, it will be much more profitable to avoid any discussion, because it is sure to be useless, and may be harmful. Some rules will be stated to be followed before, during, and after a written or oral discussion.

1. **Before.** — "Id faciam quod in principio fieri in omnibus disputationibus oportere censeo, ut quid illud sit de quo disputatur explanetur, ne vagari et errare cogatur oratio, si ii qui inter se dissenserint non idem esse illud de quo agitur intelligant" (Cicero, De Oratore, I, c. 48). This precept is very prudent, and, if it were always followed, many discussions would become needless. It often happens that, for lack of previous understanding, two bitter opponents come to find out, at the end, that they fight for almost the same ideas. Hence (1) Ascertain the meaning of the terms, especially of those that are vague and ambiguous. (2) Ascertain the meaning of the propositions on both sides. See whether they are universal or particular, or restricted in any manner, etc. (3) To avoid the *ignoratio elenchi* and the *petitio principii*, see to what school of science, philosophy, religion, etc., the adversary belongs, so as to start from principles admitted on both sides. Against an atheist I cannot suppose the existence of God. Against a rationalist I may suppose the existence of God, but I cannot argue from divine revelation, and so on with other classes of men. No discussion is possible unless it is based on principles common to both parties.

2. **During.** — Logical and moral rules are to be observed.

(*a*) *Logical.* (1) Take care that all the rules of logic are observed on both sides. Keep a close watch on all the facts brought forward and on all the principles used. Examine whether they are clear and certain. (2) Frequently facts and personal interpretation of facts are presented together as one. Keep them distinct. (3) Keep yourself and your opponent to the point at issue. A man who feels the weakness of his position frequently will tend to shift the problem to some other point, and drift away from the main question. (4) Avoid, and make your opponent avoid, verbosity, that is, an abundant flow of words making up for the paucity of ideas. Hence, after a long presentation, sum up the ideas expressed, and reduce them to stricter forms of syllogism in order to test their value more easily. See also that the same terms are always used in the same sense. (5) When contending against a view, beware of the common tendency to go too far, to fall into the opposite extreme, and to try to prove too much. (6) While following the preceding recommendations, avoid the ridicule of rigid formalism that wants to use none but perfect syllogisms, and affects pedantry.

(*b*) *Moral.* (1) Practise moderation. Avoid the anxiety to make your opinion prevail. Look for light, not for triumph. (2) Avoid anger and impatience. To abuse an adversary is not to prove the truth of one's contention; on the contrary, it is frequently a sign of weakness. Truth stands in no need of injurious and ungentlemanly remarks and abusive epithets. Moreover, passion has for its effect to blind the mind and prevent it from seeing things in their true light. (3) Avoid intolerance. All men are fallible. Practise the great principle: "In dubiis libertas." Do not try to impose your view simply because it is yours, but because you are convinced that it is true. (4) Honesty and fairness must be practised all the time. It is always dishonest knowingly to use inaccurate statements or distorted facts in order to prove one's contention. It is the more so when arguing against uneducated persons, who cannot see the falsity of such assumptions, and are more easily misled.

3. **After.** — (*a*) If victorious, practise modesty. Nothing is

more cowardly than to abuse a defeated opponent. Arrogance is a sign of conceit, and indicates that a man loves his own satisfaction more than the truth. (*b*) Be not depressed by defeat, and be honest enough to accept the truth. Always remember Cicero's maxim: "Cuiusvis hominis est errare, nullius nisi insipientis in errore perseverare" (Philipp. XII, c. 2).

ÆSTHETICS OR THE NORMATIVE SCIENCE OF THE FEELINGS OF THE BEAUTIFUL

INTRODUCTION

I. What is Æsthetics?

1. **The term "Æsthetics."** — Etymologically, "æsthetics" (*αἰσθητική*, from *αἰσθάνομαι*, to perceive) is an adjective form now used substantively, and indicates that which has reference to sensation or perception. Its meaning has been narrowed down to a special kind of feelings or sentiments, namely those originating from the perception of beauty. As an adjective, "æsthetic" has either a subjective or an objective meaning. We speak of an æsthetic taste, i.e. a just and keen appreciation or judgment of beauty; and we also speak of a thing as being more or less æsthetic. As a substantive, "æsthetic," or more frequently "æsthetics," is objective, and includes the science of beauty, the rules of taste and of art. It is the *normative science of the æsthetic feelings*.

2. **Æsthetic Feelings.** — If we examine the whole group of mental states known as feelings or the affective life, we find that the *feelings proper* — pleasure and pain — cannot be assigned any special norm. Experience and association manifest which things or uses of things are pleasurable, and which are painful. All that can be done is to seek the former and avoid the latter. To a great extent *emotions* are also subjective. In so far as they can be controlled and governed, they fall under the rules of morality, politeness, decency, sociability, etc. Besides these general norms,

no other can be assigned to either self-regarding or altruistic emotions. The will to subdue them if they are wrong or excessive, and the will to acquire them if they are good and lacking; in every case, the will to control them — as explained in psychology — is about the only rule that can be given for this class of feelings.

Intellectual, moral, and religious *sentiments* must be governed in accordance with the principles of logic, ethics, and religion.

There remain therefore the æsthetic feelings which require a special treatment here, but which can be allowed but a few pages in this elementary course.

3. **The Science of Æsthetics.** — Æsthetics is *the science which tries to determine the conditions of beauty*, to analyze the elements that constitute it and enable it to produce æsthetic feelings. Beauty may be natural or artificial; æsthetics deals with both. Because tastes and appreciations differ, it has been said that æsthetics cannot be a science, and that no rules can be given for æsthetic feelings. But the fact that, notwithstanding many divergences, there are certain objects which practically all men agree in finding beautiful, and others which all agree in finding ugly, shows that there must be some reason in the subject, or in the object, or in both, for this uniformity. Moreover, without considering how other individuals are affected, I find different types of beauty, and I may ask in what respect those different objects — a piece of music, a statue, a building, a person, a poem, etc. — agree so as to deserve the common adjective "beautiful" which I apply to them. Undoubtedly there is a science of the beautiful. Even if conclusions are not always clear and cogent, there are reasons accounting for the æsthetic feeling. Æsthetics is not a strict science like mathematics or even like physics. The rules of art cannot compare with the laws of chemical combination. Yet certain principles must be observed, although they may be applied differently, and much is left to individual conception and interpretation.

II. The Place of Æsthetics

The object of logic is the true, that of ethics, the moral good, that of æsthetics, the beautiful. Logic is the normative science of the intellect, ethics, of the will, æsthetics, of the feelings of the beautiful. This leads us to inquire into the relations of the beautiful with the true and the good.

1. **Relations Between Beauty and Truth.** — (a) *Beauty cannot be identified with truth.* Some beautiful things, like poetry, romance . . . are not true, but fictitious. Others, without being fictitious, cannot be called true, e.g. music. On the other hand, some truths are not beautiful, or may be positively ugly. We do not find any beauty in the truths "four and four are eight"; "the straight line is the shortest distance between two points"; "it rained yesterday"; "John Smith died last week," etc.

(b) Yet *there are relations between the true and the beautiful.* (1) That which is false, unlikely, and unnatural is not beautiful. A picture in which the proportions are not kept, a novel in which events appear impossible or unlikely, produce a disagreeable impression. A statue or drawing with certain defects and departures from nature will be pronounced ugly, etc.

(2) Many truths of the intellectual order, when taken together systematically, are beautiful for those who can understand and penetrate them. There may be no beauty in a geometrical axiom, yet the science of geometry, with its numerous deductions, is not without beauty. There may be no beauty in a single physical conclusion, e.g. that heat expands metals, or that matter attracts matter in direct ratio to its mass, and in inverse ratio to the square of the distances. But certainly physical sciences reveal the beauty and harmony of the material world, either in the largest bodies (like astronomy), or in the smallest (like the science of radioactivity).

(3) The effort, success, and power of certain minds in grasping the truth, in passing from truth to truth and in perceiving relations, is also worthy of admiration.

(4) The perceived beauty of a science is an incentive to its pursuit. The man who admires the laws of nature, the marvellous structures of living organisms, etc., will become more enthusiastic for the study of physical and biological sciences, because every new step discovers some new harmony and some new beauty.

(5) However, even where the true and the beautiful coincide,

the formal reason of the true and the formal reason of the beautiful are not identical, and the effects produced on the mind by these two aspects are not the same. I may perceive the truth without admiring the beauty, or admire the beauty without reference to the truth.

2. Relations Between Beauty and Goodness. — Good means (1) agreeable, (2) useful, (3) conformable to the rules of morality.

(*a*) *The sentiment of beauty is always pleasant and agreeable*, but many things are agreeable without being beautiful. The taste of an apple, a walk in the country, the smell of a rose, rest after fatigue, etc., are agreeable, yet not beautiful. Beauty is one special source of pleasure. An object is not beautiful because it is agreeable; it may be agreeable because it is beautiful.

(*b*) *The useful is not always beautiful;* instruments, tools, clothes, etc., are useful; they frequently are not beautiful. On the other hand, many beautiful things have no practical use in themselves besides satisfying man's æsthetic taste or giving him some recreation, e.g. a statue, a picture, a flower-bed, etc. Or they may be useful indirectly by reminding one of noble examples, and inciting to follow them. It may even happen that the beauty of a thing seems to make it less useful, as certain architectural ornaments, or the hart's antlers which hinder him. Even where the two coincide in the same thing, the reason why it is beautiful is not the same as that for which it is useful. Beauty is an end in which the mind rests without looking beyond. The feeling of beauty is disinterested and stops at the contemplation and enjoyment of its object. Utility is essentially the quality of a means. A thing is not useful purely and simply; it is useful for this or that end. A plain dress, a simple house may be as useful as, and even more useful than, other dresses and residences which are much more beautiful. Where beauty and utility are combined, beauty is added as something distinct from utility.

(*c*) *Not all actions morally good are beautiful.* To speak the truth, to return a lost article to its owner, to respect one's parents, to give alms, are good actions which, under ordinary circumstances, excite in us no feelings of admiration. On the contrary, certain hideous characters in a novel or a drama, moral monsters, may contribute by contrast to foster the total æsthetic satisfaction. But immorality as such cannot be beautiful either in real life or in works of art.

The close relations of beauty and morals were emphasized by the Greeks, who frequently put together the beautiful and the good. They speak of καλὸς κἀγαθός, or even in one word καλοκαγαθός. Το καλόν is frequently moral beauty or virtue, and in fact the Stoics identified the two. Without going to this extreme, the influence of artistic beauty on morals cannot be denied. The beautiful, being agreeable and attractive, is a spring of action. To represent the immoral as beautiful and attractive is therefore morally wrong. Art may be of great service in moralizing, as is clear from experience, and from the principles laid down in psychology concerning the influence of imagination and feelings on the passions, the will, and the character. Art need not always be at the service of morals, and all works of art need not be undertaken for the purpose of teaching lessons. (But at least art must never be immoral, nor represent that which is wrong under the aspect of beauty.)

By way of comparison and elimination, the preceding considerations have already given some ideas concerning the nature of beauty. We shall now proceed to a more positive analysis.

CHAPTER I

BEAUTY

Whatever is agreeable is not thereby beautiful. Yet the æsthetic feeling is one of the forms of agreeable feelings. What are its special characteristics? Both a subjective and an objective analysis will help in finding them.

I. Subjective Aspect

We shall recall and complete what has been said in psychology on the æsthetic feeling (p. 155).

1. **Several Mental Factors** contribute to produce æsthetic feelings.

(*a*) The *senses* through which the beautiful object is perceived. They are sight and hearing.

(*b*) The *imagination* and, with it, the *association of ideas* and *suggestion*. The perceived object arouses in the mind images of objects already perceived or constructed by the imagination, and ideals formed by the higher mental powers. All these give a certain coloring to the actual perception. Hence the feeling of beauty is the combined result of the actual perception and of the images and ideals which the object recalls or suggests.

(*c*) The *intellect*. The object must not only be perceived, but, to some extent, understood. Its elements must be known in their mutual relations. The harmonies of the world are beautiful only for those who understand them. The intellectual element appears also in the absolute judgment which every man, rightly or wrongly, has a tendency to pass on the æsthetic qualities of an object. When perceived, beauty seems to have such a character of evidence that one is inclined to suffer no contradiction on this point.

(*d*) *Activity*. What is so simple and obvious as to leave no room for personal activity produces no feeling of beauty. This feeling is greater when the beauty is discovered little by little, and when it requires a certain application to perceive it. If we are almost exclusively passive, to glance rapidly at a painting, or to listen distractedly to a musical composition, will produce little or no æsthetic feeling. A man must work his own way into the object in order to grasp its inner beauty.

2. **Essential Factor.** — From the preceding remarks we infer that the feeling of beauty results from *the harmonious activity of several mental faculties*. However, the fundamental, or rather essential, process seems to be the *understanding of the object*, which depends on natural endowments and on æsthetic education. Why is it possible for children, and even for a number of adults, to find the music of the street-organ as beautiful as — perhaps more beautiful than — the first-class performance of a masterpiece? Undoubtedly because they cannot understand the latter. In the same way some will derive more æsthetic satisfaction from a ten-cent picture with glaring colors than from a real work of art. The æsthetic feeling is greater in proportion as the object is understood better and as the relations of its parts among themselves and with the totality are grasped and mastered more completely.

3. **Diversity of Æsthetic Judgments.** — The diversity of these individual factors in different persons accounts for the diversity of æsthetic judgments. Appreciations vary with individuals, countries, races, degrees of civilization, and periods of time. Without referring to the caprice of fashion in dress and ornamentation, it is otherwise evident that tastes vary. The source of this diversity is to be found in the complexity of mental factors that influence the feeling of beauty. Every individual has his own ideals to which he refers objects, and his own images with their different associations. As a consequence, actual perception will arouse various ideas and images in the mind. Education, surroundings, character, habit, novelty, etc., will also exercise a marked influence on the æsthetic judgment.

II. Objective Conditions

Besides these subjective factors, objective elements must be admitted. Certain things are beautiful for all men and at all times, although their beauty may not always be fully appreciated. Moreover, men are agreed that there is a good and a bad taste. The possibility of developing the æsthetic taste means again that there are some rules for the beautiful. It was said above that the chief source of æsthetic pleasure is the understanding; but the understanding of what? Not of the truth of the object, since the beautiful is not to be identified with the true. There are therefore other aspects in the object which account for the subjective feeling. To these we now pass.

1. **Three Conditions are Required in the Object:** (1) Fulness, perfection, and completeness, (2) unity amid variety, (3) splendor and clearness.

(*a*) To be beautiful, an object must not lack any of its essential parts, functions, or elements. *It must possess a certain perfection, completeness, energy, and life*, varying of course with the type to which it belongs. Incompleteness and deformity are always ugly and displeasing. The application of this is clear in the natural order. See why one horse is pronounced beautiful, and another not; why a fertile cornfield, or a forest with abundant vegetation, or a high mountain, etc., are beautiful, whereas the field with brambles or a few corn-stalks, the small elevation and hill, produce no such impression. We rather call pretty (not to say *cute*) that which is of small proportions. The elements or aspects of the whole object may be considered apart, and found beautiful, e.g. the façade of an edifice, the face of a hunchback, etc., but then they are considered as complete in themselves. Again, and for the same reason, an ugly person may perform a beautiful action; in an ordinary composition there may be found beautiful passages, etc. What is true of material objects is true also of intellectual and moral beauty. It requires some perfection, power, or special greatness.

(*b*) *Variety* means a multiplicity of parts, or a successive change. There is variety in an edifice because it has several parts, several ornaments, windows, doors, columns, etc. There is variety in poetry or in a novel because different ideas, events, circumstances . . . are evolved successively. There is variety in music because there is at the same time a multiplicity of combined sounds, and successive changes of sounds, tempo, rhythm, etc. Generally, monotony, sameness, and lack of change are tedious and disagreeable. The variety and number of parts must be in proportion to the nature of the object, and must not be exaggerated. Too many parts, too many successive changes, a superfluity of ornaments, decorations, and colors are also opposed to beauty, because generally they are obstacles to the unity which is also required.

It is not enough to have many elements, *they must harmonize together in some unity*. Many disparate things, unconnected parts and incoherent details, are not beautiful; there must be symmetry, proportion, order, and adaptation. A common centre, a unity of action and of plan are required to prevent the attention from being diffused. This harmony must be found not only between the parts of the object, but also between the object and its surroundings. A statue or ornament will produce a different effect according to the objects found around it. High-flown eloquence is out of place in conversation. A beautiful frame may not be adapted to a certain painting, etc.

(*c*) Finally, a certain *splendor*, *neatness*, or *clearness* is required. The qualities mentioned above must be sufficiently apparent. There must be enough light to see a picture or a drawing; its lines and colors must be visible without too much strain, etc. The unity amid variety should be perceived without too great an effort and tension.

2. **There are Various Types of Beauty.** — (*a*) *Ideal beauty* is a type or, as the word itself indicates, an ideal according to which beautiful concrete objects are judged, or which the artist strives to realize and express. *Real beauty* is that which is found in existing objects. It is more or less perfect according as it realizes more or less completely the conceived ideal.

(*b*) *Beauty is natural or artificial* according as it is found in nature without man's intervention, or, on the contrary, is the work of man. The sea, mountains, animals, the songs or colors of birds, are natural. Statues, buildings, music . . . are artificial. Man may embellish nature, and the result is partly natural and partly artificial.

(*c*) *Physical beauty* is expressed in matter; *intellectual beauty* results from the exercise of reason; *moral beauty* depends on the mode of exercise of free activities.

(*d*) Finally, we mention again the distinction already explained in psychology between the simply beautiful, the sublime, and the pretty (p. 156). We need not discuss the question whether these objects produce more or less intensive forms of the same feeling, or specifically distinct feelings.

CHAPTER II

THE FINE ARTS

I. Nature of the Fine Arts

1. **Meaning of Art.** — In general, art means a collection of rules or of activities necessary for the skilful production of certain works. *Art* is frequently contrasted with *nature*, and artificial with natural. The former is produced by human activity, the latter without it.

Art is also opposed to *science*. The fundamental difference between them is that science refers to knowledge; art, to practice. Hence arise two other points of difference. (1) True science is based on universal laws, and is valid for all men and at all times. Art is more personal, and more changeable according to times and places. (2) Science is acquired by study; art, chiefly by practice. Science also, it is true, may have a practical purpose, and in fact certain sciences, e.g. logic, medicine, etc., may also be arts, but the formal difference remains. As sciences they deal with what is, with the truth, and with the reasons of things. As arts they deal with the production of what does not yet exist, with the practice and the action. A man may have the complete science of medicine without ever applying it. He knows the causes and remedies of diseases without using this knowledge. On the contrary, a man may possess only the art of medicine. His own experience or that of others may have taught him the value of certain plants or remedies which he may use to good effect without knowing the reasons why they are beneficial.

2. **Meaning of Fine Arts.** — Arts are divided into useful or mechanical, and æsthetic or fine arts. The former tend to the production of something *useful;* the latter to the production of something *beautiful*. The artisan will select materials such as wood, steel, or stone in order to make something useful, a table,

a saw, or a house. This object itself is destined to serve a purpose; it is a means to something else, not an end in itself. The artist tries to produce something which is *an end in itself*, and not simply a means. It is often difficult to draw the line between the two because the beautiful is also frequently useful, e.g. a building; but, as already indicated, the two aspects must be distinguished.

From what precedes it may be inferred that eloquence is not, strictly speaking, one of the fine arts, for it aims at persuading others. The same is true of the history of heroic deeds, and the lives of the saints, which are written for the purpose of instruction. However, these may become arts if the grace of the gestures, the harmony of vocal inflections, the charms of the style and composition, etc., are intended. Fine arts tend primarily to the production of beautiful works without regard to any other purpose except the satisfaction of the mind's aspirations toward beauty.

II. Art and Nature

1. **Realism and Idealism.** — Beauty is found both in nature independently of human intervention, and in art, that is, in works which are intentionally produced by man. Moreover, we have said that beauty always supposes two elements, one sensible and real, the other ideal and intelligible. Hence the questions: Must artificial beauty be a simple imitation of natural beauty? Must it reproduce the real and the sensible of nature as closely as possible? Or, on the contrary, must the artist overlook nature so as to form higher and independent ideals? Realism chooses the first alternative; idealism, the second. In their extreme forms, both are to be rejected, and the true answer is found between them. Works of art must be based on nature and inspired from it. Yet they must not be mere imitations or copies, but idealized representations.

(*a*) *Art borrows its materials* — sounds, colors, etc. — *from nature*. Moreover, what is against nature is never beautiful, e.g. a statue without due proportions. Finally, pure idealism tends to abstraction, i.e. to the absence of reality and life, and therefore has less power to arouse æsthetic feelings.

(*b*) But *art cannot be a sterile imitation of nature.* (1) Music is not a mere imitation of natural sounds; nor architecture, of natural forms. Painting and sculpture are not the same as photographing and casting. (2) Nor can art, if it merely imitates nature, be as beautiful as nature, for, in many cases, it is incapable of representing the details, greatness, life, and movement that are found in nature. It represents only some of the realities of nature. (3) Not everything in nature is beautiful; nor is any object perfectly beautiful, for none realizes completely the type of beauty of the class to which it belongs.

(*c*) Art, therefore, must borrow its materials and objects from nature, but also idealize, purify, and refine them, making abstraction of certain features and emphasizing others.

2. **Advantages of Art over Nature.** — Art cannot reproduce all the realities of nature. Thus sculpture reproduces forms, but not colors. Art, however, has several advantages.

(*a*) It is not subject to the same laws of space and time that are found in nature. A landscape covering in reality many square miles, which cannot be embraced at a single glance, may be represented on a small canvas where its harmonious beauty will be grasped at once. A multitude of events which would require a long period of time may be condensed in a theatrical play. The deterioration which occurs in nature, especially in living organisms, is avoided in art, etc.

(*b*) Art is not subject to the physical laws which prevent nature from realizing a complete and perfect type. Art supposes abstraction, and represents only certain features which it idealizes.

III. The Production of Works of Art

We shall examine the conditions required in the *work* itself and the processes by which the *artist* produces it.

1. **Qualities Required in the Work.** — The object must be one, true and good, and, in general, have the qualities of the beautiful.

(*a*) We have already spoken of *unity in variety* as one of the conditions of beauty. Thus, in an edifice we require the unity of style and architecture, and the proportion of the various parts, for if the style is not the same, or if the parts are out of proportion, the result is not harmonious. In a play or a novel we require the unity of composition — one plot around which other events are centred. In a picture we require things that are not disparate, but can associate together to form one complete whole. In a volume of essays we do not expect one unit, but several. We expect a sequence throughout a novel.

(*b*) *Truth* does not mean that the work of art must be a mere imitation of nature, for art idealizes nature. Yet it must be what we generally call natural or likely. Thus a personage supposed to be gifted with a certain quality, to have a certain character, or to be subject to a certain passion, must be made to speak and act naturally, i.e. in conformity with these endowments. To fail in this, or to exaggerate beyond measure, shocks the æsthetic feelings. The statue or painting of a man need not represent any man who exists or ever existed, but it must represent a human form with all its essential features.

(*c*) *Vice and immorality as such cannot be beautiful.* If they cause pleasure, it is either on account of the skill of the artist, or because of the passions of those who perceive such works. It is not allowable to represent as beautiful and worthy of admiration that which is in opposition to the rules of morality. But, with due caution, it may be represented as an object of aversion which, by contrast, makes virtue more beautiful.

2. **The Realization of Beauty.** — The artist must form an ideal, find the means of expressing it, and use these.

(*a*) *The conception of an ideal* is based on the study of nature. Before applying the colors to the canvas, the painter must have in his mind the representation of the figure or the objects which he wants to paint. Before starting to write, the poet, novelist, or playwright must know what human passion he will describe, what plot he will unravel, and what circumstances he will represent. This ideal is higher or lower according to the artist's power to understand the beauties of nature, rise above them, and abstract the beautiful features from the common, insignificant, or ugly features with which they are mixed. The nature and loftiness of the ideals and interpretations will vary with the personal qualities of the artist.

In their relation to nature, the artist and the scientist have an altogether different attitude. The scientist's aim is to know what is, and his mind must, as far as possible, grasp the whole reality in all its complex details. He must express his knowledge accurately, neglecting nothing, and describing facts, events, and things in their various aspects. In scientific books, illustrations are not necessarily beautiful, they may even be positively repugnant, for instance in books on medicine, but they must be true to nature. The artist selects only what suits his purpose, and is free to change and adapt the materials found in nature. He is original, and supplies something out of his own mind. In this process of conception, imagination, sensibility, and artistic taste are the most prominent factors.

(*b*) The artist must find the *means and materials best adapted to express his ideal*. He follows general rules already mentioned, and more special rules like those of concord and discord, rhythm and tempo in music; unity, rhythm, and rhyme in poetry, etc. In this process of finding and choosing the means, the main faculties necessary are imagination and memory, association, attention, sensibility, and the æsthetic taste which directs the selection.

(*c*) *Execution* is the *expression itself of the ideal*. To a great extent it is a question of practice and of the proper use of instruments. The artist's purpose is to reproduce in matter that which he has conceived in his mind, and the perception of which will produce in others the same emotions and arouse the same ideals. Hence, as far as possible, the work of art must be animated, resplendent, and have a soul that reveals itself through sense-perception.

IV. Classification of the Fine Arts

1. **General.** — (*a*) It is difficult to give a satisfactory classification of the fine arts; difficult also, and even impossible, to give a complete enumeration of them, for it is not always possible to establish a clear distinction between several minor subdivisions; nor is it always possible to determine whether a given art should be counted among the fine arts.

(*b*) It is generally admitted that there are *five principal fine arts*: architecture, sculpture, painting, music, and poetry. Among the secondary or auxiliary fine arts, mention may be made of dancing, which is subordinate to, though widely different from, music; acting, which is auxiliary to poetry; embroidery, pottery, jewelry, gardening, park-making, dress-making, house-ornamenting, cabinet-making, etc., which are subsidiary to painting, sculpture, and architecture. We shall not attempt to give any definition of these several arts, still less their special technical rules. Their mutual relations will be shown best by indicating the most important principles of classification which have been proposed.

2. **Principles of Classification.** — (*a*) The first and most common distinction is derived from the senses by which the work of art is perceived. These are vision and hearing. Hence there are: (1) *Visual arts* — sculpture, architecture, and painting. (2) *Auditory arts* — music and poetry. Acting and dancing are visual and also auditory, since they are subsidiary to music and poetry.

(*b*) In a similar way are distinguished: (1) *The arts of repose*, plastic or formative, in which all the parts may be perceived simultaneously. (2) *The arts of motion and speech*, in which the parts are successive and can be perceived only after one another. The former have reference chiefly to space; the latter, to time.

(*c*) Considered in their relation to nature, arts are either *imitative* (representative), or *non-imitative* (presentative), according as they imitate natural objects — painting, sculpture, poetry, drama; or are in a stricter sense creative — music and architecture.

(*d*) We have seen above that *beauty* is essentially distinct from *utility*. Yet, although the special point of view of beauty is always different from that of utility, the two may be combined in the same object. A new principle of classification may be derived from this fact. Architecture is generally serviceable. Even if there are exceptions for certain monuments, its object is generally to build that which is both useful and beautiful. The other principal arts are primarily non-serviceable. Of the minor arts, many are serviceable, like pottery, embroidery, jewelry, glass-making, dancing, and many others which tend to produce or ornament objects which have a practical use.

ETHICS OR THE NORMATIVE SCIENCE OF THE WILL

INTRODUCTION

I. THE MEANING OF ETHICAL SCIENCE

I. Facts

Certain facts of internal and external experience with which ethics is concerned must first be mentioned.

1. **The Ethical Aspect of Human Actions.** — (*a*) Besides their psychological aspect, i.e. their nature as processes and the mode of their actual production, human actions have other important aspects or relations. Besides the manner in which they are performed and *actually take place*, there is the manner in which *they should take place* in order to reach certain ends, and to have certain qualities that are considered as good or advantageous. In other words, *there are rules or norms of action.*

In the ball player, it is not so much the psychological or physiological processes that are of interest as their special adaptation to the end in view, which is to score or help team-mates to score runs, and to prevent the opposing team from scoring, according to the rules of the game. The value of the complex actions performed on the diamond is judged by this standard. We speak, not only of what is done, but of what should be or should have been done. Again, to be successful, the merchant must act according to certain principles. We call men good or bad in their respective occupations, fit or unfit for their business, prudent or imprudent in their transactions, when we compare what they do with what they ought to do, and when we examine their action to see whether it is adapted to the end which they have in view.

(*b*) There is another sense — the *ethical* or *moral* sense — in which actions are called good or bad, right or wrong, praiseworthy or blameworthy. Whatever this may mean — a question to be examined later on — it does not appear at first sight to have an immediate reference to utility or advantage, at least not in the same sense as the actions mentioned above. However useful it may happen to be for an individual, stealing is wrong, and helping those who are in need is right, even if giving alms imposes some sacrifice. I do not consider in the same light the failure to avail myself of a good business opportunity, and the failure to keep my contract made with, or even my word given to, my fellowman.

(*c*) All actions which, considering all circumstances, are wrong must always be omitted. I must never commit perjury or act unjustly. But all right actions do not appear obligatory. Some, it is true, seem to impose themselves on man in such a way that to omit them is to fail in one's duty. Others, on the contrary, seem to be optional; to perform them is good; to omit them is not wrong. Thus, even if I do not comply with the obligation, I consider myself obliged to restore that which is clearly somebody else's property, and to abide by my valid contract. I do not feel obliged in all cases to give alms to every poor man whom I meet on the street, or, if I have the means, to endow hospitals or educational institutions, although all this is good.

(*d*) The question here is not: Which actions are good, and which are bad; which are obligatory, and which are free? The standards vary with the different degrees of culture and with different classes of persons. History also shows that there has been a great diversity in the past. The question is: Are some actions morally good, and others morally bad? The fact is universally true that man, everywhere and at all times, recognizes the distinction of right and wrong, and has a sense of duty.

The consequence of this sense of obligation is the feeling of remorse or satisfaction which is experienced according as one has acted wrongly or rightly, and the bestowing of blame or praise on other men.

2. **Moral Law.** — From what precedes, the common notions of good, obligation, and duty are sufficiently clear as facts. Now

there is no obligation without a *principle of obligation*, without a *law*, and consequently without a *lawgiver*. At this point, if asked for an explanation, the ordinary man, and very frequently even the most learned, will hardly be able to give a satisfactory answer. Of course it is wrong to exceed the speed limit with your motor car and to sell certain articles without a license. But wrongness here means rather imprudence and liability to the penalty provided by the law in such cases. I do not mean the same when I say that it is morally wrong for me to set fire to my neighbor's house, or to steal his purse.

Hence what is commonly called the law, namely the civil law, is not always assumed and accepted as the standard of moral obligation. Who then is the judge of this moral obligation? What is its standard? And when you tell another man: You must not do this, it is morally wrong; or when you accuse him of being unjust, on what authority do you pronounce? How do you know that it is so? What is your standard? And is your standard necessarily the same as his, or any other man's? Is it universal and must it be accepted by all? In a word, what is the supreme court that is to decide on the question of right and wrong? This is an important problem suggested by obvious facts.

3. **Conscience.** — It is clear that, in order to make its decisions known, the law or supreme tribunal, whatever it may be ultimately, must do so *through the human mind*. When applied to human actions, the decision must always appear in human consciousness in the form of a judgment. This is what we call conscience, the application to a concrete action of the general principles concerning its moral character. *Conscience is the actual judgment regarding the morality of actions*, and every individual man has his own conscience just as he has his own understanding. In the same way that, if I do not see, I may rely on, and be guided by, those who do, and that my eyes may be treated by the oculist, and my errors corrected by others or by my own deeper study and reflection, so my moral judgment may be based on another man's authority, changed, improved, and corrected; but I can no more judge with another man's conscience than I can see with his eyes.

4. **Meaning of Morality.** — The special relation of an action to the rules of right and wrong is what we call its morality. "Moral" comes from the Latin "mos" (plural, "mores"), which signifies habit. Applied to actions, it means, (1) that which has relation to the rules of duty and obligation, (2) that which is in conformity with these rules.

(*a*) In the first sense, *moral is opposed to non-moral*, that is, to that which has no reference whatever to any rules of right and wrong. Only human actions are called moral. A stone or bullet that kills a man is not blamed, but the man who wilfully threw the stone or fired the pistol is considered as having done wrong. Morality supposes some psychological conditions which are not found in beings inferior to man. Nor are all human actions moral, but only those of which man is truly the cause and the free agent, and which he commits with sufficient knowledge and freedom. The man who is under coercion, and, for instance, is carried to a certain place against his will, is not the real agent; the action is not his, and, for him, is not moral. (Cf. p. 167 ff.) There is no morality in the actions of a man who accidentally falls and kills himself, or who speaks and walks in his sleep. Such actions are non-moral.

(*b*) In the second sense, *moral is opposed to immoral*, that is, to that which is in opposition to the rules of morality and therefore is bad and wrong. In order to be moral in the second sense, or immoral, it is clear that an action must be moral in the first sense.

II. The Science of Ethics

1. **Nature of Ethical Science.** — (*a*) Ethics (from ἦθος, character) means the same as moral science, namely, *the science of right and wrong*, or the science of right conduct. It endeavors to account for the facts which have been indicated above, and to explain their nature, origin, and bearings. It also endeavors to direct human actions, to find the general moral laws by which they should be governed, and to apply these laws to the various circumstances of life. Hence ethics includes two parts, or has two functions; one is essentially practical, and tries to determine what

we should do and avoid; the other is more speculative, and tries to determine why ultimately we should do or avoid it.

(*b*) From this it follows that, as a whole, ethics is a normative science. It deals with human actions, to find out, not how they are actually performed, but *whether and how they should be performed*. History and psychology are not directly normative sciences. They simply state what takes or took place, and how events or processes occur or occurred. Ethics passes a judgment on the moral value of these actions and determines whether they are right or wrong.

(*c*) The term "law" does not apply to human actions and to physical events in the same sense. *Physical laws* are abstractions for the facts; they are not rules to which events ought to conform, but to which we see that events do in fact conform. And when what was thought to be a law is found to conflict with facts that are certain, the law has to be abandoned or modified. Not so with *moral laws*. They are ideals to which human actions do not necessarily conform, but to which they should conform in order to be good.

2. **Importance of Ethics.** — From the scope of ethics its importance may be inferred. In order to live well, perform his duty, and shape his conduct aright, man must first know in what these consist. It is true that there is innate in every man a certain moral sense which tells him his duty, but, on many points, it is vague, and, even where it is clear, one must examine whether and why its dictates are legitimate. It is not enough to *feel* that an action is right or wrong, one must *know* that it is so. Moreover, the moral feeling, precisely because it is a feeling, is often uncertain and misleading. It has to be interpreted, justified, and directed. Although knowledge is insufficient for good conduct, — one may know the good and fail to practise it — it is an essential condition of morality.

3. **The Relations of Ethics to Other Sciences** will now be understood easily.

(*a*) *Physical sciences* have only a remote relation to ethics, inasmuch as the knowledge or ignorance of physical laws may change the morality of an action by modifying the intention, motives, and foresight of the agent. Thus, according as one is, or is not, aware of the poisonous nature of a certain substance, the morality of giving it to a fellowman to swallow will differ. Biological sciences also are indirectly connected with ethics. Many obligations refer to human life and health, but generally they may be known and discussed without any detailed physiological knowledge.

(*b*) *Psychology* is much more closely related to ethics, and for this reason a few pages will be devoted to the psychological implications of morality. At present we shall limit ourselves to pointing out the difference between psychology and ethics. The psychologist studies human actions as processes, to find out how mental functions are related. The moralist tries to regulate human actions. Psychology gives to ethics its materials, but ethics does not place the same value upon all. The psychologist is like the botanist who studies the growth, nature, and characteristics of all plants. The moralist is more like the gardener who arranges certain plants according to an order, cultivates some and carefully excludes others. No action is moral which is not also in some way psychological.

(*c*) *Pedagogy* and ethics should also be kept in close contact. A complete education trains the whole man, and moral character is essential to man. Man must be accustomed not only to think consistently, but also to act rightly.

(*d*) *Æsthetics* and *logic*, although different from ethics, agree with it in being normative sciences, or in dealing with ideals and standards, the first with the ideals of beauty, the second of truth, the third of moral goodness. Frequently terms are transferred from one science to another. A man who is true to himself is one who acts according to his principles; a beautiful soul or character is one that includes certain moral characteristics, etc.

(*e*) *Sociology* is also related to ethics, since it considers man in his social aspect, which is the source of many duties. Society is an important factor in the morality of individuals on account of the laws by which it is ruled and of the mere fact of men associating with one another.

N.B. We shall see later that ethics is also related to metaphysics and religion.

4. **Division of This Treatise.** — Ethics will be divided into two parts; the first more speculative and more formal, dealing with *duty in general*, its nature and conditions; the other more practical, more detailed, and dealing with the *various duties and obligations*. Before passing to these, however, it is necessary to indicate the main psychological conditions of moral life.

II. PSYCHOLOGICAL CONDITIONS OF MORALITY

Psychological conditions and influences may be grouped under the three headings of knowledge, feeling, and will.

I. Knowledge

1. **Knowledge Necessary to Morality.** — In general, from what was said above and in Psychology on the relations of intellect and will, it is evident that knowledge is a condition without which an action cannot be voluntary. A man cannot be morally bound by an obligation unless this obligation is known to him. It is impossible to conceive that a man should be responsible for failing in a duty of which he has no knowledge. Moreover, a man must be aware of what he is doing. For instance, he is not responsible for an action performed automatically during sleep. The killing of a man by the accidental discharge of a pistol which was thought to be unloaded may be the result of imprudence, but, as such, it is not morally imputable. Hence a twofold knowledge is required, (1) of what one is doing, (2) of the relations of this action to the rules of morality. These general principles need a little further explanation.

2. **Effects of Ignorance.** — (*a*) Ignorance may be involuntary or voluntary. It may be unsuspected and unavoidable, when sufficient care has been taken to know one's duty; or it may, to some extent, be due to negligence in investigating one's duty when there was a suspicion of it, or, worse still, when the investigation was omitted precisely in order to act more freely and without restraint. The action due to *involuntary ignorance* is itself involuntary, and the will has no share in it. The action due to *voluntary ignorance* is not voluntary in itself, yet the will has a share in

it inasmuch as the ignorance from which it proceeds was voluntary. Hence such an action is called voluntary in its cause. Thus the physician who is aware of his incapacity and incompetence, either in general or in special cases, is accountable for the lives he loses since he knows that he lacks the sufficient knowledge of his art. It is clear that the amount of diligence to be used depends on the importance of the interests in question, the time at one's disposal, the qualifications and opportunities for investigating, the urgency of the action to be performed, and so on.

(*b*) The effects of ignorance are the same whether it affects the nature and consequences of an action, or the existence of a law which commands or prohibits it. I may speak an untruth in good faith thinking that it is the truth — *ignorantia facti* — or may fail to see that in the present circumstances lying is wrong — *ignorantia iuris*.

(*c*) In order to prevent possible confusion, it must be noted that we speak here of the moral obligation, and not merely of the obligation to obey the civil law in any concrete case. When duly promulgated, the civil law is supposed to be known by all the citizens for whom it is intended. Hence a penalty may be inflicted on a man for breaking a law of which he was *bona fide* ignorant. But if the ignorance is involuntary, there is no moral wrong, although the civil law may be the source of a moral obligation and bind in conscience.

II. Feelings

Feelings exercise a great influence on the intellect and the will. Among them the most important in the present question seem to be love, fear, and anger. A great love or passion blinds the mind more or less completely. The fear of losing that which one loves, or the anger caused by a sense of injury, frequently influences man to take a certain course of action. This action is less voluntary than it would be if performed coolly and deliberately. It will perhaps be performed with greater vehemence and stronger inclination, but this inclination proceeds from feeling, not from reason. In the case of the fear of an impending danger, however, a man may freely and deliberately choose a less evil, e.g. promise a liberal reward to his rescuer, although he would not otherwise do so. How far, in concrete instances, responsibility is lessened by passions and emotions is frequently impossible to determine exactly. Their influence varies from the slightest, and even imperceptible, impulse to a complete blinding of the mind, absence of mastery over oneself, and consequently of freedom and responsibility.

III. Will

1. **Coercion.** — An action may be due to violence or coercion. Instead of proceeding from the command of the will, it may proceed from some external power opposed to the will. Such an action is therefore *involuntary*. The real agent is the external power, and if this be a person, he alone incurs the responsibility. Thus a man may be dragged to a forbidden place, or compelled to perform unjust actions. Provided of course that he resists as much as the nature of the case allows, the action cannot be attributed to him. The gravity of the obligation to offer resistance varies with the nature and circumstances of the case, the chances of success in overcoming the violence, and the necessity of showing one's opposition and reluctance. If the possible resistance is not offered, the action is voluntary to some extent, and the responsibility remains in varying degrees. The physical violence of which we speak here is actual, and must not be understood in the sense of a mere fear referring to the future, which, as said above, generally leaves the action voluntary.

2. **Habit.** — (*a*) As explained in Psychology (p. 175 ff.), habit produces uniformity of action, facility and pleasure in acting. Hence it lessens the control of the will, both because the action proceeding from a habit is frequently performed without consciousness, or at least without distinct consciousness, and because, even if there is distinct consciousness, the impulse toward the action is greater, and consequently more difficult to overcome, in proportion as the habit is stronger and more inveterate. The influence exercised by habit varies in nature and intensity according to the nature, origin, and strength of the habit.

(*b*) A habit may be (1) acquired and preserved wilfully; (2) acquired wilfully and preserved unwilfully, when one is making serious efforts to overcome it; (3) acquired and preserved unwilfully. The "wilfulness" in all these cases is itself more or less perfect.

In the first instance the morality of the habitual action is not diminished by the fact itself of habit. "Qui vult causam vult et effectum"; the actions due to habit are rightly attributed to the man who consents to the good or bad habit from which they proceed. In the second, the morality is lessened in various degrees according to the strength of the habit, the actual consciousness and consent, and the amount of effort made to resist and uproot it. In the third, the morality is still more reduced, and may even be totally destroyed. The liquor habit may be given as an illustration of these various cases. A man may acquire this habit knowingly and freely, and indulge in it although he realizes that it is bad. Or he may acquire it almost without noticing it, owing to physiological conditions, to circumstances, to the presence of alcohol in medicine which he had to use, etc. As soon, however, as he becomes aware of it, he is under the obligation of resisting it and of taking the proper means to overcome it.

(*c*) Habit is a very complex factor in human actions, and it is frequently impossible to trace back all its antecedents in all their details and ramifications. A habit may be so strong as to be almost invincible. But generally it can be overcome by good resolutions and the use of proper means. Even when the individual declares it invincible, in most cases his "I cannot" is to be interpreted as meaning "I do not want to." The man who is not willing to try seriously and use his best effort shows that, in reality, he consents to the habit.

3. **Freedom** is an indispensable condition of the moral character of human actions. This has been indicated already in Psychology (p. 180 ff.), and only a few considerations will be added here.

(*a*) At all ages and in all places mankind has recognized two distinct orders of facts. *Some are necessary* and worthy of neither blame nor praise. *Others are free*, and their agents are held accountable for them. A man is not blamed for being sick or for accidentally hurting himself. He is blamed for wilfully killing his fellowman, stealing his neighbor's property, indulging in vices which caused the disease or accident.

(*b*) *Obligation* supposes the power to do or omit the obligatory action, and hence postulates freedom. There can be no obligation if human actions are necessarily determined and are ruled by laws as necessary as those which are found in the physical world. Obligation is an absurdity if man is not the master of his own actions, and if all are strictly and necessarily determined.

(*c*) The same consideration applies to the notions of right and duty as correlative. A man has a right when he can exact something from his fellowman; he has a duty when he ought to give that which is exacted. The right to exact and the duty to give suppose the actual power to give what is exacted.

(*d*) Responsibility, merit, virtue or vice, self-satisfaction and remorse suppose freedom.

(*e*) Hence *freedom is at the very basis of the essential factors of morality*. Without it, the terms "obligation," "responsibility," "right" and "wrong," are meaningless, and every action takes place with the same necessity with which the stone falls to the earth and obeys the law of gravitation. Such actions can neither be prescribed nor forbidden; they are neither right nor wrong, and deserve neither blame nor praise. It is true that some actions performed by man are necessary, but neither does he feel himself responsible, nor is he held responsible for them. If they are bad, he regrets them as he would regret an unavoidable misfortune or bodily deformity, not in the same way that he is sorry for an action known to be wrong, and yet freely committed. On this point the practice of determinists agrees with the practice of those who admit freedom. The inconsistency of the former is a sign of the connection which exists between the fact of freedom and the facts and elements of morality.

CHAPTER I

FUNDAMENTAL ETHICS

The object of this chapter is to indicate the bases on which morality rests, and to discuss briefly the problems suggested by the obvious facts mentioned above. Although this chapter is rather theoretical, its practical importance is evident, since, in order to be effective, the rules of morality must rest on secure foundations.

ARTICLE I. THE MORAL NORMS OR LAWS

The idea of obligation supposes that of a law to which actions should conform, and of a rule which they should follow. This *rule* may be considered in its *external reality*, as a law properly so called, and in its *internal application* or conscience.

I. LAW

I. Definition and Divisions

1. **Meaning of Law.** — In general, law signifies a constant or uniform rule according to which actions take place. A distinction is to be made between physical, civil, and ethical laws. The first apply only to material beings, the second and third to men as intelligent and free agents.

(*a*) *Physical laws* are abstract expressions or formulæ for the constant, necessary, and uniform mode of happening of phenomena; thus the laws of gravitation, attraction, chemical affinity, etc. Ethical laws do not express what necessarily and constantly happens, but what should happen. They are not indicative, but imperative formulæ.

(*b*) When asked why I have certain documents signed before

a notary public, or why I do not build a house without a permit from the city authorities, I answer that it is the law, and that its violation would make me liable to a penalty. This answer refers to what is called the *civil law*, i.e. a set of rules promulgated by competent authorities, varying with different countries and governments, and the violation of which is punished in different ways. Were I in another state or country, or at another time, I would not have on this point the same obligations under which I am now.

(*c*) If asked why I do not steal my neighbor's property, or kill my innocent fellowman, I may also answer: Because the law forbids it. But I feel that the meaning is not the same as above, that the obligation is of a higher character, that it would follow me everywhere and at all times, and that it would continue to exist even did the civil code make no mention of it and inflict no penalty for its transgression. It is based on human nature itself, and for that reason called *natural law*.

(*d*) The civil law supposes the natural law. In certain cases it is only the expression or enforcement of what human reason itself dictates, as when it forbids to kill. In other cases, it is reason again that requires obedience to any just command of the civil power, and to any law enacted by the proper authority for the welfare of the subjects.

2. **The Natural or Moral Law** in the strict sense is that which imposes a universal and strict obligation. It indicates an ideal to be realized, and, although one may fail to submit to its commands, yet, in failure, one always has the consciousness of a disorder and of a lack of harmony between what is done and what should be done. As the term indicates, the natural law is derived from our rational nature itself; it is based on man's essential relations to other beings, and manifested by the light of reason. Some of its fundamental and general precepts are self-evident, like: "Do good and avoid evil;" "Do unto others as you would like to have others do to you." Others are less general and already touch upon something concrete like: "Honor thy father and thy mother"; "Thou shalt not kill"; "Thou shalt not bear false witness." Other points, finally, are very complex, and, in many concrete cases,

their morality may seem doubtful, e.g. lying to procure a great advantage; committing suicide to avoid shame, etc.

Natural law and moral law have almost the same meaning, yet the latter term seems to have a greater extension, for civil laws may also impose a strict moral obligation. But, even here, this obligation is based on the natural law commanding to obey superiors when they give just orders. The civil law rules only on matters that refer to the public material welfare. The moral law reaches a number of other actions, even internal feelings like hypocrisy, dissimulation, and evil desire; and some external actions like ingratitude, egoism, gluttony, which the civil law does not consider. What follows applies strictly to the natural law.

II. Characteristics of the Moral Law

The moral law is given in consciousness with the following characteristics.

1. **Obligation.** — The moral law is not, like physical laws, the expression of what happens fatally and unavoidably, not merely a generalized fact. It is a rule which does not register a fact, but commands, although, even when acknowledging this rule, man may depart from it and disobey. Obligation is distinct both from the determinism of the laws of nature, and from a mere attraction, desirability, or counsel, which does not command strictly in the form of a "Thou shalt . . . ." In a word, *it is an imperative.*

2. **Absoluteness.** — The moral law is a categorical, not a hypothetical, imperative. A law is conditional when it enjoins a certain means to reach an end. It is absolute when it enjoins a thing *as an end* in itself independently of any condition. In the former case the obligation may be shirked by renouncing the conditioning end. In the latter, the obligation, even if not complied with, is unavoidable. Thus, "Thou shalt not steal," "Thou shalt not kill," are absolute commands. But if I say: "You must work in order to preserve your health, or to become rich," or "Avoid defrauding others if you want to increase your business," I use a conditional form, and the command depends on a supposition which may or may not be verified. The moral imperative imposes itself

simply because it is good and necessary, and because doing otherwise is acting against one's nature, reason, and conscience. I may not feel obliged to be a healthy or rich man, but I feel obliged to act as a man. This is expressed by the proverb: "Do your duty, come what may."

3. **Universality.** — (*a*) The moral law is independent of individual character, persons, countries, and times. It may prescribe different things according to different circumstances, but it is independent of personal interests and passions. Its principles are unchangeable, since they are based on human nature itself. Interests, pleasures, and desires vary with every individual. Not so the moral law which Kant sums up in this maxim: "So act that the maxim of thy will can at the same time be valid as the principle of universal legislation," i.e. act in such a manner that all men can act in the same manner; or again, in a more personal way: Do unto others as you would have them do unto you. Thus even if it were my own interest to steal, I do not wish others to steal from me. I know the law, and may not wrongfully make an exception in my own favor.

(*b*) It is true that practical applications vary almost endlessly with times and places. The law: "Thou shalt not kill," may be interpreted in many ways, and admit of many excuses. Moreover, it may seem to conflict with other principles and thus become obscured. Thus in certain tribes it is deemed lawful to kill parents in old age so as to avoid their falling into the hands of the enemy, or to shorten their sufferings. These excuses are understood as applications of the law which obliges us to love parents and do them good. Variations in practice are accounted for by (1) the misinterpretation of certain principles; (2) the real or apparent conflict of several principles; (3) the difficulty in agreeing on some points of morality which are obscure in themselves; (4) the depravity of the will which makes it disobey known laws; (5) habits and customs which modify or deprave the moral sense.

III. Existence of the Moral Law

In the second article we shall speak of the basis on which the distinction between right and wrong rests. For the present we want to show that such a distinction exists. Two points must be established, (1) that this distinction is recognized in consciousness; (2) that it is valid.

1. **Testimony of Consciousness.** — To formulate the moral law and explain its characteristics is already to demonstrate its existence. The distinction between right and wrong conduct is as natural and as evident for man as the distinction between true and false assent. Both impose themselves with the same cogent force, and neither can be denied without renouncing human reason itself. Let us, however, sum up a few facts which will illustrate this conclusion.

(*a*) *Everywhere* and *at all times* we find this distinction recognized, praise or blame bestowed, honor or disgrace attached to certain actions. In all languages expressions are found for these ideas. Standards differ, it is true, yet the fact at issue is admitted, for we are not concerned at present with the practical determination of what is right and what is wrong, but only with the fact that there are right and wrong actions.

(*b*) The testimony of *individual consciousness* is equally clear. The consciousness of freedom is inseparable from the consciousness that freedom is restricted by the moral law which it may transgress. Sometimes at least, before acting, there is a feeling that one of two possible courses of action is right and honorable, the other wrong and dishonorable. After acting, feelings of self-approval or self-blame are experienced. These feelings are not merely feelings of joy and regret, such as might be experienced on the occasion of some fortunate or unhappy event, success or failure, luck or accident. In these latter cases, unforeseen circumstances, or even personal imprudence, may be deplored, but we do not feel that our real value, moral worth, intrinsic and genuine honorableness, have been lost or lessened.

From being rich a man may become poor, and in consequence receive less external honors; he may regret the loss of wealth, advantages, and honors, but he may feel nevertheless that his own personal worth remains what it was before. On the contrary, the man who, from being poor, becomes rich by using unjust means, may receive honors; yet he has lost some of his essential worth, and feels it unless he has stifled his moral sense by depraved habits of thought and will. It is possible to hush the voice of conscience and become hardened against its warnings. Monsters are found in the moral as well as in the physical world, men who commit the greatest crimes without experiencing any shame or remorse. A man may be born sickly, or deprived of some external sense; or disease and the loss of a sense may develop later. So also a man may be born a moral monster owing to organic or mental defects; or he may little by little allow his moral sense to be destroyed. These are exceptions, and no more proofs against the reality of the moral law than the existence of insane or sick persons is a proof against the reality of sanity and health.

2. **Attempts to Explain Away This Fact.** — How will these feelings or data of consciousness be accounted for? Can we ascribe to them an artificial origin, or must we say that they are natural, innate, and rooted in human nature itself? Some facts are important and must be admitted.

(*a*) *Education* contributes to develop and direct the moral sense. According as the child is taught by word and example, he will in life consider certain things as right or wrong. The influence of education on morality is an obvious fact.

(*b*) Owing to *habit* and *custom*, actions which, at first, shock the moral sense in time appear quite natural and indifferent; or actions performed previously without any sense of wrong-doing appear blameworthy. Hence attempts have been made to explain the moral law by education, habits, surroundings, and by the existence of the civil law.

(*c*) According to the schools of positivism and associationism, all actions are *originally indifferent*. Some become indissolubly associated with pleasurable or displeasurable feelings and with useful or harmful results. Gradually such associations of actions with their consequences cause men to look upon the actions as good or bad in themselves. These estimates of the value of actions are transmitted by education. Parents, instructed by their own experience, give orders to their children, and rulers lay down laws for their subjects; or contracts are made by which men bind themselves to behave in certain ways toward their fellowmen. These associations become necessary and indissoluble, and thus are explained the universality and absoluteness of the moral law.

3. **The Preceding Explanation is Insufficient.** — (*a*) *Education* may make the child look upon certain actions as good, and upon certain others as bad. It may direct the moral sense, but *supposes* already in the child's mind the *distinction between right and wrong*, between praiseworthy and blameworthy actions. It influences it, strengthens it, and directs it, but does not create it. The animal may be "educated," or trained, but it can be taught only the utilitarian expediency of certain actions, because it lacks the necessary foundation for morality. Moral education is not simply a matter of prudence, expediency, or interest. These are at most hypothetical imperatives, not moral laws. Moreover, wherefrom would the educator derive the idea of obligation, morality, and responsibility? No associations can change the idea of useful into that of right, nor the idea of harmful into that of wrong. As a matter of fact — at present we deal with morality only as a fact — consciousness refuses to identify these two aspects of human actions. Education is for morality what logic is for the intellect. Logic supposes the distinction of truth and falsity, but does not create it. Moral education also supposes the distinction of right and wrong.

(*b*) We need not insist on the supposition that the sense of obligation arises from *contracts*. It is clear that contracts presuppose the obligation of observing them. What is the use of giving my word, if I feel that it is indifferent to break it? Justice alone, i.e. moral law, can unite human wills in one common agreement.

(*c*) Finally, the *civil law* gives no satisfactory explanation. (1) The civil law may be just or unjust, tyrannical or advantageous; it may respect or disregard individual rights, etc. To say this is to appeal to a higher law as criterion. (2) The authority of the civil law is derived from the natural law, which tells us that it is good and obligatory to obey legitimate authorities. If obedience is not already due to a civil law, it ceases to be a law at all. (3) There are good and evil actions, both internal and external, about which the civil law says nothing. (4) If morality is derived from the civil law, the door is opened to all forms of tyranny, since, in this case, there is no higher standard of morality than this law.

(*d*) In conclusion, if morality had an artificial origin, the notion of moral obligation would vanish from the mind as soon as one would come to know this fact. On the contrary, it always persists, thus showing that it comes from human nature itself.

II. CONSCIENCE

I. Nature of Conscience

What has been said so far applies as much to conscience as to moral law. Even if the moral law is imposed on man from without, — a question which is out of consideration here, — it remains certain that it cannot reach and affect man except through the knowledge of it, that is, through conscience. And the arguments which prove the existence of the moral law do so by proving at the same time the fact of moral conscience. What then is conscience?

1. **Conscience Implies Two Elements**, one belonging to the intellect, the other to the feelings.

(*a*) Conscience appreciates the moral value of human actions. This judgment is not merely logical, it is imperative. It does not simply state what takes place, it dictates what should take place.

(*b*) Conscience produces feelings of joy or blame according as the recognized obligation has been complied with or not. This element is the consequence of the former, which is the more important.

(*c*) Hence conscience may be defined as *the practical judgment which dictates what is good and what is bad, what is obligatory and what is optional, in every individual case*. Such at least is the strict meaning of the word. But frequently it is used to denote, not so much the *act* of judging as the *habit* of forming correct judgments on the morality of actions. Thus we say of a man that his conscience is erroneous on certain points, meaning that he habitually has misconceptions of their moral aspect. Sometimes also conscience refers to the agreement between a man's conduct and his principles. To say of a man that he has no conscience generally implies that he knows what he ought to do, but fails to act accordingly. Conscientious and conscientiousness refer also to the same idea.

2. **Conscience and Reason.** — From what precedes, conscience is not simply, nor even primarily, "moral feelings," or "moral sense." An action is not primarily looked upon as good or bad because it is attractive or repulsive, or because it produces feelings of self-approval or self-blame, but rather these are felt because the action is judged to be good or bad. Moral judgment, or conscience, is an *intellectual judgment* proceeding from reason, based on implicit or explicit, actual or habitual, deliberation, comparison, and reasoning, and capable of truth and error. In order to answer the question: Is this action which I propose to do right or wrong? I appeal to reason and try to solve my doubt by making use of higher, better known, and more certain principles. All this is essentially the function of reason.

II. Value of Conscience as the Rule of Actions

1. **In General,** since conscience is a function of reason, *its dictates are not necessarily true.* The very fact that judgments on the morality of the same action vary with times and places indicates that some must be false. Sometimes also personal experience shows clearly how difficult it is to reach a conclusion, and how uncertain this conclusion may remain after the most careful investigation. But from these facts it cannot be inferred that conscience has no value at all, and that its dictates are always arbitrary and never to be relied on. To reason this way is no more justifiable than to disclaim the validity of all scientific conclusions because some are false, or to deny absolutely that highly probable conclusions have any value because they are not certain.

In some cases duty is certain, and conscience manifests it clearly. As to the variations in moral estimates, they do not apply to the first principles of morality, such as the distinction of right and wrong, the obligation to avoid moral evil, and so on. The differences in their practical applications are due to habits, circumstances, modes of life, civil law, and chiefly to the real or apparent conflict of duties. The murder of enemies taken as prisoners may seem legitimate to tribes which are constantly at war; weak children or old people may be looked upon as hindrances to public welfare, etc. (cf. p. 295).

2. **Various Kinds of Conscience.** — Conscience may be true or false; ignorant, doubtful, or probable. It is important to note the difference between speculative and practical reason. The solution of a problem of mathematics or natural science may be postponed indefinitely, or even never be reached. But action cannot always wait. In a concrete circumstance, I must do one thing or abstain from it, perform one action or another. To doubt is possible; to do nothing is not always possible, and may be wrong.

(*a*) *If conscience is certain*, leaves no doubt, and shows clearly what should be done, it must be followed. What it commands must be done; what it forbids must be omitted; what it allows may be done or omitted. This is true even in the case of unsuspected or invincible error. When a man, after taking all prudent available means — available means will of course vary with the intellectual capacity and special disposition of the agent, and with the urgency of the action — judges *bona fide* that he should do so or so, he is obliged to follow his conscience, since it is the only rule he can apply to his actions. Nor is absolute certitude required such as would exclude completely every doubt, but only such as would exclude every prudent doubt. In moral questions it would be useless to look for mathematical certitude. A greater certitude is required in actions which have more serious consequences.

(*b*) *Where no certitude is possible* and yet it is necessary to take a course of action, man must do his best. An obligation which is strictly doubtful cannot be said to be a real obligation and therefore to bind. In such cases, especially where great interests are at stake, the best rule is to take the course which appears the safest and least likely to injure anybody's rights and interests. But it is always necessary to ascertain carefully which course should be pursued, and, if possible, to delay until this has been done. How is it to be done?

3. **The Formation or Education of Conscience** is general or special. (*a*) The *general* education of conscience consists in the habit of forming correct practical judgments. Besides the external helps, such as studying, reading, consulting, inquiring on ethics

in general or on special matters, it is important for the individual to be careful about the acquisition of intellectual, volitional, and emotional habits, since all these, as explained previously, influence moral judgments.

(*b*) *In special cases*, when a man doubts whether a given action is right or wrong, he must, as far as time allows, reflect, consider, and consult. Especially when one's own interests are engaged, and when, in consequence, there is danger of passing a less correct and less impartial judgment in one's own cause, the consultation of trustworthy and prudent persons is preferable to reflection. We may and must consult competent moralists as we may and must sometimes consult a physician, lawyer, or scientist. The more important the action, the greater must be the diligence in ascertaining its morality.

4. **Determinants of Concrete Morality.** — From the preceding doctrine it follows that the morality of a concrete action depends on several factors, the nature itself of the action, the intention, and the circumstances.

(*a*) Since certain actions in themselves are good, and others bad, it is clear that morality depends on the *nature of the action itself*, that is, on its relation with human reason. From this exclusive point of view a number of actions are neither good nor bad in themselves, but indifferent, or, rather, non-moral, like walking, sitting, singing, etc. But they become moral, i.e. good or bad, owing to the intention of the agent and the circumstances in which they are performed.

(*b*) For instance, walking to relieve a poor man is good; walking to commit a theft is wrong. It may even be said that the *intention* is the primary determinant of concrete morality, since conscience is the immediate norm of human actions. The final purpose, being that on which the will is fixed, is really the directive principle of everything else. This must not be understood in the sense that the end justifies the means, or that any means, even those that are wrong, may be taken in order to reach a good end, but in the sense that means known to be indifferent in themselves derive their morality from the end in view.

(*c*) *Circumstances* of time, place, person, quantity, quality, etc., may also increase, diminish, or change the morality or immorality of an action. We often hear the plea of aggravating or extenuating circumstances. To kill unjustly is wrong; to kill in self-defence is lawful. To give alms is right in general; to give alms when a bad use will certainly be made of it is wrong.

ARTICLE II. THE MORAL STANDARD

I. THE QUESTION STATED

I. The Object of the Present Article

1. **Necessity of a Rule.** — The proximate rule of morality is the actual dictate of conscience. But on what basis does this dictate itself rest? Or rather, on what basis should it rest? Men act for certain motives, and in order to secure certain ends, and yet some of these motives and ends are approved as good, noble, and moral, while others are condemned as bad, base, and immoral. A man who always acts for his own personal satisfaction, in whose conduct no place is found for a disinterested motive and for self-sacrifice, will generally be looked upon as a low type of morality to be shunned and despised. There are therefore rules that govern conscience and guide it in pronouncing on the morality of the end which a man proposes to himself. There is a standard to which we do and must refer human actions, motives, intentions, and ends. Why are some actions morally good, and others morally wrong?

2. **What is a Rule?** — (*a*) In a material sense, a *rule* or ruler is a straight-edged instrument used as a measure, or as a guide in drawing straight lines. A *standard* is a measure or value established by law or by universal consent, to which other things are referred. By analogy these material meanings are applied to immaterial things, and especially to human actions. In the school, the child uses his ruler to draw a straight line. If the pen or pencil fails to follow it, the line is no longer straight; it becomes crooked or curved. So also the action which deflects from the rules of morality is crooked and wrong. Measures are referred to a stand-

ard. The length of all foot-rules must agree with the standard foot accepted by law.

(*b*) When we speak of morality there is no positive law, nor universal agreement establishing a moral standard. In fact, we shall see that philosophers have proposed different systems. This is not to be wondered at, as we deal here with ideals, the determination of which is influenced by many circumstances, and especially by the whole complex psychology of the individual. Sometimes also, apparent contradictions are only at the surface, while at bottom there is essential agreement. Some divergences may be radical; others may come either from the incomplete expression of a view, or from laying too much stress on what is only a secondary aspect of the question. Thus theories become one-sided.

3. **Conditions Required in the Standard.** — The moral standard *cannot* be: (1) A mere *consequence* of morality. Thus remorse and self-approval are only effects of moral actions, and cannot be the standard we are now looking for. (2) Something *variable* and changing. Morality is not something dependent on individual peculiarities, interests, or character. There is not one morality for one man, and another for another man. The ultimate standard of morality is universal. (3) Something merely *optional* which man can accept or renounce. The laws of morality are frequently obligatory. In some cases, it is true, they are permissive, but in others, man is not given the moral choice between doing or omitting; he is under the obligation of acting so or so, and of omitting such or such an action.

II. Different Views Classified

1. **Logical Classification.** — It is almost impossible to give a logical classification of the various systems of morality. They merge insensibly into one another.

(*a*) In the first place one may claim that we have a *direct apprehension*, or *intuitive knowledge*, or *feeling*, of morality. But evidently, if a man claims to *know* in the strict sense, he may be asked for the grounds of his knowledge, and unless he appeals to immediate evidence — in which case he will be in near agreement with some feeling-theory — he will appeal to some form of reasoning.

If, on the contrary, a man claims that he *feels* an action to be right or wrong in the same way that he feels an impression to be pleasurable or painful, no more questions can be asked him, although such an assertion may be discussed.

In the second place, morality may be determined by a *calculation of*, or *reasoning upon, the fitness of an action to reach a certain end* which is conceived as a *bonum in se.* From this point of view it is clear that the discussion of the criterion of morality centres around the end itself which determines the morality of actions.

(*b*) Looking at the question from another point of view, all will agree that, in acting, man always looks for *some good*, since by all it is admitted that morality enables us to classify actions as good or bad, and goodness is the quality which all must strive to realize. This good may be (1) the satisfaction of *the senses* or that of *reason;* (2) *my own good* (egoism) or *the good of others* (altruism). Hence the following synopsis.

I. According to the *mode of knowledge* of morality. The distinction between right and wrong may be known

- (1) immediately. *Intuitionalism*
  - *emotional*
  - *intellectual*
- (2) mediately
  - by reason. *Rationalism*
  - by experience. *Empiricism*

II. According to the *good* which morality must realize. This good is

(1) the pleasure of the senses. *Sensualistic ethics*
(2) the satisfaction of rational aspirations. *Rational ethics.*

In either case one may seek

(1) personal good. *Egoism*
(2) the good of others. *Altruism*
} *Utilitarianism*

2. **Order of the Following Questions.** — Combining these different aspects and points of view, we shall examine successively (1) the true nature and foundation of duty and moral obligation, and we shall try to determine the true standard and criterion of morality; (2) the other systems, which contain only a part of the

truth, or one aspect of the answer, and which, therefore, may be false in their exclusiveness, i.e. not so much in what they assert as in what they deny. Here we shall consider the theories basing morality on (*a*) feelings; (*b*) pleasure and utility; (*c*) reason. (3) Finally, we shall attempt to determine the ultimate foundation of morality.

II. THE QUESTION DISCUSSED

I. Positive Determination of the Moral Good

1. The Notion of End. — (*a*) All actions which belong to morality are *purposive*, and frequently the reason why they are good or bad is that the purpose is good or bad. The purpose or end toward which an action is directed may be objective, or subjective, or both. Thus an action may be wrong because it leads of itself to some bad result, or because the agent intends to produce some result which he looks upon as bad; and if this estimation is correct, the action is both objectively and subjectively wrong. The science of ethics determines objective morality. It cannot reach subjective morality, which depends on psychological, and therefore individual, factors.

(*b*) Since morality is determined by the nature of the purposive action, *the notion of end is essential* in the question of the moral good. If an action, by its very nature, deprives my fellowman of an essential right, this result makes the action wrong. Thus, loading a pistol and firing are wrong, if the result of it is murder by which an individual is deprived of his essential right to live. In this case, the several actions leading to the final result are coördinated by a preconceived mental purpose.

(*c*) To answer the question: What is the standard of morality? it is necessary to answer this other question: What are the legitimate ends of human actions? To what final result must they tend? Ends may be proximate or remote according as they are reached immediately or only after a succession of coördinated actions. One may eat to support the body, thereby to make mental work possible in order to acquire riches and finally enjoy oneself. For the present we shall limit ourselves to natural ends, attainable on this earth, as our previous studies do not yet entitle us to speak of God as the natural end of man, still less of the supernatural end to which man has been raised.

2. **Morality Relative to Human Nature.** — Whenever man acts as a man — that is, uses his faculties with a sufficient knowledge of what he is doing, and a sufficient consent of the will — what he seeks is always the satisfaction of some of his aspirations and desires, i.e. the reaching of some end. But human aspirations correspond to human faculties and, like them, are very complex. Man desires happiness, but this may be the happiness of sensual pleasure or that of reason; it may be his own selfish happiness or also that of others. For, not only is man complex within himself, but living, as he does, amid complex social surroundings, many new relations arise from this social aspect of life. It is impossible to satisfy all human faculties because frequently they stand in opposition to one another. Reason and the senses are in many cases antagonistic, reason dictating duties which impose a restriction on the senses, and the senses craving for gratifications which reason condemns. If man had only *one* faculty, the development and perfection of this faculty would be his duty and the source of his legitimate happiness. In the real *complexity* and frequent opposition of his faculties, what is he to do? To "follow nature" may be a good precept, but what is it to follow nature when nature is so complex?

(*a*) *Human nature is human owing to that which distinguishes it from other natures.* It possesses certain properties identical with or analogical to those of other beings. Like the stone, the human body obeys the law of gravitation. Like the plant, it assimilates foreign substances, grows, etc. Like the animal, man sees, hears, remembers, etc. These faculties, therefore, are not special to man; they do not make of man a being distinct from other beings. As we proceed upwards in the scale of beings, we find that every superior degree shares in the properties of the preceding one and adds something to them. *The perfection of every being consists primarily in the degree of perfection of its specific properties and faculties.*

(*b*) The perfection of man consists, therefore, not in the satisfaction of such faculties as he possesses in common with lower beings, but of such as are *special* to him, that is, *reason* and *will*, together with the sense of obligation and duty which is based on these. The body, the senses, and the feelings have their claims, it is true, but they must always be subordinated to those of reason, and, in case of conflict, the former, not the latter, must yield. Whatever man does he does in order to complete and perfect his nature, since he does it in order to satisfy a desire and an aspiration, i.e. in order to fill a deficiency. Every desire and aspiration is essentially the avowal of the lack of something. A man can desire only what he does not yet possess, and his actions tend to acquire it.

(*c*) Hence the *primary duty of man is to preserve in himself the essential harmony and subordination of his faculties.* Both in the individual and in society reason discovers a certain order which imposes itself. Every faculty in the individual and every member in the society have their proper nature and place. Reason commands us to respect this order, and to give to every faculty and to every fellowman their dues. From this general principle are derived the complex duties relating to self or to other men. Concrete moral good includes both that which is necessary and that which is permitted according to the general principle just mentioned.

3. **Morality is not Obedience to Law**, whether external or internal. This is a consequence of what has been said above, since law, whatever it may be, is itself the expression of a good, and obligatory only in so far as it commands some good. Obedience to law is itself dictated by reason, and hence not primary. Moreover, laws, divine or human, contain points which are evidently of unequal importance, and which may come to conflict with one another. Thus the law forbidding homicide may conflict with the duty of self-preservation. This is true not only of external law, but also of the internal law or conscience, for conscience is largely a matter of education, feeling, and habit, and these may conflict with reason. If, however, by conscience be meant reason itself as applied to a line of conduct, we come back to the solution given above. In practice the separation of reason from other

mental faculties is never perfect; hence the diversity of moral standards.

To sum up: *The moral good for man is to live in accordance with his specific nature*, to perfect it as much as possible, to respect the nature of other beings, to treat his own faculties and every other being according to the place which they occupy. This is the ideal which one cannot conceive without feeling the obligation of realizing it as far as possible. Whatever system does not take all this into consideration will be false or incomplete, as will appear more clearly from the following discussion.

II. Morality Based on a Special Sentiment

1. **Importance of Feelings.** — (*a*) Undoubtedly feelings are very *important* in morality. Merely to perform one's duty, or to perform it reluctantly, hesitatingly, and faint-heartedly, is less easy and less noble than to love it and perform it with readiness. Not that all duties are agreeable, but the sense of duty and the love of whatever is known to be right make man fulfil it with the pleasure of doing right, and the satisfaction of obeying conscience. When duty is found agreeable, this feeling can in no way destroy the value of the action by which it is accomplished. Man is not merely a rational being, but a feeling being as well, and even if the ideal of morality does not consist in acting for pleasure, yet the pleasure found in right conduct is a sign that the principles of morality are interwoven with other elements in the human mind.

Feelings *increase the energy*, and make it possible to accomplish actions that would otherwise be above human strength. St. Augustine's words express a truth which is daily experienced: "Ubi amatur non laboratur, aut si laboratur labor amatur." A cold idea has but little motor power, but it derives much strength from the feeling that accompanies it. All noble and heroic actions proceed from the idea of duty, the will to accomplish it, and also a certain passion that impels to it. To try to eliminate all feelings from morality, and look upon them as obstacles to be removed, as the Stoics and Kant did; to look upon duty as being by its very nature a burden to be carried painfully and by dint of effort; to place the ideal of man in a state of perfect calmness and rest undisturbed by any feeling or emotion, is to misunderstand human nature, to overlook human psychology, and to give a rule unfit to guide men, since it fails to take men as they are essentially.

(*b*) But if feelings play an important rôle, this rôle must not be exaggerated. (1) *Feelings are blind;* they must be controlled and guided, and hence cannot be the *standard* of morality. (2) They *attract*, but *do not command* or create any obligation. (3) They are not universal, but *vary with every individual*. (4) What is agreeable to all men is not thereby obligatory. (5) It must be noted especially that *moral feelings presuppose the idea of morality*. Why do we experience moral pleasure, if not because we know that we are doing right? Why do we experience moral displeasure, if not because we know that our actions are against our duty? Why do we love duty, if not because duty appears to us as good? Feelings do not explain the moral standard, but presuppose it. They are not its basis, but its derivatives. Yet certain theories propose feelings as the very basis of morality. To these we now pass.

2. **Moral Sense.** — (*a*) Some philosophers like Shaftesbury, Hume, and especially philosophers of the Scottish school, after Reid, assert the existence of a *special moral sense* which intuitively distinguishes right from wrong in about the same way that the sense of taste distinguishes bitter from sweet, and the sense of vision, blue from red. It is a kind of natural instinct which reveals what is good and what is bad. It may also be compared to the æsthetic sense or taste which at once makes us find certain objects beautiful, and others ugly. Among Greek philosophers we already find the identification of the good with the beautiful, and it must be admitted that ethics and æsthetics have many points of contact. Some actions are beautiful or sublime on account of their moral excellence and they cause feelings of admiration akin to purely æsthetic feelings.

(*b*) *Criticism.* — It must be admitted that the habit of respecting the moral law, and the spirit of obedience to it, contribute to develop in man something like an instinct, a kind of moral taste, or moral sense, by which, in ordinary cases, he is guided in the choice between right and wrong actions without any effort of reasoning. Education and social surroundings create in man a second nature, moral as well as psychological.

But, precisely because it is a *second* nature, *it cannot be looked upon* as *primary*. It depends on something else. As it is neither obligatory nor constant, this taste cannot be the moral standard. Still less can it decide which of two feelings must prevail in case the same action is both agreeable or disagreeable from different points of view. Thus a physician may have to choose between self-sacrifice in relieving the sufferings of a man having a contagious disease, and the love of his own life and of his family. In such cases appeal must be made to some other norm and ideal. In other words, we may speak of moral taste, but *a rational explanation of it must be given*. It must be determined why certain actions are in conformity with, and others in opposition to, the moral sense. Thus it becomes possible to criticize the actions of others, and to refer them to certain rules which are not, like individual feelings, subject to endless variations. In fact, all admit that there is a depraved and a correct moral taste, and therefore refer it to some higher norm.

3. **Benevolence.** — (*a*) According to Hutcheson, man is moved by two kinds of affections, self-love and benevolence. In case of conflict between them, the moral sense decides in favor of benevolence, for it approves actions which follow from a desire to do good to others without regard to any personal advantage to be derived from them.

(*b*) *Criticism.* — This is only one side of the question. It leaves out the *duties toward self*, and fails to account for the *obligatory character of the moral law*. If self-abnegation is sublime, its foundation should be the more secure, since the principle of obligation must be more certain in proportion as the sacrifice imposed is greater. And are there no duties toward those with regard to whom no benevolent feelings are experienced, but who excite feelings of antipathy, often unexplainable?

4. **Sympathy.** — (*a*) Adam Smith proposes the feeling of sympathy as fundamental in ethics. By sympathy is meant the ten-

dency to share the feelings of others, to suffer when they are afflicted, and to rejoice when they are joyful. It is a fact that man naturally sympathizes with other men, and chiefly wants them to sympathize with him. According to Smith, sympathy is *not only a fact*, but *a principle of morality*. To approve or condemn the actions of others is simply to recognize that we are, or are not, in sympathy with them, and that we also should feel right or wrong if we performed the same actions. The sentiment of obligation is simply the fear of exciting antipathy in others. Hence one must endeavor to have the sympathy of the greatest possible number of men. As those who judge the value of actions may be more or less depraved and prejudiced, and as the danger of prejudice is greater when a man passes a judgment on the value of his own actions, an appeal must be made to an *ideal onlooker*, disinterested and impartial. It is his sympathy which man must try to deserve.

(*b*) *Criticism.* — Sympathy as the rule of moral conduct is insufficient. (1) Like all other feelings it *varies* with individuals and their surroundings. Those who live in corrupt company would win their fellowmen's sympathy by doing wrong. (2) It is not *obligatory*. It is at most a fact, not a law. To make it a guide is to expose oneself to the danger of going astray, for not all forms of right excite sympathy, nor all forms of wrong, antipathy. (3) To appeal to an *impartial onlooker* and judge is hardly consistent with Smith's theory. This ideal judge is precisely one in whom abstraction is made of the feelings of sympathy and antipathy. He is a judge who bases his judgment on *deliberate reasonable evidence.* Hence the criterion of feeling is abandoned for that of reason. How can I know that my action will be approved by an ideal and impartial onlooker? The only means is to reason out for myself whether it is worthy of praise or of blame, that is, to find out *by reason* whether it is morally good or bad.

5. **Honor.** — (*a*) What has been said so far applies also to all theories which base morality on a sense of honor. Honor is a vague term, but, in its most common meaning, it applies to a man's reputation as based especially on social relations. Every

condition of life has its own special line of honor. The soldier's honor, the gentleman's honor, the citizen's honor, nay, even the thief's honor, are not according to the same standard. These meanings, however, are not strictly ethical — not all, at any rate — but conventional. They are based on custom, etiquette, habit, etc. If they are ethical, they do not refer to the *basis of morality*, but only to certain *applications* of it, to some special virtue or behavior characteristic of this or that profession. Hence honor is neither a universal nor a constant norm. Nor is it obligatory in all cases; frequently one feels that its precepts are not at all moral obligations, but simply rules established by custom and convention. There is also the danger of making of this sense of honor a purely external affair, and of paying no attention to *secret* wrong-doing as long as *reputation* is intact.

(*b*) This, it is true, is a false and hypocritical sense of honor. True and genuine honor is based on human dignity. It refers to self-approval and is not satisfied with merely external decorum. As such again, it is not fundamental. True honor is distinguished from false honor by *reason*, not by *feeling*. To live according to true honor and true human dignity is to live according to duty and reason. The sense of honor, although it must be inculcated and cultivated as early and as carefully as possible, will always remain something *accessory* and require another basis.

III. Morality Relative to Pleasure and Utility

1. Theories Outlined. — (*a*) There is no *a priori* reason to *oppose* duty and morality to pleasure and utility. There seem to be no contradictory elements in these two notions. Nor is there any reason *a posteriori*, i.e. from experience. The accomplishment of duty is frequently pleasurable, and may become so by practice and habit. Even when the action is difficult and cannot be performed without checking some natural tendency, it produces the nobler and purer happiness resulting from the satisfaction of the sense of duty, whereas acting in a contrary manner will produce the painful feeling of remorse and self-condemnation.

(*b*) From this it does not follow that pleasure and duty are *identical*. There are many kinds of pleasure, all of which perhaps are not in conformity with duty. Even if it should be proved that in all circumstances duty is pleasurable, the two notions would nevertheless be distinct. Duty imposes itself as an obligatory end; pleasure does not. Even where right conduct is pleasant, consciousness testifies that it is not right because it is pleasant, but pleasant because it is right.

(*c*) *Hedonism* (ἡδονή, pleasure) is a doctrine identifying the moral with the pleasurable, and holding that actions are good or bad according to their pleasurable or painful results. It has two main forms: (1) *Egoistic* or *individual hedonism*, which considers only the agent's personal happiness. (2) *Altruistic* or *universal hedonism*, which considers the happiness of others, or of the greatest number of men. This latter form has been called *Utilitarianism* by Stuart Mill, its chief exponent.

2. **Egoistic Hedonism.** — (*a*) We need not insist on systems looking upon morality as an affair of personal pleasure, chiefly of sensual pleasure. These systems have come to be condemned universally as lowering man to the level of the brute. (1) In antiquity, Aristippus of Cyrene gives as a rule to look only for the present and immediate pleasure to be derived from an action. The end of man is happiness, and, as the future is uncertain, man must always follow the instinct that prompts him to strive after the greatest sum of pleasure in the present. The same doctrine found advocates among the French materialists of the eighteenth century. (2) Epicurus insists more on the happiness of life as a whole. True happiness does not consist so much in sensual pleasure as in the calmer, purer, and more lasting pleasure of the soul. Hence, although pleasure is the end of man, not all pleasures are to be placed on the same level, because many pleasures are followed by pain, and pain is often followed by pleasure. Prudence and judgment are necessary to know which pleasures are to be chosen, and which pains are to be avoided. Hence, also, the necessity of virtue, temperance, honesty, justice, etc., which are conditions of true pleasure. This moral principle is much higher and nobler than that of Aristippus.

(*b*) *Criticism.* (1) To identify rightness with the pleasure of the senses is to *vilify human nature*, to look merely at its lowest aspect, and to neglect its highest aspirations. (2) *Pleasure is not an end but a means;* not a principle but an effect. The end of man is to act in conformity with his nature, and thus to exercise his activity and develop his faculties. Pleasure may result from this, and the desire of pleasure may stimulate it, but it is not the end. (3) Consciousness shows that pleasure is not obligatory, absolute, and universal, hence *not a standard* of morality. Frequently pleasure is followed by remorse of conscience. (4) To apply this principle of hedonism is to open the door to all *abuses*. If pleasure is the end, it has to be sought and enjoyed at whatever price, and in whatever circumstances. No room is left for disinterested motives and self-sacrifice. Personal pleasure may be procured, even should pain be thereby inflicted on others.

3. **Bentham's System** is fundamentally egoistic and secondarily altruistic. His main principles are the following:

(*a*) Pleasure is the only good; pain, the only evil. From this principle is to be derived the only standard of the value of actions. An action is useful, and consequently good, when the sum of its pleasurable consequences is greater than the sum of its painful consequences.

(*b*) Pleasures are to be chosen prudently. Attention must be paid to their (1) intensity; (2) duration; (3) certainty or uncertainty; (4) propinquity or remoteness; (5) fecundity, i.e. capacity of producing other pleasures; (6) purity, according as they are, or are not, mixed with pain; (7) extent, i.e. the number of persons who enjoy them. On these bases Bentham builds an arithmetical determination of good and bad actions, of virtues and vices, according to the quantity of pleasure and pain that results.

(*c*) Personal and universal utility are inseparable. Man cannot live and be happy except in society. Hence it is necessary to procure pleasure for others in order to receive some from them. Altruism is a condition of true egoism.

Criticism. — (*a*) To this system are opposed all the reasons given against making pleasure the standard of morality. Personal interest is not: (1) *Obligatory absolutely*, but only hypothetically. In order to succeed, perhaps the merchant must be honest, but he is not obliged to succeed. (2) *Absolute and universal.*

It is hardly possible to find anything more changeable according to persons, conditions, times, and places. (3) *Practical.* Often the consequences are unforeseen before acting, and yet it is from them alone that the action is supposed to derive its whole value. (4) *Safe.* If personal utility and pleasure are always the goal of man, it will not always be true that "honesty is the best policy." It will be true only when the lack of honesty would be known to others so as to become a source of pain.

(*b*) Bentham's arithmetic of pleasures is *impossible* because there is no common measure applying to all. Pleasures vary with individuals. Consequently Bentham's calculations to show, for instance, that drunkenness is immoral because, notwithstanding the pleasures which it procures, the pains of which it is the source are more numerous, will fail to convince a large number of individuals who will calculate on a basis different from that of Bentham. This whole arithmetic is *a matter of personal taste.*

(*c*) *From egoism it is impossible to derive altruism.* Even if praise and reward, or blame and punishment are sources of pleasure and pain, and if man must seek the former and avoid the latter, the following facts remain. (1) Secret actions, like theft or murder, would be good if productive of pleasure. (2) If self-interest is primary, it is primarily worthy of praise. Frequently a man knows his action to be right or wrong before being praised or blamed for it. (3) Why should men be so inclined to praise self-sacrifice and benevolence? Benevolence or altruism is not to be derived from a purely egoistic starting-point. In this view, it always remains a means toward egoism and toward securing personal pleasures. It is at most an indirect altruism in the service of egoism.

4. **Stuart Mill.** — While admitting also that happiness is the end of man and the supreme test of morality, Stuart Mill modifies the hedonistic doctrine on two important points.

(*a*) It is not enough to pay attention to the *quantity* of pleasure, as Bentham had done, but pleasures also differ in *quality*. Some are higher, nobler, and more refined, and hence to be preferred to others, not because they are greater, but because they are superior in quality. This qualitative determination depends both on the pleasurable object and on the faculty in which the feeling resides. "It is better to be a human being dissatisfied than a pig satisfied; better to be a Socrates dissatisfied than a fool satisfied." (Utilitarianism, ch. II.)

(*b*) It is not true that individual and general interests are inseparable; they may conflict. The aim of man is to work, not for any personal interest, nor even for the private interest of a family or a nation, but for the general good of humanity. The standard of morality is the greatest and truest happiness taken altogether. Hence "to do as you would be done by, and to love your neighbor as yourself, constitute the ideal perfection of utilitarian morality." (Utilitarianism, ch. II.)

(*c*) Mill's system of morality must be taken together with his psychological doctrine of associationism. Moral feeling, duty, conscience, self-approbation, remorse, etc., result from the associations of certain actions with the subsequent feeling of pleasure or displeasure. Hence actions performed at first for the sole motive of personal interest, are little by little considered as good. Morality is thus largely, if not exclusively, dependent on association and habit, and consequently arbitrary and artificial, varying with times, places, and other circumstances.

Criticism. — This conception of morality is nobler than that of Bentham, and, on many points, will give a satisfactory line of conduct. Yet *it is insufficient.*

(*a*) To appeal to a distinction between the *quantity* and the *quality* of pleasure is to renounce the principle that pleasure is the end of man and the norm of morality. Some pleasures are said to be more desirable than others, not on account of their pleasantness, but on account of their purity, nobleness, disinterestedness, beauty, etc., i.e. on account of something else which is itself *primarily* desirable. How shall we know which pleasures are qualitatively superior *unless we appeal to reason*, which, independently of the pleasant character of experiences, pronounces that the satisfaction of some faculties and aspirations is preferable to that of others? How shall we convince the thief and the sensual man that their pleasures are inferior in nature to other pleasures unless we go beyond the hedonistic principle?

(*b*) If interest is the only standard, why should an individual prefer the general good to his own private advantage? This cannot be shown to be obligatory without introducing again some higher standard. If pleasure is the end of man, *my pleasure* is *my end*, and it is what *I am entitled to reach*, even if I do not thereby foster the happiness of mankind. *On a mere utilitarian basis*, nobody can show me that I am, in any circumstance whatsoever, obliged to sacrifice myself for the good of others. It is necessary in this case to show that there is an absolute order, an ideal of reason, and a duty different from pleasure. The principle of altruistic utilitarianism throws no light on the duties of man toward himself. Even with regard to altruistic duties, it is far from clear, for it is difficult to estimate what will be the good of mankind in general.

(*c*) Undoubtedly the *association of ideas* is an important factor in ethics, and on it, to a great extent, current ideas of morality depend. But it is insufficient. (1) Certain principles of morality are demonstrable, and based on *reason*. As was shown in Psychology mere habitual sequence will not of itself produce the feeling of "oughtness" any more than it can produce a universal and necessary judgment. When I reflect on it, the habit of lying does not destroy the conviction that it is wrong, even though lying should bring me some advantage. On the other hand, the habit of washing one's face and hands every morning, of smoking tobacco, etc., produces no feeling of moral obligation. Moral obligation, therefore, rests on something else. (2) If habits are the very starting-point of morality, they are *of themselves* indifferent or non-moral. Hence I may change them as I please. Thus it becomes perfectly lawful to stifle the voice of conscience and to refuse to heed remorse, since all these are simply results of non-moral associations. Conscience will disappear by the same means which gave rise to it, and with equal right.

5. **Spencer's** addition to utilitarianism, namely, the position he gives it in his general scheme of universal evolution, does not remedy its intrinsic weakness. According to him, primitive man is exclusively egoistic. Soon he perceives that his own personal interest will gain by associating with others, and doing them good.

Little by little, altruistic feelings arise and struggle with egoism. This is the present state of humanity, but the day will come when altruism will have conquered, and be natural to man. Then, and only then, will Comte's fundamental principle of ethics be realizable: "Live for others."

This system does not explain the character of obligation. It tells us *what* conscience dictates; it cannot tell us *why* it has the right to dictate. Moreover, as was remarked against Mill, if the moral views which man has to-day are the artificial products of evolution and of adaptation to surroundings, man cannot be obliged morally to respect them. There can be at most a certain organic and mental necessity resulting from habit. All that man can do is to follow blindly his hereditary tendencies, good and bad, and this is precisely against true morality.

6. **Solidarity.** — A word must also be said of solidarity. It is a fact that no man is independent. All men form one body, and receive advantages from the other members of society. Hence man is obliged to return these, to work for others as others have worked for him, to behave, not merely as an individual, but as a part of a whole. He must respect others, as well as himself.

There is much that is true in this view; but it presupposes a deeper basis. Even if solidarity is a *fact*, it is not a *duty* until appeal is made to higher principles of justice which oblige a man to return what he receives. And even this justice and obligation must rest on some other principle of reason antecedent to the fact of solidarity.

IV. Morality Dependent on Reason

Morality is dependent on reason, but how? We have now to examine briefly the various systems proposed in this direction. "Morality for its own sake, and independently of the results which the moral action may have," such would be the motto of those moralists whom we are to study. They stand at the opposite extreme of those according to whom, as we have seen, morality depends primarily on the results of human actions. The moral action is an end, not a means subordinate to something else, as hedonists assert. Resulting pleasure and utility have nothing to do in the determination of the moral aspect of an action. The norm of morality is reason alone with its practical dictates.

1. **Stoics.** — (*a*) According to the Stoics, virtue, i.e. action in conformity with the laws of human nature, is the only good, and vice, i.e. action against the laws of human nature, the only evil. (1) Since human nature consists essentially in reason, which differentiates it from other natures, *virtue is a mode of action in conformity with reason.* (2) *Virtue must be sought for its own sake*, and is its own reward and the only happiness. To act for any ulterior end and any other reward or happiness is wrong. (3) All other things, sometimes called good, like health, reputation, pleasure, etc., are not really so; nor are pain, disease, ignominy, etc., real evils. They are given no attention by the wise. (4) *All feelings and emotions are opposed to reason.* To subdue them, and reach a complete apathy is the duty of man. The wise man is not subject to, or rather not affected by, pleasure or pain, fear or desire, etc. Even the pleasure found in the practice of virtue should never be an end, but only a consequence of virtue.

(*b*) This view, however much truth it may contain, is based on an incomplete psychology. Virtue is necessary to happiness, but other conditions are also required. The man who suffers physically or mentally is not completely happy. Pain is a true evil, although not a moral one. Moreover, human nature includes emotions no less essentially than it includes reason. That feelings should be controlled is true. That they should be suppressed is against reason itself, which must recognize them, and finds in them, sometimes enemies, it is true, but sometimes also allies.

2. **Kant.** — The essential points in Kant's fundamental ethics may be summarized as follows:

(*a*) The existence of the moral law is a *primitive fact* of consciousness, universal and necessary. "Oughtness" manifests itself clearly to the mind. It is not derived from any motive like pleasure or happiness, but is autonomous, and imposes itself for its own sake, independently of anything else.

(*b*) Hence the moral law is a *categorical imperative.* An *imperative* because it does not merely advise or recommend, but commands strictly, and imposes an obligation. A *categorical* imperative because it is unconditional. A conditional imperative would make the command dependent on a condition, as "Transact this business in such or such a way *if* thou wouldst be successful." But the categorical imperative is subject to no condition, and, for instance, without any restriction or ulterior end, commands: "Thou shalt not lie."

(*c*) The only moral action is that which is performed *out of respect for the moral law itself*, and disregards all other ends and results. "Good-will," i.e. the will to act in conformity with duty, is the only real good. Goodness or rightness is not antecedent, but consequent to obligation. An action is not obligatory because it is good, but it is good because it is obligatory and performed out of respect for the moral law.

(*d*) *The two most important principles* which must be kept in mind for the concrete determination of moral actions are: (1) "So act as to treat humanity, whether in thine own person or in that of any other, in every case as an end withal, never as a means only." Reasonable and free will is that which constitutes essentially human personality, and since it is absolute, it should never be made an instrument destined to gratify passions or desires. (2) "So act that the maxim of thy will can always at the same time hold good as a principle of universal legislation," i.e. Never perform an action which thou wouldst not allow to be performed by everybody else. Thus, in my individual case, breaking a promise is wrong, because, if it were admitted to be right for me, it should be right for all men. Hence there could be no faith at all in promises. Promises themselves would therefore cease to be made, and the maxim that promises may be broken lawfully would thus destroy itself. Hence, since it is not lawful for all men to break promises, it is not lawful in my individual case. This principle is the practical test of morality, and its application will lead to the realization of the supreme moral ideal, a "republic of ends," in which men will respect and help one another out of pure respect for the moral law.

Criticism. — Kant's system contains a great number of true and noble principles. He brings duty to the foreground instead of making it a mere result derived from utility, and subordinated to it. He shows the dignity of the human person and insists on its intrinsic value. Without showing here the place of ethics in Kant's whole system of philosophy, we shall limit ourselves to some remarks concerning his moral teaching.

(*a*) Human nature, precisely because it is *reasonable*, will always ask for the *reason* why any command should be obeyed. To obey blindly a law which man finds within himself, without inquiring if the law is valid and binding, is not reasonable. The law must exhibit its claim to man's obedience. To examine this claim is to examine *something anterior to the law*, some good which the law presupposes but does not create. The principle that this law makes the goodness of actions is therefore in contradiction with reason. Far from being *autonomy*, as Kant calls it, it is pure *despotism*.

(*b*) Moreover, if the will is autonomous, it is so for all men, good or bad; for all consciences, right or wrong; and Kant has no means of proving the existence of the categorical imperative which he experiences to another man who does not experience it. Even when the categorical imperative is accepted, since man is autonomous, and since the will is the only principle of obligation, he may transgress its commands without any injustice. Hence Kant's categorical imperative is really hypothetical: "Obey duty *if* thou wilt live conformably to reason." Why should I treat humanity in myself and in others as an end, and not as a means, if not because this is *recognised as good* before my practical reason *commands* it?

(*c*) Good-will, says Kant, is the will of performing duty for its own sake, independently of any feeling. This exclusion of pleasure as vitiating morality is *excessive*. A mother attends to her sick child because she loves him. Who will condemn her on that ground? And who will say that the philanthropist is not performing moral actions, or that his will is not good, when he helps his fellowmen out of sympathy and pity?

(*d*) Kant's ethics fail to distinguish between the obligatory and the non-obligatory good. There are things which I *may* do, although I am *not obliged* to do them, like helping the ordinary poor man on the street, or giving him more than he strictly needs. Even if the categorical imperative clearly commands or forbids certain actions, conscience does not merely command; sometimes it permits or counsels, and this is no less an immediate fact than the categorical imperative. To fulfil all strict obligations is only one aspect of morality. Many morally good actions are not obligatory.

(*e*) The norm of the morality of individual actions, namely, the possibility of their being universalized into general principles, good as it is as a *negative* guide telling what to avoid, is insufficient as a *positive* guide telling what to do. In short, Kant has not taken a complete view of man and of all the exigencies of human nature.

V. The Ultimate Foundation of the Moral Law

1. **Human Nature.** — The moral good consists essentially in the *conformity of an action with human nature* considered both in itself and in its relations with other men. Human nature is not merely reason, nor feelings, nor will, and on this ground we reject the systems mentioned above. All contain some truth, but consider only one aspect of human nature. Their point of view is too narrow. Emphasizing the claims of the feelings, utilitarians neglect those of reason. They fail to see the intrinsic value of actions, and look only at the value of their results. Kant, on the contrary, considers only reason and will, and has no regard whatever for the results of actions.

The view which was explained above recognizes the claims of both. It is more complete, and more in accordance with human nature as a whole. It alone accounts for the distinction between that which is obligatory and that which is good without being imposed, because certain things are strictly required by human nature, while others are in accordance with it, but not necessary. Right and wrong are known by comparing actions with the exigencies of man's rational nature. This is the true norm or standard according to which the morality of actions should be judged.

2. **Reason Not Autonomous.** — Hence morality rests on human reason as the *standard* according to which the value of human actions is measured. But is reason the ultimate and self-sufficient foundation of morality? To this question we must answer that, while reason *manifests* what is right and what is wrong, what is obligatory and what is optional, it does not *make* it so. It shows

in what direction we should act, but does not create the obligation. We have here something similar to what takes place in the knowledge of truth. Reason is not free to declare certain things true or false, but it must conform to evidence. It perceives truths that exist independently of itself. In the same way, the moral good is not made, but only perceived, by reason. Hence in neither case can *reason be called autonomous*, since *it must conform to the nature of things*.

3. **The Ultimate Basis of Morality.** — (*a*) Can we say that the *will* is *autonomous* and, of itself, obliges man to act according to the dictates of reason? In other words: Why is the moral good, in some cases at least, *obligatory?* Whence comes the *strict duty* of acting in conformity with our rational nature? No man can give me a binding order without showing his credentials, and without being my superior. I will not consider a law as valid unless it is enacted by the proper authority. There is no law without a lawgiver. Who is the lawgiver in the moral order? (1) Some answer that obligation results from the very nature of the moral good, which is sufficient to give rise to a strict duty. (2) Kant, on the contrary, asserts that duty is the primitive fact, and that an action is good because it is prescribed. (3) In both cases, reason is looked upon as independent of any higher authority, and as the sufficient and ultimate source of obligation.

(*b*) This view cannot be accepted. *The moral law is not explainable finally without rising above human nature* to God Himself as the author of human nature and of every reality, and as the supreme ruler of the world. Duty necessarily implies two terms, an authority and a subject, a superior who imposes the law and an inferior who must comply with it. Hence *man cannot be his own lawgiver*. An obligation which would arise primarily from human reason or will leaves man alone with himself, and consequently ceases to be a real obligation. "It is good" does not mean the same as "You ought." An action is good because it is in conformity with human nature, but the duty to live in conformity with human nature supposes a superior intelligence as the source of the moral order, and a superior will as the lawgiver who commands us to respect this order.

(c) We are thus led to this dilemma: Human reason either *makes* the law or *simply perceives* it. In the first supposition, the law ceases to be authoritative and stable. What reason has done it can undo and modify; duty no longer exists. We must therefore accept the second supposition, that reason knows a law which is universal, superior to the reason that perceives it and to the will on which it is imposed; and which, consequently, comes from God Himself. It is in my power to break the moral law, but I know that it persists even when it is violated. If the moral order does not rest on God, it is but an *abstraction*, an *idea of the human mind*, and why should we bow before it? Shall we be accountable to a mere idea for our actions? If this idea is able to rule, and to impose an obligation, it is because it is the *idea of God Himself*, the source of the moral order.

(d) Hence God is not necessary as the *criterion* of our knowledge of right and wrong, but as the only *foundation* on which the moral law can rest ultimately. Without knowing God, I may *know* my duty, but I cannot *account for* it. God's law is not given *from without* — except in the case of positive divine law, with which we are not concerned here — but *from within*, through our reasonable nature. Yet this natural law must rest on, and derive its validity from, the eternal law, i.e. the wisdom of God ordering all things, and the will of God commanding that this order be preserved. The binding force of conscience can come only from the fact that it is the voice of God within ourselves.

4. **Summary.** — We may therefore conclude that psychological analysis alone does not suffice to furnish us with the ultimate foundation of morality. Good as far as it goes, it necessarily leaves something unexplained. *Human reason gives only the contents or material elements of morality:* namely, it tells us what is right and what is wrong. *The formal element of morality*, or duty, which is *known* through reason, *can be derived only from God*. Hence ethics is intimately bound to metaphysics and religion. An *immanent obligation*, i.e. an obligation which is recognized within oneself, supposes a *transcendent ruler*, i.e. a superior being distinct from human reason and will. To discover a true law, a true

obligation, is *ipso facto* to find oneself in presence of a higher intelligence and will, in presence of God Himself.

VI. Conclusion

1. **Responsibility.** — From the existence of duty follows responsibility, i.e. *the imputability to the agent of the actions which he performs*. Responsibility presupposes the knowledge of the morality of an action, and freedom in performing it. Hence responsibility varies with the degree of freedom and knowledge. Whatever affects these conditions affects also responsibility. As these conditions are not known to any one but the agent, it follows that others, while being justified in passing judgment on the value of an *action* in itself, should abstain from passing judgment on the *agent*. "Judge not," since you have no sufficient data to judge others. You know what they do, but you are ignorant of the hidden springs that prompt them to act.

2. **Virtue** is the habit of doing right; vice, the habit of doing wrong. Virtue has many degrees. It may stop at that which is strictly obligatory, or may extend to actions that are good, but not prescribed. In every case, it must avoid extremes. The principles "Ne quid nimis" and "In medio stat virtus" express an important truth. In all things, not only defect, but also excess, is reprehensible.

3. **Sanction.** — (*a*) Every law must have a sanction; rewards for those who respect it, and penalties for those who violate it. A sanction is a necessity of justice, since, without it, the law can be violated with impunity. To be perfect, it should be universal, i.e. reach all men and all actions, and be proportionate to the degree of merit or demerit.

(*b*) The main sanctions of the moral law are: (1) The *legal* sanction, i.e. that which, in some cases, comes from the civil law. (2) The *social* sanction, i.e. of public opinion. (3) The *natural* sanction, i.e. the various physical, physiological, and mental advantages and disadvantages resulting from the observance or neglect of moral laws. (4) The *moral* sanction, i.e. satisfaction and remorse.

(*c*) That none of these sanctions is sufficient is almost self-evident, for they are neither universal nor proportionate. *Human justice* can reach neither all men nor all actions, and is sometimes mistaken. The same is true of *public opinion*, of *natural sanctions*, and of *satisfaction and remorse*. Their value depends on habit and on the delicacy of one's conscience. Nor are such sanctions in proportion to merit. Hence, if there is a true sanction, if ultimately all things are to be righted, there must be a final sanction beyond this life. Otherwise the moral world lacks rationality and order. And here again we are led to *God as the Supreme Judge*, who alone, in His infinite science and justice, can give to every man what he has merited by his deeds. It is not to himself, nor to other men, but to God, as the author of the moral order, that man is ultimately accountable for his actions.

CHAPTER II

APPLIED ETHICS

We shall now endeavor to indicate man's most important duties, and this determination will be based on the principle enunciated above, namely, the exigencies of the rational nature of man as the basis of his rights and duties. First, however, it is necessary to say a few words about rights and duties in general.

Right and Duty

1. **Meaning of Right and Duty.** — All men and societies insist on their rights. Disputes, lawsuits, and wars are undertaken in order to protect real or imaginary rights. Less, perhaps too little, is heard about the correlative of right, namely, duty, and we are more prone to assert our rights than to think of our duties. As a substantive, *a right is the moral power which a person has to do, omit, or exact certain things*. Duty corresponds to right. Whenever a man has a right, others have the duty to leave him free in the exercise of it. *Duty*, therefore, *is the moral obligation to do or omit certain things.*

A right is called a *moral*, not a physical, power. Yet rights may be exacted; and the power of coercion, especially by legal authority, is a consequence of the moral power. Duty is also a *moral* obligation, not a physical necessity. Man is free to fulfil it or not. A right is *inviolable*, i.e. even if another man fails to respect it, it nevertheless remains; for instance, stolen property continues to belong to the original owner.

2. **Division of Rights and Duties.** — (*a*) Rights are:

I. (1) *natural*, i.e., resulting from human nature itself, and the essential order of things; hence they are equal in all men. They are the rights
- (*a*) *to be*, i.e. to life and the necessaries of life.
- (*b*) *to do*, i.e. to the free exercise of one's faculties within due limits.
- (*c*) *to have*, i.e. to the possession of the means of living.

(2) *acquired*, e.g. the right to own a determined property, to exact certain work from a hired servant, to exact wages for one's labor, etc.

II. (1) *absolute*, which involve duties on the part of all other persons, e.g. the right of ownership of a certain property.
(2) *relative*, which involve duties only on the part of some, e.g. the rights of parents with regard to their children, of a buyer with regard to the vender, etc.

III. (1) *real*, i.e. to possess a thing already acquired.
(2) *personal*, i.e. to acquire a thing by compelling a person to give it.

In the former case, the object is mine, in the latter, I can force a person to do certain things in my behalf.

(*b*) Duties are:

I. (1) *positive*, when they command what must be done.
(2) *negative*, when they forbid what must not be done.

N.B. Many duties may be expressed in both a positive and a negative way. Positive duties bind to act in such or such a way only at the time for which the action is commanded. Negative duties oblige at all times. For instance, it is never lawful to steal, whereas a man is not bound to give alms all the time. Negative duties are more elementary; they simply forbid evil. Positive duties command to do good.

II. (1) *natural*, based on natural rights.
(2) *positive*, depending on positive laws.

Note the two meanings of positive, one opposed to negative, the other to natural.

III. (1) *personal*, toward self.
(2) *social*, toward others.

IV. regarding (1) *external* goods (property).
(2) *bodily* goods (e.g. life, health).
(3) *spiritual* goods (e.g. truth, dignity, freedom).

N.B. The duties toward God, which are the most important, should occupy the first place here. As, however, they suppose some knowledge of the nature of God and of the relations of man to God, it will be more convenient to speak of them in Theodicy.

3. **Relations of Rights and Duties.** (*a*) *In the same person*, right and duty are intimately connected. A right is generally based on a duty, and man has the duty before he has the right. In other words, the reason why man has rights is that their exercise is necessary to fulfil certain duties. Thus the rights of parents are based on their duty to educate their children; the rights of civil authorities are based on their duties toward society, etc. All rights are based on the fundamental duty of every man to reach his rational end.

(*b*) *In different persons*, right and duty are correlative, in such a way that a right is prior to the corresponding duty, since the duty is the obligation to respect the rights of others. To all rights correspond duties. To all duties do not necessarily correspond rights in the strict sense, but only to duties based on justice. Thus it may be my duty to give alms, yet another man has not, on this ground, any right to my property, nor can he, for instance, exact it before the courts.

(*c*) Rights are *subordinated*, not opposed. Hence in the case of apparent conflict, one predominates, namely, the stricter — e.g. life compared to property; the more extensive — e.g. social compared to individual good; the clearer — e.g. parents have a clearer claim to be helped by their children than strangers. The same is true of duties. Sometimes they seem to be opposed and cannot be fulfilled at the same time. In this case, their relative value or excellence and their extension must be considered, and the more important must prevail. Thus moral is to be preferred to temporal good, life to riches, etc.

4. **The Subjects of Rights and Duties** are only persons, i.e. intelligent and free agents. Rights and duties suppose a capacity for moral obligation and moral power. Hence, strictly speaking, animals have no rights, and man has no duties toward them. However, man owes to himself and to his reasonable nature to treat animals according to their nature, not to ill-treat them or make them suffer uselessly, etc.

The two following articles will deal with personal and with social ethics.

ARTICLE I. PERSONAL ETHICS OR DUTIES TOWARD ONESELF

Existence of Duties toward Oneself

1. **Has Man any Duties to Fulfil toward Himself?** — (*a*) Since man is obliged to act in conformity with reason, and to respect in himself the dignity of the moral person, he is obliged to use his faculties in the manner which reason dictates. As Kant expresses it, he must treat human nature, wherever found, as well in himself as in others, as an end, not as a means.

(*b*) Some duties toward others suppose duties toward oneself; for instance, unruly passions like anger, intemperance, sloth, carelessness, are obstacles to the fulfilment of duties of justice and charity toward others.

(*c*) The objection that man, being identical with himself, cannot be obliged toward himself has no value, for man is bound always to act reasonably. Nor can man renounce all his rights, as some of these are essential, and to renounce them is to renounce his own reason. Nor, finally, can it be said that man, by failing in his duties toward himself, injures himself alone, and is at liberty to do so. On account of the law of solidarity among members of a society, on account also of heredity, scandal, etc., the harm of one member is also the harm of others. Moreover, the neglect of duties toward self tends to make man incapable of fulfilling duties toward others, as was said above. Finally, the moral law does not merely forbid to injure oneself, it commands us to perfect our own nature. It may be added that these duties are closely related to, and based on, man's duties toward God, for man owes it to God to make good use of the faculties received from Him.

2. **Basis of These Duties.** —The primary root of man's duties toward himself is the duty of *self-respect*. *Self-love* is a natural fact which cannot be eradicated; but self-love must be according to reason. Man is a very complex being, and he must love in him-

self that which is loveworthy, and in the relative degree in which it is loveworthy. "Charity begins at home" is a very ill-used proverb, yet it is true that, unless we first know, revere, and perfect human nature in ourselves, we shall never do so in others.

I. DUTIES REFERRING CHIEFLY TO THE MIND

I. Personal Dignity

1. **Self-Respect.** — (*a*) By his reason, will, and freedom, man is superior to other beings. He must always keep in mind this dignity, and not lower himself, nor suffer himself to be lowered, to their level. Hence self-respect will always make man place duty before pleasure, reason before the senses, and the will before the lower appetites and tendencies. It will prevent him from being arrogant and proud, and from exacting from his fellowmen more than is due to him, and even from claiming every possible advantage and pleasure which he may think himself entitled to. It is in conformity with human dignity to forbear and overlook a great many things. This shows better man's mastery over himself. But there is one thing which it would be against his essential dignity to surrender, namely, the right and freedom to perform his duty, whatever it may be. This right, man must vindicate against all who would prevent its exercise.

(*b*) Due self-respect and self-esteem will proceed from *self-knowledge*. Cicero says: "Illud Γνῶθι σεαυτὸν noli putare ad arrogantiam minuendam solum esse dictum, verum etiam ut bona nostra norimus" (Epist. ad Q. Fratrem, III, 6). Self-knowledge makes man aware of what is respectworthy in himself, chiefly his moral nature, and prevents him from lowering or allowing anybody to lower his human personality. At the same time it prevents him from glorying in small advantages which neither come from him nor add anything to his real worth. Pride and vanity not only cause men to place their dignity in those advantages in which it does not consist, but tend to make them "trust in themselves and despise others," and thus neglect in others the esteem due to their human dignity. Bodily advantages, wealth, dress, etc., should be of small importance to a man who knows himself and his true value. Both in yourself and in others, respect and esteem the human person. Humility is truth, and while making man aware of his own weakness, failings, and defects, it must not make him forget his prerogatives.

2. **Honor and Reputation.** — "A good name is better than great riches" (Prov. xxii, 1). Man must be jealous of his honor and good name. He must not do anything that would lessen the good opinion others have of him. We speak here of true honor, that is, of the homage due primarily to genuine excellence, secondarily to old age, excellence, authority, etc. We do not speak of the worldly praise bestowed too often on external and vain advantages. Frequently the sense of honor degenerates into a base human respect which makes one pay undue attention to prejudices and fashions, and even, in consequence, omit what is known to be one's duty. At times human judgments are based on appearances, wealth, etc., while the real value is overlooked. Hence too much attention is not to be paid to the opinions of men. Perhaps a man will not be honored when he deserves it, but he must be honorable. His endeavor, according to St. Thomas, must be "ut studeat facere ea quae sunt honore digna, non tamen sic ut pro magno aestimet humanum honorem" (Summa Theologica, II-II, Q. 129, Art. 1 ad 3).

II. Intelligence

1. **In General.** — Since intelligence is a fundamental prerogative of man, and on it depends his whole reasonable conduct, it is important to cultivate it, both negatively and positively. *Negatively*, by avoiding everything that would tend to obscure it and prevent its legitimate exercise, like the undue influence of passions or imagination. *Positively*, by exercising the intelligence, developing habits of attention and reflection, and acquiring the science of general duties common to all men, and of duties special to every man's vocation. All men need not and cannot have the same instruction, but all men must know (1) the general duties of all men toward God, themselves, and their fellowmen, (2) the special duties incumbent upon them on account of their

condition in life, e.g. the duties of a lawyer, physician, professor, etc. The more a man knows, the better able he is to discharge his obligations, and be useful to his fellowmen. (Cf. p. 133 ff.)

2. **Veracity, Sincerity, Intellectual Honesty,** must always be practiced. Man ought not to deceive others, still less deceive himself, by his imprudence and temerity. Avoid temerity in assenting, dissenting, and doubting; in thinking and reading. Above all, avoid stifling the voice of conscience, and making up your mind that your action is right and legitimate simply because you want to perform it.

As to veracity toward others, it is not necessary in every case to speak the whole truth, still less to try by all possible means to make one's opinions prevail, but dissimulation and lying make a man abominable in the eyes of others, and should make him abominable in his own eyes. On this duty more will be said later.

3. **Prudence** is essentially an intellectual virtue which enables man to know where his true interests and those of others are to be found. It supposes habits of deliberation, discernment, and rectitude of judgment. It excludes rashness and precipitation. The greater the interests at stake, the more prudent should one be in finding out the means to safeguard them. Intuitions of genius are rare. In most cases the rule is that man does not at once see the path to be followed, but has to reflect, consult, and deliberate. Little by little the mind acquires habits of perspicacity, sagacity, and sound judgment. The subordination of interests is always to be kept in mind, so that lower interests will be subordinated to higher ones. (1) Prudence makes man foresee. It is not enough to see present advantages or disadvantages. Attention must be given to consequences so as to compare the present with the future, and, later on, to have no occasion to be sorry. (2) Profit by every experience, happy or unhappy, so as to compare the present issue with past success or failure.

III. Will

The will must always follow reason, hence avoid precipitation and obstinacy. It is above the senses, the passions, and the imagination, hence let it guide and rule them. Its main prerogative is freedom, hence it must not allow itself to be enslaved by external surroundings and human respect, nor by internal influences like passions and lower tendencies. (Cf. p. 185 ff.)

1. **The Will must be Strong.** — The coward who fears to assert himself when duty requires it, and has not enough courage to follow the dictates of his conscience, is despicable if his weakness is voluntary, and worthy of pity if it is not voluntary.

(*a*) *Courage* is necessary not only to the soldier on the battlefield, nor is it the exclusive virtue of some classes of men; it is necessary everywhere, since everywhere there are duties to perform, and obstacles to overcome in order to fulfil these duties. To resist corruption and bribery, to attend to one's duties notwithstanding perhaps the attacks and mockery of others, to resist the temptation of human respect, to acknowledge one's mistakes and wrongs, to watch constantly and resist energetically the lower tendencies of human nature, in a word, to proceed manfully along the path of duty in spite of all contrary influences, requires courage at every instant, a courage which is not the result of a transitory impulse or of the hope of glory, but of a calm deliberation, a determined will, and strong moral habits. In every condition of life, courage and strength of will are indispensable.

(*b*) Courage is needed also, not merely to act, but to suffer. *Patience*, *equanimity*, and *strength in adversity* are signs of a strong mind. The will must strive to create better conditions, but the inevitable cannot be remedied. The will shows courage in accepting it with resignation.

(*c*) *Perseverance* in spite of difficulties is an enduring courage, both in action and resignation. Courage and perseverance are not obstinacy. If a man comes to see that he is wrong, his duty is to come back to the right path, and, at times, this also may require an uncommon courage.

2. **Moderation and Equality of Temper** are signs that the will controls the lower tendencies. Irascibility and passion show that man is subject to, and ruled by, them. Exuberant joy in prosperity and depression in adversity indicate the undue influence of external circumstances on the will.

Temperance, both in its most general sense as the avoidance of every form of excess, and in its more special application as the avoidance of excess in drinking, is an indispensable virtue. Nothing is more degrading to man than the abuse of intoxicating beverages which ruin his health, obscure his mind, weaken his will, are sources of innumerable evils both individual and social, and lower him to the level of the lowest brute. "Principiis obsta," for, chiefly on account of the physiological effects of alcohol, the habit of excess is easily contracted. Gradually a need is created which soon becomes too strong for the will. "Moderation in all things" should be the principle guiding all men, since lack or excess are opposed to the dictates of reason.

3. **Self-Control.** — All the duties concerning the will may be reduced to mastery of and control over oneself. The man who is even-tempered, whom prosperity, favor, praise, and success do not blind or make proud and arrogant; whom adversity, contradiction, and failure do not make impatient, angry, or discouraged; the man who tries to overcome all obstacles that oppose his progress on the road of duty; the man who truly possesses his own soul and mind and is his own master, this man is truly great and worthy of the admiration of all.

IV. Conclusion

1. **Realization of a Moral Ideal.** — One must have a high moral ideal, and constantly keep it before his eyes. It will be realized, or at least approached, by constant effort and work. Work, mental or bodily, is both a pleasure and a necessity, and the idle man is a danger to himself and to society. Idleness lessens the will's strength, and leaves it unprepared for the time of struggle. Like tools which become rusty for lack of use, the faculties become dull for lack of exercise. All men have duties to fulfil, and to fulfil them requires work and effort. In themselves all useful works are noble, and all occupations, intellectual or manual, praiseworthy. The first place must be given to necessary work, then to useful work, and finally leisure may be employed in agreeable work, in healthy and becoming recreation which rests the mind and the body, and prepares them for further labor.

2. **Self-Examination.** — It is necessary for success to keep business accounts. It is no less necessary to keep ethical accounts. Know how you stand with regard to your duties and resolutions; verify your gains and losses so as to repair mistakes and prepare the future. Examine your conscience frequently, and always strengthen your will more and more by new resolutions and by fidelity in keeping them. Know your principal defect, and courageously lay the axe to the root of the tree. Resist your evil habits, and endeavor to contract only those that are praiseworthy. Know yourself, and always keep your eyes turned on the feelings and desires of your heart.

Thus by constant attention in cultivating his faculties and perfecting his nature will man rise higher and higher, and enjoy the happiness which comes from the satisfaction of fulfilling his duties, and from the feeling that he is truly the master of all that is in himself.

II. DUTIES REFERRING CHIEFLY TO THE BODY

These duties do not refer to the organism independently of the mind, but in so far as the organism is the necessary condition of life, and therefore of the fulfilment of all duties. Health, strength, and life are valuable as instruments of the human person. Duties referring to the body are negative or positive.

I. Negative Duties

The chief negative duty of man is to avoid taking his own life by suicide.

1. **Suicide** is direct and intentional self-murder committed on one's private authority. We say "direct and intentional" to indicate that the natural result of the action is the destruction of life, and that, in fact, no matter what reason or motive one may have, such is the purpose for which the action is performed. Hence it is not suicide for a man to endanger his own life when there is a sufficient reason to do so, or a higher duty to fulfil. The soldier on the battlefield, the physician treating contagious diseases, the man who exposes his life in order to save that of another, do not

directly kill themselves, but indirectly, by exposing themselves to danger. Nor do they intend to do away with their lives, but they have in view the good of their country and of their fellow-men, which requires this sacrifice. In some cases this sacrifice is obligatory, namely, when required by one's strict duty. In other cases it is praiseworthy, and may be an act of heroism. Suicide, instead of proceeding from noble feelings of self-sacrifice on behalf of others, generally proceeds from egoism, fear, weakness, and false honor. It has been excused by the Epicureans, the Stoics, and some modern philosophers, as at least a remedy against the evils of life. When life becomes unbearable, they say, man is at liberty to renounce it.

2. **The Reasons Against Suicide** are of two kinds. Some may be used as arguments *ad hominem* because they are suited to the frame of mind and principles of certain individuals. Others are more fundamental and apply to all men. Among the former may be mentioned the following. For the Christian, this life is but a preparation for a future endless life. Man must not pay too much attention to the transitory sufferings of this life which are means of purification for his immortal soul. Moreover, man is not the master of his own life. It belongs to God who gave it to him, and reserves for Himself the right of life and death. He has assigned a post to every man, and man has no more right to abandon it than the soldier has the right to abandon the post assigned to him by his superiors. Frequently, also, suicide may be shown to be an act of cowardice; the motives that prompt to it may be proved to be valueless, and the need which others have of one's life may be pointed out.

The following reasons apply to all. (*a*) The natural wish to live, which is experienced by all, prevents man from committing suicide as long as life is enjoyable. Suicide is committed in order to avoid shame, misery, or suffering of some kind. But to leave man free to take his own life in such cases is to constitute him a *judge in his own cause*,— and no man can be a good judge in his own cause — and therefore permit suicide whenever, for any reason, a man is tired of life.

(*b*) Man's life has a *moral purpose*, and the moral law is absolute and categorical. Suicide withdraws man from all these duties, and therefore makes the moral law merely hypothetical; it commands if man does not choose to shirk its obligations. Man thus fails to respect in himself the moral person; he makes it a mere instrument; a thing instead of a person.

(*c*) To commit suicide is to *injure others*, for it is a bad example; it deprives society of one of its members who might still be useful, were it only as an example of courage, patience, and resignation.

The main reasons against suicide are derived from religious considerations, as God positively forbids it. Those we have just given will be made clearer by answering the main objections.

3. **Objections.**—(*a*) Suicide is a courageous action.—*Answer.* In reality it is cowardice, for it is a sign that man lacks strength and energy to bear the trials and difficulties of life. The suicide avows himself vanquished since he abandons the struggle.

(*b*) Life is miserable; sufferings are too great; the disease is incurable, or the failure irretrievable. In short, life is an unbearable burden for the individual and for society.—*Answer.* The purpose of this life is not immediate happiness. Moreover, suffering is made intolerable largely because it is thought to be so. The patience of a number of men amid the greatest and most excruciating pains and afflictions shows that, with courage, everything is possible. As St. Paul wrote (II Cor. vii, 4): "I exceedingly abound with joy in all our tribulation." And such patience is always a great edification for others, while for the sufferer it is a source of moral perfection.

(*c*) Death is preferable to shame.—*Answer.* Suicide adds another shame to the former. If a man has done nothing wrong, the testimony of his conscience is enough, and life will give him the means of proving his innocence. If he has committed some blameworthy action, life will be an expiation, and will enable him to give an example of repentance and of effort toward a better life.

(*d*) Man may desire death, therefore he may cause it.—*Answer.* It is true that in some cases death appears as a deliverance; but as the soldier may wish to be relieved from a certain duty, and yet is not free to leave it, so man cannot, on his own authority, renounce his own life.

4. **The Main Causes of Suicide** are: (1) *Insanity*, perpetual or temporary. The mind may be so disturbed as to lose its freedom. This insanity make take the form of despondency and melancholia, which deprive the mind of energy; or that of exaltation and passion, which blind the mind and deprive it of the power of reflection. Ordinary dispositions and character, temperament, nervous diseases, as well as other special circumstances, may lead to suicide. A good moral education of the intellect and the will, a physician's care, bright surroundings, healthy exercise and distraction, sound advice and encouragement, will be useful to do away with ideas of suicide. (2) A *sensual life*, which looks for present happiness, prefers it to duty, and makes man too weak to bear disappointment and suffering. (3) The *example of others*. Suicides, especially sensational suicides, when published, are generally followed by others. It becomes like a contagious disease. Avoid sensational reading.

To counteract these, religious and moral education showing the true value of life both in its present and future aspects, the cultivation of the will by the practice of true virtue and courage, will prove auxiliaries.

5. **Self-Neglect.** — For the same reasons for which suicide is immoral, any mutilation of the body and unjustified danger of death are also forbidden. Hence temperance, sobriety, moderation, etc., are duties based on the duty of self-preservation. There are cases, however, where it is necessary to remove a part of the body in order to save life; and there are circumstances in which the temporary loss of reason, e.g. by the use of anæsthetics, is also necessary. The body is the instrument of the soul, and must be treated as such, i.e. preserved in its integrity and normal condition unless the higher interests of life require that a part of it be sacrificed. Nor is this duty opposed to the discreet and prudent use of mortification and austerity by which the will is strengthened, and the spirit of self-renunciation and self-sacrifice is acquired. A little violence to one's natural inclinations, even if they are not bad, prepares man for the greatest acts of virtue.

II. Positive Duties

1. **Care of Life.** — Man must not only avoid whatever would injure his health, he must also preserve it by hygiene, cleanliness, exercise, etc. He must take ordinary care and precaution when sick. Extraordinary means, such as very expensive cures or dangerous operations, are not obligatory. Two extremes must be avoided: (1) excessive care and fear, which make one indulge in every little comfort, and dread the slightest privation and inconvenience; (2) excessive carelessness and negligence, which make one abuse one's strength by intemperance, privation of sleep, unnecessary exposure to heat and cold, etc. In all things, the body is to be treated according to its nature, as inferior to the mind, and as an instrument which must serve the mind, but also as the mind's auxiliary, and as the condition necessary for the mind to fulfil its duties.

2. **External Appearance.** — What is true of the health of the body is true also of its external appearance. Extremes are to be avoided by the practice of modesty and moderation. If neglect, carelessness, and lack of cleanliness are to be avoided, to put one's pride in external advantages and ornaments is no less to be blamed. The mind manifests itself in these details. Show that yours is orderly and careful, yet withal simple, unostentatious, and that its first care is for internal beauty and nobleness, in which man's real worth consists.

ARTICLE II. SOCIAL ETHICS OR DUTIES OF MAN TOWARD OTHER MEN

Existence and Nature of These Duties

1. **In General.** — Man does not and cannot live alone. From his necessary intercourse with his fellowmen a great number of duties arise, some toward all men in general, others toward members of the same group or society. The former may be called social duties, social indicating a special reference to all men. It is better, however, to refer to them as duties toward individual men

irrespective of the various groupings, and to reserve the term "social" for duties that arise from such groupings. Since all men have the same essential nature, all have the same essential rights. Too often man is inclined to look upon himself as a privileged person, insisting on his own rights and on the duties of others, forgetting that he must also consider their rights and his own duties toward them. These duties may be summed up in the two fundamental maxims: (1) "Do not to others what you would not have them do to you." (2) "Do to others what you would have them do to you." These two maxims are but the application of the Christian precept: "Thou shalt love thy neighbor as thyself."

2. **Justice and Charity.** — (*a*) The first maxim refers especially to duties of justice. *Justice* is the respect of the strict rights of others, and rests on the equality of all men. The duties which it commands are chiefly *negative*, and *determined:* "Thou shalt not injure thy neighbor" is their general expression. They forbid any action which would be against the rights of others, and hence are strictly binding, always, in every case, and toward everybody; and as a consequence they can be exacted.

(*b*) The second maxim refers especially to duties of charity, which rest on the community of nature of all men, and on human brotherhood. *Charity* consists in helping others and giving bodily and spiritual assistance. Its duties are chiefly *positive* and *indetermined*. "Thou shalt help thy neighbor" is their general expression. They prescribe some action, but do not oblige always, nor in every case, nor toward everybody; and as a consequence, they cannot be exacted. For instance, justice forbids killing or stealing; charity commands to help a sick man and to give alms. In the former case, I am forbidden to be an obstacle preventing my neighbor from exercising his essential rights. In the latter, I am bound to help him although he has no strict right to exact this help from me or from any determined man. I must pay my debts exactly and at the appointed time. There is no fixed amount or time for my obligation of giving alms. However, as noted already, the same duty may be both positive and negative from different points of view. I am obliged to pay a debt (positive action) because I must not keep my fellowman's property (negative). Moreover, there are also positive duties arising from justice, and negative duties arising from charity.

(*c*) Distinct though they are, justice and charity are in close relation. Charity supposes justice. Before helping others, it is necessary to do them no harm; a man cannot steal in order to give alms. A strict and determined obligation comes before a general and indetermined one. Even in the exercise of charity there may be some kind of justice or equity; certain persons, e.g. members of the same family, have a special title to be assisted in their needs. On the other hand, justice is not complete without charity. Strict rights should not always be exacted, because in some cases other men's rights would thereby be injured. Thus for the rich man to refuse food to the hungry, or for the employer to exact too hard or too long a labor from the workingman, is a real injustice. Justice must always be tempered by equity, which, before applying the strict rights of justice, considers all circumstances of time and person. In this sense Cicero quotes the axiom: "Summum ius, summa iniuria" (De Officiis, I, c. 10). To be strict to the extreme in matters of justice is to become unjust.

It may be noted that what is a duty of charity for one may be a duty of justice for another on account of his special position. An ordinary man is not bound in justice to prevent a criminal from wrong-doing, but this is the strict duty of the policeman.

3. **Love.** — (*a*) "He that loveth his neighbor hath fulfilled the law" (Rom. xiii, 8). We do not speak here of the special love due to some individuals who are "nearer" or more strictly "neighbors" than others (cf. p. 151), but of the love due to all men in general simply because they are men having the same nature as ours, and moral persons enjoying the same prerogatives. Hence this duty extends even to enemies, because of their human nature with its inalienable rights, though not in the sense that we must love their depravity or offences. The love of others excludes hatred and the spirit of revenge, although a man may by lawful means seek redress for the wrongs he has suffered. It also excludes scandal, bad advice, and in general whatever would lead others to harm themselves in any manner.

(*b*) There are several *degrees of love*. 1. *Negative:* (1) Not to return evil for good, i.e. not to be ungrateful. This is the minimum and the lowest degree. (2) Not to injure those who have not injured us, i.e. to avoid injustice and cruelty. (3) Not to return evil for evil, i.e. to avoid vengeance; a man's wrong-doing is not excused or justified by that of others. — All these duties refer to strict justice. 2. *Positive:* (1) To return good for good — gratitude. (2) To do good to those who have done us neither good nor evil — charity and benevolence. (3) To return good for evil. It is the most sublime degree of virtue. — These duties refer to charity.

I. DUTIES TOWARD INDIVIDUAL MEN

These duties may refer to their persons and personal faculties, or to their property.

I. Duties Toward the Person of Others

1. **Life.** — The first right of man, and the condition of all other rights, is the right to live. Hence the taking of human life on one's private authority, and apart from the necessity of self-defence, is always an injustice.

(*a*) This does not apply to the killing of another man *by public authority*, as in the case of the executioner, or of soldiers during war. If the state has the right to inflict the death penalty and to protect its rights by war, it also has the right to the necessary means. The individual acts as the agent or instrument of public authority.

(*b*) In the case of *self-defence*, the principle: "Prima sibi charitas" may be applied. As public justice would be too late in protecting my life and property, I may protect it myself, provided the two following conditions be verified: (1) There must be actual danger. If the danger is passed, there is no longer self-defence, but homicide and vengeance. (2) The violation of the rights of others must be as limited as possible. Whatever is not necessary is unjustified; it is intentional wrong-doing. An adversary who can no longer do any harm because he is wounded or without power, ought not to be killed. This right of self-defence extends — in justice — not only to the protection of life, but also to that of great interests, fortune, freedom, or property; and — in charity — to the defence of others.

(*c*) *Duelling* is the meeting of two parties in order to fight with weapons apt to kill, after a private agreement as to the time, the place, and the weapons. The motive of duels is generally to avenge an insult. But this reason has no value whatever, and a duel is a most unjust and unreasonable action. It can decide at most which of the two adversaries is the more skilful or the stronger. It can never decide on whose side right and justice are found. It is an act of vengeance, which makes of justice a private affair, and constitutes a man a judge in his own cause. It exposes him to the danger of suicide by exposing his own life without reason, and to that of homicide by exposing himself to the danger of killing another on his own authority.

N.B. What has been said of the life of others applies also, in varying degrees, to any action by which their body would be injured, or their health impaired.

2. **Dignity and Freedom.** — The respect for essential human dignity forbids any action by which others would be deprived of the legitimate use of their freedom.

(*a*) *Slavery*, which makes of man the thing or property of another in such a way that the master may dispose of his slave as he pleases, and almost without any restriction, is against morality. It lowers man to the level of animals, and even of inanimate tools, deprives him of his essential dignity, and prevents him from being a truly human person.

(*b*) Man has the *right to work*, to choose his own profession, exercise it, and enjoy the fruit of his labor, since work is but the extension and product of his own faculties.

(*c*) *Conscience*, which applies in every case and for every man the laws of morality, must not be violated. In things which are not otherwise against the rights of other men, or against public order, the individual is entitled to freedom of conscience. He may be shown that he is mistaken, but, after due investigation, the voice of his conscience is for him, and must be for others, sacred.

(*d*) *Freedom of thought* cannot mean that human intelligence is free to accept anything as true or false as it pleases, but that man has the right to use his faculties in order to discover the truth, to examine the foundation of his beliefs, and to stand by his conclusions. It even implies the spreading of his opinions by publication. But this right is limited, because certain opinions, even if adhered to honestly and *bona fide*, would be injurious to society, for instance, when they encourage immorality or excite to crime directly or indirectly.

3. **Honor and Reputation.** — Man has a right to his honor and reputation. *Honor* is based on excellence, and hence varies with individuals. The same marks of honor are not due to a stranger and to a high public official. Yet to all men some honor is due. *Reputation* or good name is acquired. Hence, although some honor is due to a stranger, he has no reputation with those by whom he is not known.

Detraction, which reveals the real defects and faults of a man to those who do not know them, and *calumny*, which falsely attributes defects or faults to others, are opposed to the right which all men have to their reputation. Calumny is never lawful. In some cases, and for serious reasons, it may be justifiable to reveal the real wrong-doings of others, e.g. for the sake of good order, to preserve the innocent, etc.

Rash judgment is against both the good use of our faculties and the rights of others to our good opinion of them. A little reflection will suffice to convince man that many of his judgments concerning others are without sufficient basis, and therefore rash, for man is ignorant of all the subjective conditions which influence the conduct of others. Only by one who would know all the hidden motives and springs of action could an equitable judgment be passed. Nobody can determine how far another man is personally responsible for his actions, and how much must be attributed to his surroundings, education, native disposition, and in general to circumstances that do not depend on him. This should make man very careful in judging, and especially in expressing unfavorable judgments.

4. **Truthfulness.** — (*a*) Man owes it to himself and to others to speak the truth. *To himself*, because it is a disorder to use words that express ideas contrary to those that are present in the

mind. *To others*, because social relations and contracts are impossible if man is allowed to lie. A man may deceive others in good faith when he is himself mistaken. This is not a lie; to lie is to speak intentionally against one's mind.

(*b*) The obligation to speak the truth does not always imply the obligation to speak the whole truth. *Discretion* is also a necessary virtue, and frequently a man would be wrong if he told all he knew. Things are to be kept secret (1) on account of their *nature*, when their revelation would be injurious to others, and when the person whom they concern is known to be opposed to their manifestation; (2) *by promise*, when the engagement has been taken not to reveal a certain imparted information; (3) *by trust*, when the information is given only on the expressed or implied condition that it will not be communicated. Such are professional secrets, e.g. of lawyers and physicians. All secrets must be kept unless there should be serious reasons, proportionate to the nature of the case, which make it obligatory to reveal them.

(*c*) Whenever a man speaks untruly without being questioned he is guilty of lying. He also lies when he deceives those who have the right to know the truth. But, for good reasons, the truth may be concealed by giving the questioner to understand that we are not at liberty to speak, or by using expressions which are understood by all. Thus a servant answers that his master "is not at home," meaning that he is not at home to receive visitors in general, or this visitor in particular. Expressions even more misleading may be used if the circumstances justify it. In the conflict of two rights, the right of my neighbor not to be deceived, and my right to keep a secret, the former must yield, since, as we suppose, my neighbor has no strict right to know the truth, whereas I have a strict duty to keep a secret. But in all things acquire habits of rectitude and truthfulness. You may not say everything you think, but generally let everything you say be the true expression of your thought.

II. Duties Toward the Property of Others

1. **Fact of Ownership.** — (*a*) Men look upon certain things as their property (*proprium*, one's own exclusively). They claim and

exercise the right to use these things and dispose of them as they please. This right is called the right of ownership, and the limits of its exercise are determined by the natural laws of justice and charity, and by civil laws such as those concerning contracts, wills, etc.

(*b*) Ownership is *private* or *public* according as the property belongs to the individual or to the community (municipality, state, nation). Public property is sometimes used for specified purposes and by certain individuals only (e.g. certain public buildings and offices). Sometimes the free use of it is allowed to all (e.g. streets, parks).

(*c*) Private ownership extends to whatever is useful or pleasurable and capable of being appropriated. It does not extend to those things which are necessary to all and the supply of which is sufficient for all, like air, the heat and light of the sun, etc. *Objects of ownership* may be reduced to (1) natural products, independent of man's industry (e.g. fruit, fish, game); (2) the products of labor and industry (e.g. machinery, manufactured articles); (3) mixed products (e.g. domestic animals, vegetables in a garden, land which is improved by culture). From another point of view the objects of ownership are either non-productive, when they are owned simply for the enjoyment which may be derived from them; or productive (capital), when they are used as means of production.

As a matter of fact such objects have been appropriated; whether justly or not remains to be seen.

2. **Socialism.** — It is needless to speak of the extreme views of communism according to which not only should private ownership be abolished, but the state should have perfect control of everything, including labor, religion, social relations, marriage, etc. Such theories are commonly abandoned to-day, even by the adversaries of private ownership, whose views are generally included under the general term of socialism.

But it is very difficult, not to say impossible, to give a definition of socialism because of the many forms which it takes. In general it is *the tendency to reduce individualism* and to increase the rights of the community *in matters referring to ownership*. It denies all or some forms of private ownership. In general it allows it for objects that are non-productive, e.g. books, pictures, food and drink, etc. On the contrary, capital, that is, all means of production, such as mines, canals, railroads, mails, telegraphs, land, machinery, factories, etc., should be owned collectively, and managed by the rulers of the community. Some, however, would allow the private ownership of everything except land.

Thus primarily socialism advocates economical reforms. But in many instances, it has also advocated moral and religious reforms, and manifested unequivocal hostility to Christian beliefs and practices. With these extreme views we have nothing to do at present.

3. **Foundation of Private Ownership.** — The following rights are natural to man, and must always be respected.

(*a*) Man has a strict right to the necessaries of life, not only for the present, but also for the future. (1) Sickness and want may come, and old age will certainly come. The prudent man foresees and prepares the future in a stable and permanent manner. (2) Moreover, the healthy man's work is not always actually remunerative. Time is required for planning, trying, and experimenting. During this interval it is necessary for man to have the means of subsistence. To permanent needs must correspond permanent resources. (3) Finally, progress requires a certain freedom from need, and even from the care concerning the means of living. Frequently the best works of art "don't pay," and even the most useful inventions are not recognized at once. Happiness requires some leisure and freedom. If following always one's own good pleasure is not the highest ideal, the other extreme, doing always what pleases others, is still farther from giving satisfaction to human aspirations.

(*b*) What is true of the individual is true also of the family. Man must not only provide for himself, but for his wife and children. To this end he needs property which he can keep permanently and of which he can dispose.

(*c*) Any theory of property must safeguard these rights. It seems evident that some kind of private ownership is required, since otherwise man does not obtain the full value of his labor, laziness and crime are encouraged, and it becomes impossible to provide for one's own welfare. This is commonly accepted by moderate socialists, who admit the private ownership of commodities, but reject the private ownership of capital. The question thus becomes chiefly a social and economical problem which cannot be discussed at length here. Only a few indications will be given.

4. **Discussion.** — By *capital* is meant any source of wealth and any means of production. That the state may own some of these goes without saying. The state owns land. Monopolies are restrictions of the rights of individuals to manufacture and sell certain articles. Whether, how far, and in regard to what articles state-monopoly is expedient is a question to which no general answer can be given, as expediency varies with times, places, and conditions. But the question is whether all means of production should be common property administered by the state authorities.

(*a*) ***With regard to production***, better care is taken of what is one's own than of what is common property. More labor will be given, and greater diligence will be used by the individual, if the products are to remain his own than if they are to be shared in common. The hope to turn again the fruit of one's labor into new capital is a great incentive to work and application. Capital is generally transformed labor. It is a surplus which the individual does not need, and which belongs to him as the product of his own faculties. Competition, notwithstanding its disadvantages, serves a good purpose in stimulating activity and inventiveness.

(*b*) ***With regard to consumption and distribution***, common ownership is open to many objections. Will the products be divided among all equally, or according to merit, or according to need? (1) Equality will tend to make man lazy. Moreover, it seems unjust to treat all men alike, whether they be diligent or careless. (2) On the other hand, who will pronounce on respective merits and needs? Here the door is open to innumerable abuses. How can the merits be estimated? On the quantity or the quality of the work? In both cases there will be dissatisfaction.

(*c*) ***With regard to the work to be done.*** Some kinds of work are agreeable; others disagreeable. Some are looked upon as noble;

others as menial. How will it be possible to give satisfaction to everybody? There is too much room for discrimination and favoritism.

(*d*) The same arguments apply to *land*. Even if it is not totally the fruit of labor, it has been improved by labor, and of itself would produce very little. In many cases land has been acquired with one's earnings. It must also be noticed here that the common right to live does not mean the right to the same means and mode of living. It is true that ultimately everything necessary to life comes from the land, but man can live without actually owning any land, for he can procure its products by exchange.

5. **Conclusion.** — (1) In conclusion we may note that socialism tends to lessen individual freedom. (2) If the exclusive right of ownership is unjust, socialism, which advocates state-property, is also unjust. Even then property is held exclusively by a certain group of men, and the same inequality which socialism seeks to remove recurs on a larger scale. Logically socialism leads to the abolition of national ownership. (3) Finally socialism supposes falsely that, according to the doctrine of private ownership, the rights of owners are unlimited, that the owner can use, misuse, and abuse his property. It insists on present social evils which cannot be denied, but suggests an extreme and dangerous remedy, worse perhaps than the evil itself. Inequality and dissatisfaction will always be found, and perfection is not attainable.

Moreover, it is important to distinguish between (1) getting rich by making others poorer, e.g. by theft, open or concealed; (2) getting rich without changing the condition of others; (3) getting rich while helping others, e.g. manufacturers, railroad companies. Laws must be made to prevent the first of these modes, which is strictly unjust, and to protect the interests of the working classes. Present conditions may be bettered by wise legislation and by the prudent intervention of the state. Owners must be reminded of their duties of justice and charity. Generally a sound view is to be found between extreme and radical theories.

6. **Main Rights and Duties of Proprietors.** — (*a*) *Rights:* (1) To give, exchange by contract, and bequeath by will. This right is not unlimited, but restricted by the natural laws of justice and

charity, as well as by civil laws enacted for the common good. (2) To exclude others. Hence theft, open robbery, fraud, cheat, are against justice. (3) These rights must be exercised according to reason, and with due respect for the rights of others.

(b) *Duties:* (1) All men have a strict right to live. Hence in case of extreme necessity they may appropriate what they strictly need, and this help cannot be refused without injustice. (2) In labor contracts both parties must stand by their mutual agreement. The workingman must respect his employer's person and property, and use diligence in fulfilling his duties. The employer must give a just salary to the workingman, respect his human dignity, and consequently give him necessary rest, as well as the time and opportunity to fulfil all his duties. (3) Charity commands almsgiving and beneficence. (4) Those who are rich and influential are more strictly obliged to give good example.

II. SOCIAL DUTIES

Society in General. — (a) Social duties result from man's condition as a member of society. As understood here, society is the permanent union of several men working together to reach a common end. (1) Members of the society supply the capital, will, energy, activity, etc., necessary to the common purpose. (2) The permanence that is required varies with the different kinds of societies. A mere fortuitous meeting and coöperation do not constitute a society. (3) The community of end brings about the union, but this union cannot subsist without some authority which will preserve it, prevent abuses, keep the members together, and give to all a uniform direction. Without it, individual members could never coöperate effectively.

(b) Societies differ: (1) According to their *origin*. They are natural when required by human nature itself, like the family; conventional when based on a free agreement, e.g. a scientific or industrial association. (2) According to their *purpose*. They may be religious, moral, scientific, benevolent, commercial, etc. (3) According to the *mode of union*. They may be based on justice, when the members have strict rights, e.g. partnership, insurance companies, etc.; or on merely friendly or charitable relations, when the union can be broken without injustice because the members have no strict rights.

Here two societies only deserve our attention, the family and the state, which are natural societies. The others are more arbitrary, and depend on special free agreements.

I. The Family

1. **Nature.**—(*a*) Sometimes the term "family" denotes a group or succession of persons connected by blood relationship, and includes even distant relatives and ancestors. It may even be restricted to a distinguished and ancient lineage. Properly it means a natural group of persons consisting of parents and children, especially children who still live with their parents.

(*b*) A family is constituted by *marriage*, i.e. by a contract which unites a man and a woman for the special purpose of raising children. (1) Marriage is a union contracted freely, to which neither party is compelled. (2) In most civilized countries marriage is contracted between one man and one woman. Polyandry or plurality of husbands is not practised. Polygamy or plurality of wives is recognized in a few nations, but is opposed not only to peace and harmony in the family, but to the dignity of the woman, who is bound where the man is free.

(*c*) Marriage is a *lasting* and *permanent* union, for both parents are necessary to the welfare and education of their children. *Divorce*, however, is not strictly, essentially, and in all cases, opposed to the essential purpose of marriage. (1) Indissoluble marriage is better, and almost indispensable for the nurture and education of children. (2) The possibility of divorce suggests the adoption of the means necessary to secure it. (3) Most domestic troubles would be adjusted if divorce were impossible. Marriage would not be looked upon as so light and easy an affair, nor contracted so carelessly. (4) Divorce is a source of dissension among families; it lowers the sense of duty and responsibility.

N.B. Looking at marriage as a sacrament under the legislation of the Church, absolute divorce with the freedom to marry again is unlawful.

2. Duties of the Members of the Family. — (*a*) *Duties of married persons.* (1) *Before marriage* great care must be taken by them to know each other well, and not to be prompted by mere motives of passion. They must also preserve their health and purity, and do nothing which they would be ashamed to have the other party know. (2) *After marriage* they must keep the mutual faith which they have pledged to each other. Disguised or secret polygamy is an injustice for both the husband and the wife, who have the same rights. They also owe to each other mutual love and assistance. The husband, because he is stronger, contributes more to the material means of living and to the protection of the family. He is the head, but must remember that the wife in her household duties, does a work equally essential, that she is not a slave, but a companion equal in rights and dignity. Finally, husband and wife must always keep in view the essential end of marriage and do nothing that would be opposed to it.

(*b*) *Duties of parents.* Children require the care of their parents for their physical, mental, and moral development. Hence the natural duties of parents are to give to their children the necessaries of life, instruction, moral and religious education. They must remember the importance of good example and of the early education of both the intelligence and the will. On these the child's future depends. The authority of parents decreases as the child grows older and better able to guide and direct himself.

(*c*) *Duties of children.* Children owe their parents (1) love, respect, and gratitude; (2) obedience, except where the command would be opposed to morality and the dictates of conscience; (3) help and assistance in their need. Moreover, duties of charity bind children of the same family among themselves in a special manner.

II. The State

1. Nature. — (*a*) *Obvious facts.* (1) Men live in certain groups determined by territories with natural or conventional limits, by community of language and of interests, etc. (2) Some of these groups are under the same government. They vary in size, population, and form of government. (3) A state is one of these groups, with a certain number of men, in the same territory, and under the same authority.

(*b*) *Explanation of terms*. The Greeks used the word πόλις for both the city and the state. (Cf. "policy," "politic," and derivatives.) The Roman "civitas" was the body of citizens, and also the city as the nucleus of the state. (Cf. "citizen," "civil," and derivatives.) The *res publica* referred to the good of the state in general, and did not, like our term "republic," mean a special form of government distinct from monarchy. (Cf. the English term "commonwealth.") To-day the term "state," which originally means any condition, is appropriated to mean the political organization, and chiefly those who exercise authority. "Nation" refers to all aspects of the state's collectivity, and "people" to the persons living in the same state. These terms, however, are frequently used for one another. Other terms like "empire," "kingdom," "republic," "country," "land," "fatherland," have a more restricted meaning.

(*c*) *The essential elements* of a state are: (1) A plurality of men and families, the number of which varies greatly. (2) A unity and cohesion under the same common authority and with the same organization. (3) A fixed territory. Nomadic peoples are not — or rather were not — perfect states. (4) Independence and freedom in administration and government. Colonies are not perfect states, and, as in our Republic individual states have only a limited autonomy under the same constitution and the same federal authorities for points determined by their mutual agreement, the "United States" is the true and perfect state and nation.

2. **Origin.** — Without discussing at length the various theories concerning the origin of civil society, it may not be without interest and utility to mention briefly the most important.

(*a*) Hobbes, in England, and Rousseau, in France, are the most conspicuous advocates of the theory according to which the origin of civil society is not to be sought in human nature itself, but in a free agreement or *social contract*.

Starting from the principle that the end of man is pleasure and happiness, and that every man is the judge of what makes him happy, Hobbes infers that man has a natural right to whatever is conducive to happiness. Hence all men have natural rights to all things. This necessarily creates an antagonism, or "the war of every man against every man." Such an individualism is natural to man, and the state of society is against nature. This condition, however, being an obstacle to happiness, men, by mutual agreement, surrender their rights and establish a power which must be strong enough to paralyze individual forces. Hence the stronger, the more extensive, and the more absolute the power of the state, the better will it be able to fulfil the purpose for which it was instituted. Thus are justified the most absolute despotism and tyranny which man can no longer resist or change, since he permanently renounced his rights.

According to Rousseau, all men are equal by nature, and no man has the right to command another. Society which supposes superiors and inferiors cannot therefore be natural. It originates from a free contract by which men surrender their individual rights to a common authority constituted, not necessarily by all men unanimously, but by the majority. Hence Rousseau's conclusion is diametrically opposed to that of Hobbes: Authority is binding only as long as the individuals want it. What the majority has done it can undo at will, and the state is complete and absolute democracy.

(*b*) What is to be thought of these views? (1) *Historically* they are *gratuitous* — for there is no record of such a contract; and false — for history shows that man, at all times and everywhere, lived in society, and traces back the state to an extension and a development of the family. (2) The *assumptions* of the system are either *contradictory* or *impossible*. Thus the right of every man to everything amounts to the negation of rights, since a man cannot have a right unless other men have the duty to respect it. That all men are born equal is true only if we speak of an equality of nature; but is there equality of health, intelligence, will, capacities, power, etc.? That all men are born free is true of psychological freedom, not of moral freedom. The very nature of man imposes duties on him. (3) *Such a contract is impossible*, or rather invalid, both because the parties did not know the extent of the obligations which they were assuming, and because, in order to be binding, a contract supposes at least some general duties of justice, and the general obligation of abiding by contracts. But this is impossible if, as it is claimed, the social contract is the principle of all determined rights and duties. (4) The *consequences* of the system are either despotism (Hobbes), or anarchism (Rousseau).

(c) *To live in society is natural to man*, i.e. required by man's very nature. (1) At all times, history shows man living in society. (2) Social organization is needed for the complete physical and mental development of the individual. Otherwise the individual and the family are left to their own private resources, which are uncertain and frequently insufficient. In other words, human progress requires organization, diversity and subordination of functions, analogical to those which take place in the human organism. (3) Freedom, far from being destroyed by the social organization, is really preserved. Without such an organization, the weaker is at the mercy of the stronger; his life and property are insecure. (4) The social feelings of love, sympathy, etc., manifest the nature of man. Progress and civilization in their various aspects result from combined efforts.

3. **Civil Authority.** — (a) As civil society is natural to man, so also is civil authority, for there can be no organization without a directive power. The persons in whom such authority will be vested are designated by the community. The methods of designation and of transmission of power vary with the different political constitutions, the power being sometimes hereditary, sometimes elective. The people are not the government, but simply indicate those who will govern.

(b) There are *three elementary types of government:* (1) *Monarchy*, when the authority resides in one man. (2) *Aristocracy*, when it resides collectively in several citizens. (3) *Democracy*, when all the citizens take a more or less direct part in the government. These elementary forms may be combined in varying manners and degrees. Absolute monarchy has disappeared from the civilized world. The monarch's power is limited by a constitution, and by parliaments composed of the people's representatives. Every one of these forms has its advantages and disadvantages, and consequently it is impossible to determine universally which is the best. It depends on the aptitudes, aspirations, traditions, etc., of the various nations.

(*c*) The government includes the *legislative power*, i.e. the power to make laws; the *executive power*, which enforces these laws and takes the means to have them respected; the *judicial power*, which applies the laws to particular cases and punishes the offenders. (See the Constitution of the United States.)

4. **Functions and Rights of the State.** — (*a*) *The function of the state* is twofold: (1) To protect the rights of individuals and families by imposing the respect of these rights, determining them when they are uncertain, and settling the various conflicts of rights. (2) To help and promote public interests in the intellectual and the economic order.

(*b*) *The state has the rights* necessary to the exercise of these two functions, namely, the rights: (1) *To impose certain conditions* respecting contracts, sales, wills, etc., and to make other regulations for the public good; to settle disputes, e.g. between capital and labor; and to determine and protect the rights of all. (2) *To promote public welfare* by encouraging private enterprises, and by undertaking what is impossible for individuals, e.g. roads, canals, etc. (3) *To help parents* in the fulfilment of their duties referring to the physical, intellectual, and moral education of their children. (4) *To punish all infractions* of laws by inflicting just penalties, proportionate to the gravity of the offence, and capable of protecting society. As far as possible penalties must be of such a nature as to deter others, repair the wrong caused, and give the offender chances and opportunities to amend. Whether or not the death penalty is advisable depends on how far it is necessary to prevent crime. (5) *To protect the rights of the whole nation by war*. But war being a duel of nations, the same objection already given against the duel applies here also. War manifests the strength, wealth, and military organization, not the moral right or wrong, of a nation. Moreover, the harm done by war is incalculable, and for this reason, war, especially offensive war, is not to be undertaken except for the gravest reasons. It is to be hoped that some other means of settling international disputes will soon be universally agreed upon.

(*c*) What are the *limits of the rights of the state?* How far must it allow individual liberty? This question cannot be given an answer applying to all nations. It must vary with the circumstances, traditions, degrees of civilization, modes of government, and a number of other influences. What would be looked upon as tyranny in one nation may be the wisest course in another.

5. **The Rights and Duties of Citizens** are especially the following:

(*a*) *To obey laws* and respect the authority of those whose duty it is to enforce them. A law is for the common good, and enacted by those to whom the people themselves have delegated the legislative power. The only exception is for obviously unjust and tyrannical laws.

(*b*) *To pay taxes.* The state needs resources to protect the rights and freedom of the citizens, and to foster their welfare.

(*c*) *To show their patriotism,* both in time of peace and in time of war; to love and revere the flag which is the emblem of the nation.

(*d*) *To take part in government affairs* as much as the constitution allows; hence, in a democratic state, to vote for worthy officers and representatives.

Although, in general, obedience is due to civil authority, resistance becomes lawful when the government is habitually tyrannical and unable to fulfil its functions. However, there must be a chance of success, and all possible moderation is to be used. A government which is no longer fit to fulfil its mission, which destroys instead of building up, is no longer for the good of the people. (Cf. Declaration of Independence of the United States.)

CONCLUSION

The faithful fulfilment of all his duties increases man's moral worth. Acting according to the dictates of his conscience cannot fail to make man better. This increase constitutes essentially what is called *merit*. Merit is also frequently used to mean the right to the retribution due to good and to bad actions. The degrees of merit vary in proportion to (1) the importance of the duty which is fulfilled and of the good which an action realizes; (2) the difficulty of the duty and of the effort which it requires; (3) the intention of the agent. Thus it is more meritorious to sacrifice oneself for common than for private interests; to give alms out of pure charity than out of vanity; to resist a strong passion than to do good without effort, etc. It is more blamable to kill than to hurt a man; to hate one's parents than to hate strangers; to fail in one's duty through malice and wickedness, than to do so out of weakness and human respect, etc.

Virtue is the habit of acting according to the dictates of conscience. It is not merely an external appearance, but an intrinsic reality. It does not make man act well "in order to be seen by men," but out of respect for the moral law; not because otherwise he would be punished, but because the dictates of his conscience are higher for him than anything else. The moral law extends farther than the civil law, and governs even the hidden motives and secret thoughts. The virtuous man does not ask himself whether human justice can and will reach him. He simply acts according to what he knows to be his duty. Virtue is susceptible of progress, and, since the noblest prerogative of man is his moral nature, his highest ambition should be to become greater, worthier, more and more perfect, and to be instrumental in helping others toward the same end.

From what has been said in psychology and in the present treatise, the student will easily infer the importance of giving an early attention to the moral nature of man, and the most important means by which this should be done. The facts of imitation and example, the influence of early impressions, the necessity of consistency between a man's principles and his conduct, cannot be insisted upon too strongly. The good should not only be known, but loved and practised. Let every man work constantly; effort strengthens the will and increases the energy. Let the effort be generous; it cannot fail to bring its reward.

EPISTEMOLOGY OR THE THEORY OF KNOWLEDGE

INTRODUCTION

I. THE NATURE OF EPISTEMOLOGY

1. **The Aim of Epistemology.** — (*a*) Among the various manifestations of conscious activity psychology numbers cognitive processes, and examines their nature and development. Logic deals with the rules to which such processes must conform in order to avoid contradiction and reach valid conclusions. But neither psychology nor logic touches upon the question of *the relation of ideas and judgments in the mind to the reality of things outside the mind*. Both remain confined within the mind itself. They do not examine whether knowledge, which they assume to be objective, is so in reality; whether, how far, and under what circumstances we may be said truly to know extramental objects; whether the facts and principles which are looked upon as true are anything but a dreamlike mental play, a product of our own faculties, springing from the very nature of our minds; whether, in other words, we do not know things as *we* are rather than as *they* are.

(*b*) Both in the course of ages as well as at the same period of time, the ceaseless contradictions of men on almost every point of science and philosophy, the changes of opinion that take place in the same mind and on the same subject, the numerous illusions of both senses and intellect, the influence of a multitude of circumstances, especially of intellectual surroundings and education, on all our judgments, arouse in the mind the suspicion that perhaps knowledge in its totality, not only needs a thorough revision, but is only an illusion of the mind that mistakes for objective realities that which is merely subjective. *The purpose of epistemology is to ascertain the validity of knowledge and the conditions of this validity.*

2. **The Term "Epistemology."** — Etymologically, epistemology (ἐπιστήμη, knowledge or science, and λόγος, speech or thought) means the science of knowledge, i.e. the part of philosophy which deals with the value of human knowledge. It is also called the "Theory of Knowledge," "Criteriology," or "Critical Philosophy," because its aim is to criticise the faculties of knowledge and to indicate the signs or criteria of valid knowledge. The names of "Applied," "Material," or "Critical Logic" are unsatisfactory because logic, as understood to-day, deals exclusively with the formal laws of thought. Nor is epistemology to be identified with metaphysics. It is rather an introduction to metaphysics which studies reality in order to determine its true nature. Epistemology completes psychology and logic, and leads into metaphysics, since the value of knowledge can hardly be examined without saying something on the objects of knowledge. Here epistemology will be treated as a transition from the subjective to the objective world.

3. **The Importance of Epistemology** can hardly be overestimated, although, as a special science, it is of comparatively recent origin. Partial discussions are found in older philosophers, but Locke is the first clearly to state the problem, and Kant the first to attempt its solution on epistemological and critical principles.

In the beginning of philosophical speculation, as well as in the beginning of the individual man's cognitive life, knowledge in general is accepted as valid without any discussion. Soon, however, contradiction, error, conflicts of opinion, the necessity of discarding as worthless some assents formerly looked upon as valid, lead the mind to compare, test, and revise these assents. If what was thought to be a truth is later on proved to be an error, it becomes necessary to find out whether there is any kind of knowledge which is certainly valid, and what are the tests of valid truths. This is the fundamental problem of epistemology and the basis of every investigation, rational or religious. That opinions change on a great number of points is undeniable. A truth for one is an error for another. A truth at one time is an error at another time. Does everything change? Are there truths the assent to which is and always should be unanimous? If so, what are they?

II. FACTS AND PROBLEMS

I. Facts

All men desire to know, but not the same things, nor through the same means; there is no man whose curiosity is not frequently aroused, and who is not eager to see, hear, understand, obtain information, reach the truth, do away with doubt and perplexity. In order to be understood, this fact supposes some definitions of truth and certitude — not final and forever settled definitions; this is impossible now — but definitions of the terms as commonly understood by all men.

1. **Truth.** — The term "truth," clear as it may seem at first, is difficult to define, and has several meanings. Thus we say of a man that he is a true orator; of a metal that it is true or genuine gold; of a man that he knows the truth, i.e. that his ideas correspond to reality and are such as they should be; of a man that he is truthful, i.e. that he speaks according to what he thinks. We are thus led to distinguish three kinds of truth, every one of which consists in *the relation of something extramental to something mental.*

(*a*) *Moral truth*, referred to in ethics, is the conformity of the expression with the thought. We need not stop to consider this meaning.

(*b*) *Ontological truth* is a relation of conformity between a thing, as existing outside the mind, and the representation of it in the mind. True wine is for me what I consider as essential to wine, namely, a certain composition, certain properties, etc. True gold is a substance corresponding really to the definition given by the physicist. I may mistake an adulterated product for wine, or another metal for gold, or an imitation for a precious stone. The error will be in the mind, yet the thing itself will be truly what it is.

(*c*) *Logical truth* is the conformity between the subjective or mental representation and the objective reality or ontological truth. Thus, if adulterated wine is offered as true or genuine, and I accept it as such, my judgment is false; if I recognize it as an adulteration, my judgment is true. If I believe that true gold is only an imitation, I am mistaken; if I admit its genuineness, I judge truly.

(*d*) Thus *ontological* truth resides primarily *in things; logical* truth, primarily *in the mind*. The former, however, implies the comparison of a concrete object with something mental, namely, with a definition, an abstract type, and certain characteristics conceived by the mind as essential. The latter implies the comparison of a concrete idea with things themselves as known, for instance, by the manufacturer in the examples given above. A true photograph or statue represents faithfully the features of the original; a true Murillo is a painting which is really the work of this artist; true wine is really made of grapes, etc. True in this sense may be synonymous with such terms as genuine, original, faithful, etc. It always implies that a thing is what it should be when judged according to a certain mental standard or ideal, which, of course, may vary indefinitely. A true judgment is one that corresponds to the fact or the thing as it is. Thus I buy a picture as a true Murillo, and if it is so in reality my judgment is true.

(*e*) *The epistemological problem* goes farther than these simple facts. Epistemology investigates whether our standards themselves have anything objective, and how much; whether what we conceive as true is in reality what it seems to be. Soluble or insoluble, this problem has been raised and must be examined.

(*f*) From what has been said it follows as a conclusion that both forms of truth consist in a certain *conformity between external things and the mind*, a relation which goes from things to the mind in ontological truth, and from the mind to things in logical truth. Primarily ontological truth is found in things; logical truth, in the mind. With regard to the logical truth contained in a given judgment, mental attitudes vary greatly and include many degrees of confidence or distrust. The assent or dissent may be more or less firm and stable. There may be certitude or incertitude. In other words, the attitude of the mind varies.

2. **Mental Attitudes.** — (*a*) Before a question or fact is presented to my mind: "Is it so or not so?" I am in the state of complete *ignorance* concerning such a question or fact. "I don't know," and I am not even aware of my ignorance on this special point, since, in order to be aware of it, I should at least be aware that such a question or problem may be raised.

(*b*) As soon as the question is asked, I may have no reason to affirm or deny; I answer again: "I don't know." Properly speaking, this is *negative doubt*, frequently also called ignorance, the state of a mind totally ignorant of the reasons pro and con, and hence unable to give any assent owing to the lack of evidence on both sides.

(*c*) Reasons may be given in favor of one alternative, which would sway the mind in this direction, were it not for reasons equally strong on the opposite side. As it is, reasons pro and con balance each other, and again the same answer is given: "I don't know." Although I do know a great deal, perhaps even all that can actually be known on the subject, I cannot give my assent either to the affirmation or to the negation. This is *positive doubt*, a state of suspense because the mind is unable to pronounce on account of the equal weight of reasons for the opposite alternatives.

(*d*) The reasons on one side may clearly outweigh those on the other. The latter, however, retain some force, and, when I give my adhesion to the former alternative, it cannot be an unlimited and perfectly secure adhesion. I may answer that "I know," but, strictly speaking, I should answer that "I think it is so," or that "I believe it." This is *opinion*, the state of a mind assenting to a proposition (which is called probable), knowing that the opposite proposition has also good reasons in its favor, and, in consequence, fearing lest the judgment it pronounces be erroneous. Frequently this will be expressed by saying: "I think so, but have some doubts about it."

(*e*) Finally, I may see the truth clearly and evidently. There are no reasons against my adhesion, or these reasons have lost their value so completely that they can in no way influence my assent. Now properly I say: "I know it is so," or "I am certain and sure," "It is beyond doubt." This is *certitude*, the state of a mind assenting unreservedly, fearlessly, without thinking that it is possible for it to be mistaken.

3. **Various Kinds of Certitude.** — (*a*) I say that "I am certain," and also that "Something is certain." "Certain" applies both to the mind or subject, and to the proposition or object. Thus a first distinction is to be made between *subjective certitude* or simply *certitude*, and *objective certitude* or rather *certainty*. Compare the three statements: "It is true"; "It is certain"; "I am certain that it is true," and see their relations.

(*b*) I may be certain either spontaneously or after mature reflection. Hence certitude is *direct* or *reflex*. Reflex, philosophical, or epistemological certitude is the certitude to be examined here, for reflection changes many spontaneous certitudes into incertitudes. Frequently spontaneous certitude is hardly a certitude at all, but an assent which may be changed readily. Thus I have no doubt about the news which I read in the morning newspaper, although I am ready to disbelieve it if denied in another paper, or in a later issue of the same paper.

(*c*) Certitude is *immediate* or *mediate* according as it is obtained immediately — as when I say: "This is my friend John," because I see him; or mediately — as when a conclusion is reached through a process of reasoning.

(*d*) Finally, certitude, although always excluding the fear of error, has *various degrees* according to the nature of the objects to which it applies. All objects are not capable of the same evidence, and, in a long series of reasonings, the evidence may become less and less clear. I may be certain, on the one hand, that two and two are four, that the whole is greater than any one of its parts, or that the man I see is John; and, on the other, that a personal God exists, that Napoleon campaigned in Egypt, or that honesty is the best policy. Yet, owing to the nature of the mental processes by which I know the truth of the latter propositions, I feel that there is a difference in the assent given to them, and the assent given to the former.

4. **How the Epistemological Problems Arise.** — As a fact, spontaneous certitude must be accepted. It is the natural

tendency of the mind. Doubt arises only later through reflection. But is certitude justified? Such is the question suggested by many facts equally certain, and already mentioned in Psychology and Logic (pp. 117 ff. 256 ff.). Whatever is mental depends on many psychological variations due to heredity, education, environment, etc. We think as we are, and, to a great extent, we are what circumstances and surroundings have made us. What is truth for one individual is error for another; and what is accepted at one time of life is rejected at another time. Even the senses, on which the whole mental life depends, are subject to illusions, and always depend on the physiological conditions of the organism. Defects of vision, such as color-blindness, long or short sightedness, etc., prevent a man from seeing things as others do. Certain diseases, drugs, or conditions will change the trend of mental life, and affect assent and dissent, certitude and incertitude. Hence arise epistemological problems.

II. Problems

Since, in many known cases, the mind is certain where it should not be, is it not so in every case? Since frequently it tinges reality with its own coloring, does it not always do so? Since the subjective mingles so closely with the objective, is not all knowledge subjective? And where shall we stop? Where and how shall we draw the line between the objective and the subjective? We distrust the man who has deceived us several times. Should we not distrust our faculties that have also misled us? It may be the very nature of the mind to represent things as it does, and to picture them, not as they are, but after its own fashion. Even the normal mind, apart from external influences, always mixes its own activity with objective reality, and in a proportion which cannot be determined. What we are aware of is always a mixture of subjective and objective elements, and, in a mixture, the proportion of the elements cannot be determined unless the elements are known separately. Here we know only the total result, or combination of the two elements. The object can never be known except in the subject.

(a) The first question then is: *Does reflection justify certitude?*

Is man capable of certain knowledge? In a general way, dogmatism answers, "Yes," scepticism, "No," while agnosticism endeavors to define the limits of the knowable beyond which lies the unknowable.

(*b*) This leads to a second problem: *Which certitudes survive the scrutiny of reflection?* If there is any valid knowledge, how can it be acquired, and what kind of knowledge is valid? The data of experience alone are declared valid by empiricism, while the claims of reason are urged by rationalism.

(*c*) Strange as it may seem to have postponed this question so far, we have now to ask: *What is knowledge?* Since knowledge as a mental function is within the mind, yet with a peculiar essential relation to some extramental reality, it becomes necessary to examine the value of this representative aspect. Idealism claims that it is merely the result of the mind's inner activity, while realism admits some external reality which is reflected in the mind. And, if such an external reality exists, what can be known about it? What is the relation between the idea in the mind and the thing outside?

(*d*) Even if knowledge — some knowledge at least — is valid, since error is also undeniable, how will truth be distinguished from error? How shall we ascertain which certitudes are justified? *What are the signs or criteria of truth?* Such systems as intellectualism, mysticism, pragmatism, traditionalism, etc., offer different answers.

Before studying these problems, a few words on the method to be followed are necessary.

III. METHOD

1. **Positive Starting-point.** — (*a*) Epistemology starts with *the obvious fact of spontaneous certitude*, which cannot be denied. By a critical and reflective analysis it endeavors to find out if this certitude is legitimate. Unless we start with this fact, no solution can ever be reached. But we neither affirm nor deny that this certitude is valid, or that our mind can reach objective truth. Nor do we pretend to investigate whether the mind can know things-in-them-

selves, as they are in reality, and apart from their mental representations. First to isolate the mind from external reality, and then ask how it can nevertheless come in contact with this reality, makes the problem forever insoluble.

(*b*) Hence Locke's principle that "knowledge is conversant only about our ideas" is opposed to facts. *Knowledge is essentially representative.* The idea imposes itself as the idea of some reality. Knowledge becomes conversant with ideas later, by reflection. For any unprejudiced mind, *knowledge is conversant primarily with external things.*

(*c*) To speak of things-in-themselves, i.e. apart from the ideas we have of them, is nothing short of an absurdity, since evidently the mind can only reach things-in-the-mind, i.e. things as represented. As the Scholastics so often repeat, knowledge, being an act of the mind, partakes of the nature of the mind: "Cognitum est in cognoscente ad modum cognoscentis." The idea is one thing; the object represented is another; but the object is never reached by the mind except through the idea. Hence the question is whether the idea, though conforming to the nature of the knowing mind, conforms also to the nature of the known object, or whether, on the contrary, it is a mere mental product.

2. **Descartes' Universal Doubt.** — (*a*) In order to examine the problem of certitude, Descartes begins by emptying the mind completely of all that it had formerly accepted as valid knowledge. Reflecting that we are frequently mistaken, he rejects every form of knowledge as uncertain, so as to be sure that the mind, being emptied of all its contents, will be free from every source of error. This universal doubt, it is true, is not real, final, or sceptical, but methodical. It is an expedient in order to find a safer basis for certitude. This basis Descartes finds in the undeniable fact that he thinks and therefore exists: "Cogito, ergo sum."

(*b*) This method has for its most serious defect that *it makes any subsequent certitude impossible.* In fact it is only through a glaring inconsistency that Descartes emerges out of his doubt. Like everything else, the fact of thought may be a dream, and the necessary connection between thinking and existing may be illusory. How in fact can such a necessity be asserted without assuming the principle of contradiction which, with every other principle, has been rejected by Descartes? Consistent thinking can never take place without supposing the laws of thought. If the facts of thought and personal existence lawfully emerge out of a universal doubt, a number of other facts have the same right, because their evidence is no less clear. And if the necessity of the connection between existing and thinking is admitted, a number of other necessary principles must also be accepted. As it is, Descartes' method necessarily goes around in a circle (circulus in probando).

Starting then from the obvious fact of spontaneous certitude, we shall examine successively the problems mentioned above.

CHAPTER I

IS CERTITUDE JUSTIFIED?

The fact has already been pointed out that a distinction is to be made between the spontaneous or natural certitude of the mind and its reflective certitude which persists even after its value has been tested. Reflection may show that the mind was mistaken, and that assent has to be refused to propositions to which it had been given formerly. More frequently it will be found that former certitudes are only opinions; truths, only probabilities. Generally speaking, mankind is misled, not by too much doubt, but by too much certitude, or rather by states of mind which man spontaneously calls certitude, and which even a summary analysis reveals to be only more or less firm opinions, accompanied by a great deal of doubt. Both for speculative, and chiefly for practical, truths, man has to be satisfied in the majority of cases with assents that fall short of perfect certitude, and that may be called either highly probable opinions, or perhaps "moral" certitudes. Assents are morally certain when they are warranted by sufficient evidence, although there is some very remote possibility of their being given wrongly. Thus opinion gradually merges into certitude, and no strict line can be drawn between them.

The questions to be examined now are not: Of what truths can we be certain? Are they many or few? Which certitudes are justified? and the like; but simply: Is the state of mind called certitude ever justified? Can we be certain of anything? Strictly speaking, only two answers can be given: (1) "Yes," and (2) "No"; or rather, since even a negative answer implies the certitude of the impossibility of certitude, (1) "Yes," or "No," and (2) "I do not know." For the present we shall speak briefly of Scepticism, Agnosticism, and Dogmatism, but many questions referring to these systems will necessarily have to be left over for subsequent chapters.

I. Scepticism

1. **Meaning.** — (*a*) The many uses of the terms "scepticism," "sceptical," etc., make it almost impossible to give any definition of them. I call a man sceptical when he does not believe my present assertion of which I am certain. Again I call sceptical a man who is generally hard to convince, requires strict proofs, and discusses every point before he gives his assent. I also call sceptical the man who says that nothing is certain, disbelieves everything, is inclined to disregard the opinions of other men, and is generally ready to answer "I don't know," to every question.

(*b*) Etymologically, "scepticism" is a Greek word (*σκέψις*, doubt, from *σκέπτεσθαι*, to look at carefully, to scrutinize), which even in philosophy has more than one meaning. In general it is opposed to dogmatism, and denotes the doctrine denying the aptitude of the mind to reach truth, or at least to be aware that it has reached it, so that *no certitude can be justified.*

(*c*) Theoretically, we may imagine a man who professes to be certain of nothing, not even of his existence, of the first principles of reason, of the distinction between the state of sleep and the state of wakefulness, nor of his own doubt. This, however, is merely an abstract supposition. The existence of such out-and-out sceptics seems impossible, and no instance justifies it historically. As it presents itself in history, scepticism is only relative. It admits some facts and principles as certain, otherwise thought and speech are utter impossibilities. The very fact that sceptics argue, discuss, and write, shows that they pretend to know something, were it only that knowledge is not possible. Scepticism, however, is distinct from agnosticism. The latter admits the validity of some forms of knowledge, but draws a strict line beyond which everything is unknowable. The former attacks knowledge and certitude in general, and tries to show the incapacity of all cognitive faculties, senses as well as reason.

2. **Historical Outline.** — (*a*) The Sophists, especially Protagoras and Gorgias, point to the contradictions of earlier philosophers,

and reach the practical conclusion that, in regard to any question, both the negative and the affirmative answers are equally plausible.

(*b*) Pyrrho professes that real things are inaccessible to human knowledge because, on the one hand, the senses manifest only appearances, and on the other, reason rests on custom, habit, and education. Hence man must abstain from pronouncing on anything. To abstain from defining and judging (ἐπέχειν) will give peace to the mind (ἀταραξία), and hence true happiness.

(*c*) Arcesilaus and Carneades also reject the possibility of knowledge and certitude, but admit that some probability, sufficient in practice, may be attained. Since, according to them, the criterion of truth is perception, and perception may be irresistibly false, it follows that unreserved assent must always be refused.

(*d*) The main school of scepticism is that of Alexandria, with Ænesidemus, Agrippa, and Sextus Empiricus, who systematize scepticism, and, under the name of tropes, classify the reasons leading to doubt. All conclude that assent should always be withheld. Scepticism proper is restricted almost entirely to Greek philosophy. Elsewhere doubt assumes a special character, and applies only to certain forms of knowledge.

3. **Criticism.** — Nothing could be said to a man whose answer to every question would be: "I don't know." A common ground which is indispensable for every discussion could never be found. It may be added that any such sceptic could be placed in constant contradiction with himself, both in his practical life and in his theoretical views. The man who knows nothing has no right to think or speak. Finally, as the fact of spontaneous certitude is undeniable, it suffices briefly to examine the objections of scepticism against the validity of knowledge.

(*a*) *Fact of error.* It is certain that sometimes man mistakes falsity for truth, and adheres to error with the same tenacity with which he adheres to truth. Both the senses and reason are sources of transitory or permanent error.

Answer. — To this it may be answered that *error supposes truth.* Since these two ideas are correlative, if nothing is true, nothing is false. If sometimes man recognizes that he errs, it is a sign that sometimes also he knows that he does not err. From the fact that we sometimes err nothing can be inferred, except that we should be prudent in affirming and in giving our unreserved assent.

The same is true for *probability*. It is a participation of, or an approach to, certainty; and the certainty of some propositions is the only ground for affirming that others are more or less probable. Thus the certitude that a bag contains more red than white balls is the only ground for affirming that the probability of drawing a red ball is greater than the probability of drawing a white one. There could be no participation if there was nothing to be participated in, no justifiable probability if there was no justifiable certitude.

(*b*) *Facts of contradictions and of the diversity of human opinions;* in space — different contemporary individuals; in time — succession of opinions; in objects — science, politics, religion, morality, etc.; in the same individual — changes in his views. All are convinced that they possess the truth, yet it is certain that some do not, since contradictories cannot be true at the same time.

Answer. — (1) *There is agreement* on certain general truths, principles, axioms, and facts. Thus men have in common the perceptions of color, solidity, etc. All are certain of their own existence and of the immediate data of consciousness. All admit some principles of reason; for instance, all look for the causes of whatever happens (principle of causality). There is also agreement on many points of abstract sciences, e.g. of mathematics. (2) As stated elsewhere, on many questions, especially in practical matters, we have to be satisfied with *more or less probable opinions*. Contradictions are more numerous in proportion as these questions are more complex and more influential on practical life.

(*c*) *Diallelus*, or *Circulus in Probando*. The reliability of human faculties cannot be proved except by using these same faculties whose validity is still doubtful. Some reason must be given for admitting the value of human faculties. This reason itself, since it proceeds from the same faculties, must rest on another reason, and so on *ad infinitum*.

Answer. — (1) *This argument leads to absolute and universal scepticism*, which is absurd. The sceptic uses his reason to prove the weakness of reason, and hence also supposes its validity. To be consistent, he must doubt even his own doubt. (2) *The objection assumes wrongly that demonstration is the only source of certitude.* Demonstration is only an indirect means of throwing light on a hidden truth. Where there is full light, such a means is unnecessary. While most propositions do not at first clearly appear as true or false, others have in themselves the stamp of truth or error, which is obvious to all men. It must be admitted that the reliability of human faculties cannot be proved, but it need not be. In some cases the use of them is its own justification.

II. Agnosticism

1. **Meaning.** — (*a*) Like the term "scepticism," the term "agnosticism" is vague, and applies to different views and systems. Etymologically it means the attitude of one who does not know (α and γνωστικός), and thus would denote something even more radical than scepticism, since the sceptic is simply one who "examines." As used to-day, however, agnosticism is a milder term than scepticism, and, whereas scepticism is looked upon as a term of reproach, many pride themselves on being called agnostics.

(*b*) The term "agnosticism," coined by Huxley in 1869, has been applied to the views of thinkers whose opinions were and are greatly at variance on many points. The feature common to all is an attitude of doubt or denial toward certain objects of knowledge. The agnostic assigns *limits* to the mind's knowing powers, beyond which lies an unknowable region. There is light up to a certain point *which can be determined*, and beyond which the human mind finds itself in complete darkness. *The recognition of some unknowable* seems to be the essential feature of agnosticism. But the dividing line between the knowable and the unknowable occupies different places according to different agnostics.

(*c*) Thus, in its mildest form, agnosticism joins hands with gnosticism — this term being taken here in its etymological signification — since every man must confess that many things are beyond the human grasp. The man who says: "I do not know," and chiefly, "I cannot know," or, "Nobody can know," assigns limits to human faculties of knowledge. The agnostic goes farther.

He has found the exact boundaries of the realm of the knowable, and the range of human faculties. Beyond the knowable objects there are others which the mind cannot reach.

(*d*) For all agnostics, that which is primarily unknowable is the Absolute, the First Cause, the unconditioned Reality, God. Hence sometimes agnosticism has been identified with atheism. Yet they are distinct. An agnostic, Spencer for instance, may admit the existence of the Absolute, although he denies the mind's power to know its nature. Frequently also agnosticism coincides with positivism and empiricism. It admits the value of empirical science, and denies that of every form of metaphysics.

2. **Critical Remarks.** — A thorough criticism of agnosticism would include the whole of epistemology, together with metaphysics and theodicy. Here we shall limit ourselves to a few remarks of a general nature.

(*a*) The agnostic attitude is attractive on account of its *apparent humility*. In reality it includes a *great presumption*, that of determining exactly how far human reason can go. There is some humility in saying: "I do not know," but it is quite different to say: "It is unknowable."

(*b*) In fact, how can one say of a thing that it is unknowable without having made a comparison of it with the capacity of the human mind, and therefore without having already *some accurate knowledge*, not only of the mind's power, but also of the object which is supposed to transcend this power?

(*c*) Can we know the *existence* of a thing, and at the same time be utterly ignorant of its *nature?* Do not the facts by which it manifests its existence necessarily manifest also something of its nature? The same mental processes used in natural science will necessarily lead higher into metaphysics. The knowledge of physical causes will lead to the First Cause, and so on.

III. Dogmatism

1. **Meaning.** — (*a*) As understood here, dogmatism is opposed to scepticism, and means the system that admits some principles or facts as certain, or more generally, *the possibility of certitude.* In a more restricted sense, which is in frequent use, dogmatism

applies to systems or assertions that are altogether uncritical, make unnecessary assumptions, and fail to give proofs where they are needed. In this sense dogmatism is a term of reproach, whereas in the former sense, which alone will be used here, it simply stands for the admission of valid knowledge.

(*b*) Dogmatism *does not claim that everything can be proved*, for this would involve an endless regressive process of demonstration. It *admits that certain principles or facts need no proof*, but stand on their own merits. To prove is to borrow light from principles, so as to throw it on the conclusion which otherwise would remain in the dark. These principles either have light in themselves or derive it from some other source. Ultimately principles must be reached whose light is not derived from any other principle, which shine of themselves, are clearly seen by the mind, and shed their light around on other objects. We say: "It is as clear as daylight," to mean something which everybody must admit. We are certain of these principles because their truth manifests itself directly and immediately to the mind, and because it manifests itself in the same way to all men.

(*c*) Nor can it be said that, in such cases, the mind knows things, not as they are, but as it is, and that cognition is determined only by the mind's nature. We are conscious that such truths are imposed on the mind from without. My judgment must agree with the reality of things, otherwise it is pure fiction, and all men make the distinction between fiction and reality. The present question, however, is not that of the nature of knowledge, but that of certitude. No matter whence this certitude comes, reflection, as well as spontaneous adhesion, justifies it. Why?

2. **Two Classes of Judgments are Pronounced with Certitude.** Some are *facts*. Thus I say: "I am as sure as if I had seen it with my own eyes," or "I am certain that I did or said so and so." Others are *principles*. Thus I say: "I am as certain of this as I am of the proposition: two and two are four." In both cases I oppose my knowledge, as true, to something fictitious. I appeal to propositions which everybody must accept, to a standard which all men admit and on which all are agreed.

These facts and principles are true because I see that they are, because they shine to my mind like daylight to my eyes. No amount of reflection can ever make me depart from them. To deny them is to commit mental suicide, and to place oneself in the absolute incapacity of ever thinking and speaking. That I exist, think, and act; that two and two are four; that the whole is greater than any of its parts, etc., are truths that are certain and beyond the possibility of any doubt, although men may dispute as to the real meaning of such propositions, and examine what correspondence is found between the mental representation and the objective reality. This is a different question, which will be raised later on, when we shall examine the nature of knowledge. At present the fact of certitude stands the test of reflection. If the extent of certitude has been questioned, we may say that its existence has never been doubted seriously. All men hold some truths as certain, nor can they be thinking men without certitude.

CHAPTER II

CERTITUDES

I. Facts

1. **Existence of Certitude.** — (*a*) Upon reflection many spontaneous certitudes resolve themselves into higher or lower probabilities, that is, into incertitudes. The absence of doubt was due to the fact that the value of the evidence had not been weighed with sufficient accuracy, or evidence to the contrary had been neglected, or the possibilities of error overlooked. But, as was said in the preceding chapter, there are certitudes which persist, and which even the most radical sceptic cannot but imply in his very denials. These certitudes belong to two groups: *Facts of experience* and *principles of reason*. In any scientific investigation, both are combined in varying degrees. Thinking is not a merely mental function, proceeding independently, and free to follow its own caprice. It must conform to something which is extramental. I am not free to think that two and two are four. This truth imposes itself on my mind from outside. I do not make it, but recognize it.

(*b*) *Truth is the right which a certain proposition has to be accepted*, and this right, like the right of ownership, persists even when it is ignored or violated. In some cases this right is not clear, and, even after a diligent investigation, may not become evident. In other cases, it is in itself shining for the mind, and immediately manifest. *Facts*, i.e. concrete experiences, both internal and external, and *principles*, i.e. self-evident propositions, are the necessary bases of thought. If they are rejected, nothing is left but to stop thinking altogether or go to an asylum.

Not that some propositions may not at first seem self-evident without being so; nor that facts may not be investigated to distinguish true immediate experience from the interpretation which the mind may rashly add to it. But even after this sifting is done, there is left a residue of facts and laws, of concrete experiences and abstract principles, which are absolutely certain, and about which no other state of mind is possible but certitude.

(*c*) Later on we shall have to examine whether and how far the mental representation corresponds with external reality. For the present we simply observe that the mental attitude is one of *absolute and unreserved certitude* which nothing can shake. "Two and two are four"; "a straight line is shorter than a curve uniting the same two points"; "the same thing cannot at once be one way and the contradictory way"; "I am now thinking and writing"; "the paper on which I am writing is white, and the ink I use black;" "I experience a headache," etc., are so many assertions of which I am so certain that, should any one try to destroy or even weaken this certitude, I should at once suspect his seriousness or his mental sanity.

2. **Facts of Experience and Principles of Reason.** — (*a*) Under certain conditions, *inferences from self-evident facts and principles lead to unreserved certitude*, while, in other cases, the conclusions are accepted with more or less fear of error. In many circumstances, I may be certain that my fellowmen do not deceive me in what they claim to have seen, heard, or experienced. Although the fact itself to which they testify is not directly evident for me, I can entertain no doubt about it. Again, once the demonstration is understood, I am certain that the sum of the three angles of a triangle equals two right angles, because the connection of this assertion with self-evident principles is clear. Once I have studied physics and chemistry, I cannot doubt that this pure water, which I have not analyzed, and which I have never seen frozen, is composed of oxygen and hydrogen in the proportion 1 : 2, and that it will freeze at 32 degrees Fahrenheit. Should the event prove otherwise, it would be a sign for me that the water is not pure, or that my thermometer is at fault. Few perhaps are the laws established beyond doubt, but the certainty of some cannot be denied.

(*b*) The mind proceeds, and this very advance supposes *something fixed and settled*, both as a starting-point and as a guiding light. Remove these, and science becomes at once an impossibility, man must renounce thinking, since every step would involve him in a contradiction. Or rather there is no vagary which could not be indulged in, since there would remain nothing to go by, no directive principle. Whether we proceed from experience — as in the sciences of nature — or from self-evident principles — as in geometry — the starting-point must be stable, firm and certain. In its inductive and deductive processes, the mind has to avoid contradiction and be guided by the sidelights of truth and facts already ascertained. Certitudes of abstract principles must always be verifiable in all concrete instances, and facts must be organized with the help of principles.

But are facts and principles irreducible to each other? If so, will either one suffice, or are the two necessary?

II. Empiricism

1. **Meaning.** — As its name indicates, *empiricism derives all valid knowledge from experience* (ἐμπειρία), either internal or external. It is opposed to innatism, which admits innate ideas independent of experience, and to rationalism, which admits that the mind possesses some knowledge, which, even if it depends on the senses, is irreducible to sense-knowledge. According to empiricism, the knowledge of universal and necessary principles is simply a strong association which, by repetition, has become indissoluble. Every form of knowledge is ultimately reduced to concrete experience, the laws of the mind being alone responsible for their abstract, general, and necessary character.

2. **Criticism.** — (*a*) In Psychology we have shown the irreducibility of the concept to the image (p. 94 ff. 102 ff.) and of necessary judgments to associations. (p. 112 ff.). Only a few words will be added here. The perception of *what is* cannot give the certitude of *what must be*. Knowledge of *what happens* cannot give the knowledge of *what will necessarily happen*. The empiricist takes it for granted that concrete knowledge alone is true knowledge. But this a priori assertion is far from self-evident, and no argument is forthcoming to demonstrate it. There are, on the contrary, self-evident principles which we do not even think of testing

by experience, because their certitude is immediate. Two and two are known to be four as soon as the terms are understood, and this assertion is at once accepted as applying universally, at all times and everywhere. It is known simply by comparing the predicate with the subject.

(*b*) To become orderly and scientific, *experience constantly needs principles* which are not given in experience, like those of contradiction, causality, etc. Experience and reason are not used *successively*, that is, reason does not only continue, surpass, and transcend experience. In any science, the use of the two is *simultaneous*, and they compenetrate each other at every step. Scientific experience is impossible without the use of principles transcending experience.

III. Rationalism

1. **Meaning.** — We are certain of concrete facts, but there is another certitude, namely, that of principles, which is acquired as the result of a direct intuition of the intellect. As understood here, rationalism is opposed to empiricism, and denies that every form of knowledge can be reduced to experience. It admits the radical difference between the concrete and the abstract, and refuses to identify the universal with the collective. It asserts that *the certitude of principles is not the direct result of experience*, but of an intuition of the understanding. It is the theory explained in Psychology when we spoke of the origin of necessary principles (p. 112 ff.).

Hence rationalism here does not mean the abuse of rationalism, which consists in relying exclusively on reason and neglecting experience, or in relying exclusively on human reason and denying the possibility, fact, or usefulness of a divine revelation. Rationalism may or may not admit the innateness of ideas and principles. This is an independent question which has been answered in Psychology. Rationalism is not opposed to the legitimate use of experience, but admits the certitude of principles transcending experience. The union of the two is indispensable in science.

2. **Value.** — Rationalism is the only satisfactory explanation of the certitude which we have of principles. (See Psychology.)

Nor does it lessen the value of knowledge, since it does not profess to create anything new, but simply to apprehend aspects of reality which are already found in sense-experience, hidden, as it were, under the concrete envelope which limits such reality in space and time. Reason goes deeper, to the core itself, which, once the outer envelope is removed, is no longer restricted to one individual.

CHAPTER III

WHAT IS KNOWLEDGE?

So far we have simply analyzed our certitudes and shown that the human mind cannot possibly remain in the state of doubt, but that, even in its denials, it implies the power to know with certitude. There remains the crucial question of epistemology: What is it to know? And what is the value of the relation established in knowledge between a knowing mind and a known object?

I. FACT OF KNOWLEDGE

1. **Nature of Knowledge.** — (*a*) Knowledge is essentially *the awareness of an object*, i.e. of anything — fact or principle — which may in any manner be reached by our cognitive faculties. The existence, size, and color of the tree out there, a geometrical theorem, the existence of God, etc., may be so many objects of knowledge. Knowledge always implies both *the antithesis of a knowing activity and of a known object*, and *their close union*. The known object must in some way be present within the knowing subject. I can know the tree out there only in so far as it acts on me, and thereby contributes to produce in my mind a representation of it. Any activity which may be conceived as purely subjective can never be a cognitive process, and any attempt to identify the *object of knowledge* with the *subjective experience* by which it is known, leads to destroying the fact itself of knowledge, which implies the object as essentially as it does the subject.

(*b*) This objective relation is expressed in an implicit or explicit *judgment* by which the perception or intuition is referred to the object. Thus in sense-perception, there is implied the assertion that my sensations refer to this or that object. "I see a tree out there" means that the color-sensations which I experience are referred to an object with certain characteristics, which I call a tree, and which is located in a certain direction, and at a certain distance. (Cf. Psychology, p. 62 ff.).

2. **Truth and Certitude are Conditions of Knowledge.** — (*a*) A man may be under the irresistible illusion that he knows, when he mistakes error for truth, and gives an unconditional assent to a false statement. Here we have only the appearance of knowledge. The man thinks that he knows, but a better informed man is aware of the mistake. Even if the error is common to all men, it remains true that the knowledge is not real, but only apparent.

(*b*) As long as a serious doubt remains in his mind, a man cannot say that he knows. "I think so" is far from meaning "I know it is so." The mental attitude of a man who "thinks so" is that of opinion, not that of certitude, and for this reason he does not strictly *know*. He passes a judgment on an object, it is true, but a judgment which is always subordinated to the implicit condition: "If I apprehend this object correctly."

II. VALUE OF THE REPRESENTATIVE ASPECT OF KNOWLEDGE

There is agreement on the fact that knowledge as a conscious process is essentially objective, as has been explained above, but the questions remain: What is the meaning of "objective"? What is the object of knowledge? What is the value of the claim of the knowing mind that it apprehends an extramental reality?

I. In General

1. **The Question Stated.** — As remarked already, the object of knowledge may be something concrete — internal or external, — or something abstract — either a physical law, found and verified through experience, or a self-evident principle admitted simply because of the rational intuition of its truth. This object seems to exist apart from the knowing process, to impose itself on the mind from without, and to have an existence and a nature independent of the fact that it is known. On the other hand, the knowledge of an object depends also on the mind. Otherwise how would the fact of error be explainable, and how would it be

possible to change one's judgment? These facts have led to theorizing on the real meaning of the "object of knowledge," and the solutions that have been proposed may be reduced to three: Idealism, Criticism, Realism.

2. **Idealism.** — It is almost impossible to define idealism. It presents so many varieties — sometimes hardly reconcilable with one another; it receives so many qualificatives which indicate every individual author's point of view, that any attempt to give a definition is sure to fall short of embracing the various meanings of the term.

(*a*) If we proceed etymologically, "idealism" applies primarily to Plato's view, according to which this world which we perceive with the senses is only a shadow of the real world, or world of *ideas*. In the world of ideas, the *types* — like beauty, goodness, virtue — of which the concrete realities of our world are only *dim participations*, are really existent. This, however, is realism par excellence, recognizing the true and exclusive reality of objective, absolute, and self-existent ideas.

(*b*) It is on *our own* mental and subjective ideas that idealism insists. Its motto is Berkeley's: "Esse est percipi." The whole reality of a thing consists in the idea which we have of it. It starts from Locke's principle that "knowledge is conversant only with ideas," or that "the mind in all its thoughts and reasonings hath no other immediate object but its own ideas which it alone does or can contemplate" (Essay concerning Human Understanding, IV, I, i). Hence the idea, it is true, has a character of objectivity, but, as the object is within the knowing subject, and as the subject cannot go out of himself, it follows that *human knowledge is necessarily limited to the knowledge of the mind's ideas.*

(*c*) Should ideas have any objects outside of the mind these objects could never be reached by the mind, since the mind is necessarily confined within its own sphere, and can never go outside of it. Ideas are objective, but the object itself has no reality outside of the idea. What we call the external world is a mental idea, or rather a system of ideas; and what we call truth is the consistent working of the mind in this complexity of ideas. Whatever we know, we know in and through the mind. To know a thing is to have an idea of it. But as *the idea is the only reality we are aware of*, no matter what it represents or claims to represent, it follows that knowledge is only a series of conscious representations. There is nothing else, for, what reason could there be to assert the existence of what we know absolutely nothing about? Not only is the mind active in knowledge, but it alone is active.

3. **Realism.** — (*a*) Realism admits that *objects exist outside the mind*, and that *ideas represent them*. Not only in the mind, but also in nature, the tree is green and occupies such or such a place. Not only in the mind, but in reality also, two and two — whatever objects they may be applied to — are four. It is true that my knowledge is in myself, that it is a part of my mind; but what I know exists independently of the fact that I happen to know it. Its "esse" is not its "percipi." It would *be*, even if it were not *perceived*. In this case it would not be *for me*, since it would have no relation to my mind, but it would be *in itself* as an external reality.

(*b*) Realism does not claim that we know things in their *absolute* reality — for, evidently the known object must be *in relation* with the mind — but that we really know things which, in addition to their *mental existence* as ideas, have also an *existence outside the mind*, and that, finally, the fact of its being known does not *make* or *change the object of knowledge*. There is an external world which we really perceive in experience — how and how far will be seen later. And there are absolute truths which the understanding apprehends by a direct intellectual intuition.

4. **Criticism.** — (*a*) Criticism is the name given to the philosophy of Kant. In itself it signifies neither realism nor idealism, but a method which consists in criticising our faculties of knowledge in order to test their objective value. Kant speaks of his own system as "transcendental idealism," and also as "empirical realism," thus indicating that it partakes of both idealism and realism. In fact Kant admits the *existence* of something external, but this is, and will forever remain, *an unknown X*, because it cannot be reached except through a priori mental forms or categories. *The mind does not conform to things*, but *our knowledge of*

things conforms to the mind. We do not think objects according to *their laws*, but according to *the laws of our minds.*

(*b*) Whatever appears necessary and universal in knowledge cannot come from experience, which is always contingent; it comes from the mind itself. Thus space and time, which are necessary and universal elements of sensation, are not real attributes of things-in-themselves, but a priori forms of sensibility. Facts given in experience are coördinated and unified in thought by the categories, or a priori forms of the understanding, which establish relations, — e.g. of causality, inherence, etc. — between the various phenomena given in sensation. Hence *knowledge is always a synthesis of two elements*, one of which is given from outside and the other is an a priori mental form through which the former is perceived. The result is the "phenomenon," or thing-as-it-appears, the only thing that we can know. The "thing-in-itself" is forever unknowable, since we cannot think except through the mind's a priori forms.

II. The External World

1. **The Problem.** — Knowledge begins with the senses, and the senses are commonly assumed to manifest the existence and properties of an external world. All men agree in making a distinction between their own bodies and other bodies; to both they attribute reality and materiality. Solid matter around us is believed to manifest itself primarily through the sense of touch, and later by association, through other senses, especially sight. To fall on the ground, to receive a blow, to strike some part of one's body against something else, show with clearness the hardness and resistance of both. Through the other senses this matter manifests itself as colored, sonorous, hot, etc. Are these perceptions manifestations of real objects and qualities? Sense-perception is in the mind. It is a conscious state, and how can a conscious state represent anything material, when the antagonism and irreducibility of mind and matter are facts admitted by all?

2. **Arguments for Realism.** — The arguments on which realism is based are but an emphasis of the fact itself of knowledge as manifested in consciousness. Even if this fact is mysterious;

even if no good account of it can be given, it cannot for this reason be denied.

(*a*) Both common and scientific *experience* make a distinction between *ideas* and *things*, between the mental and the physical world. (1) There is a real book here on the table, nine by six inches, with a red binding, near another book, etc. When I grasp it, I grasp something real. When I read it, I believe that the black characters are really printed on the white paper. (2) The scientist always assumes that his studies are about real matter, and that the laws which he discovers or applies — e.g. the laws of gravitation or of chemical composition — are not mere mental formulas, but expressions of the way according to which things really happen in nature. Science can foresee and generalize, not on mental laws, but on natural laws.

My idea of a foot is not longer than that of an inch. Yet every man with his senses knows that the foot is twelve times as long as the inch. The association of ideas in the mind produces expectation, but the expected result takes place in nature. It is to physical, not to mental, realities that knowledge is referred in perception, and every man is convinced naturally that his mind comes in contact — it may be difficult for him to say how — with material objects outside of it.

(*b*) *Mental processes are essentially private.* They may even differ in regard to the same object. But *objects are common.* Even if my idea of an object which we are now looking at is different from yours, it will never occur to anybody to say that we are not looking at the same object. Even if other minds do not perceive exactly as I do, they nevertheless perceive the same world. No amount of effort can ever make two men walking together think that they are not perceiving the same objects with their respective minds.

(*c*) *The distinction between percepts and images* is an evident one. My images are largely dependent on my will. By imagination I may travel where I please, as I please, with more or less rapidity; or I can see and hear things which I choose to recall to my mind, and as I choose to recall them. Perception is independent of me. I must travel where and when the train carries me, and my various perceptions are dependent on something external which determines what I shall see, hear, or experience. I cannot, by taking thought, change the color of the paper before me, nor the sound of the church bell. I light the fire, place a kettle of water on it, go away, and come back a little later. During my absence, while I had no perception of it, there was a real action of the fire on the water, which is now boiling. Independently of perceptions, material beings persist and act upon one another. Before there was any human mind at all, these beings were evolving toward their present condition, as astronomy, geology, and other sciences now teach.

(*d*) In perception, consciousness testifies that the mind is *passive*, i.e. acted on by something else. This can be accounted for only if there is something outside the mind, capable of *acting* on it.

(*e*) Unless I fall into absolute solipsism, and deny the existence of any mind except my own, — a step which no sane man will be willing to take — I must admit that I am not alone. Besides myself *there are other men*. How do I know it? Minds do not communicate with one another immediately, but only through the organism, by speech, writing, or gestures. If I admit that there are other men, with bodies like mine, I admit also that the report of the senses which manifest their bodies is valid. The senses therefore give me valid information about the external world, of which the bodies of my fellowmen are a part.

(*f*) Psychology — whether of realists or of idealists — admits a certain correlation between *mental processes* and *brain processes*. The brain and its processes are assumed by the idealist to be mere representations in consciousness. For him, to say that mental processes depend on cerebral processes simply amounts to saying that a conscious process, e.g. a sensation, depends on another conscious representation, e.g. of a motion or change in the idea called brain. This surely is not the meaning of psychologists, who distinguish the relations of mind and organism from a mere association of ideas, and claim that the organism is really the physical instrument of sensations.

3. **Objections.** — It seems to be almost a defiance to common-

sense to reject these arguments for realism. Yet the objections of idealists oblige us to emphasize them. We shall briefly examine some of the objections of idealism, and thus see how a man may come to contradict so openly common-sense and experience.

(a) The main argument of idealism is the supposed impossibility for perception, as a *conscious process*, to reveal anything *external to the mind*. The mind is aware only of its own contents, i.e. of ideas. And since it can no more step out of its own mental limits than the organism out of its skin, it follows that we are forever restricted to the awareness of conscious processes, which are *toto coelo* different from any external and material reality.

Answer. (1) Were the fact unexplainable, no right would be given thereby to deny it. Here *the fact is obvious*. When, for instance, I shake hands with, and speak to, a friend, I cannot doubt his real presence; I feel his touch, and he feels mine; I hear him and he hears me.

(2) The mind perceives external objects *through the organism* with which it is united intimately. Obviously man is not a pure spirit separated from the organism, but a living organism united to a mind. What we perceive as external is not only extramental, but also extraorganic.

(3) *The mind does not know only its own ideas*. It does not even know them primarily, but through reflection. What I am aware of primarily in perception is an external reality, and subsequently, by reflection, I consider the mental process of perception.

(4) The perception of external objects is *immediate* because external objects act on the organism. The organism is not simply a physical reality, but matter animated by the soul. To a great extent idealism is the outcome of the Cartesian doctrine relegating the soul to some part of the brain, and thus cutting it off from everything external. But, in fact, the "action" of the external object is at the same time the "passion" of the organ. Both are one, since they are united in this common process, and the "patiens" need not go out of himself to perceive the foreign action which is in himself at the time of sensation. The abyss between the subject and the object is imaginary. Imaginary also, therefore, the need of a bridge which idealism declares to be an impossibility.

This fact is clear in perceptions of touch, but from psychology we know that the other senses also require some immediate contact. The organic stimulation is not a mere mechanical process, for the soul is wherever the animated organ is, as we shall see in the Philosophy of Mind (p. 480 ff.).

(5) Consciousness, it is true, takes place only when the external impression has been conveyed to the brain through the sensory nerve. Yet it is the hand that feels, the eye that sees, etc. The brain is *necessary*, but of itself *insufficient* for sensation. The complete organ includes the peripheral apparatus, the afferent nerve, and the brain centre.

(6) If it were not so, the *objectivation or exteriorization of sensations*, i.e. the fact that they are spontaneously referred to an external reality, would be *unexplainable*. (a) The habit of exteriorization supposes a first exteriorization, which is impossible. (b) The association of internal images can never give anything but complex internal images. (c) An inference, by which ideas would be referred to some external object as their only adequate cause, already supposes the knowledge of an objective cause, and of the existence of something real, external, distinct from the mind, material, and capable of acting. — Hence these three theories which have been proposed to account for the fact are insufficient.

Briefly: It is true that *the external world is not known except through sensations*, but it is true also that *a sensation is always an experience of the external world.*

(*b*) *Mental dispositions influence perception.* Perception is different according as the organs are in a normal, or in a more or less abnormal, condition. It varies with mental attitudes, feelings, actual contents of the mind, etc.

Answer. (1) Even then sensations are always referred to external objects. (2) The mind has its share in determining the nature of perception, but is not the only factor. (3) In most cases we can point out the physiological or mental causes that modify perception. Moreover, we are not concerned here with determining where and when the senses are trustworthy.

(*c*) What appears in consciousness as color, sound, heat, etc., is reduced by physical science to vibrations of ether, air, and molecules, differing in length and number, and totally *unlike the sensations.*

Answer. (1) At present we are concerned only with the *existence* of the external world, not with the *nature* of the properties manifested in sensation. This is a task for inductive science. But it is clear that if there is movement, there is something moving, and that if there are vibrations, there is something vibrating. (2) It is by *using their senses* that scientists come to know the real nature of physical qualities. To admit the validity of this objection is, therefore, sheer contradiction for the idealist. (3) Other qualities, like resistance, relative size, etc., cannot be reduced to something depending on the percipient organism. I see plainly that a foot is longer than an inch. For all men it is true that water is composed of oxygen and hydrogen.

4. **Kant's View.** — A few words will suffice on Kant's view of external perception. According to him, two elements are found in external perception, one varying with every perception, the other necessary and common to all perceptions, namely, space. The same is true of the consciousness of every mental process, the invariable element being time. Hence the ideas of space and time are not derived from experience. They are conditions of experience, and a priori mental forms. The ideas of space, extension, geometrical figure, etc., cannot be derived from the perception of bodies; nor those of "before" and "after" from the consciousness of mental processes. Things and processes cannot be perceived without these spatial or temporal relations, which are therefore in the mind as a priori forms antecedently to sensations.

Answer. (1) The "where" and "when" are given in perception, and spontaneously *attributed to things and events.* This event took place at such a date, before this, and after that. Historical events are not given their dates by the mind. It is not through any a priori form that President Taft succeeded Roosevelt, or that the discovery of America took place before George Washington commanded the troops of the United States against the forces of England. Again, this object is really square, higher or lower, on the right or on the left of this other object; its relative position is independent of the mind. Such, at any rate, is the universal consent of men.

(2) That sensations necessarily manifest things in space and time may be accounted for by the fact that things really *are* always in space and time, as well as by any a priori forms. Both are possible explanations, and the former is the one which experience suggests.

(3) In fact, we make a distinction between *objective* space and time and our *perception* of it. I want to measure a stick with a real objective foot. The same for time: my perception of duration may differ greatly from objective duration.

(4) Kant fails to distinguish space and time as (a) real, i.e. the spatial relations of a body and the real successive duration of a movement; (b) ideal, i.e. the general concepts of space and time; (c) imaginary, i.e. imagined to exist before or after there was or will be any real succession, or beyond any real occupation of space. In perception, real space and time are given; the concepts of space and time are elaborated by the mind; imaginary space and time are altogether unreal, as we shall see in Cosmology (p. 449 ff.).

III. Ideal Truths

1. **Analytic and Synthetic Judgments.** — (*a*) The difference between analytic and synthetic judgments was explained in Psychology (p. 109). The former are obtained by the analysis of the terms themselves, which leads to the immediate intuition of their relation. Such judgments are not adhered to because they are verified in experience. They are pronounced to be true *independently of their application to concrete objects*. Even if there were actually no divisible substances, it would still be true that the whole is greater than any of its parts. Even if there are no perfect geometrical triangles, the sum of the angles in any triangle equals two right angles. A synthetic judgment *depends essentially on experience*. Analyzing its terms will not reveal their relation, but it is necessary to perceive concrete existing objects. The judgments: "Water boils at 212 degrees"; "birds are oviparous"; "Havana tobacco is good," etc., are synthetic.

(*b*) Analytic judgments are very important, not only in rational sciences, like mathematics, which, starting from them, derive other judgments equally necessary and analytic, but also in empirical sciences which, as was explained above (p. 383), require principles transcending experience. Here we shall not speak of synthetic judgments, as they have been dealt with in the preceding question on the knowledge of the external world (p. 389 ff.). Nor need we come back to empiristic theories concerning analytic judgments, as they have been discussed in our second chapter (p. 382), and in Psychology (p. 112 ff.). A few words must be said on Kant's views, but we shall first establish the value of analytic judgments, so as to dispose of idealistic subjectivism, which claims that such principles are not objective, but simply laws of the mind.

2. **Objectivity of Analytic Judgments.** — Analytic judgments are objective, that is, in accepting them, the mind knows truths which are independent of the mind itself, and which it *does not create* according to the laws of its own nature. The analysis of the conscious process itself is the proof of this assertion. When I say: "The whole is greater than any of its parts," I do so because I see clearly the relation between the subject and the predicate of this proposition. The understanding of the terms is enough to perceive that such a proposition is true, certain, and necessary, and that objectively the whole cannot be equal to, or smaller than, but must be greater than, a part. I do not merely see that it is so, nor is any other relation simply inconceivable and incomprehensible, but it is clearly impossible, and contradictory to the terms themselves of the proposition. "The sum of the angles in a triangle equals two right angles," or "$8 \times 13 = 104$." These propositions may not at first be accepted as true. But as soon as they are analyzed, the agreement of the subject with the predicate becomes clear, and the assent is given in consideration of this objective evidence. As long as I have not perceived this objective evidence, I refuse my assent. Or the evidence may appear gradually, and the mind passes from doubt to certitude through varying degrees of opinion.

3. **Kant's View.** — Kant admits two kinds of universal and necessary judgments: analytic and synthetic. The former are those in which the predicate is contained in the comprehension of the

subject. They have no scientific value, since they manifest nothing new; they are mere repetitions or tautologies. Synthetic judgments may be simply matter-of-fact, contingent, a posteriori and empirical, like: "This man is tall." Or they may be necessary and a priori like: "7 + 5 = 12" (mathematical); "the straight line is the shortest distance from one point to another" (geometrical); "through all changes in the material world the quantity of matter is constant"; "in every transmission of motion, action and reaction must be equal to each other" (physical); "everything that begins to exist has a cause" (metaphysical).

These judgments, according to Kant, are *not analytic*. They really combine or synthetize a subject with a predicate taken outside of the comprehension of the subject. Hence they are *synthetic*. As, however, the synthesis is not given a posteriori, i.e. from experience, — since experience cannot give universality and necessity — they are *a priori*, and suppose in the mind the existence of categories or a priori forms of the understanding. Such judgments are the most important in science, which is universal and necessary.

Criticism. — (*a*) An analytic judgment is not merely that in which the predicate is already contained in the subject, but also that in which, from the analysis of the subject and predicate in their essence and essential properties, their *necessary relation* is perceived by the mind. (Cf. Psychology, p. 109.)

(*b*) Such judgments are not acquired from experience alone, but by the mind abstracting and generalizing, i.e. elaborating the data of experience.

(*c*) With his a priori forms, Kant cannot explain the fact that sometimes we arrive at the knowledge of analytic truths little by little and through various stages of opinion. The only explanation of this fact is that the objective light is seen more or less clearly.

(*d*) There is no room for *synthetic a priori* judgments. All judgments are either analytic, a priori, and independent of their empirical verification; or synthetic, a posteriori, and dependent on experience. The examples given by Kant do not prove his contention. (1) The judgment "7 + 5 = 12" is *analytic*. It does not mean, as Kant claims, that $7 + 5$ is a sum which experience alone can verify to be 12, but it means that $7 + 5$ and 12, when compared together, are necessarily found to be equal. In fact, it means $(1 + 1 + 1 + 1 + 1 + 1 + 1) + (1 + 1 + 1 + 1 + 1) = 1 + 1 + 1 + 1 + 1 + 1 + 1 + 1 + 1 + 1 + 1 + 1$, which shows the judgment to be analytic and pronounced on objective evidence. (2) "A straight line is the shortest distance from one point to another" is also *analytic*. It means that, compared to other lines, the straight line is the shortest, and this is evident when we consider that not to go straight is to cover more space. In the straight line we have only one spatial relation and the same direction throughout, whereas in the curve the direction changes at every point, and, in the broken line, at every angle. (3) Both principles taken from physical science are *synthetic*, but not at all a priori. There is no a priori contradiction in denying them. As far as they are to be admitted, these principles are verified by experience. (4) The principle of causality is *analytic*, and based directly on the principle of identity, "A = A," which means that, of itself, a being is always itself, and that there must be some foreign addition or subtraction to make it more or less. Thus when we have $0 = 0$, we cannot have $0 = 1$ unless to 0 we add a new factor, $0 + x = 1$. The predicate is not contained formally in the subject, but is seen to be essentially and necessarily connected with it.

4. **Objectivity of Concepts.** — Ideal truths express the relations of agreement or disagreement between concepts. What is the value of concepts? For Kant, the intelligible object is unreal because the activity of the mind consists precisely in creating appearances or phenomena. As long as judgments are referred only to *phenomena*, they are correct, but the *noumena* or things-in-themselves are unknowable. In Psychology we have discussed the theories proposed to explain the concept (p. 98 ff.). From the conclusions reached there it may be inferred that concepts are not mere names (*nominalism*) or labels to which no idea corresponds in the mind; nor merely collective and associated perceptions (*associationism*); that concepts are not simply ideas in the mind without any corresponding reality (*conceptualism*); that concepts do not correspond to realities as they exist outside of the

mind (*exaggerated realism*); but that nevertheless some reality corresponds to concepts (*moderate realism*).

Concrete reality is determined and individual, while, owing to mental abstraction, concepts are abstract and universal. When the notes which individualize an object are mentally removed, what remains is abstract, and no longer restricted to one individual. The concrete is real, and really contains the object of our concepts. This man, with all his concrete determinations, is a being, a substance, a living organism, etc. Hence the objects of these abstract concepts are really found in the concrete man, but under a multiplicity of other characteristics.

IV. Summary and Corollaries

1. **What is Knowledge?** — (*a*) *To know is to be aware of an object*, concrete or abstract, individual or universal, which does not exist in the mind alone, but is a reality independent of the fact that it is known. The mind does not make the truth, but becomes aware of it; facts and laws are imposed on it from without. That knowledge is a conscious process is true, but it is only a part of the truth. Knowledge is *a mental process conditioned by external evidence*. The right of a proposition to be accepted as true persists even when the mind fails to accept it. The law of gravitation was true before it was discovered by Newton.

(*b*) Knowledge may be intuitive or discursive, more or less certain, and more or less immediate. The really objective may be difficult to disentangle from subjective influences. Yet it is there, and under proper conditions may be found. To be known, the object must be present in the mind, but ideas and judgments truly represent objects. The mind contributes its share in the act of knowledge, but is not the only factor.

2. **The Relativity of Knowledge.** — Knowledge is necessarily proportioned to the *capacity of the mind* and the *manifestation of the object*.

(*a*) Owing to native and acquired dispositions, *minds* — both senses and intelligences — differ in keenness, perspicacity, and power. Not all men have the same keenness of vision or hearing, nor the same intellectual aptitudes. Certain animals are endowed with keener senses than those of man. We may imagine senses much more perfect than those with which we are acquainted. We may even imagine that the material world is endowed with properties which none of our senses is adapted to perceive. Understandings more powerful than ours would discover laws and relations of which we are ignorant.

These limitations do not invalidate the knowledge which we acquire with the faculties with which we are endowed, any more than a man's horizon, or the presence of fog which bounds his view, prevents him from seeing more or less distinctly the objects found within his range of vision. The fact that *we do not know all things* is no justification for the assertion that *we know nothing*.

It is true also that knowledge depends on subjective conditions, but this must not be exaggerated. Men *agree* on many propositions both of the ideal and of the empirical order. They *differ* not so much on objects of knowledge as on objects of opinion; not so much on what they really know as on what they think they know; not so much on immediate evidence as on more remote conclusions reached after difficult and complex processes of inference. In immediate sense-perception or intellectual intuition, the "fringe" of consciousness may vary with the different mental attitudes and acquired dispositions, but the "focus" is essentially the same for all minds.

(*b*) *Reality manifests itself in different ways.* Sometimes it is bright in itself. Sometimes light must be thrown on it from elsewhere by reasoning, analogy, etc. One professor may give clearer explanations than another. Text-books on the same matter are not equally suited to meet the needs of students. A landscape is seen better on a clear day than through a misty atmosphere. The manifestation of the object must be adapted to the mind. A demonstration which is clear for one mind may not be sufficient for another. Some truths are hidden and to be sought for. In a word, truths are more or less easily accessible.

3. **The Limits of Knowledge.** — Knowledge is limited. We do not and cannot know everything. Nor can we know any object perfectly, in all its relations, and with all its properties. Human knowledge is always inadequate. But, with the agnostic, to assign

clearly defined limits to our power of knowing is unjustifiable. Without break we gradually pass from one object of knowledge to another. The limits of both the range and the perfection of knowledge vary with every individual mind. Yet the same principles which the agnostic uses in acquiring what he admits to be valid knowledge will necessarily lead him higher into regions to which he arbitrarily applies the name of unknowable. Starting from self-evident facts or principles, we may proceed, inductively or deductively, as far as we can. As we go along, the progress will become more and more complex and difficult; dangers of error will be greater. Hence greater caution will be needed. But no one has the right to say: "Thus far shalt thou go and no farther." Objects of knowledge are common property, and we may always go farther in exploring them.

CHAPTER IV

THE CRITERIA OF VALID KNOWLEDGE

The Meaning of Criterion. — (*a*) The human mind is naturally qualified to know. As, however, the facts of error, of change in the successive assents of the same mind, and of dissent among several individuals, are undeniable, there must be a *standard* or *test* by which truth is distinguished from error. In fact, we make a constant use of such tests. I say: "Such a man is tall, black-haired; his voice is deep, etc." — "How do you know?" some one asks. — "Because I saw and heard him." Again: "Water freezes at 32 degrees." — "How do you know?" — "Because I have observed it in a sufficient number of cases and conditions to warrant this general assertion." Again: "The sum of the angles in a triangle is equal to two right angles." — "How do you know?" — "Here is the demonstration." And so on.

A *criterion* (κρίνειν, to judge) is necessary as *the distinctive sign of truth*, and as the basis on which it rests. In the instances just given, different criteria were used: the testimony of the senses, induction, and demonstration, which justified my assertions. But why are these criteria accepted? Are they self-sufficient, or do they themselves rest on something else?

(*b*) This leads us to distinguish *two kinds of criteria*, one supreme, ultimate, universal, and applicable to all kinds of truths; the other derived, proximate, and applicable only within a restricted field. How do I know that Peking is a city of China? Because witnesses have told me. Why do I believe them? Because they are trustworthy. Why are they trustworthy? Because they know and would not deceive me. Why? . . . Why? . . . In a series of "whys" the ultimate criterion is the answer to the last. All the others, like senses, induction, demonstration, derive their value from it. It is common to all, and, without it, proximate criteria would serve no purpose. Hence the division of this chapter.

I. THE ULTIMATE CRITERION

Three theories or groups of theories are to be examined. Some claim that the supreme criterion is to be found outside both the knowing subject and the known object. Others place it within the subject, but outside the object. Others finally make it both subjective and objective, intrinsic to both the knower and the object of knowledge.

I. Theories of a Criterion Extrinsic to both the Knowing Mind and the Object known by this Mind

1. **Traditionalism.** — Various systems, which we may group together under the name of traditionalism, agree in asserting the radical incapacity of *personal reason* for knowing with certitude either any truth at all, or at least the truths of the metaphysical, religious, and moral order. Hence appeal is made to tradition, i.e. to *universal reason*, to the consent of mankind, or of the majority of men, which manifests a primitive divine revelation made to man. The ultimate criterion is a divine revelation. According to Lamennais the sign of this revelation is the common agreement of men, i.e. general, as opposed to individual, reason. De Bonald argues from the fact that man has the power of speech. According to him, speech is indispensable to, and precedes, thought, and consequently could not have been acquired by man. It must have been revealed by God together with the ideas which it expresses.

2. **Criticism of Traditionalism.** — It is true that divine revelation is a great help to the human mind in acquiring moral and religious truths. True also that in many cases individual reason feels uncertain, whereas the agreement with other men increases its confidence, and, under certain conditions to be mentioned later, may become a sign of truth. Actual knowledge is the accumulated wisdom of preceding ages. Man's plight would be a sad one, could he not avail himself of the results obtained by those who have

gone before him. Yet tradition cannot be the ultimate criterion of truth.

(*a*) *In general.* (1) This system is opposed to the testimony of consciousness, which certifies that, in some cases at least, knowledge is acquired independently of any external teaching. (2) Certitude cannot be based on faith in a divine revelation. This faith is either certain or uncertain. In the latter case, it cannot be the criterion of certain knowledge. In the former, it supposes the certitude of God's existence, of His knowledge and truthfulness, and of the fact itself of a revelation, hence of reason by which these are demonstrated. (3) This criterion, even if admitted, is not universal. It does not apply, for instance, to conscious facts, actual experiences, historical events, etc. Hence all other criteria are not participations of this one. No authority, divine or human, can be the final test of truth.

(*b*) With De Bonald we may admit that without speech thought would be very difficult. But it does not seem true to say that it would be absolutely impossible. Moreover, if it were not associated already with the thought it expresses, language would be a mere physical sound. Hence *thought precedes language.* (Cf. Psychology, p. 126 ff.). Finally, even if God revealed language, He would not necessarily reveal ready-made propositions. Language may express error as well as truth.

(*c*) *Common consent*, however useful it may be, cannot be the criterion we are now looking for. Even if it is a criterion, it is derived, not ultimate. (1) It supposes the reliability of the senses through which a man is aware of the existence of other men, and the certitude that, under some circumstances, and under these only, the unanimous consent of man is an infallible source of truth. Hence personal reason precedes universal reason as a test of truth. (2) The reason of all men is but the sum of the reasons of every individual. If all individually are incapable of certain knowledge, how can the collection give certitude? (3) How can this unanimity or quasi-unanimity be ascertained? A whole lifetime would be spent before any truth would be known with certitude. Must it be understood of all men at all times? Then the task is utterly impossible. Must it be understood of all men living together at the same time? Then history shows that common and universal errors are possible.

II. Theories of a Subjective Criterion, Intrinsic to the Knower, but Extrinsic to the Object

Traditionalism failed to recognize the fact that, since the mind knows by its own faculties, the criterion must be intrinsic to the mind. We pass now to subjective theories.

1. **Common Sense and Feelings.** — (*a*) Some philosophers have appealed to a blind impulse or instinct which prompts man to accept spontaneously the truthfulness of his faculties. It is a common law of our nature, and no account of it can be given. Reid speaks of a "common sense," i.e. of an invincible propensity common to all men; Jacobi, of a "feeling," or affective disposition of the mind, which makes it assent to the reality of what the senses and reason manifest.

(*b*) *This criterion is insufficient.* Everybody, even the sceptic, admits this natural impulse, but the question remains *whether it is justified or not.* If it is not, it cannot be a criterion. If it is, an appeal must be made to something else by which it is justified. This view is rather a refusal to meet the epistemological issue than a solution of it. The fact manifested in consciousness is that we are certain, not because a blind impulse makes us assent, but because we see the truth. While we may be aware of impelling motives within us, we are also aware that we are not only impelled from within, but also drawn from without. Many subjective motives, like interest, utility, habits of thought, education, etc., may impel man to accept error, and there must be something whereby he may recognize the object itself as true or false.

2. **Clear Idea and Divine Veracity.** — (*a*) Descartes emerged from his methodical doubt through the affirmation: "I think, therefore I am," which he accepts because, in the fact of thinking, he clearly sees the necessary implication of being. Hence the general rule that "whatever things we conceive very clearly and very distinctly are true." According to Descartes, the guarantee of truth is ultimately the perfection, wisdom, and veracity of God, who cannot be the cause of error, and cannot endow us with

faculties that would deceive us. Ontologists asserted that all things are seen in God, who is known to man immediately.

(*b*) *Criticism*. (1) The clearness of an idea as such cannot be the criterion of truth. It is merely subjective, and varies with individuals. It is not primitive, but must itself be tested. Moreover, if clear means certain, nothing is explained. If it means distinct, the fact that we may be certain of things which we do not perceive distinctly and adequately is overlooked. (2) The guarantee mentioned by Descartes is insufficient. The existence and perfections of God are not known intuitively, but by demonstration; and demonstration must be based on principles that are certain. If the certitude of these principles is said to depend also on God's veracity, we are involved in a *petitio principii*. If it is said to depend on something else, certitude may be derived from our own faculties. (3) The same applies to ontologism. We do not see God immediately, but know Him only by a process of reasoning.

3. **Consistency, and Inconceivability of Negation.**—(*a*) *Consistency*, i.e. the harmony between judgments, has been proposed as the criterion of truth by certain philosophers imbued with idealistic or agnostic tendencies. If knowledge is limited to our own mental states, what other criterion can be given? Spencer writes: "There is no mode of establishing the validity of any belief except that of showing its entire congruity with all other beliefs. . . . If, by discovering a proposition to be untrue, we mean nothing more than discovering a difference between a thing expected and a thing perceived, then a body of conclusions in which no such difference anywhere occurs must be what we mean by an entirely true body of conclusions." (First Principles, § 40.)

Yet Spencer himself goes farther, and gives another criterion, namely, the *inconceivability of the negation of a proposition*. This inconceivability comes from hereditary associations, so strong that the associated ideas can no longer be thought of as separated. "To assert the inconceivableness of its (a cognition's) negation is at the same time to assert the psychological necessity we are under of thinking it, and to give our logical justification for holding it to be unquestionable." (Principles of Psychology, § 426.)

(*b*) *Criticism.* — *Inconsistency* is a sign that one of the inconsistent propositions is false. Consistency is a useful, but secondary, test of validity. Nor is it infallible. *A whole system of errors may be consistent*, the falsity being at the starting-point. Consistency shows that the rules of logic have been observed, not that knowledge possesses objective validity. If it must be the criterion of validity, it must have something else to rest on. Moreover, several facts or principles may be perceived separately, so that their consistency will not be known. They may nevertheless be true.

As to *inconceivability:* (1) Sometimes Spencer confounds it with the incapacity for *imagining*. Many things are conceivable for the intellect without being imaginable, e.g. a polygon with a thousand sides. And the impossibility of imagining the contradictory of a statement is no sign of the truth of that statement. (2) *Intellectual inconceivability* may be subjective or objective, i.e. it may depend on the mind's lack of power to unite both terms of a judgment, or on the fact that these terms are mutually exclusive. In the former case, it is purely negative and proves nothing. The incapacity to see how a thing could be otherwise than it is conceived does not prove that it cannot really be otherwise. What is inconceivable for one mind may be conceivable for a more perfect mind. In the latter case, the inconceivability is positive, and we see why a thing cannot be otherwise. In this supposition, inconceivability is a criterion of truth, but not the *first* criterion. It supposes that we know the necessity for the object of being as it is conceived. Two and two are four, and it is inconceivable that it should be otherwise. Why inconceivable? Because I perceive the necessary equality of "two plus two" and of "four." The truth of this statement is not tested by the inconceivableness of its opposite, but *this inconceivableness results from the clear perception of the truth.*

4. **The Exigencies of Practical Life.** — (*a*) The conclusion of Kant's "Critique of Pure Reason" is the mind's utter incapacity to acquire valid knowledge. We must be satisfied with knowing things-as-they-appear, and they appear in consciousness according to the mind's a priori forms or categories. Kant, however,

does not stop at this sceptical conclusion, but emerges out of his doubt in the "Critique of Practical Reason." On the fact of the categorical imperative as a foundation (see Ethics, p. 320 ff.) Kant builds up again three central truths: the freedom of the will, the existence of God, and the immortality of the soul, which are necessary postulates of the categorical imperative as given in consciousness. Of these truths Kant professes to have a true certitude which nothing can shake, but not a scientific certitude reached by demonstration. He calls it "moral" certitude, faith, or "belief of reason."

(*b*) The many contradictions of thinkers have led some modern philosophers to doubt the ability of human reason to reach certain knowledge. There is a wide-spread tendency to follow Kant in attributing to *practical reason* a superiority over *pure reason*. This tendency manifests itself in various ways which are more or less divergent, but all of which start from the same assumption of the weakness of reason, and tend to the same end of reconstructing knowledge on a practical basis; on action rather than intellect, on practice rather than speculation. Since all this is dynamic and ever-changing; since, moreover, the mind's relations to objects of knowledge may change, the term *belief* rather than the term *knowledge* is held by many to express the mind's attitude in regard to truth.

(*c*) The main aspects of this general tendency are the following: (1) Since the intellect is unable to give certitude, and yet moral life has imperious exigencies, the *will* is the main cause of our assents. Such is the position of Neo-criticism, with Renouvier, and of many who advocate a voluntaristic as opposed to an intellectualistic primacy. (2) Not only the will, but all the complex exigencies of human nature lead man to assent, and a great prominence is given to the satisfaction of *human feelings* and *aspirations*, especially of the need of belief and certitude. (3) *Action* may also be made the central element. Thought, they say, cannot reach objects, because it is immanent in the mind. But action reaches external reality, and establishes the contact with it, which is impossible to reason. The consciousness of activity leads to the knowledge of objects. This view is completed again by the theory of the primacy of the will. (4) Somewhat along the same lines, Pragmatism claims that the criterion of truth consists in *practical results*. By these are meant not only external useful results, but also subjective satisfaction, consistency, good influence on moral life, etc. An assertion is worth its results. It is to be tested by its effects; and its meaning itself can be expressed only in terms of its practical results.

Criticism. — (*a*) Kant's attempt at reconstructing certitude with practical reason alone is a failure. In practical as well as in speculative matters, *the same reason* judges and decides. There are not two reasons in man, but only one reason with a twofold function, speculative and practical. If liberty, immortality, and God are realities, the categorical imperative on which they rest must itself be, not only an appearance, but a reality, and the nexus between these truths and the imperative must also be real. How is all this perceived with certitude? The postulates of practical reason resort naturally and necessarily to the logic of pure reason. Morality cannot be blind; it must be enlightened and reasonable. If the noumena are not accessible to the pure reason, they cannot be accessible to the practical reason.

(*b*) We shall not discuss the general question of the primacy of will and intellect. It has too many points of view from which it may be considered, and according to which the answers must vary. In epistemology, when we speak of the test of truth and certitude, and of the justification of our assents, it is impossible to give our preference to will, action, or practice. We always find ourselves in the same dilemma: Either these are enlightened or blind. If blind, they can give no certitude of the truth. If enlightened, tested, and shown to be correct, where is the light, and where is the test? Of itself, the will is blind, and what we mean by mental light is the knowledge of the "why" of an assent, i.e the objective reason of its truth, not the subjective motives of the assent.

(*c*) The intellect is falsely declared incapable of giving any certitude. Few, perhaps, are the legitimate certitudes, but it has been shown that, in some cases, they are possible. Moreover, why should the *will* impose on the mind's assent inevident certitude? Experience teaches that we are not free to think as we please. Our assents are motived by something which is not within us, and the will cannot force us to accept the uncertain. Certain truths are accepted because they are evident for the intellect.

(*d*) It must be admitted that truth satisfies the exigencies of human nature. We need certitude. Scepticism is opposed to the very nature of the mind. But it is also the nature of the mind to require that this certitude be justified intellectually. At times, truth, even opposed to feelings, imposes itself on our acceptance. Why, if not because it has rights which we may be forced to recognize, and because *primarily our assents are rational?*

(*e*) We have discussed already the postulate that thought is immanent in the mind, and cannot reach external reality. How can *action*, which alone is supposed to place the mind in contact with external objects, be taken cognizance of, if not by an intellectual process of reflection and thought? Here again the intellect must be called in as the ultimate test, unless we rest satisfied with a blind assent.

(*f*) Pragmatism seems to identify truth with goodness or usefulness, and this is, to say the least, a gratuitous postulate. Moreover, granting that truth always *has* good results, it does not follow that it is to be *identified with* them, but rather that it is distinct from them as a cause from its effects. *A statement is not true because it is useful*, but rather *it is useful because it is true.* Many subjective influences impel us to believe or assent. But reflection is not satisfied with spontaneous assents. In order to test their value, the mind endeavors to rid itself of these influences and to consider the object on its own merits. It may be added that, in order to know which results and consequences are good, a test distinct from them, or another criterion, is required. Finally, self-evident statements are accepted independently of whatever results they may have, simply because they are seen to be true.

5. **Conclusion.** — The conclusion seems now justified that subjective criteria, whatever they may be, are insufficient as tests of objective truth, and cannot produce more than probable beliefs. In fact, among those who propose them, many claim no more

than a higher or lower degree of probability for all our knowledge. However, it must be recognized that these various systems which insist on practical reason, will, action, etc., rightly emphasize the great influence of subjective dispositions on all assents, and the necessity for man of seeking the truth with his whole mind. If we deal with practical truths, it is not enough for the intellect to accept them, the whole man must comply with them. Will, action, feelings, too frequently prevent man, not only from acting according to his knowledge, but even from seeking or accepting the truth. All this, however, is the psychological, not the epistemological, point of view. (Cf. p. 117 ff.) When applied as tests of truth, these systems fail. They do not show where the truth is, but only why, how, and by what process we accept certain things as true.

III. Theory of a Criterion Intrinsic to the Object and, in a Certain Sense, also to the Knower

As the criterion which we seek must be the distinctive sign of truth, it must be *in the object* which it distinguishes from others, and on which it imprints the characteristic stamp of truth. It must also be somehow *in the subject*, since it is the motive justifying certitude. This is possible if we look upon knowledge as the vital union of subject and object in the cognitive act.

1. **Nature of Evidence.** — (*a*) Evidence (*e, videre*) etymologically refers to the light of truth, and hence to its visibility. Many current expressions are borrowed from the sense of vision. After giving an explanation, a man asks: "Now do you see?" that is, do you *understand?* Or one says: "See how this tastes," or "Let us see how these men sing, play, etc.," i.e. let us *hear*, etc. To see is used of every sense-perception and of every function of the understanding. Evidence is the property of truth — fact, principle, or argument — by which it is enlightened so as to be perceived by a knowing power. It includes three elements: an object, its light, and the mind's perception of such light. *Evidence is the object itself, shining and manifesting itself to the mind* so as to determine the mind's assent.

(*b*) Evidence may mean the *proof* by which a claim is established, or *a claim which needs no proof* because it is self-evident. In other words, it may be mediate or immediate, according as the object possesses full light in itself, or must borrow it from other sources. In any discursive process, the self-evident must ultimately be reached, and there are different degrees of evidence according as a statement is more or less closely connected with something self-evident, and the nexus itself perceived more or less clearly.

2. **Evidence is the Criterion of Truth.** — (*a*) This is hardly more than a corollary of the preceding pages in which scepticism, idealism, and various theories of criteria were discussed. Subjectively we know that our assents must be justified, and rest on some foundation distinct from ourselves. We feel that we have to conform, not only to the *laws of thought*, but also to the *laws of things*. We are compelled to accept truth as it is. Objectively we perceive clearly at times the necessity of truth. We see it because it is shining, and we can no more see it otherwise than we can see as red the wall which is white.

(*b*) Hence it is always to evidence, mediate or immediate, that we appeal when asked to give an account of our assents. To justify a statement, I may say: "It is so because I see that it cannot be otherwise, because it clearly manifests itself." Or I may answer by a series of "becauses," the last one of which will be something self-evident. The mind may see more or less clearly, and the firmness of its assent should be in proportion to the degree of evidence. But surely we need not ask ourselves why we see in broad daylight. We see because we have the power of vision, and the proper external conditions are verified. Asking the reason of self-evidence would be tantamount to asking to light a candle in order to see the light of the sun.

3. **Difficulties Examined.** — This will be made clearer by answering a few difficulties.

(*a*) *Evidence may be apparent and illusory*, as it is in hallucination and delusion. A man may mistake subjective phenomena for objective facts and truths, and invincibly believe that he has full and satisfactory evidence.

Answer. — These are abnormal cases in which the causes of

error are frequently known and traceable to some definite organic defect. They may be corrected by other evidences. For instance, a visual hallucination may be corrected by using the sense of touch, or even the sense of vision itself when it recovers its normal condition. The problem here is psychological rather than epistemological.

(*b*) *How, then, can the mind be sure of objective evidence?* As noted already, evidence cannot be proved; it is perceived. (1) One must be careful not to exaggerate it. Frequently rashness impels to assents which objective light does not warrant. (2) It must be ascertained that the object perceived is really external. Judgment must control the data of the senses, and the understanding must proceed with caution. (3) A complex object must be analyzed, and every one of its elements examined. As remarked in Logic, one small error at a given point of the process may ultimately lead far astray.

(*c*) If evidence is the test of truth, *how can there be error?* Differences of opinions, as remarked elsewhere, are chiefly on matters in which we have only probabilities, and they depend on innate and acquired dispositions. On evident truths there is agreement. We are not concerned at present with their number. Even if they are few, they are accepted because of their evidence. Error may come from rashness, and from subjective dispositions which blind man, and impel him to assent without sufficient evidence. This will happen especially in questions which have a practical bearing. Moreover, owing to the complexity of the object, the need of long demonstrations, the difficulty experienced in extricating various elements of a complex process, the mind may be led astray without being aware of it. But the progress of science consists largely in ascertaining, verifying, and correcting conclusions already reached.

In many cases we must rest satisfied with a greater or smaller probability, and admit the possibility of error. He is a wise man who does not give to his assents more firmness than evidence entitles them to, and knows how to doubt when there is not enough light.

Error may be caused by the nature of the object, or by influences within the subject. It is a judgment which exceeds that which is really given in intuition or reasoning. But the fact that all men speak of error indicates that all have a test of truth. Error could never be mentioned if truth were unknowable. The process of detecting error always consists in applying evidence, in its various forms, as the criterion of truth.

II. DERIVATIVE CRITERIA

As the ultimate criterion, evidence manifests itself to different faculties, and in various ways. We shall now speak of these derived criteria. They may be reduced to two groups according as the truth is reached by one's own personal effort and seen in itself, or, on the contrary, is reached only through mediate contact, i.e. through another mind that has perceived it in itself.

I. Personal Faculties Coming in Direct Contact with the Known Object

1. **Senses.** — (*a*) The reliability of the senses has already been asserted against idealism. They rightly testify to the existence of our own body and of an external world. The subject and the external object being united in the "action" of the object which is at the same time the "passion" of the subject, no bridge is necessary between the two, and no transformation of the physical cause into a psychical result.

Each sense manifests only some aspects of objects. Knowledge is thus acquired in a fragmentary way, but the intellect combines these fragments and reaches a more complete knowledge of reality. It is true also that individual perceptions may differ owing to the condition and the degree of perfection of the senses, but this does not invalidate perception. The distinction must also be remembered between what is actually perceived and what is imagined or inferred. We naturally interpret and complete perceptions. (See Psychology, pp. 62 ff., 79 ff., 118 ff.)

(*b*) *Some conditions are necessary* for the trustworthiness of the senses. (1) Each sense is fully reliable only within its own special sphere, for what has been called in psychology its *sensile per se proprium*. The *sensile commune* should be ascertained by more than one sense. As to the *sensile per accidens*, it may be the occasion of many errors. Wrong habits and accidental causes of error are frequent; hence great caution is required in inferring the nature of objects. The eye may mistake salt for sugar owing to their common whiteness. The ear may mistake one man's voice for another man's owing to their likeness, etc. (2) The *object* must be within due limits of distance, intensity, etc., and there should be no obstacle between the object and the sense. Owing to its distance, the moon looks like a disk, and not like a sphere. Owing to a refracting medium, a stick half-dipped in water, not perpendicularly, appears broken to the eye, and rightly so, since, in fact, the rays are refracted. (3) The *organ* must be in a normal condition. Many physiological influences modify perception. Error is due to rashness in judging hastily that sensations are objective.

(*c*) Induction must complete the immediate data of the senses to ascertain the physical nature of the perceived qualities, correct illusions, and verify the reports of an "educated" sense by those of another. The evidence in sense-perception is sometimes direct and intuitive, sometimes indirect and mediate.

2. **Consciousness**, by which we become aware of our own internal states, ideas, emotions, volitions, etc., is an infallible criterion. I may err in referring these processes to wrong causes, but, as far as consciousness manifests my present subjective experiences, e.g. my feeling of pain, my thinking, imagining, doubting, etc., its evidence is intuitive, and can be denied by no one, not even by the out-and-out sceptic. Illusions and hallucinations are real for consciousness; the images are really present in the mind. The error consists in referring them wrongly to external objects, and in *judging* that they are faithful representations of external reality. Consciousness also apprehends vaguely the ego or subject, but not its nature.

3. **Memory**.—(*a*) Memory includes both the recall of the past and its recognition as past. Its *veracity* is to be admitted, and in many cases can be verified. I may, for instance, note my impressions, and later on compare what my memory recalls with what

I have written. Or I may compare my impressions with those of others who have perceived the same object. Without memory, comparing, identifying, distinguishing, reasoning, etc., would be impossible. The validity of memory is thus shown in its very exercise, and may be tested by experiments proving its agreement with past perception.

(*b*) However, it has its *limitations*. We do not recall at will everything we have perceived or known; and we may recall an image of the past without recognizing it. But these limitations are negative, and do not affect the trustworthiness of memory, as far as memory goes, any more than the ignorance of certain things affects the validity of the knowledge one possesses.

(*c*) It is also to be admitted that there are not only limitations, but also *positive errors* of memory. Memory may combine a reproduction of the past with fanciful additions and changes, and yet we may be led to think that the whole is a faithful copy. This simply shows that an imprudent use of memory is possible, and that, owing to habit, lack of care, of exactness and reflection, one fails to verify the elements of an image before passing a judgment on its value. Because of the close relation between memory and imagination, great caution is necessary. But, if proper care is taken, in normal conditions at least, the evident testimony of memory is reliable. If it remains doubtful — and frequently it should be held as such — assent must be suspended until further research by means of the laws of association brings full light.

4. **Reason.** — Enough has been said on the objective value of concepts and of intuitive necessary judgments. As to judgments derived by inductive or deductive reasoning from self-evident facts or principles, the degree of their validity depends on the necessity by which they are connected with the self-evident starting-point. The nearer such judgments are to self-evidence and the more necessary their connection, the greater also is their evidence, and consequently the firmer should be the mind's assent. Here, as well as in the use of other cognitive faculties, error does not come from the instrument itself of knowledge, but from the bad use that is made of it. In inference we connect facts and principles with other facts and principles. Not only must these be certain

and valid, but the application of them must be made with prudence. In a series of inferences, principles that are not demonstrated, and yet that are far from self-evident, are sometimes used or implied, and the rules of logic also may be violated. (Cf. Psychology, pp. 115 ff.)

II. Indirect Relation of the Mind with the Known Object

1. **Authority.** — (*a*) Agreement with others always strengthens personal conviction. But there are cases in which the testimony of others does not merely strengthen, but also is a valid motive of, assent. A truth may not have been perceived directly by me, yet I accept it because it has been perceived by others who tell me, i.e. I accept it on their authority. For me, the evidence is not in the object itself, since none of my cognitive faculties has come in direct contact with it. What must be evident is (1) that those who tell me really know, and (2) that their testimony is reliable. By far the greater part of human knowledge is acquired on the authority of others. Not only is history in all its branches dependent on it altogether, but even the majority of contemporary facts, events, and circumstances are known from the relation of others. Personal experience is restricted within narrow limits, and would give but little knowledge, if it were not possible to profit by the experience or science of others who live at present or have lived in the past. Personal experience lasts only a short time and extends to only a small space.

(*b*) In practical as well as in scientific life, man must believe his fellowmen. The physician believes the chemist; the chemist trusts the physician's knowledge; the physicist accepts the conclusions of the mathematician, and so on. Even the greatest scientist and philosopher is obliged to believe his cook on many points. All records of transactions between individuals or nations depend on testimony. The decisions of courts are given in view of the testimony of witnesses. At all its stages, education depends on the authority of parents and teachers. History is essentially based on human testimony. Faith in other men is implied in every endeavor of life, and without it progress would be an impossibility. Who can estimate the influence of the daily newspaper or the magazine on human assents and on human conduct? Think a moment of the number of things which we have to take on authority, and of the number of things which we do take on authority so as to save ourselves the trouble of ascertaining them.

(c) (1) *Belief* is the assent given to testimony. It may be certain, but frequently is more or less probable. (2) *Testimony* is the communication of some information by a witness. (3) The *authority of a witness*, or his reliability, is based on the fact that he knows, or is not deceived, and that he speaks the truth, or does not deceive. (4) The *matter of his testimony* may be a universal law —e.g. that water is composed of oxygen and hydrogen; a permanent fact—e.g. that Washington City is on the Potomac; or a transient fact,—e.g. an eclipse, a battle, an earthquake. (5) These facts may be *contemporary* or more or less *remote*. (6) The witness may be an *eye-witness* (immediate), when he has been present at the occurrence which he relates, or he may rely on the testimony of *others* (mediate witness). (7) Finally, the testimony may be given in speech, writing, or in the form of monuments, coins, statues, etc.

2. **On Questions of Fact.** — (a) *The nature of the fact* itself must be taken into account, and compared with the competence of the witness to observe it. The observation of some facts and experiments requires a special training of the observer's mind. Furthermore, if the fact is unlikely and extraordinary, a higher authority or a greater number of witnesses will be required.

(b) If there is only *one witness*, his qualifications must be ascertained. Some men lack the power of attention, judgment, and memory. Others have it only along certain lines. Hence the special aptitudes and dispositions of the witness must be considered in reference to the special fact which he relates. His veracity is also to be ascertained. To this end it may be necessary to know his moral character, to find out whether he had any interest in deceiving, etc. When there is only one witness, greater severity is required in testing his authority.

(c) *Several* unanimous and independent witnesses give a greater certitude than one witness. If they disagree, it is necessary not so much to number those on each side as to weigh their authority. *They must be independent*, i.e. not prompted by the same interests or passions, nor following the same original witness, for otherwise there is really only one testimony Frequently the impossibility of deception is certain, for instance, when witnesses relate important contemporary events, and their testimony has not been contradicted. In general, the greater the number of witnesses, their independence, and their competence to observe the fact, the greater also the certitude.

3. **On Questions of Doctrine,** human authority has less value than on questions of fact, because the human mind is more fallible in its deductions and inductions than in ordinary easy observations, and because there is less agreement among men. Yet in every discussion, men appeal to authorities, and rightly so, for a specialist has more chance to reach the truth in his special branch than another man. However, the general principle to be applied here is that *the authority of a man is worth the reasons which he gives*, at least for one who can understand these reasons. As to those who cannot understand, they must accept the statements with more or less reserve according to the qualities, fairness, prejudices, etc., of the man who makes them. The common consent of mankind, in questions on which man in general is competent, shows, not only the propensity of human nature, but also objective evidence.

4. **Oral Tradition is** a difficult criterion because it is too variable. By passing from man to man, the same fact may become gradually distorted by additions, subtractions, and changes. Experience shows that if the same fact is narrated by one person to another, by this one to a third, and so forth, the narration made by the tenth person may be greatly different from the original. Hence the greatest care must be used in distinguishing truth from legend. Yet, as a rule, even after a long time of oral tradition, there remains a nucleus of truth which may be disentangled by controlling oral tradition with the help of written documents, and comparing one line of oral tradition with other lines independent of it. If the tradition happens to be mentioned in writing,

the circumstances of the writing are to be taken into consideration. Moreover, the nature of the fact must be examined, as also the customs and characteristics of the people by whom the tradition has been preserved. When the tradition is a popular one, known to all, adulterations are less likely to occur, because the statement of one man is corrected by the statement of others on the same point.

5. **Written Documents.** — The conditions required in a written document are its authenticity, integrity, and veracity.

(*a*) The *authenticity* or genuineness of a book, that is, the fact that it has been written by the author whose name it bears, is established by (1) *internal evidence:* its style as compared to the style of works that are certainly genuine; the agreement of its contents with the time and place at which it is supposed to have been written; the agreement of its contents with the author's views and opinions, etc.; (2) *external evidence:* the testimony of other writers, oral tradition, the silence of those who would be interested in denying its authenticity, etc.

(*b*) The *integrity* of a book, that is, the freedom from additions, subtractions, or changes, is proved by different circumstances: the multiplicity of independent editions, the comparison with manuscripts, the difficulty of introducing interpolations or mutilations, the importance of the contents, the comparison with other documents, etc.

(*c*) The *veracity* is ascertained by showing the author's knowledge and fairness, and by comparing the book with other documents.

N.B. A general principle to be observed in the application of the criterion of authority is that one must always guard against both excessive credulity and exaggerated scepticism. Few sciences are more difficult than history, which endeavors to find out the truth of facts related in written documents or oral traditions.

To discuss here the question of the authority of divine revelation would be to anticipate a number of conclusions on the existence and the attributes of God, and on the criteria of revelation. All we can say at present is that, granting God's omniscience and sanctity, and also the fact of revelation, divine faith gives to man the highest possible certitude.

CONCLUSION

The conclusion of this treatise is that certitude is possible for man, but that it requires some conditions. Not only is certitude possible, but it is the indispensable condition of thought. Knowledge is a complex process. It always needs correction and readjustment, but its bases are secure. Man's endeavor should be to build as strong and as high an edifice as possible on the twofold foundation of facts and principles that are certain. He must know the limitations, and imperfections of his own mind, and hence be satisfied with opinion and even doubt where certitude is not justified. He must also proceed cautiously, and use all possible tests of his knowledge. But the field to be explored has no limits, and, provided the mind starts from evidence and proceeds with evidence, there is no reason to assign any border line beyond which would lie the unknowable. What is unknown for the science of to-day may be known for the science of to-morrow.

COSMOLOGY OR THE METAPHYSICAL STUDY OF THE PHYSICAL WORLD

INTRODUCTION

1. **General Introduction to Metaphysics.**— (*a*) The name "metaphysics" owes its origin to the arrangement of Aristotle's works by Andronicus of Rhodes (first century B.C.), who gave the general title of τὰ μετὰ τὰ φυσικά to all the treatises that followed Aristotle's treatise on Physics. The name given by Aristotle himself was that of "First Philosophy." Metaphysics means the science which rises higher than physical sciences, and considers things from a more abstract, hence more general, point of view.

All sciences are more or less abstract, and all suppose general principles. But physical sciences use experience as their chief instrument, and call upon experience to test and verify their conclusions. Moreover, every science considers only certain classes of beings, and from a special point of view. Metaphysics endeavors to complete special sciences by a higher unification. Thus all physical sciences deal with material substances; but what is matter which is common to all? They use the principle of causality; but what is a cause? and so on. Physical sciences are empirical; the present science is metempirical or metaphysical. Its conclusions cannot be verified directly by experience, yet must be based on it and harmonize with it. Metaphysics is not, and cannot be, divorced from physical science.

(*b*) That its *object is real* has been shown in epistemology, and those who claim that metaphysics is an impossibility, or deals with the unknowable, do so on account of preconceived ideas on the nature of knowledge. In a series of subordinated "whats" the mind is not satisfied till it reaches the last. What is ice? . . What is water? What are oxygen and hydrogen? . What is an element? . . . What is matter? . . . And although it is more abstract, the object of metaphysics is nevertheless real. Hence metaphysics is not a mere science of words and ideas, and the discredit into which it has fallen is due to agnostic tendencies, and also to the abuse which has sometimes been made of metaphysics, by asking and trying to solve idle questions, or by making it a purely a priori and ideal construction.

(*c*) The *objects of metaphysics* may be reduced to three main groups: the physical world, the human soul, and the ultimate ground of all things. Hence we shall have three parts: Cosmology, Philosophy of Mind, and Theodicy. The method will be both inductive and deductive, i.e.,proceed from experience and from self-evident principles. But everywhere we shall keep in touch with concrete reality.

2. Cosmology (*κόσμος*, *mundus*, universe) is *the philosophical science of the physical world.* (1) It deals with the *physical world*, and, in this respect, its object is the same as that of natural sciences, with this difference, however, that it deals with all physical realities, while each of them is concerned only with certain groups. (2) It is a *philosophical science*, and, in this, its point of view differs from that of the other sciences. Thus physics deals with the common properties of matter; chemistry with its changes; mineralogy with the description and classification of minerals; geology with the formation of the crust of the earth, etc. None touches upon the higher questions of the intimate and ultimate constitution of matter. They assume that matter exists, and they show its various properties and activities, but do not consider its essential nature.

Cosmology, therefore, completes natural sciences. It endeavors to answer questions which they do not answer. Yet it evidently depends on them, since it tries to explain the real world. Its method is chiefly inductive, starting from common experience or from scientific conclusions, and rising to higher generalizations, by the use especially of the principles of causality and of sufficient reason.

3. **Division of Cosmology.** — (*a*) To be complete, cosmology should include the following subjects: (1) Inorganic beings; their properties and nature. (2) Organic beings; life in general; plants, and animals. (3) Man; his activities and nature. (4) Genesis and evolution of the world, both of the individual beings that compose it and of the universe as a whole; of life and of the various forms of life; of man. (5) The end or purpose of the world. (6) The cosmos, or the universe considered as a whole, and the relations by which its unity is realized.

(*b*) Of these questions, however, some, like the question of evolution, belong chiefly to natural sciences, and cannot receive a full treatment here. Others, like the ultimate efficient or final cause, will find a more suitable place in Theodicy. The questions referring to man, owing to their special importance, will be the special object of the next treatise. Hence we shall have the four following chapters: (1) Inorganic beings. (2) Life. (3) Origin and evolution. (4) The Cosmos.

CHAPTER I

INORGANIC SUBSTANCES

I. PROPERTIES

The properties of inorganic substances may be reduced to two groups, passive and active properties, or extension and energy.

1. **Extension.** — (*a*) All material substances are endowed with extension. Such, at any rate, is the constant *testimony of the senses* of touch and vision. Such also is the *assumption of sciences*, like mechanics, physics, and chemistry. Psychology itself would be at a loss to account for the perception of extension, if extension were a reality neither in the external world nor in the organism. For the present it is enough to note that the phenomenon of extension is undeniable. Whether extension be real or not, its appearance at least will have to be explained.

(*b*) However, extension cannot constitute the whole essence of bodies, as Descartes claimed. He based this conclusion on the fact that, even if all qualities — temperature, shape, resistance, etc. — of a material substance be changed, its extension always remains. But (1) when, for instance, a stone is broken into several parts, every part has the same essential nature as the whole, although not the same extension. Large or small, it has the same essence. (2) When we want to distinguish one substance from another, we never do so by its extension alone, but by other properties, which, therefore, are more characteristic than extension.

(*c*) In consequence of their extension, bodies occupy a certain space, have a multiplicity of parts distributed in this space, and although, in a continuous body, such parts are mutually exclusive, they exist only potentially before an actual division takes place. The right is not the left, but actual division alone makes a determined number of parts.

2. **Activity.** — Material substances act, i.e. are endowed with

forces and energies by means of which they cause changes in other substances. Thus electricity, heat, etc., are powerful agents; the forces of attraction, resistance, repulsion, etc., are constantly at work. Substances act upon one another in a multitude of ways, and man strives to master and control these forces so as to make them subservient to his ends. That these forces are real is evident from the testimony of consciousness, for we are aware of the actions — heat, resistance, electricity, etc. — of external bodies on our own, and from the testimony of external senses which manifest the interaction of all material substances. These forces are distinct from extension, and physicists commonly oppose matter to energy.

II. CONSTITUTION

I. The Question Stated

1. **The Problem.** — The present problem is that of the ultimate constitution of material substances in general; not of this or that special substance, but of all bodies. Chemistry resolves certain substances, called compounds, into others which can be analyzed no further, and are called simple substances or elements. Both physics and chemistry agree in admitting that material substances are not continuous, but composed of distinct molecules (smallest units of compound), and atoms (smallest units of elements). And even what until recently was looked upon as the atom, i.e. the indivisible unit, is now, owing to the discovery of radio-activity, looked upon as made up of a number of corpuscles or electrons.

Our point of view here is different from that of physical and chemical sciences. The element is a specific material substance. The atom or electron is also a physical reality. Hence concerning both the element and the atom the questions may be raised: What are they? What is their nature? These questions cannot be answered by natural sciences, for their methods will always lead them to something physical, and what we want to know is whether, starting from physical facts, reason cannot proceed farther in the mental analysis of substances, and discover principles which, although they may be inseparable, are nevertheless distinct.

2. **Theories.** — The theories may be reduced to three, two of which advocate one single principle, whilst the other advocates a twofold principle. One insists on quantitative properties, admits extension, and denies real energies. The other insists on energy, and denies real extension. The third tries to account for extension, energy, and specific properties.

(*a*) As a philosophical system, *atomism* not only admits the physical reality of atoms endowed with extension, but asserts that we can proceed no farther in our rational analysis. The atom is the ultimate reality of matter. Atomism is a very ancient theory, advocated in Greece by Leucippus, Democritus, and Epicurus, and in Rome by Lucretius. These philosophers hold that atoms are eternal, infinite in number, and that their fortuitous meeting formed the various substances. Gassendi modified the theory on minor points in order to reconcile it with Christian dogmas, but admitted also a pure atomism. To-day, owing to the discredit into which metaphysical investigation has fallen, there is a tendency to stop at the atoms as physical units, without pushing the analysis any further. Atomism may attempt to explain everything with atoms of the same kind, endowed with various motions (mechanical atomism), or it may admit different kinds of atoms, with specific properties (dynamic atomism).

(*b*) *Dynamism* in general holds that matter consists essentially of simple, and consequently indivisible, units or forces. Extension is not real, but only apparent. The first vestiges of dynamism may probably be found in the school of Pythagoras. It is only later, however, that this doctrine is held explicitly by some Arabian philosophers. In more recent times, Leibniz claims that matter is composed of "monads," i.e. of simple substances without parts or extension, all dissimilar, and endowed only with an internal activity. Matter can never act on other matter. Boscovich reduces matter to an aggregate of homogeneous points without extension, which, by their different numbers, groupings, distances, and interaction, produce the diversity of so-called material substances. To-day many scientists advocate an electrotonic theory of matter according to which matter is ultimately reduced to electrons which have no real extension. Under the name of energetism, an attempt is also made to reduce the concept of matter to that of energy.

(c) *Hylomorphism*, or physical dualism, holds that no theory can account for all the properties of matter by one principle only. It admits a twofold principle, matter, or rather primary matter (ὕλη), and form (μορφή). This applies to all substances, even to the "elements" of chemistry, and the "atoms" of physics and chemistry. *Matter* is the principle of quantity, but is of itself indetermined, the same in all substances, and incapable of existence apart from the form. The *form* is the specific or determining principle, the source of all determinations. The *union* of both principles, each of which is incomplete in itself and inseparable from the other, gives the complete specific material substance. The two always go together, and cannot be perceived separately by the senses. What we call matter in the usual sense is always primary matter together with the substantial form with which it is intimately united. This theory was proposed by Aristotle. It was the common doctrine of the scholastics in the Middle Ages, after which it was almost forgotten until recently.

II. Discussion of the Systems

1. **Atomism** has the general defect of not answering the question proposed. To say that what we call matter, and what appears to the senses as one material substance, is in reality composed of a multitude of smaller bodies leaves the problem without solution, for this problem refers to the smallest body or atom as well as to the largest. Physical division cannot here substitute itself for reasoning. The atom is one and supposedly indivisible. Yet, however small it may be, it occupies space, has different parts, and a point on its surface is not the same as another point. Atoms are real, but their reality must be explained.

(a) If different forces and properties are admitted, one may ask: Where do these come from? What is their ultimate source? If the atoms are of different size, why are all equally indivisible?

(b) Mechanical atomism rejects all specific properties, admits that atoms are all of the same nature, and tries to explain all the facts by their different motions. But it fails in this attempt. To mention only a few facts: (1) Chemical affinity, in virtue of which certain elements combine only with certain others, and always in definite proportions, supposes laws which the atoms invariably obey, and which their motions alone cannot account for. (2) Whatever explanation be given of the difference between a chemical mixture and a chemical compound, this difference implies in the elements the presence of specific properties which do not manifest themselves in a simple mixture, but only in a combination. If the elements have been completely altered in the compound, how do they always reappear in the analysis? If they have not been altered, where do the new properties come from? (3) Affinity, cohesion, molecular and molar attraction, cannot be explained satisfactorily by mechanism. They suppose an internal principle of tendency. (4) In a word, chemical and physical laws are not reducible to mere mechanical movements. (5) Even if they were, mechanism would still be inadequate, for motion itself cannot be communicated without supposing intrinsic forces. The communication of a movement supposes in the mobile an aptitude and power which is actualized by the impulsion of the motor. When the actual impact of the two has taken place, and the mobile keeps on moving, its motion cannot actually come from the motor, with which it is no longer in communication. It is therefore the unfolding of an intrinsic energy. (6) In general, as will be explained later, there is in every substance an internal principle of tendency. (Cf. pp. 452, 455.)

2. **Dynamism.** — (*a*) Dynamism cannot explain real extension. It is clear that a multitude of "naughts" of extension put together can never give a positive quantity. If points without extension are supposed to touch one another, all necessarily coincide in the same point. If they are supposed to be at a distance from one another, it becomes necessary to admit an *actio in distans*, the possibility of which is generally denied by physicists. Moreover, this would not give real, but only apparent, extension, and it is difficult to understand this appearance or illusion of extension, if there is no extension anywhere, not even in the sense-organs.

(*b*) It is true that matter does not manifest itself to the senses except through its activities (radiations, vibrations, resistance, heat, etc.), but it does not follow that real extension is to be denied. Without matter it is difficult to understand energy, for in this case, what is it that moves, rotates, vibrates?

(*c*) The recent discoveries in radio-activity are not given the same interpretation by all. Some deny, while others admit, that the electron has extension, and it is difficult, if not impossible, to answer this question from the physical standpoint.

3. **Hylomorphism.** — (*a*) We distinguish the matter and form — i.e. the materials and shape — of any object, e.g. of a marble statue. We may go farther, and ask what the substance which we call marble is itself composed of. We shall find that it is composed of carbon, calcium, oxygen, etc. These may be variously combined with other elements so as to form new compounds, with properties different from those of the former compound, and from those of the component elements themselves. The element has in itself a principle which may indifferently be this or that specific substance, and which is called "primary matter" as opposed to "secondary matter" (marble or any other substance). That by which it is determined as marble, and not anything else, is the "substantial form," as opposed to "accidental forms," i.e. the various determinations like shape and physical properties, which the marble may receive.

Thus physical matter is composed of a deeper reality, indetermined, and capable of being indifferently one substance or another (primary matter), and of a determining principle by which it is a special kind of substance (substantial form). The many changes which the same elements undergo in forming different compounds lead to the admission of a twofold principle. The element itself always has a principle of indetermination, and a determining principle; a principle common to all substances, and a specific principle which differentiates one substance from another; a principle of passivity capable of receiving successively different modifications, and a principle which makes it to be what it is.

(*b*) It is true that, understood in this way, matter and form are only abstractions. They do not exist separately as physical realities, and cannot be perceived by the senses. But, like all abstractions, they are not purely mental products; they are realities that compose the physical substance and cannot exist apart from each other.

In fact, even atomism and dynamism are obliged to admit that homogeneous units, by their movements, groupings, and activities, form substances that are widely different in their properties. Hence they must admit some kind of a form or law according to which these differentiations take place. Should various substances ultimately consist of only one kind of elements, that is, should it be ascertained that the elements of chemistry are reducible to identical units like the electrons, it would still be necessary to explain how these ultimate identical materials are what they are, and how they unite to form the various substances. They always obey certain laws which indicate a true determination or formal principle. Hence this would always lead to a dualism of the indetermined and the determinant, of the common and the specific, of a substratum and its superstructure, of matter and form.

CHAPTER II

LIVING BEINGS

I. THE CHARACTERISTICS OF LIFE

I. In General

1. **Common Idea of Life.** — (*a*) A distinction is made by all men between certain beings — animals and plants — which are called living, and certain others which are called lifeless. It may not always be possible to indicate which beings have life, and which are deprived of it — especially in the case of micro-organisms where the biologist himself is not always able to make this distinction with certainty — yet a sharp distinction is always recognized between living and dead, and between organic and inorganic matter.

(*b*) The common basis of this distinction is the presence or the absence of movements or changes which *originate within the being*, that is, the principle or cause of which is not, or at least does not seem to be, external. Thus an animal is distinguished from an automaton because the latter must be pushed or "wound up." Were not this necessary condition known, the automaton would easily be mistaken, e.g. by the child or ignorant man, for a living being. An animal or a man ceases to live when he ceases to move, when the respiratory process stops, when the heart ceases to beat, etc. A plant ceases to live when the sap no longer circulates, when ordinary changes in the growth, foliage, etc., no longer take place. Many metaphorical expressions are derived from this fact. We speak of a living fountain as opposed to stagnant water; we say of a man, animal, or plant that they are full of life when they change rapidly. (Compare such expressions as "lively imagination," "living faith," "live wire," "live coal," "the company was alive," etc.)

To live, therefore, is to move, and to undergo changes due to an internal principle, although an external stimulus may be present, as in the case of a rabbit running away from a dog. In the same circumstances, lifeless matter would not move or change. It must be pushed or acted upon by some mechanical force.

(*c*) The changes that are most commonly taken as *signs of life* are local movements of the whole being, or of some of its parts (heart, head, arms, etc.); the functions of nutrition and growth, and various modifications in the general appearance (foliage, flowers, fruits, etc.); a certain shape, size, and organization; and consciousness, which some of these changes manifest.

2. **Scientific Conception of Life.** — The following points summarize the differences which biological science observes between living and inorganic substances.

(*a*) *Chemical composition.* Evidently living matter as such cannot be analyzed, since the process of analysis deprives it of life. The analysis of an organism yields primarily the following elements: carbon, oxygen, hydrogen, nitrogen, sulphur, and phosphorus. In living beings, the elements unite to form proteids, and these compounds are always highly unstable and constantly changing. A mere glance at the formulæ of organic and of inorganic chemistry shows how much more complex the former are than the latter, and how many more atoms are required.

(*b*) *Shape and structure.* (1) Whereas the organism always has a special *determined shape* according to its kind, the mineral has *no determined shape*, except in crystals. The shape of crystals is always angular; angles are generally excluded from the shape of the whole organism and of its elementary structures. The outlines, both of the organism and of its parts, are generally curve lines. (2) The mineral is *homogeneous;* the organism is *differentiated*. This is clear for higher organisms, in which a cross section will reveal a multitude of different tissues. It is true of the lowest also, for the cell, which constitutes the whole of unicellular organisms, and which is the last unit in multicellular organisms, is itself already heterogeneous and very complex in its structure. Its natural shape is spheroidal, and it possesses the essential properties of nutrition, growth, multiplication, irritability, etc.

(*c*) *Origin.* Life cannot be produced in the laboratory. The rule is general: "Omne vivens ex vivo," or "Omnis cellula ex cellula." A crystal is but a special regular arrangement of a substance under certain conditions.

(*d*) *Nutrition, growth, duration*. (1) Living substances alone have the power of *assimilation*, i.e. they manufacture proteids out of inorganic matter, and elaborate foreign substances which they incorporate into their own. (2) Minerals are *stable*, and inorganic matter always tends to the most stable equilibrium. Living matter *changes* constantly. A continual decay and a continual repair take place within it. Living matter returns to the inorganic world, and, from the inorganic world, new living substances are formed. (3) The *growth* of minerals is not limited to any size or shape. Living matter has a maximum for every species, and is always shaped according to a specific type. (4) The growth of minerals — crystals included — takes place by *accretion*, i.e. *juxtaposition* of particles; that of living beings takes place by *intussusception*, i.e. *assimilation*. (5) Inorganic substances, of themselves, have no limited or definite *duration*; they change only when they are acted upon by external agents. In living substances, the period of growth and of life itself is subject to laws varying with the different species.

3. **Philosophical Notion of Life.** — If we now try to find out the essential characteristics of living beings, all the special properties of living beings have the following points in common. (1) They imply changes that are constant and uninterrupted, owing to the unstable equilibrium of living matter. This is the fundamental characteristic of nutrition which is the first vital function. (2) They are immanent, i.e. they modify and perfect primarily the living substance itself. There are many transitive activities, but the final term of these is within the organism itself. Inorganic substances, on the contrary, (1) tend to the most stable combination and equilibrium; (2) act only on one another. They do not modify or perfect themselves, but other substances.

II. Manifestations of Life

1. **Hylozoism** (ὕλη, matter, and ζωή, life) asserts that matter is essentially living, and hence that even so-called inorganic matter

possesses a very low degree of life. This name is sometimes restricted to the system according to which, not only some degree of life, but also some degree of consciousness, must be attributed to all forms of matter. Proposed in various forms by ancient philosophers, this view has been advocated recently under various names like the German "Allbeseelung" (all-animation), or Panpsychism.

From the point of view of science, this assertion is evidently *gratuitous*, and even *contrary to facts*. It is advocated on a priori grounds, such as monism, or the assumed identity of all things; evolution, or the assumed necessity for life and consciousness to have originated from lower forms of matter; and the endeavor to exclude every intervention of God. The main differences pointed out above between living and non-living substances show their irreducibility to each other.

2. **Plants and Animals.** — Living beings may be divided, according to their complexity, into unicellular and multicellular; according to their size, into visible and miscroscopic. But the main division, according to their functions, is into plants, animals, and men. The reason for assigning to man a special place will be given in rational psychology. There are many differences between plants and animals. The main difference, however, consists in *the absence or the presence of consciousness*. Animals, at least the higher forms of animals, give unmistakable signs of consciousness. They have sense-organs, and respond to stimuli in the same way as man. By analogy, we know that they experience sensations, that they have imagination, memory, feeling, and instinct. Otherwise their behavior is unexplainable. Plants, on the contrary, give no signs of consciousness. They have no nervous system, with which consciousness is always connected in animals, and there is no reason whatsoever to attribute to them what they do not manifest. Sometimes, it is true, the scientist may not be certain whether a living being (especially among microbes) is a plant or an animal, but this can in no way be given as an objection against the distinction of both kingdoms. The degrees of consciousness vary greatly in animals, but the question may always be asked, if not answered: Is consciousness present? Then we have an animal. Is consciousness absent? Then we have a plant.

II. NATURE OF THE LIVING BEING

I. Theories

Sometimes a distinction is made between living beings that are endowed with consciousness and those that are deprived of it. As consciousness has characteristics irreducible to those of matter, it must also require a distinct principle. This conclusion seems correct, but, for the present, we limit ourselves to the lowest degree of life, vegetative life, the main manifestations of which have been described above.

(*a*) Some refuse to admit the existence of a special principle of life. Life is explained adequately by the *general properties of matter*, either by its mechanical motions, or by its physical and chemical properties, which manifest themselves in various ways according to the adaptation of the various organs. But the point on which all agree is that life results simply from the greater complexity of matter in living beings, and from the natural play of its mechanical, physical, and chemical energies.

(*b*) Others admit that *special forces* are necessary to explain life. These vital forces are distinct from, irreducible and frequently antagonistic to, the ordinary properties of matter. As inorganic forces rather tend to destroy life, vital forces must constantly resist them. Some look upon this special energy as a spiritual, intelligent, and directive force (Stahl); others, as inherent in matter, but yet superadded to its ordinary properties (vitalism). All agree that organized matter and the vital principle are two distinct realities, irreducible to each other.

(*c*) Others finally take a middle course. Life is not merely the result of mechanical forces; nor does it require any special forces. The living substance is composed, like every other material being, of a twofold principle, *matter* and *form*. The form, or vital principle, is united with matter, and, together with it, constitutes only one complete living substance.

II. Discussion

1. **Physical Energies in Living Beings.** — Not only does life depend on the various energies of matter, but there seems to be no

necessity for admitting in the organism the presence of any energies *distinct from* ordinary physical energies, still less for admitting energies *antagonistic to* these. There is no real opposition or struggle between vital phenomena and physico-chemical phenomena. On the contrary, we see the physical and chemical properties of matter utilized by the living substance, and working together to maintain life. In every vital process, the chemical laws of affinity, attraction, cohesion, combination, etc., and the physical laws concerning heat, gravity, osmosis, capillarity, levers, etc., are obeyed, and numberless applications of them could be made to the processes of digestion, assimilation, respiration, circulation, etc. As biology proceeds farther in its explanation of vital processes, it succeeds better in showing that these processes presuppose no forces distinct from the ordinary properties of matter. The general laws of the conservation of matter and of the conservation of energy seem to hold in the organic as well as in the inorganic world. Nothing is created; nothing annihilated. In the living substance, and in the laboratory, changes obey the same laws of equivalence, and are subject to the same conditions. The distinctive property of life, therefore, is not the presence of special forces, but the *special mode* according to which these converge to the same end which is the life of the individual.

2. **Their Insufficiency.** — (*a*) Life is not explained by mechanical, physical, and chemical energies alone. Even in the lowest organism, they are many and complex; and yet all serve the same purpose, the life of the organism. It is precisely this *harmony* and this *unity of direction* which suppose a directive principle. How, for instance, do these forces work together so as to form a highly differentiated organism, with very complex parts (eye, ear, digestive apparatus, etc.), out of one single primitive cell with which all organisms begin? How are the physical materials elaborated so as to furnish every organ with the elements it needs? This requires a guiding principle; *a principle of unity*, presiding over the functions of the whole organism; and *a principle of formation*, presiding over the development of the organism itself. And here it would serve no purpose to appeal to the elaboration of organic substances in the laboratory. Organic they may

be called, but they are not living, and they lack the essential principle of life.

(*b*) This principle of unity, directing and subordinating the various organs and functions, is not distinct from the living being itself. It is an *internal principle*, tending to the creation and preservation of the organism. The living being is one, but, like the inorganic being, it is composed of a twofold principle, matter and form. The substantial form, principle of determination, unity and activity, is, in the living being, the "soul," as Aristotle called it, i.e. the vital or animating principle. It is not something extrinsic to living matter, guiding it as the pilot steers his vessel, but it is an intrinsic determining principle of matter, which together with it forms *one complete living substance*. (Cf. pp. 428, 430.)

CHAPTER III

ORIGIN AND EVOLUTION

I. THE QUESTION STATED

One of the most striking tendencies of modern science and philosophy is to take a *dynamic* and *genetic* rather than a *static* and *descriptive* view of things. Attention is given to the questions: What can a thing do? How does it come to be what it is? Things are looked upon as moving, changing, becoming. The passage from the simple to the complex is followed closely. This tendency manifests itself, for instance, in biology, by the questions concerning the origin of life and of the different forms of life; in astronomy and cosmology, by the questions of the formation of the earth and the universe; in the various branches of psychology, by the study of mental development, and the genesis of various mental manifestations. This tendency is one of the characteristics of the nineteenth century, and continues to manifest itself in the twentieth.

1. **The Problems.** — (*a*) The problems of the origin and development of the universe are partly scientific and partly philosophical. Both contributions may be completed by information from a higher source, namely, divine revelation, which we have not to deal with here. (1) *Science* records many changes. It also examines the origin, natural or artificial, of many things, inorganic and organic, and follows their development. In many cases it can form, and, to a certain extent, test hypotheses. (2) Science always presupposes the existence of matter and its energies. The very first origin of things belongs to *philosophical* research.

(*b*) The problem may refer to (1) the world as a whole; (2) the earth as a whole, its origin and formation; (3) life on the earth, either the individual living beings, or the first origin of life, or the various differentiated forms of life as they exist to-day.

(*c*) It will be useful here to recall a few methodological remarks. (1) Many arguments being analogical, it is important that the analogy should not be carried farther than the facts justify. (2) All aspects of the beings under consideration must be examined. (3) Care must be taken to distinguish the facts from the interpretation which they may receive (e.g. the fact of the successive appearance of the forms of life from its interpretation as filial descendance). This is necessary especially when an author is known to have preconceived ideas. (4) Ascertained conclusions of all sciences must be kept in mind. (5) The problems, and chiefly the theories, are still young, and many are still under discussion. Enthusiasm is frequently a characteristic of youth; hence rash assertions must be guarded against.

2. **Meaning of Evolution.** — It is important at the outset to define the term "evolution" (*e-volvere*, to unfold), which is so frequently met with, and which is applied to a great number of different things.

(*a*) Formerly it was used in the sense of "preformation" to mean the theory according to which the living germ already contains, in miniature proportions, all the organs of the fully developed individual. This is opposed to the view now scientifically established of "epigenesis," according to which the organs become differentiated little by little out of a primitive cell. This meaning — preformation — of evolution is universally abandoned to-day.

(*b*) At present evolution refers not so much to the individual as to a successive group of individual substances or processes, the complexity and differentiation of which go on increasing from the first to the last. It implies succession, becoming, filiation, descent. Thus we have cosmic evolution, organic evolution, evolution of morality, of religion, etc.

(*c*) Sometimes, it is used for "monism," i.e. for the theory of the substantial unity of all things, deriving life from inorganic matter, and man from lower forms of life, and rejecting any intervention at any stage, of a supramundane agency, both as the first origin and cause of the world, and as a factor in its evolution.

(*d*) Frequently it is applied more particularly to organic evolution. In this sense, it is synonymous with "transformism" or the "theory of descent." "Evolution" refers to the race (phylogenesis), whereas "development" applies to the individual (ontogenesis).

(*e*) Hence evolution is not, as sometimes popularly misunderstood, the theory according to which "man originated from a monkey." Nor is it the same as atheism, for God may be admitted as the first cause of the existence of beings, and of their tendency to evolve. Nor is it the same as Darwinism, which is only one of the theories concerning the mode of evolution. Nor, finally, is it the same as universal progress; in some cases evolution may be regressive.

II. THE INORGANIC WORLD

We shall merely mention the question of the evolution of the inorganic world, which belongs to natural sciences (physics, chemistry, geology, astronomy). Our earth was at one time an incandescent mass which, together with the other planets, was detached from the original matter forming the solar system, and the crust of which little by little cooled off and became solid. As to the solar system, its matter was originally spread throughout the space it now occupies. It had a very low density, and as yet formed no special bodies. It was endowed with a movement of rotation, and parts of it separated, forming groups independent to some extent, and yet in constant relation with the others (movement, gravitation, etc.). Little by little these separate groups cooled off and formed solid bodies, while the central portion, the sun, is still incandescent. This nebular hypothesis, which, in its essentials, is commonly received, is extended to all stars, which are so many suns. This theory leaves without explanation the first origin of matter, of the laws by which it is governed, and of its first rotary motion. We pass now to the origin of living beings on the earth.

III. THE ORGANIC WORLD

Two questions must be distinguished: the origin of life itself, and the origin of its various forms.

I. The Origin of Life

1. **At Present.** — (*a*) *Common experience* shows that at least the higher organisms invariably come from parents of the same species, but it does not extend to all forms of life (parasites, insects, infusoria, etc.). On the other hand, *science* teaches that many organic products can be manufactured in the chemical laboratory, and that the analysis of protoplasm yields only a few inorganic elements. Hence the questions: Does life always originate from life? Does a living being always originate from a living being of the same species, or can parasites, for instance, originate from a different organism? Can dead matter give rise to inferior forms of life?

(*b*) In antiquity and in the Middle Ages, spontaneous generation and generation from dead matter were commonly accepted as facts. Recipes were given to generate such highly organized beings as mice, birds, snakes, etc. In 1668, Redi of Florence showed that meat, if exposed to the air, is soon full of maggots, but that, if it is screened, no maggots are produced. The reason is that their germs have been excluded. Little by little the production of other animals, such as parasites and others, was also traced back to germs. The discovery of bacteria revived the problem, which, however, was definitely solved by Pasteur (about 1860), who showed that, when germs were effectively excluded, no life appeared.

(*c*) Hence the law is accepted to-day: "Omne vivens ex vivo," and to this rule no exception is known. Notwithstanding all efforts, no transitional form from the inorganic to the organic world has ever been found. The modes according to which generation takes place are different according to the diversity of organisms, but "biogenesis," or the origin of every living organism from a living organism of the same kind, is the universal law. There is no "spontaneous generation."

2. **First Origin of Life.** — How far can we go back in this regressive process, i.e. how far can we trace back the ascending series of ancestors? Somewhere we must find an absolute beginning, for we know that life did not always exist on the earth, since at one time the earth was incandescent, and therefore unfit for life and for

the preservation of any germs of life. To say, with Lord Kelvin, that germs were brought down from stars or planets through cosmic dust or aerolites, is no solution. How did life originate there?

Some evolutionistic monists, however, claim that what does not take place to-day, namely, spontaneous generation, must have taken place in the past. Otherwise, how could life have arisen? And Haeckel describes at length the origin and evolution of the "moneron" or primitive form of life. This assertion is anti-scientific, and rests on the preconception that there is no personal God, that the world is not His work, and that spontaneous generation is the only possible way of accounting for the existence of life. As far as science goes, the origin of life is a mystery. Even should life ever come to be produced artificially, only a minor advantage would be gained by monism, for the existence of a Creator does not hinge on this point.

II. The Origin of the Various Forms of Life

1. **The Problem.** — (*a*) That the forms of life are manifold is evident. (1) Plants and animals constitute two distinct kingdoms, and within each kingdom the greatest diversity is observed as to size, shape, organization, etc. (2) A still greater diversity is observed if the present is compared with the past. The science of paleontology, which deals with fossil remains of organisms, shows that the species actually existing did not always exist, and that many species now extinct have succeeded one another in the past. (3) Although living organisms are generated by organisms of the same kind, the offspring differs more or less from the parents, and certain features are transmitted by heredity. Gardeners and breeders constantly use this fact to improve races and create new varieties. Hence the questions: How did successive species arise? How did life come to be differentiated as it is to-day? Are successive species new creations (theory of the fixity, constancy, or immutability of species), or are they, not only the successors, but also the descendants of former species (theory of organic evolution, descent, or transformism)?

(*b*) The *fact* itself of transformism must be distinguished from the *theories* by which this fact is explained. There may be agreement on the fact without agreement on the influences that caused it. And the fact may stand even if it cannot be explained.

(*c*) For the present we shall not speak of monism, which not only admits transformism, but asserts that life originated from inorganic matter, and that the passage from the lowest to the highest forms of life, man included, took place without any extramundane intervention. We cannot speak of man until we know his nature, and this will be considered in our next treatise. As to the passage from the vegetable to the animal kingdom, from the absence to the presence of consciousness, it is impossible. No reality comes from nothing. From unconsciousness consciousness cannot arise. So we limit ourselves to transformism within each kingdom. Scientists are not agreed as to the number of original types. Some admit only one (monogenesis); others, several (polygenesis). As to the mode of evolution, some admit slow variations; others the sudden appearance of new features.

2. **Historical Outline.** — Only the most prominent names will be mentioned here. The history of transformism begins with the nineteenth century. Before this time we find only hints and vague suggestions which have no scientific basis.

(*a*) Lamarck denies the fixity of, and the sharp limits between, species. Changes in the environment create new needs. New needs call forth new activities and create new organs to meet these needs. The use of organs perfects them, while their disuse allows them to become atrophied. These various modifications are transmitted by heredity.

(*b*) Geoffroy Saint-Hilaire, as partisan of the mutability of species, and Cuvier, as partisan of their fixity, opposed each other, the latter being victorious over his adversary.

(*c*) In his "Origin of Species" (1859) Charles Darwin advocates the theory of organic evolution by *natural selection*. The variations which occur in certain cases, if useful to the individual, give it an advantage over its competitors in the "struggle for life." Hence such an individual survives, while others become extinct. It is the "survival of the fittest." Later Darwin admitted also other factors. In his "Descent of Man" (1871), he applies the theory of transformism to man. Among other prominent transformists of the same period must be mentioned Wallace, Huxley, Spencer, and Haeckel.

(*d*) To-day the fact of evolution is commonly accepted, and is hardly ever discussed, although this position seems to be somewhat rash and premature. The main discussions are on the modes and factors of evolution. Darwinism (i.e. the theory of natural selection) is generally looked upon as inadequate.

3. **The Reasons for Transformism** will only be indicated here. Their study belongs to natural sciences.

(*a*) *Living organisms are plastic*, and become modified under the influence of (1) surroundings, climate, food, etc.; (2) artificial selection, especially in domestic plants and animals; (3) natural selection, which accentuates useful variations; (4) unknown causes which sometimes produce in the offspring sudden variations or mutations. To this it is added that, in the beginning, organisms must have been more plastic, and the causes of change more active owing to greater geological disturbances. Moreover, the divisions of races within the same species are arbitrary, and many races would be looked upon as distinct species, were not their common origin known (e.g. the various races of dogs).

Remarks. — This variability is limited, moves around a certain fixed average, and frequently a modified type tends to return to the primitive type. Moreover, as even with the best efforts, only varieties are produced artificially, how could new species arise naturally? There is no proof that a new species has ever been produced in this way. And if it had, have we the right to extend the fact to all species? Hence this argument does not prove the fact of transformism, but offers only a possibility.

(*b*) *Mutual affinities of organic beings.* (1) *Morphology.* The various groups (e.g. vertebrates) are built according to the same plan, and, from the lowest class to the highest, a gradual increase in complexity is observed. The reason is that all have developed by successive differentiations from less differentiated types.— *Remarks.* — The analogies must not make one overlook the differences. Moreover, it remains to be proved that a closer resemblance is due to a closer relationship by descent. (2) *Embryology.* During the period of embryonic development, higher forms of life pass successively through inferior stages resembling lower forms of life, and little by little become more differentiated. Hence ontogeny, or the development of the individual, is a recapitulation of phylogeny, or the evolution of the species. — *Remarks.* — In many cases, the resemblance of the embryo with lower forms of life has been grossly exaggerated (especially by Haeckel). Moreover, resemblances are to be expected in the development of organisms of the same type, since all begin with a simple cell and develop in similar surroundings. (3) *Rudimentary organs*, and incipient or nascent organs. In many higher forms of life organs are found which are now useless because they are too small and undeveloped, e.g. the eyes of the mole, the rudimentary hind legs of boas and whales, etc. These must be remnants of organs once fully developed and useful. — *Remarks.* — The conclusion might be true without proving transformism. The ancestors may have been of the same species, though with certain organs more developed than those of actual forms. Moreover, the uselessness of all such organs at all stages of life is not demonstrated.

(c) *Geological distribution* or *paleontology*. Paleontology shows that various species have succeeded one another on the earth. Although the geological record is very imperfect and difficult to decipher, owing to numerous perturbations in the strata of the earth, in a general way the lower forms of life appeared first, and little by little more differentiated forms succeeded them. In some cases, especially that of the horse, a series of closely allied forms can be traced back, leading progressively to actually existing species. As research progresses, "missing links," forming transitions between different species, are discovered.

Remarks. — Sometimes also, forms of life are found which do not progress in one sequence, but, as it were, in parallel lines. Nor can succession, when verified, be identified with descent; paleontology gives only the fact of succession. Moreover, this progressive succession is established only in very few cases of species closely similar. When we try to apply it to larger groups, evidence is lacking, and there is not even a semblance of proof which would allow us to connect together all forms of life. To appeal to the imperfection of the record and the difficulty of the task is no proof. Conclusions can be based only on the data at hand, not on data which possibly may — or may not — be gathered in the future.

4. **Conclusion.** — *Philosophy* has nothing to say for or against evolution. It is a *scientific* question to be answered by a patient investigation of the facts. As a scientific conclusion it is, as yet, not demonstrated. It is a hypothesis, which, on the strength of established facts, extends only to closely allied species. To make evolution a universal law by which all forms would ultimately be differentiations of one primitive type, is to proceed far beyond the conclusions justified by actual evidence.

CHAPTER IV

THE COSMOS

Introductory

1. **Unity and Multiplicity in the World.** — There is plurality and variety in nature, yet, in many cases, multiplicity is reduced to unity. According to the point of view from which it is regarded, the same reality may be spoken of as one or as many. The process of unification has degrees, and is more or less inclusive. Thus I speak of the earth as one when I oppose it to other planets or heavenly bodies. From the point of view of geography, many mountains, valleys, oceans, are on the one earth. From the point of view of geology, many rocks of different nature form one mountain. Every rock in turn may be looked upon as composed of many elements, and ultimately reduced to atoms. The same is true of the one human organism composed of many organs, every organ composed of many tissues, etc. Thus according as we look at things in one way or another, the same reality is called one or many. We know that some processes of unification are only mental or logical. The genus under which species are classified exists only in the mind. Other processes of unification are based on real relations of causality, dependence, influence, subordination, etc. The *many existing beings* in some way form *one universe*.

2. **Terms Defined.** — (1) *Cosmos* (Greek equivalent of Latin *mundus*) means the world conceived as an orderly and harmonious system of many things, and is opposed to chaos, disorder, or lawlessness. (2) *Universe* means the collection of all material things, and indicates completeness and all-inclusiveness. Sometimes it is used so as to include even God. (3) *World* may generally be used for cosmos or universe, but its meaning is more vague. Frequently it is made to apply especially to our earth, or to what is

nearer to us on the earth. Frequently also it is restricted to special systems, not necessarily material, e.g. the living world, the world of art, religion, literature, fashion, etc. (4) *Nature* has several meanings. It applies either to the whole universe or to the individual beings that compose it. We speak of nature in general, e.g. the works of nature, or of the nature of this or that being. Nature always has a special reference to *dynamic* principles which enable beings to act in various ways and to modify other beings. It is *the intrinsic principle of activity.*

The many form one, not through an identity of substance, but through their many interrelations which prevent them from being isolated. The most important of these relations are space, time, causality, teleology, and the various laws of nature. Hence the following titles.

I. SPACE AND TIME

Few notions are more usual than those of space and time. We speak daily of things as occupying a definite part of space, and of events as occurring at a certain time. Yet, simple and clear as they seem to be, these notions become difficult to explain as soon as we try to give an accurate definition.

I. Space

1. **Place.** — Space and place are closely connected. When we are asked in what place an object is located, we answer by assigning a determined portion of space which it occupies, or by referring it to other objects the place of which is known, i.e. by defining its spatial relations. Place then is a determined part of space. We may distinguish the external and the internal place.

(*a*) When I say: "The fish is in the water, and the water is in the jar," I assign the place of the fish and of the water in reference to something *external* to them, namely, in reference to the immediate surface of the water that surrounds the fish, or of the jar that contains the water. Not the whole water is, strictly speaking, the *locus* of the fish, but only that which comes in immediate contact with it. This is the *locus proprius.* Sometimes a *locus communis* is assigned, as when I say that the chair is in the room — together with many other things.

(*b*) I may consider the space occupied by an object without reference to anything external, but simply as the space occupied *within* the object's limits and dimensions, as when I say that the volume of a body is so many cubic feet. This is the *locus internus*, which remains the same even when, owing to some motion, external spatial relations change. The fish occupies the same space, whether in the water or out of it.

2. **Space.** — (*a*) In general, space implies (1) *distance;* thus we say that there is so much space between two objects, or that the train flies through space; (2) *capacity* and *aptitude to contain;* as when I say that the room is very spacious, or that the stars are scattered in space; (3) *relative emptiness;* thus I say that there is no more space in the room, i.e. its capacity is already exhausted because it is completely occupied. This emptiness is only relative to the use which is to be made of space.

Space, therefore, supposes bodies with distances between them, and consists essentially in the interval, the distance, the capacity, the volume occupied. It almost coincides with place, except that the term "place" emphasizes the bounding surface, while "space" emphasizes the voluminal capacity.

(*b*) (1) *Concrete space* is thus a relation of distance in a threefold dimension, or a voluminal distance. It is not the body itself, but a special aspect of it. It may refer to individual bodies, but is frequently applied to the immense receptacle in which all things are contained, i.e. to the sum of all individual spaces. (2) *Ideal space*, or the concept of space, is an abstract idea. It does not refer to this or that space, with such or such dimensions, but only to an indetermined distance, capacity, or volume. Like all abstract and universal concepts, it exists only in the mind, but is based on the concrete perception of space. (3) *Imaginary space* is the space which we imagine to exist beyond the limits of the real world — if the world be limited — and which we suppose to extend *ad infinitum* even where there is nothing.

(*c*) Hence real space is not an a priori form of external sensibility (Kant), but an aspect of real extension; nor the divine attribute of immensity (Newton, Clarke), for God has no extension and is not material; nor a distinct reality, an immense receptacle independent of bodies (Gassendi); nor finally the extended body as such (Descartes). *Real space is a special relation based on the threefold dimension of matter.* It does not exist independently, as a special reality in itself, but is directly based on reality, namely, on really existing bodies which have a real extension.

II. Time

1. **Nature of Time.** — Time has many analogies with space. We may state immediately that time, like space, is not an independent existing reality, but that it is based on something really existing. Whereas *space* is based on *extension* and *co-existing* parts, time essentially implies *succession*, and is always *moving on*. Its parts — if it may be said to have parts — never co-exist. Another obvious fact is that what we commonly call *time* is measured by *spatial* relations, e.g. of the sun, the hands of a watch, etc.

(*a*) In the realities of the world we find *duration* and *change*, *permanence* and *succession*. Things endure, and yet undergo successively many modifications in place, quantity, and qualities. It is in this *fact of succession* that we find the idea of time which represents a continuous flowing, which never stops, but proceeds uniformly while the real changes are not always continuous for the senses, and do not take place uniformly. Hence time is the same reality as movement or change, but viewed from the special aspect of succession, i.e. of an "after" and a "before." The perception of time evidently supposes in the mind the power of memory.

(*b*) Thus conceived, time is composed of the past, present, and future. The *present* alone exists actually; it is an indivisible point constantly moving and becoming past. The *past* has been, the *future* will be, the present instant constantly moves into the future, and as soon as we try to think of it, it is already passed. Psychologically, however, we give to the present a greater or smaller duration.

2. **Various Meanings of Time.** — (*a*) The various meanings of time are analogical to those of space. (1) *Intrinsic concrete*

time is the time based on varying concrete changes of concrete realities. Every substance has its own time. (2) ***Extrinsic concrete time*** is the one which has been adopted as a standard unit to measure other durations, namely, the revolutions of the earth around its own axis (day), and around the sun (year). This time is divided into years, months, weeks, days, hours, etc. Although it is in itself no more real than intrinsic time, it is, owing to its regularity and constancy, more obvious for us, and hence is understood as time par excellence. Psychological time is the apparent duration as perceived by the mind. (See Psychology, p. 88.) (3) ***Abstract*** or ***conceptual time*** is the idea of time apart from all determinations with which changes occur concretely in the beings of the world. (4) ***Imaginary time***, in the supposition that the world had a beginning and will have an end, is the time which we imagine to be prolonged *ad infinitum* both before the world existed and after it will have ceased to exist.

(*b*) Hence real time is not an a priori mental form (Kant), but is based on something objective; nor the divine attribute of eternity (Newton, Clarke); nor a reality independent of changing concrete realities (Gassendi); nor the successive duration as such (Descartes). It is not a reality as such in itself, but is directly based on ***the real succession of the changes which take place in the various beings of the world.***

II. THE LAWS OF NATURE

I. Meaning and Properties

1. **Meaning.** — (*a*) A law means either a norm for human actions, or the constant mode of action of physical agents. (Cf. p. 292.) Here we deal with *physical laws*. A law indicates the behavior of certain beings in various circumstances. It reduces every manifestation of their activity to more or less comprehensive formulæ which apply in all cases.

The term "nature" has special reference to the dynamic aspect of beings, and means the substance inasmuch as it is a principle of action. Sometimes it applies to individual beings, as when we say of a thing that it is natural for it to act so or so, and that every being acts according to its own nature. Sometimes it applies to the whole universe, as when we speak of the beauties of nature, the order of nature, etc. A law of nature means a uniformity — more or less comprehensive — of physical activity in a given being or in the whole universe.

(*b*) The *existence of natural laws* needs no demonstration. The uniformity of action in nature is both an obvious fact and a condition of science. We daily see that the same agents, in the same conditions, produce the same effects, and the endeavor of science is to formulate the laws according to which these results occur. Were there no laws, science could not foresee and predict results.

"Accidental" effects prove nothing against the existence of natural laws, for, although they are not constant and uniform, they result from an unforeseen meeting of several causes, every one of which acts according to its own laws. Man may act intentionally, and, in order to realize his purpose, he uses the "natural" activities of various instruments and materials. Physical beings act naturally in the same way. But if several physical beings combine to produce a result both unusual, because this combination seldom occurs, and unforeseen, because unusual, we call this result accidental, although it is due to natural causes. Thus death in a mine explosion is an accident, although it results from natural activities, the presence of which was unknown. The killing of a man with a bullet, when the shooter was not even aware of his presence, is also called accidental, although it happens in perfect accordance with natural laws. Accidental is therefore a relative term which applies to results due to an unfamiliar and unforeseen concourse of circumstances.

2. **Properties.** — Natural laws are necessary and yet contingent. We shall explain briefly these two apparently conflicting properties.

(*a*) The laws of nature are *necessary*, i.e. invariable and immutable, as appears both from experience and from reason. *From experience*, because, for instance, everywhere at sea level pure water boils at a temperature of 212 degrees, and will always be analyzed into the same constant proportions of oxygen and hydrogen. A stone thrown up in the air will always fall down. Fire always burns, etc. *From reason*, because the mode of activity must correspond to the very mode of being, and hence every individual nature is so determined as to exercise a certain kind of activity.

This activity requires certain conditions, and unless these are verified, the result does not follow. Thus conditions of contact, temperature, pressure, etc., are necessary for oxygen and hydrogen to combine into water. If a piece of wood be covered with asbestos, fire will not consume it. If the stone be held up in the air, it will not fall down, etc. Thus the necessity of the laws of nature is not absolute, but hypothetical. The conditions must be verified.

(*b*) Yet these laws are *contingent*. They have no absolute a priori necessity, but are discovered by experience. They might be otherwise than they are. In geometry, reason will discover certain properties, — e.g. of triangles — which are absolutely necessary, and cannot be otherwise. But, in physics or chemistry, no analysis of gunpowder will ever show that it is necessary for it to have the power of exploding; and no analysis of oxygen will ever reveal a necessary affinity for hydrogen in certain proportions. Moreover, we can see no necessity why things themselves should exist, and, in fact, if certain conditions had not been verified, this individual man, horse, stone, water, etc., would not have existed. If certain other circumstances had been realized, other individuals would have existed. The laws of nature, therefore, are not derived from the essence of things, but rather the essence of things is inferred from their properties and laws.

N.B. From this we may simply hint at the possibility of an intervention of the Creator and Ruler of the world, who can supply or withdraw the conditions necessary to the activity of various substances, and thus produce miraculous events.

II. Efficiency and Teleology

The chief laws of nature refer to the mode of activity or efficiency of physical agents, and this in turn implies teleology. Hence the present question.

1. **Efficiency.** — (*a*) The senses perceive only the succession of phenomena, i.e. antecedents and consequents; hence for empiricism causality is nothing but succession. As soon, however, as

we observe a regularity of succession, and an invariability of sequence, we are led to admit that there is not only a *succession*, but a *real influence* of the antecedent on the production of the consequent. If the consequent did not depend on the antecedent, there would be no reason why it should not appear without it, or after any other antecedent. As it is not so, the conclusion imposes itself that the consequent depends on the antecedent, and that the antecedent, by its activity, is the cause of the consequent.

(*b*) There may be a series of subordinated causes; hence the distinction between proximate and remote causes. Causes may exercise a more or less direct influence, but the existence of true efficiency is attested for man by his own consciousness, and for other beings by the rational interpretation of external experience. Many causes may and do contribute to the same result. Which will be called the cause will depend frequently on the point of view one takes. Thus, the photographer, the film, the light, the object, etc., are causes of the photograph. The decomposition of the blood, the bullet, the powder, the firing, the murderer, etc., are causes of death. Any effect is thus the result of a series of causes which contribute their share in various ways. The complete causation includes both a number of causes, and of conditions without which their activity could not be exercised.

2. **Teleology.** — (*a*) Teleology or finality is opposed to mechanism. It affirms the existence of final causes, that is, of ends, or purposes, which efficient causes tend to realize. Mechanism affirms that everything is simply the result of mechanical forces acting without any presupposed direction. (1) The question is not whether there are efficient causes *or* final causes, but whether, *in addition to* efficient causes, there are also final causes; that is, whether the activity of efficient causes is directed to certain ends. The aeroplane flies because it is constructed in such or such a way; from this point of view, flying is but a *result* of mechanical causes. But at the same time, the aeroplane is built in this way *in order to* fly; from this point of view, flying is an *end*. The same is true of the works of nature, e.g. the wings of birds. (2) Again, the question is not that of conscious and intelligent finality such as is revealed in human purposive activities, but of physical

finality, which is revealed by the constancy of the manner in which physical beings act.

(*b*) Finality is *extrinsic* when the activity of a substance produces results that are useful to other substances. Thus the mineral is utilized by the plant, the plant by the animal. Or again, the heat of the sun is a source of growth and development. But we cannot see everywhere such an adaptation of means to an extrinsic good, for the good of one is frequently an evil for another. The plant is destroyed by the animal that eats it. The thriving of microbes may result in the death of the organism. Yet, in a general way, the order and harmony of the universe cannot be denied. But this order is realized by individual beings *acting according to their own nature.*

(*c*) Hence primarily finality is *intrinsic* or *immanent.* This means that every being is endowed with an internal tendency to realize its own end, and to strive for its own good and perfection. This finality manifests itself clearly in the organic world, where we see the ovum or primitive cell developing according to the general type of the species, and little by little evolving into the complete organism. It also manifests itself in the struggle which the organism undertakes against destructive or harmful agents. Even in the inorganic world, the constancy of the laws of nature shows that nothing happens at random or by chance, for chance cannot explain stability, but that there is *an internal principle of direction and orientation* which is no other than the nature of every being. The existence of final causes is required to account for the orderly and harmonious sequence of phenomena, and for the convergence of diverse activities toward harmonious results which persist notwithstanding the manifold changes that take place in the world.

CONCLUSION

Cosmology leaves many questions without an answer. It assumes the existence of things, but why, how, and whence are they? What is the ultimate ground of reality, i.e. of things individual and of the totality of things? The beings of the world are many and diverse, and yet compose one universe. Every being exists only in dependence on other beings, for nothing in the world is absolute and self-sufficient. Since unity cannot come out of manifoldness without some principle which is itself one, where must we look for the principle of order and harmony? What is the ultimate reason of the laws of nature, and of the internal teleological principle which they manifest? How have differentiation and order arisen from the primitive nebular chaos? How have highly differentiated organisms evolved out of more general types? How did life itself arise?

Thus many questions spring from the study, scientific or philosophical, of the material world. In general, has the world in itself a sufficient reason of its existence and laws, or must we look for a sufficient reason in some higher being above the world? When things have been explained by their immediate causes, there remains to explain these causes themselves. Hence the necessity to proceed to Theodicy, and examine whether the ultimate reality, the Absolute, or First Cause, is immanent in the world, or transcends the world. The method will be to go from the world to God: "For the invisible things of Him from the creation of the world are clearly seen, being understood by the things that are made; His eternal power also and divinity." (Rom. i, 20.)

RATIONAL PSYCHOLOGY OR PHILOSOPHY OF THE HUMAN MIND

INTRODUCTION

1. **Subject-Matter of This Treatise.** — Psychology deals with the empirical study of the mental functions of cognition, affection, conation, and describes the various mental processes. We must now inquire about the *nature of the principle* of these functions. Mind and matter, subject and object, consciousness and motion, have irreducible characteristics, and yet are connected intimately. Hence the questions naturally arise: What is the mind? How is it related to the organism? On the solution of these two problems will depend the answer to be given to the questions: What is the origin of the human mind or soul? What is its destiny?

Hence the following division: (1) Is the mind a substance? (2) Is it spiritual? (3) How is it united to the organism? (4) What is its origin? (5) Is it immortal? It is needless to insist on the importance of such questions, both from a merely speculative, and from a practical point of view.

2. **Method.** — (*a*) The knowledge of the nature of the mind is not intuitive but must be inferred from facts of experience. Hence the method to be followed is chiefly inductive. It starts from facts, and assigns to them an adequate explanation. But once the nature of the soul is known, we may proceed deductively, in part at least, and base on its nature conclusions concerning its origin and destiny. The main principle to be used is that of sufficient reason. A cause must be assigned which will be sufficient and strictly required to explain all the facts. To avoid imperfect and one-sided conclusions, all facts must be considered. Erro-

neous views may arise from considering exclusively conscious processes, or exclusively physiological functions. This caution is important here owing to the great complexity of the subject-matter.

(*b*) We cannot agree with Spencer and other agnostics when they assert the unknowableness of the nature, origin, and destiny of the mind, and consequently the futility of the present investigation. It must be granted that our knowledge of the mind remains imperfect, but the same principles that are used in all other sciences will be used here, and will carry us beyond mere empirical facts. No science is possible without the use of the principle of causality and of sufficient reason, and it is this principle which we shall constantly appeal to: The effect is a sign of the power and nature of its cause.

CHAPTER I

SUBSTANTIALITY

The existence of mental states, manifold and varied, is an obvious fact of experience which has been the subject-matter of psychology. These processes are spontaneously ascribed to one mind as their permanent and active centre. What is the correct interpretation of the facts? Is the mind a reality distinct from the mental states, or is the collection of mental states the whole mind? *Phenomenalism* asserts that the mind is but a common name, a *genus logicum*, an abstraction. The only reality is the series of mental processes. Whatever else we may add to these is illusory. *Substantialism* asserts that the mind is a deeper concrete reality of which mental states are only the surface. It is this latter position which we shall now explain and defend.

I. Meaning of Substantiality

1. **What is a Substance?** — (*a*) Beings are divided into substances and accidents, i.e. into beings existing in themselves, and beings existing in others. Some realities are, as it were, weak; they need a support in which they are and to which they are attributed. This character belongs to mental processes; a mental process does not exist in itself, but in the mind. It is mine, or yours, or his, etc. Other realities stand by themselves, exist in themselves, are not attributed to any other, but are supports of qualities or accidents. There is no "white" in itself, but "white" is a quality attributed to some substance (paper, cloth, paint, etc.).

(*b*) Hence primarily *substance means that which subsists in itself*. It also has secondary characters. (1) It is a *principle of activity*. A substance without activity would be altogether unknowable, meaningless, and unthinkable. If it is necessary to conceive the substance as a strong being, as a support, it is also necessary to conceive it as a power, an active principle, which manifests its energies. (2) It is something more or less *permanent*, although this is not so essential. Here permanence means that the mind endures and remains identical notwithstanding the constant flux of processes.

2. **Further Determination.** — To complete this explanation, it is necessary to make a few remarks as to what the assertion "the mind is a substance" does not mean.

(*a*) The present question is not to be identified with other questions to be examined later: What is the nature of the mind-substance? Is it material or spiritual? What are its relations to the organism?

(*b*) To assert that the mind is a substance is not to assert that it is a hidden substratum, inert and permanent, under the visible surface of conscious processes, or that it is a concrete being distinct from concrete accidents, and separable from them. *There is only one concrete being* composed of substance and accidents, and the mind-substance is known only through its accidents or activities. The mind and its modifications are perceived in the same experience. To argue, with Spencer (Principles of Psychology, §59), that we can never know the *unmodified* substance of the mind is correct, but substantialists never made such a claim. According to them, what is known is the *modified* substance of the mind. The surface is, as it were, transparent, so that to perceive actions at the surface is to perceive at once the mind as acting. In general, to perceive the accidents is also to perceive at once the substance in which they inhere and from which they proceed.

II. Proofs of the Substantiality

1. **Facts.** — We may first insist on some psychological facts which imply the substantiality of the mind.

(*a*) Consciousness clearly testifies that I am the *subject* of sensations and of other mental processes, that I am the *agent* which produces certain actions, that I am *distinct* from everybody and everything else, and that I *subsist in myself*. That is, not only does consciousness manifest the surface, or mental processes, it also manifests that all converge to, and start from, the same *identical centre*, notwithstanding the manifoldness and the changes at the circumference. The same intuition reveals both the *processes* — walking, thinking, feeling, etc. — and the *subject* to which they are attributed — *my* walking, thinking, and feeling. And not only the present, but the past, and, to some extent, the future are referred to the same substance.

(*b*) Consciousness testifies that I am *active*, that I am the *cause*, not merely the witness, of certain activities; not a simple spectator, but an agent and an active source of energy. "I did this, and I shall do that, etc."

(*c*) The mind is *identical* and *permanent*, as shown by the fact of memory. Mental processes succeed one another rapidly, yet memory preserves, reproduces, and recognizes them. Without a permanent subject, this would be impossible, for the reference of a present image or perception to a past experience supposes that the same mind is the witness of both. The act of memory implies the consciousness of *self-identity*, that is, of the sameness of the mind under the perpetual flux of its processes. The same conclusion is reached from the various modes of thought which imply succession, and consequently memory. In judging and reasoning, the mind thinks successively several terms or propositions, and holds them together so as to perceive their relations.

2. **Reality of the Substance of the Mind.** — (*a*) These psychological facts cannot be looked upon as illusory without falling into out-and-out scepticism. Since they are *real*, they require not merely an *apparent* or *logical subject*, but a *real subject;* not indeed a subject separable from conscious processes, but nevertheless a subject underlying the processes through which it is known. The "permanent possibility of sensations," of which phenomenalists speak, is a fact, but, as this possibility is real, it supposes some real being on which it is based. There can be no possibility without an agent on which the possibility depends. To say that an event is possible is to say that there are causes capable of producing it.

(*b*) The concrete reality of the mind is therefore a substance plus its modifications, the two being indissolubly united both in reality and in our knowledge of them, yet being distinct. To refuse to accept this conclusion is to make of the processes themselves so many substances, proceeding from no agent, inhering in no subject, and self-subsisting. It is to overlook the essential fact of the unity of the mind under its many processes. It is to make the supposed illusion of a substantial reality impossible, since this illusion itself presupposes the real unity of the onlooker.

III. Phenomenalism

The foregoing view will be made clearer by discussing phenomenalism in its various forms. In general, as its name indicates, phenomenalism is the theory reducing the mind to phenomena or appearances, and denying its substantial reality. It is a very common view to-day, owing to the prevalent fear of "metaphysical entities." A mind-series is substituted for the mind-substance. The mind is reduced to the collection, aggregate, or succession of mental states.

1. **The Present Mental State.** — The mind cannot be merely the present mental state. (1) This state itself must be explained, and there can be no thought without a thinking principle, no action without an agent. (2) The present state is transitory, and the facts of memory and recognition require something permanent to account for the possibility of recall. (3) As far as experience informs us, we do not always think, but sometimes thought seems to be interrupted, e.g. in sleep, swoons, etc. Yet something must remain, since the past is known again when consciousness reappears.

2. **The Series of Mental States.** — The mind cannot be merely the series of mental states, whether it be described as a "bundle" or "collection of different perceptions" (Hume), or as the "sum of our inner experiences" (Höffding), or as "a thread of consciousness supplemented by believed possibilities of consciousness," "a series of feelings with a background of possibilities of feelings" (Stuart Mill). Many modern psychologists hold similar views. Ebbinghaus illustrates his position by the following comparison. As the plant is composed of various parts (roots, branches, leaves, flowers, etc.) united into a whole, each one supported by, acting and depending on, the others, and their totality constituting the

plant, which, however, is not a substance distinct from these parts, so the mind is simply a system of numerous realities of consciousness, closely united, and causally related. James speaks of the mind as a stream of consciousness, in which the ego is nothing but the "real, present, onlooking, remembering, judging thought," which appropriates and embodies in itself all past experiences.

(*a*) A series implies three things, a *multiplicity* of elements, their *succession* in time or space, and the *connection*, real or logical, of the several units. One thing cannot form a series; nor is a bundle or heap of things a series; nor finally do disparate and disconnected things form a series. (1) The mind-series *has to be explained*, and, with it, the facts already mentioned of personal identity, memory, judgment, reasoning, etc. Each unit of the series requires a support and an active principle, since it is not a self-subsisting reality. (2) *The awareness of the series* as such supposes a permanent and identical subject, witness of the present and of the past. If there is no mind-substance, not only the series, but even the possibility of speaking of the mind as a series, is to be denied, since the awareness of manifoldness, succession, and connection supposes something distinct from the units that form the series. We do not deny that there is a mental series of processes, but at the same time we assert that something else is required to make it possible. (3) The addition of a "permanent possibility" is not enough, since possibility means *the presence of an adequate cause* by which certain effects become possible. There must be a reason for every possibility.

(*b*) Taine says that, as two or three horses may be able to draw a cart which one horse is insufficient to draw, so several states together may stand without a support or substance, even if one alone cannot do so. Or it may be said that, although one blade of grass by itself cannot stand up straight, a bundle of them will stand. Ebbinghaus's comparison mentioned above belongs to about the same type. (1) Horses taken individually are real powers, and each blade of grass has some power of resistance. The parts of the plant are material and substantial, and thus can support one another. But mental states are transitory processes, and in the line of substance *every one of them is a zero.* To add them will not make them able to stand by themselves. If a certain quantity is required to obtain a given result, the addition of positive quantities will eventually give the necessary amount. But the addition of ciphers will never give a positive quantity. (2) The plant is a "complex," as Ebbinghaus says, but not so much a complex *of processes and functions* as *of parts or organs.* So also the mental processes and functions do not form the "mental complex," except through the unity of the mind whose functions they are.

(*c*) The mind *may* be a "stream of consciousness," but it *must* be more. (1) It cannot be proved to be an everflowing and never-interrupted stream. If it is interrupted, something must remain in the interval to connect the section preceding the interruption with the section that follows it. (2) The comparison with a stream would lead us to admit a *source* from which the stream originates. (3) To say that a mental state, i.e. a function, appropriates all those that have taken place before is to give it a substantiality which of itself it has not. It is true, as James says, that the same herd may be transmitted rapidly to different owners. But the difference between this and our case is that the herdsman and the cattle co-exist, whereas here the mental states are successive. Moreover, the herdsman is a substance distinct from the cattle, not a mere process. (4) Appropriation, even if possible, would not yet be memory and recognition, and would offer no sufficient explanation of them.

In conclusion we may state that phenomenalism, which may be sufficient for the *psychologist,* is not an *ultimate or philosophical explanation.* Either it cannot account for all the facts of mental life; or, against the testimony of consciousness and the common consent of psychologists, it makes of mental states so many substances; or finally it surreptitiously introduces in fact what it denies in words, a mind-substance or something which is supposed to fulfil its functions.

IV. Multiple Personality

1. **Facts.** (See Psychology, p. 197). — (1) In some abnormal cases, persons have, as it were, two, or even more, different, suc-

cessive, and apparently independent existences which we may represent as *A*, *B*, *A*1, *B*1, *A*2, *B*2, *A*3, *B*3, etc., the series *A* forming one continuous existence, and the series *B* another. In the state *An*, the subject remembers the whole series *A*, but knows nothing of the series *B*. In the state *Bn*, the series *B* is remembered, while all the *A* periods are so many blanks. In each series mental dispositions may be widely different; *A* will speak of *B* in the third person, etc. Hence the natural conclusion: The mind cannot be one substance identical with itself at all times. (2) The same conclusion is inferred from certain conditions in which two "persons" seem to appear simultaneously. Thus while a man is wholly intent on a rational conversation, his arm will write something else, also very rational, and the person himself will not even be conscious of this action. There are two groups of intellectual activity proceeding independently.

2. **Explanation of the Facts.** — The facts themselves must be accepted. As to their explanation, it requires some general and some more special remarks.

(*a*) *General remarks*. (1) It is admitted by all that these facts are extraordinary, rare, and abnormal. We must always be careful in basing any theory on such facts, and in leaving the clear testimony of *normal* consciousness for the obscure testimony which it may seem to give in *abnormal* cases.

(2) The *fact* (ontological) of identity must be distinguished from the *consciousness* (psychological) of identity. There may be a real, yet unperceived, identity, i.e. there may be at the surface different manifestations of the same deeper reality. The ego must be distinguished, although it cannot be separated, from the states of the ego.

(3) We may compare these abnormal cases with normal cases to see if any hints can be found leading to the understanding of the former. (*a*) In normal cases, the conscious conflict of tendencies, and the ensuing struggle, rather go to prove the identity of the ego who witnesses the two impulses, and who experiences the conflict. (*b*) There are slow and gradual changes in character, and sometimes we may say of a man whom we knew formerly that he has changed completely, that he has reformed, that he is

no longer what he used to be, etc. (*c*) There are also more sudden and more radical changes for better or for worse, sudden conversions and downfalls. (*d*) Many things are forgotten, either individual experiences or whole series of experiences. (*e*) At times, we may even assume different "personalities" which are illusory, e.g. in dream, somnambulism, hallucination, hypnotism. (*f*) Actions and experiences during hypnosis may be forgotten altogether in the normal state, but recalled in subsequent hypnosis. The hypnotizer may suggest different "personalities" to the subject.

(*b*) *More special remarks*. (1) Even if the consciousness of identity disappears, we have reasons for saying that the fact itself remains. (*a*) Frequently in one of the series there is the memory of some of the things that have been experienced in the other. (*b*) Sometimes one of the series predominates and includes the knowledge of what happens in the other. (*c*) These series are not altogether strangers. Generally there is something common to both (knowledge of language, persons, objects, or localities). (*d*) Frequently also *A* will speak of *B* as a stranger and in the third person, and this is a sign that *A* knows *B* and is aware of the change. (*e*) The fact that $A2$ is linked with $A1$ after an interval during which *B* has appeared shows that something has persisted to link the present with the past. (2) Simultaneous manifestations are automatic and due probably to the dissociation of certain cerebral or spinal centres from the others. (3) Hence what we have here is in reality a disease of memory with illusions and hallucinations. These phenomena are due to organic causes which cannot as yet be assigned definitely. (4) What has disappeared is not the ego, but only the consciousness of identity. There are indications that the surface only has changed, not the deeper reality.

Hence from these facts no objection can be derived against the unity, permanence, and substantiality of the mind. The term "personality" is wrongly applied here, and psychologists generally have come to recognize that, from these abnormal facts, nothing can be inferred against the unity of the mind. We adhere therefore to the testimony of normal consciousness, and hold that the mind is not only the collection or series of conscious states, but their common centre, subject, and agent, *a real substance known by the same indivisible act of consciousness which manifests the surface or circumference, i.e. the processes or accidents.*

CHAPTER II

SPIRITUALITY

I. The Question Stated

1. **Its Importance.** — It is not enough to know that the human mind is more than the series of mental states, and that it is a substantial and permanent principle. We must now examine its nature more closely. That it is bound to, and dependent on, the organism is an obvious fact. For the present we shall not examine the nature of this union, but only the question whether the mind itself is some form of matter or of material energy, and whether, in all its processes, it acts with the intrinsic coöperation of the organism. This question is of primary importance, for on it depends the answer to the questions of the origin and destiny of the soul. If in some of its actions the soul is found to act by itself, and not through the organism, it will not necessarily share all the vicissitudes of the organism.

2. **Meaning of the Terms "Material" and "Immaterial."** — (*a*) A thing is material when it has extension and is composed of several parts. This is matter itself. Or a thing is material when, although it is not matter itself, it cannot exist and manifest itself except through matter. Physicists oppose matter to energy, although, in this latter sense, energy itself must be called material since it is the energy of matter. The vital principle, as seen in Cosmology, must also be called material in this sense, since all functions of the living organism are exercised in and through matter.

(*b*) Hence immateriality may mean: (1) *Simplicity*, i.e. the absence of composition, of parts, and of quantity, even though there be an essential dependence on matter for existence and the exercise of activity. (2) *Spirituality*, i.e. simplicity plus independence from matter, or the aptitude to exist and act without matter. It is important to keep this distinction in mind, for a thing may be immaterial in the first sense, and yet altogether dependent on matter in every respect. The characteristic features of the mind are generally accepted to be irreducible to those of matter. The physical and the mental are acknowledged to be altogether different. Yet, without identifying mind and matter, many psychologists do not admit a spiritual soul, independent of the organism in some of its activities.

II. Simplicity of the Soul

Little space will be given to the simplicity of the soul because it is not the exclusive characteristic of the human soul, and, while differentiating the soul from matter, it does not show whether or not it is so essentially bound to matter as to be unable to exist and act except in and through the body.

1. **Ideas.** — (*a*) Thought is simple and indivisible. There is no half idea or third of an idea. The idea as a whole is either present in or absent from the mind. Even when it is composed of several logical elements, the idea is indivisible. If one of its essential elements be absent, the idea ceases to be. The idea of "man" or "triangle," for instance, may be acquired and perfected by various mental processes; it is a synthesis of several essential notes. But, whether it be complete or imperfect, as an idea it is a single and indivisible mental process.

(*b*) Were the mind composed of parts, this would not be possible. Suppose these parts to be *A* and *B*. Either *A* and *B* singly would apprehend the whole idea, and in this case there would be two ideas. Or *A* would apprehend some, and *B* other elements of the same idea, and this again is contrary to experience which testifies that the idea is one and indivisible, as well as the process by which it is made present in the mind. Even if this latter supposition were accepted, we must go farther and deeper beyond *A* and *B*, to a simple and indivisible unity which gathers these elements into a single perception and apprehension.

2. **Judgment and Reasoning.** — The same argument holds for judgment, reasoning, and volition. The same mind, or simple

reality, must apprehend both the subject and the predicate, and their relation of agreement or disagreement. The same mind also must apprehend three judgments, and see that the conclusion follows from the premises. The act of choice is one and simple, although several alternatives are present in consciousness.

3. **Reflection** shows that the mind is not composed of parts. A material substance is not capable of reflecting upon itself. A part may come in contact with, and act on, another, but not reflect totally upon itself.

4. **The Mind, not in Space.** — Wherever there is matter, there are also spatial relations. But conscious processes are not in space. An idea or feeling is not on the right or on the left of another. It is not taller or shorter, greater or smaller, similar or different in shape, etc., because it is free from all quantitative determinations.

SPIRITUALITY OF THE HUMAN SOUL

Not only the human, but also the animal mind is immaterial, for consciousness can never be reduced to matter. To examine the question whether the human soul is spiritual necessitates a comparison with the animal mind so as to ascertain if these two differ essentially, for we hold that the human mind alone is spiritual.

I. Specific Human Activities

1. **General Remarks.** — (*a*) Great caution is necessary in interpreting the behavior of animals. Even when their actions are similar to human actions, it would not always be justifiable to suppose that they are prompted by the same motives. A dog may show signs of "remorse" because it remembers past experiences of punishment, whereas in man remorse springs from moral and religious ideas. Again, the so-called education of animals is the result of sensory associations, whereas human education is due to personal effort and the possession of universal ideas. The difficulty of knowing the animal mind is greater owing to the absence of language, for we know the mental processes of other men chiefly

from what they tell us. The principle to be applied is that no faculties are to be attributed to animals unless they are necessary to explain their mode of activity.

(*b*) We need not stop to consider the theory of Descartes, who denies that animals have any consciousness, and considers them as pure physical mechanisms. The presence of consciousness in animals is as clear as its presence in men other than ourselves. Although they cannot speak, they give unmistakable signs of perception, feeling, memory, etc., and by analogy we conclude with certainty that they are endowed with consciousness. Their organism also presents many analogies with the human organism, especially in regard to the nervous system, which is the physical accompaniment of consciousness.

(*c*) The primary and fundamental difference between man and animal is the presence in the former, and the absence in the latter, of *abstract, universal, and necessary knowledge.*

2. **That Man Possesses Such Knowledge** is evident from psychology. (1) No man, however ignorant and uncivilized, fails to recognize certain universal and necessary *principles*, e.g. the principle of contradiction, or the truth that two and two are four. (2) *Language* is not the expression of concrete feelings, but of thought and of universal ideas. However imperfect and, from our point of view, ungrammatical, such expressions may be, and even if they are but simple gestures, they nevertheless manifest universal ideas. They are rational in their origin and character. (3) *Progress*, realized by passing from principles to consequences, from laws to facts, from causes to effects, etc., manifests itself in many ways. Civilization, science, both speculative and practical, etc., are the results of combined processes of induction and deduction. (4) Man is not a mere automaton. Even in many activities that are common to him and to animals, he can use *self-control* derived from reflection. (5) *Morality* and *religion* suppose the knowledge of fundamental principles, of universal laws, the sense of obligation, the demonstration of God's existence and of man's relations with Him.

3. **That Animals Do not Possess Universal Knowledge** is evidenced by the following facts: (1) They have no *language*.

Although some are capable of articulate sounds, it is clear that the manner in which they use the few sentences which they have learned from man manifests only concrete associations. They do not know the meaning of what they say, but simply remember the result which is wont to follow. No other kind of rational communication, e.g. by gestures or the use of signs and symbols, is ever used by animals. Their cries and movements express only concrete ideas and feelings. (2) The behavior of animals, their "progress" and "education," manifest no *reason*. They adapt means to ends, but there is not the slightest indication that they do so from any abstract knowledge of the end and of the aptitude of the means to reach it. Everything can be accounted for by sense-perception, memory, and association. The wonderful tales of animal "intelligence" never require the power of reasoning, nor any abstract knowledge of cause and effect. (3) Moreover, animals act in a *uniform manner* according to their species. They do not use tools or instruments, nor sow to reap a harvest, and, after many attempts to teach them, they do not even know how to light a fire to protect themselves from the cold. To a certain extent they may adapt themselves to their environment, but man alone knows how to adapt his environment to himself. (4) They manifest no *morality* or *religion* of any kind, no freedom, and, in fact, we do not hold them morally responsible, nor attribute to them right or wrong, virtue or vice, etc., in the moral sense of these terms.

4. **Conclusion.** — Hence, after a period of great enthusiasm in favor of animal "intelligence," during which all human faculties, at least in a rudimentary form, were attributed to animals, a more accurate study of their behavior has led the most serious investigators to conclude that animals do not reason, that they have no "intellect," no abstract and universal ideas. We are therefore justified in saying that between the cognitive faculties of man and those of animals, there exists *not only a difference in degree*, but a *difference in kind*. Similar in many respects, and having many activities in common, man and animal differ radically on some essential points. If, on this account, certain prerogatives must be attributed to man, they need not belong to animals.

II. Spirituality of the Human Soul

Two groups of activity, namely, intellect and will, show that the soul is spiritual.

1. **Intellect.** — (*a*) It has been shown in Psychology that the fundamental function of the intellect is *abstraction*, and that the abstract nature of the concept is the source from which its other characteristics — necessity, universality, independence of space and time — flow (pp. 92 ff.). It has been shown also that this abstraction cannot be identified with a mere association or fusion of images by addition or subtraction. Now this function cannot be the function of a material organ. A material organ can perceive only that which acts upon it, i.e. that which is material, concrete, determined in space and time. It cannot perceive the abstract, universal, and immaterial, or the object divested of its material concrete conditions of existence. To the *concrete function of a material organ* can correspond only a *concrete object*. No material organ can perceive the general ideas of triangle, man, virtue, justice, beauty, love, friendship, freedom, relation, possibility, etc., because these cannot act upon the organ. Still less could a material organ perceive an object purely spiritual like God or the human soul.

(*b*) The existence and nature of *necessary judgments* has also been examined in Psychology (p. 112 ff.). Now a material organ can perceive only what is. The necessity and universality of knowledge, the logical sequence of a reasoning, cannot be derived from concrete perceptions. Necessary judgments are not the result of material activity.

(*c*) The human mind is *self-conscious;* it knows its own knowledge and its own knowing activity; it thinks its own thought and the thinking subject itself. Self-consciousness cannot be organic. A particle of matter acts on another particle, but not on itself. It cannot fold itself back so as to perceive itself and its own activity. It cannot penetrate itself so as to be conscious of itself. Self-consciousness is therefore essentially spiritual, since it is directly opposed to what we know of matter.

(*d*) The *mode of exercise* of the intellect is different from that of the senses. If stimulated by too great a stimulus (light, sound, heat, etc.), the senses are so fatigued as to become dull or impaired. The intellect never finds the evidence, clearness, or brightness of a conception or truth too great.

2. **Will.** — (*a*) The will does not tend only to concrete goods, but primarily to abstract good, i.e. to the *ratio boni* incorporated in every concrete good; not only, for instance, to an individual good action, but to the general class of good actions. This tendency, like the corresponding knowledge in the intellect, is a sign of spirituality, for an organ could only tend to concrete sensible good.

(*b*) The will tends to the *immaterial*, the possession of truth, virtue, justice, patriotism, etc. These are man's noblest aspirations which cannot be rooted in the organism and exercised through an organ. The fact of conscience, the sentiment of an obligation, also transcends every form of sense-experience.

(*c*) *Freedom* is a sign of spirituality, for matter is governed by necessary laws, and the sequence of causes and effects is invariable. Hence a free volition, a choice, cannot be the function of a material organ. The freedom of the will, known as a fact from psychology, finds its only possible explanation in the spirituality of the soul.

3. **Summary.** — The human mind transcends matter. It has activities which are not merely *different from* those of matter, but are *in opposition to* the known properties of matter, and therefore are not exercised through the material organism. These are therefore spiritual, and since every being necessarily acts as it is, and according to its own nature, that is, since there must be a proportion between a being and its activities, it follows that the soul which exercises certain activities independently of matter is itself *independent of matter* or *spiritual*. The nature of this spirituality, however, must now be explained more accurately, by indicating exactly what the above arguments prove.

4. **Nature of This Spirituality.** — (*a*) The spirituality of the soul is not manifested by all its operations, but only by those of *intellect* and *will*. Consciousness in general is no sign of spirituality, because certain forms of consciousness are essentially and intrin-

sically bound to the organism so as to be the functions, not of the mind alone, but of the organism as well. Later on we shall see how the soul is related to the organism.

(*b*) Even for intellectual and volitional activities, spirituality does not mean *absolute* and *complete independence* of the soul from matter. As was explained in Psychology (p. 98 ff.), intellectual processes start with the data of the senses which they elaborate. Common experience shows the influence of the organism even on the highest mental functions. (Cf. p. 190.) The intellect is, as it were, a new faculty grafted on the senses, and giving new products for which the senses are inadequate. Hence the spirituality of the soul means that the subject exercising the operations of intellect and will is not material, and consequently not organic; that its dependence on the organism is not a subjective, intrinsic, or immediate one, but a mediate and extrinsic dependence, due to the intellect's necessity of *deriving its materials from the senses.*

III. Psychological Materialism

1. **Meaning.** — (*a*) Materialism in general asserts that there is no other reality than matter and its essential forces. In psychology, materialism rejects the existence of the soul as a distinct reality, and claims that all mental processes are functions of the organism. The cruder and older forms of materialism denied even the simplicity of the mind. The more recent are satisfied with denying its spirituality. There are many forms, not only of obvious and avowed, but also of disguised, materialism, and to-day many theories that go by other names are materialistic. They assert an intrinsic dependence of the mind on the organism, especially on the brain, a dependence which is affirmed as the conclusion of scientific facts.

(*b*) In ancient times may be mentioned Leucippus and Democritus, Epicurus and Lucretius. The French materialism of the eighteenth century is represented especially by De La Mettrie, Helvetius, D'Holbach, and Cabanis. According to the latter, "thought is a secretion of the brain." The German materialism of the nineteenth century is represented especially by Vogt, who holds that brain secretes thought as the liver secretes bile and as the kidneys secrete urine; Moleschott, who holds that thought is an inexplicable motion of brain matter; and Büchner, who denies that thought is anything material like a secretion, but claims that it is the activity itself of the brain. To-day this crude materialism is commonly rejected; the irreducibility of mind and matter is recognized, and thought is not conceived as anything material, or as a product, movement, or activity of matter. We shall see later on, however, that some systems, like epiphenomenalism, parallelism, monism, are frequently materialistic.

2. **Criticism.** — The fundamental argument of materialism as applied to the mind is as follows: Where there is no brain there is no thought. Where there is a brain there is thought. Variations in consciousness depend on the quantity and quality of brain matter, and whatever affects the brain affects also even the highest forms of intellectual thought. Moreover, certain forms of thought are localized in certain portions of the brain. What more, according to the rules of induction, is required to justify the conclusion that thought is essentially and intrinsically dependent on the brain? that it is a function of the brain? that the brain is the organ of thought?

We shall begin with a few remarks on the general value of this argument. (1) If by *function of the brain* is meant "mathematical" function, i.e. concomitance of variations, we may allow the expression, although even then a strict concomitance may be questioned and cannot be proved. If "physiological" function is meant, i.e. production, nothing proves that thought is a function of the brain. On the contrary, sound reason disproves it. (2) The assertion that *the brain is the organ of thought* is true of sensitive functions, not of intellectual functions as such. Yet, even in this latter case, the brain is the organ which furnishes the intellect with the materials necessary to the exercise of its spiritual activity. (3) *Concomitant variations*, even if they were proved to be always verified — they are not — show a dependence, but not necessarily an immediate and intrinsic one. The instrument by itself does not produce the music, and yet the quality of the music depends on the quality of the instrument, that is, of the materials which are at the musician's disposal. In order to prove that thought is material it is not enough to show that it has material antecedents, concomitants, and consequents; its nature must be examined in itself. Beware of the fallacy: "Post hoc, ergo propter hoc." We may now come to the more specific assertions of materialism.

(*a*) Although we must admit that, in a general way, *intelligence depends on the brain*, this fact, as already indicated, proves nothing in favor of materialism. Moreover, no strict parallelism can be asserted. Attempts to make the amount of intelligence dependent on the *quantity* of brain matter have failed miserably, both for the whole animal series and for different men. Intelligence is in proportion neither to the absolute weight of the brain, nor to its weight compared to the total weight of the organism, or of the nervous system, or of the encephalon; nor finally is it in proportion to the dimensions of the brain. This is recognized to-day by all physiologists. The same is true of the attempts to make intelligence essentially dependent on the *qualities* of the brain, e.g. (the amount of phosphorus; the number, depth, and variety of the convolutions). No equation is to be found.

(*b*) The influence of the organism, especially the brain, on the intellect is certain, and has been outlined in Psychology (p. 102). It is accounted for by the fact that changes in the brain affect the quality of the materials offered to the intellect.

(*c*) Psychophysics and physiological psychology measure only the physiological concomitants of mental states.

(*d*) Cerebral localization applies only to movements, and to sensory functions on which the intellect depends and from which it cannot be separated. In fact, higher mental functions are localized nowhere in the brain.

3. **Conclusion.** — Hence we may conclude that the arguments of materialists are not proofs against the spirituality of the soul. They were known to all spiritualists, even those of the Middle Ages. Thus it is Saint Thomas who wrote that "it is necessary for man to have a brain larger in proportion to his body than all the other animals." Why? "To facilitate the activity of internal senses that are necessary to intellectual activity" (Summa Theol., I, 91, 3 ad 1). He knows that if, owing to organic troubles,

memory or imagination be impaired, intellectual faculties are also impaired, even with regard to the use of the knowledge already acquired (I, 84, 7). All this, because "the organism is necessary to intellectual activity, not as the organ through which such activity is exercised, but on account of the materials on which it is exercised" (I, 75, 2 ad 3). These expressions sum up the main ideas and arguments of the present chapter.

CHAPTER III

THE UNION OF THE SOUL WITH THE BODY

That the human soul is in some manner united with an organism, and that mind and body exist together and in mutual dependence, are obvious facts. The nature of this union and its consequences are the problems to be examined in the present chapter.

II. THE UNION ITSELF

I. The Question Stated

1. **Union Defined.** — Several things are said to be united when, in some respect, they may truly be called one. According to the nature of the resulting unity there are several kinds of union.

(*a*) If we consider the *place* in which things are located, their mere juxtaposition produces some unity; thus many stones or bricks together form one heap. This unity is more striking when the juxtaposition realizes a plan, like that of the stones or bricks which are used to build one house.

(*b*) If we consider their *activities*, several things may again be united in several ways. (1) There may be several actions, all of the same kind, and, as it were, on the same level, and tending to the same result. Thus several horses unite their strength to pull a heavy wagon. (2) The several actions tending to the same end may be on different levels and subordinated. Thus we have the pilot steering his vessel, or the rider guiding his horse. (3) The union may consist in an interaction, each substance acting on the other. Thus the fire communicating its heat, or a man struggling with another. (4) There may be similarity or parallelism of action, due to the fact that both actions result from, or are influenced by, the same causes. Thus the hands on several dials may be moved by the same clock-mechanism. (5) Causality and dependence also produce some unity, e.g. one family, one dynasty, etc.

(c) If we consider the *perfection* or *complement* which one reality receives from another we have two kinds of union: (1) The union of a quality or attribute with a substance, e.g. the shape of a material substance, the science or virtue of a man. (2) The union of two principles to form only one substance, e.g. matter and form, as explained in Cosmology, or two elements forming one chemical compound.

(d) Here the problem will be restricted to this: Are body and soul united substantially, i.e. in such a way that only one substance results from their union? Or are they united accidentally, i.e. in such a way that, being two distinct substances, they are united merely by their juxtaposition or their interaction? It is clear that this question is identical with the question: What is man? Is he primarily (1) a spirit united accidentally with an organism? Or (2) an organism with an accidental adjunct of consciousness and intelligence? Or finally (3) both mind and organism united by interaction, or by a substantial union, or by the fact that both are only appearances or modes of the same deeper reality?

2. **Theories.** — The opinions concerning the nature and mode of the union of body and soul are chiefly the following:

(a) According to Malebranche (Occasionalism, or Theory of Divine Assistance) and Leibniz (Preëstablished Harmony), the union is more apparent than real. Both agree on the general principles that body and soul are two distinct and complete substances, and that no created substance can ever act on another.

According to Malebranche, the apparent interaction is due to God's intervention in each and every case; according to Leibniz, to the internal evolution of body and mind respectively, an evolution which at every step corresponds in both substances, and proceeds harmoniously owing to the Creator's infinite wisdom. For Malebranche, soul and body proceed together like two independent clocks that keep the same time because, whenever the hands of one move, God moves the hands of the other correspondingly. On the occasion of some organic processes, God produces in the mind the corresponding conscious process, and, on the occasion of some volition, God produces in the organism the corresponding change. For Leibniz, soul and body proceed together like two independent clocks that keep the same time because from the beginning they were so constructed, so regulated, and endowed with such an initial motion that they always agree, and that all the movements of both correspond. The soul and the organism have been set and regulated together from the beginning, and their apparent interaction is but a harmony, and a perfect agreement preëstablished by God, the creator of both.

To-day, psychophysical parallelism is the offspring of these views. Body and mind, or rather the bodily and the mental series, — parallelists are also phenomenalists — proceed like two parallel lines, keep the same pace, and yet never come in contact by any interaction. Parallelism, as a psychological theory, is generally explained philosophically on a monistic basis: Body and mind are only appearances or modes of the same underlying reality.

(*b*) According to Descartes, man is essentially the soul or spirit. The soul is essentially thought, and matter is essentially extension. How are body and soul united? Descartes's answer is not always consistent. (1) Sometimes, especially when answering objections, he speaks of this union as substantial. (2) Sometimes also he speaks of the interaction of two distinct substances. The soul, located in the pineal gland, receives impressions from the various parts of the organism, and sends back responses. (3) Sometimes, unable to understand the possibility of an interaction between spirit and matter, he seems to give up the problem as hopeless. To-day by those who admit the substantiality and spirituality of the soul, interactionism is frequently given as the bond of union, although it is not explainable.

(*c*) A few philosophers, like Cudworth (1617–1688) and Leclerc (1657–1736), advocate a third substance, or plastic medium, as a means of union. It partakes of both the spiritual and the material nature, and serves to unite these opposites. To-day, some spiritists also assume a body composed of a very subtle matter, which they call the astral body.

(*d*) Psychological monism admits only one substance, which

manifests itself in two ways, consciousness and extension. These are only modes and appearances of one and the same reality which is unknown and unknowable, and which is neither body nor mind. Some, however, give preference to the mind: The one substance must be conceived rather as mind than as matter. Others give preference to the organism, which is a conscious automaton, and would act in exactly the same way, even without the accidental adjunct of consciousness which is an epiphenomenon, or a light thrown off by certain activities of the nervous system. Suppress this adjunct, and the world will go on just as before, since consciousness cannot act on the organism.

(*e*) Aristotle and the scholastics hold that body and soul are two principles united in one complete substance, as matter and form. Like every other material being, man is a composite substance, neither body nor soul separately, but the one substance resulting from the intimate union of both. This one substance is not, as in monistic theories, a primitive unknown substance with two manifestations, but the result of the union of two co-principles. This view is monistic in admitting a unity of substance; dualistic in admitting two principles necessary to constitute this substance. (Cf. above, pp. 428, 430, 436 ff.).

II. Man One Composite Substance

1. **Man One Substance.** — (*a*) Among the functions and activities which man calls his own some are *unconscious*, at least generally, like digestion, secretion, and circulation. Others are *conscious*, either purely spiritual, or psychophysical, i.e. either independent of, or dependent intrinsically on, the organism. All these are attributed to the same subject: I live, walk, eat; I see, hear, feel; I think, understand, reflect. I speak of my body and of my mind, thereby implying that neither is my complete being. This fact of consciousness shows that the complete man is not simply the organism, nor simply the soul, but something *one* resulting from the *union of both*. It may be admitted that the soul is the nobler part, but to say that it is the whole man, using the body as an instrument, guiding and directing it, is to overlook one part of the truth, for when we speak of ourselves or of other men, we

also refer to the organism. The fact that all functions, material and spiritual, belong to the same person is inexplicable if the ego, including body and soul, is not one.

(*b*) Moreover, the *harmony* of bodily and mental functions, and their mutual *dependence*, suppose that man is one being composed of body and soul, one nature tending to develop all its activities for the good of the whole ego. Why should an intense mental function affect organic processes, and vice versa, if mind and organism are distinct substances? Why should mental work after a meal interfere with the digestion if bodily and mental energies are altogether distinct?

(*c*) These facts are overlooked by all theories of two distinct substances. (1) We need not stop at the theories of *occasionalism* and *preëstablished harmony*. Both are based on the false assumption that creatures are incapable of activity. The marvellous structure of the organism becomes meaningless, and all the facts of physiological psychology are unexplainable. (2) A *plastic mediator* will not restore man's substantial unity. Furthermore, it is an impossibility, for, in order to serve as a binding link between matter and spirit, it should be both spiritual and material, and this involves a contradiction. (3) As to *interaction*, superior though it is to the other theories, it does not explain man's real unity, and it makes of the body an instrument of the soul instead of an intrinsic part of man. Moreover, there is the insuperable difficulty of understanding how a spiritual substance and matter can act on each other, since no contact is possible between them. The soul, therefore, is not united to the organism like the musician to his lyre, or the pilot to his vessel (Plato), and man is not simply an intelligence that uses an organism. The union of body and soul is more intimate, so as to form *one substance* which is *man*.

2. **Union of Body and Soul.** — (*a*) The only mode of union which will account for this fact is that according to which the soul is the substantial form of the body. If body and soul are two complete substances, they may be brought close together, and conceived as acting upon each other, but they will always remain two distinct beings. Hence body and soul must be looked upon

as substantial principles, as primary matter and substantial form, each one incomplete in itself, and calling for the other.

(*b*) Between the human composite and other material beings, however, there is an important difference. In man the "forma substantialis" is itself a spiritual substance, which is not altogether, and for all its operations, intrinsically bound to matter. Other forms, and inferior "souls," i.e. the vital principles of plants and animals, exercise no activity except in and through matter. All the activities of plants and animals are functions neither exclusively of matter nor exclusively of the vital principle, but of both together, i.e. of the animated organism, or, if you choose, of the animating soul.

But, while the whole energy of the human body comes from the soul as substantial form, the soul is not altogether immersed in matter. In addition to vital and sensory activities which are exercised through the animated organism, the soul has also spiritual activities which are not exercised through any sense-organ. However, even for its spiritual activities, the soul is not a pure spirit. It requires the organism, since the senses are necessary to supply the materials of spiritual activities. (Cf. p. 475.) This union is not against, but in strict conformity with, the nature of the human soul.

3. **Double-Aspect Theory.** — (*a*) Descartes estranged body and mind from each other, and united them only by an interaction. Spinoza made of them two attributes of one and the same substance, and to-day monism or new Spinozism advocates the same view. There is, and there can be, no interaction of mind and matter. Yet, as science shows the correspondence of both series of processes, they must be called parallel. As they are different in nature, they can never come in contact with each other. So far this view is *psychophysical parallelism*, at which many *psychologists* stop without going farther.

(*b*) But *philosophy* asks the reason of this parallelism. The answer is given in the *identity-hypothesis* or *double-aspect theory*. Neither the body nor the mind are substances; they are only appearances of the same two-sided reality. They are like the two aspects of the same curve, which is concave from within and convex from without, or like the same story told in two languages, or the same sum of money which is a debt for one man and a credit for another. This psychophysical monism is connected with panpsychism, universal monism, evolutionism, and agnosticism. Frequently also it is but a covert materialism, when the one reality is identified with some form of matter, and when a dependence is admitted of the mind on the organism, but not of the organism on the mind.

Criticism. (*a*) The expression "psychophysical parallelism" is *objectionable;* how can we speak of two utterly different series as being parallel? They cannot be so in space since mental processes are not spatial, and nothing proves that they are so in time, since nothing proves that the mental series is continuous. If to every mental process corresponds an organic process, there are apparently many organic, and even cerebral, processes that are not accompanied by any consciousness. Many parallelists inconsistently admit that the psychical series is determined by the physiological. Moreover, if it is completed by the identity-theory, parallelism admits that parallels do meet in the unity of their common substance.

(*b*) As to the "double-aspect" theory, it has to answer the question: Is the double aspect universal for all kinds of matter, or is the mental aspect to be found only in certain beings? If, with some monists, we admit panpsychism — without a shred of evidence — we have nevertheless to explain how two irreducible series can come from the same principle. If, with others, we reject panpsychism, the appearance of the psychical aspect remains unexplained.

(*c*) To make of man a conscious automaton is opposed to consciousness, which testifies that certain movements are undertaken in consequence of visual, auditory, etc., perceptions, and of other states of consciousness. Moreover, the evolution of the individual and of the race, civilization, inventions, etc., are due to the desire of producing certain pleasurable feelings of comfort and pleasure, and of avoiding painful feelings. Finally, the existence of other minds is known only indirectly from the various organic expressions that are supposed to manifest mental states.

(*d*) The expression "identity-theory" is also to be rejected. I am not conscious of a universal substance, identical with the one substance of all other things, but of my own substance, including body and mind. And I distinguish this substance from all other inanimate or animate substances. Here monists take refuge in an agnostic position. The one substance of all things is unknown and unknowable, and when safely intrenched there, monists are proof against all attacks, for no question can be asked them concerning what they declare to be unknowable. But is it logical to make the unknowable account for things known? Many things are in reality unknowable, but the unknowable must not be made contradictory either with itself or with known facts and the clear testimony of consciousness. This whole question will have to be touched upon again from a more general standpoint when we speak of monism as a world-wide theory.

II. CONSEQUENCES OF THE UNION

1. **Only One Soul in Man.** — The arguments presented above not only show that man is one substance, and that the soul is the substantial form of the body, but also that there is only one soul in man, which is at once the principle of spiritual activities, of sensitive processes, and of vegetative, i.e. vital functions. Some philosophers hold that there is a special *vital principle*, distinct from the *principle of consciousness*. This seems to break the substantial unity of man as manifested in consciousness, and to offer no satisfactory explanation of the intimate relations between the two lives. A violent emotion may disturb the organism, and even destroy life. In a number of ways the dependence of life on the mind, and vice versa, is manifest. (See Psychology, pp. 190 ff.) This strengthens the testimony of consciousness that one and the same substance lives and is also conscious.

2. **The Seat of the Soul.** — We cannot speak of the *locus*, place, or seat of the soul in the same way that we speak of the place which a material being occupies, because the soul, being spiritual, has no spatial relations (right, left, between, surrounded by, etc.). Hence, when we ask where the soul is, we do not speak of a

material localization, or of a contact, but simply of a substantial and active presence, which cannot be imagined — since the soul cannot be perceived by the senses — but only understood, and even this imperfectly, owing to our habits of thinking of everything in terms of matter.

Since the soul is the substantial form and the principle of life of the human organism, it follows that it is not only in one part of the body, but *in the whole body which it animates*, not as water in a sponge, or blood in the veins, but as a co-principle, an indivisible substance exercising its activity through the organism. The soul, however, does not exercise its whole activity through the whole organism. Different functions require different organs, and hence are localized in these respective organs: vision in the visual, hearing in the auditory, organs; memory in the brain, etc. As to the spiritual activities, they are not exercised through the intrinsic coöperation of the material co-principle, but by the soul alone, as explained above.

3. **Faculties.** — (1) The soul is one and, together with the organism, forms the human substance. (2) As it is simple and indivisible, faculties cannot be parts of the soul. (3) As it is the principle of all determinations and activities in the body, faculties cannot mean distinct agents, independent of the soul, acting and reacting upon one another like so many substances. But without meaning this, faculties may mean more than mere classifications or labels of functions. They mean *the various modes of activity of the soul*, exercised either by the soul alone — spiritual faculties — or by the soul and the organism united in one common principle — faculties of the *compositum*.

From what has been said on the seat of the soul in the organism, it is clear that organic faculties are *classified* according to the various functions of different organs. Hence some persons have the exercise of faculties lacking in others. Vision is absent in the blind because the necessary conditions are not verified. If these were restored, the radical faculty would become capable of exercise. It is impossible to determine the number of distinct faculties; we can only group them according to different points of view. Thus from one point of view we may have vegetative, sensitive, and intellectual faculties; from another, knowledge, feelings, and will; from another, faculties of immanent or of transitive activity, etc.

4. **Mutual Dependence of Organism and Mind.** — In Psychology (p. 190 ff.) mention was made of the reciprocal influences of body and mind. We understand now how they must be conceived. Not as if body and mind were two distinct substances, or two distinct agents, *acting upon each other*. They rather *act together*. Their union does not consist in an *interaction*, or mutual influence, but *their mutual influence is the result of their substantial union*. We have not so much an interaction as a "simulaction," since body and mind form one man and one complete principle of activity. Owing to this intimate union, whatever affects one also affects the other.

5. **Definitions.** — (1) *The human soul* is not only thought, or the power of thinking, as Descartes claimed. It has other functions equally essential. It is a spiritual substance, in the sense already explained, destined, however, to be essentially united with, and to give life to, the body. (2) *Man* is not merely a spirit or intelligence; nor simply an organism, but the one substance composed of two principles. He is *body and mind united in one complete substance*.

CHAPTER IV

ORIGIN OF THE SOUL AND OF MAN

The Problem Stated. — (*a*) In the problem of origin several questions must be distinguished. Owing to its spiritual nature, the soul's origin must be studied apart from that of the organism. Moreover, the problem may refer either to the origin of individual men — organism or soul — now, in the present condition of man; or to the origin of the first man. Hence the following questions: (1) Origin of the human organism. (2) Origin of the human soul. (3) Antiquity and specific unity of mankind.

(*b*) The main suppositions that can be made are the following: (1) The first man was created by God, both as to his body and as to his soul. At present, however, the organism arises by way of generation, and the soul (a) arises also by generation, or (b) is directly created by God. (2) The first man's soul was created by God — and subsequent souls originate in either way mentioned above. His organism was the result of an evolution from lower forms of animal life. (3) The whole man, body and soul, is a product of evolution.

I. THE HUMAN ORGANISM

It is clear that actually the human organism arises by a process of generation similar to that which takes place in other living beings. Arising from a primitive cell, it gradually develops into a complete organism. Hence the present question refers only to the appearance of the first human organism. We know that man did not always exist. Did his organism arise by a direct creation of God, or by an evolution from other types which existed before man appeared on the earth?

I. The Evidence

N.B. Transformists do not claim that man evolved out of any actually existing type, but that man and the higher apes, known as anthropoid, sprang from a common ancestor less differentiated than either man or ape.

1. **Arguments for Descent.** — It must be admitted that many of the arguments brought forward in Cosmology in favor of the theory of transformism apply also to man, and the remarks made there on the value of these arguments must be kept in mind. Thus there is a *morphological resemblance* — on the main lines — between the human and other vertebrate organisms. A *similar chemical composition* of the blood and the tissues may also be pointed out. *Rudimentary organs* may be indicated. *Embryology* may show that the human organism develops in a manner closely resembling that of other vertebrates. When all this has been done — and it has frequently been done in a one-sided way in order to prove a thesis — the fact of descent remains unproved, and transformism, when applied to man, as well as in the case of many other forms of life, is a mere hypothesis.

2. **Difficulties.** — (*a*) Resemblances must not make us overlook differences, among which may be mentioned the vertical attitude, and the adaptation of the lower limbs for this purpose; the relative length of arms, much shorter in man than in the ape; the general morphology of the head; the absence of hair, etc.; and especially the quantitative and qualitative development of the brain.

(*b*) The main stumbling-block of the theory of descent is the absence of paleontological evidence, notwithstanding the fact that man is of comparatively recent origin, hence that remains of forms of transition should be found more easily, and that diligent research has been made in this direction, in order to find the much sought for "missing link." That such "missing link" between man and ape does not now exist is admitted. As to its existence in the past, much ado has been made about the discovery of certain fossils, especially skulls, which, however, more calm and reflective science has shown to belong certainly either to apes or to well-developed races of men.

II. Conclusions

1. **Scientifically**, i.e. judging only from the facts at hand, the theory of descent as applied to the human body is not proved,

but remains a mere hypothesis with insufficient evidence. This is acknowledged by the best scientists, who are not led by a priori conceptions, but want their conclusions to rest on established facts. To give more or less vivid pictures of "primitive man," and of his evolution out of inferior organisms to the present form, to indulge in numberless suppositions, is to pass from the realm of science to that of imagination, and to take dreams for realities.

2. **Philosophically** there is nothing contradictory or unlikely in the theory of descent as applied to the human organism any more than in the general theory of evolution. It is a question of fact which is not to be answered a priori.

II. THE HUMAN SOUL

By zoölogists man is classified — and rightly — as a vertebrate and a mammal with certain anatomical and physiological characteristics. Rightly, I say, because zoölogy considers only one aspect of man, namely, his organism. But there is something more in man. The reason for differentiating him essentially from animals is not his organism, but his soul. Zoölogy is not competent to pass a final judgment on the place of the whole man in nature, for it leaves out of consideration man's nobler part, namely, his mind.

I. The First Human Soul

1. **Not a Result of Evolution.** — (*a*) Starting either from zoölogical considerations or from monistic views of a universal evolution, certain philosophers are led to assert that the whole man, body and mind, is the result of evolution. Hence, for them, the necessity of admitting between the human and the animal mind, not a specific difference, but only a difference of degree. Animals must have at least rudiments of whatever mental manifestations are found in man. Either the human mind is animalized, i.e. lowered so as to show that all its activities are reducible to sensory activities, and that, in consequence, it is not spiritual; or the animal mind is humanized, i.e. raised so as to show that it possesses — at least in some degree — the specifically human activities. By this twofold process the human mind is successfully (?) linked to the animal mind, and the obstacle to evolution removed.

(*b*) But, as was shown when we spoke of the soul's spirituality, to interpret the actions of animals *humano modo*, i.e. to assert that animals act in the same way, and from the same motives as man, should not be done when we have evidence to the contrary. To any fact only the minimum of necessary cause should be ascribed, since the surplus, i.e. that which is over and above the strict requisite, is asserted gratuitously. After a great deal of talk about animal intelligence, it is commonly accepted to-day that the power of abstract and universal thought remains the fundamental distinctive feature of the human mind. It constitutes an impassable gulf between animal and man.

2. **Created by God.** — How could this gulf be bridged over? How could a difference in kind arise? How could the first man's spiritual soul be produced? Some simply assert that they do not know, and that some cause unknown to science must have been at work. This is a strictly *scientific* position. Others, from the point of view of *philosophy*, recognize the intervention of God's creative power. Only an infinite cause can bring to existence something out of nothing. The spiritual cannot arise from the material. Hence, whatever be said of the human organism, the human soul at least is the direct work of God. This view supposes, of course, what will be said in Theodicy concerning God's existence and nature.

II. Subsequent Human Souls

1. **Various Opinions.** — If God's creative act was necessary for the production of the first human soul, is it so for subsequent human souls? Or can the parents transmit to their offspring, not only organic life, but also the spiritual soul which animates the organism, and yet in some of its activities is independent of it? This problem is distinct from the preceding, for in the present case the parents are endowed already with a spiritual soul. Two main solutions are offered: (1) Every individual soul is created directly by God. (2) The soul of the offspring comes from the parents either (*a*) by the material organic process of generation, or (*b*) by a kind of spiritual generation in which the offspring's soul is derived from the parental soul. Of these solutions (1), or

creationism, is commonly accepted by Catholic philosophers and theologians; (2, *a*), or traducianism, was held by Tertullian; (2, *b*), or generationism, was held by a few Catholic theologians, especially Froschammer, who was reproved by the Church.

2. **Criticism.** — (*a*) (1) *Traducianism* is impossible. Either it denies the spirituality of the soul; or, if it admits it, it does not assign to the soul an adequate cause, since spirit cannot arise from matter. (2) *Generationism* is also impossible. A spiritual semen would suppose the division of the parents' soul, and this is opposed to the very spirituality and indivisibility of the soul. (3) Hence, since the soul cannot originate from any preëxistent reality, whether material or spiritual, the only possible mode of production of the soul is a production out of nothing, i.e. a *creation*. Is there any other possibility which the necessity in which we are of thinking of spiritual substances according to material analogies prevents us from knowing? To this no answer can be given.

(*b*) We may note that (1) the divine creation of every individual soul is not a miracle, but an action strictly in accordance with the laws of nature, since it is the nature of the soul to be unproducible in any other way; (2) the parents are really parents since their action is the cause of a human being, just as we say that the murderer kills a man although he does not destroy his soul, which, as we shall see, is immortal; (3) heredity is easily explained by the dependence of the mind on the organism.

3. **Time of Origin.** — At what time does the soul begin to exist? Some suppose that souls exist before the organism. Thus Plato, many Origenists, and Leibniz. This theory of preëxistence is frequently held in connection with metempsychosis (Pythagoras), or the doctrine of reincarnation advocated by Eastern thinkers, and by theosophists. But we say that the soul is produced only at the time of its union with the organism. Preëxistence is a purely gratuitous assertion without the slightest evidence. Moreover, since the soul is naturally the form of the body, it follows that it must begin to exist when the time comes for it to "inform" the body. When is this time? Is it immediately at conception, so that the first principle of life is the spiritual soul? Or is it some time later so that at first the principle of life is of an inferior kind,

and animates the organism until it is sufficiently developed to receive the spiritual soul? This cannot be determined, but the former opinion is the more common to-day.

III. MANKIND

The questions of the specific unity and antiquity of mankind are to be answered by geological, ethnological, and anthropological sciences. Here we shall simply give the main conclusions without entering into the detailed account of the facts on which they are based.

I. Specific Unity of Mankind

The question of the specific unity of mankind is not identical with the question of the community of origin from the same first ancestors. Both questions, however, are closely connected. If all men belong to the same species, it is at once, if not demonstrated, at least highly probable, that all come from the same first parents. And, in fact, historically the two questions have been looked upon as correlative.

1. **Races.** — Some differences are always found between individual men. Much more striking are the differences between certain groups of men forming what has been called different races — e.g. differences in color, size, relative development of certain parts, hair, etc. Many attempts have been made to classify the various races of mankind according to some characteristic feature. As a basis some have taken the color of the skin; others the facial angle; others the peculiarities of the hair; others the geographical distribution; others the language, etc. It is admitted that none of these classifications is perfectly satisfactory, as there is no clear-cut distinction between the many human types.

However, such classifications are useful, and among the main ones may be mentioned the following. Blumenbach distinguishes five races: Caucasian (white), Mongolian (yellow), Ethiopian (black), American (red), and Malay (brown). Cuvier distinguishes three races: Caucasian (white), Mongolian (yellow), and Negro (black). Huxley admits four races: Australioid, Negroid, Mongoloid, and Xantocroic (white). Others have admitted many more distinct races, while those who admit a smaller number are obliged to subdivide them.

2. **Unity of Species.** — While we must admit several races or varieties of men, there is absolutely no reason for admitting several species. Facts, on the contrary, show the specific unity of mankind.

(*a*) All men have the same *anatomical organisation* and *physiological functions* (upright attitude, blood temperature, number of teeth and bones, general structure, etc.). *Interracial fecundity* is also general, and the offspring of parents belonging to different races are also prolific. Finally all have the same essential and fundamental *characteristics of intelligence*, e.g. language, use of tools, religion, capacity for progress, etc.

(*b*) The differences between human races are less important than the differences within certain animal and vegetable groups the common origin of which is beyond doubt. These differences can be explained easily by the influence of surroundings, climate, food, isolation from, or association with, other men, etc. The main differences between men do not indicate a specific diversity. Everywhere and at all times *man is truly man*, and has the same essential characteristics.

II. Antiquity of Man

1. **The Question.** — History cannot tell us how long man has existed on the earth, because it always refers to groups of men already in existence. Moreover, the chronology of early historical documents is most uncertain. Hence recourse must be had to natural sciences, especially geology, so as to find traces of man in the form either of fossil remains or of tools and results of human activity. This can never lead to an accurate chronology, because geologists differ widely as to the time necessary for the formation of the various strata of the earth. The existence of man in the tertiary era is, to say the least, very doubtful. The first unmistakable signs of the existence of man are found at the beginning of the quaternary era. How long a time has elapsed since then it is impossible to determine. Some give as high a number as 250,000 or 300,000 years, but without sufficient foundation, as this lapse of

time does not seem necessary to explain the transformations of the earth. Nothing certain can be said on this point.

2. **Primitive Man.** — There is no evidence that the primitive state of man was a state of savagery, but rather that the state of savagery is one of degradation and degeneration from a higher condition. Evolutionists generally hold the contrary. For them, the savage is the backward man, less evolved, nearer to primitive man, and therefore to animality. It is impossible to reach any general law applicable to all cases. We may, however, state the following facts.

(*a*) Through the successive ages of man's existence, no essential physical differences are observed in human fossils, and the differences between races now extinct and those existing to-day are not greater than the differences between the various actual races.

(*b*) Unmistakable signs of true intelligence, and of a truly human mind, are found wherever primitive man existed. That he did not have so much science, comfort, or what we call civilization, is certain; but it is no less certain that he had the use of reason as well as we have, based on the same power of abstract and universal knowledge. And even to-day, whether a child will be a simple countryman or a great scientist depends greatly on circumstances, and the countryman may have more intelligence than the scientist, even if he lacked the opportunity to develop or manifest it. Hence neither on the organic nor on the mental side can any transitional type be found between man and animal.

(*c*) Some of the savage races actually existing are known historically to have come from more civilized races (e.g. the Fuegians, Bushmen). Others give clear signs that they are degenerates, either by the traces of an ancient civilization (monuments, paintings, etc.), like those of the American Indians, especially in Mexico; or by their language, which, like that of the Australians and the Fuegians, is very rich in words, declensions, and grammatical forms. When thrown into unfavorable circumstances, the most highly civilized man returns promptly to a kind of savage condition.

CHAPTER V

IMMORTALITY OF THE SOUL

The last problem to be examined is that of the destiny of man, and especially of his soul. After stating the question, we shall examine successively the possibility and the fact of immortality.

I. THE QUESTION STATED

I. Death

1. **The Law of Death.** — Common experience shows that, after a longer or shorter time, organisms cease to live. The law of death applies to all living beings, at least to all those that are more highly differentiated. Certain unicellular beings are reproduced by simple fission. Death does not occur, but the mother-cell, by fission, gives rise to two independently living cells. This, however, cannot be called true immortality, because nothing proves that the individual mother-cell persists in its own life; it may disappear when giving rise to two different individuals. At any rate, although this kind of immortality would be "natural," death would result from a number of accidental causes. Limiting ourselves to higher organisms, and with special reference to man, we see that, sooner or later, life disappears, and the organism becomes a corpse.

2. **The Duration of Life** varies greatly with the different species of organisms, both vegetal and animal. Although there is more constancy within the same species, yet, even there, great variations are observed. It must also be noted that physiologists agree that comparatively few men die a natural death. The majority die of some special disease before the system is worn out. If we ask why, apart from accidental death, one man lives longer than another, we find that the length of life depends on many

factors. Among the most important are natural endowments and heredity: a man is born with a strong or a weak constitution; the struggle for life (climate, food-supply, labor, struggle against micro-organisms, etc.); the mode of life (kind of work, use and abuse of certain foods and drinks, drugs, pleasures, etc.); mental life in its various aspects; the rest or unrest of organic and mental activity: some live "faster" than others.

But when this has been said, the question remains: Why is death a necessity of nature? Why cannot the same organism that has grown and developed hold its own instead of decaying? Why cannot the same vital principle or soul continue the work which it was formerly capable of doing? It must be confessed that death, like generation, is a mystery. When we have said that it is a law of nature hardly anything more can be said. We simply note that no objection can be drawn from this fact against the existence of the vital principle or soul. Vital functions are essentially dependent on matter. It is matter that lives, and the difficulty confronts not only those who admit a principle of life, but also those who try to explain life simply by physical and chemical forces. Why cannot these forces do always what they do in the beginning?

3. **The Main Signs of Death** are the lividity of the face; the coldness and rigidity of the muscles; the absence of certain reflexes (e.g. of the contraction of the pupil when a light is brought near the eyes); the absence of muscular contraction, respiration, and circulation; in a word, the cessation of characteristic vital functions. These signs, however, are not infallible, for there are cases in which life remains latent without manifesting itself; hence the precise time of death cannot be determined. The only certain sign of death is the decomposition of the organism, first into cells that may for some time continue to live independently, and lastly into inorganic particles, which again may enter into the composition of new organisms. In the first stage, certain vital functions may still be performed: secretion, digestion, reflexes, nutrition (e.g. by blood transfusion), growth of hair and nails, etc. But the principle of unity in the organism is absent, and after a relatively short time all manifestations of life cease.

II. The Question of Immortality

1. **Meaning of Immortality.** — (*a*) At death, the principle of life in plants and animals disappears, since it was only an essential part of the compositum, and had no existence or activity except in and through matter. It simply ceases to be, as the spherical shape of a wax ball disappears when the wax is given another shape, or, more properly, as the substantial form of any substance disappears when this substance is changed into another. Hence the present question of immortality applies only to the human soul.

(*b*) The assertion that the human soul is immortal means that the soul does not cease to exist with the body, but that, after death, it *continues to exist forever as an active and conscious reality*. (1) We are not satisfied, therefore, with the poor substitute offered by materialists and positivists who admit only a *metaphorical* immortality, consisting in a man's enduring works, his influence, glory, good name, the love and admiration of mankind. What is, for us, the use of all this, if *we* are no longer? And can we say that future glory given by posterity is in proportion to man's worth? (2) Nor are we satisfied with the *pantheistic conception of immortality*, according to which, it is true, the soul survives forever, but without its consciousness and personality being absorbed in the Great All, a part or emanation of which it is, or engulfed in the great ocean of unconsciousness and inactivity like the Buddhistic Nirvana.

2. **The Attitudes Regarding Immortality** are affirmation, negation, and doubt.

(*a*) The *affirmation* of immortality may be based on (1) purely *rational* grounds: the nature of the soul, and its aspirations; (2) chiefly *ethical* grounds: the fact of morality and the necessity of a future sanction; (3) *religious* grounds: the existence and nature of God, and (4) the fact of a divine revelation; (5) *empirical* grounds: the facts of spiritism, in which the departed souls are supposed to manifest themselves. The first two lines of argument go together. The third also completes them as far as the rational knowledge of God is concerned. The argument from divine revelation, which does not belong to philosophy, is distinct altogether. So also is the empirical argument.

(*b*) The *denial* of immortality may be based on an analogy with the general laws of nature, e.g. the law of death for every organism; the nature of the soul, its dependence on the organism, and its consequent incapacity to exist and act by itself.

(*c*) The *agnostic position* is an attitude according to which neither the affirmation nor the negation of immortality is sufficiently justified. We do not know; at most we may be allowed to have hopes. This view may be based on many grounds, among which the positivistic claim that nothing is certain except what experience can verify.

N.B. (1) The present problem is closely related to ethical problems and to the existence and nature of God. Here we assume the theistic position which will be justified in Theodicy, that is, the existence of a personal God, creator of the world, infinitely wise, good, and just. (2) The various reasons for immortality must not be considered separately as complete and independent arguments, but rather as forming together one whole and complete argument.

II. POSSIBILITY AND FACT OF IMMORTALITY

I. Possibility

1. **Dependence of the Soul on the Organism.** — (*a*) An objection is suggested immediately by the fact that the soul is the substantial form of the organism, that the two together form only one complete nature, and have only one existence. How, then, can the soul survive the organism? Moreover, does not the soul share all the organic changes and vicissitudes? It begins with the organism, grows with it, becomes old with it. It must also cease to exist with it.

(*b*) We must remember that, if the soul is the substantial form of the organism, it is nevertheless a *spiritual* substance. All that the organism is, it owes to its union with the soul. But it is not true to say of the human soul that all it is, it owes to its union with the organism. This is true of the soul only as the principle of life and sensation, not as the principle of intellectual and volitional activities which, in themselves, are spiritual. In this sense alone is it true to say that the soul shares the fate of the organism. Owing to their dependence on the senses, intellectual activities seem to grow with the organism, and they may be impaired for the same reason. But frequently intellectual activities are exercised as perfectly as ever when the organism has become old, weak, and diseased.

2. **Activities of the Soul.** — (*a*) The dependence of the soul on the organism, whether it be extrinsic or intrinsic, must make it impossible for the soul to act at all once it is separated from the organism. If it remains, it cannot be said to survive, that is, to outlive the organism, since life, i.e. activity, consciousness, intellection, becomes impossible. And what would be the good of such a bare and dead persistence?

(*b*) We admit that such a persistence is not what we seek, nor what we claim. We want a *living* and *active* survival. It is certain also that the functions which the soul exercises in common with the organism cannot remain, except, we may say, "in radice"; i.e. the soul retains these faculties as mere "potentiæ." Supposing that the essential conditions of their exercise be verified again, the soul will be able to exercise them.

But what about its own spiritual activities? The soul separated from the body cannot acquire ideas in the same way that it does now, by elaborating materials furnished by the senses; nor can it express ideas by language. We must remember that the dependence of the spiritual soul on the organism is only extrinsic, and that intellectual activity itself is spiritual. Hence if materials can be secured elsewhere, this activity can be exercised.

Where can these be found? The soul can preserve ideas acquired in the present life. Moreover, by reflection it can know itself and its own processes, and from these acquire many ideas. By the elaboration of these ideas many others may be inferred. Finally, by communication with other souls and spirits, much knowledge may be acquired. The love of the good, and admiration for perfection, will follow knowledge. Moreover, it may safely be said that, if God keeps the soul in existence, He will give it the means of knowing all that interests it, even things and events of this world. Of course, reason alone cannot carry us very far, since our knowledge of spiritual substances is very imperfect. It can show only that it is not impossible for certain activities of the soul to be exercised, although we do not understand positively the manner of this exercise, nor the mode of communication between spirits.

II. Proofs of Immortality

The proofs of immortality may be reduced to three: teleological, ethical, and ontological. To these some secondary proofs are added.

1. **Teleological.** — The end, purpose, and destiny of any being are known from its structure, aptitude, tendency, and activity. Man has capacities, aspirations, tendencies, and activities which are not realized or fulfilled in this life. Therefore they point to a future life.

(*a*) The major of this argument is the *principle of teleology or finality*, which is used extensively, especially in biological sciences. It states the universal law that a being's destiny is known from its activity. In organisms there is always a correlation between an organ and its function and the mode of this function. The presence of an organ is always taken as a sign of an appropriate activity, and of an adaptation of all other organs in conformity with this activity. From one single fossil bone, the structure of the whole animal to which it belongs may be inferred by the naturalist. If one organ is modified, others are modified accordingly. The organization manifests the mode of life, the kind of food used, the various instincts, and so on. Man must be included in the same law, and his destiny will be known from his activities.

(*b*) The minor of the argument states that man has aspirations which are not fulfilled here on earth. It rests on *psychological facts* of intellect and will.

(1) *Intellect.* In the first place human thought is not enclosed within any temporal or spatial limits, nor within the limits of contingent, actual, finite beings. It rises above space and time.

Beyond the present it foresees the future, and has the idea of an endless duration. It longs for what is *perfect*, *necessary*, and *universal*. It conceives the possibility of a life free from the many physical and moral evils of the present life. Moreover, the human intellect seeks for truth, and will never be satisfied with fragments of truth. And yet how little is known now! The knowledge which we acquire moves a little farther the boundaries of our ignorance, but opens new unexplored regions and increases our desire to know. *Sciences* are not sufficient, we want *science*, full, complete, and perfect, free from incertitude, and all-embracing. If the human intellect has a destiny, it is the possession of such truth.

(2) *Will*. Man inevitably seeks happiness, not partial, but complete. No *goods* satisfy him; he wants the *good*, the perfect and unmixed good, the fulness of life, the satisfaction of all human desires. Evidently such happiness is found nowhere in this life. Neither wealth, nor art, nor science, nor anything else can give it. We find only aspects or parts of happiness, which increase our craving for a more perfect happiness.

(*c*) (1) The conclusion is that, if man's mind moves in the perfect, the eternal, and the infinite, it is because it is *destined to the perfect, the eternal, and the infinite*. Otherwise man is an exception on the earth. The animal's instincts and cravings find their own satisfaction in nature. How can man's highest aspirations be baffled? Is he alone in creation endowed with aimless tendencies and with needs which he cannot satisfy? (2) The argument is more forcible if we consider that these higher aspirations are stronger in proportion as man is more perfect. As man acquires more knowledge and happiness, it would seem that he should be better satisfied, and that his cravings should decrease. We know that the reverse takes place. The greatest scientists, artists, and saints are those whose aspirations and desires are the strongest for truth, beauty, and virtue. (3) This merely rational consideration is strengthened when we look upon God as the author of human nature. Since He is all wise and all good, He must satisfy the yearnings which He has given to man.

(*d*) This argument points to a future life, conscious and personal, and without end — since no happiness is perfect if there is the fear of losing it. It does not apply to infants, and applies less perfectly to men whose minds are less developed. It also leaves out of consideration the punishment for the wicked, whose aspirations after happiness will never be satisfied if their chastisement is eternal. Here, however, we touch upon the ground of apologetics and theology.

2. **Ethical.** — There is a moral order. This order requires a future life. Therefore the soul survives after death.

(*a*) The existence of the moral order, including the sense of obligation, the essential distinction of right and wrong, the categorical imperative, the fact of conscience, etc., has been shown in Ethics.

(*b*) How does this order require a future life? (1) Because otherwise it would not be order, but disorder; not a rational, but an irrational condition. Obedience to the dictates of conscience cannot ultimately have an evil result. Compliance with the moral law cannot ultimately result in man's unhappiness; otherwise man would be a contradiction to himself. Right conduct cannot be man's condemnation to misery. The accomplishment of duty cannot be the cause of man's unhappiness. In other words, honesty and dishonesty, the practice of justice and of injustice, virtue and vice, cannot have the same final issue, otherwise morality itself is but an illusion, and the natural conclusion is: "Enjoy yourself here on earth, no matter by what means; the rascal's and the saint's final condition is the same." The sacrifices which a man has to impose on himself to obey the voice of conscience cannot make his lot worse than that of the debauchee. (2) We have seen in Ethics that no satisfactory sanction is found in this life. Yet, if there is justice and reason in the world, good must be rewarded and evil punished.

(*c*) Hence the conclusion that, if the moral order is rational, a future life is necessary. This conclusion becomes still more forcible in the theistic conception of an infinitely just God on whom ultimately morality rests, and who will not fail to give to every man according to his merits.

(*d*) This argument shows the necessity of a future life, conscious and personal, but it does not show that such a life must be endless. Temporary rewards and punishments might suffice. Nor does it apply to infants, or to those who, owing to mental defects, are not capable of morality.

3. **Ontological.** — The human soul, either in itself or on account of its dependence on the organism, has no principle of destruction. Moreover, no external cause will destroy it. Therefore it will endure forever.

(*a*) In itself the soul is a *simple* and *spiritual substance*, hence not divisible. It cannot be resolved into parts or principles. Its dependence on the organism is not intrinsic. Being spiritual, the soul can exist and act without the organism. It does not, therefore, perish on account of its union with the organism. This is but a consequence of what was said above (pp. 501 ff., 474 ff.).

(*b*) The only external cause that could destroy the soul is God. Although this is, absolutely speaking, possible to God, we have reasons to assert that it will not take place. In His wisdom, He will not annihilate a substance which He has made incorruptible by nature. In His goodness, He will not frustrate man's highest and noblest aspirations. In His justice, He will not leave man without retribution for his deeds. In His holiness, He will not suffer vice to be finally equal to virtue.

(*c*) This argument shows the soul's ability to survive the organism, and when completed by considerations from theodicy, psychology, and ethics, it acquires its full force.

4. **Secondary and Insufficient Proofs.** — (*a*) Notwithstanding the lack of empirical evidence for immortality it is a fact that belief in it is universal among men, past and present, civilized and barbarous, ignorant and learned, as their writings, practices, funeral rites, etc., show. This belief is a sign of truth, as it can be explained only by the naturalness and necessity of immortality. This consideration is important, but only secondary, because this common belief is ultimately based on the arguments given above, explicitly or implicitly recognized. Moreover, the unanimity is only moral. Numerous individual exceptions are to be found, and some nations, especially in the East, do not seem to admit a personal, perhaps not even a conscious, immortality.

(*b*) The organism is not annihilated; how can the nobler part of man perish? It is true that the law of the conservation of matter must be admitted, but the organism as such is destroyed. Its elements are changed and enter new combinations. To be worth anything, this consideration must be based on the soul's substantiality and spirituality.

(*c*) The proof from a natural desire of perpetual life is included in the proof from the aspirations of man.

(*d*) Plato's argument from the eternal preëxistence of the soul must be rejected, as has been said when speaking of the origin of the soul.

(*e*) We cannot admit the empirical proof given by spiritists, as the nature of spiritistic manifestations is far from known. Do any spirits manifest themselves, and, if so, who are they? These questions are not answered satisfactorily at present.

5. **Cumulative Value of the Arguments.** — We cannot here speak *ex cathedra* and state what absolute value these arguments have, and how they must be received by everybody. Evidently they produce no mathematical certitude. They do not give a direct and immediate knowledge of the soul's immortality. But, when taken together, they give more than a mere probable hope. The more we look upon it, the more wisely and rationally constructed this universe seems to be, and the more impossible it appears that the soul should perish. It may be added that the three main arguments presented separately show the same thing from different angles, namely, the nature of the soul; hence all centre around the ontological proof to which they may be reduced. There is, however, a reason for distinguishing them, as the first two are more easily understood, and do not presuppose so many abstract reasonings on the nature of the soul. They seem to be more living and more practical.

6. **Conclusion.** — But how many questions these arguments leave without answer, especially concerning the future state of the soul. They show that this life is only a preparation; but a preparation for what? What is the nature of the happiness which the soul is destined to enjoy, and of the retribution for the good and the wicked? Here divine revelation completes the proofs of reason, and tells us what reason cannot see. The very dogma of the

resurrection of the body is in perfect accordance with the exigencies of the human soul as the substantial form of the organism. God has lifted the veil that covers the great beyond. We know whither we are going, and the meaning of this life becomes clearer. It is a time of trial and probation, short, and yet all-important. Time is a preparation for eternity. We now live in the shadows, grasp only parts and fragments of the truth, enjoy only partial happiness, meet unjust treatment, etc. None of our highest faculties is fully satisfied. The full reality will come in the possession of the Infinite Truth, Goodness, and Justice.

CONCLUSION

HUMAN PERSONALITY

As we concluded Psychology by some general considerations on character and personality, we may also conclude this treatise by a more accurate definition of the meaning of person and personality. Strictly speaking, although the distinction is not always observed, person and personality stand in the same mutual relation as white and whiteness, animal and animality, etc. One is concrete; the other, abstract. Personality includes the distinctive characteristics of a person.

(*a*) *For common experience.* (1) Person is practically the same as, and coextensive with, human being. Only men are persons, and all men are persons. Infants are looked upon as persons in somewhat the same manner that a tiger-whelp is looked upon as a carnivorous animal, i.e. inchoatively. (2) Hence a person includes both body and soul. A wax figure or a corpse is not a person; nor is a disembodied soul a person, at least completely. Yet some current expressions refer chiefly to the body, and others to the mind (e.g. personal charms, a strong personality). (3) Personification consists in attributing to things distinctly human features, especially mental features. Might and power (thunder), usefulness or necessity (sun), mysteriousness (automata), motion and apparent purpose (animals), order and harmony (nature), are among the most important causes of the process of personification.

(*b*) *In psychology*, which insists on the mental factors of personality, the main elements of a person are (1) self-consciousness; (2) self-conscious memory, i.e. the awareness of personal identity; (3) activity, purpose, and will.

(*c*) *In ethics*, a person is (1) an agent, (2) having the knowledge of right and wrong, and (3) a certain autonomy, freedom, and responsibility. Hence not all men are persons, since not all have these faculties (e.g. children, insane people). Nor are all actions of persons always personal (e.g. actions performed during a blinding passion).

(*d*) *In law.* (1) Person includes both body and mind (e.g. murder and assault, slander and calumny are personal wrongs). (2) Infants are persons, at least for certain rights which they possess (e.g. life, property). (3) Some men are not persons with regard to certain rights (e.g. outlaws). (4) Several men together may be looked upon as one person in certain cases and for certain purposes (e.g. corporations).

(*e*) *Philosophically* a human person is not merely consciousness and memory, for these are personal activities, and hence already suppose a person as the agent. It implies (1) a concrete human nature, i.e. body and soul united in one complete substance, together with the activities springing from this nature; (2) an incommunicability of essence, i.e. the distinction from everything and from every other person.

THEODICY OR THE STUDY OF GOD

INTRODUCTION

1. **Subject-Matter of Theodicy.** — (*a*) We must now rise above the visible or sensible world to the ultimate cause, principle, and lawgiver of the world. We see that beings depend on one another, are caused by one another, rest on one another, and this naturally suggests the question: What is the first source of dependence and causality? Is it in the world itself, or outside of it? This is the problem of God, for by God has always been meant the independent being, the cause and the ruler of the world.

Analogically with the names of many other sciences, this investigation would aptly be called "Theology" (θεός, God, and λόγος) were not this term applied almost exclusively to a special mode of the study of God and of divine things, namely, that which is based on a revelation from God himself. The present investigation is carried on with the exclusive light of reason. It may be called "Rational," or "Natural Theology," but is more frequently called "Theodicy" (θεός, and δίκη, justification or judgment). It starts from facts, and with the help of principles, establishes (1) the existence of God, (2) His nature, (3) His relations to the world.

(*b*) It is impossible at the outset to give a definition of God, since this would suppose already the knowledge of God. We want to find the sufficient and necessary explanation of the world, to determine whether it must be looked for within or without the world, and what nature belongs to this first principle. To start with the supposition that God is an infinitely perfect being, distinct from the world, is to limit the range of the question, and also to anticipate the answer. Moreover, the only reason that could justify such a starting-point would be the common use of the term "God," and we know that the meaning of this term has not always been the same, and is not always the same to-day. The gods of ancient and modern polytheism, the god of India, the God of Christians, etc., are not identical. Hence, as the term "God" is not univocal, we abstain now from giving a definition. Here God means *the ultimate explanation of the whole universe of matter and mind.*

2. **The Importance of Theodicy** is evident from the nature of its subject-matter, for, as long as we have not reached the ultimate cause of the world, we have no final explanation. It completes the sciences of the world of matter (physical and cosmological), and of the world of mind (psychological and ethical), and indicates the duties of man toward God.

Theodicy is a branch of metaphysics, and supposes what has been said above on the possibility of metaphysics, and on the theory and value of knowledge. Positivists and agnostics deny that such an investigation is of any utility, since they claim that no knowledge is possible except that of phenomena which is acquired through experience. But we know that positivism is a one-sided view, and that, while admitting the validity of experience only, it is unable to account for this experience without implying and using principles transcending experience. Science is the arrangement and interpretation of experience by reason. Physical science, not only leads to, but essentially implies in itself, some metaphysics.

N.B. This treatise should be supplemented by courses in Apologetics and Religion. For this reason we shall limit ourselves here to the statement and explanation of the most fundamental principles.

CHAPTER I

THE EXISTENCE AND NATURE OF GOD

These Two Problems are Closely Related. — (*a*) The two questions of the existence and of the nature of God are intimately related to each other, and can hardly be considered separately. If the world is self-sufficient and self-explaining, there is no reason for asking either question. Both become useless, and the various physical sciences give the final answer to the problems which a complete explanation of the world suggests. But, if it is found that science does not give an ultimate explanation, and that the existence and laws of the world postulate something beyond the visible world itself, it seems impossible that the same principles and arguments which lead us to admit the existence of a first cause and lawgiver should not also manifest something of its nature. In other words, the answer to the question of the *nature of God* is but the unfolding of the conclusions by which *His existence* is known.

(*b*) And, for this reason, an essential inconsistency is found in the agnosticism of the Spencerian type, admitting the existence of the unknowable. We shall see later in what sense we may admit the unknowableness of God, but we remark now that we can, neither directly nor indirectly, acquire the knowledge of the existence of any reality without acquiring at the same time some knowledge — however limited and vague — of its nature. The "power behind the phenomena," to use Spencer's expression, must have some proportion to the phenomena. I may not know who rings the door-bell, but I know that, in the causal series ending with the ringing of the bell, every consequent has its *raison d'être* in the immediately preceding antecedent, and, no matter how far back I go in this regressive series, that every antecedent — the person who rings the bell included — is a cause which must be adequate to explain the subsequent phenomenon. In every line of thought by which God's existence is inferred, some aspect of His nature, power, causality, intelligence, or will is also manifested.

(*c*) For clearness' sake, however, we shall first examine the existence of God, and secondly make the conclusions concerning His nature and attributes more explicit. Let us keep in mind that this is only a logical expedient and that the two questions are in reality intimately connected.

I. EXISTENCE OF GOD

I. The Question Stated

1. **Meaning of the Question.** — (*a*) The question of the existence of God is not merely the question whether all phenomena in the world must be given a satisfactory explanation, for this is admitted by everybody. But the question is whether the material and mental world, both of the plain man and of the man of science, finds *in itself* a sufficient explanation, i.e. whether we are compelled or not to go *beyond science* in order to find, in the world itself or out of the world, some reality which science cannot reach with its methods, and which is nevertheless necessary to account for scientific facts and laws.

(*b*) So again the question is not whether science leaves an unexplained residue; or whether, beyond its own field, there are found unexplored regions; or whether science must leave certain problems without solution. This leads simply to the unknowable of the agnostic. But the question is whether the *known facts and laws of science* do or do not require some other specific reality without which they could not themselves exist.

That scientific equations include many an unknown *X* is admitted by all. As science progresses, the value of these unknown quantities becomes known little by little; the limits of science are widened, and beyond these ever-receding limits is the unknown. This is not enough. What we want to find out is whether all scientific equations, with their many *X*'s, do not of necessity imply some higher reality without which the equations themselves, with their known and unknown quantities, could not be given.

(*c*) Hence it is seen that the question of the existence of God is that of the existence of a reality superior to the world of phenomena with which science deals, either immanent in it or transcending it, i.e. either identical in reality with the phenomena the substance of which it would be, or distinct from both the phenomena and their substances. The question of identity or distinction will be examined later.

Atheism denies the existence of God, and asserts the self-sufficiency of the scientific universe. *Pantheism* and *monism* assert that God is in reality the one substance of the world. *Theism* admits the existence of a personal God distinct from, superior to, and ruler of, the world.

N.B. The question of atheism is an unimportant one. The problem to-day — as at all times — is not so much whether there is a God, as what God's nature is, and whether God is distinct from the world. Atheism has sometimes been understood as the negation of a personal God distinct from the world, and then it seems that pantheism and atheism coincide although the terms are etymologically opposed.

2. **Method.** — (*a*) The method to be used is the inductive method, starting from facts and interpreting them with the help of the essential principles of reason. We shall not renew the discussion with scepticism, empiricism, and criticism; we presuppose the validity of rational knowledge as vindicated in epistemology. We shall use chiefly the *principle of causality* without which empirical science itself cannot advance one step. To reject this principle is to fall into contradiction with the fundamental laws of thought. It is to make, not only metaphysics, but physical science itself, impossible. And with sceptics no argument is possible.

(*b*) The existence of God is not known directly, immediately, and intuitively. It is true that the mere contact with the external world and its succession of phenomena governed by constant laws, as well as the aspirations and feelings of the mind, easily lead to a spontaneous ascent of the mind to God. This, however, is not intuition, but *demonstration*, at least implicit, and our present task is to make it explicit, i.e. to test by reflection the spontaneous admission of God's existence.

(*c*) A fact confronts us, namely, that many phenomena formerly ascribed to the direct intervention of divinities now come within the range of scientific explanation. Will not God be pushed, as it were, farther and farther, and finally disappear from the world as a useless agent, postulated formerly owing to the ignorance of real scientific explanations? We repeat again that it is *not from the unknown* that we prove God's existence, but *from the known*. His existence is inferred *not from the supposition of an unexplored beyond, but from facts and laws of which we are certain*. That ignorance has caused men to see the direct action of God where it was not will be for us a warning not to argue from our ignorance of causes, but, on the contrary, from the causes and laws which we know. We shall not say: "The action of God is seen behind phenomena which we cannot explain"; but: "The action and presence of God are seen in phenomena themselves whose scientific explanation — as far as it can go — is at hand."

II. The Argument

1. **General.** — (*a*) The terms "actus" and "potentia" were used by the scholastics to translate Aristotle's ἐνέργεια or ἐντελέχεια and δύναμις. No single word in English is an adequate rendering of either. "Actus" includes the meanings of act, action, actuality, perfection, determination; "potentia," those of potency, potentiality, faculty, power, capacity. In general *potentia* means an aptitude to change, to act or be acted upon, to give or receive some new determination. *Actus* is the fulfilment of such an aptitude, the actual exercise or possession of that which before was only *in potentia*. In a word, both in the physical and the mental world, *potentia* is the determinable being, *actus* the determined being. Since *potentia* means the actual non-existence of some determination and the capacity for acquiring it, it follows that it cannot be known in itself, but only through the corresponding *actus*. The aptitude to see, walk, understand, melt, solidify, etc., has no meaning until the *actus*, vision, walking, etc., is known.

(*b*) A change of any kind whatsoever is the passage from *potentia* to *actus* and vice versa, and the existence of manifold changes in the world is an obvious fact. Beings come to existence or disappear, and those that exist undergo many changes as to size, place, color, shape, temperature, activity, etc. Hence in every being there are *actus* and *potentia*, i.e. actual determinations or perfections, and capacity for further determinations and perfections.

(*c*) It is true that *in the same being* the state of potentiality precedes that of actuality. Before acquiring a determination, a being must be capable of acquiring it. But, *absolutely speaking*, *actus* must precede *potentia*, for, in order to change, a thing must be acted upon, or actualized, i.e. it supposes a being which is *in actu*. In other words, nothing passes from potency to act of itself, but only under the influence of something else. Hence change supposes an antecedent *actus*.

(*d*) Now, since no being in the world has in itself a sufficient reason of the *actus* which it possesses, if the world is to be explained at all, we must proceed to another being *in actu*. If this being is also mixed with potentiality, and subject to change, we must go higher till we reach an "actus purus," without any potentiality. For, since no individual phenomenon or change has in itself its *raison d'être*, but is always "relative" to something else, the whole series cannot have within itself such a *raison d'être*. It remains not only unexplainable, but impossible and contradictory until somewhere, — behind, under, or above the changes, — we find the unchangeable; beyond the imperfect, the perfect; beyond the relative, the absolute; beyond potentiality, the "actus purus."

(*e*) This general argument, in some form or other, is generally admitted. But there are many controversies concerning the nature of the Absolute and *actus purus*. We shall now indicate a few applications of the general argument.

2. **Causality.** — (*a*) There are in the world many kinds of efficiency, activity, movement, and causality. The appearance of every new reality, whether substantial or accidental, is always conditioned by, and dependent on, something else. Hence nowhere in the world do we find a self-sufficient reality; nowhere consequently a sufficient explanation. Therefore, since in the world causes are only intermediary, i.e. caused as well as causing, we

must reach an unconditioned and independent reality, a *first uncaused cause.*

(*b*) This is true, no matter how great the number of intermediary causes may be, no matter how far back in the past we may proceed. The length of a river does not dispense with the necessity of a source, and to push back a difficulty farther and farther is not to give a solution. Science refers us back to a primitive nebula out of which the world evolved. The fact remains that there was *activity*, hence *a first source of activity;* there was *dependence*, hence somewhere the *independent;* there were *relations*, hence somewhere the *unrelated;* there were *conditions*, hence somewhere the *unconditioned* and the *absolute.*

(*c*) The world, they say, is eternal; from all eternity the same processes went on, and these processes originate in the very nature of things. We have nothing to do here with the eternity of the world; nothing to say against its eternity. But to lengthen time is not to assign a cause. If the time during which the cosmic processes have been taking place had a beginning, the existence of a first cause to explain their appearance is, of course, an absolute necessity. If it had no beginning, the first cause is required from all eternity, since, without it, there can be no other causes, and consequently no sufficient reason for existing realities. A being, or a series of beings, no matter how long it may be, which is not self-sufficient, requires a self-sufficient principle, for its existence always remains contingent and conditioned.

(*d*) We know from science that certain forms of existing realities had a beginning. Life did not always exist, and man appeared a long time after other forms of life. We have seen elsewhere that life has no sufficient explanation in the preëxistence of inorganic matter, nor consciousness in unconsciousness, nor the spiritual soul in any material activity (pp. 442, 492 ff.). Some higher principle, therefore, is required to explain these new appearances which cannot be explained by antecedents in nature.

N.B. This argument again is general, and special aspects of it might be emphasized, e.g. movement, origin, contingency, etc., and these new proofs would proceed in a direction parallel to the one just indicated.

3. **Teleology.** — (*a*) There is order and harmony in the world; the universe is not a chaos, but a cosmos. (See Cosmology, pp. 448, 455.) The various beings that compose it act according to determined laws, and from this manifold interaction results a permanent order. We do not speak here so much of extrinsic finality, that is, of the usefulness and adaptation of one being to another, as of intrinsic finality, that is, the determination of a being by its own nature to unfold its specific energies, every part contributing to the existence and functions of the whole. Examples could be multiplied in the inorganic as well as in the organic world, from the smallest atom, and chiefly the cell in the organism, to the harmony of heavenly bodies.

Efficient causes, it is true, explain the world, but only from one point of view. They are not *opposed to*, but *completed by*, final causes, ends, and purposes, as explained in Cosmology (p. 455). Everywhere in the world we find manifold interaction, and the more science progresses, the greater also the evidence for the existence of order. The world, therefore, manifests an intention, a design, hence an intelligence, a mind. Otherwise, what explanation can be offered?

(*b*) They say: The cosmos is a *result*, not an *end;* it is what it is, and acts as it does, because of the necessary laws that govern it. True; but there is no opposition between the result of efficient causes and the end or realization of a plan. The clock keeps time as a result of its mechanism, and yet keeping time was the end the clock-maker had in view in making it. Without ends and purposes efficient causes acting at random will not produce stability and order. Without ends and purposes the world will act as it does *supposing it to be what it is*, but why is it what it is? Laws govern the world, it is true, but a law is not an explanation; it is only a systematic expression, or a formula of the facts.

We need not stop to consider the position that order is the result of hazard or chance. Chance is but an avowal of ignorance as to the coming together of several causes. It is without laws, and essentially without stability, constancy, and regularity.

(*c*) There are also apparent *disorders*, it is true. I say *apparent*, because they may belong to a more general and wider plan and order. But even if they are *real*, they are exceptions, and simply prove that the world, though orderly, is not perfect. One misprint does not destroy the order of the letters in the whole page; and dissonant chords, when resolved properly, contribute to the beauty of the harmony.

(*d*) Again many say: The world is harmonious, and progresses harmoniously, because of the general law of evolution. This law is universal; it is the great ruler which dispenses with any higher intelligence. Let us repeat here that *a law is not a cause;* that *evolution is not a source,* but only the mode according to which the stream runs. And precisely this progressive and orderly evolution from a primitive nebula supposes a directive principle of evolution. Evolution or no evolution, a principle of order is required. If it is said that the world evolves unconsciously, like the plant which grows and develops into an organism out of a simple seed, we reply that unconscious finality is itself possible only on condition that there be somewhere a consciousness of the plan to be realized.

(*e*) Appeal to nature and to natural laws is always legitimate; science can go no farther. But nature and laws are not self-sufficient, and must find elsewhere their explanation. We *discover* meaning in the world, and do not *put* it there. The scientific and philosophical study of nature is in fact a constant attempt to find this meaning. If there is meaning in nature, there is a mind distinct from our own, with which our own tries to come in contact. (Compare, for instance, the meaning of speech, of works of art or machines for the student who, through them, endeavors to know the author's mind.)

4. **Morality.** — As a special application of the preceding considerations, we may say that the moral order also is not self-sufficient. Man, as was seen in Ethics (323 ff.), is not his own lawgiver, and yet is subject to the moral law which it is not in his power to change. The author of the moral order is therefore elsewhere. Moreover, a sanction is required, and, as no sufficient sanction is found in this life, there must be a judge to whom man is accountable. God is the ultimate principle of the moral order as He is the principle of human nature itself and of the physical world.

5. **Universal Consent.** — A last, but secondary, argument is taken from the consensus of mankind in admitting the existence of God. Everywhere and at all times, the existence of God is and has been admitted, although the conceptions regarding the nature of God vary greatly. This shows at least the natural propensity of the human mind to rise from the world to the cause and ruler of the world.

6. **Conclusion.** — In conclusion we may say that the material world as known by common experience and scientific investigation, and the mental and moral world, are not self-sufficient. The universe requires a ground on which it may rest, which is inaccessible to experience and to physical science, and is a self-sufficient reality. In this there is scarcely any dissension among philosophers. But divergences become accentuated when questions concerning the nature of God, and His distinction from the world, are raised.

II. THE NATURE OF GOD

We shall now endeavor to outline — it can only be a short outline — the main points concerning the nature and attributes of God. We shall first examine the distinction of God from the world; secondly, His primary attributes, i.e. those that are looked upon by us as constituting the divine nature; thirdly, the secondary attributes. Then we shall vindicate our conclusions against the attacks of agnosticism. Hence the four following sections.

I. The Distinction of God from the World

1. **The Question Stated.** — (*a*) When we assert that God is distinct from the world, we do not mean that God is estranged from the world, far away from it, and that He has nothing to do with it. The omnipresence of God, and His providence — to be mentioned later — imply that God is present and acts everywhere. But nevertheless His being is not to be identified with that of the world. The world is not the whole reality, and the being of God is transcendent.

(*b*) The two opposed systems here are Theism and Pantheism or Monism. *Theism* admits the existence of a personal God, distinct from, yet cause and ruler of, the world. *Pantheism* in general identifies God's being with the being of the world, so that God and the world are one and the same substance. Hence the term *Monism* (μόνος, one only), by which it is frequently called to-day. Historically it had many forms and expressions which cannot be discussed here. We shall limit ourselves to those forms which are found at present.

(*c*) Monism is idealistic or realistic. (1) *Idealistic monism* denies the objectivity of the conception of God as absolute and infinite. God is an ideal which the world, through its successive evolutions, little by little realizes without ever reaching it. He is not to be found at the beginning of the world, but at the end; not in the past, but in the future. Starting from indetermination and imperfection, i.e. from a minimum of reality, the world progresses, and tends toward determination, perfection, and maximum of reality, i.e. toward the realization of God. (2) *Realistic monism* admits the actual existence of the absolute, but identifies it with the universe, asserting either that the material elements of the world are self-existing, and obey essential and self-sufficient laws (materialistic and mechanical monism); or that the world as we know it is only the surface, the phenomena, the modes or aspects of the one common underlying substance (pantheistic or monistic evolutionism).

(*d*) It may be noted here once more that extremes meet. Pantheism is close to atheism; to identify God with all things is very nearly the same as to deny His reality. Pantheism must naturalize God or divinize nature.

(*e*) The main reasons advanced by monism are the impossibility of creation, the necessity for the infinite of including all things in itself, and the existence of evil in the world, for evil cannot come from a supposedly all-perfect and all-good cause.

2. **Idealistic Monism.** — The assertion that God is merely an ideal is directly opposed to the proofs for the existence of God, since these, starting from real facts, show the real existence of a first cause and of an *actus purus*, whereas the ideal God is primarily *potential*. To start from indetermination or *potentia* is to fall into the impossibility of ever reaching an *actus*, since the

passage from *potentia* to *actus* supposes a previous *actus*. The progress and evolution of the world, its manifold changes, and its activity require a sufficient principle, an *actus purus*, which exists not only in the mind, but in reality. Becoming supposes being. The order of the world requires a mind which unfolds a plan. We need not be detained longer by this view which to-day is looked upon by most philosophers and scientists as a dream, a confusion of the logical with the real order, and a contradiction in terms and in reality.

3. **Mechanical Monism**, which admits only material elements and their "actual" motions, has already been touched upon in the proofs given for the existence of God, and in Cosmology (pp. 428 ff., 436 ff., 454 ff.). The main objections against it are the following: (1) What is self-existing and necessary cannot change, and all material elements are subject to many changes. (2) The atom or material element is always dependent, relative, and conditioned. Its location, the exercise of its activity, its movement, etc., are contingent, since they constantly change dependently on external conditions. The dependent, the conditioned, and the relative suppose the independent, the unconditioned, and the absolute. (3) The atom is indifferent in itself to this or that combination, this or that motion, and as a consequence to this or that result. How were the primordial chaotic elements — I say chaotic in comparison to what they are now — of the nebula determined to arrange themselves so as to form the present world? How were they placed in such positions, and endowed with such movements as to lead to the present order? (4) If atoms exist from all eternity, the present state of the world should have been realized sooner. Why only now, and not yesterday or last year? Or why did not the first differentiations of the nebula take place earlier? (5) Mechanism looks only at efficient causes and neglects teleology which is also real. (6) It is unable to account for the origin of life, and chiefly for the origin of intelligence which is spiritual. Mental ideals, true morality, freedom, etc., find no place in such a system.

4. **According to Pantheistic Evolutionism, or Monism**, the absolute, unconditioned, and necessary substance actually exists. It

is *the only substance*, and the various beings of the world are its *phenomena* or *manifestations*. This substance is the one cause of all realities, the one principle of energy, unfolding itself in diverse ways — especially as matter and as mind — not intelligently or freely, but according to its own essential, necessary, and intrinsic law of evolution, like the germ evolving into the complete organism. Against common experience and scientific evidence, this doctrine must deny all forms of interaction between bodies, and between body and mind, since the *One* is also the *whole* energy. (Hence the theories of parallelism and of double-aspect, with their consequences, as mentioned in the Philosophy of Mind, pp. 481 ff.)

(*a*) If the term "substance" is used to mean that which is necessary and self-existing, it is clear that there is only one substance, namely, the Absolute or God. But this is not the usual meaning of substance. Substance is not that which exists *from* itself, or *a se*, but that which exists *in* itself, or *in se*. As such it is opposed to accidents which require a subject in which they inhere. It denotes a being which, although it is dependent, conditioned, and relative, yet is not inherent in something else. In this sense there may be many substances.

(*b*) Among substances is found the human person, as consciousness clearly testifies. Its *esse-in-se*, and *non-in-alio*, appears as a fact, as well as its activity and autonomy. Distinct personality and freedom find no place in monism.

(*c*) The absolute, self-existent, and necessary being cannot be identified with the world because it is necessarily all that it is, and hence cannot change, whereas changes in the world are evident facts, and every change implies a dependence on certain conditions necessary for it to take place.

(*d*) Why are not the cosmos and the actual order of the world eternal? The only answer of science is that the *conditions* of the present state were not always verified. But we cannot speak of anything external *conditioning* the *one* reality. Since this reality is the only one, it can depend on nothing different from itself. Since then the absolute has in itself the *totality* of being, why did it begin with the *part?* i.e. since it has the superior reality, why did it begin with the inferior? Why is evolution a law of the world?

(*e*) The comparison with the seed that develops into a complete organism does not favor the monistic position. The germ is not the whole plant. It has the power to develop into a plant, but always *dependently*, for it requires other substances external to itself which it assimilates, the influence of light, heat, moisture, etc. Without these the evolution of the germ would be impossible. The germ's change and development become intelligible precisely by reason of this manifold dependence on external agencies. Either the world depends on external conditions, and then it is not the one substance, nor the absolute; or it is the absolute and necessary substance, and then to speak of its change and evolution is contradictory.

(*f*) Perhaps it will be said that the condition is not extrinsic, but intrinsic to the one substance; that it is to be found in the very nature of the absolute; that the obstacle is not from without but from within. This supposition introduces into the one substance a *dualism* of antagonistic and irreconcilable tendencies: the essential tendency to the realization of a state, and the essential obstacle to such a realization. Here, therefore, *monism* seems to depart from its fundamental position.

We may conclude that the being of God is not to be identified with that of the world, and that the first cause is not identical with the world, but transcendent.

II. Fundamental or Primary Attributes

1. **Self-Existence.** — The proof of the existence of God shows that there must exist an absolute being, i.e. a being existing by itself, *a se*, as the scholastics used to say, and independently of any higher principle. A dependent cause cannot be the adequate explanation of its effect, since that on which it depends also contributes to it. The absolute, independent, and unconditioned cause alone can be the final explanation of all things. All others are inadequate. And the absolute cause is self-existing, necessary, and eternal, otherwise it would necessarily depend on something else for its existence, and would involve a contradiction. Its only

sufficient reason is in itself. In one word again, God is the *actus purus*, without any admixture of potentiality or dependence.

2. **Perfection.** — (*a*) God is perfect and cannot acquire more perfection, otherwise He would be ***in potentia*** with regard to the perfections which He actually lacks. Moreover, God, as the first cause, must possess in Himself all the perfections found in the world, since He is their source. As we shall see, these perfections need not be found in God in the same way as in beings of the world where they are always accompanied by imperfection. But God must possess at least something ***equivalent*** or ***analogical*** to the perfections of the world. Finally, as the *actus purus* and the plenitude of being, God must be ***infinite***. He cannot be limited by any other being without implying dependence on them; nor by Himself, since He is essentially and from Himself all that He is.

(*b*) But if God is not all, how can He be really infinite? The world is a reality, and if God is not the very substance of the world, there are realities other than God. Hence a God who does not include all things is not infinite, since His reality would be increased if the beings of the world were added to Him.

This difficulty rests on a misunderstanding, which itself is due to our incapacity of understanding the nature of God completely. We use the same expression "to be" of God and of creatures, but "being" does not apply univocally to God and to the world. God alone "is" *fully*, i.e. *by himself:* "I am who am" (Exod. iii, 14), that is, *God is the fulness of being and of perfection.* The world "is" as *a participation, a derivation, a shadow of the being of God.* Hence we cannot speak of the addition of the world to God, since units of different kind cannot be added to each other. God stands alone as the fulness of being, surpassing infinitely everything else, containing all perfections eminently, and this infinite perfection is precisely what isolates God and forbids His identification with the world. They are not on the same plane, nor in the same genus even remote, but God stands alone on a higher plane, as the first absolutely independent cause. With the addition of the world, were this possible, there would be more "beings," but there would not be more "being."

We have here something similar to the imparting of a science to ignorant pupils by a great scientist. After they have learned a few imperfect rudiments, there are more "knowings," but there is not more "knowledge," and the addition of the pupils' science to that of the master would not increase it, but rather make it less perfect. The Infinite is transcendent. He is neither increased nor decreased by the existence or non-existence of other realities to which He gives their derived being.

3. **Simplicity.** — There can be no composition in God; He is absolutely simple. Hence He is not material, but a pure spirit. The reason is that every composition implies potentiality which must be excluded from God. (1) God cannot be *material* because the changes in matter always occur in dependence on some agent, whereas God is the first cause. (2) God cannot, like man, be composed of *two co-principles*, matter and form, or body and soul, because matter is essentially a potential and determinable principle. (3) Nor can God be composed of *substance and accidents*, because accidents rest on the substance and are dependent on it. The human soul, for instance, has certain capacities which it exercises successively. By the passage from *potentia* to *actus* it acquires new perfections, and this is not possible for God.

Briefly, wherever there is composition there is also potentiality and subsequent determination. The compound always depends on its components and on the cause of their union. All forms of potentiality must be excluded from the *actus purus*. We have to speak of God and of His attributes as if they were distinct, but this is owing to the imperfection of our understanding which cannot grasp at once God's one and simple reality.

4. **Unicity.** — God is one, because if there were several gods, none of them would be the plenitude of being and perfection. One would have some being not possessed by the others. The tendency to unity is so marked to-day, both in philosophical and natural sciences, that it is useless to insist on this point. No one ever speaks of the "absolutes" in the plural. If there were several first causes, the question would immediately be raised: How did they act as one, and harmoniously, unless there were a higher cause and principle of unity on which all others depended? These several causes therefore would not be first causes, and we would be

led back to one first cause. The existence of evil, which is sometimes alleged as a proof for the dualism of causes, will be examined later.

III. Derived or Secondary Attributes

1. **Negative.** — (*a*) God is absolutely *unchangeable* or *immutable*, because change implies acquisition, or loss, or both. Hence it implies composition, since something remains permanent while something is added to, or subtracted from, the substance. It also implies potentiality with regard to the new acquired condition. But both composition and potentiality are excluded from God.

(*b*) God is *eternal*, not only in the sense that He had no beginning and will have no end, but in the sense that, existing at all times, His existence is not, like ours, subject to a successive series of elements, changes, activities, etc., i.e. to past and future, because succession implies change and potentiality. God is free from all temporal relations.

(*c*) God is *immense*, i.e. free from spatial relations. Being a pure spirit, God cannot be "localized" like material substances. He is omnipresent in the sense that His being and activity cannot be restricted or limited. He is present wherever there is something, present to every existing reality, for, wherever there is something contingent and potential, there is required also its necessary support, the absolute and pure *actus*.

These negative attributes exclude from God all "relations," since relative and absolute are essentially opposed.

2. **Positive.** — (*a*) God is *intelligent*, because (1) He is not only the principle of the material world, but also of the world of minds; (2) we have seen that the world manifests an intelligence. But God does not know like man by successive processes which imply imperfection, but intuitively and without acquisition or passage from *potentia* to *actus*.

Hence God's science is not (1) the exercise of an activity, but it is identical with the activity itself, which, in turn, is not really distinct from God's being, which is simple; nor (2) dependent on the objects of knowledge, for there can be no dependence in the absolute being; nor (3) discursive, for this implies successive acquisition.

God knows perfectly and intuitively His own essence, and, in it, everything that was, is, will be, or can be, since all finite existences are but participations of the divine essence. In His eternal present, God knows all things, past, present, and future, although He knows them actually with their temporal modality. To say that God acquires the knowledge of things only when they come to pass would again introduce succession, dependence, and potentiality. God, therefore, knows everything from all eternity.

(*b*) The same reasons that oblige us to attribute intelligence to God also oblige us to attribute a *will* to Him. (1) The existence of man, intelligent and free, requires that the first cause should also have these perfections. (2) The world is a realized plan. As the object of the will is always the good, the object of God's will is primarily His own essence, which is the infinite goodness, and, secondarily, whatever is a participation of the divine goodness. God's freedom does not imply, as it does for us, changeableness, fickleness, caprice, or disorder, but exists together with immutability, sanctity, the knowledge of all things, and omnipotence.

(*c*) God is *omnipotent*, i.e. whatever is not intrinsically impossible can be done by Him. Things that have no reality at all, like a square circle, a triangle whose angles taken together are not equal to two right angles, are intrinsically impossible, and, hence are called impossible for God because in themselves they involve a contradiction; and as *they have no potential reality*, it is clear that *they are not actually realizable*. Since God is infinitely perfect, He is also infinitely powerful. Since He is absolutely simple, His power is identical with His will.

IV. Value of These Conclusions

What is the value of our conclusions? It is objected that our finite minds cannot know the Infinite (agnosticism), and that to speak of it at all is necessarily to apply to it our human finite concepts, and to conceive God as a perfected man (anthropomorphism). A few remarks on these objections will make the preceding doctrine clearer.

1. **Agnosticism.** — (*a*) The absolute exists, says Spencer, and the belief in it "has a higher warrant than any other whatever"; but nothing more can be said of it, since human knowledge is essentially relative. It "cannot in any manner or degree be known in the strict sense of knowing." Yet its existence is certain as the "fundamental reality which underlies all that appears," "the reality which is behind the veil of appearance," and as the "omnipresent causal energy or power of which all phenomena, physical and mental, are the manifestations." It is the "inscrutable power manifested to us through all phenomena." (First Principles, p. I, ch. 3, 4, 5.)

(*b*) It must be admitted that (1) God cannot be known *perfectly* or *comprehensively*. What we claim to know about God is infinitely inferior to the reality. Our knowledge is largely *negative*, i.e. the knowledge of what God is not and cannot be. In its *positive* aspect this knowledge is *analogical*, i.e. we know that there must be some proportion between the cause and the effect. (2) God cannot be known apart from His manifestations, and we know Him only *in so far as He manifests Himself in the world*. All other aspects of His reality are unknown to us. (3) God is known by our finite minds *successively*, *disjunctively*, and *relatively*.

Hence we must admit that the little knowledge which we have of God is as nothing when compared to the being itself of God. Yet we claim that our concepts *truly* represent, though very *imperfectly*, something of the divine reality. "That which is uncaused cannot be assimilated to that which is caused," and there is between them "a distinction transcending any of the distinctions existing between different divisions of the created." (First Principles, § 24.) We admit this. But without assimilating God as "uncaused," to the world as "caused," we may compare God as "cause" to the world as "caused," and thus acquire some knowledge of God from His works.

(*c*) Spencer's *inconsistency* is glaring. God cannot manifest Himself without manifesting some aspect of His reality. A "power" behind the phenomena implies continuous *efficiency*. A "first cause" means *self-existence*, eternity, and activity. And, if the same reality is behind both physical and mental phenomena, how can Spencer speak of it merely as *power*, and not also as *consciousness*, *intelligence*, and *will?* If God manifests Himself as power or energy in the physical world, He must also manifest Himself as mind through the mental phenomena.

(*d*) So God, it is true, is not definable. But between comprehensive knowledge and unknowableness there is an intermediary term, namely, true, though imperfect and analogical knowledge. Human works manifest some of the attributes and thoughts of their authors; imperfectly, yet truly; incompletely, yet without essential alteration. In the same way, the world bears the trace of God's attributes, and, no matter how far beneath the reality our interpretation must remain, it leads to the knowledge of God.

Spencer professes that he does not know whether the first cause is conscious because it might have an attribute distinct from both unconsciousness and consciousness, and infinitely superior to both. But between consciousness and unconsciousness there is no middle term; we have to choose between the one and the other. God must have something analogical to consciousness, though infinitely above *our* consciousness. The only name we can give it is consciousness, but we recognize that it applies to God without the imperfections found in ourselves, and in a manner which we cannot understand.

2. **Anthropomorphism.** — (*a*) The agnostic urges again: What do you do in all this but conceive God as a magnified man, and attribute to Him human perfections, even if you do enlarge them? You call them infinite, but cannot, with your finite mind, know even the meaning of this term. In other words, we are accused here of anthropomorphism: we predicate of the infinite essentially *human concepts*, finite, and out of proportion to God. "Is it not just possible that there is a mode of being as much transcending intelligence and will as these transcend mechanical motion?" It is an erroneous assumption to suppose "that the choice is between personality and something lower than personality; the choice is rather between personality and something higher." (First Principles, § 31.)

(*b*) It must be admitted that, in our mode of conceiving God, anthropomorphism is a real danger which has not always been avoided with sufficient care. Sometimes human passions and emotions, for instance, have been attributed to God without sufficient discrimination. Moreover, *some anthropomorphism is unavoidable*. As we have no direct knowledge except of the external world and of our own conscious states, it follows that we can think only with the concepts acquired from these realities.

(*c*) However, when the philosopher applies these concepts to God, he is aware that he cannot do so *univocally*, but only in an *analogical* way, and that they are realized in God in a manner which is transcendent and supereminent, yet not altogether unlike the manner in which they are found in finite beings. He does not simply enlarge the finite, but also recognizes a qualitative difference which he can neither express nor conceive. The agnostic's concepts of force, power, and cause are also derived from experience, and yet applied to the absolute; this objection, therefore, applies to him as well as to us. But the analogy used by Spencer starts only from the lowest beings, those of the physical world, instead of including also, as it should, the highest beings, those endowed with intellect, will, and personality.

3. **The Personality of God** is but a corollary of what precedes. But it must be attributed to God only in an analogical way. It is the best conception we can form of God's being; yet His personality is as far above ours as His other perfections are above all those of the world. Why is man a person? Because he is a complete substance, *sui iuris*, and a conscious free agent. Now, God is *the* Substance, distinct from other beings, it is true, yet supporting them. Complete in His fulness of being and of perfection, absolutely independent and unconditioned, He realizes in Himself the plenitude of perfection. Infinite mind and free agent, He has in Himself all that is required to be called personal, but personal in a transcendent and incomprehensible sense, distinct from everything else by His very infinity.

How poor are the substitutes that are offered for a personal God. First, we are offered *the Divine*, i.e. a pure psychological feeling to which nothing real corresponds; an adjective without a substantive. How absurd to speak of the Divine, as some do, if there is no God! Or will God be replaced by *Nature*, personified with a capital initial, or by an *indefinite World-Ground*, or some similar term? Of course nature and its laws explain the world, but also need explaining. They give an immediate, not a final explanation. Or shall we speak of the indefinite, the indetermined, progress, evolution, and what not? All these are insufficient, as we have seen. God exists, distinct from the world, infinite in all perfections, perfectly independent; and yet, while acknowledging our incapacity to name Him, with the full consciousness that the expression applies to Him in an infinitely superior degree than it is possible for us to conceive, we rightly speak of Him as a personal God.

4. **Conclusion.** — (*a*) The knowledge we have of God is *imperfect* in many respects. (1) We have been obliged to *analyze* that which is one and simple, and, owing to the very nature of our mind, to consider as distinct, attributes which are in reality identical with the divine essence. (2) We have reached chiefly a *negative knowledge*, the knowledge of what God is not, and we admit that our positive knowledge of His nature is very imperfect. (3) We have tried with our *finite ideas* to reach the infinite, but evidently these ideas remain infinitely distant from their object.

(*b*) This knowledge, however, is not without value. Although it is only analogical, it manifests something of the divine reality. We have a positive starting-point, the perfections of the world, and we know that the first cause must be adequate to account for all these. This gives us a *positive*, though *inadequate* knowledge. No matter how great we conceive God's perfections to be, we must always remember that our conception remains infinitely beneath the reality of the divine perfection. Yet there is in God "something like" these perfections. As St. Gregory says: "Balbutiendo, ut possumus, excelsa Dei resonamus." Here below we have to be satisfied with a knowledge which St. Paul calls "through a glass," and "in a dark manner," but we live in the hope of one day seeing God "face to face," and "as He is."

CHAPTER II

GOD AND THE WORLD

We rise to God from the visible world. There now remain to be examined two questions: (1) What are the relations of God to the world? and (2) What are and must be the relations of the world to God?

I. GOD IN RELATION TO THE WORLD

Two points of view may be considered, being and becoming, i.e. the being of God compared to the being and to the becoming of the world. Hence two questions: (1) Those referring to the "esse," especially the distinction of God from the world. (2) Those referring to the "fieri," i.e. the origin and government of the world. As the distinction of God from the world has already been established, there remain only the questions of Creation and Providence.

1. **Creation.** — (*a*) The distinction of God from the world leads to the conclusion that the world was created by God. Pantheism makes of the world a manifestation of God, i.e. God produces — if we can use the word "produce" — the world out of His own substance. We have said already that this substantial identity is impossible.

(*b*) *Philosophical dualism*, admitting eternal and increated matter, coexisting with God, who thus becomes simply an intelligent designer and architect using preëxisting materials, is also impossible, and finds no advocates to-day. The essential characteristics of matter, its contingency and dependence, show that it cannot be self-existent. In the dualistic hypothesis, God would no longer be unconditioned, since His activity would depend on preëxisting matter.

(c) Hence there remains only *creation*, which means *the production of a thing out of nothing*, i.e. the production of a thing which is not simply a modification of some preëxisting reality, but which begins to exist as a reality. The workman or artist requires apt matter on which to exercise his activity. Everything that is produced now in the world, either by nature or by art, is produced out of preëxisting materials endowed with certain potentialities. From nothing, nothing comes. When it is said that creation is a production out of nothing, it is not meant that "nothing" is the material out of which something is made, but simply that in His creative act God is independent of any preëxisting matter and potentiality.

We cannot, it is true, comprehend the act of creation, but we find an analogy in works of art, in which the artist realizes his mental ideal. The greater the art and skill, the more perfect also is the result obtainable from the same matter, and hence the less the dependence on matter. We are thus led to conceive of a supreme cause, and an infinite art of God, who is altogether independent of matter.

2. **Providence.** — After creation, God does not abandon His works, but "provides" for His creatures the necessary conditions for being and acting, and governs them. This divine government is chiefly what is meant by Providence. It has been rejected by Deists, who deny that, after creating, God has anything to do with the world.

(a) Even when existing, the creature is *contingent* and *dependent*. The first moment of its existence does not necessarily imply the second and those that follow. Hence every being in the world is at all times dependent for its very existence on the first *self-existent* being. Not for its existence alone, but also for the exercise of its activity, the creature depends on God. The *motor secundus* depends on the *motor primus immobilis;* and the contingent activity, on the first cause.

(b) Divine providence or God's government of the world is but a consequence of what was said above. In the cosmos, everything has its place in harmony with the rest, its own end in harmony with the general end of the world. This place and end are assigned to it by the wisdom of the Creator, who thus realizes the plan of creation. The infinite mind does not act without a plan and purpose, and the infinite power is adequate to realize this plan in all its details. So every being individually is subject to God, who assigns to it its place and rôle.

But, if we speak of the actual direction or government of the world, it must be said that God's action is rather general and mediate with regard to individuals. God governs beings by one another, subjects by superiors, physical beings by general laws which contribute to produce and preserve order and harmony in the world. The order of the world results immediately from the efficiency and intrinsic finality of secondary causes. (Cf. pp. 454 ff.)

3. **Evil.** — The existence of evil in the world is urged as an objection against creation, for, how can God, infinite in goodness and power, produce or allow evil? and against providence, for, how can a wise ruler tolerate evil which it is in his power to eliminate? (Cf. above, teleological argument for the existence of God.)

(*a*) The *existence of evil* cannot be denied, at least from our narrow point of view. There are destructions of inorganic and organic substances by others. There is suffering in conscious beings. There are uneasiness, affliction, and unsatisfied desires in the human heart. There are disorder, perversity, and sin in the human will. In general, it may be noted that evil manifests the good, that disorder is a derogation from order, and hence that evil supposes good, order, and harmony.

(*b*) Moreover, evil is seen frequently to serve a good purpose, namely, a general higher order. For instance, if the reproductive functions in plants and animals always obtained their results, if the majority of seeds were not wasted, the means of subsistence and co-existence of all living organisms would not be found. Yet this co-existence is itself a perfection and a harmony. Again, the animal, simply by walking, may destroy a number of plants and insects, but walking is life, activity, and perfection. Where there is manifold activity, there is antagonism, and can we say that a lifeless, inactive, crystallized world would be better than a living and active world? *Evil is thus subordinated to a higher good.*

(*c*) Evil is an *inevitable result of imperfection*, and a creature is necessarily imperfect. The finite is essentially imperfect, and the present order freely chosen by God, good and harmonious though it may be, could not be realized without imperfection and evil. For instance, the death of some is the *sine qua non* of the existence of others.

(*d*) More specifically, *suffering* is the inevitable lot of sensitive beings whenever antagonistic activities are exercised on them. Frequently suffering is caused by man's disorderly conduct, and by the wrong exercise of his faculties. Finally, suffering has its advantages; it is a warning against impending or existing disease; it atones for sin, fortifies, purifies, and elevates the soul to higher purposes, to a higher destiny, to God himself, since this life is only a preparation for a future life.

(*e*) *Moral evil* is the consequence of freedom, which is a perfection. It is not God's, but man's, doing. Without freedom, man is incapable of sin, but also of merit and virtue. Freedom is a good which it is in man's power to use or misuse, but self-direction is superior to determinism.

(*f*) Could not God have created a world in which there would be less evil, less suffering, and less sin? We do not know. Let us admit the mystery, and confess our ignorance of the divine plan. God reigns supreme. The world, man, society, depend on Him, and we have no right to investigate His secret ways. The world is good without being the best possible. It has evils without being the worst possible. God chose the present order; let us try, as far as lies in our power, to preserve it. We know little of the whole universe, and our knowledge of the divine plan, like that of God himself, is only fragmentary. An ignorant man might find fault with the most ingenious mechanism, and criticise some details from his limited point of view. This would be due to his ignorance of the complete plan and harmony. He would be an object of ridicule for those who know better. And yet he would have more reason for finding fault with human works than any man has to find fault with the works of God.

II. THE WORLD IN ITS RELATIONS TO GOD

We shall briefly examine here the general relations of the universe, and more especially those of man, to God.

I. The Universe

The various relations of dependence and subordination have been indicated already. The world holds its existence from God as its ultimate principle, and its preserver. It obeys the laws given to it by the Creator. Only one more question may be touched upon rapidly: The various beings of the world have tendencies, and work toward ends. What is the ultimate end of the universe as a whole? It may be summed up in these words: "The Lord hath made all things for Himself" (Prov. xvi. 4), and "The heavens shew forth the glory of God, and the firmament declareth the works of His hands" (Ps. xviii. 1). The only end which is worthy of God is God Himself. The world, it is true, adds nothing to God's perfection, excellence, and intrinsic glory. Yet it is an external manifestation of the divine attributes in which creatures participate.

But the tribute which creatures give to God, except that which is given through man, is, as it were, dumb in itself. Man is the spokesman of creation. His intelligence leads him from the consideration of the world to the knowledge of the Creator. And as he is endowed with reason and will, he can and must effectively recognize the glory of God and his own dependence and subjection. Hence we must speak now of his main duties toward God.

II. Man

1. **General Duties Toward God.** — However imperfect our knowledge of God may be, it suffices to show that we have certain duties toward Him. These duties constitute what is called *religion*. God is known as creator, providence, ruler, goodness, wisdom, sanctity, etc., and this is enough to create in man certain corresponding obligations. It is true that God needs nothing and is ever self-sufficient. But we need God, and must obey the dictates of reason. The natural order of things requires that

we should know our place in the world, and fulfil our duties toward God.

As He is the supreme being, infinitely perfect, we must recognize our dependence. We must adore Him and revere His name, love Him as the infinite good, respect Him as the infinitely great, be thankful for what we have and are, since all comes from Him, respect and obey conscience which is the divine voice within ourselves, try to know God, the infinite truth, place Him above all creatures in our thought, will, and love. Above, infinitely above all creatures is His real place, and it is the place which must always be assigned to Him in our minds and hearts.

2. **Prayer.** — By prayer the soul rises to God to adore and thank Him, to ask His help and assistance and to beg forgiveness of offences.

(*a*) However natural it may seem for man to have recourse to the infinite goodness and power of God, this aspect of prayer has been objected to on the ground that (1) God knows all our needs, (2) He is infinitely good, and must give the needed assistance without being asked, (3) He is immutable, and prayer cannot change His eternal decrees.

To this we answer: (1) We do not pray to God simply to make our needs known to Him, but to acknowledge our insufficiency and God's supreme power. This recognition of our dependence is an expression of the truth, and therefore agreeable to God. (2) God is infinitely good, but He requires our activity, intelligence, will, and freedom, which are means and conditions of merit. God does not work alone; He requires our humble coöperation. (3) God's decrees are eternal and immutable, but formed in prevision of the free actions of men, among which are his prayers.

(*b*) Prayer, then, in its general sense, is the natural and universal manifestation of man's feelings, the communion of man's will with God's will, by which man submits to the decrees of the infinite wisdom; acknowledges this wisdom even when it seems to hide itself; accepts suffering and affliction in the hope of future happiness; asks God to help him to wipe away sin and destroy its evil consequences.

3. **External Worship.** — (*a*) The internal worship of our intel-

ligence, feelings, and will naturally manifests itself by external actions, attitudes, gestures, vocal prayers. It is a law of psychology that mental attitudes tend to express themselves through the organism. Moreover, these bodily actions tend to foster and develop corresponding mental attitudes. Finally, not only the mind, but the whole man, body and soul, must acknowledge God's supremacy and excellence.

(*b*) It may be added that man, being essentially social, must worship God, not only privately, but as a member of society. Individual religion is strengthened by association with others. Public worship unites men, places them above earthly things by making them recognize more fully their community of origin and destiny, and profess the supreme authority of God not merely over individuals, but also over societies.

CONCLUSION

We need not repeat how little we know about God. Before the Infinite, the proper attitude of the human mind is that of awe, as it feels incapable of formulating the little knowledge it possesses; and that of astonishment at God's greatness and its own littleness. This ought to make us readier to accept the manifestations of God, not merely through the mirror of His creatures, but through His own revelation. Faith helps human reason, and manifests in what way God wants to be served. We have spoken only of natural religion; positive revealed religion completes it. As the infinite truth, God must be believed; as the infinite ruler, He must be obeyed.

The little knowledge which we have of God shows enough to make us understand that the greatness of God is above all that we can think. It is much even to acknowledge that God is incomprehensible and ineffable. Chiefly negative, this knowledge contains, nevertheless, positive data concerning God's nature, and it would be unreasonable to look upon it as valueless because it is not complete.

God is the necessary solution of the enigmas of the world, the supreme principle of truth and goodness, the necessary basis of morality, the fulfilment of the aspirations of the human heart.

OUTLINES OF HISTORY OF PHILOSOPHY

INTRODUCTION

1. **Importance.** — The history of philosophy is the natural complement of a course in philosophy, because it shows the progress of human thought in regard to both the statement and the solution of philosophical problems, and it reveals the various influences at work in the development of philosophy. Philosophy is not crystallized, but living. It grows, and modifies its points of view. Hence it is important to see the causes of this growth and development, and the various relations of philosophical systems to one another. Moreover, this study, while revealing the many struggles of thinkers, will enable the student to understand better the different systems of philosophy, to see the part of truth which they include, and to judge where error begins, and what causes led to it. We shall find frequent instances of the axiom that extremes meet, that thought passes easily from one extreme to another, and that here, as in physical science and in political history, action brings about an equal reaction, till later the equilibrium is reëstablished.

2. **Method.** — (*a*) Only a short outline of the history of philosophy will be given. The principal names alone will be mentioned, and the main systems examined. While learning this general summary, the student will do well to complete it by collateral reading from the best historians of philosophy. This is only a sketch, a skeleton. The various parts must be connected, so as to give life and fulness to this outline. Our purpose is merely to enable the student to place historically the various names and systems mentioned in this course.

(*b*) The method followed will be both logical and chronological. Logical, tracing out the relationship and filiation of the various systems. Chronological, following generally the successive appearance of schools and philosophers.

(*c*) We shall divide the history of philosophy into three chapters: (1) Ancient philosophy. (2) Mediæval philosophy. (3) Modern philosophy.

CHAPTER I

ANCIENT PHILOSOPHY

I. ORIENTAL PHILOSOPHY

Oriental philosophy is originally and essentially religious, i.e. connected with religious beliefs and practices. Speculation, especially in India and China, developed from mythological legends and religious tenets.

1. **Egypt.** — The Egyptians had two sets of doctrines: one esoteric, hidden from the people and known only to the priests — what this mysterious wisdom consisted in is not known; the other exoteric, common and public. According to this, there was a multitude of gods; yet in this polytheism many indications of an essential monotheism are found. One of the gods, different according to different centres, was held to be superior to, or even the principle of, the others. The world is their work, and various gods produced various classes of beings. Besides his body and soul, man also includes some kind of genius which after death dwells in the statue or mummy of the dead, and receives the offerings of the living. After death, the human soul is judged according to its good and evil deeds, and either receives its reward, after due purification, or is sent back to the earth into other organisms, human or animal, or even into inanimate objects, to again go through a series of migrations. This doctrine of metempsychosis is connected with the animistic beliefs of the Egyptians which made them attribute souls to the various objects of nature, and also with their fetichism and animal-worship. The moral precepts of the Egyptians seem to have been of a high character, and recommended the practice of virtue, both internal and external.

2. **Babylonia and Assyria.** — In Mesopotamia, as in Egypt, under polytheistic forms of worship may be found a form of mono-

theism. Among the Babylonians, Anu exercises dominion over the other gods, and when Assyria had conquered Babylonia (about 1300 B.C.) Ashur was looked upon as the king and father of the other divinities. The divinities participate in different ways in the creation and government of the world. As early as twenty-two or twenty-three centuries B.C. the Babylonians had a code of high morality, the code of Hammurabi.

3. **Persia.** — The sacred books of the Persians, still preserved and used by the Parsees of Western India, form the *Zend Avesta* (*Avesta* = sacred text; *Zend* = commentary). They were not all composed at the same time, and their date is uncertain. A part of them must be ascribed to *Zoroaster* or *Zarathustra*, the great priest and reformer, who lived in the seventh and sixth centuries B.C. A number of good and evil spirits were admitted, which constantly struggle to prevail, the result being the many antinomies and oppositions of elements in the inorganic and the organic world. Zoroastrianism reduces this multitude to a stricter dualism. The chief deity is the principle of good, Ahura Mazda (Ormuzd or Ormazd; hence Mazdeism), who is the god of light, goodness, and holiness. The principle of evil is Añra Mainyu (Ahriman), who is the spirit of darkness. From both proceed a number of spirits, among which the evil ones produce moral and physical disorder and suffering. The conflict will come to an end after twelve thousand years, when the good will triumph, the world will be purified, and a new era will begin. The human soul is judged after death, and rewarded or punished for longer or shorter periods of time according to its deeds.

4. **India.** — (*a*) Among the *sacred books* of the Hindus the most important are the Vedas (Rig-Veda, Sama-Veda, Yagur-Veda, and Atharva-Veda). They include Hymns (Mantras), ritualistic treatises (Brahmanas), and philosophical commentaries (Upanishads). The commentaries were not composed at the same time, but the oldest parts of the Vedas seem to date from fifteen or twenty centuries B.C., although they were not written till much later, being first transmitted by oral tradition. The philosophy contained in the Vedas is based on a cosmic pantheism. (1) Brahma or Atman is the absolute and infinite being who gave

rise to all other beings by an emanation from his own substance. He is the only reality, so that everything conceived outside of Brahma can only be an illusion. (2) The soul is immortal, and, after death, migrates from one organism into another. Any human deed (or karma) has an eternal value, and its consequences endure forever. Every man is thus the maker of his own condition which corresponds to his deeds. (3) Ultimately the soul and every other being are reabsorbed in Brahma, and again merged into his universal being. Mortification and asceticism are necessary as a preparation for this reabsorption. (4) Men are divided into four classes or castes: priests (who came from the head of Brahma); soldiers (from his chest); merchants (from his abdomen); slaves (from his feet). The rights and duties of every one of these differ according to their relative dignity.

(*b*) From these doctrines arose several *schools* of rational and speculative philosophy, which are based on the Vedas and try to interpret them. The Sutras are maxims or aphorisms which sum up these philosophical doctrines. There are found six main schools of philosophy, which, however, go two by two, 1 and 2, 3 and 4, 5 and 6, thus forming three distinct groups, and both schools of each group having essential points in common. (1) The Purva-Mimamsa (= prior investigation), attributed to *Jaimini* (place and date uncertain), is chiefly a system of apologetics referring to the authority of the Vedas and to casuistic ethics. (2) The Uttara-Mimamsa (= posterior investigation) or Vedanta (= Veda-end), composed or compiled by *Badarayana*, with commentaries by *Çankara* (eighth and ninth centuries of our era), is even to-day the most important system, and adheres closely to the Upanishads. It admits the identity of all things, and especially of the soul, with Brahma; the illusory nature of our knowledge of the phenomenal world; the transmigration of souls, and the final absorption in Brahma. (3) The Sankhya, whose Sutras bear the name of *Kapila* (place and date unknown), in its present form, dates from the fourteenth century of our era. It recognizes the essential dualism of spirit and matter. The world is real and pluralistic, and knowledge (sense-perception, induction, authority) is valid. This philosophy tends to, and perhaps professes, atheism.

(4) The Yoga of *Patanjali* (probably second century B.C.) is rather theistic. (5) The Vaiceshika, attributed to *Kanada* (of whom nothing is known), is essentially a philosophy of nature, recognizing six padarthas (= world-things), or categories: substance, quality, action, genus or community, species or particularity, and coherence or inseparability. Substances are composed of eternal, indivisible, and unalterable atoms. (6) The Nyaya (= going back, hence syllogism), attributed to *Gotama*, is essentially a system of logic, destined to lead man to happiness by the possession of knowledge.

(*c*) *Buddhism* was founded in the sixth century B.C. by *Gotama*, a member of the Sakya clan, whence his name Sakya muni (muni = solitary). Buddhism became popular largely owing to its abolition of castes, but was finally driven out of India about the fourteenth century. It flourishes chiefly in China, Thibet, Mongolia, etc. Although it denies the divine authority of the Vedas, it borrowed largely from the atheistic Sankya of Kapila, and from other common brahmanistic doctrines. Its main distinctive philosophical tenets are the following: (1) A pessimistic view of life. Suffering comes from the illusion of personal and separate existence which inclines man to satisfy his personal desires. (2) Hence the natural craving for individuality must be eradicated by ascetic practices. (3) The supreme end to which man must tend is Nirvana, which, if it is not complete annihilation, is at least the loss of personality and individual consciousness.

(*d*) We simply mention the Jains, who still form a community in India, and whose doctrines have many points of contact with Buddhism and with the Sankya and Vaiceshika philosophies.

5. **China.** — In the earliest traditional religion of the Chinese, the supreme source of all things is the animated sky (Tien), personified under the name of Shang Ti, or supreme ruler. Many spirits were also worshipped, especially those of ancestors. The two great philosophers of China, Lao-tsze and Kong-fu-tse, or Kong-tse (Confucius), were almost contemporary.

(*a*) *Lao-tsze* (born about 604 B.C.) insists on the doctrine of Tao (= way, hence course of nature). The Tao is the one substance, neither conscious nor unconscious, neither personal nor impersonal, but transcending both modes of existence. He is the source of all things, and also the moral type or ideal. To-day Taoism is a popular form of religion in China, implying many superstitious practices.

(*b*) *Confucius* (551–478) was a religious and political reformer. He revised the sacred books of kings and composed some himself. He insisted on the old Chinese traditions and developed an essentially conservative system of ethics referring to the relations of man with his fellowmen. His doctrine is still prevalent among the higher classes of China.

(*c*) Among other Chinese philosophers must be mentioned *Yang-chu* (fifth century B.C.) who advocates the ethics of pleasure; *Mih-tsze* (fifth century B.C.), who recommends a universal love of men; *Meng-tsze* (Mencius, 372–289), who contributed much to the influence of Confucianism.

II. GREEK PHILOSOPHY

We shall leave out the first rudiments of philosophy found in the poems of Homer and Hesiod, and begin with the appearance of philosophy proper. Greek philosophy may be divided into three periods. (1) Pre-Socratic, devoted exclusively to the study of the external world. (2) Socratic, adding subjective studies, i.e. psychological and ethical. (3) Post-Aristotelian, neglecting almost entirely the philosophy of nature and giving predominance to ethical problems.

N.B. The Romans did not develop any original philosophy, but borrowed from the Greeks. The few names to be mentioned will come under the respective schools to which they belong.

I. Pre-Socratic Schools

The early speculations of Greece were cosmological.

1. **Early Ionian Philosophy.** — The earlier Ionians (Ionia, a Greek colony of Asia Minor) endeavor to give an answer to the question: What is the ultimate substance of things? They agree that matter is endowed with some kind of life (hylozoism), and

attempt to determine the nature of this first or primordial matter. *Thales* of Miletus (born about 640 B.C.) claims that it is water. *Anaximander* of Miletus (born about 610 B.C.) admits an eternal and infinite matter from which all things were produced by processes of condensation and rarefaction. For *Anaximenes* (born about 588 B.C.), the primordial principle of all things is air, which is an infinite substance from which all things come and to which all return.

2. **Pythagoreans.** — *Pythagoras* (sixth century B.C.) was born at Samos, and founded, at Crotona in the Greek colony of Italy, a school in which he taught his religious and scientific doctrines. The basis of all things is number, and the whole world is a harmony of odd and even numbers, which are all derived from the unit. The one, unit, or monad, is God, from whom emanates the dyad, i.e. matter and spirit. Pythagoreans admitted the transmigration of souls, and their doctrine included an elaborate code of morality. Little is known with certainty about the meaning of the Pythagorean theory of numbers, as we have but scant, fragmentary, and second-hand references.

3. **The Eleatic School.** — The Eleatic school takes its name from Elea, a city of southern Italy (then a Greek colony). Eleatics tend to identify the world with God and hence to attribute to the world unity, eternity, and unchangeableness. *Xenophanes* (born about 570 at Colophon in Asia Minor) admits only one God, whom he identifies with the world. Hence the substance of the world is immutable, and the changes affect only its surface. *Parmenides* (born about 540 at Elea) denies the fact of change; the testimony of the senses on this point is illusory. Real being is one and absolutely immutable and unproduced; hence becoming and change are impossibilities. *Zeno* (born about 490 at Elea) was the disciple of Parmenides, and by his dialectics defended his master's position.

4. **Later Philosophers of Nature.** — (*a*) *Heraclitus* (born about 500 at Ephesus) opposes Parmenides. Far from being absolutely unchangeable, the world is on the contrary always changing and perpetually flowing. Nothing is, everything is becoming. The primordial element is fire, out of which all things were made.

This is the turning-point in Greek speculation, shifting the problem of nature from the question: What are things? to the question: How did things come to be what they are?

(*b*) *Empedocles* (born about 495 at Agrigentum, Sicily) admits four elements: earth, water, air, and fire. Two antagonistic forces, love and hatred, tend to combine and dissociate these elements; hence the becoming.

(*c*) *Anaxagoras* (born about 500 at Clazomenæ in Ionia) admits an infinite number of elements which at first formed a chaos. But the Spirit or Mind, endowed with knowledge and power, gives them their orderly and harmonious motions.

(*d*) *Leucippus*, and *Democritus* of Abdera (about 460–370), profess a mechanistic atomism. Atoms are homogeneous in nature, dissimilar in size and shape, infinite in number, and indivisible. They move in an infinite vacuum, and, by their motions, everything, even thought, must be explained.

5. **Sophists.** — (*a*) The name "sophist," which etymologically signifies a wise man, was at first honorable, but later, owing to the abuse of dialectics leading to scepticism, it acquired a disreputable meaning. The sophists dwelt little on metaphysics and science, but chiefly on grammar, rhetoric, and logic. They came to dispute in order to prove any proposition, lost sight of objective truth, and were led to scepticism. On the contradictions found among early philosophers they based their arguments to show that nothing can be known with certitude, and that the only useful science is that which enables us to convince others. This method already included a beginning of reflection on the value of knowledge. It accustomed the people to philosophical discussions, and thus formed a transition to the following period.

(*b*) The most important sophists are *Protagoras* of Abdera (born about 480) and *Gorgias* (about 480–375). According to the former, human knowledge deals only with appearances and is essentially relative, since what is true for one man is false for another. According to the latter, nothing exists really; if anything existed, we could not know it; and, supposing that we knew it, this knowledge could not be communicated to other men, since the word or sign, which is different from the idea, is the only thing that can be perceived by others, and they interpret it according to their own minds.

II. Socrates, Plato, Aristotle

These three names represent the most perfect epoch of Greek philosophy.

1. **Socrates.** — (*a*) Socrates of Athens (469–399) opposed the Sophists and showed the method of true knowledge. He left no writings, and we know his method and doctrine especially through his disciples, Plato and Xenophon. His method is essentially inductive, starting from concrete data, and from them leading to a general idea or definition. He frequently consulted men of all ages and conditions, and in his discussions with them employed a twofold process: one destructive (irony), consisting in showing that a definition given by an adversary led to absurd and ridiculous consequences; the other positive or constructive (maieutic), consisting in finding the true definition by an analysis and comparison of common concrete ideas. His doctrine is no longer concerned with nature, but primarily with man, and is chiefly ethical. Man is created for happiness, and he must first ascertain where true happiness is to be found, for, as no man does wrong knowingly, to know the right is to be virtuous. Virtue is knowledge.

(*b*) Socrates exercised great influence, both by his example and his teaching. Among the philosophers who were influenced by him must be mentioned *Antisthenes*, *Diogenes* of Sinope, and the other *Cynics*, who claimed that man must live according to nature, practice virtue, and neglect conventional culture and customs; *Aristippus* of Cyrene and the other *Cyrenaics*, who advocate hedonism, i.e. the theory that pleasure is the sole basis of morality; *Euclid* of Megara and the other Megarian philosophers, who used, developed, and frequently abused the Socratic method. In metaphysics they continue the tradition of the Eleatic school.

2. **Plato.** — (*a*) Plato (427–347) is the most illustrious disciple of Socrates. After his master's death, he travelled through Egypt, Sicily, Italy, etc., and went back to Athens, where he taught philosophy in the gymnasium of Academus. Hence the name of "Academy" given to his school. He wrote a great num-

ber of works, in the form of dialogues. His doctrine may be classified under the three headings of dialectics, physics, and ethics.

(*b*) *Dialectics*. (1) True science deals not with the world of the senses, which is concrete, changing, and unstable, but with the universal, common, and unchangeable essences, independent of their concrete realization in space and time. (2) These essences or ideas are the real prototypes which concrete beings participate. There are, for instance, individual beautiful beings, persons, statues, landscapes, etc.; therefore there must exist from all eternity a beauty-in-itself which these objects participate. Again, a triangle may disappear, but the nature and properties of the triangle are eternal and unchangeable. To every one of our ideas corresponds a real prototype. (3) The world of suprasensible ideas exists really, since sensible objects are real, and the sensible world is but a reflection of the intelligible world. There could be no good, virtuous, just, beautiful, etc., objects or actions, if there did not exist really goodness-itself, virtue-itself, justice-itself, beauty-itself. Thus universal ideas as such are objective; they are principles not only of knowledge, but also of existence. (4) How does the mind pass from sense-knowledge to intellectual knowledge? Since the ideas are not realized in the sensible world, the mind cannot find them there. Plato explains true knowledge by the theory of reminiscence. Before being imprisoned in the body, the soul has preëxisted in the suprasensible world of ideas, from which it was expelled in consequence of some sin. Sense-perception is the means by which the soul is led to recall some of the ideas acquired before its union with the body. (Cf. p. 100.) (5) The highest idea is God, the supreme good and source of all perfection.

(*c*) *Physics* (including the science of the human soul). (1) The three principles of the world are God, the soul of the world which participates the divine nature, and matter which is eternal, and is the principle of limitation and multiplicity. Matter is also described as the immense receptacle of sensible phenomena. (2) The soul is immortal, and its union with the body is against its nature. (3) In addition to the intelligent soul, Plato seems to have admitted two other souls, the sensitive and the vegetative.

(*d*) *Ethics*. (1) The supreme good is the contemplation of pure ideas, the true, the good, and the beautiful. (2) Virtue is identified with knowledge. (3) The individual exists for the state, and the state has absolute rights over the citizen.

(*e*) Plato and his immediate disciples form the school known as the *Old Academy*. The *Middle Academy* shows a tendency to scepticism. It is represented especially by *Arcesilaus* (about 316-241), who claims that true knowledge or certitude is impossible. In the *Third Academy*, *Carneades* (about 210–129) asserts that certitude is impossible, and that man must be satisfied with probability. The *New Academy* (second and first centuries B.C.) with *Philo* of Larissa and *Antiochus* of Ascalon returned to Plato's dogmatism, which they combined with Aristotelian and Stoic doctrines.

3. **Aristotle.** — (*a*) Aristotle (384–322) was born at Stagyra in Chalcidice, a Greek colony in Macedonia (hence the name of Stagyrite frequently given him), and for twenty years studied under Plato. In 342, Philip of Macedon called him to his court and intrusted him with the education of his son Alexander (the Great). In 335, Aristotle returned to Athens and, in the Lyceum, opened a school of philosophy known as the *Peripatetic School* (περιπατεῖν, to walk about) from the master's habit of walking with his disciples while teaching. Aristotle wrote a large number of works, logical, metaphysical, physical, and ethical. He agrees with Plato in defining the scope of science, which is to deal with the universal, the eternal, and the unchangeable, but differs from him in claiming that these characters can be found by the mind in the sensible world. Hence his philosophy is more inductive and more scientific.

(*b*) *Logic*. Aristotle is the founder of scientific logic, and, apart from the development which is given to induction owing to the growth of empirical science, our logic to-day is essentially that of Aristotle. (1) Scientific demonstration based on the syllogism tends to find the universal causes and principles of things. (2) It assumes some indemonstrable principles, which are not innate, but acquired from the consideration of the world, and applies them to concrete facts. (Cf. p. 383.) (3) Categories are the general concepts under which we classify our knowledge. There are ten categories (cf. p. 211), namely, substance, and nine accidents. The categories are not simply classes of concepts, but also classes of things.

(c) *Metaphysics.* (1) In every reality of the world there is being and becoming, something stable and something changing. (2) Change is the passage from one state to another. It implies the distinction of "act" (ἐντελέχεια) or actual possession of a determination, and "potency" (δύναμις) or capacity for acquiring such a determination. (3) The universal and necessary as such has no existence apart from individual and contingent realities in which it is found, not "actually," but "potentially." Actually it exists only in the mind which elaborates sense-perception. (4) There are four causes, material, formal, efficient, and final. The first two are intrinsic and constitute the being itself; the latter two, extrinsic, the productive cause calling forth a being from potency to act, and the end being the motive for which the agent exercises its activity. (5) Act precedes potency, for, although in an individual being the capacity for acquiring a determination precedes the acquisition of it, yet the passage from potency to act always requires a preëxisting act. (6) Hence Aristotle is led to admit the existence of the "Actus purus." (Cf. pp. 516 ff.)

(d) *Physics* (including the philosophy of mind). (1) All material substances are composed of two principles, primary matter and substantial form. (Cf. pp. 428 ff.) (2) The soul is the substantial form of the human body. (Cf. pp. 483 ff.) (3) It is endowed with five faculties, nutritive, sensitive, intellectual, appetitive, and locomotive. (4) Intellectual knowledge reaches the object apart from its individual features in space and time. (5) The intellect is immortal.

(e) *Ethics.* (1) The supreme good of man is happiness. It consists essentially in the harmonious development of all his faculties, especially of the highest, i.e. the intellectual. (2) Virtue is a habit consisting in avoiding excess and defect. (3) The highest virtues are intellectual virtues.

(f) Among the most important peripatetic philosophers must be mentioned *Theophrastus* of Lesbos, contemporary of Aristotle, and later *Apollonius* of Rhodes (first century B.C.) who edited Aristotle's works.

III. Post-Aristotelian Philosophy

1. **Stoics.** — The main Stoic philosophers (from στοά, porch, the place where Zeno taught) are *Zeno* of Citium in the island of Cyprus (born about 340), the founder of the school; *Cleanthes* (born about 300), his immediate successor, and *Chrysippus* (born about 280), who, by his dialectics, contributed to the defense and spread of the school. Later, the Stoic doctrines were propagated among the Romans, especially by *Seneca* (3–65), *Epictetus* (died about 117), and *Marcus Aurelius* (121–180).

According to the Stoics, (1) The only principle of knowledge is sensation. (2) Matter alone is real, and what we call spirit — God and the soul — is but a form of more subtle matter. (3) God is the soul of the world, and must be conceived as a primordial fire, principle of all activity and intelligence. The human soul is but a transitory emanation from the divine spirit, or a spark of the divine fire. (4) The whole world, including man, acts according to an absolute determinism. (5) Virtue for man consists in living according not only to his rational nature, but also to all cosmic laws. This is man's end and true happiness, the only good and its own reward. The wise man must be absolutely apathetic, i.e. indifferent to all motives of action which do not spring from pure reason. All passions and emotions, therefore, must be subdued and annihilated. Bear patiently and without feeling what cannot be avoided. Abstain from everything distinct from pure reason: *Abstine et sustine*, sums up this ethical doctrine. (Cf. p. 320.)

2. **Epicureans.** — *Epicurus* (342 or 341–270) opened a school of philosophy at Athens. His disciples added nothing important to the master's doctrines, which were soon propagated in the Greek and Roman world, their main representative at Rome being *Lucretius* (95–51). The aim of philosophy is to procure happiness for man, and everything is subservient to this end. (1) As the world obeys necessary laws, man need not fear the gods. They exist, but have nothing to do with the world or with man. The

deliverance from this fear will contribute to man's happiness. Epicurus admits the essential principles of the mechanical atomism taught by Democritus. (2) Knowledge is reduced to sensation, and sensation is the only test and criterion of certitude. (3) The soul is a subtle form of matter, originating and ceasing to exist with the body; hence death is not to be feared. The will, however, is free. (4) Personal happiness and pleasure is the supreme good. It does not consist so much in anything positive as in the absence of pain and the repose of the mind. Sensual pleasure must be tempered and guided by reason. Not only the present enjoyment, but also the future, must be considered. (Cf. p. 314.)

3. **Sceptics and Eclectics.** — (*a*) The earlier *sceptics* of the third and second centuries agree with the Stoics and Epicureans that the chief purpose of philosophy is to show the way to happiness, and that happiness consists essentially in the peace and repose of the mind. Hence man must abstain from researches and studies, since they are not necessary to practical happiness, and disturb the mind. The main sceptics of this period are *Pyrrho* of Elis (about 360–270), who holds that the wise man abstains from passing judgment on anything; *Arcesilaus* and *Carneades*, already mentioned as leaders of the Academy. (Cf. pp. 373 ff.)

(*b*) The *Eclectics*, like the Sceptics, do not pretend to reach speculative certitude, but only to frame a working hypothesis on which a system of practical conduct may be based. The knowledge which they claim to have is sufficient for practical purposes; it is felt instinctively rather than based on demonstration, and is therefore more subjective than objective. Among the most important eclectics are *Seneca*, already mentioned as a Stoic; *Philo* of Larissa (of the Academy); *Andronicus* of Rhodes (of the Peripatetic school), and, to some extent, *Cicero* (106–43).

(*c*) Eclecticism led again to *scepticism*, represented by *Ænesidemus* (first century B.C.), who denies the value of both sensitive and intellectual knowledge, and asserts that all our mental representations are subjective, and by *Sextus Empiricus*, who gathered in his treatises all the objections of sceptics against certitude.

III. GRECO-ORIENTAL PHILOSOPHY

The main centre of this period is Alexandria, where the western world had frequent intercourse with the eastern world. Although this movement occurred in the beginning of the Christian era, it belongs to ancient philosophy, as Christianity had no influence on it. In the present period, the most important doctrine is Neo-Platonism, but we must speak first of Neo-Pythagorism and of the Greco-Jewish philosophy that preceded Neo-Platonism. The feature common to these is a mystical tendency to an ecstatic union with the Divinity.

1. **Greco-Jewish and Neo-Pythagorean Philosophy.** — (*a*) The Jews endeavored to harmonize the views contained in their sacred books with those of Greek philosophy. They had recourse to an allegorical interpretation of the Scriptures in order to find therein symbols and figures of the Greek philosophical doctrines. The main attempt was made by *Philo*, an Alexandrian Jew (30 B.C.–50 A.D.), according to whom (1) God, the first cause, so transcends the world that, although we can know His existence, nothing can be known of His nature and attributes. He is, however, good and almighty. (2) The world was created by God, not immediately, but through certain intermediary "powers," which may be identified with ideas, angels, demons, etc. They proceed from God, yet are distinct from Him. (3) The primordial divine "power" is the Logos, a kind of world-soul the nature of which is not explained clearly. (4) The human soul is a divine principle, or angel, united with a body which is a hindrance to its higher activities. (5) By withdrawing itself more and more from the influences of the organism, the soul may enter into immediate communication with God by a mystical ecstasy.

(*b*) *Neo-Pythagoreans* also took their doctrines from the Greek schools of philosophy, and combined them with the Pythagorean symbolism and mystical aspirations. The main representatives of this movement are *Plutarch* of Chæronea (about 46–120), *Maximus* of Tyre, and the works collected under the name of *Hermes Trismegistus* (end of the third century).

2. **Neo-Platonism** develops the doctrine of religious mysticism, or the union of man with the Infinite, based on a pantheistic monism, God being the source from whom all things proceed by emanation. With Plato's teachings as a basis, it combines doctrines from the main Greek schools.

(*a*) *Plotinus* (205–270) holds that (1) All things emanate from the One, i.e. the supreme being, world-transcending, indetermined principle, without any attributes, without even intelligence and will. (2) The first reality which emanates from the One is the Mind (νοῦς), or pure intelligence; from this intelligence emanates the soul of the world; from the soul of the world, particular souls; and from these, matter. (3) The human soul is free and immortal, but goes through a series of transmigrations. (4) The soul finally returns to God by successively purifying and almost annihilating itself, and ascending to the contemplation of the Mind, and the ecstatic union with the One. *Porphyry* of Tyre (233–304) was Plotinus's immediate disciple, and spread his master's doctrine.

(*b*) *Iamblicus* of Syria (died about 330) also holds a theory of emanation with a polytheistic and demonistic doctrine.

(*c*) At Constantinople the chief representative of Neo-Platonism is *Themistius* (latter half of fourth century). At Athens, *Proclus* (410–485) and *Simplicius* also teach the doctrine of a series of emanations from the One.

CHAPTER II

MEDIÆVAL PHILOSOPHY

Transition. Patristic Philosophy

The Fathers of the Church are primarily apologists. They endeavor to explain Christian dogmas and to defend them against both heresy and paganism. Hence whatever philosophy is found in their writings is not presented systematically, but scattered here and there as circumstances require. Two periods may be distinguished. The first, ending with the council of Nice (325) includes the first three centuries, during which the main dogmas were established and defined. The second extends to the seventh century, during which time theology became more systematic, and consequently more attention was given to philosophy as an auxiliary.

1. **First Period.** — (*a*) The question of the origin of evil gave rise to two heresies, Gnosticism in the second century, and Manicheism (founded by Manes in the third century). *Manicheism* holds an essential dualism of principles, one of good, the other of evil, and a doctrine of emanation. *Gnosticism* had recourse to a supposed esoteric doctrine of Christ, higher than revelation and to which the name γνῶσις was given. According to this (1) God is the principle of all good, and from God emanates a series of Æons. (2) Matter is the principle of evil, and the world results from the union of the divine with the material principle. (3) All things will ultimately return to God. (4) The Scriptures are to be interpreted allegorically. It is easy to see in this teaching a mixture of elements borrowed from Philo and Plotinus.

(*b*) Among the Fathers of this period must be mentioned two names, both belonging to the Christian school of Alexandria: *Clement* of Alexandria (died about 216) and *Origen* (185–254). Both insist on the doctrine that God is not to be identified with, but transcends, the world. The world is not an emanation from God, but was created by Him. The soul is spiritual and immortal.

2. **Second Period.** — (*a*) We simply mention in passing the names of *Gregory of Nyssa* (331–394), *Basil* (died 379), *Ambrose* (340–397), and *Gregory Nazianzen* (born 330).

(*b*) *Saint Augustine*, born 354 at Tagaste in Numidia, was converted by St. Ambrose. He became bishop of Hippo in 395, and died in 430. The following works especially are of interest for philosophy: "Confessiones"; "Retractationes"; "Contra Academicos"; "Soliloquia"; "De immortalitate animae"; "De anima et eius origine"; "De libero arbitrio"; "De civitate Dei."

Augustine borrows from the Greek philosophers, especially from Plato, but adapts their teaching to Christian dogmas. (1) God exists as the one supreme being, simple, eternal, omniscient. He is the creator of all things, and brought them out of nothing according to His plan, ideas, or exemplars. (2) The soul is spiritual and immortal. (3) Its main activity is intellectual knowledge. Certitude is possible, and Augustine defends it against the probabilism of the Academy. God is the source of all truth, and the first light which illumines the human mind. (4) God is the supreme good, hence man's ultimate end. Virtue is essentially the conformity of the human with the divine will, the fulfilment of God's law, especially the law of love, in view of man's eternal destiny.

(*c*) Some works formerly attributed to Dionysius the Areopagite, the disciple of St. Paul, are now known to have been written at the end of the fifth or the beginning of the sixth century. The philosophy of *Pseudo-Dionysius* is essentially Neo-Platonistic, and reproduces the mysticism of Neo-Platonism, although it rejects its pantheism.

Mediæval or scholastic philosophy (thus called because it was taught in the schools), although it was frequently systematized along with theology, is nevertheless distinct from it, as it proceeds on merely rational grounds. We shall divide it into three periods: (1) The period of formation and growth (from the ninth to the end of the twelfth century). (2) The period of perfection (thirteenth century). (3) The period of decline (from the fourteenth to the sixteenth century).

I. FIRST PERIOD

I. Beginnings

1. **The Schools.** — (*a*) Before Charlemagne, the invasion of the barbarians and the dismemberment of the Roman Empire made it impossible to acquire and develop any branch of learning. From the time of Charlemagne schools were founded: (1) *palace schools*, at the court of rulers, especially of the French kings; (2) *monastic schools*, annexed to monasteries, for the education of both the religious and strangers; (3) *cathedral schools*, established in the most important diocesan sees. The seven liberal arts were taught in these schools, namely, the *trivium* (grammar, rhetoric, and dialectic), and the *quadrivium* (arithmetic, geometry, astronomy, and music). Little by little natural sciences, history, theology, and philosophy were added. Among the first "scholastici" or masters of the schools may be mentioned *Alcuin* (735–804) at the court of Charlemagne, and *Rhabanus Maurus* (784–856) at the Benedictine school of Fulda.

(*b*) The teaching in the schools was chiefly in the form of *commentaries* on the works of Greek philosophers (mostly in Latin translations) and of Latin philosophers. Among these works the most important were the *Organon*, i.e. the logical works of Aristotle, part of which only was known then; the *Timaeus* of Plato; the *Isagoge*, i.e. the introduction to Aristotle's Categories, by Porphyry, and other commentaries of Plato and Aristotle; some of the writings of Cicero, Seneca, and Lucretius; those of St. Augustine, Pseudo-Dionysius, and some Fathers.

2. **John Scotus Eriugena** (born between 800 and 815) is the first who tried to systematize philosophy. The doctrine contained in his main work "De divisione naturae" is a mixture of Christianity, Oriental pantheism, and Alexandrian mysticism. There is only one being, namely, God, from whom all things proceed by emanation. God remains the one substance of all things. In this process of emanation, four stages must be distinguished.

(1) Uncreated and creating nature, i.e. God as the origin of all things, unknowable both for us and for Himself. (2) Created and creating nature, i.e. God as the principle and exemplar of all things. (3) Created and not-creating nature, i.e. the world of phenomena in space and time, all of which are participations of the divine substance, and theophaniæ, i.e. manifestations of God and of the divine becoming. (4) Neither created nor creating nature, i.e. God as the end of all things, to whom all things ultimately return.

Other important names of this period are *Remi of Auxerre* (died 904) and *Gerbert* (died 1003).

II. The Problem of Universals

1. **The Problem Stated.** — (*a*) Toward the middle of the eleventh century the problem of universals becomes the centre of scholastic discussions. It is not the only problem, as we shall see; from it radiate other psychological and metaphysical inquiries, but it is the chief one. Nor is the discussion of this problem an idle one, for it is the very question of the value of our universal ideas, a question which, in some form or other, reappears throughout the whole history of philosophy, and is still a vital one at the present time.

(*b*) A passage in Porphyry's *Isagoge* which, in Boethius's translation, was the text-book of logic used in the schools, was the starting-point of the discussion. Porphyry asks whether genera and species exist *in themselves* as realities, or only *in the mind* that conceives them. Are they objective things or mental abstractions? Hence two answers are suggested. (1) *Absolute realism:* Universal concepts as such correspond to objective extramental realities, which are universal independently of the mind. (2) *Conceptualism:* The idea alone is universal, and there is no extramental reality corresponding to it. Later on, a distinction was made and two new systems were evolved. (3) *Nominalism*, more radical than conceptualism, denies even the conception of the universal by the mind, and attributes universality only to the common name. (4) *Moderate realism* answers that, as such, the universal exists only in the mind, that existing things are always individual, but that there is in things a "fundamentum" for this universality, namely, their essence which the mind, by a process of abstraction, may conceive apart from individual features. (Cf. p. 398.)

2. **Realism.** — (*a*) *Scotus Eriugena* and *Remi of Auxerre*, already mentioned, were realists.

(*b*) In the twelfth century, *William of Champeaux* (1070–1120), a disciple of St. Anselm and of Roscelin, whose teaching he opposed (see below, p. 564), held — according to Abelard, his opponent, on whose authority we have to depend for this account — that universals are present in individual things. Hence individuals are identical as to their essence and differ only in their accidents. In other words, the essence of man, for instance, is one and identical in all men, and contained totally in every individual man. In consequence of the ridicule heaped on this doctrine by Abelard — who objected that in this case Socrates at Rome, since he contains the whole human essence, should also be at the same time at Athens, where Plato, who also contains the whole human essence, is — William modified his view, and finally seems to have abandoned realism altogether.

(*c*) A more reserved realism, called *indifferentism*, was taught by *Adelard of Bath* (in the beginning of the twelfth century) and *Gauthier (Walter) of Mortagne* (died 1174). In every individual we must distinguish two classes of realities. Some constitute its essential differences; others are specific and generic, i.e. common to all individuals (*indifferentes*), hence universal. It would seem then that, according to the point of view one takes, the same being may be looked upon as individual and as universal, but the theory, as presented, is vague, and may receive various interpretations.

(*d*) The school of Chartres — *Bernard of Chartres* (died about 1125), *Thierry of Chartres* (died 1155), *William of Conches* (about 1080–1154), a disciple of St. Bernard — teaches an absolute realism similar to that of Plato. The true reality is universal, and the sensible world is composed only of fleeting shadows. However, this doctrine endeavors to avoid pantheism, and admits creation.

3. **Anti-Realism.** — (*a*) At the end of the eleventh century, *Roscelin of Compiègne* affirms that reality belongs primarily to the individual, and that universals are only names, "voces" (nominalism), or at most mental conceptions to which nothing real corresponds.

(*b*) In the twelfth century *Abelard* (1079–1142), a disciple of Roscelin and of William of Champeaux, is the main figure in philosophical and theological discussions. (1) He opposes both the realism of William of Champeaux and the nominalism of Roscelin. He does not seem to look upon universals as mere mental ideas without any reality whatsoever in things. While he claims that individuals alone exist, his doctrine seems to be that of a moderate realism not yet formulated clearly. (2) He is essentially a rationalist, even in regard to Catholic dogmas and mysteries which, he claims, can be understood and demonstrated by reason. (3) In his "Sic et Non" he presents pros and cons on a number of questions, but stops at these statements without giving any positive answer. (4) He also gives some attention to cosmological, psychological, and ethical problems.

(*c*) *Gilbert de la Porrée* (1076–1154) admits that universal essences exist only in individuals, and become universal in the mind when the similarities between them are discovered by a process of comparison.

4. **Saint Anselm** (1033–1109) deserves special mention on account of the many questions which he touched upon, and of his efforts to systematize the results reached by his predecessors. He was influenced greatly by St. Augustine. (1) Faith is superior to reason, yet reason is an independent source of knowledge. (2) The real existence of God is proved by the idea which we have of an infinitely perfect being, to whom, therefore, existence, as a perfection, must belong. (This argument has been discussed and found wanting as passing from the ideal to the real order.) (3) Truth is eternal and unchangeable, and therefore based ultimately on God. (4) Universals exist in things; yet St. Anselm does not seem to teach an absolute, but a moderate realism. (5) Abstract ideas are not innate, but have their origin in the data of the senses.

5. **Eclectics and Synthetics.** — Efforts to sum up and coördinate various doctrines were made by *John of Salisbury* (died 1180), and *Alanus of Lille* (about 1128–1202). The former is a humanist, historian, critic, and philosopher. The latter insists on dialectics and applies himself chiefly to cosmology, psychology, and metaphysics.

III. Mysticism and Pantheism

1. **Mysticism.** — In general mysticism admits that, at least under certain conditions, there is for man a mode of knowledge of God and of divine things higher than logical demonstration, namely, the direct communication and union of the soul with God through contemplation and love. The purpose of life is to develop these higher faculties, and to make the immediate union with God closer and more perfect. The main mystics are found in the abbey of *Saint-Victor* (Paris), and among them especially the two abbots, *Hugh* (1096–1141) and *Richard* (died 1173). Without despising reason and dialectics, they look upon them only as a step to contemplation which alone gives true science.

2. **Pantheism.** — In the latter half of the twelfth century there was a revival of pantheistic doctrines. (1) The pantheism of the school of Chartres is represented by *Bernard of Tours*, who, about 1150, wrote his "De mundi universitate," in which he follows the Neo-Platonistic doctrines, and admits a theory of emanation. (2) The pantheism of *Amaury of Bènes* and his disciples admits that God is immanent in all things, and that all things are substantially identical with God. (3) The materialistic pantheism of *David of Dinant* asserts that God is the primary matter identical in all things. Three classes of substances are distinguished, God, the soul, and matter, but they are only one and the same being.

IV. Oriental Philosophy

1. **Arabian Philosophy** is based chiefly on Aristotle, whose works were translated into Arabic from Syriac versions. Naturally such translations were very defective. Arabian philosophers also

borrow doctrines of emanation and ecstasis from Neo-Platonism. In the discussions which were raised about the Koran toward the end of the eighth century, the Mutazilites were rationalists, the Mutakallimun defended orthodoxy, and the Sufis gave prominence to mysticism. Arabian philosophy proper is divided into eastern and western.

(*a*) *Main oriental Arabian philosophers.* (1) *Alkendi* (died about 870) wrote on logic, physics, metaphysics, medicine, magic, etc. (2) *Alfarabi* (died 950), at the school of Bagdad, wrote commentaries on Aristotle's logical works. In metaphysics he admitted an emanationistic pantheism. (3) *Avicenna* (*Ibn Sina*, 980–1036) wrote a great number of works in which he abandons many of the Neo-Platonistic interpretations of Aristotle, but still admits a theory of emanations or processions from God. The last emanation is the "intellectus agens," which governs our world. Matter is eternal and increated. (4) *Gazali* (*Algazel*, 1058–1111) opposed the philosophers and stood for the Koran. He was one of the Sufis or mystics.

(*b*) *Occidental Arabian philosophers* lived in Spain. The most important was *Averroës* (*Ibn Roshd*, 1126–1198), born at Cordova; died at Morocco. He wrote many commentaries on Aristotle's works, and also original works on philosophy, medicine, and astronomy. (1) Primary matter is eternal and contains all forms in a germ-like fashion. (2) Human reason is impersonal, one and identical in all men. Hence there is no personal immortality.

2. **Jewish Philosophy** developed chiefly in Spain under the influence of Arabian philosophy. *Avicebron* or *Avicebrol* (*Ibn Gebirol*, 1020–1070), born at Malaga, reproduces many tendencies of the Neo-Platonists. God is one and unknowable. All things, even spiritual, are composed of matter and form. The soul must unite itself to God by contemplation. *Moses Maimonides* (1135–1204) tries to combine the teachings of Aristotle with Judaism. On many points he agrees with the interpretation of Aristotle by Averroës. Matter is not affirmed to be eternal. The human intellect is partly innate (one and the same for all) and partly acquired (personal and individual).

II. SECOND PERIOD

I. General

1. **Influences.** — The thirteenth century is the period of perfection of scholastic philosophy. An attempt is made to coördinate all preceding doctrines in a complete synthesis. The main influences at work were the introduction of hitherto unknown philosophical writings, especially those of Aristotle; the foundation and growth of universities, and the institution of religious orders.

(*a*) Before this time only the logical works of *Aristotle* were known to the schoolmen. Now his other philosophical and scientific works were translated into Latin, sometimes directly from the Greek, more generally from Arabic translations. The translations from the Arabic were frequently very imperfect, and, together with Arabian commentaries, were causes of the misrepresentation of the master's doctrine in a way which was often irreconcilable with Catholic dogma. Hence prohibitions to read Aristotle's works were enacted by the provincial council of Paris (1210) and by the Pope's legate (1215). This prohibition, however, applied only to the University of Paris. Little by little, when Aristotle became better known through more accurate translations, this prohibition ceased to be applied, and Aristotle became the undisputed master in the University.

(*b*) *Universities* gave to philosophy an important place in their teaching. The University of Paris was founded early in the thirteenth century, or rather grew out of the union of the cathedral schools. The University of Oxford, which already existed, was definitely organized in the thirteenth century, and, to a great extent, modelled after that of Paris. The University of Cambridge was founded in the latter half of the thirteenth century.

(*c*) It is also at this time that the *Dominicans* and *Franciscans* were founded. Their teaching, both in their monasteries and in universities, had a stimulating influence on account of the learning of the men who gave it, and of the controversies which arose between seculars and regulars, and between the various religious schools.

2. **Division.** — We shall consider successively (1) the philosophy of the earlier part of the thirteenth century; (2) Thomistic philosophy; (3) Scotistic philosophy; (4) some other more or less independent schools and philosophers.

II. Philosophy in the Earlier Part of the Thirteenth Century

In general, the beginning of the thirteenth century is a period of transition. The influence of Aristotle is already very important, but far from exclusive. Many elements are borrowed from other sources, especially from St. Augustine. (1) *William of Auvergne* (died 1249), professor at the University of Paris, and later bishop of Paris, attempts to reconcile Aristotle with Plato and St. Augustine. (2) Among the Franciscans must be mentioned *Alexander of Hales* (died 1245) and *St. Bonaventure* (1221–1274). Alexander's philosophy is essentially Aristotelian, although it still retains some traditional Augustinian elements. St. Bonaventure was Alexander's disciple. In his metaphysics, psychology, theodicy, etc., the growing influence of Aristotle is manifest. He also taught a form of mysticism akin to that of the Victorine school. The world presents to the mind the "vestiges" of God, and the soul is an "image" of God. The knowledge of God's vestiges and image must lead to the immediate contemplation of God Himself.

III. Thomistic Philosophy

1. **Albert the Great** (1193–1280), a Dominican, professor at Cologne and Paris, was St. Thomas's master, and began the great synthesis completed by his disciple. He contributed to spread the influence of Aristotle. Remarkable as a theologian and philosopher, Albert is still more remarkable as a scientist. He was familiar with all the sciences of his time, zoölogy, botany, physiology, medicine, geography, astronomy, mineralogy, and even alchemy. His philosophy, except on some minor points, is essentially the same as that of St. Thomas, but less perfectly elaborated.

2. **Saint Thomas** of Aquino or Thomas Aquinas, called the Angelic Doctor (1225–1274), entered the Dominican order in 1243,

was the disciple of Albert the Great at Cologne and Paris, began his public teaching at Paris about 1257, and later taught at Rome, Bologna, Perugia, Naples, and other places.

(*a*) Besides a number of commentaries on Holy Scripture, Aristotle, etc., he wrote "Opuscula," "Quodlibeta," "Quaestiones disputatae," and especially "Summa contra gentiles" and "Summa theologica." These constitute a theological and philosophical encyclopædia in which Aristotelian philosophy and Catholic dogma are harmonized. Thomistic philosophy is essentially Peripatetic, but on many points Aristotle's doctrine is modified. Reason is a source of knowledge distinct from revelation, but allied with it, and St. Thomas always distinguishes natural from supernatural truth, and philosophy from theology.

(*b*) We shall mention only the fundamental points in the philosophy of St. Thomas. (1) Material substances are composed of matter and form, potentiality and actuality. (Cf. pp. 426 ff.) The world was created by God. (2) Man is also composed of matter and form (cf. pp. 480 ff), but the form or soul is substantial and spiritual, hence directly created by God and immortal. (3) The soul has faculties, some of which it exercises through the organism, while others are spiritual. The intellect is spiritual, but depends extrinsically on the senses. From sensory knowledge we arise to intellectual knowledge by the abstractive activity of the *intellectus agens*. (Cf. pp. 98 ff.) Intellectual or universal knowledge alone constitutes true science. Universals exist in things "fundamentaliter," i.e. in their concrete essence, but in the mind "formaliter." (Cf. p. 398.) (4) The existence of God is known a posteriori from the world, as also whatever may be known concerning His nature. But no finite mind can ever have a comprehensive knowledge of God. (Cf. pp. 529 ff.) (5) The ultimate end of man is perfect happiness which is to be found in the possession of God, the infinite good. The moral character of actions is to be derived from their relation to the ultimate end.

3. **Thomists and Adversaries.** — Some of St. Thomas's doctrines were opposed very strongly, and the opposition succeeded even in having some of them condemned at Paris and Oxford. But, in 1278, the whole Dominican order accepted Thomism, which

thenceforth gained in favor. Among the main opponents of St. Thomas are the Dominican *Robert Kilwardby* at Oxford and the Franciscan *Richard of Middletown* at Paris. Among his main partisans on the controverted questions are *Giles of Lessines*, and some philosophers who were eclectics, but kept Thomism as a central doctrine: *Godfrey of Fontaines*, *Giles of Rome*, and *Henry of Ghent*.

IV. Scotistic Philosophy

John Duns Scotus, the Doctor Subtilis (1266 or 1274–1308), a Franciscan, taught at Oxford (1294), Paris (1304), and Cologne (1308), where he died. His philosophy is primarily critical and negative, secondarily constructive. He attacks the main contemporary systems of St. Bonaventure, St. Thomas, Giles of Rome, Henry of Ghent, and others. (1) Philosophy and theology not only are distinct, but may be opposed. The field of reason is narrowed more than in St. Thomas. (2) All created beings are composed of matter and form. Even spiritual substances have a common and homogeneous substratum, the *materia primo-prima*. As to the substantial form, it is not necessarily one in the same being, but there may be together several subordinated forms. (3) Scotus defends a moderate realism. However, the individual as such is not made individual by its matter, as St. Thomas asserted, but by a special reality called *haecceitas* or "thisness." In general, under the name of formalities, Scotus distinguishes a number of principles within the same individual, to which he attributes reality, although their distinction seems merely logical. (4) Both in God and in man, the will is superior to the intellect. It may be noted that, notwithstanding the differences, Scotus's philosophy agrees with that of St. Thomas on many fundamental points. It found many exponents and defenders, especially among Franciscans, but Scotus's influence never equalled that of St. Thomas, who remains the greatest of all scholastics.

V. Other Schools and Philosophers

1 **Averroism.** — The commentaries on Aristotle by Averroës were introduced at Paris at the same time as Aristotle's works.

Condemned in 1210 and 1215, Averroism revived especially with *Siger of Brabant* (died at the end of the thirteenth century), and was again condemned in 1270 and 1277. At this period, Averroism holds that the active intellect is impersonal and identical in all men. Hence there is no personal immortality. It also denies the providence of God and asserts a mediate creation, God having first created separate intelligences who, in turn, created material substances. Finally it divorces reason from faith, so that a philosophical truth may be a falsehood in theology, and vice versa.

2. **Roger Bacon** (about 1210–1294) was a Franciscan who taught at Oxford and Paris. He attaches great importance to natural sciences and uses experimental methods. He appeals to observation and experience against authority and a priori deductions. His learning was very extensive and embraced physics, mathematics, geography, astronomy, alchemy, and linguistics. In philosophy he borrows from Aristotle, early Franciscan traditions, and Arabian philosophers. His violent polemics against acknowledged authorities contributed to lessen his influence.

3. **Raymond Lully** (1235–1315) was also a Franciscan, and opposed Averroism. He held that reason and faith, far from being opposed, always go together. Faith is essentially rational, and reason can demonstrate all revealed truths. Thus the difference between the natural and the supernatural is suppressed. His "Ars Magna" contains a kind of logical mechanism in which various letters and symbols representing ideas are combined in different ways so as to lead to formulas and conclusions that are supposed to correspond to reality.

III. THIRD PERIOD

1. **General Causes of Decline.** — The third period of scholastic philosophy, including the fourteenth and the first half of the fifteenth century, is a period of decline. Several causes contributed to this decline. As, on the one hand, Albert the Great and Roger Bacon had failed in their attempt to foster the scientific spirit and develop experimental methods; and as, on the other hand, the work of harmonizing philos-

ophy and theology, reason and faith, had been perfected, philosophers indulged in mere verbal questions, abused dialectics, and discussed idle subtleties. They ceased to think for themselves, and limited themselves to commenting on the works of their predecessors. Hence frequently arose animated discussions on points of little or no importance. Moreover, these obscure thoughts were often expressed in more obscure terminology. All this contributed to a general decline of studies, and the high level which universities had attained in the thirteenth century was considerably lowered. Two main movements characterize this period, the revival of nominalism and of mysticism.

2. **Terminism.** — (*a*) The formalism of the Scotistic school multiplied metaphysical entities, and led to an extreme reaction in which everything was simplified as much as possible. Thus was revived nominalism which had generally been abandoned in the preceding century. *Durandus of St. Pourçain* (died about 1332) and *Peter d'Auriol* (*Aureolus*, died 1322) are the precursors of *Ockham* (about 1280–1347), who taught at Paris and was the true author of the revival of nominalism. According to him, only individuals exist, and to universal notions no reality whatever corresponds in nature. Ideas are signs or terms of the things which they signify, but intuitive knowledge alone represents things that have any reality outside the mind. Abstract concepts have no objective value whatsoever. They are *termini*, conceptions of the mind, and substitutes for a number of individual realities. This theory is neither Roscelin's nominalism nor Abelard's conceptualism, but rather terminism. In addition to this, Ockham manifests sceptical tendencies, and professes an extreme voluntarism.

(*b*) Ockham's terminism was in great favor during the fourteenth and fifteenth centuries. Notwithstanding many prohibitions by the University of Paris, it became predominant at Paris, Vienna, Cologne, and Heidelberg. The most prominent followers of Ockham were *John Buridan* (died about 1358), rector of the University of Paris, *Marsilius of Inghen* (died 1396), rector of the University of Heidelberg, and *Peter d'Ailly* (1350–1425).

3. **Mysticism.** — The abuse of dialectics brought about, as a reaction, a revival of mysticism and the distrust of reason. Among

those who professed a mysticism consistent with Catholicism are *John Ruysbræck* (1293–1381), *Gerard Groot* (1340–1384), *Thomas a Kempis* (1380–1471), *Denys the Carthusian* (1402–1471), and especially *John Gerson* (1364–1429), chancellor of the University of Paris, whose doctrine has many points in common with that of St. Bonaventure. Among those who professed a mysticism inconsistent with Catholicism, on account especially of a leaning toward pantheism, are *Eckhart* (about 1260–1327), who holds that God is the very existence and actuality of the world, but tries to defend himself from accusations of pantheism; *Henry Suso* (about 1300–1366); *John Tauler* (1290–1361).

CHAPTER III

MODERN PHILOSOPHY

Transition. Renaissance

1. **General Features.** — The philosophical doctrines that succeeded scholasticism have little in common besides an opposition to scholastic philosophy. They develop in many different directions, show much confusion and little originality. Some tendencies, however, manifest themselves; a separation of philosophy from dogmatic teaching, a complete independence of theology and revelation, an alliance of philosophy with natural sciences, and a return to antiquity.

Among the *causes* which brought about this break with the past the most important were the following:

(*a*) The movement known as *humanism*, i.e. the study of Greek and Latin classics, especially from the point of view of the perfection of the form which was contrasted with that of the scholastics. Naturally this artistic renaissance affected philosophical thought, for it is not possible to attend to the form without feeling the influence of the ideas. The contact of Italy and the western world with Greece contributed to develop this tendency, especially as a number of learned Greeks fled to Italy when Constantinople was captured (1453) and Europe was threatened by the Turks. The invention of the art of printing facilitated the spread of literature.

(*b*) *Religious reformation*, which implied essentially a doing away with the authority of the Church, and an advocating of the supremacy of individual thought.

(*c*) *The progress of natural sciences*, in which new discoveries gave rise to new problems. The heliocentric system replaced the geocentric view (Copernicus, 1473–1543; Tycho-Brahe, 1546–1601; Kepler, 1571–1631; Galileo, 1564–1642). The laws of the movements of heavenly bodies were discovered. Anatomy, physiology (Vesalius, 1514–1564; Servet, 1509–1553), and mathematics (Galileo, Tartaglia) made a rapid advance. America was discovered, etc. All these opened new horizons, suggested new questions, and necessitated the use of new methods.

(*d*) *The formation of nationalities* out of a formerly united Christian empire, and the abolition of the feudal system. Hence questions concerning individual and national rights and liberties grew in importance.

(*e*) *The failure of scholastic philosophy*, which had weakened considerably in its period of decline, to adapt itself, as it could and should have done, to these new circumstances and needs. Its dry verbal discussions could not withstand the opposition which raged against it. Many important problems had been raised, and there was no time to lose in idle discussions.

2. **Revival of Greek Schools.** — (*a*) The revival of *Platonism*, favored by the beauty of form and diction found in Plato's writings, was encouraged especially by the Platonic Academy of Florence founded by Cosmo de' Medici in 1460. Plato, frequently with a Neo-Platonic interpretation, was preferred to Aristotle, especially by *Gemistus Pletho* (1355–1450), a Byzantine scholar, Cardinal *Bessarion* (1403–1472), and *Pico della Mirandola* (1463–1494), who combined Neo-Platonism with the Jewish Cabala.

(*b*) *Pomponatius* (1462–1524) is the chief *Aristotelian* of this period, but Aristotle's doctrine is frequently misinterpreted, and becomes again the subject of many discussions.

(*c*) *Stoicism* finds a great number of advocates, especially *Justus Lipsius* (1547–1606). *Epicureanism* in its essentials is revived by *Gassendi* (1592–1655).

3. **Naturalism.** — The study of natural sciences was based largely on observation. But at this early stage of scientific investigation, whenever real causes were not at hand, occult forces were frequently called in to explain facts. Hence a tendency to magic and astrology. A tendency to pantheism was favored by the admiration of the order of nature. (1) *Bernardino Telesio* (1508–1588) is an opponent of Aristotelian philosophy, and devotes his life to the study of natural sciences. According to him, the uni-

verse results from the combination of matter with two immaterial forces, heat and cold. The principle of life, or spiritus, is a manifestation of heat. (2) *Tommaso Campanella* (1568–1639) was influenced chiefly by Telesio, and added metaphysical and political doctrines to his master's teaching. (3) *Paracelsus* (1493–1541), a physician, mingles science with alchemy, magic, and astrology. (4) *Nikolaus of Cusa* (1401–1464) manifests a tendency to mysticism, and his doctrine, although it avoids pantheism, contains the germs of it. (5) *Giordano Bruno* (1548–1600) teaches that the universe, infinite in time and space, is but an unfolding of the being of God. The universe is one living organism, vivified by an intelligence or *anima mundi*. There is no freedom and no personal immortality.

4. **Mysticism.** — The private interpretation of Scripture, which is a fundamental tenet of Protestantism, cannot fail to lead different individuals to contradictory beliefs, which, in turn, must be harmonized with philosophical ideas. Hence the rise of Protestant philosophies and mysticism. *Luther* (1483–1546) irreducibly opposes reason, as a function of the flesh, to faith, as a function of the spirit, and thus professes an exaggerated psychological dualism. *Zwingli* (1484–1531), in his pantheistic doctrine of the immanence of God in all things, combines Neo-Platonic and Stoic elements. *Melanchthon* (1497–1560) follows chiefly Aristotle. The mystics proper are *Sebastian Franck* (1499–1542) and *Jakob Bœhme* (1575–1624). The latter explains the existence of evil by assuming that in God Himself the opposition of good and evil is essential and necessary.

5. **Political Philosophy.** — (1) *Niccolo Machiavelli* (1469–1527), in Italy, professes a sort of political utilitarianism. The ethical distinction of justice and injustice, of right and wrong, is not valid. Whatever means are useful to the state must be adopted. Not only Christian ethics, but even natural law is worthless. (2) *Thomas More* (1478–1535), in England, besides advocating a kind of communistic view of property, professes the mutual independence and indifference of church and state. (3) *Hugo Grotius* (de Groot, 1583–1645), in the Netherlands, claims that human society originated from a social contract by which individuals

transferred their rights to the state. Natural rights are those which reason discovers to be essential to man.

6. **Scholasticism.** — Among the scholastic philosophers of this period are the commentators of St. Thomas, *Ferrara* (1474–1528) and *Cajetan* (1468–1534); the Spanish philosophers *Bañez* (1528–1604) and *John of St. Thomas* (1589–1644), both Dominicans; the Jesuits *Fonseca* (1528–1597) and *Suarez* (1548–1617). But, notwithstanding their efforts, scholastic philosophy soon lost all prestige and succumbed to the attacks directed against it. It failed to adapt itself to new needs, to keep abreast of scientific progress, to modify itself according to new discoveries. Hence its downfall.

7. **Scepticism.** — The confusion of ideas and contradictory systems soon brought about a revival of scepticism represented by *Montaigne* (1533–1592), *Charron* (1541–1603), and *Sanchez* (1562–1632). All this in turn opened the way to the philosophical reforms of Bacon and Descartes.

In the modern period of philosophy, the work of construction begins anew. New systems appear, and original syntheses are completed. The break with the past and with dogmatic authority becomes more and more accentuated; problems and schools are multiplied.

We shall divide the history of modern philosophy into two periods. (1) The Pre-Kantian period, in which a rational current starts from Descartes, and an empirical current from Bacon. (2) The Kantian and Post-Kantian period, in which criticism, i.e. the problem of the origin and value of knowledge, becomes central.

I. FIRST PERIOD

I. Bacon and Descartes

With Bacon and Descartes originate two distinct movements which, in a more or less direct manner, influence subsequent philosophy, namely, empiricism and rationalism, the supremacy of experience and the supremacy of reason.

1. **Francis Bacon** (1561–1626), baron of Verulam, after occupying several high political positions, was condemned for receiving bribes, and deprived of his office. His two works, "De dignitate et augmentis scientiarum," and "Novum organon" (the latter incomplete), were the first two parts of the *Instauratio magna* which he had planned. After proposing and expounding a classification of sciences based on a tripartite division of mental faculties (memory, imagination, and reason), he insists on the necessity of method, and opposes his *Novum organon* to the *Organon*, or logical works, of Aristotle.

The method which he proposes consists essentially of the following points: (1) The syllogistic method is absolutely worthless, and experience alone is a sure criterion (cf. p. 382); respect for antiquity is an obstacle to progress. (2) The sources of error, or "idols," must be eliminated, namely, "idola tribus," based on human nature itself and common to all men; "idola specus," arising from individual tendencies; "idola fori," arising from the contact with other men through language; "idola theatri," arising from the various systems of philosophy and the authority which they exercise. (3) The constructive work is based on scientific induction, in which facts are classified in three groups, called *tabulae praesentiae, absentiae, graduum*. From the facts, gradually, and always with great caution, the passage is effected through theories and probabilities to certitude as to the causes of the facts. One must beware of prejudices, and all judgments must be based only on the comparison of facts.—N.B. Most of these rules were applied before Bacon without being formulated; Bacon was the first clearly to state the inductive methods.

2. **Réné Descartes** (*Cartesius*, 1596–1650) travelled extensively, and entertained relations with the most prominent scientists of his time. His main philosophical works are the "Discourse on Method"; "Meditationes de prima philosophia"; "Principia philosophiae."

(*a*) *Method.* (1) Descartes begins with a universal methodic doubt bearing on whatever knowledge he had acquired previously, and looks for a truth the evidence of which is so clear that doubt about it will be impossible. (Cf. pp. 243, 369 ff.) (2) He finds this truth in the intuition of his own thought, and consequently of his existence: "Cogito, ergo sum." As this idea imposes itself as true on account of its clearness, he infers that, in general, the clearness of an idea is the criterion of its truth. (Cf. p. 405.) (3) Finding in his mind the idea of an infinitely perfect being, Descartes concludes that God exists, because existence, being a perfection, must belong to the Infinite, and also because this idea itself of the Infinite can come only from God Himself. Moreover, the idea of an infinite perfection includes that of infallible veracity. Hence God, being the principle of all things, cannot deceive man who invincibly believes in the reliability of his faculties. The perceptions of the mind are therefore truthful. (4) Descartes is now ready for his constructive work, which he undertakes with the help of four guiding precepts: Require clearness and evidence; proceed first by analysis; then by synthesis; always proceed gradually and cautiously.

(*b*) *Psychology*. (1) From his starting-point: "Cogito, ergo sum," Descartes infers that he is a thinking spiritual substance, the essence of which is thought. (Cf. p. 489.) (2) Ideas are of three kinds, innate (especially that of God), acquired, or formed by the imagination. The first two classes are objective. (Cf. pp. 100, 102 ff.) (3) The organism is a mere automatic machine which the soul, located in the pineal gland, moves, and from which it receives external impressions.

(*c*) *Cosmology*. (1) Matter consists essentially in extension, and is thus opposed to thought or spirit. (2) Movement is always mechanical, and we know nothing of final causes. Its first source is God, who in creating the world endowed it with a certain quantity of movement which remains invariable.

II. Development of British Empiricism

1. **Thomas Hobbes** (1588–1679), a friend and disciple of Bacon, advocates Bacon's empiricism. Yet his philosophy is also influenced by Descartes, with whom he became acquainted at Paris. His main works are "Leviathan" and "Elementa philosophiae." (1) Sensation is the only source of knowledge; hence whatever exists is material, and universals are only names. As a conse-

quence, science and philosophy can deal only with matter. (Cf. pp. 380 ff.) (2) Qualities perceived by the senses have no reality outside of the mind. They are simply mechanical motions in things and in the brain. (3) The natural condition of man is not to live in society, but to live in a state of war against everybody else. The disadvantages of this condition brought about a social compact by which individuals transferred absolutely all their rights to the authority of the state. This authority is therefore absolute and unlimited. Right and wrong result only from positive laws. (Cf. pp. 355 ff.)

2. **John Locke** (1632–1704) in the four books of his main work, "An Essay concerning Human Understanding," examines the human faculties of knowledge. (1) There are no innate ideas, since there are no ideas that are present in the minds of all men. All ideas are acquired by experience. (2) This experience is two-fold: sensation, i.e. the mental representation of the external world, and reflection, i.e. the consciousness of mental activities. By combining simple ideas derived from these two sources, the mind forms complex ideas. (Cf. pp. 99, 103 ff.) (3) The qualities which are attributed to bodies are either primary, like extension, figure, motion, etc., or secondary, like color, odor, sound, etc. Primary qualities exist really in things; secondary qualities exist only in the mind. (4) We do not know directly external things, but mental representations or ideas. (Cf. pp. 369, 387.) (5) Among complex ideas is found that of substance. Substances exist (bodily, spiritual, and divine), but their nature is unknown and unknowable. (6) Generality and universality belong only to names. (7) Reason alone cannot prove the spirituality of the soul.

3. **George Berkeley** (1685–1753), bishop of Cloyne in Ireland, in his "New Theory of Vision," "Principles of Knowledge," and "Dialogues between Hylas and Philonous," starts from Locke's assumption that we know directly only our ideas, and, from this, endeavors to refute scepticism, materialism, and atheism. (1) Not only secondary, but also primary, qualities are mere ideas. For instance, the shape (primary) is known through visual sensations, and is no more objective than color, which is perceived through

the same sensations. Extension, far from being the essence of matter, as Descartes held, is not objective at all. (2) All ideas, even abstract and universal, are derived from concrete impressions which are products of the mind alone. (3) Matter is not perceived directly by the senses, for these perceive only qualities; nor is its existence known by demonstration, since, on the one hand, passive matter cannot be the active cause of sensations, and, on the other, ideas cannot result from an inert substance such as matter. Matter is a contradictory notion leading to scepticism. (4) The external world, therefore, is not material. The cause of its order and harmony is God, since this order shows that the world is but an idea of God manifesting itself to the human mind. The world is a mental representation — *esse est percipi* — it is not matter, but spirit. (Cf. pp. 387, 389 ff.)

4. **David Hume** (1711–1776), especially in his "Treatise on Human Nature," and his "Enquiry concerning Human Understanding," carries the consequences of empiricism to their extreme limits. (Cf. pp. 98, 113, 382.) (1) Nothing exists except what is given in experience, and as experience manifests no substances at all, it follows that no substance exists. Hume denies not only the existence of material substances, as Berkeley had done, but of spiritual as well. As matter is but a collection of phenomena, so the mind is but a collection of mental states. (Cf. pp. 460, 463 ff.) (2) As experience does not manifest any causality, but only the succession of phenomena, the idea of cause is not objective, and the regular sequence of cause and effect is not one of ontological dependence. It is owing to habit that we expect this sequence. Hume's position is thus phenomenalistic and sceptical. (Cf. p. 454.)

5. **Moralists.** — As a reaction against Hobbes, many moralists admit a universal moral law, natural to all men, and altruistic as well as egoistic. Among them are *Ralph Cudworth* (1617–1688) and *Richard Cumberland* (1632–1718). Others base morality on a special innate feeling (cf. pp. 309 ff.), which is either an æsthetic sense (*Shaftesbury*, 1671–1713), conscience (*Joseph Butler* 1692–1752), or a moral sense distinct from reason (*Francis Hutcheson*, 1694–1747). Others, finally, apply empiricism to morals (cf. p.

311) and are led to utilitarianism (*Mandeville*, 1670–1733; *Adam Smith*, 1723–1790).

III. Development of Cartesian Rationalism

1. **Direct Influences.** — From Descartes's principles *Arnold Geulincx* (1625–1669) and *Nicolas Malebranche* (1638–1715) deduce the doctrines of occasionalism and ontologism, which, however, are neither so clearly expressed nor so fully evolved in the former as in the latter. According to Malebranche, (1) God alone can be a cause; hence the activity of creatures is only apparent. In the various changes that occur there is only a coincidence which is due to God's direct intervention. This also explains the union of body and soul (occasionalism; cf. p. 481.) (2) Since finite beings do not act, our ideas cannot be caused by them. They come from God, in whom we see everything (ontologism; cf. p. 405).

2. **More Remote Influences.** — Spinoza and Leibniz are influenced by Cartesianism, but introduce many new elements and develop the system in new directions.

(*a*) The main works of *Baruch Spinoza* (1632–1677) are "Ethica more geometrico demonstrata," "De intellectus emendatione," "Tractatus politicus." In them is revealed the influence of Cartesianism, Neo-Platonism, and of the pantheism of Bruno and Maimonides. (1) The Cartesian substantial dualism, and opposition of extension and thought, is reduced to a dualism of attributes of one and the same substance, namely, God. (2) The divine substance, indetermined and unknowable in itself, unfolds itself through attributes, two of which are known to us, viz., extension and thought. (Cf. pp. 521 ff.) (3) These attributes are manifested through a number of modes, which are the finite determinations of the divine infinite substance. (4) Everything in the physical and the mental world takes place necessarily, and there is no room at any stage for freedom.

(*b*) *Gottfried Wilhelm Leibniz* (1646–1716) is an eclectic who borrows from Descartes, Plato, Aristotle, and adds many personal ideas. His main works are "Essais de theodicée," "La monadologie," "Nouveaux essais sur l'entendement humain" (an answer to

Locke's Essay). (1) Descartes was wrong in identifying spiritual substances with thought, and material substances with extension. There are in the soul perceptions which are almost unconscious, and which cannot be called thought in the Cartesian sense. As to extension, it is the principle of multiplicity and composition. But composition ultimately supposes simple and indivisible units. Substance means essentially a principle of activity, a force. Thought and extension are modes of substances. (2) The substantial unit is the monad, immaterial, eternal, and active. Bodies are aggregates of simple monads, while souls are simple monads. (3) The activity of the monad consists essentially in representation, i.e. every monad is like a mirror reflecting the whole universe more or less perfectly according to the degree of its perfection. In the lowest monads this representation is unconscious; in the highest it is conscious, and the degrees of clearness vary with the perfection of every monad. God, the increated monad, knows everything perfectly. (4) Monads do not act on one another; their development is only from within, every monad unfolding its own energies. The order of the world is the result of a divinely preëstablished harmony, (cf. p. 481) working in the best possible world, since God, infinitely perfect, would have acted without a sufficient reason if He had not created the best possible world. (5) Every monad is different from every other. There is a gradual transition by infinitesimal differences from one degree of perfection to another. (6) There are no innate actual ideas; yet, in a certain sense, all ideas are innate, namely, in the innate power of acquiring them. (Cf. pp. 100 ff.)

Christian von Wolff (1679–1754) expounded and systematized the philosophy of Leibniz.

3. **A Reaction against Rationalism** was due largely to the influence of British empiricism, and contributed to the changes which took place at this time in French political and religious conditions.

(*a*) *Etienne Bonnot de Condillac* (1715–1780) follows Locke and teaches a psychological sensationalism. Instead of two sources of ideas admitted by Locke (sensation and reflection) he admits only one. External sensation is the primitive mental fact which by various successive modifications gives rise to the most complex mental states. (Cf. pp. 98, 103 ff.)

(*b*) ***Materialistic empiricism*** is represented by ***La Mettrie*** (1709–1751), who attacks especially the existence of the soul, and by the ***Encyclopedists*** (editors of, or writers in, the Encyclopédie), namely, ***Diderot*** (1713–1784), ***d'Alembert*** (1717–1783), ***d'Holbach*** (1723–1789), ***Cabanis*** (1757–1808). (Cf. p. 476.)

(*c*) These views opened the way to ***atheism***, or at least ***deism***, which is represented especially by ***Voltaire*** (1694–1778).

(*d*) ***Ethical sensualism***, which reduces morality to egoistic pleasure, has for its main advocate the materialist ***Helvetius*** (1715–1771).

(*e*) ***Political philosophers*** of this period are chiefly ***Montesquieu*** (1689–1755) and ***Jean-Jacques Rousseau*** (1712–1778). The latter refers the origin of society to a social contract. (Cf. pp. 355 ff.)

II. SECOND PERIOD

I. German Philosophy

1. **Kant.** — *Immanuel Kant* (1724–1804), born at Koenigsberg, was successively a student and a professor in the university of his native city. In the first period of his philosophical life, he studied and taught the leading ideas of Leibniz, Wolff, Newton, and later became acquainted with the writings of Locke and Hume. Owing to these manifold influences, Kant's own doctrine was evolving gradually. It was made public in the second period of Kant's life, by the publication of his main works: "The Critique of Pure Reason," (1781), "The Critique of Practical Reason," (1788), "The Critique of the Faculty of Judgment" (1790). Here we shall deal only with this latter period, or period of Kant's critical philosophy, in which, he says, he was aroused from his dogmatic slumber by Hume's scepticism.

(*a*) *Critique of pure reason.* Knowledge consists essentially in judgment, not analytic, since in analytic judgments the predicate is already contained in the subject, and therefore such judgments have no scientific value; nor synthetic a posteriori, since such judgments refer only to concrete experience, and therefore cannot give the universal and necessary knowledge, which alone is scientific. It consists in synthetic a priori judgments, in which the predicate is neither contained in the subject, nor affirmed of the subject simply on the ground of experience, but on account of the very structure of our faculties, hence necessarily and universally. (Cf. pp. 101, 106, 109, 395 ff.) Kant passes now to the three parts of his work, transcendental æsthetic, transcendental analytic, and transcendental dialectic.

(1) *Transcendental æsthetic* (i.e. study of sense-knowledge). External objects always appear to us in space, and internal experiences always in time. Space and time are a priori forms of our minds, and cannot be applied to things-in-themselves (cf. p. 394). Things are only the matter of knowledge, unknowable in themselves, since, in order to be known, they must reach the mind, and can reach it only through its a priori forms.

(2) *Transcendental analytic.* Sense-knowledge is elaborated by the understanding which perceives manifold relations between various sense-experiences, and thus makes them scientific. These relations also depend on a priori forms or categories, twelve in number: unity, plurality, totality (referring to the quantity of judgments), reality, negation, limitation (referring to their quality); subsistence and inherence, causality and dependence, reciprocity (referring to their relations); possibility, existence, necessity, and their opposites (referring to their modality). Here again the conclusion is that we know only phenomena, but not noumena, i.e. things-as-they-appear, but not things-in-themselves. (Cf. pp. 396 ff.)

(3) *Transcendental dialectic.* This knowledge in turn is reduced by reason to three ideas, the world, the soul, and God, which are also a priori ideas. To take them for realities leads to antinomies or contradictions.

(*b*) *Critique of practical reason.* The critique of pure reason led Kant to assert the impossibility of knowing the noumena. He turns now to practice and action, which is different from, and independent of, pure reason. (1) The moral law is absolute, universal, and necessary. It is expressed in conscience by the categorical imperative that dictates independently of any condition and of any utilitarian or agreeable motive. (Cf. pp. 320 ff.) (2) The existence of the moral law postulates freedom, since "Thou must" implies "Thou canst"; immortality, since virtue requires an adequate sanction; and the existence of a personal God as perfect holiness and justice. (3) Although these are noumena or things-in-themselves, and although they are unknowable for pure reason, they are nevertheless certain, because without them the moral law is impossible. (Cf. pp. 407 ff.)

(c) *Critique of the faculty of judgment.* This faculty is intermediate between pure reason and practical reason. It applies to the phenomena of pure reason some a priori forms of practical reason, special to free agents. (1) Teleological judgments refer external phenomena to a purpose, and look upon them as adapted to an end. They serve to order and unify experience. (2) Æsthetic judgments refer external phenomena to our own subjective feelings of the beautiful and the sublime. All these judgments depend on the structure of the human mind.

(d) *Influence of Kant; immediate disciples and opponents.* Of all the influences exercised on philosophy in the nineteenth century that of Kant is certainly the greatest, and most of the currents of thought that subsequently appeared were either developments of the Kantian theories or reactions against them. Among the immediate disciples of Kant are *Reinhold* (1755–1823), and the poet *Schiller* (1759–1805), the latter upholding especially Kant's æsthetic doctrines. Among his opponents are *Herder* (1744–1803), and *Jacobi* (1743–1819).

(e) Kant admitted two elements in knowledge, one material, the thing-in-itself; the other formal, the a priori form or category. But how can the phenomenon come from the noumenon? How can the objective and the subjective be reconciled? This dualism gave rise to two currents, critical idealism reducing even the thing-in-itself to a mental product, and critical realism reasserting the existence of the thing-in-itself.

2. **Idealism.** —Three names especially are prominent, Fichte, Schelling, and Hegel.

(a) *Johann Gottlieb Fichte* (1762–1814) places the whole reality in the subject, which is essentially activity and consciousness. (1) The ego, i.e. the universal self-consciousness, posits itself, that is, knows itself as existing and self-identical (thesis). (2) By reflection on its own activity, the ego posits the non-ego within itself, merely as an object of mental representation (antithesis). (3) The ego is aware that it is limited by the non-ego, and that the non-ego is limited by the ego (synthesis). In this whole process, the ego is the only reality, since the non-ego is but a modification of the ego.

(*b*) *Friedrich Schelling* (1775–1854) taught at Jena with Fichte. His thought varied in the course of his life, and he seems to have defended successively no less than five different systems. The most important and characteristic of these is the philosophy of identity, in which the subject and the object are identified in the same common reality, or Absolute, which is of itself indifferent to both the objective and the subjective point of view, and evolves into both.

(*c*) *Georg Wilhelm Friedrich Hegel* (1770–1831) was Schelling's disciple at Jena, but soon abandoned his master's doctrine to develop his own absolute idealism. The object is not derived from the ego, as Fichte supposed, but from the absolute. This absolute is not indifferent, as Schelling claimed, it is thought and idea, since the rational element is the whole reality of things. This idea, however, is not necessarily, but only accidentally, conscious. In its abstract state it is the object of logic; in its exteriorization, the object of the philosophy of nature; in its self-conscious aspect, the object of the philosophy of mind, which studies the individual manifestations of the universal spirit, the evolution of mankind and society (objective mind), and art, religion, and philosophy (absolute mind). Everything becomes, and the Idea or Spirit unfolds its potencies according to laws that are absolutely necessary.

Among Hegel's followers some belong to the right party (*Goeschel*, *Rosenkranz*, *Erdmann*), and admit the existence of a personal God and the soul's immortality; others belong to the left (*Strauss*, *Feuerbach*), and are pantheists.

3. **Realism** reasserts the existence of the thing-in-itself. (*a*)

Herbart (1776–1841), professor at Göttingen, teaches the existence and irreducible manifoldness of things. One of these Realities (*Realen*) is the individual human soul whose essential function is representation. Things external are unchangeable and identical. It is the mind alone that establishes between them the many relations which we perceive. Prominent among the Herbartians are *Drobish*, *Steinthal*, and *Lazarus*.

(*b*) *Arthur Schopenhauer* (1788–1860), professor at Berlin, admits a priori forms of knowledge, namely, space, time, and causality. The thing-in-itself is essentially will, which is one and independent of a priori forms. In everything the fundamental reality is the will-to-be, or the will-to-live, and this will unfolds itself through existing things. In addition to this, Schopenhauer develops a pessimistic philosophy. One of his most important disciples is *Von Hartmann*.

4. **Materialism**, as a reaction against idealism, was defended by *Karl Vogt* (1817–1895), *Jakob Moleschott* (1822–1893), and *Ludwig Büchner* (1824–1899), while *Ernst Hæckel* (born 1834) defends an evolutionary monism. (Cf. pp. 476, 521.)

5. *Lotze* (1817–1881) and *Paulsen* are Neo-Kantians, and *Trendelenburg* (1802–1872) tends to Aristotelianism. *Baader*, *Froschammer*, *Günther*, *Görres*, who flourished in the middle of the nineteenth century, were Catholic philosophers, though they differed on many important points. The distinctly neo-scholastic movement is represented by *Kleutgen*, *Stöckl*, *Tilmann Pesch*, etc., in Germany.

II. Scottish Philosophy

Like Kantian philosophy, Scottish philosophy was a reaction against Hume's scepticism and Berkeley's idealism. Scottish philosophers base their dogmatism and their ethics on some innate sense or instinct, and claim that we know external things. *Thomas Reid* (1710–1796) asserts that "common sense" is the basis on which philosophy must be built, and common sense is not compatible with scepticism or idealism. *Dugald Stewart* (1753–1828) holds essentially the same view, as also *Thomas Brown* (1778–1820) and *James Mackintosh* (1765–1832). *William Hamilton*

(1788–1856) tries to combine the doctrines of Reid with those of Kant. (Cf. pp. 405, 310.)

III. French Philosophy

1. **Spiritualism and Eclecticism.** — The French materialism of the latter part of the eighteenth century was followed by a spiritualistic reaction. The distinction of reason from sense-knowledge, the spirituality of the soul, the existence of a personal God, and the spiritual basis of morality were recognized. The main representatives of this school were *Maine de Biran* (1766–1824), who emphasizes the importance of the will; *Royer-Collard* (1763–1845), who introduced into France the leading principles of the Scottish school; *Victor Cousin* (1792–1867), who sought to combine the main systems of philosophy into one harmonious synthesis, and hence gave a prominent part to the history of philosophy. He was thus the head of the school known as Eclecticism. Among his main followers were *Théodore Jouffroy* (1796–1842), *Damiron* (1794–1862), *Garnier* (1801–1864), *Paul Janet* (1823–1899).

2. **Traditionalism** was a Catholic reaction against materialism and rationalism. It minimized the value of personal reason and advocated the common consent of mankind, based on a divine revelation, as a safer basis of certitude. *Joseph de Maistre* (1754–1821) dealt chiefly with political and religious problems. *De Bonald* (1754–1840) is looked upon as the founder of the traditionalistic school. Besides expounding the Catholic doctrine of society in opposition to the principles of the French Revolution, he claimed that language is absolutely prerequired for thought, and as a consequence, that it must have been revealed by God, and together with it, the truths which it expresses. Hence the criterion of truth is tradition based on primitive revelation. *Felicité de Lamennais* (1782–1854) holds that the criterion of truth is universal tradition or collective reason. Traditional principles, sometimes in a mitigated form, were also held by *Bautain* (1796–1867), *Bonnetty* (1798–1879) and others who mingled it with some tenets of ontologism, that is, of a system developed chiefly in Italy, and according to which we know all things in God. (Cf. pp. 105, 126, 403.)

3. **Positivism** is but a slightly modified form of sensationalism and empiricism, insisting chiefly on the epistemological aspect of knowledge. Its founder is *Auguste Comte* (1798–1857), who, in his "Cours de philosophie positive," claims that human thought passed through three successive stages: (1) The theological stage, in which phenomena are explained by the activities of divinities and supernatural agents. (2) The metaphysical stage, in which they are explained by abstract principles, such as essences, causes, substances, forms, souls, etc. (3) The positive stage, in which they are explained by their concrete antecedents and laws. This is the only valid knowledge, limiting itself to facts and their relations. Metaphysical, religious, and moral questions are idle when they try to transcend facts. Later on, Comte founded a positive religion, or religion of humanity. Among the main positivists are *Littré* (1801–1881) and *Taine* (1828–1893).

4. **Various Tendencies.** — (1) *Social questions* are in the foreground to-day. Among the precursors of modern socialism (cf. pp. 347 ff.) may be mentioned *Saint-Simon* (1760–1825), *Charles Fourier* (1772–1837), *Pierre Leroux* (1797–1871), who propose more or less radical, social, and industrial reforms. (2) *Neo-scholasticism* finds many representatives, and its influence is felt even where it does not predominate. (3) *Neo-criticists* (*Renouvier*, *Sécrétan*, etc.) modify Kant's doctrine in a dogmatic direction, at least with regard to certain metaphysical truths.

IV. Italian and Spanish Philosophy

In Italy, *Galuppi* (1770–1846) professed a kind of criticism which, on many points, is akin to that of Kant. *Rosmini* (1797–1855) teaches that the intuition of the ideal and universal being is the form of thought. Hence it does not come from experience, but is innate. Although Rosmini rejects ontologism and pantheism, his system seems to lead to these consequences. Ontologism is the doctrine that we have a direct primitive intuition of God, by means of which all other things are known. It is represented especially by *Gioberti* (1801–1852). Among the pioneers of *neo-scholasticism* are *Liberatore* (1810–1892), *Cornoldi* (1822–1892), *Sanseverino* (1811–1865).

In Spain, *Balmes* (1810–1848) and *Donoso Cortes* (1809–1853) defend spiritualistic philosophy, and harmonize philosophy and religion.

V. English and American Philosophy

1. **Associationism.** — Among associationists are *David Hartley* (1705–1757) and *Joseph Priestly* (1733–1804), whose doctrine shows a marked tendency toward materialism; *James Mill* (1773–1836) and his son *John Stuart Mill* (1806–1873); *Alexander Bain* (1818–1903). All reduce even the highest forms of knowledge to associations of images. (Cf. pp. 96 ff., 99, 112 ff.) As we can know nothing which is not given in experience, associationism leads to empiricism and positivism. (Cf. p. 382.) Moreover, whatever transcends experience is unknowable; hence agnosticism. In addition to their theory of knowledge, Stuart Mill and Bain advocate a utilitarian morality, as had been done before by *Jeremy Bentham* (1748–1832). (Cf. pp. 315 ff.)

2. **Evolutionism.** — The theory of evolution started with *Laplace* (1749–1827) for the inorganic world (nebular hypothesis), and *Lamarck* (1744–1829) for the organic world. Both were French. But it was in England that the main impetus was given to transformism (cf. pp. 444 ff.) by *Charles Darwin* (1809–1882) and his followers, *Alfred Russell Wallace* (born 1822), *George Romanes* (1848–1894), *Thomas Huxley* (1825–1895), *Saint George Mivart* (1827–1900) and *Herbert Spencer* (1820–1903).

Spencer, in his "Synthetic Philosophy," covers a far wider ground. (1) Under the phenomena lies an unknowable reality, whose modes only are knowable (agnosticism. Cf. pp. 376, 513, 530.) (2) The same universal force manifests itself throughout all phenomena. Sensation is ultimately a nervous shock, and the highest knowledge is but an association of ideas (associationism. Cf. pp. 96, 99, 112.) (3) Not only are physical and mental processes results of a universal evolution, but to evolution must also be reduced all social moral, and religious developments (evolutionism).

3. **Idealism** is represented by *Thomas Carlyle* (1795–1881), *John Caird* (1820–1898), *Thomas Green* (1836–1882).

4. **American Philosophers.** — Among American philosophers, exclusive of those now existing, mention must be made of *Jonathan Edwards* (1703–1758); *Benjamin Franklin* (1706–1790); *James McCosh* (1811–1894) who defended a theory of knowledge akin to that of Reid; *Noah Porter* (1811–1892), who also adheres to many tenets of the Scottish School; *Orestes Brownson* (1803–1876), who, after being successively a member of several Protestant denominations, became a Catholic; *John Fiske* (1842–1901), who adheres to cosmic evolutionism.

CONCLUSION

(*a*) The history of philosophy, presenting, as it does, a succession of so many systems, frequently completing one another, frequently also antagonistic and irreconcilable, might well make one doubt whether philosophical truth can ever be reached. Are so many efforts fruitless? Is the human mind condemned forever to seek the truth without ever finding it? From this point of view it is true that the constant conflict of philosophical schools is rather disheartening. But there is another point of view. Light comes from the friction of two stones. So also in philosophy, the conflict of systems tends to show in what respect they may be defective or exaggerated, and to make the element of truth which they contain more secure. Without asserting that every error is but an incomplete truth, it may safely be asserted that every erroneous system contains a great many truths.

(*b*) Notwithstanding, or rather owing to, the incessant clash of systems, philosophy progresses, and, slow as it is, its advance is nevertheless real. Throughout the ages, the same problems come back incessantly, and the attempts to solve them present the same divergences. Any actual system or theory can be traced back to past systems and theories, but every reappearance of a view and tendency shows a development. The human mind does not turn around like a squirrel in its cage to come back to exactly the same point. Its movement is rather spiral-shaped, always widening, embracing more and more, and yet ever turning so as to face again the same problems.

(*c*) Will philosophy ever be one? Will philosophers ever agree at least on a group of essential principles? If we forecast the future by what we know of the past, this is not likely. Too many influences are at work. As the highest science, philosophy receives contributions from too many sources, and these respective contributions affect different minds in too many different ways to make the epoch of philosophical agreement one whose near advent can be predicted. Conflict will remain as a proof of the weakness of the human mind, but also as an element of progress. It contributes to the accuracy of expression, and to the revision of opinions which were not sufficiently examined nor subjected to a thorough criticism.

(*d*) Hence historical contradictions, while showing errors of the human mind, should also be a source of encouragement toward a sincere and honest search for truth. They can frequently be traced back to prejudices, one-sided views, and exclusive attention to one aspect of a complex problem. To recognize the source of an error is the first step toward correcting it. To free the mind from error, to proceed farther and farther, and to rise higher and higher, must be the aim of every man. The unwearying search for truth must be the endeavor of every human intelligence, with the help of the "true light which enlighteneth every man coming into this world."

GENERAL CONCLUSION

The problems outlined in this course of philosophy are so numerous, so complex, and so varied that it is impossible to view them at one glance. Yet it is interesting to retrace the general lines of this vast panorama. The observer on the top of a hill has on all sides a wide horizon within which a number of objects are visible: a forest, a town, a road, a field, a meadow, etc. But only the main outlines are seen, and in a general way; the details cannot be perceived. The observer may go down, and observe a group of objects more in detail, e.g. the general appearance of the forest or city, by moving around or through it. Again, one tree may be selected for a more special examination; then each part of it, till, through the help of the microscope and other instruments, its finest details are known. What we want now is to observe from the summit of the hill, so as to glance at the most general outlines of the philosophical horizon, including the physical universe, man, and God.

I. The Universe

1. **Unity Amid Diversity.** — How little man knows about the universe, about those millions of worlds in which our earth is but an atom! To look at the stars fills the mind with amazement, and yet we see nothing of their details, and a great number are altogether invisible. How little we know even about the planet on which we live! We see only its surface. Its past and future are hidden from us, and every one of the various beings that compose it, or live on it, includes countless mysteries.

Yet what we know is enough to manifest at the same time a most harmonious variety and a most diversified unity. Variety in the inorganic and the organic world. Unity because we see everywhere harmonious action and interaction, and gradual transitions.

Far as it is from the other planets and from the sun, the earth is in close relation with them and with the rest of creation. Nothing in the world is isolated, but everywhere all things are related. On the earth these relations are seen more in detail. Things change more or less rapidly, but they change constantly. Inorganic matter is assimilated by organisms to return again to the inorganic world. Everything serves a purpose. Everywhere activities are exchanged.

2. **Laws and Causes.** — All changes take place according to fixed laws which govern their occurrence. These laws are expressions of the mode of causality of various beings. What is a cause? It is a being applying, consciously or unconsciously, its energy to the production of some result. Here again, how narrow the point of view of man who is obliged to place certain stops in the uninterrupted flux of things. Why did *A* die? Because *B* shot him, we say, and we are satisfied with the answer. Yet the immediate cause of death was the internal hemorrhage, or some other similar organic result due to the presence of the bullet. The pulling of the trigger, the explosion of the powder, the impulse given to the bullet, etc., are so many intermediaries between the murderer and death. And beyond the murderer, in his feelings at the time of the deed, and away back in his past, in his early education, in the dispositions which he inherited, etc., many causes have contributed to the present result.

The same is true of every occurrence. We are obliged to look at things from the point of view from which they interest us most, and according to the limitations of our knowledge as to time and space; limitations which make man incapable of seeing all influences, of tracing back the series of causes in nature, and of following all their results. The list of "whys," "wherefroms," "wheretos," even of the smallest events is inexhaustible, and hence our necessity of stopping without ever knowing anything completely.

Natural laws and causes are utilized by man for his own purposes. Freedom does not change them, but simply adapts them. Art always supposes and is based on nature, without ever modifying its intrinsic energies and laws.

II. Man

1. **In Himself.** — Not only does nature present many mysteries to man; man is the greatest mystery to himself, so complex in structure, so manifold in activity, that the study of self is a never-ending task, and yet the condition of true progress. Physiological and mental functions, lower and higher faculties, organic and mental complexity, make of him one harmonious whole, different from everything else. Faculties of knowledge, feeling, and activity are intimately correlated, all originating from the same substantial unity composed of matter and spirit. Earthly by his organism, heavenly by his soul, man is obliged to cling to the earth, and yet cannot help feeling that his destiny is higher and nobler than that of other organisms.

2. **In the Universe.** — The earth is small when compared to the rest of the universe; man is small on the earth. What is one man among the countless men who now exist or who have existed in the past? Yet how great when we consider his faculties, and his spiritual soul which is a spark of the Eternal Light. Man, it is true, is the plaything of nature, powerless in the face of its tremendous energies. And yet man is able, in many things, to conquer and subdue natural agencies, and make them serve his own ends. Rising above space and time, his intelligence reaches abstract and universal laws, and it is this mode of knowledge which is the basis of specifically human activities. Similar to animals in his physiological functions, he is different from them because some of his activities escape the determinism of matter. Hence man alone is capable of morality, for he alone can know the distinction between right and wrong conduct, and he alone is responsible for his actions. And all these activities point to the fact that this life on earth is not complete, but calls for a complement hereafter. It is chiefly this hope which in all circumstances gives to life its full value, and truly makes it worth living.

III. God

1. **Supreme Cause.** — (*a*) God is the *first cause of nature* and of its laws, distinct from it and transcending it. And not only

must He be placed at the beginning of the world, but He is still governing and ruling His works whose activity and energy suppose His, and are derived from His. Whatever exists in the universe, whatever is real, is a derived reality, and this derivation from the common source of all things leads man to some knowledge of God's perfections, however imperfect such knowledge must remain. Yet the beauty and perfections of the effect must evidently be attributed to the cause, even when this cause is so far above its effects that these present only dim indications of its infinite perfection.

(*b*) God is the *first principle of truth*. Not in the sense that truth depends exclusively on God's will, as Descartes claimed, in such a way that if God had willed it otherwise, two and two would not be four; but in the sense that *true and real are identical*, and that God being the principle of reality is also the principle of truth. God could not make two plus two to equal five because this supposed relation expresses nothing real. It *is not* so, and hence cannot be derived from the principle of reality. God knows Himself first, and in Himself, the various realities or truths that are finite realizations of the divine mind's exemplars.

(*c*) It is also God who is the *first principle of the moral law*. All essences, including man, are ultimately based on the divine essence. The moral law, therefore, which governs man according to his rational nature, is based on God, the author of nature, and the infinite good from which every other good is derived.

(*d*) Finally, God is the *cause of the social order*, since man naturally lives in society, and society requires an authority. Yet no man has of himself the right to give orders to his fellowmen. For a man to obey another man is to debase himself. But "let every soul be subject to higher powers, for there is no power but from God, and those that are ordained by God" (Rom. xiii. 1). When those who command are looked upon as representatives of God, submission to them becomes honorable.

2. **Ultimate End.** — In creating, God could propose to Himself no other end but Himself. "The heavens shew forth the glory of God." Even inanimate creation manifests the divine perfections, but man is the spokesman of creation. He can know

his maker, and must entertain toward Him the feelings of reverence, praise, thanksgiving, etc., which are due to Him. Reason shows only in an imperfect way the final relations of man to God, but revelation completes the data of reason; the supernatural order is added to the natural, and perfects it; man knows his higher destiny and is given the means to reach it. Of the whole universe in general, and of man in particular, God is the First Cause and the Ultimate End, "Alpha and Omega, the first and the last, the beginning and the end" (Apoc. xxii. 13).

APPENDIX

IT is important that the student's mind should be trained to personal thinking. For this reason the following thoughts are suggested as topics for papers and discussions. Many of them are true; others are false; all must be explained and interpreted. A number of other subjects can easily be found in connection with the different lessons of the text-book. Some of those that are given here may be found too difficult, but, however imperfect at first the student's attempt to treat them may be, they will oblige him to think for himself, and thereby contribute to his mental development.

From time to time the whole class may be given the same subject, thus affording an opportunity for the comparison of different viewpoints. Generally it will be found profitable to assign the paper to one student — perhaps two — who should be given ample time to think it out and write it. He should then read it in class and, under the professor's direction, the other students should express their views on both the paper and the subject itself.

Special attention should be given to clearness of thought and expression, logical sequence of ideas, careful preparation of the plan, etc.

1. Studium philosophiae non est ad hoc quod sciatur quid homines senserint, sed qualiter se habeat veritas rerum. — St. Thomas, *In lib. I de Coelo*, lect. XXII.

2. Nec vero probare soleo id quod de Pythagoreis accepimus: quos ferunt, si quid affirmarent in disputando, cum ex eis quaereretur quare ita esset, respondere solitos: Ipse dixit; "ipse" autem erat Pythagoras. — Cicero, *De nat. deor.* I, 5.

3. Errare malo cum Platone quam cum istis vera sentire. — Cicero, *Tusc. Quaest.* I, xvii, 39.

Though both [Plato and truth] are dear to me, it is my duty to prefer truth. — Aristotle, *Eth. Nic.* I, vi, 1.

4. I think . . . I can make it plain . . . that there are at least six personalities distinctly to be recognized as taking part in that dialogue between John and Thomas.

Three Johns.
1. The real John; known only to his Maker.
2. John's ideal John; never the real one, and often very unlike him.
3. Thomas's ideal John, never the real John, nor John's John, but often very unlike either.

Three Thomases.
1. The real Thomas.
2. Thomas's ideal Thomas.
3. John's ideal Thomas.

— O. W. Holmes, *The Autocrat of the Breakfast Table*, III.

5. Noli nimis in sensu tuo confidere, sed velis etiam libenter aliorum sensum audire. — *Imit. Christi*, I, ix, 2.

6. Qui bene seipsum cognoscit sibi ipsi vilescit. — *Imit. Christi*, I, ii, 1.

7. Illud γνῶθι σεαυτόν noli putare ad arrogantiam minuendam solum esse dictum, verum etiam ut bona nostra norimus. — Cicero, *Ad Q. fratrem*, III, 6.

8. Ita natura comparatum est ut altius iniuriae quam merita descendant, et illa cito defluant, has tenax memoria custodiat. — Seneca, *De benef*. I, 1.

9. Things without all remedy
Should be without regard; what's done is done.

Shakespeare, *Macbeth*, III, 2.

What's gone, and what's past help,
Should be past grief.

Id. *Winter's Tale*, III, 2.

10. Pleasure and action make the hours seem short. — Shakespeare, *Othello*, II, 3.

11. A man should never be ashamed to own he has been in the wrong, which is but saying in other words that he is wiser to-day than he was yesterday. — Swift, *Thoughts on Various Subjects*.

12. Tell (for you can) what is it to be wise?
'Tis but to know how little can be known,
To see all others' faults, and feel our own.

Pope, *Essay on Man*, IV, 261.

13. Non enim tam auctoritatis in disputando, quam rationis, momenta quaerenda sunt. Quinetiam obest plerumque iis qui discere volunt auctoritas eorum qui se docere profitentur. — Cicero, *De nat. deor*. I, 5.

14. (Hi non viderunt) hominem ad duas res, ut ait Aristoteles, ad intelligendum et ad agendum esse natum. — CICERO, *De fin.* II, 13.

15. I find the great thing in this world is not so much where we stand as in what direction we are moving. — HOLMES, *The Autocrat of the Breakfast Table*, IV.

16. Onerat discentem turba [librorum], non instruit; multoque satius est paucis te auctoribus tradere quam errare per multos. — SENECA, *De tranquil. an.* IX.

Non refert quam multos [libros], sed quam bonos, habeas; lectio certa prodest, varia delectat. — Id. *Epist.* 45.

17. Read not to contradict and confute; nor to believe and take for granted; nor to find talk and discourse; but to weigh and consider. — BACON, *Essays*, *Of Studies*.

18. A man may have a great mass of knowledge, but if he has not worked it up by thinking it over for himself, it has much less value than a far smaller amount which he has thoroughly pondered. — SCHOPENHAUER, *Essay On Thinking for One's Self.*

19. Homo autem (quod rationis est particeps per quam consequentia cernit, causas rerum videt, earumque progressus et quasi antecessiones non ignorat, similitudines comparat, et rebus praesentibus adiungit atque annectit futuras) facile totius vitae cursum videt, ad eamque degendam praeparat res necessarias. — CICERO, *De offic.* I, 4.

20. Scilicet et fluvius, qui non est maximus, ei est
Qui non ante aliquem maiorem vidit; et ingens
Arbor, homoque videtur, et omnia de genere omni,
Maxima quae vidit quisque, haec ingentia fingit.

LUCRETIUS, *De rerum nat.* VI, 674.

21. Neque hoc quidquam est turpius quam cognitioni et perceptioni assensionem approbationemque praecurrere. — CICERO, *Acad.* I, 12.

22. The heart has its own reasons of which reason has no knowledge. — PASCAL, *Pensées*, P. II, art. xvii, 62.

23. Causarum ignoratio in re nova mirationem facit; eadem ignoratio si in rebus usitatis est, non miramur. — CICERO, *De divinat.* II, 22.

24. A great mistake: for a man to think himself greater than he is, and to value himself less than he deserves. — GOETHE, *Maxims*.

25. There is danger in showing man his equality with animals without showing him his greatness. There is danger also in insisting too much on his greatness without showing him his littleness. There is a still greater danger in leaving him in the ignorance of both. But

there is a great advantage in showing him both. — PASCAL, *Pensées*, P. I, art. iv, 7.

26. Quid importat sollicitudo de futuris contingentibus? . . . Vanum est et inutile de futuris conturbari vel gratulari quae forte nunquam evenient. — *Imit. Christi*, III, xxx, 2.

27. Past, and to come, seem best; things present, worst. — SHAKESPEARE, *II Henry IV*, I, 3.

28. With regard to the estimation of a man's greatness, mental nature obeys a law which is the reverse of that of physical nature. The former is increased, the latter decreased, by distance. — SCHOPENHAUER, *Parerga und Paralipomena*, II.

29. Self-love . . . is not so vile a sin as self-neglecting. — SHAKESPEARE, *Henry V*, II, 4.

30. To business that we love we rise betime,
And go to 't with delight.

SHAKESPEARE, *Anthony and Cleopatra*, IV, 4.

31. If all the year were playing holidays,
To sport would be as tedious as to work.

SHAKESPEARE, *I Henry IV*, I, 2.

32. Two principles in human nature reign:
Self-love to urge, and reason to restrain.

POPE, *Essay on Man*, II, 54.

33. Communi fit vitio naturae ut invisis, latitantibus atque incognitis rebus magis confidamus, vehementiusque exterreamur. — CÆSAR, *De bello civ.* II, 4.

34. Plus dolet quam necesse est qui ante dolet quam necesse est. — SENECA, *Epist.* 95.

35. Suave, mari magno turbantibus aequora ventis,
E terra magnum alterius spectare laborem.
Non quia vexari quemquam est iucunda voluptas,
Sed quibus ipse malis careas quia cernere suave est.

LUCRETIUS, *De rerum nat.* II, 1.

36. Hoc modo magnanimitas est circa honores, ut videlicet studeat ea facere quae sunt honore digna, non tamen sic ut pro magno aestimet humanum honorem. — ST. THOMAS, *Sum. theol.* II–II, Q. 129, art. i, ad 3.

37. Male enim respondent coacta ingenia; reluctante natura, irritus labor est. — SENECA, *De tranquillit. animi*, VI.

38. Maiora cupimus quo maiora venerunt . . . ut flammae infinito acrior vis est quo ex maiore incendio emicuit. Aeque ambitio non

patitur quemquam in ea mensura honorum conquiescere quae quondam eius fuit impudens votum. . . . Ultra se cupiditas porrigit, et felicitatem suam non intelligit, quia non unde venerit respicit, sed quo tendat. — SENECA, *De benef.* II, 27.

39. Endeavor to conquer yourself rather than fortune, and to change your desires rather than the order of the world. — DESCARTES, *Discours de la méthode*, P. III, 3d maxim.

40. Obstinacy is the result of the will forcing itself into the place of the intellect. — SCHOPENHAUER, *Essays*, *Psychological Observations*.

41. Men's thoughts are much according to their inclination; their discourse and speeches according to their learning and infused opinions; but their deeds are after as they have been accustomed. — BACON, *Essays*, *Of Custom and Education*.

42. Qui blandiendo dulce nutrivit malum
Sero recusat ferre quod subiit iugum.
SENECA, *Hippolytus*, I, 134.

43. For every animal, and more especially for man, a certain conformity and proportion between the will and the intellect is necessary for existing or making any progress in the world. — SCHOPENHAUER, *Essays*, *Psychological Observations*.

44. Efficiendum est ut appetitus rationi obediant, eamque neque praecurrant nec propter pigritiam aut ignaviam deserant, sintque tranquilli atque omni perturbatione animi careant. — CICERO, *De offic.* I, 29.

45. Yet he who reigns within himself, and rules
Passions, desires and fears, is more a king.
MILTON, *Paradise Regained*, II, 466.

46. Resiste in principio inclinationi tuae, et malam dedisce consuetudinem, ne forte paulatim ad maiorem te ducat difficultatem. — *Imit. Christi*, I, xi, 5.

47. Ad istud diligenter tendere debes . . . ut sis dominus actionum tuarum et rector, non servus nec emptitius. — *Imit. Christi*, III, xxxviii, 1.

48. Use almost can change the stamp of nature,
And either curb the devil or throw him out
With wondrous potency.
SHAKESPEARE, *Hamlet*, III, 4.

49. A little fire is quickly trodden out,
Which, being suffered, rivers cannot quench.
SHAKESPEARE, *III Henry VI*, IV, 8.

50. Certa viriliter; consuetudo consuetudine vincitur. — *Imit. Christi*, I, xxi, 2.

51. 'Tis education forms the common mind;
Just as the twig is bent, the tree's inclined.
POPE, *Moral Essays*, I, 149.

52. The will of man is by his reason sway'd. — SHAKESPEARE, *A Midsummer Night's Dream*, II, 3.

53. Naturam expellas furca, tamen usque recurret,
Et mala perrumpet furtim fastidia victrix.
HORACE, *Epist.* I, x, 24.

54. He that complies against his will
Is of his own opinion still.
BUTLER, *Hudibras*, III, 3, 547.

55. Principiis obsta; sero medicina paratur
Cum mala per longas convaluere moras.
OVID, *Remed. Amor.* 91.

56. Discipulus est prioris posterior dies. — PUBLIUS SYRUS.

57. Viamque insiste domandi
Dum faciles animi iuvenum, dum mobilis aetas.
VERGIL, *Georg.* III, 164.

58. A man's nature is best perceived in privateness, for there is no affectation; in passion, for that putteth a man out of his precepts; and in a new case or experiment, for there custom leaveth him. — BACON, *Essays*, *Of Nature in Men*.

59. Vita hominum altos recessus magnasque latebras habet. — PLINY THE YOUNGER, *Epist.* III, 3.

60. No man can justly censure or condemn another, because indeed no man truly knows another. — BROWNE, *Religio Medici*, P. II, 4.

61. Children have neither past nor future; but, as scarcely ever happens to us, they enjoy the present. — LA BRUYÈRE, *Caractères*, II.

62. Oportet te igitur aliorum graviora ad mentem reducere ut levius feras tua minima. — *Imit. Christi*, III, xix, 1.

63. They say best men are moulded out of faults. — SHAKESPEARE, *Measure for Measure*, V, 1.

64. Some are born great; some achieve greatness, and some have greatness thrust upon them. — SHAKESPEARE, *Twelfth Night*, II, 5.

65. Men are the sport of circumstances, when
The circumstances seem the sport of men.
BYRON, *Don Juan*, Canto V, St. 17.

Man is not the creature of circumstances. Circumstances are the creatures of men. — DISRAELI, *Vivian Grey*, B. VI, ch. 7.

66. Ita vita est hominum, quasi cum ludas tesseris;
Si illud, quod maxime opus est iactu, non cadit,
Illud, quod cecidit forte, id arte ut corrigas.

TERENCE, *Adelphi*, IV, vii, 21.

67. The fire in the flint shows not till it be struck. — SHAKESPEARE, *Timon of Athens*, I, 1.

68. Thoughts are but dreams till their effects be tried. — SHAKESPEARE, *Lucrece*, St. 51.

69. The moon being clouded presently is missed,
But little stars may hide them when they list.

SHAKESPEARE, *Lucrece*, St. 144.

70. Indeed man is a being wonderfully vain, complex and vacillating. It is difficult to find in him a basis for a constant and uniform judgment. — MONTAIGNE, *Essais*, I, 1.

71. (Montaigne recommends travelling in order that we may) "rub and polish our brains against the brains of others." — MONTAIGNE, *Essais*, I, 24.

72. Nimium altercando veritas amittitur. — PUBLIUS SYRUS.

73. 'Tis with our judgments as our watches; none
Go just alike, yet each believes his own.

POPE, *Essay on Criticism*, 9.

74. What's in a name? That which we call a rose
By any other name would smell as sweet.

SHAKESPEARE, *Romeo and Juliet*, II, 2.

75. Give every man thine ear, but few thy voice;
Take each man's censure, but reserve thy judgment.

SHAKESPEARE, *Hamlet*, I, 3.

76. Veritatis simplex oratio est. — SENECA, *Epist.* 49.

77. It is not enough to have a good understanding; the main thing is to apply it properly. — DESCARTES, *Discours de la méthode*, I.

78. Nescire quaedam magna pars scientiae. — PUBLIUS SYRUS.

79. Videndum est non modo quid quisque loquatur, sed etiam quid quisque sentiat, atque etiam qua de causa quisque sentiat. — CICERO, *De offic.* I, 41.

80. Idem enim vitii habet nimia quod nulla divisio; simile confuso est quidquid usque in pulverem sectum est. — SENECA, *Epist.* 89.

81. One must know how to doubt where necessary, affirm where

necessary, submit where necessary. To do otherwise is to misunderstand the rôle of reason. — PASCAL, *Pensées*, P. II, art. vi, 1.

82. If a man will begin with certainties, he shall end in doubts; but if he will be content to begin with doubts, he shall end in certainties. — BACON, *Proficience and Advancement of Learning*, B. I.

83. Where men of judgment creep and feel their way,
The positive pronounce without dismay.

COWPER, *Conversation*, 145.

84. The will is one of the main instruments of belief; not that it is the source of belief, but that things appear true or false according to the point of view from which they are seen. — PASCAL, *Pensées*, I, vi, 13.

85. Veritati aliquid extremum est; error immensus est. — SENECA, *Excerpta*.

86. Quod fere libenter homines id quod volunt credunt. — CÆSAR, *De bello Gall*. III, 18.

87. Veritas visu et mora, falsa festinatione et incertis valescunt. — TACITUS, *Annal.*, II, 39.

88. Words are wise men's counters; they do but reckon by them; but they are the money of fools. — HOBBES, *Leviathan*, I, iv.

89. Nothing is so easy as to deceive oneself, for a man readily believes what he wishes, but this belief is frequently in opposition with the facts. — DEMOSTHENES, *Olynth*. III, 19.

90. Be calm in arguing; for fierceness makes
Error a fault, and truth discourtesie.

G. HERBERT, *The Temple, The Church Porch*.

91. Qualis unusquisque intus est, taliter iudicat exterius. — *Imit. Christi*, II, iv, 2.

92. The fool doth think he is wise, but the wise man knows himself to be a fool. — SHAKESPEARE, *As You Like It*, V, 1.

93. Sic est vulgus: ex veritate pauca, ex opinione multa aestimat. — CICERO, *Orat. pro Q. Rosc. Com*. X.

94. Quid maiore fide porro quam sensus haberi
Debet? An ab sensu falso ratio orta valebit
Dicere eos contra, quae tota ab sensibus orta est?
Qui nisi sint veri, ratio quoque falsa fit omnis.

LUCRETIUS, *De rerum nat*. IV, 483.

95. Ut necesse est lancem in libra ponderibus impositis deprimi, sic animum perspicuis cedere. — CICERO, *Acad*. II, 12.

96. Non enim tam auctores in disputando quam rationis momenta quaerenda sunt. — CICERO, *De natura deor*. I, 5.

97. Assiduitate quotidiana et consuetudine oculorum assuescunt animi, neque admirantur, neque requirunt rationes earum rerum quas semper vident; proinde quasi novitas nos magis quam magnitudo rerum debeat ad exquirendas causas excitare. — CICERO, *De nat. deor.* II, 38.

98. Ipsa consuetudo assentiendi periculosa esse videtur et lubrica. — CICERO, *Acad.* II, 21.

99. Duo cum idem faciunt, saepe ut possis dicere:
Hoc licet impune facere huic, illi non licet;
Non quod dissimilis res sit, sed quod is qui facit.

TERENCE, *Adelphi*, V, iii, 37.

100. Nescimus saepe quid possumus, sed tentatio aperit quid sumus. — *Imit. Christi*, I, xiii, 5.

101. Mane propone, vespere discute mores tuos. — *Imit. Christi*, I, xix, 4.

102. Saepe malum facilius quam bonum de alio creditur et dicitur; ita infirmi sumus. — *Imit. Christi*, I, iv, 1.

103. Nam qualitercumque ordinavero de pace mea, non potest esse sine bello et dolore vita mea. — *Imit. Christi*, III, xii, 1.

104. When men are friends there is no need of justice, but when they are just, they still need friendship. — ARISTOTLE, *Eth. Nic.* VIII, i.

105. If our virtues
Did not go forth of us, 'twere all alike
As if we had them not.

SHAKESPEARE, *Measure for Measure*, I, 1.

106. The ruling passion, be it what it will,
The ruling passion conquers reason still.

POPE, *Moral Essays*, Ep. III, 153.

107. There is some soul of goodness in things evil,
Would men observingly distil it out.

SHAKESPEARE, *Henry V*, IV, 1.

108. Reputation is an idle and most false imposition; oft got without merit, and lost without deserving. — SHAKESPEARE, *Othello*, II, 3.

109. To thine own self be true;
And it must follow, as the night the day,
Thou canst not then be false to any man.

SHAKESPEARE, *Hamlet*, I, 3.

110. Fine art is that in which the hand, the head, and the heart go together. — RUSKIN, *The Two Paths*, lect. 2.

111. Omnis ars imitatio est naturae. — SENECA, *Epist.* 65.

Art is the perfection of nature. — BROWNE, *Religio Medici*, I, 16.

112. Beggars mounted run their horse to death. — SHAKESPEARE, *III Henry VI*, I, 4.

113. Were man but constant, he were perfect. — SHAKESPEARE, *The Two Gentlemen of Verona*, V, 4.

114. Striving to better, oft we mar what's well. — SHAKESPEARE, *King Lear*, I, 4.

115. Know thou this, — that men
Are as the time is.

SHAKESPEARE, *King Lear*, V, 3.

116. There is no vice so simple but assumes
Some mark of virtue on his outward parts.

SHAKESPEARE, *Merchant of Venice*, III, 2.

117. That in the captain's but a choleric word
Which in the soldier is flat blasphemy.

SHAKESPEARE, *Measure for Measure*, II, 2.

118. Insani sapiens nomen ferat, aequus iniqui
Ultra quam satis est virtutem si petat ipsam.

HORACE, *Epist.* I, vi, 15.

119. The laws of conscience, which we say are born of nature, are born of custom. — MONTAIGNE, *Essais*, I, 22.

120. Est modus in rebus; sunt certi denique fines
Quos ultra citraque nequit consistere rectum.

HORACE, *Sat.* I, i, 106.

121. Quot homines tot sententiae; suus cuique mos. — TERENCE, *Phorm.* II, iv, 14.

122. Gloria nostra est testimonium conscientiae nostrae. — ST. PAUL, *II Cor.* I, 12.

123. Mea mihi conscientia pluris est quam omnium sermo. — CICERO, *Ad Attic.* XII, 28.

124. Lex quaedam regula est et mensura actuum. . . . Regula autem et mensura humanorum actuum est ratio. — ST. THOMAS, *Sum. theol.* I–II, Q. 90, art. i.

125. Omnino si quidquam est decorum, nihil est profecto magis quam aequabilitas universae vitae tum singularium actionum; quam conservare non possis si aliorum naturam imitans omittas tuam. — CICERO, *De offic.* I, 31.

126. Actio recta non erit nisi recta fuerit voluntas; ab hac enim est actio. Rursus voluntas non erit recta nisi habitus animi rectus fuerit; ab hoc enim est voluntas. — SENECA, *Epist.* 95.

127. Maximum hoc habemus naturae meritum quod virtus in omnium

animos lumen suum permittit; etiam qui non sequuntur illam vident. — SENECA, *De benef*. IV, 17.

128. Aequam memento rebus in arduis
Servare mentem, non secus in bonis
Ab insolenti temperatam
Laetitia.

HORACE, *Odes*, II, 3.

129. Ira furor brevis est; animum rege, qui, nisi paret,
Imperat; hunc frenis, hunc tu compesce catena.

HORACE, *Epist*. I, ii, 62.

130. Non est, crede mihi, sapientis dicere: vivam.
Sera nimis vita est crastina; vive hodie.

MARTIAL, *Epigr*. I, 16.

131. Ut quisque est vir optimus, ita difficillime esse alios improbos suspicatur. — CICERO, *Ad Q. fratrem*, I, i, 4.

132. Felix qui potuit rerum cognoscere causas. — VERGIL, *Georg*. II, 490.

133. Prudens interrogatio quasi dimidium scientiae. — BACON, *De augmentis scientiarum*, V, 116.

134. Tamdiu discendum est quamdiu nescias, et, si proverbio credimus, quamdiu vivas. — SENECA, *Epist*. 76.

135. It is much easier to detect error than to find truth. The former lies at the surface, and therefore is easily got at; the latter lies in the depth, and to search for it is not every man's business. — GOETHE, *Maxims*.

136. Errors like straws upon the surface flow;
He who would search for pearls must dive below.

DRYDEN, *All for Love, Prologue*.

137. Nil ideo quoniam natum est in corpore ut uti
Possemus; sed quod natum est, id procreat usum.

LUCRETIUS, *De rerum nat*. IV, 833.

Nature adapts the organ to the function, and not the function to the organ. — ARISTOTLE, *De part. animal*. IV, xii.

138. What we train is not a soul, nor a body, but a man; the two must not be separated. — MONTAIGNE, *Essais*, I, xxvi.

139. Ratio et oratio. . . . conciliat inter se homines, coniungitque naturali quadam societate. Neque ulla re longius absumus a natura ferarum. — CICERO, *De finib*. I, 16.

140. Sufficit ad id natura quod poscit. — SENECA, *Epist*. 90.

141. Modus quo corporibus adhaerent spiritus omnino mirus est,

nec comprehendi ab homine potest, et hoc ipse homo est. — St. Augustine, *De civitate Dei*, XXI, 10.

142. Ipsi animi magni refert quali in corpore locati sint; multa enim e corpore existunt quae acuant mentem, multa quae obtundant. — Cicero, *Tuscul.* I, 33.

143. Mutat enim mundi naturam totius aetas,
Ex alioque alius status excipere omnia debet;
Nec manet ulla sui similis res; omnia migrant;
Omnia commutat natura, et vertere cogit.

Lucretius, *De rerum nat.* V, 826.

144. Intrandum est in rerum naturam, et penitus quid ea postulet pervidendum. — Cicero, *De finib.* V, 16.

145. Non est causa efficiens, sed deficiens mali, quia malum non est effectio, sed defectio. — St. Augustine, *De civitate Dei*, XII, 7.

146. Omnia profecto cum se a coelestibus rebus referet ad humanas, excelsius magnificentiusque et dicet et sentiet. — Cicero, *De Oratore*, XXXIV, 119.

147. The course of Nature is the art of God. — Young, *Night Thoughts*, Night 9.

148. 'Tis but a base ignoble mind
That mounts no higher than a bird can soar.

Shakespeare, *II Henry VI*, II. 1.

149. A little philosophy inclineth man's mind to atheism; but depth in philosophy bringeth men's minds about to religion: For while the mind of man looketh upon second causes scattered, it may sometimes rest in them, and go no further; but when it beholdeth the chain of them, confederate and linked together, it must needs fly to Providence and Deity. — Bacon, *Essays*, *Atheism*.

150. Thy desire, which tends to know
The works of God, thereby to glorify
The great Work-Master, leads to no excess
That reaches blame, but rather merits praise
The more it seems excess.

Milton, *Paradise Lost*, III, 694.

INDEX

INDEX

Made in the USA
Middletown, DE
29 February 2020

85586014R00358